To
Michelle

Enjoy three
memories

[signature]

Profiles of POWER & SUCCESS

Profiles of POWER & SUCCESS

Fourteen Geniuses Who Broke the Rules

GENE N. LANDRUM, Ph.D.

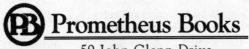 **Prometheus Books**

59 John Glenn Drive
Amherst, New York 14228-2197

Published 1996 by Prometheus Books

00 99 98 97 96   5 4 3 2

Library of Congress Cataloging-in-Publication Data

Landrum, Gene N.
    Profiles of power and success : fourteen geniuses who broke the rules / Gene N. Landrum.
        p.   cm.
    Includes bibliographical references and index.
    ISBN 1–57392–052–5 (cloth : alk. paper)
    1. Success—Case studies. 2. Achievement—Case studies. 3. Gifted persons—Biography. 4. Genius—Case studies. 5. Nature and nurture. I. Title.
BF637.S8L346   1996
155.2—dc20
                                                        95–54002
                                                        CIP

Printed in the United States of America on acid-free paper

To Tammy

Moxie and Mania Move Mountains—Follow Your Bliss

Contents

List of Figures

Acknowledgments

The Naples, Florida, library staff and in particular the reference personnel should be commended for their assistance with the subject research. Ruth Sawyer of the International College Library was also of substantial help in retrieving critical research data for this effort. This book would not have been possible without the interlibrary loan system, which located esoteric and long-out-of-print books and periodicals. The editing and grammatical integrity of the work was enhanced by the diligent and comprehensive work of Mary A. Read and Steven L. Mitchell of Prometheus Books. Whatever objectivity exists in the work is due to the dutiful editing by my loving wife, Diedra, who also contributed to the Jungian personality profiles assigned to each of the subjects. The author is indebted to Bill Dorsey and many others who contributed to the subject research.

Preface

This book follows the theme of my first two *books, Profiles of Genius* and *Profiles of Female Genius,* in using the technique of psychobiography to ferret out "what makes the great tick?" This work differs in that it is written with self-help in mind for those readers interested in emulating the successful and powerful. My objective is to unearth the specific qualities and methodologies that these fourteen individuals utilized in their march to the top of their field, and to discover any similar patterns in their approach. This book is also dedicated to overcoming the myth that money, brains, formal education, and societal influence have *anything* to do with success. The bottom line is that too much money, education, or IQ is counterproductive to achievement, which is validated in the findings on these super-successful people. This book will confirm that "behavior, not genes" is the formula for any great achievement in life. I will attempt to prove that anyone with slightly above normal intelligence can become a powerful leader or creative genius through hard work, tenacity, and risk taking.

These fourteen visionaries confirm that supersuccess is more a function of the heart than of the brain, of emotion than genetics, and of freedom than structure. Drive in the form of psychic energy has been coined in the text as a "manic success syndrome" due to the inordinate role it played in the rise to power of these wunderkinds. It's not what we *are,* but what we *think* we are, that defines us. The more deluded we are in our dreams and fantasies, the more successful we can become.

The psychobiographies of these subjects clearly illustrate the fallacy in Francis Galton's claim that genetics and family heritage are the derivation of all success. It also disproves the "cognitive elite" theory proposed by Charles Murray and Richard Herrnstein in *The Bell Curve* (1994) that all success and power is a function of intelligence, education, and socioeconomic status. These visionaries clearly demonstrate that great success and power are learned and not inherited. All came from average families, had few forebears of any note, and their middle-class households provided little or no influence in their adult successes. There was no evidence of genius found in their immediate families. In fact, the fathers of Amelia Earhart, Pablo Picasso, Frank Lloyd Wright, Edith Piaf, Isadora Duncan, and Walt Disney were miserable failures. The only two who had fathers of note were Howard Hughes and Rupert Murdoch and their fathers only realized a modicum of success in one market area. The other six subjects had parents who were quite ordinary.

Formal education wasn't a factor in their power or success. Napoleon graduated forty-second of fifty-eight students from the École Militaire in Paris but went on to achieve enormous success as the world's greatest military genius. Isadora Duncan had but four years of formal schooling, but Auguste Rodin called her the "greatest woman the world has ever known" due to her literary prowess and vast knowledge of the arts and dance. Isadora is universally acclaimed as the mother of modern dance yet, aside from one hour of ballet instruction, had no formal training in the discipline. Edith Piaf was recognized as Europe's greatest chanteuse despite being illiterate until age twenty-one and incapable of reading one note of music. Picasso's father, Don Jose Ruiz, was his mentor and also a journeyman painter. He influenced Picasso's desire to paint but was otherwise a nonfactor in Picasso's success. Picasso was a miserable student and only graduated primary school because his father bribed the officials to pass his son. All of these subjects clearly demonstrate that *life-experiences* and not genes, and *drive* and not education are keys to achieving great power and success.

Selection Criteria

One hundred candidates from the past three hundred years were studied, and fourteen powerful and super-successful individuals were selected from the arts, business, entertainment, humanities, politics, and science. The objective was to select the greatest and most powerful person in each profession. Candidates were chosen from works such as *The One Hundred: A Ranking of the Most Influential Persons in History* by Michael Hart and *The Creators: A History of Heroes of the Imagination* by Daniel J. Boorstin, in addition to substantial research on the six professions. Psychobiography was used in order to best analyze environmental and early childhood experiences relative to adult achievement. It is the methodology best suited for examining historical data and heuristic learning relative to personality and behavior. This approach was first used by Sigmund Freud, who studied the childhood experiences and dysfunctions of Leonardo da Vinci to ferret out the major clues to his later success. This book uses a similar technique in attempting to isolate the personal behavior characteristics responsible for the derivation of power and success in creative geniuses. Through a process of elimination I arrived at the final fourteen, using these specific knock-out factors:

Father/mother of industry or changed the world. The individual must have had a material impact on society or be universally acknowledged as the father/mother of the industry or field (e.g., Picasso and cubism, Isadora Duncan and modern dance, Frank Lloyd Wright and architecture, Walt Disney and cartoons).

Pinnacle of power and influence. The subject must have been the very best in their profession during their era or considered the very best by more than one source (e.g., Howard Hughes in business and Rupert Murdoch in publishing).

Ten-year dominance. Once on top, the subject must have stayed there for at least ten years. They could not have been a flash in the pan (e.g., Robert Maxwell).

Negative success. Two subjects were purposely chosen for their nihilism to see what, if any, similarities existed in people successful in gaining power and success through destruction. (Adolf Hitler and Napoleon Bonaparte, and Howard Hughes and Pablo Picasso turned out to fit the model.)

Worldwide influence. The person had to have had a worldwide and not merely a regional or local influence (e.g., Amelia Earhart, Nikola Tesla, Edith Piaf, and Helena Rubinstein).

Originality. The individuals had to have been responsible for creating their own success and not have married or inherited it. Kings born into power like Peter the Great or a woman who married into power like Eleanor Roosevelt were eliminated.

Who Qualifies as a Creative Genius?

This brings us to the definition of creative genius. I have elected to use the definition of genius throughout this text in its *qualitative* (achievement) not *quantitative* (IQ potential) sense. The world has become enamored with numbers where "genius" and "gifted" require a minimum Scholastic Assessment Test (SAT) score of 1400 or an IQ score of 140 to qualify. This book will demonstrate that great achievement has little to do with scores on a test, but more to do with performance on the stage of life. Jules Henri Poincaré scored at the imbecile level on Alfred Binet's IQ test at a time when Poincaré was universally acknowledged as the world's foremost mathematician. Skid row is littered with people touting 150 IQs. *Webster's Dictionary* defines a genius as "a person who influences another for the good or bad" or who has "an extraordinary intellectual power especially as manifested in creative activity" or "a marked capacity or aptitude [IQ]." Creativity is likewise defined as "bringing something new into existence." I am using the following definition of creative genius fashioned from the above definitions: "Creative genius is any person who influences another for the good or bad by bringing something new into existence (which changes the world in some dramatic way)."

SUBJECTS SELECTED

The fourteen selected include five women and nine men in six different professional categories: artistically powerful (Frank Lloyd Wright and Picasso); business tycoons (Helena Rubinstein, Howard Hughes, and Rupert Murdoch); powerful entertainers (Isadora Duncan, Walt Disney, and Edith Piaf); socially powerful (Marquis de Sade and Amelia Earhart); powerful politicians (Napoleon Bonaparte and Adolf Hitler); and scientific powerhouses (Nikola Tesla and Maria Montessori). Eight were European by birth (only six of these achieved major success in Europe), five American, and one Australian. All were Promethean spirits (intuitive-thinkers) except Duncan and Piaf. The subjects came from diverse cultures and religious backgrounds, yet proved to be quite similar in behavioral characteristics and operating methodologies. Figure 1 lists the fourteen by their greatest achievement and key success trait.

FIGURE 1
MANIC ACHIEVERS AND POWER BROKERS   Edimonlogy

Creative Genius	Achievement	Key Success Trait
Napoleon Bonaparte	Greatest military genius in history	Intuitive vision
Walt Disney	Built dynasty in family entertainment	Tenacity
Isadora Duncan	Revolutionized modern dance	Independence and rebellion
Amelia Earhart	Pioneered air travel and women's rights	Inspirational risk taking
Adolf Hitler	Almost conquered the world	Psychic and charismatic energy
Howard Hughes	Billionaire power broker	Lived on the edge in all things
Maria Montessori	Revolutionized childhood education	Supreme self-confidence
Rupert Murdoch	World media tycoon in TV, news, radio	Type A workaholic
Edith Piaf	Rose from gutter to penthouse of song	Perseverance beyond belief
Pablo Picasso	Greatest artist of twentieth century	Prodigious self-image
Helena Rubinstein	First innovator of beauty in a jar	Workaholic
Marquis de Sade	"Most absolute writer who ever lived"	Renegade sexual intellectual
Nikola Tesla	Arguably the world's greatest inventive genius	Psychic energy incarnate
Frank Lloyd Wright	Greatest architect in history	Promethean intuition

CONSIDERED BUT NOT SELECTED

Many worthy subjects were considered but rejected. Two books were read on Mao before rejecting him for Napoleon and Hitler. Robert Maxwell was dropped since Rupert Murdoch was far more effective in the same profession. Georgia O'Keeffe was replaced by Picasso because he better defined art in the twentieth century and his influence was far greater. Alexander Graham Bell has had an enormous impact on communications but Tesla's contributions seemed more critical to the solution of electrical power distribution. Those seriously considered but not selected were:

Alexander the Great	Charles Darwin	Sigmund Freud
Steve Allen	Charles Dickens	Galileo Galilei
Honoré Balzac	Fyodor Dostoevsky	Genghis Kahn
Ludwig van Beethoven	Werner Earhard	Ruth Ginsberg
Alexander Graham Bell	Thomas Edison	Martha Graham
Rachel Carson	Albert Einstein	Timothy Leary
Catherine the Great	Henry Ford	Martin Luther

Marshall McLuhan	Marilyn Monroe	Elvis Presley
Malcolm X	J. P. Morgan	Janet Reno
Nelson Mandela	Isaac Newton	Joseph Stalin
Mao Tse Tung	Frederich Nietzsche	Peter Ilyich Tchaikovsky
Karl Marx	Florence Nightingale	Leo Tolstoy
Margaret Mead	Georgia O'Keeffe	Leonardo da Vinci
Andrew Mellon	Juan Perón	Barbara Walters

Trait Chapters—Psychohistories

Most subjects were endowed with all seven traits found important in achieving great success—drive, risk taking, charisma, rebellion, self-confidence, tenacity, and vision—but one trait always jumped out as clearly most responsible for their rise to fame and fortune. Each subject was placed in a "trait chapter" that was most indicative of their acquisition of power and success. These chapters illustrate the role played by all subjects but highlight just two subjects (for example, "Risk Taking" with Amelia Earhart and Howard Hughes). In this case a risk-reward curve illustrates how risk is used to gain power. In the chapter on intuition (Napoleon and Frank Lloyd Wright) the Promethean personality is described relative to the importance of right-brain decision making and planning via macrovision. Each trait chapter contains a brief biographical history of the subject. The derivation of their driven personality and power traits is emphasized relative to their early experiences and environmental influences. Included are early life experiences, successes, crises, acquisition of power and influence, manic propensity, and self-destructive tendencies. The chapters are organized for easy use by the reader. The organization allows one to turn to any chapter for specific advice on that particular trait or to any individual to delve into that profession.

If a reader is only interested in discovering how risk taking can be used to gain power and success, they may proceed right to that particular chapter and learn how Howard Hughes and Amelia Earhart acquired their power and influence by living on the edge. Anyone interested in discovering how a Promethean temperament (intuitive-thinking personality) affects creative success can turn to that chapter. Likewise anyone interested in hard work or the Type A behavior and its influence on success can turn to the chapter "Work Ethic," which features Helena Rubinstein and Rupert Murdoch. Those readers interested in hypomania, obsessiveness, or psychic energy should read the "Obsessive Will/Manic Energy" chapter where the charisma and psychic energy of Hitler and Tesla are analyzed in depth. The first three chapters and the last one summarize the findings on everything from birth order to dysfunctional behavior relative to high achievement and self-actualization. These chapters cover crises, hierarchy of power, and a manic success syndrome in respect to that particular nuance of achieving power and success. The whole

---

FIGURE 2
FOURTEEN VISIONARIES WHO CHANGED THE WORLD

ARTISTS—PASSION AND POWER

Pablo Picasso (Spanish). Arguably the greatest artist of the twentieth century. His art documented the psyche of a troubled world and defined his macho mentality. The most prolific painter in history who violated all rules of decorum and behavior and left a trail of death and destruction—in both art and women. His destructiveness led two wives and a mistress to commit suicide.

Frank Lloyd Wright (American). The world's most acclaimed architectural genius. He was a renegade who designed radically different structures that he called "organic architecture"—designs based on nature. He had a romantic flair where poetic forms and philosophic intent were paramount. He left a heritage of splendor based on a Promethean spirit of freedom and form.

BUSINESS ORIENTED—CREATED DESTRUCTION

Rupert Murdoch (Australian). This Type A workaholic became the tycoon and tyrant of the information age through a unique vision of the global village and satellite communications. Dominant in Australia, England, and the United States, his power pervades the newspaper, radio, TV (Fox), and book publishing industries, the catalysts for creation of the world's most influential communications dynasty.

Helena Rubinstein (Polish). The first woman to innovate beauty in a jar and who did it effectively on three continents with panache, bravado, and class. An entrepreneurial visionary who used hard work and a positive attitude to conquer the world of business. *Life* magazine described her as the "world's most successful businesswoman." Work made her the richest self-made woman in the United States.

ENTERTAINMENT—DRIVEN TO SEEK POWER

Isadora Duncan (American). The mother of modern dance was a self-made woman who single-handedly created a unique style and form of dance. Duncan used an intransigent and renegade nature and passion to change the world of dance. Her life was a Greek tragedy. The sculptor Rodin described her as "the greatest woman the world has ever known"—a testimony to her power and influence.

Walt Disney (American). Violated all traditions of movie production in creating a dynasty in children's entertainment. He hated art but ironically made cartoons into an art form by turning his childhood fantasies into a viable business enterprise. Traditionalists and adversaries refused to accept his concepts but Disney persevered to alter family entertainment to fit his image of the world.

Edith Piaf (French). Born in a gutter, this optimistic singer survived to become a legend in her own lifetime. Her self-destructive nature required drugs and alcohol to cope with the ups and downs of life. She used an internally generated passion and a unique power on stage to become Europe's most famous chanteuse.

---

issue of nature versus nurture (born or bred) is covered in chapter 1 in addition to intelligence, formal education, and socioeconomic status, plus a detailed analysis of dysfunctional behaviors and their concomitant for success. The last chapter summarizes all the traits and other factors such as gender that appear to have contributed to success and power.

SOCIAL CONSCIOUS—ALTRUISTIC POWER

Amelia Earhart (American). An off-the-scale risk-taker and the prototypically independent female. She competed with men on their terms and on their turf and was eminently successful in the process. Earhart broke numerous aviation speed records, started an airline, operated her own fashion business, and like most in this book was destroyed by her very strengths.

Maria Montessori (Italian). A medical doctor who revolutionized the education of small children by allowing their self-esteem and holistic natural freedom of thought to prevail. Confidence and truth led her to the top of her chosen profession. Discovered that a child's natural propensity for work was instrumental in their personality development in contrast to play.

Marquis de Sade (French). An aristocrat who became the alter ego of the French Revolution. A rebel who sacrificed his "self" to demonstrate to the world that behavior cannot be legislated. His power was based on an iconoclastic need to satiate his own passions while defying religious and social dogma. A talented writer who spent 50 percent of his adult life in jail due to his refusal to recognize authority over his mind.

POLITICIANS—MESSIANIC MANIA AND POWER

Napoleon Bonaparte (Corsican). Acknowledged as the world's greatest military genius, he conquered the world as a Frenchman even though he was not French. His macrovision and internal belief system elevated him above his peers and made him the consummate charismatic leader. He was responsible for the deaths of millions due to his obsession with power.

Adolf Hitler (Austrian). Austrian madman who used a mesmerizing charismatic vision to gain tyrannical power over Germany—a nation he led based on nationalism while not having one drop of German blood. Responsible for the deaths of approximately forty million people based on his nihilistic view of the world and a magnificent and hypnotizing rhetoric.

SCIENTISTS—INQUISITIVE POWER

Howard Hughes (American). He violated all the rules and took enormous risks in his drive to become the richest and most powerful man in the world. His live-on-the-edge mentality was instrumental in changing the airline industry, and affected his love affairs and the creation of a Las Vegas real estate and casino empire.

Nikola Tesla (Hungarian). Arguably the greatest inventor in history, inventing the AC induction motor and alternating current distribution systems. He was consistently ahead of his time in electronics, robotry, computers, missile science, and communications. A gifted creative genius who used psychic energy to create and invent, he was obsessed with achievement.

Controversy over Subject Selection

Any selection process is always subject to second-guessing by academia, publishers, readers, and the author. There is little agreement on the definition of power, influence, and success in both the academic and nonacademic world. Therefore the claim of someone as the most powerful, greatest, or best will always be open to criticism. Power and influence are in themselves subjective words. They conjure up controversy since they often mean something different to each reader. Chapter 3 depicts "power" as an evolutionary factor in success and goes through a "hierarchy of power" that encompasses physical, financial, knowledge, titular, and charismatic power, and a will-to-power.

Was Napoleon truly the greatest military genius in history? Many historians have called him such although selecting him as the greatest who ever lived is sure to be controversial. Was Frank Lloyd Wright the most influential architect in history? Many people think so, including social scientist Lewis Mumford. Many others, including the *New York Times,* called Wright the "Anarchist of Architecture" and "Frank Lloyd Wrong." Hitler is probably the most controversial subject selected even though most people would acknowledge that he was highly influential in the course of twentieth-century history. Hitler was selected not only for his enormous power and influence but also because he achieved more success with less talent than anyone in history. I felt it was important to show that his rise to power employed many of the identical traits and behavior characteristics of Walt Disney and Amelia Earhart. It is shocking that such a no-talent could rise to absolute power by little other than charismatic speech. Is he unusual in this? Not really. Napoleon, Wright, and Montessori were equally eloquent and mesmerizing. Jim Jones, David Koresh, and other cult leaders have utilized mesmerizing dialogue to lead disciples to their deaths. These individuals took advantage of vulnerable people with promises of salvation and were able to deceive the weak into believing they were divine. Hitler was indisputably the most tyrannical beast who ever lived, but discerning what made him tick might give some insight into his methodology for gaining power.

Calling Maria Montessori the preeminent female in primary education will surely prove controversial. Maria was included for two reasons. She not only met the criteria for creative genius but her Montessori method of teaching and philosophy of learning were found to be shockingly consistent with the early life experiences of all these subjects. Her beliefs that teaching is "social engineering," that "the subconscious is much more important than the conscious," that "liberty and freedom is power," and that "education is liberty in the prepared environment" were crucial concepts in the personality formation and rise to success of these fourteen visionaries. Montessori claimed that "no one can be free unless he is independent," which is the theme of chapter 7 in this book and one of the key success traits of creative genius. Her most profound finding is also strangely consistent with the findings on these power brokers: "It is only in persons of exceptional power—the geniuses—that this love of work persists as an irresistible impulse." This tenet is the basis of chapter 9. Her hypotheses that "education is acquired not by listening but by experiencing the environment" and "it is by work, not play, that the child organizes his personality" were found pervasive in the early lives of all these subjects. Her thesis of "empirical learning" is also fundamental to super achievement.

Montessori successfully trained "uneducable 'idiot' children" to perform normally, giving credence to the "nurture" not "nature" theory. She then replicated that feat by doing the same for culturally deprived children from a Rome ghetto.

Just as I have discovered that heuristic (trial and error) learning was critical to the success of these fourteen, Montessori demonstrated that educational success was based on empirical learning in an enhanced environment. This book will show that the Promethean personality and resultant entrepreneurial success were the by-product of the same type of learning. The fourteen subjects in this book were not supposed to have succeeded, just as Montessori's children were not expected to be capable of reading and writing. Yet they did succeed despite their genetic and socioeconomic heritage, just as Montessori's "idiot" children had done. Further research is needed to validate Montessori's methods relative to adult overachievement, but it is shocking to find such coincidental findings. These alone were justification for inclusion of Montessori in this text.

Subjects by Profession

Common patterns found in the creative and entrepreneurial personality were:

1. All were self-starters and prodigiously productive.

2. They did not *get* ulcers, they *gave* them.

3. Most had few friends but many disciples.

4. They were not generally loved but universally respected.

5. Most were not admired by their peers or bosses (allegiance came from below not above).

6. Their persona instilled fear in associates and family (people sensed a ticking time bomb ready to blow at the least provocation).

7. They reached the top but never remembered or enjoyed the journey.

8. Most were their own worst enemy (their strengths became their weaknesses).

9. Most were dysfunctional personalities (in such a hurry to gain power, they never even saw, let alone smelled, the roses on the road to success).

10. All were impatient, impulsive, and intolerant.

11. Most were loners who only listened to their own council.

12. They had a childlike imagination and lived life as a fantasy.

Figure 2 categorizes these creative geniuses by profession, including a brief description of their methodology for success and their dominant trait. This outline should help the reader decide which subjects are the most interesting to read or which best fit a personal or professional interest. All success and power comes with a high price, which not everyone is willing to pay. These individuals were willing to repeatedly pay that price both personally and professionally. They are classic examples of the Promethean personality type.

Introduction: Paradoxes of Power

Many who achieve great things are amazed at their own accomplishments. Eminent innovators, entrepreneurs, and creators are usually so immersed in their own driven need to achieve that they are not aware of the amount of money, knowledge, and authoritarian or charismatic power they have. Power is paradoxical. The more it is desired, the harder it is to get. New Age psychologists believe the only way to obtain more power is to forget about power itself and use the will to pursue the principles of power. In the words of Ram Dass, a mystic and a spiritual leader: "The most exquisite paradox . . . as soon as you give it all up, you can have it all. . . . As long as you want *power,* you can't have it. The minute you don't want *power,* you'll have more than you ever dreamed possible" (McClelland 1978, p. 204).

Paradoxical Intention

Most people try too hard to achieve and their intensity becomes counterproductive to the process. They are so focused on the goal that they are incapable of functioning in a way best suited for success. The path to excellence and power is relaxed concentration, which can be attested to by any world-class athlete. Psychiatrist/writer Viktor Frankl labeled this concept "paradoxical intention," which maintains that concentrating too much on anything is counterproductive to the objective. He derived this theory of self-control or behavior modification in his work on psychotherapy and neuroses. Frankl founded a school of psychotherapy called logotherapy and wrote a book, *In Search of Meaning* (1959), in which he explained his hypothesis of paradoxical intention, which maintains that concentrating too much on anything is counterproductive to the objective. In Frankl's words, "fear brings about that which one is afraid of and hyperintention makes impossible what one wishes." Frankl came upon this accidentally in his experimental work with patients he was treating for various forms of neuroses. He found perfectionism to be a factor in failure in areas like impotence, stuttering, and excessive perspiring. Those who tried too hard were less capable of performing than those who were relaxed and focused.

Frankl discovered "paradoxical intention" while working with impotent patients. He found they were only able to have an erection by not trying to have one. The harder they tried to have an erection, the more difficult it became; their minds got in the way of their ability to perform. Tennis players, golfers, and skiers can cite similar examples in their performance. Frankl confirmed his hypothesis by working with a teenager who had stuttered from childhood. When the boy concentrated too hard on stuttering he was unable to stutter, when he tried not to stutter he did. Frankl then reinforced his theories by working on perspiration. He found people who were unable to perspire even when they tried on a hot day. If they did not try, they perspired profusely. Frankl further illustrated the concept through handwriting experiments where he found it impossible to perfectly replicate cursive handwriting. Try writing your name three times in cursive with exacting precision. It is impossible. But when you relax you can write your name exactly the same every time. In Frankl's words, "try to scribble" and you will write better. "Try to write better" and there is a good chance that you will scribble. Frankl's conclusion was:

> Don't aim for success—the more you aim at it and make it a target, the more you're going to miss it. For success, like happiness, cannot be pursued; it must ensue . . . as the unintended side effect of one's personal dedication to a course greater than oneself. (*In Search of Meaning* [1959], p. 146)

PARADOX OF POWER

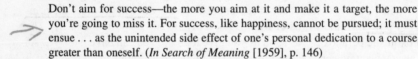

Frankl's principle of paradoxical intention is pervasive in the lives of great people. Most of these fourteen did not try to make a lot of money but became very rich. If they had tried, the chances are they would have failed. They had huge goals and dreams and never lost sight of them, but once they were established these goals were relegated to the background while they focused on the fundamentals for success. An example is the paradox of frenetically searching for romance. Most great romances occur accidentally. Edith Piaf spent her life attempting to find love. Her intensity guaranteed her failure. Attempting to get rich quick will end in the same futility. Successful individuals concentrate on the fundamentals in a microway while keeping the macrogoal in the background. To achieve great success it is important to set a goal, then forget it and concentrate on the fundamentals for achieving that goal. Winning a tennis match should be subordinate to serving well and hitting the ball correctly. If these are achieved there is a good chance of achieving the primary objective. If one thinks of the goal while performing, he or she is incapable of becoming proficient in the fundamentals. The "mind" must be removed in skiing, sex, tennis, and in all professional pursuits. These fourteen visionaries did just that. They became the best they could become and power, fortune, and fame were the by-products of their focus.

Examples in history are rampant. Columbus was looking for the Indies and found America. Darwin was a trained minister whose inquisitiveness created the theory of evolution. Bell was looking for a cure for hearing disorders and invented the telephone. Einstein was a postal clerk when he propounded the theory of relativity. The Marquis de Sade lived his whole life as a paradox. He was a dedicated atheist living in a Roman Catholic country, a nobleman in Revolutionary France, and a sadomasochist during the height of the Enlightenment. His bizarre behavior caused him to spend his life in jail, but had he not gone to jail he would never have become a famous writer-philosopher or a symbol for the surrealist movement. Both Napoleon and Hitler were paradoxes of the first order. Both rose to dictatorial power in politics where all power comes from a constituency. The power is given from below, it is not taken by force, except in rare cases like Attila the Hun who lived in an era devoid of other power sources. Both Hitler and Napoleon used their charismatic powers to convince an unhappy and distraught electorate to give them total power. What is amazing is that neither one of these men were of the same nationality as the electorate which gave them power. True empathy with those whom they led was impossible, so these two driven men were forced to use other means of persuasion. Napoleon used Austrian and British threats while Hitler utilized the threat of communism and starvation to gain power and influence. Such success demands an awesome amount of moxie, guts, and charisma. Both of these despots had these traits in abundance.

The danger in giving cultlike leaders such power is that they virtually never give it back. In a December 1994 article in *Parade* magazine, Carl Sagan wrote about the frightening menace of cultists. He said, "Once you give such a charlatan power over you, you almost never get it back." The paradox of Napoleon and Hitler is that both were able to gain dictatorial power on a platform of passionate nationalism. The irony is that the Corsican Napoleon (of Italian heritage and speaking broken French) and the Austrian Hitler were both able to take over nations steeped in a nationalistic ideology. They overcame these obstacles through the power of their wills. Napoleon convinced the French people to crown him emperor at age thirty-three based on his military success in Italy. Hitler assumed dictatorial power in Germany as its führer (leader) in 1933 based on his promise to save the nation from Jewish exploitation and Communistic threats. Once in power he led millions of Germans to their death based on Aryan supremacy and the dream of establishing a master race. Hitler, like Napoleon, never allowed the truth to get in the way of his objective, and once in power never relinquished it. His power of persuasion resulted in the deaths of forty million people.

Many paradoxes surround the lives of successful people. Montessori was a medical doctor who hated the idea that the only professional opportunity for her was in education, yet she ultimately revolutionized the world of education. Isadora Duncan rejected ballet after signing up for one lesson and quit to found her own school of modern dance. Helena Rubinstein was asexual and never even dated until her thirties—long after she started her business based on making women seductive. Walt Disney so hated art that he never allowed the word to be used at Disney Studios, yet he revolutionized the artistry of the cartoon character. Similarly,

Picasso detested art schools, yet became the father of his own school, cubism. Frank Lloyd Wright is probably the greatest paradox. This child of a Baptist minister violated every principle of the church when he abandoned his business, wife, and six children for a wild fling with the wife of one of his clients. The paradoxes of these fourteen visionaries are illustrated in the following list.

Paradoxes of Power

How could a Corsican immigrant, who spoke broken French, use nationalism to become emperor of a foreign nation and lead millions of Frenchmen to their death?

How did a mediocre cartoonist, who hated artists, build the most creative animated art works in history?

What allowed a fifth-grade dropout, who never took a dance lesson, to create modern dance and revolutionize the art?

How was an average female pilot able to gain the reputation as the "Goddess of the Air" and become the world's most famous aviatrix?

How could a loser who never held a job in his life before age forty become the most tyrannical dictator in the twentieth century when he wasn't even a citizen of this powerful nation?

How could a risk-oriented man like Howard Hughes, who was willing to risk his life and fortune with total abandon, be petrified of germs and flies?

What motivated a woman who detested teaching as a profession to spend her life revolutionizing that profession?

How could a puritanical fundamentalist become rich and famous by building a newspaper empire through the use of blatant, salacious, and pornographic reporting?

How could a woman who could not read a note of music become Europe's greatest chanteuse?

How was Picasso able to create a whole new school of art—cubism—when he hated all art schools and the art establishment with a passion?

How could an asexual woman, who needed no man, become the First Lady of Beauty by making women seductive?

How did being raised in a Jesuit abbey mold the man who created "sadism" and spawn the world's most famous sexual intellectual?

Why would a life-long pacifist create destructive death rays and earth-splitting oscillators capable of annihilating mankind?

Why did the creative masterpieces of the world's greatest architect leak? And what motivated this fundamentalist to abandon his wife and six children plus a thriving business during the height of his career?

1

Nature vs Nurture: Creativity and Power

Many things that are attributed to biological prewiring are not produced by self-ish, determinist genes, but rather by social interactions under nonequilibrium conditions.

—Alvin Toffler, *Order Out of Chaos*

No human quality is beyond change.

—Jerome Kagan, Harvard psychologist

Drives and Dreams vs Genes and Means

This book is about power and personality. It is not about genetic endowments. It is about fourteen people who used average attributes to attain super power. Silver spoons, Ivy League educations, MENSA IQs, and social-register status are not essential to acquiring and maintaining power. Superpowerful people are able to "take" power because they truly believe they deserve it. These visionaries believed in themselves and their belief endowed them with the attributes that led them to enormous power.

Instant power, like instant gratification, is an exercise in mental masturbation. Great power emanates from years of sweat and toil and cannot be attained overnight. It is the by-product of enormous mental, emotional, and physical struggle. True power comes from within. Knowledge and authoritarian and charismatic powers are merely the external manifestations of an indomitable internal belief system. Even when one's beliefs are deluded, the pack is willing to follow, which will be illustrated in the chapters on Napoleon, Hitler, and Hughes.

Mozart was an anomaly and Forrest Gump was not just a Hollywood fantasy. Superstars and creative geniuses are ordinarily endowed people with abnormal drives. They are obsessed with "actualizing" their own internal dreams and self-images. Such people are bred, not born. History has given us numerous examples of people with few genetic gifts who attained power. The great learned to be great. Muhammad was a common camel driver who turned Mecca into a citadel because of a spiritual revelation that inspired him to write the Koran. Columbus had few redeeming qualities other than a vision that he was driven to fulfill. A bolt of lightning transformed Martin Luther from a law student into a religious reformer. Fear and imagination led him to great religious power. Loss of hearing became the motivation for Beethoven's greatest symphony—the Ninth. Being born a cripple was not a detriment to Lord Byron—it was his inspiration.

Thomas Edison parlayed three months of formal education into the most prolific inventive career in history. Einstein violated all traditions in a dogmatic field like physics. He visualized the concept of relativity in his early teens and admitted to never having another truly original thought after adulthood. He said: "Once you are sophisticated you know too much—far too much." Einstein always ignored the experts and changed the world in the process. He advised: "The gift of fantasy has meant more to me than my talent for absorbing positive facts." Abraham Lincoln was so simple and basic that he was a perennial loser. Tenacity and drive allowed him to become one of America's greatest presidents. The name Stalin means "steel" in Russian. Joseph Stalin grew up to fulfill his childhood destiny by exacting a despotic revenge on a weak constituency. Stalin learned violence from a drunken and abusive father, which nurtured a revolutionary spirit even though he was being groomed for the ministry. All of the above are examples of successful people inspired to fulfill their internal images and fantasies and in so doing achieving enormous power and success.

Talent Is of Little Import

Failure imprints an indomitable resolve in certain people. Milton Hershey turned adversity into drive, which led to a dynasty in chocolate. Handyman Will Kellogg was afraid of being fired when he forgot to refrigerate wheat dough. Instead of throwing it out, he put it through the roller and it flaked into a cereal fortune. Elvis Presley ignored a horrid reputation as a gospel singer to become the "king" of rock 'n' roll. "Mad Henry" Ford failed repeatedly in business but realized his dream of building a car for the average man (the Model T), thereby revolutionizing automobile mass-production techniques. Even Freud, the man primarily associated with "sex," was an asexual individual who stumbled on psychoanalysis by accident while treating emotional problems.

It took a Siberian prison to transform Dostoevsky from a disillusioned journeyman writer into a great author. John D. Rockefeller turned moxie into money just as Ernest Hemingway utilized a distorted imagination to create provocative novels. Andrew Carnegie rose from the gutter with little raw talent. Drive and inspiration transformed him into a great entrepreneur and philanthropist with twenty-five hundred libraries as testimony to his greatness. Mother Teresa created the Sisters of Mercy out of a passion for nurturing the sick and not out of any need for power, yet it has made her into the most powerful woman in the Catholic church. Ray Kroc was a middle-class milk-shake salesman who transformed a dream into the miracle called fast food. Ty Cobb and Pete Rose are the quintessential examples of baseball players with mediocre talent who rose to the top. They utilized an average talent for hitting a baseball into the most hits in baseball history—a case of mind over muscle or will over genes. There is little question that drive and dreams win out over talent and genetics every time as illustrated by the above superstars. It is not so important the hand we are dealt, but the desire and obsession with which we play that hand. Will and drive are far more important than all the talent in the world.

Born or Bred?

Francis Galton ascribed all great genius to genetics. He spent years attempting to validate his premise that ability was inherited through genes. His work *Hereditary Genius* (1892) was a self-aggrandizing effort to prove that genes were responsible for his cousin Charles Darwin's genius. Intellectuals and academia are wont to believe Galton's premise that all success is a function of family heritage. Such people are determinists, convinced that successful people are living out a preordained destiny. They believe that nature, not nurture, is the secret ingredient for all creative success. On the contrary, based on the family histories of these fourteen visionaries, heritage had little or nothing to do with their success. They were programmed early in life with unique personality traits that appear to have been critical to their success. They had *Drive, Tenacity, Vision, Work, Confidence, Risk Taking,* and a *Renegade Nature.* These traits were acquired and not inherited. Individuals with these traits are those who make it to the top in creative and entrepreneurial ventures despite the lack of genetic gifts.

POWER AND SUCCESS ARE LEARNED

Napoleon graduated forty-second out of fifty-eight graduates from the École Militaire in Paris. Historians have commented on his early mediocrity. How did a man with such average credentials, reared in an average family of seven average brothers and sisters, become the greatest military genius in history? Even more remarkable, how did the son of a perpetually unemployed minister become the most renowned architect in history? Frank Lloyd Wright's father was so inept that he was never able to keep a job more than one year in twenty years. Based on the genetic theory of creative genius, one would think Disney's forefathers would have been steeped in creative talent. Walt Disney's father was even more inept than Wright's. He failed in running a motel and a Florida orange grove, and as carpenter, farmer, and manufacturer. Did Amelia Earhart become the "Goddess of the

Air" from inherited genes? Did she inherit her temerity and style from a drunken father or a submissive mother? No way! Amelia adored her father but admitted that he was a failure in every professional venture he ever undertook, and Amelia nurtured her mother from middle age on.

Did Picasso inherit his painting skills from an artist father? No chance! Picasso's father was a mediocre artist at best and failed in every responsible position he ever held. The only major contribution Don Jose Ruiz made in Picasso's education was to bribe Spanish officials to get young Pablo through grade school. How did Edith Piaf, abandoned, illiterate, and unable to read one note of music, rise to become the greatest chanteuse in Europe? It certainly wasn't genes. Even Howard Hughes was an enigma relative to his heritage. He inherited Hughes Tool from an entrepreneurial father and paranoia from a hypochondriac mother. When his father died, he left young Howard $650,000 after a lifetime of hard work. Howard then demonstrated true entrepreneurial flair in parlaying the inheritance into a billion-dollar empire encompassing many industries. Howard certainly benefited from an entrepreneurial heritage, but his success was the result of the driven personality he developed along the way.

SUCCESS AND FAILURE IMPRINTS

These subjects learned to be powerful and successful during their impressionable youths or through some metamorphosis, crisis, or other experience that molded them with the key traits for success. Daniel Goleman in *Emotional Intelligence* (1995) said: "Emotional learning is lifelong . . . and can have a profound impact on temperament, either amplifying or muting an innate predisposition" (p. 221). Jerome Kagan, the eminent Harvard psychologist, has studied childhood development and believes all infants are born with a proclivity for being timid, bold, upbeat, or melancholy. But he found that those predispositions are often altered even while in the crib. In his study he found that "the emotionally competent . . . children spontaneously outgrew their timidity." Goleman observed that "we are not necessarily limited to a specific emotional menu by out inherited traits. . . . Our genes alone do not determine behavior; our environment, especially what we experience and learn as we grow, shapes how a temperamental predisposition expresses itself as life unfolds" (p. 224).

Harvard pediatrician T. Berry Brazelton found that infants in a crib learn "success" and "failure" by interacting with their environment. In a study where children were taught to place blocks together in their cribs, Dr. Brazelton found they were either imprinted with a "greatness" or a "hangdog" image of themselves, depending on their success or failure in the block experiment. He said those who failed would express their failure in their demeanor and take on an expression which said, "I'm not good. See. I've failed." Brazelton's children had what I refer to as a "failure imprint," which results in a losing persona that continues on into adulthood unless modified with a "success imprint." Brazelton observed that those children who experienced "success imprints"—putting blocks together successfully—would beam with a bright-eyed look of omnipotence that communicated, "Tell me how great I am." Success begets success and failure begets failure, making it critical to imbue oneself with successful experiences instead of failure experiences, both of which are destined to be replicated later in life.

ACQUIRED MANIA

Nothing in the genetic histories of these fourteen visionaries indicated they were destined for future success. They were certainly bright, aggressive, and reasonably healthy. Beyond inheriting a slightly above-normal intelligence (115–140 IQ), a fair share of testosterone (competitive and thrill-seeking drive), and normal physical bodies, they were normal people with abnormal drive and energy. Their particular genetic gifts are found in many millions of people who do not achieve beyond the norm. Then what made *them* great? *Mania* for pursuing their dreams was one overwhelming factor. Another was their *dysfunctional personalities.* Most were driven from some internalized need to be the very best and to pursue their dreams with a passion seldom seen in the normal population. Was this mania learned or inherited? Substantial evidence indicates it was learned. Were these fourteen what one would call well-adjusted personalities? Not in the classic sense. They were abnormally driven to achieve and were hypomanic in their methodology. All but one had a Type A personality and they all exhibited various forms of dysfunctional behavior. Most were manically driven, which often resulted from some great trauma in their early lives.

What was their secret? How did they acquire such a strong work ethic, tenacity, intuitive skills, and temerity? What made them so different and driven? Intelligence certainly was not the key variable. And none started with as much money as they ended with. None were born with Mozart-like precociousness. Most were reared in average middle-class families. So what allowed them to gain such incredible power and influence? One of the major factors I have coined is a "Manic Success Syndrome." All exuded a kind of manic need to succeed at any cost. They were driven people who would not allow anything or anyone to interfere with the realization of their dreams. Rupert Murdoch biographer Thomas Kiernan searched for factors that could have molded Murdoch into such a driven man. He interviewed one of Murdoch's school friends at Geelong Preparatory School in Melbourne, Australia, which gave him some insight into this media mogul's drive. The school friend said, "I don't think Rupert was born with the traits that have sullied his reputation as a grown-up. He developed them out of his desperation to encourage his father's approval when he was growing up. . . . If you ask me, the Rupert Murdoch of today is very much a creation of his father" (Kiernan 1986, p. 19). This is a common finding in the rest of the fourteen, although the men were more influenced by their mothers and the women by their fathers.

EXPERIENTIAL IMPACT

What drove Picasso to become the most prodigious artist in history, producing in excess of fifty thousand works of art? Why would Nikola Tesla, a millionaire by age thirty-three, sleep only two hours a night in a mad need to solve the mysteries of science? What drove Walt Disney to sleep in his studio for months to produce *Snow White,* almost destroying his health and marriage in the process, when he had already created Mickey Mouse, Pluto, and Donald Duck? I hope to give a plausible explanation in this and the next chapter.

One truth is self-evident from these psychohistories. It is not money, family background, intelligence, formal schooling, or other mysterious talent that account for success. It appears that the critical traits for success were acquired by these fourteen during lifetime experiences through interaction with early role models, mentors both real and imagined, and the many crises that armed them with a frenetic need to achieve. In other words, they learned to be great from an inner need that had been imprinted and conditioned, not inherited.

Francis Galton's theory that genius is a function of inherited intelligence set the stage for the controversial book *The Bell Curve* (Murray and Herrnstein 1994), which attempted to correlate all success with intelligence. Both Galton and *The Bell Curve* used a deterministic hypothesis to suggest that all great achievement emanates from intelligence, which in turn is preordained by one's genes. To some degree Galton was justifying his own heritage, having been related to Charles Darwin. Biologist Edwin O. Wilson disagrees: "Genes *do not* determine behavior, but only produce a tendency that can be ignored or controlled" (Leman 1985). Reviewing the psychohistories of these fourteen subjects, none descended from a powerful ancestry or successful parents as Galton suggested. In fact, the fathers and grandparents of Disney, Duncan, Earhart, Picasso, Piaf, and Wright were considered failures. The fathers of Napoleon, Hitler, Montessori, Rubinstein, Sade, and Tesla were average middle-class individuals who provide no clue to the creative genius and achievement bent of their famous offspring.

LEARNED SUCCESS

The only two subjects born of successful parents were Howard Hughes and Rupert Murdoch. Both had successful fathers whose success paled in comparison to their famous sons. Hughes's father was a successful entrepreneur who started the Hughes Tool Company which Howard inherited in 1924. Within twenty years young Howard had parlayed his $650,000 inheritance into $1 billion. Howard, Sr., never achieved success outside of Houston, Texas, and was never completely solvent due to a turbulent life of wine, women, and song. Howard, Jr., assumed control of his father's business at age nineteen and used it as a springboard in building a worldwide empire of movies, airlines, casinos, silver mines, and real-estate holdings.

Rupert Murdoch inherited one small newspaper in Adelaide, Australia, at age twenty-one. His father, Keith Murdoch, was a prominent publisher in Australia. Murdoch is the only subject who had a successful father in the same profession. His father was a successful freelance writer and entrepreneur early in his career, prior to becoming a powerful corporate newspaper magnate in Melbourne. Keith's power was based on his position in a corporate hierarchy. Rupert, on the other hand, took his inheritance (one small marginal newspaper) and developed it into the most powerful worldwide media empire in history. His influence and power dwarfs that of Pulitzer or Hearst and encompasses four continents in various industries: newspapers, television, publishing, and airlines. In November 1994 *Forbes* magazine estimated Murdoch's worth at $4 billion. Not bad progress for a twenty-one-year-old who started with a small town daily paper worth $500,000 in 1954.

EVEN ARTISTS ARE MADE

Some will argue that Picasso inherited his talent for painting from his artist father. Not so! Picasso's father was a mediocre artist at best. His impact on Picasso was not genetic but emotional. Don José Ruiz was dedicated to making Pablo into a great painter. He himself was unable to keep a job, but he did exercise enormous influence over his son's emotional need to paint. Don José instilled the passion for art in Picasso. One indication is Pablo's ability to paint before he spoke. His first word was *piz* for pencil and his reward was sweets for producing a drawing. His behavior and schoolwork were not rewarded, which motivated Picasso to disregard everything but painting. Picasso and his father were exact opposites, physically, emotionally, and mentally. Don José was a tall, thin, and elegant man who was well mannered and pleasant. Picasso was short, squat, abusive, and an arrogant tyrant, oblivious of the feelings of others. Picasso was raised by indulgent aunts, sisters, and a mother who told him as a young child, "If you become a soldier, you'll be a general. If you become a monk, you'll end up as pope." The egoistic Picasso responded by creating mystical and godlike art to match his internal vision of himself. His great success was learned, not inherited. His egomania knew no bounds, which was illustrated by the painting he created for his family when he left for Paris at age nineteen. Picasso's self-portrait was signed "I the King." His die was cast.

EVEN SCIENTIFIC GENIUS IS BRED

Nikola Tesla purportedly inherited a phenomenal memory from his mother. At least he gave her the credit in his autobiography. Tesla's father was an Orthodox minister and his mother an illiterate housewife with a photographic memory. Tesla was a precocious child but driven with an obsession for perfection. Nikola was certainly bright, probably the brightest of these subjects, but his memory, intuition, and intelligence were not that different from millions of others. These gifts were hardly the causal factor for the person who has been called the greatest inventive genius in history. Both Picasso and Tesla were manic personalities with a herculean work ethic. They were both driven and endowed with a psychic energy that could not be denied. They also shared many similar behavior patterns and personality traits (intuition, work ethic, independence, obsessional drive, and a Promethean temperament) all common to the other subjects and the real basis for their consummate success and power.

Common Personality Traits

Seven key behavior traits appear to have been responsible for the supersuccess and power of these fourteen visionaries: *Intuition* (vision), *Self-Esteem* (confidence), *Risk-Taking Propensity* (temerity), *Rebellion* (independence), *Obsessive Willpower* (drive), *Type A Work Ethic* (energy), *and Tenacity* (perseverance). These traits were recurrent themes during the research on these subjects and are universal patterns found in most entrepreneurial and creative geniuses.

EXPERIENTIAL DERIVATION OF TRAITS

How were these traits acquired? In these subjects it was early childhood experiences and traumas that imprinted the key traits and formed their unique personalities. Early experiential factors also led to their various abnormal behavioral characteristics, which also contributed to their success and power. Most were so different that they were labeled dysfunctional by their friends and often megalomaniacs by their enemies. Unique and at times bizarre behavior—hypomania, obsessive-compulsiveness, manic depression, and Type A behavior—appear to have contributed greatly to their success in life. The most common intrinsic or causal factors that appear to have been responsible for molding their characters were: birth order, transiency, little formal education, mythological hero mentors, early traumas, positive role models, and permissive family environments. Each of these proved instrumental in the formation of the unique personalities that ultimately made these subjects great.

Birth order	Firstborns are groomed for a life of perfectionism, leadership, and drive, and have the responsibility of wearing the family mantle of leadership.
Frequent travel/transiency	Instills self-sufficiency, independence, perseverance, temerity, and ability to cope with the unknown. Children learn how to effectively deal with ambiguity.
Little formal education	Instills the need to overachieve. Insecurity makes children try harder. Boarding schools instill autonomy, independence, and self-confidence.

Fantasy hero mentors	Imprint children with an unconscious feeling of omnipotence and remove all limits for potential achievement. Great role models for achievement.
Early traumas	Early crises indelibly imprint children with unusual resolve and endow them with higher than normal risk-taking propensity and drive.
Positive role models	Independent and self-employed fathers instill autonomous spirit and demonstrate ability to make it in the world outside a corporate womb.
Permissive families	Instill temerity and independence. Freedom to risk and err without remorse builds coping skills and positive/optimistic views of the unknown.

"Manic Success Syndrome" and the Dysfunctional Personality

High energy emanates from the mind, not the body and is often the by-product of a driven personality. The lives and experiences of these subjects clearly demonstrate that abnormal drive or high energy is conducive to superachievement. Anyone interested in launching the greatest breakthrough product, producing the most universally renowned art, revolutionizing social systems, creating a whole new scientific paradigm, or becoming a superentertainer must have high energy. Such individuals often are viewed as frenetic overachievers and social deviants. Rock stars must have greater insight on this issue than most as they lead reckless lifestyles and pride themselves on being different—both important to great achievement. Great entrepreneurs also exhibit high energy and tend to be different. Leaders are never normal by any barometer. That is not surprising since all great breakthroughs demand what Harvard's Joseph Schumpeter called "creative destruction." This premise suggests that anything "new" cannot be created without a willingness to destroy the "old." One must be prepared to sacrifice the "existing present" to create an "opportunistic future." These visionaries certainly qualified on the creative destruction definition and were also culturally diverse in the context of society's norms for behavior. I have categorized these manic successes into four divergent personality types that appear to contribute to success. These four are: *Type A, manic-depressive, obsessive-compulsive,* and *hypomanic personalities* (see figure 3).

IT PAYS TO BE A LITTLE CRAZY

Experts on the subject of dysfunctional behavior agree that the majority of creative geniuses are abnormal personalities. In 1931 Ernst Kretschmer wrote *The Psychology of Men of Genius* in which he concluded that manic depression was a necessary factor in all genius. He said, "The spirit of genius . . . is no free-floating, absolute power, but is strictly bound to the laws of blood chemistry and the endocrine

FIGURE 3
PERSONALITY DYSFUNCTIONS OF CREATIVE GENIUS

Definitions (American Psychiatric Glossary based on *Diagnostic and Statistical Manual of Mental Disorders* [*DSM-IV*]):

Mania:	A mood disorder characterized by excessive elation, inflated self-esteem, and grandiosity, hyperactivity, agitation, and accelerated thinking or speaking.
Obsessive-Compulsive:	An anxiety disorder characterized by obsessions, compulsions, or both.
Manic-Depressive:	A mood disorder featuring a *manic* episode and/or recurrent episodes that are manic or depressive in nature (also known as bipolar disorder).
Type A Behavior:	A temperament characterized by excessive drive, competitiveness, a sense of time urgency, impatience, unrealistic ambition, and need for control.

Creative Genius	Manic	Obsessive-Compulsive	Manic-Depressive	Type A
Napoleon Bonaparte	Yes	No	Yes	A+
Walt Disney	Yes	Yes	Yes	Yes
Isadora Duncan	Yes	No	No	No
Amelia Earhart	No	No	No	A–
Adolf Hitler	Yes	No	Yes	Yes
Howard Hughes	Yes	Yes	Yes	Yes
Maria Montessori	No	No	No	A–
Rupert Murdoch	Yes	No	No	A+
Edith Piaf	Yes	No	Yes	A–
Pablo Picasso	Yes	No	No	A+
Helena Rubinstein	No	No	No	A+
Marquis de Sade	Yes	Yes	Yes	Yes
Nikola Tesla	Yes	Yes	Yes	A+
Frank Lloyd Wright	Yes	No	No	Yes
TOTALS	11	4	7	13

glands." In the *Key to Genius* (1988) D. Jablow Hershman and Julian Lieb concluded that "manic depression is almost indispensable to genius because of the advantages it can supply, and that if there have been geniuses free from manic depression, they have been a minority" (p. 11). They argue that "mania bestows abnormal energy," which leads to creative genius. Anthony Storr in *The Dynamics of Creation* (1993) said that "Einstein provides the supreme example of how schizoid detachment can be put to creative use" (p. 83). These fourteen subjects were all viewed as a little crazy by the media, and operated with an abnormally high level of manic energy that became a catalyst in their success.

ABNORMALITY AND SUCCESS

Individuals with *normal* aspirations and goals typically achieve normal success and those with *abnormal* aspirations and goals typically achieve abnormal success. Normal individuals fit into the middle of the distribution curve. Their success in life hardly ever places them in the two extremes of distribution where great success and abysmal failure reside. Their normal aspirations ensure normal success and guarantee that they will avoid terrible failure, but predestine them to mediocrity. Conversely, it is virtually impossible for the abnormal visionary to end up in the middle of the distribution curve where mediocrity presides. The visionary either makes it very big in life or becomes a miserable flop. These fourteen were abnormally driven and therefore ended up as eminent successes. Virtually all people with abnormal dreams and drives end up either like these visionaries or on skid row, which prompts the aphorism, *Supersuccess and power emanate from the impossible dreams of abnormal people.* Great success demands deviance from the norm and also requires great temerity. Those who are afflicted with "rushing sickness" are better equipped to succeed.

TYPE A PERSONALITIES

Abnormal personalities may be the creative geniuses and innovators but they are difficult to deal with both personally and professionally. All but one of these fourteen subjects were Type A personalities (see figure 3). Type A personalities make impossible bosses, tending to be tyrannical and demanding. Both Rubinstein and Murdoch were hated and considered ruthless and overaggressive by their employees. Type As typically justify unrealistic expectations of others since they also demand such results of themselves. While such individuals do not make the ideal boss or employee, they do successfully perform and meet impossible goals. They typically outperform their peers because of their competitive natures and maniacal need to succeed. Anyone desirous of enormous achievement must be willing to tolerate the Type A personality. As the old adage goes, "If you want something accomplished, give it to a busy person." The reason "busy" people are capable of producing instant results is that they have an internal need to fit more and more into less and less time.

DRIVE AND SUPERACHIEVEMENT

Driven personalities are compelled to satiate an internal need for achievement independent of any external rewards. Such individuals should be given the necessary resources and left to their own devices. There is no need for monitoring their work as they are self-motivated. They achieve because they "have" to emotionally, not for the organization, but for their own personal ego gratification. These individuals are self-driven and will work passionately, if not pathologically, to succeed at any cost. No price is too great for them to pay either personally or professionally, which begs the aphorism, "Successful performance demands employing a Type A or Hypomanic personality. Conformity demands employing a Type B personality." Some of the personalities in this book were more A than others. Napoleon, Rupert Murdoch, Picasso, Helena Rubinstein, and Nikola Tesla were off-the-scale Type A+s. They were impatient, intolerant, impulsive, workaholics with short attention spans, and obsessed with winning at life. They were in such a hurry that I tagged them with a "rushing sickness" label in chapter 9. Eight of the subjects were Type A−, as they were less driven than the above five. Of the fourteen subjects, only Isadora Duncan was not classified as a Type A personality, but even she was driven.

MANIC DEPRESSION AND SUCCESS

Seven of the subjects (Napoleon, Disney, Hitler, Hughes, Piaf, Sade, and Tesla) were manic-depressive personalities who vacillated between states of mania and depression. Kay Jamison, an authority on manic-depressive disorders, has done extensive research on manic-depressive creative artists. Her work *Touched with Fire* (1993) defined the manic-depressive personality as having "many features of hypomania—such as outgoingness, increased energy, intensified sexuality, increased risk taking, persuasiveness, self-confidence, and heightened productivity—have been linked with increased achievement and accomplishments" (p. 87). Her research was based only on artists. The manic subjects in this book confirm Jamison's findings. Their enormous success appears to have been a direct result of the manic side of their disorder, not the depressed side. Unfortunately these subjects were not always in their manic state. Lord Byron, a classic manic-depressive, said, "I can never get people to understand that poetry is the expression of *excited passion,* and that there is no such thing as a life of passion any more than a continuous earthquake, or an eternal fever." Jamison found that when manic-depressive personalities are in an "intensely creative episode," they exhibit "high enthusiasm, energy, and self-confidence." Napoleon, Disney, Hitler, Hughes, Sade, and Tesla had similar experiences that elevated them to greater achievements. Their success instilled confidence, which gave them still more success until they became megalomaniacs, so confident they were convinced they were infallible. Jamison also believes manic depression is an inherited disorder. The seven individuals in this book (Napoleon, Disney, Hitler, Hughes, Piaf, Sade, Tesla) indicate no such genetic influence.

OBSESSIVE-COMPULSIVES

Four of the subjects were obsessive-compulsive. Walt Disney went through periods of continual hand-washing and had a lifelong affliction with facial tics and eye-twitching similar to Howard Hughes. Hughes's bouts with obsessive-compulsive behavior were common knowledge. He ate twelve peas—no more and no less—at each meal for many years. He watched the same movies hundreds of times as a compulsive voyeuristic sexual fantasy. One of his more bizarre obsessions was with flies. Hughes hired three permanent body guards just to catch flies so they would not land on his food (Tesla would throw away a whole meal if a fly just landed on his table). His greatest obsession was with germs. Any dish or plate used by a guest would be broken after the meal and new ones purchased. Howard refused to open any door without the use of gloves or tissues. Hughes's obsessive-compulsive behavior was a by-product of his perfectionism, which was his greatest asset in business. In life it became his greatest liability.

It is hard to believe but Nikola Tesla was even more obsessed than Hughes. Tesla had a compulsion to finish whatever he started no matter the cost in time or energy. He read a hundred volumes of Voltaire in one semester while in college, wanting to quit after the first volume but unable to do so. If he started walking in one direction around a block, he couldn't stop and would have to walk all the way around even if he knew it was the wrong way. He compulsively computed the cubic contents of every meal and used exactly eighteen napkins at each meal for recleaning the table utensils. Tesla refused to stay in any hotel room whose number was not divisible by three. Women's earrings and hair created a horrid anxiety for Tesla. No wonder he never ate a meal alone with a woman in his whole life or ever married. Tesla had the same compulsions for work, which is what made him famous, although his compulsions forced him to live alone and die a virgin.

Freud would have classified Sade as the consummate anal-retentive personality. The Marquis de Sade was so obsessed with sodomy (anal sex) that he wrote volumes on the subject. Before his imprisonment, Sade would write erotic but professional plays where he could play the protagonist and thereby act out his wildest fantasies. These plays were the cause of his initial incarceration when he created a scene utilizing aphrodisiacs and was accused of poisoning the prostitutes-turned-actresses. Sade was never able to control his basic obsessions and knew he would never be able to, telling his political adversaries, "Kill me or take me as I am, because I will not change" (Lever 1993, p. 313). Both Sade and Tesla had a mysterious obsession with numbers and devised bizarre numerical systems which only they understood. Wright had a similar obsession with numbers.

HYPOMANIA

Hypomania is a mood disorder characterized by excessive elation; inflated grandiosity; hyperactivity; agitation; and accelerated thinking, speaking, and working. Eleven of the fourteen subjects were "manic" personalities. They were not always in a euphoric state of mania but vacillated between normal states and a mania state depending on the importance of their undertaking. Only three individuals were not inclined to mania—Amelia Earhart, Maria Montessori, and Helena Rubinstein—but even these women were Type A personalities. All of the men were hypomanic. Helena Rubinstein was driven to produce more and more and has been selected as the prototypical Type A personality for this book along with Rupert Murdoch. Figure 3 categorizes all the subjects into one or more of the four dimensions of abnormally driven behavior. All were driven to be the very best in their profession although in different ways. They all were willing to sacrifice marriage, family, or personal happiness for the redemption of their dream. Hitler, Montessori, and Tesla never bothered to marry because they felt such a relationship was contrary to fulfilling their professional dreams. Hitler finally married just prior to committing suicide in the Berlin bunker but did so after his professional destiny was sealed. Isadora Duncan married later in life and it had nothing to do with a permanent relationship. Those who married only did so out of convenience (Rubinstein, Earhart, Sade), to salve some psychological need (Hughes, Piaf, Duncan), or to have children to carry on their heritage (Napoleon, Wright, Disney, Picasso). Those who did enter into traditional marriages tended to give their spouses second or third priority in their lives. One common denominator in their personal lives was a manically induced single focus to follow their dreams, never allowing anything or anybody to interfere with their lives until those dreams were realized.

IQ Scores/Intelligence

Howard Gardner, a Harvard researcher on types of intelligence and the creative process, said, "It is clear that psychometric creativity is independent of psychometric intelligence, once a threshold IQ of 120 has been reached" (*Creating Minds,* 1993). Neil McAleer wrote in *Omni* magazine (April 1989): "No correlation between measured IQ and creativity exists. Intuition, more than rational thought, appears to be vital to the creative thinking process." A long-term researcher on the creative personality, Frank Barron wrote in *Creative Personality and Creative Process* (1969): "For certain intrinsically creative activities a specific minimum IQ is probably necessary to engage in the activity at all, but beyond that minimum which is often surprisingly low, creativity has little correlation with scores on IQ tests." Herrnstein and Murray, in their controversial book *The Bell Curve* (1994) espoused the opposite view. They did a very comprehensive and commendable job in demonstrating the role of intelligence for society in defining a "cognitive elite" who are emerging as the movers and shakers of the world relative to organizational power. They predicted that "the twenty-first century will open on a world in which cognitive ability (intelligence) is the decisive dividing force" and maintain that "intelligence is fundamentally related to productivity" followed by "success and failure in the American economy, and all that goes with it, are increasingly a matter of the genes that people inherit" (p. 91). I find their work exacting and important research to consider. However, their findings are absolutely and unequivocally not in synch with the derivation of creative and entrepreneurial success. The psychobiographies of the world's greatest innovators, creators, and entrepreneurs prove that *intelligence is way down the list of important criteria for high achievement or attaining power in virtually any profession.* As Derek Bok, president of Harvard, said in

1985, "Test scores have a modest correlation with first-year grades and no correlation with what you do in the rest of your life."

IQ, SCHOOL GRADES, AND SUCCESS

Years of research by the Institute of Personality Assessment and Research—Berkeley (IPAR) shows that intelligence is not an important variable for success. The fourteen subjects in this book indicate creative genius is in no way correlated to high intelligence. *The Bell Curve* confirms that intelligence is highly correlated to school achievement and especially to acceptance in prestigious schools. High IQ also has fringe benefits such as gaining entry to Mensa groups and other intellectual organizations. But it is wrong to elevate a "cognitive elite" or anyone with high SAT or IQ scores to positions of eminence. Those positions are earned through hard work and other factors. Herrnstein and Murray and others in the "cognitive elite" are inclined to self-propagate their only quantitative position of power and intellectual pedigrees to a place of eminence. The truth is, very high IQ scores (intelligence) are usually counterproductive to great success in virtually every profession.

IQ AND BUREAUCRATIC POWER

Professors, psychometrists, economists, nuclear physicists, and the like are certainly highly correlated to IQ scores. Becoming a great artist or entrepreneur is definitely not correlated to intelligence. The reason is that superintelligent people tend to "intellectualize" when they should be "implementing." They are the individuals most guilty of "analysis paralysis" and "overmanaging." They tend to allow their intellects to affect all actions, to overintellectualize everything. Individuals who are too bright tend to overthink, overmanage, and overrationalize. They allow their intellectualizing to interfere with performance. Any great athlete knows that thinking is detrimental to performance. The thinking should take place before the match, prior to hitting the ball and before skiing down the mountain. Once the action is in process, thinking can only negatively impact performance. Getting to the very top in art, business, entertainment, humanities, politics, and science is similar to sports. It requires focus on action, not thinking. The reverse is true in bureaucratic environments.

INSECURITY BREEDS GREATNESS

Why are individuals who are not specially endowed or gifted the ones to achieve greatness? Have you noticed that the best athletic performances often occur when the protagonist has the flu or is otherwise less than healthy? The reason is that expectations are low and motivation high. Relaxed concentration is the formula for all great achievement in any profession. Low potential demands high performance, which dictates high drive for achievement. Ty Cobb and Pete Rose hold all of the hit records in baseball despite the fact that both were considered only average in skill or talent. It was their drive and need to achieve that made them great, not their genetic endowments. Those without a lot of formal education have a similar predilection for accomplishment. They know they must try harder and do so. The same holds true for those without 1400 SAT scores or a 140 IQ. None of the fourteen visionaries in this book were considered intellectually brilliant with the possible exception of Nikola Tesla, and even he admitted his success was based on his intuition and manic energy, not mental ability. According to Catherine Cox (*The Early Mental Traits of Three Hundred Geniuses*), Napoleon had a 140 IQ. If she was correct, his intelligence was certainly an asset in his becoming the most powerful man in Europe, but it certainly was not even close to being the critical variable that was responsible. Napoleon's drive, Promethean temperament, work ethic, comfort with high risk taking, and obsessional willpower were the basis for James McKeen Cattel labeling him the "most eminent personality in Western civilization" (Simonton 1994, pp. 217, 246). Although a smart driven leader will usually outperform a dumb driven leader there is no proof that Napoleon's intelligence in any way impacted his rise to glory. In fact, the findings in this book would indicate his "manic success syndrome" was far more important to his success than intelligence.

The Bell Curve Is a Graph—Success Is Earned

The Bell Curve argued that intelligence is more important than money or social station and that "the twenty-first century will open on a world in which cognitive ability [which the authors use interchangeably with "intelligence"] is the decisive dividing force in determining where an individual will end up in the social scale." In other words, they argue that the "cognitive elite" are destined to become the power brokers of the world who will dominate the "custodial state" and determine the future of the "underclasses" who are classified as the "cognitive deficient." On the contrary, I believe intelligence is antithetical to rising to the very top of any profession. Great power and success are a function of the many other traits that have been described in the psychobiographies of these fourteen wunderkinds. Intelligence can help up to a certain point after which it becomes counterproductive to the process. Other factors like the Seven Key Success Traits are far more critical to eminent achievement than high intelligence. Intelligence-quotient test scores may be highly correlated to school success and getting hired in bureaucratic organizations or accepted in Mensa, but are not critical to attaining great power or achievement on the street.

IQ AND BUREAUCRATIC SUCCESS

Dean Keith Simonton writes in *Greatness* (1994): "Mensa gatherings seem to amass the biggest collection of misfits and underachievers on this planet" (p. 220).

IQ scores are excellent barometers for success in institutional-type organizations and terrible barometers of success in any dynamic environment. *The Bell Curve*'s thesis that IQ and success are universally correlated is way off base. Real power will never emanate from any bureaucratic institution. Power and success emanate from creators, entrepreneurs, and innovators—not intellectual pedigrees. *The Bell Curve*'s "cognitive elite" may be destined to be the movers and shakers in governments and educational institutions but not in any dynamic business environment. Murray and Herrnstein even suggest that a "cognitive elite" or "overclass" will create a "custodial state" to manage the welfare state comprised of society's less intellectually gifted. Their suggestion that high-tech Native-American reservations will be created to control the "underclasses" of the "expanded welfare state" understandably irritated many people. These authors have lived their lives in a bureaucratic environment where great power is pyramidal and hierarchal due to authoritarian position. Bureaucratic institutions promote and propagate a mentality that attracts the intellectually elite. The "cognitive elite" are not effective in a dynamic world where change is pervasive and survival paramount. They tend to become the "self-preservation" mentalities who gravitate to the top by caretaking and protecting the asset base, the key attributes of bureaucrats. Such executives end up as high-pedigreed administrators who have sold their souls to the organization and survive by flaunting high IQ, and SAT scores or Ivy League educations to secure their places of positional power. Temerity, work ethic, tenacity, and risk-taking propensity are far more desirable traits than intellectual pedigrees.

PEDIGREES AND SUCCESS

Let's assume that Murray and Herrnstein are correct in their claim that blacks as a group are intellectually inferior to whites (they found a one standard deviation difference, 15 IQ points or 85 vs 100), and that social standing and education are also highly correlated to intelligence. So what? Most of the fourteen subjects in this book could never have gained entrance to an Ivy League school and if eligible would not have attended. Eleven of the fourteen came from the lower or middle classes which would have made them persona non grata to the upper echelons of the "cognitive elite" organizations. Eight never made it through high school (Disney, Duncan, Hitler, Hughes, Picasso, Piaf, Rubinstein, Sade) and only three graduated from college (Napoleon, Montessori, Murdoch), but all rose to the top of their professions. These fourteen were probably intellectually inferior to almost any graduate of an Ivy League school, yet achieved far more than any "cognitive elite" could ever hope to achieve.

The controversy over a "cognitive elite" dominating society and "intelligence" as the requirement for professional power is a waste of energy. High SAT and IQ scores may buy you entry into an Ivy League school and will assist you in highly competitive chess and scrabble games. A cognitive elite label will not make you a success and cannot make you a failure. It may keep you out of an elitist college but will have no bearing on your success either professionally or personally. A prime example of this tenet is Jules Henri Poincaré's scoring at the imbecile level on his friend Alfred Binet's intelligence test at a time when Poincaré was universally acknowledged as the world's greatest mathematical genius. John Kennedy scored 116 on an IQ test; Madonna scored a 140 on her high school IQ test. Should Madonna have had any greater success in a political career than Kennedy, or become an international diplomat or scientist? Intelligence scores of slightly above average appear important for anyone who desires to reach the very top of their profession. Lower and higher scores are probably detrimental to success. Otherwise intelligence should be admired but not revered.

Sociocultural Influence

Social standing in the community has little to do with achieving great success and power. Napoleon spoke halting French since he was of Corsican (Italian) heritage. Hitler was an Austrian with an inclination for Bohemian behavior as a young adult and never held a legitimate job until he was appointed führer of the German National Socialist Party in his mid-thirties. Both men ascended to the very top of foreign nations and led them to war based on a platform of nationalism. How were they able to convince a foreign constituency of their nationalistic ideology? It certainly wasn't their family heritage, social influence, or contacts. They were both notorious loners who selected and used people, then discarded them. Their success had absolutely nothing to do with sociocultural background or economic influence and was due to variables other than social status. The only pertinent family factor was having a self-employed father who espoused self-sufficiency.

SUCCESS COMES FROM MASSES, NOT CLASSES

Only three (Sade, Hughes, Murdoch) of the fourteen visionaries were raised in a privileged environment but in none of these cases was their background a factor in their later success. Only Rupert Murdoch's background could be construed as a factor in his early success. All three were born into well-to-do families with influence and connections. They had early economic advantages and attended private boarding schools, but these advantages appear to have had little or no effect on their later success. The one exception is that there appears to be a positive element in attending boarding schools, which instills independence and self-sufficiency. Napoleon did gain some important political connections at the Ecole Militaire, which allowed him to associate with the upper classes although they detested him. Three of the individuals (Duncan, Disney, Piaf) were raised in lower-class environments. Disney was not destitute, but was quite poor and forced to work as a child to buy candy and art supplies. Duncan was destitute as a child. Frequent evictions caused her to change schools like most kids change clothes. As a child Duncan became the family emissary to beg the butchers and bakers for food. At age ten the precocious girl from the streets quit school to start her own dance school. In her autobiography she wrote that these early experiences molded her into becoming a great dancer. Edith Piaf's early life is a classic rags-to-riches story. She was born in the streets of Paris and never knew a normal family life. Her only home was a brothel run by her paternal grandmother. The Great Piaf never learned the value of money because she had never had any, and only perceived it as a means to acquire the necessities of life. The majority of these subjects were better off than Piaf and raised in middle-class environments. Figure 4 summarizes their sociocultural and economic backgrounds by category.

FIGURE 4
SOCIOCULTURAL/ECONOMIC STATUS

Creative Genius	Sociocultural Background	Economic Status
Napoleon Bonaparte	Noble heritage	Middle class
Walt Disney	Blue-collar agrarian	Poor
Isadora Duncan	Professional musicians	Very poor
Amelia Earhart	White-collar working class	Middle class
Adolf Hitler	White-collar working class	Middle class
Howard Hughes	Affluent socialite mother	Wealthy upper class
Maria Montessori	Professional	Middle class
Rupert Murdoch	Affluent executive	Upper class
Edith Piaf	No class	Impoverished
Pablo Picasso	Professional artist	Middle class
Helena Rubinstein	White-collar business	Middle class
Marquis de Sade	Noble heritage	Upper class
Nikola Tesla	Professional clergy	Middle class
Frank Lloyd Wright	Professional clergy	Middle class

Birth Order

The first sixteen astronauts were firstborn children, as were over 50 percent of the U.S. presidents. Over half of all "notable creators, leaders, and celebrities of the twentieth century" are firstborn (Simonton 1994). What bearing does the order of birth have on creative genius? Firstborns have an internal need to achieve because it is instilled quite early that they are the torch-bearers for the family heritage. They become laden with the responsibility to achieve and are conditioned with a kind of perfectionism. Firstborns and only children have a better-than-average chance of winning a Nobel Prize and envision themselves as the "center of the universe" (Leman 1985). Simonton (*Greatness,* 1994) said, "Primogeniture implies intellectual superiority. . . . The first born is stimulated by the social interactions of mature adults; the later-borns grow up in a home increasingly inundated by the immature activities of older siblings." Kenneth Leman wrote in the *Birth Order Book* (1985): "firstborn and only-born children are preconditioned to a life of su-

perachievement. . . . They are superreliable and superconscientious." He added
that only children tend to be "impatient" and "intolerant" of others—a trait repeatedly found in these subjects. It appears from Leman's analysis that firstborn
boys are labeled "crown prince," which he says puts far more pressure on firstborn
males than on firstborn females to succeed. Only children tend to be "critical, pam-
pered, spoiled, and self-centered."

FIRSTBORN PERFECTIONISTS

Nine of the fourteen subjects were either only children (Sade, Hughes, Piaf,
Montessori) or firstborn (Hitler, Wright, Earhart, Rubinstein, Picasso). Three others were reared as firstborns for varying reasons (Tesla, Murdoch, Disney). Only
two were exceptions to the rule. Isadora Duncan was last-born with two older
brothers and two older sisters, and Napoleon was the second of eleven children
with one older brother, Joseph. It appears from this research that those children
born first or raised as if they were develop leadership qualities. They envision
themselves as out in front of the pack (siblings) and perform as leaders. This early
imprinting and expectation conditions them to act superior and to suffer fools
poorly. They are often seen as arrogant due to their high expectations and standards
for both themselves and others. They are alone but like the seclusion.

Rupert Murdoch's older sister Helen described Rupert as a "bit of a cat who
walked alone." Walking alone and assuming huge responsibility is important for
anyone desirous of leadership and power. Life at the top is a lonely vigil and learning the role early is a big advantage. Murdoch was not the firstborn, but as the first
male born in a chauvinistic society he was considered an *alpha male* (dominant
male) in the anthropomorphic sense. Walt Disney was also not the firstborn, but
his closest sibling Roy was eight years his senior. Psychologists have shown that
an age difference of over six years imbues the child with the same qualities as a
firstborn. It can also instill additional qualities due to the role models provided by
the older siblings, which was the case with Freud. Nikola Tesla was also raised as
a firstborn since his only older brother Dane died when Nikola was five. Even
more telling is the evidence of Nikola pushing his brother down a flight of steps,
causing his untimely death. Tesla's history of nervous afflictions, compulsions, obsessions, and manic behavior give credence to his guilt over his brother's death,
which will be addressed in more detail in chapter 2. Figure 5 lists the birth order
and sibling status for these subjects.

BOOKS AS COMPANIONS

Most of the fourteen subjects used books as substitutes for siblings or friends, especially the firstborn or only children. It was from books that they learned to fantasize and search for knowledge. Most were self-educated and it was books that
became their source of knowledge. Books ensured them of a far greater knowledge
than their formal education indicated, but voracious reading was often a function

FIGURE 5
BIRTH ORDER AND SIBLING ANALYSIS

Only Children

Howard Hughes	Father absent, mother hypochondriac	Sibling died before birth
Maria Montessori	Father absent, mother doting	
Edith Piaf	Raised in brothel after abandonment by mother	Stepsister Simone
Marquis de Sade	Father absent, mother indifferent	Sibling died year before birth

Firstborns

Amelia Earhart	Father absent, mother housewife	Younger sister
Adolf Hitler	Father abusive, mother doting	Younger sister
Pablo Picasso	Father and mother doting	Two younger sisters
Helena Rubinstein	Father and mother supportive	Seven younger sisters
Frank Lloyd Wright	Father absent, mother doting	Two younger sisters

Raised as Firstborn

Walt Disney	Father abusive, mother doting	Closest sibling, Roy, eight years older; one younger sister
Rupert Murdoch	Father older, mother permissive	One older sister; two younger sisters
Nikola Tesla	Father strict, mother mentor	Older brother died when Nikola was five; older sister; two younger sisters

Lower Birth Order

Isadora Duncan	Father absent, mother permissive	Last-born of four; two brothers and one sister
Napoleon Bonaparte	Father absent, mother distracted	Second of eleven with older brother, Joseph

of their birth order. History of great creative geniuses have shown a similar propensity for finding solace and heroic role models in books. Vincent Van Gogh was so inspired. He said, "I have a more or less irresistible passion for books, and I continually want to instruct myself, to study if you like, just as much as I want to eat my bread." Montessori was so enamored with books that she took them with her to the theater to the chagrin of her parents. Amelia Earhart and Isadora Duncan were constantly reading. Hitler's only companion on the front lines of World War I was a book by Schopenhauer. Napoleon was an avid reader, as was Sade. Both were enamored with Voltaire and Rousseau.

Lack of Formal Education

Only three of these visionaries had college educations: Napoleon, Murdoch, and Montessori. Napoleon was educated at the École Militaire where strategy and philosophy were emphasized. He was a poor student but was able to graduate in half the allotted time due to his manic need for speed. It is important to note that Napoleon is the only individual in this book to have achieved success in the field of his formal education. Rupert Murdoch studied political science, economics, and philosophy at Oxford and barely graduated due to poor grades and total disinterest. Maria Montessori was by far the most educated, but her schooling was in medicine and not in the psychology of education where she made her mark. In 1896 she became the first woman in history to graduate from the University of Rome Medical School. Montessori is by far the most educated of these subjects as she had substantial postgraduate work in anthropology and educational psychology. Figure 6 shows the formal education of the fourteen.

LEARNED DROPOUTS

Nine of these wunderkinds never made it through high school although Hughes, Hitler, Rubinstein, and Wright came close. Both Wright and Hughes took college courses. Edith Piaf had the least amount of education and was illiterate until age twenty-one when mentor/lover Raymond Asso took it upon himself to teach her to read and write. Isadora Duncan is a classic example of someone with virtually no formal education who was erudite through self-education. In many respects she was one of the better educated individuals in this book. Isadora never visited a city without spending days in its museums and art galleries, and read voraciously on philosophy and the classics throughout her life. She was conversant with the great works of art in writing, poetry, painting, sculpture, ballet, philosophy, and the Greek classics. Isadora Duncan left school at age ten in order to open a dance school in San Francisco. When experts asked her who taught her to dance she responded, "Terpsichore taught me." She wrote poetry and an eloquent autobiography. Picasso had less formal education than Duncan. It appears he may have been dyslexic, which could explain his deplorable school record. He could not stand school and was self-taught.

AMATEUR POETS AND WRITERS

Eight of the subjects wrote poetry as a hobby and many wanted to be philosophers. Napoleon was enamored with the philosophy of Rousseau and Voltaire, which later helped him to write the Napoleonic Code. Eight of the fourteen wrote one or more books. Earhart, Montessori, Wright, and Sade wrote more than one book, which is amazing since they were not writers by profession.

KNOWLEDGE BEGETS SUCCESS

All fourteen of these Promethean spirits revered knowledge and used their wisdom to attain the pinnacle of success. They were as knowledgeable as anyone in the world in their given profession with most of their education based on self-teaching. They also illustrate quite emphatically that too much knowledge in any field

FIGURE 6
FORMAL EDUCATION

Less than High School

Edith Piaf	Less than one year of schooling; illiterate until age twenty-one
Isadora Duncan	Dropped out of school in fifth grade, but voracious reader of philosophy and classics; wrote poetry and one book; erudite
Marquis de Sade	Middle school at College Louis le Grand, Paris; poor student, wrote poetry and many books in prison on philosophy and rebellion
Pablo Picasso	Primary school education; attended art academies in Barcelona and Madrid, wrote poetry and was an amateur philosopher
Helena Rubinstein	Dropped out of technical high school as poor student
Howard Hughes	Boarding school from age ten in Texas, Connecticut, Massachusetts, and California; dropped out of Thacher Academy, Santa Barbara, Calif.; one class at Cal Tech
Adolf Hitler	Dropped out of high school; failed entrance exam at Vienna Art Academy; voracious reader, especially of philosophy of Schopenhauer; wrote poetry and one book
Walt Disney	One year at Chicago McKinley High School; one semester at Chicago Academy of Arts
Frank Lloyd Wright	Madison, Wis., high school; one year at University of Wisconsin Engineering School; voracious reader; wrote poetry and book

High School and Some College

Amelia Earhart	Chicago high school graduate; attended Ogontz and Columbia; voracious reader who also wrote poetry and two books
Nikola Tesla	Boarding high school plus two years at Vienna Polytechnic in engineering; voracious reader; lifelong poet plus one book; taught himself six languages

College

Napoleon Bonaparte	Boarding schools from age ten; graduated from École Militaire in Paris; poor student but voracious reader of philosophy and the classics; wrote poetry
Rupert Murdoch	Geelong boarding school, age ten; Graduated Oxford in political science and economics; poor student

Graduate Degree

Maria Montessori	Rome high school, University of Rome premed and medical degree plus postgraduate psychology of education and anthropology; wrote many books

is probably a hindrance: one may attain a certain arrogance of expertise and become less and less capable of exploring new areas of thought in that field. Formal education is also notorious for setting limitations. When Nikola Tesla had the intuitive revelation for alternating current motors, his college professor informed him that such a concept was nonsense and "impossible." Fortunately for the world the irrepressible Tesla refused to believe him and within two years solved the problem which revolutionized electrical power and motors.

STUPIDITY AND INNOVATION

None of these subjects was overly trained in their disciplines. They were just stupid enough *not* to know what to do or where to go—and went there with great passion. Only Rupert Murdoch grew up in a family business—publishing—that would become his vehicle to the top. But even Murdoch refused to study journalism in school and violated all of the dogmas in an industry in which he was supposedly an expert. He approached his profession with a renegade attitude that appears to have allowed him to achieve more than otherwise would have been possible. Hughes knew nothing about movies or aviation, yet became an enormous success in each industry. Piaf couldn't read a note of music but became the "Great Piaf," claiming, "My music school is the street." Isadora Duncan refused to listen to her dance instructor when he told her standing on her toes was beautiful. She said, "It is ugly," walked out, and never took another lesson, but went on to found her own school of modern dance. Tesla taught himself six languages as a teenager. He had such a remarkable memory that he could memorize whole logarithmic tables and when a teacher would write a differential equation on the blackboard, Tesla would instantly write the answer, to the chagrin of the teacher. Amelia Earhart detested formal education because teachers insisted that she justify her solutions to problems. This intuitive woman refused and later would write, "Experimentation . . . that's better than any college education."

Maria Montessori refused to enter the teaching profession because she was told as a child that it was the only profession available to women. Ironically she lived to revolutionize the educational profession she hated as a child. Montessori had no other choice in nineteenth-century Italy, which infuriated her. She made up her mind to become a professional engineer, scientist, or doctor. She was enrolled in a science class in an all-boys school to study math in middle school, an outrage in Victorian Italy. In college she studied engineering in defiance of tradition and finally decided to pursue a medical career. When this renegade woman was unable to gain entrance to the University of Rome's Medical School, she appealed to the pope for admission and became Italy's first female doctor. It is ironic that the field she so hated as a child (education) is the field in which she made history by revolutionizing its most basic postulates.

The lack of formal education proved to be an asset for most of these visionaries. Had they been more formally educated it is unlikely they would have achieved such professional eminence. These individuals were never educated enough to know their limitations and ascended to the very top through intellectual innocence. They approached education like Mark Twain, who said, "I have never let my schooling interfere with my education."

Transiency

Frequent moves at a young age are a positive experience for young children in becoming great creative or entrepreneurial geniuses. This is contrary to the opinion of most mothers who are convinced that the instability wrought by continual relocations is a detrimental experience for their young children. The truth is that it is more of a problem for the adults than the children who benefit by the new cultures, friends, and environment. Frequent transiency instills the ability to cope with an unknown environment at a very early age. When children are moved from state to state, forced to meet new friends, enroll in new schools and cope with new teachers, and adapt to strange cultures, they are imprinted with self-sufficiency, independence, perseverance, and temerity. Napoleon, Hitler, Sade, and Tesla were forced to learn entirely new languages and cultures. Napoleon left for boarding school in France at age ten and didn't return to his Corsican home for eight years. Wright lived in six different states and ten different cities before age ten. Isadora Duncan lived a nomadic childhood fleeing angry landlords during her primary years. A quote from her autobiography gives some credence to her early life, "When I was five we had a cottage on 23rd street . . . moved to 17th . . . moved to 22nd . . . then to 10th street . . . with an infinite number of removals." She talked her mother into moving to Chicago when she was sixteen, to New York at eighteen, to London at twenty, to Paris at twenty-two, and Athens at twenty-three. What an unbelievable cultural and educational experience. No wonder she was fearless in all those foreign environments.

VAGABONDS AND INDEPENDENCE

These subjects all led a vagabond existence as children. Walt Disney lived in three different cities in two states before he was a teenager. At age fifteen he rode the rails selling soft drinks and joined the Red Cross for a two-year stint in France at age sixteen after lying about his age. Amelia Earhart attended six different high schools in four different states, which conditioned her to a life of freedom and independence. She wrote, "I grew up like a rolling stone." She became enamored with ambiguity and explained her vagabond lifestyle to reporters, "I've had twenty-eight different jobs in my life and I hope I'll have 228 more." She loved the thrill of the unknown and was content with high-risk environments. Such a temperament would have been impossible had Amelia been raised in a tightly controlled environment devoid of change. Hitler lived in four different cities prior to his teens and attended several schools in the process. Howard Hughes moved to Louisiana from Houston at age two and then back to Houston a year later. At age eight he was enrolled in the Prosser Academy boarding school in Houston. At age twelve he was enrolled in Sanford Boarding School in Connecticut, followed by Fessenden in Boston, and then Thacher in California when he was fifteen. Maria Montessori was born in Chiaravelle, Italy, then moved to Florence at age three and to Rome at age five. Later she would become a wandering international spokeswoman for the Montessori Method, living in Spain, Holland, England, and India while travelling constantly to the United States and South America. Murdoch spent his summers living alone in a tree house on a farm near Melbourne, Australia. At age ten he was enrolled in a Geelong boarding school. He was shipped off to England at seventeen to attend Oxford. The independent spirit that Murdoch acquired fighting the boarding school system has been influential in his becoming an international media tycoon.

European Gypsies

Transiency defined Edith Piaf's life. She never lived in what could be called a traditional home her whole life. Born in a gutter, raised in a brothel, and nurtured as a street entertainer from age seven to twenty, the Great Piaf was a child of the streets. Piaf lived by her wits, for years avoiding the authorities who would have placed her in a detention home or worse had she been discovered as a street urchin. Pablo Picasso was born in Malaga, Spain; moved to Corunna at age ten; to Barcelona at fourteen; to Madrid at sixteen; back to Barcelona at eighteen; and to Paris at nineteen. In between he was a gypsy in the Pyrenees Mountains. At eighteen Helena Rubinstein fled her Polish home to find refuge on the opposite side of the world in Melbourne, Australia. She took refuge with a distant uncle and within two years had fled that home to make her way in the world alone. Sade was thrown out of the Conde Palace at age four for physically attacking the prince. He lasted another year with a grandmother in Provence. At age six he was sent to La Coste to live with his uncle Abbé de Sade with whom he traveled Europe before returning to Paris at age ten. Sade, like Piaf, never had a home of his own. His father enlisted him in the military at fifteen and he became a citizen of the world. Nikola Tesla moved with his family at age six and was put in a boarding school at age twelve. He left for college in Vienna at age sixteen. He then started working in Paris and Budapest prior to emigrating to the United States at age twenty-eight.

It is amazing that not one of these visionaries lived in just one house during their formative years, which in those days was highly unusual. All experienced numerous relocations that imprinted them with a comfort for ambiguity and armed them with a resilient self-esteem. It groomed them to deal with an unknown world and imbued them with a propensity for risk taking, both critical to success in a dynamic world.

Fantasy Hero Mentors

Joseph Campbell spent his life attempting to prove that mythological myths were fantasies that could affect our conscious actions: "Myths are clues to the spiritual potentialities of the human life" (*The Power of Myth*, p. 5). He wrote in *The Hero with a Thousand Faces*: "all things and beings are the effects of the ubiquitous power out of which they rise, which supports and fills them during the period of their manifestations, and back into which they must ultimately dissolve" (p. 257). Campbell was influenced by Jung and believed, as I do, that all great achievement emanates from the unconscious. He wrote in *Hero,* "all life-potentialities are innately unconscious." Campbell had great insight into what makes great creative geniuses tick, speculating that this genius derives from "unconscious vision." His hypothesis is validated based on the findings for these subjects. They had mythical-like visions of success while young. They dreamed great dreams and/or fantasized about great heroes and heroines and reverted to those visions as adults. Most of them had a euphoric (unconscious) vision of themselves as fantasy heroes that they had formed, mostly from books, in early life. Campbell saw books as the true teachers: "James Joyce and Thomas Mann were my teachers."

FICTIONAL HEROES

Most of the subjects were voracious readers as children and often fantasized about their heroes and heroines. Their fantasies were usually larger-than-life titans like Christ, Alexander the Great, Aphrodite, Terpsichore, Nietzsche's Superman, Voltaire, Aladdin, Rousseau, or Saint Theresa. Frank Lloyd Wright's hero was Aladdin and his magic lamp. Wright's mother was convinced that young Frank was the reincarnation of the mythological Welsh god Taliesin. She envisioned her son to be destined for success as a creator of great buildings in the likeness of the god Taliesin. Wright eventually embodied his mother's dream, which helped him violate the traditional rules of architecture, by creating buildings beyond the scope of mere mortals.

IMAGINATION CREATES ITS OWN REALITY

Nikola Tesla adopted the Hungarian fictional hero called "the Son of Aba" as his hero mentor at age eight. Tesla wrote that "this book somehow awakened my dormant powers of will and I began to practice self-control," a discipline to which he later attributed his success as an inventor. As a teenager Tesla embraced Mark Twain as his hero, which carried on into adulthood when the two met and became friends in New York City. He then adopted Voltaire and proceeded to read everything the philosopher ever wrote. In college Tesla memorized Goethe's *Faust* in its entirety and was reciting lines from this epic poem when he had the revelation for alternating current motors. Sade's heroes were Voltaire and Rousseau. Helena Rubinstein chose Dr. Lyskusky, the inventor of her magic skin cream, as her hero mentor. Picasso adopted Raphael as his first artist hero, to be followed by Cézanne. As a teenager he discovered Nietzsche and his "Overman" or "Superman" ideology became Picasso's alter-ego hero. Edith Piaf adopted Saint Theresa as her mythological heroine. Piaf lost her eyesight at age three and when the doctors offered no hope for recovery she was taken on a pilgrimage to the shrine of Saint Theresa to pray for a cure. When she was miraculously cured at age seven, young Edith passionately idolized Saint Theresa the rest of her life, believing her sight had been restored by this Catholic saint. Whenever Piaf was faced with a huge new booking like Carnegie Hall, she would burn candles to Saint Theresa, believing her mentor would ensure success.

IMAGERY AND CREATIVITY

Albert Einstein was convinced that all great imagery occurs in childhood or in a person capable of returning to that freedom-oriented state. He often commented that all of his great ideas had originated in some childhood imagery, especially around the age of twelve or thirteen when he formulated the theory of relativity. Disney's life of creation gives credence to Einstein's belief. He lived his life in a fantasy where the fairy tales of his youth became the source of his adult creativity. The "innocence" of childhood pervaded all of his work. Disney spent his life recreating fantasy visions of his childhood in Kansas. His characters took on the real characteristics of those early fantasies. His pet pig Porker became the Foolish Pig in the *Three Little Pigs*. Mickey Mouse was a mouse who lived in Disney's desk in the early days in Kansas City, and Mickey's personality (see chapter 10) became the identical psychological personality of Disney, as did that of Donald Duck.

INTERNAL FANTASIES—A SELF-FULFILLING PROPHECY

Children have a way of growing up fulfilling their childhood fantasies. Real and fictitious heroes are often adopted and imprinted as part of the self-images of children and it appears from this research that they grow up attempting to emulate their heroes. Montessori worshiped the Virgin Mary and Jesus Christ but later became enamored with the more worldly works of Edouard Séguin. Rupert Murdoch identified with the fictional Citizen Hearst and the real-life hero Lord Beaverbrook. Howard Hughes idolized Charlie Chaplin's Little Tramp character and after flying became his passion, became enraptured with Baron von Richthofen, the fictional Red Baron of World War I fame. A teenaged Hitler became obsessed with Wagner's opera *Rienzi*. He attended this opera with his only friend, August Kubizek, who was shocked at Hitler's emotional reaction, recalling, "He entered a state of ecstasy and rapture with visionary power. . . . Such rapture I had only witnessed in the theater . . . as though a demon had possessed him." He described Hitler's passionate dialogue saying, "I will lead Germany out of servitude to heights of freedom." Years later when Hitler met Kubizek in 1939, he told him, "In that hour it happened." As an adult Hitler became captivated by Schopenhauer's philosophy of "will" and Nietzsche's "Superman." Isadora Duncan chose Walt Whitman as an early hero whose nonconformity led her to adopt the existentialism of Nietzsche. She then chose the Greek mythological gods Terpsichore, Aphrodite, and Prometheus as her hero mentors. Napoleon became so enamored with Jean Jacques Rousseau as a youth that he would have died for him. *The Social Contract* became Napoleon's bible during his teen years when he favored independence for his native Corsica. Voltaire and Rousseau were his philosophical mentors as Alexander was his military mentor. Napoleon went so far as to invade Egypt in a fantasy reenactment of his hero Alexander. He drove himself to conquer the world in his thirties as a tribute to his hero. Napoleon succeeded in all respects, including dying at a young age after conquering the world.

LARGER-THAN-LIFE ROLE MODELS

What is important in adopting hero mentors is not the specific individual adopted, but that the hero is larger than life. When children or young adults have such fantasies and identify with them, they remove all limits from their own lives. They see themselves in this larger-than-life role where no conquest is too large or out of reach. These subjects never doubted that they were worthy of success and power and were willing to go to any length to gain what they saw as their birthright. Visionaries like Wright, Napoleon, Duncan, Hitler, Picasso, Tesla, and Hughes were so deluded with their fantasies that they spoke in grandiose terms. Desiring to own the whole state of Nevada, Hughes called press conferences to announce plans to build the world's largest airport in Las Vegas to service the world's largest casino at a time when he had not left his bed for ten years. He fully intended to implement these projects no matter how unrealistic they became. These particular individuals had dreams which became delusions of grandeur, and they believed themselves infallible.

INTERNAL DREAMS BECOME EXTERNAL REALITIES

Nikola Tesla wrote in his autobiography that he was twice rescued from serious illness by reading of great heroes and success. One of these heroes was Mark Twain, whom he was convinced saved him from certain death at the age of eight. As a young adult Tesla once again became afflicted with a bizarre life-threatening illness that the doctors diagnosed as incurable. It was during this period that he had one of his intuitive revelations. Tesla was reading a passage about one of his great heroes from Goethe's *Faust* when he had the vision for his breakthrough invention of alternating current. He said of the experience, "The idea came like a flash of lightning and in an instant the truth was revealed." Frank Lloyd Wright's mother believed him to be the earthly reincarnation of the Welsh god Taliesin. When Wright created the breakthrough design of the Prairie House or ranch-style home, he gave it the metaphorical name "Taliesin." This home incorporated all of his innovations and doubled as his home, image, and mythological namesake. He would later use the name Taliesin interchangeably for his estate and himself. When he built a home in Arizona he called it Taliesin West. Later in life he started referring to himself as the Master Taliesin, which gives credence to the hypothesis that mythological archetypes become an unconscious reality to those so indoctrinated. Their self-portraits become confused with their fantasies. Their "inner" and "outer" realities became inextricably intertwined just as Joseph Campbell had predicted in *Hero with a Thousand Faces*:

> The standard path of the mythological adventure of the hero is a magnification of the formula represented in the rites of passage: separation-initiation-return: . . . A hero ventures forth from the world of common day into a region of supernatural wonder: fabulous forces are there encountered and a decisive victory is won: the hero comes back from this mysterious adventure with the power to bestow boons on his fellow man. (p. 30)

The above quote would indicate that Campbell was writing the legacy for these fourteen creative geniuses. These subjects had a mystical approach to seeking success and would venture into new arenas even when the experts said they were destined to fail. They had an internal belief system and mythical kind of certainty that only genius understands. Their early identity with great heroes and heroines in books appears to have had a certain validity for them. Hopefully, reading the lives of these fourteen will imbue the reader with a similar sense of internal power. Figure 7 outlines Freud, Jung, and Campbell's psychological perspective on mythological heroes. Campbell's basic tenets are outlined in the context important to this work. The only divergence from Campbell is my claim of a possible imprinting during a trauma or crisis where a person identifies with their mythological hero mentor.

POSITIVE ROLE MODELS

Fathers who work nine-to-five jobs are excellent role models for children desirous of building a life of stability and security. They are not the best role models for molding great power brokers and creative geniuses. These powerful leaders had fathers who did not work in a corporate environment and therefore were not conditioned to the traditional nine-to-five lifestyle. They had fathers who were entrepreneurs (Earhart, Disney, Hughes, Rubinstein), ministers (Tesla, Wright), government officials (Napoleon, Montessori), artists (Picasso), or were absent from the family (Piaf, Duncan, Sade, Wright). Only Murdoch and Hitler had fathers who went to an office to work. Murdoch's father had spent his youth as a freelance writer and entrepreneur and elected to climb the corporate ladder later in life. Hitler's father was a customs agent.

It appears that such self-employed parents instill a sense of adventure and freedom in the minds of children. The children see them as romantic and adventurous role models who are independent. Such children learn quite early that they can

FIGURE 7
MYTHOLOGICAL HERO MENTORS

"Myths are spontaneous productions of the psyche"—Joseph Campbell, *The Power of Myth*

Freud	The unconscious is acquired as a young child ("The motive force of phantasies are unsatisfied wishes") as a result of repressed instincts, molding a fixed cognitive behavior by the teens.
Jung	All archetypes are *inherited* from a collective unconscious ("It is not Goethe who creates *Faust* but *Faust* who creates Goethe. . . . *Faust* is but a symbol"). Life's experience then activates archetypes.
Campbell	Archetypes are acquired through identity with myths. The imagination develops symbolic experiences recording them as mythical scripts on the unconscious. The emotions and actions in life (IRMs—Innate Releasing Mechanisms) allow the innate behaviors to be manifested from the hero Imprints that have been recorded as archetypes. "Myths create heroes out of those who heed them" and the "will" of such people becomes inextricably tied to the metaphoric hero. Self-actualization emanates from "following your bliss."

Visionary	Hero Mentor and Fantasy Role Model
Napoleon Bonaparte	Alexander the Great, Voltaire, Rousseau, Paoll (Corsican revolutionary)
Walt Disney	Snow White, Alice in Wonderland, Tom Swift, Mark Twain, fairy tales
Isadora Duncan	Aphrodite, Terpsichore, Prometheus, Walt Whitman, Nietzsche, Wagner
Amelia Earhart	Susan B. Anthony, Eleanor Roosevelt, Charles Lindbergh
Adolf Hitler	Eckardt's "Thulism," Nietzsche's "Superman," Wagner's *Rienzi,* Schopenhauer's "Will"
Howard Hughes	The Red Baron (Eddie Rickenbacker), Charlie Chaplin, Charles Lindbergh
Maria Montessori	Virgin Mary, Christ, Edouard Séguin, Jean-Marc-Gaspard Itard, Frederick Froeble, Rousseau
Rupert Murdoch	Astrological signs, Citizen Hearst, Lord Beaverbrook, Arthur C. Clarke, Leonard Goldenson
Edith Piaf	Saint Theresa, astrological signs and séances, Jean Cocteau, Louis "Papa" Leplée
Pablo Picasso	Mythological Greek and African gods; Nietzsche's "Superman," Raphael, Cézanne
Helena Rubinstein	Dr. Lykusky (inventor of her magic skin cream)
Marquis de Sade	Witchcraft and black magic, Abbé de Sade, Voltaire, Rousseau
Nikola Tesla	Fictional Son of Aba—Abafi, Goethe's *Faust,* Voltaire, Mark Twain, mystical energy
Frank Lloyd Wright	Welsh god Taliesin, Aladdin and his magic lamp, Louis Sullivan

Landrum's Mythological Scripting Theory

Adults spend their lives fulfilling internal self-images acquired during childhood. Strong internal images of mythical heroes are imprinted during childhood (from Bible, books, and fairy tales) and become internalized as archetypes for successful behavior. Children with a "loser imprint" unconsciously strive to fulfill that negative image just as those with a "hero imprint" strive to fulfill that image. Even deluded scripts become archetypical scripts. Children who are taught they are "little Messiahs" by indulgent/doting parents become arrogant overachieving adults. *We all become as we think* (unconsciously) with positive imprints preordaining positive actions and negative imprints resulting in negative ones. Positive traits/attitudes like self-confidence, tenacity, indomitable will, and optimism often are the by-products of modeling one's life after a fantasy hero/mentor found in books, fairy tales, or spirituals. Mythological Greek gods, Nietzsche's "Superman," Aladdin and his magic lamp, and fairy tales like Snow White can be inspirational and guide one to great success. Real-life historical heroes such as the Virgin Mary, Mark Twain, Voltaire, Rousseau, or Alexander the Great can instill an unconscious belief system with few limitations for success in the real world. Since these heroes are larger than life, the ability to emulate them can also be larger than life. Fantasy and reality often overlap in such a scenario. Belief suddenly becomes more critical to success than reality with optimism leading one to success and pessimism leading to failure. Positive hero mentors become the guiding force for overachieving adults who tend to emulate their fictional heroes.

make it outside the corporate womb. This early insight was probably instrumental in motivating these fourteen to work outside an organized system. Their fathers were influential in this regard by prejudicing their selection of independent and autonomous professions. A parent's avoidance of bureaucratic and organizational structure demonstrates to the child that professional destiny is in their own hands.

SELF-SUFFICIENCY LEARNED FROM SELF-EMPLOYED PARENTS

Not one of these fourteen subjects worked in what could be called a normal job. Only five (Earhart, Disney, Montessori, Tesla, Wright) of the fourteen ever received a paycheck and they only did so for a short period of time. These were jobs taken during their early twenties when they were just starting out in life. The other nine subjects never held one job during their entire life. They had evidently been highly influenced by their self-employed parents and became self-sufficient in their own right. Their parents were not always successful but they were always the masters of their own destiny, which apparently appealed to their renegade children. Parents who are self-sufficient appear to instill independence and temerity in the young and prepare them for taking great risks as adults.

NEGATIVE ROLE MODELS

A few parents of the subjects, especially fathers, were negative role models, which tended to work as a reverse motivator. Hitler's father was a customs clerk, which demanded he conform to rigorous and mundane rules and punch a time clock. Such a life did not appeal to Adolf, who had been indulged since birth and had an independent spirit. Hitler's abuse by his authoritarian father also contributed to his rejecting his father as a role model. Hitler's doting mother overcompensated for the father's abuse, creating a lazy and insolent "mama's boy."

Disney's father was an authoritarian figure who beat his children regularly, probably due to the frustration of being a professional failure. Walt was beaten at the slightest provocation, which apparently contributed to his need to escape into his own contrived fantasy world. Walt's nurturing mother placated him by reading him to sleep with fairy tales. Fun, innocence, and happiness were pervasive topics in his mother's fairy tales, which were important themes in all of Walt's adult creations. Good and evil were dominant themes throughout his movies and cartoons, where good always won out over evil. He detested the dog-eat-dog world of Hollywood business where cheating and corruption were rampant and he escaped into the safe haven of fantasyland. Disney lived a surreal life fantasizing a utopian world. Even at age fifty Disney could be found riding his miniature backyard railroad whenever life at the studio became too difficult. It is quite telling that at age fifteen Disney road the rails in the Midwest selling soft drinks to earn money to buy drawing materials, and at fifty resorted to a fantasy of that same experience. Disneyland proved to be Walt's ultimate fantasy. The park was created as a place for adults to escape from the real world and return to the freedom and

innocence of childhood. This business strategy was clearly apparent in his five different fantasy lands and contributed to the difficulties he encountered in getting the
park financed. Disneyland violated all the traditional economics of an amusement
park, which is what has made it enormously successful. Disney's creative endeavors—animated cartoons and amusement parks—were merely vehicles for
his psyche to make life more pleasant and bearable both for him and his customers.
What an ironic contrast to the sadomasochism of Hitler whose fantasy revenge for
an abusive childhood was the Holocaust.

Family Influence

Comfort with ambiguity is a critical attribute for the creative and innovative.
Those interested in a pioneering lifestyle of entrepreneurship or creativity need to
learn to risk and fail without remorse. Overprotective mothers and authoritarian
fathers are the bane of creativity as they instill fear in young children and mold
them into becoming dependent adults. Those parents who do not allow their children to explore the unknown are conditioning them to worship at the altar of security. Locking a child in a room may keep the child from ever skinning his
knees, but it is guaranteed to keep him from learning to cope in a cruel world.
David McClelland, a specialist in the psychology of motivation, is an authority on
achievement and leadership power. He found that highly motivated people tend to
become so indoctrinated in tolerant family environments:

> Achievement-motivated people are more likely to be developed in families in
> which parents hold different expectations than normal families. They expect
> their children to start showing some independence between ages six and eight,
> making choices and doing things without help, such as knowing the way around
> the neighborhood and taking care of themselves around the house. (McClelland,
> *Power: The Inner Experience* [1953])

The fourteen visionaries in this work were raised in homes where expectations of
self-sufficiency were high and the children could try and fail without remorse. As
children these subjects were allowed to experiment and fail without retribution.
They could explore new frontiers and blunder without being ridiculed. Of the fourteen, only Hitler and Disney had authoritarian fathers and even these two negative
influences were neutralized by indulgent mothers. Isadora Duncan is a perfect example of a child growing up without restrictions. Isadora was reared in a home
where money was nonexistent, but where poetry, philosophy, music, and the arts
were revered. She was a latch-key child who was allowed to explore the streets of
turn-of-the-century San Francisco, and this early experience helped form her independent nature and total self-sufficiency. This training allowed her to revolutionize the world of dance since she obdurately refused to accept traditional
dances. Freedom was the operative word in Isadora's home and she credits this

early experience with her later success. Isadora was convinced that her mother's permissive attitude was the prime factor in molding her into a great artist, and that her mother encouraged independence and delighted in her free spirit: "It is certainly to this wild untrammeled life of my childhood that I owe the inspiration of the dance I created, which was but the expression of freedom. I was never subjected to the continual 'dont's' which it seems to me make children's lives a misery" (Duncan, p. 11). Isadora disdained the control freaks and overprotective parents that she encountered while giving dance lessons to the rich children of San Francisco, saying, "The finest inheritance you can give to a child is to allow it to make its own way, completely on its own two feet. . . . In comparison to the children of millionaires, I seemed to be a thousand times richer in everything that made life worthwhile"(p. 21).

OVERINDULGING BREEDS GENIUS AND ARROGANCE

Freud said of his upbringing, "If a man has been his mother's undisputed darling he retains throughout life the triumphant feeling, the confidence in success, which not seldom brings actual success along with it." Many of these individuals were "mama's boys" who could do no wrong. Napoleon, Hitler, Hughes, Picasso, Sade, and Wright were surrounded by women. Interestingly, these six grew into arrogant egomaniacs even though quite successful. Mothers who continually tell their children how great they are tend to instill enormous self-esteem but simultaneously create egotistical bores.

The mothers of these individuals were responsible for developing optimistic and powerful adults who were not likeable. These individuals became so self-absorbed that they ignored all societal rules and were labeled deviant personalities by their many adversaries. Their egomania was a positive factor in their later success but became a detriment in their interpersonal relationships. Hitler, Hughes, Picasso, Napoleon, Sade, and Wright all grew up to become sadomasochistic and destructive. Success and omnipotence were so imbued into the unconsciousness of these men by their mothers that they became convinced of their own infallibility. When individuals like Napoleon and Hitler reached the top, their egomania became so pronounced that they became convinced they were divine. It is interesting that these six, who were worshiped by women when children, grew into chauvinistic adult tyrants who had little or no respect for women.

MAMA'S BOYS

These six "mama's boys" operated with a "my way or the highway" attitude. They pursued their own dreams in total disregard of friends, family, or spouses. If they couldn't control anything or anyone they wanted to destroy it. An example is Picasso, who emotionally destroyed one wife (Olga), one mistress (Dora Maar), and had another mistress and a wife commit suicide (Marie-Therese and Jacqueline). His son Paulo became an alcoholic and his grandson and namesake

Pablito committed suicide by drinking a quart of bleach when he was barred from Picasso's funeral. Hitler was a control freak who went into violent rages when he couldn't have his way. He drove his niece and mistress Geli Raubel to commit suicide. Three other women attempted suicide over Hitler's abusive behavior and gross inattention. To Hitler women were pawns and a distraction to his ultimate egomaniacal goal in life—creating a thousand-year Reich. Sade's sexually perverse reputation is self-evident, although in his defense, Sade was far less abusive to women than Picasso, Hughes, or Hitler. Sade felt that prostitutes were fair game in fulfilling his fantasies of sadomasochism, sodomy, and blasphemy. He treated what he called normal women with great respect. Howard Hughes was the most philandering of these men. Hughes used and abused women with total disdain. He would propose marriage to women, seduce them, and then discard them. He felt he could buy anything and anyone, and actually did buy hundreds of very prominent women whom he promptly abandoned once they were his. Napoleon and Wright were capable of extreme cruelty to women, but were not in the same league as these four.

FREEDOM SPAWNED SUCCESS

It appears that power, influence, and creativity are often the by-product of a free environment. Hughes, Napoleon, Murdoch, and Tesla learned freedom in boarding schools where they were all placed at age ten. Such an environment forces the child to come to grips with his own destiny. No longer is he in a protective family where he is not required to make any of life's decisions. The rules of the pack are observed in boarding schools. Piaf learned freedom the hard way as a street urchin. Picasso spent a great deal of his teen years roaming the Pyrenees Mountains. Rubinstein was given free reign of a Polish household where she was the oldest of eight children. Such a family environment created freedom since Helena's mother didn't have the time to set hard and fast rules. Walt Disney actually lived alone for many months during his midteens when the family moved away to Chicago and he road the rails earning money at age fifteen. Sade admitted he had no parental control during his early years and said, "I was told I was the reincarnation of Jesus, a marvel, miracle, and idol." Such indulgence made him believe he could do anything to anyone—and he did. Hitler also had free rein while living alone in Vienna at a very young age. All of these individuals were allowed the freedom to explore and this molded them into independent and autonomous adults. It made them strong, endowing them with a strong risk-taking propensity while developing their self-confidence. It also made some of them into monsters.

GENDER INFLUENCE

Mothers were the major influence on the men in this work and fathers the primary influence on the women. Hughes's mother created an adult obsessed with germs due to her own paranoid delusions. She was a hypochondriac whose influence helped form Howard's paranoid obsessions. His entrepreneurial bent and ethical values were instilled by a wild, adventurous father. Picasso was raised in a family dominated by women—a doting mother, three unmarried aunts, two sisters, and a governess—which appears to have had an enormous influence on his life and art. A tribute to his mother's influence was his adoption of her name Picasso instead of his father's name Ruiz. Picasso and Sade were both raised in an environment almost devoid of men and were revered by doting females. It is ironic that these two had an identical view of women as adults. Both viewed women as either madonnas or whores, as evident in Sade's writings and Picasso's art. Hitler, Murdoch, Tesla, and Wright, like Picasso and Sade, were surrounded by women during their formative years. Most of their values were learned from females. In a moment of reflection on St. Helena, Napoleon credited his mother for much of his success: "I was very well brought up by my mother, I owe her a great deal. She instilled into me pride and taught me good sense." Sade's experience was just the opposite. He wrote, "I love my father with distraction, and feel that I hate my mother." Sade felt his childhood had been responsible for his inability to control his emotions. He said with hatred, "I was indulged and admired" and everyone "submitted to my will."

FATHERS/DAUGHTERS AND MOTHERS/SONS

The female subjects in this book were enamored of their fathers. Many had fathers who were unsuccessful but it appears this didn't affect them as long as their fathers supported them emotionally. Earhart's father was an alcoholic and failed at every business venture he tried, but she still idolized him. Helena Rubinstein attributed all of her business acumen to her father while giving her mother credit for her interest in beauty. Edith Piaf had little use for her mother or father as they both abandoned her as a young child. Duncan never knew her father but it is interesting that when she finally married late in life it was to a poet, the same profession as that of her itinerant father. Duncan admitted her mother was her role model and mentor and went on to adopt her mother's hatred of marriage, God, and the establishment. Montessori's mother was her friend and confidant during those years when she rebelled against the Italian establishment. Her conservative father never understood her and faded into the background in shock over his defiant daughter. Hughes's father imbued young Howard with the most telling ethical values of any of these subjects. Howard, Sr., bribed his son's entrance into Thacher School in Santa Barbara, California when he was fifteen. After his mother died, he wanted Howard close to him in Los Angeles and removed Howard before his graduation from Thacher. He then bribed the authorities at no less an institution than Cal Tech to have his son enrolled in college despite his having dropped out of school. Cal Tech accepted Howard which gave him a distorted prescription for getting through life. Howard's father felt that he could buy anything or anybody and those values were instilled in the impressionable teenager. Howard grew up with the knowledge that he could buy his way into industries and governments. He would later bribe presidents and prime ministers or whoever got in his way. The Watergate conspiracy became one of his legacies. Young Howard had learned well from his father, telling Noah Dietrich, "I can buy any man in the world."

Summary

Creative geniuses and successful people are bred not born. They are imbued with most of the critical traits for success from early life experiences, parental influences, and crises. Manic drive and willpower are at the seat of their success. Money, genes, formal education, or socioeconomic status are of little importance to achieving great power. Being different is far more important than normality for great achievement in life. Most of these individuals were abnormally driven from an internally motivated psychic energy. They are best described as megalomaniacs-on-a-mission. They lived on the edge in all things with a propensity for high risk that ensured them great success or miserable failure. There is no middle ground with driven people. They were mostly Type A personalities who had a kind of "rushing sickness" causing them to walk, talk, eat, drive, and think faster than normal people. These individuals were impossible to please and were difficult bosses because of their "manic success syndrome." Drive made them great but it also contributed to many of their greatest problems.

The powerbroker and creative genius are the by-products of an average family with no obvious predilection for greatness. Among these subjects none were exceptionally bright or from influential families. The majority had normal middle-class socioeconomic backgrounds. Eleven (79 percent) were firstborn or only children, which imprinted them with perfectionism and drive. High transiency in childhood molded them with feelings of self-sufficiency and independence and built resilience. Moving often taught them to cope with new friends and cultures, imbuing them with self-confidence and a proclivity for risk taking. Most were voracious readers who identified closely with fictional heroes and fantasy mentors. Their heroes and heroines were larger-than-life characters who became mythological fantasy mentors for them to emulate. These Campbellian-type heroes tend to instill feelings of omnipotence. The subjects identified with characters without limitations and their fantasies became their reality. Napoleon mimicked Alexander the Great in attacking Egypt and conquering the world by age thirty-six and Hitler adopted Nietzsche's "Superman" as a model for his Master Race.

Positive role models in teachers and parents, especially self-employed fathers, conditioned these subjects to function outside the corporate womb. They saw a regular paycheck not as security but as handcuffs. Most were raised in permissive households or latch-key home environments where freedom to risk and err was common. The most perverse and egocentric males were reared by indulgent mothers who saddled them with awesome self-esteems by raising them as little messiahs. All were frenetic and self-made. Creativity and success were imprinted quite early and nothing could keep them from passionately pursuing their destiny.

2

Crisis:
The Mother of Power and Creativity

> All dissipative structures are teetering perpetually between self-destruction and
> reorganization.
>
> —Dr. Ilya Prigogine

Chaos and Creativity

All systems in life are in a dynamic state of flux. They are in the process of going
up or down, being destroyed or recreated. Dr. Ilya Prigogine, a Russian-born bio-
chemist, won the Nobel Prize in 1977 for his pioneering work on chaos and recovery. As he put it in *Order Out of Chaos* (1980): "Every artistic or scientific creation implies a transition from disorder to order." Prigogine found that systems
which get to the point of chaos or what he labeled the "bifurcation point" either
self-destruct or rise to greater heights. It was as if he was describing great entrepreneurs and creative geniuses, most of whom have experienced some terrible crisis and trauma in their lives. Many of these fourteen saw brothers and sisters die,
others lost parents early in life, and a number have had near-death experiences or
emotional collapse. It is apparent that the crises and traumas they experienced were
contributing factors in molding their resolve and instilling key behavior characteristics which contributed to their later success. Most became enormously creative
just after a tragedy. Others appear to have been armored by the crises with an iron
resolve, comfort with ambiguity, and tolerance for taking high risk. Their conditioning took place when they were at their "bifurcation point" or at the depth of
their despair. It is at this point in a great crisis where the individual is armed with
the internal resolve to survive. Examples of this abound in history. Martin Luther
was struck by lightning, dropped out of law school, joined the church, and by the
age of thirty-four had become the Father of the Reformation. Lord Byron was born

65

a cripple, which drove him to write great poetry. Alexander Graham Bell lost both brothers to tuberculosis and was transformed from a journeyman employee to the inventor of the telephone.

FEAR OF FAILURE: A PRIME MOTIVATOR

The fourteen visionaries in this book had various crises that drove them to overachieve. Based on the crises shown in figure 8, it is apparent that the path to the top is often easier when one has been to the bottom. When a person is totally stripped of everything, life's journey becomes more clearly defined and self-motivation takes over. With mortality on the line, great risk takes on a different perspective. The journey is less arduous when there is little to lose and enormous gambles are easier options. People who are too secure and content are not willing to jeopardize the status quo. Risk taking is related to psychological need. Desperate people do desperate things. Great creative geniuses and entrepreneurs have a similar mentality when attempting to realize their dreams. They operate as in a state of desperation in order not to fail. It isn't winning they fear as much as failure. Great crisis and trauma condition a person with tremendous drive and a fearless demeanor.

TRAUMA AND CREATIVITY

Individuals who experience great trauma are imprinted and changed by their experience. Either their internal drive mechanisms are altered and put into some higher gear or they are destroyed by the experience. Scientists have confirmed that "superlearning" takes place during traumatic periods, while an individual is in the theta or trancelike state. The theta state is a twilight zone where very slow brainwaves occur similar to those just prior to sleep or waking. Such a state can also occur in transcendental meditation or when in traumatic shock. Brain researchers have shown that superlearning and creativity take place in this theta state. Thomas Budzynski of the University of Colorado says that in "the hypnagogic state—the twilight state—between waking and sleep . . . a lot of work gets done very quickly." Researchers have found that children are in the theta state most of the time, which is the reason for their superior learning proclivity. Athletes and entertainers have learned to meditate because the conditioning enhances performance. Michael Hutchison, author of *Sex and Power,* says this theta condition is "the state in which the brain can learn enormous amounts very quickly." It was in this state that Patty Hearst was totally transformed within days from a polite, middle-class, heterosexual college coed into Tania, a bisexual Symbionese Army revolutionary. She had been imprinted with the reality map of her captors. Such crises also were at work with these fourteen individuals who were transformed by traumas into driven personalities armed with a manic need to succeed.

FIGURE 8
CRISIS AS INSPIRATION

"You can't know the top without having visited the bottom"

Creative Genius	Crisis—The Mother of Creativity	Resultant Success
Napoleon Bonaparte	Backed Corsican revolution after college; exiled from native Corsica; crisis of revolution launched him into leadership role	French leadership because of Corsican crisis
Walt Disney	Bedridden with a nail through his foot at age eleven, Walt discovered comic strips; bankrupt at twenty-one, fled to Hollywood where he and Roy opened Disney Studios	Both experiences launched Disney's career in animation
Isadora Duncan	First memory of life was being thrown out of upper-story window of burning building— caught by policeman. Early life a series of crises	"No choice" childhood; insecurity bred intensity; quit school at ten to found dance school
Amelia Earhart	Potential sledding disaster as child of five taught her fearlessness, launching her into adventurous career	Risk-oriented career a direct result of her sled experience
Adolf Hitler	Blinded by mustard gas WWI; upon regaining eyesight entered politics. Beer Hall Putsch and suicide attempt launched his political career	Wrote *Mein Kampf* in prison and emerged to lead Nazi party
Howard Hughes	Both parents died in teens and he took over the reins of Hughes Tool at nineteen	Entrepreneurial flare emerged in early need to cope alone
Maria Montessori	Illegitimate child in Catholic Italy forced her to resign medical directorship, reenter school, and start over in educational psychology	Plight launched her into education of small children and Montessori method emerged from crisis
Rupert Murdoch	Father died when he was at boarding school, forcing him to return to Australia and assume control at age twenty-one	Media empire grew out of debacle
Edith Piaf	Abandoned at birth; blind from age three to seven; no family and raised in brothel and on street	Felt loss of eyesight was responsible for her singing success
Pablo Picasso	Sister Conchita died when he was thirteen; vowed to quit painting if she lived. Her death launched him into exorcism of unrelenting rage against religion and women	Greatest paintings were all of death and devastation
Helena Rubinstein	Ran off to Australia and forced to leave foster home; skin cream only choice between starvation and living	Cosmetics empire grew out of her need to survive in Australia
Marquis de Sade	Lifelong incarceration destroyed his life but made him into a writer/philosopher	Imprisonment made him famous
Nikola Tesla	Brother Dane's tragic death at age five inspired him to obsessive achievement; near death at age twenty-five and miraculous recovery induced A/C invention within days	Greatest invention in modern history—A/C motors—emerged out of deathlike trance
Frank Lloyd Wright	Madison building collapse and tragedy at age nineteen affected him for life. Taliesin burned with him on roof trying to save masterpiece; lover killed	He was like Phoenix rising from ashes of his beloved Taliesin

CHAOS AND INSPIRATION

Dr. Prigogine found "psychological suffering, anxiety, and collapse can lead to new emotional, intellectual, and spiritual strengths—confusion and doubt can lead to new scientific ideas." During World War I Hitler was in a hospital recovering from a leg wound and exposure to mustard gas when he suddenly went blind. Doctors diagnosed his blindness as hysteria, but Hitler understandably was traumatized by the event. When Hitler recovered his vision in the hospital, he felt the event to be a prophetic experience, recalling that, "Suddenly the idea came to me that I would liberate Germany, that I would make it great. I knew immediately that it would be realized." Napoleon had a similar experience after the battle of Lodi and admitted it was then that he felt destined for greatness. Tesla went through his metamorphosis after doctors told him he was incurably ill from some mysterious disease when he was in his midtwenties. He had been struggling with the solution to the induction-motor design when he was coming out of this traumatic illness and suddenly went into a "trancelike state." The solution to the induction motor "came to him in a flash." Picasso was only three when an earthquake forced his family to flee from their Malaga, Spain, home, which had caught fire. Picasso was horrified by this traumatic experience and talked about it fifty-seven years later. Harvard psychologist Howard Gardner suggests this traumatic event triggered Picasso's most famous painting *Guernica* at age fifty-six. Although such crises are not desirable episodes in anyone's life, it appears from the research that such events are the catalysts for transforming average people into overachieving visionaries.

DISSIPATIVE STRUCTURES

Dr. Prigogine labeled chaotic events in life "dissipative structures." He coined this phrase to describe systems in a state of disorder or what scientists call *entropy*. Entropy is the theory that all systems, including man, are in the process of running down or burning up in what the Second Law of Thermodynamics calls "Heat death." This law asserts that all machines, including the universe, are in a continual process of running down and moving irreversibly toward decay and disorder. This is a nihilistic view of the world that the optimistic Prigogine revised with his "dissipative structure" theory. Prigogine agrees that all systems are in a state of self-destruction—a negative concept of life—but he gave a positive twist to the process. He concocted a system where "Life emerges out of entropy [chaos] not despite it." His dissipative structure theory states that "it is out of chaos, turmoil, and disorder that higher levels of order and wisdom emerge, thus if the creative thinkers have less mental stability . . . they also experience higher levels of mental connectedness, complexity, evolution." When life becomes intolerable, Prigogine's bifurcation point is reached. Systems and man either self-destruct or metamorphose into a higher form. History has many examples of individuals who rose from the ashes to change the world. Mohammed had a traumatic near-death experience and after a vision of the angel Gabriel was transformed at age forty from an illiterate camel driver into a great sage, prophet, and conqueror. Joan of Arc went through a similar experience. Beethoven suffered catastrophe when he lost his hearing at the height of his career. He composed his last great symphony and greatest masterpiece—the Ninth Symphony—while deaf.

Crisis as Inspiration

NAPOLEON

Napoleon experienced a near tragedy that is not often written about, but which could easily have changed history. The young Napoleon was inspired by Rousseau's *Social Contract* and used that philosophical ideology to justify (in his mind) Corsica's secession from France. Napoleon was notorious for using ideas to justify his actions, just as he used his horses to reach a destination. He was just as willing to bend ideas as he was willing to kill a horse to meet his needs. His near debacle in Corsica occurred shortly after he graduated from French military school. He took an eighteen-month leave from the military to return to Corsica to fight for his native country's independence. This radical move could easily have destroyed his career. It was only the turbulence of the French Revolution that allowed him to play such a high-stakes game between his native country and his adopted one. When the Corsican revolt failed, he and his family were deported to France. Had he been successful in Corsica, Napoleon would never have returned to France and history would have been dramatically altered.

HITLER

Adolf Hitler was jailed after the Munich Beer Hall Putsch failed miserably. He hid out with a friend whose wife kept him from committing suicide. While serving his sentence at Landsberg prison in 1924 he was in a state of complete depression. This failed coup d'état and imprisonment transformed Hitler from a neophyte rabble-rouser into a methodical political revolutionary. During his imprisonment Hitler began writing his memoirs, which were published in 1925 as *Mein Kampf* ("My Struggle"). Later he characterized his imprisonment in Landsberg "as my college education." Actually he reached his "bifurcation period" or state of chaos during this period and began his inspirational quest to "save Germany." In *Mein Kampf* he wrote that "willpower is greater than knowledge," which gives credence to the internal transformation that had occurred. Hitler decided in prison that "force" (physical power) was not the way to the top. He decided to utilize his enormous charismatic power and his vital energy or willpower to rise to the leadership in his adopted nation. He became the titular head of the National Socialist German Workers (Nazi) party, which is ironic since he had never worked. A revitalized Hitler emerged from Landsberg intent on using the power of the electorate instead of force to achieve power. His new strategy took only seven years to reap dividends when he was proclaimed dictator of Germany in 1932. He had transformed himself from a whimpering suicidal loser into one of the most powerful men in Europe because of his traumatic internment.

ISADORA DUNCAN

Isadora Duncan's whole childhood was a crisis. Her first memory was of being tossed out of an upper story of a burning building and being caught by a policeman. Her family had been abandoned by an itinerant father and lived a hand-to-mouth existence during her formative years. Isadora's mother told her there wasn't a Santa Claus so as not to expect toys. She often begged for food, and the family lived a transient life running out on irate landlords. Her destitute existence was instrumental in her quitting school at age ten to start a dance school. Isadora was convinced that her traumatic childhood helped mold her into the mother of modern dance.

AMELIA EARHART

Earhart became a thrill-seeking aviator because of an early life experience that imprinted her with a passion for risk taking. Young Amelia was a tomboy. She ignored all efforts to make her dress and act like a young lady. Her early trauma was the result of her refusal to sit upright on a sled in the manner of proper girls. This tomboy behavior saved her life when at the age of five her sled went flying between the legs of a horse drawing a carriage. She would have been seriously injured had she been sitting up. By lying face down on the sled she survived the death-defying experience. Earhart liked to relate this story to reporters who wanted insight into her death-defying behavior in the air. This early experience not only imprinted Earhart with great temerity but it became a titillating experience that made her liken high risk to adventure instead of potential catastrophe.

HELENA RUBINSTEIN

Rubinstein's cosmetics empire grew out of her personal crisis. Her father had arranged for her marriage to a thirty-five-year-old widower when she dropped out of school as a teenager in turn-of-the-century Poland. Rubinstein was so incensed that she ran off to live with an uncle in Australia at age eighteen. She was without money or any means of support. When her uncle made advances toward the attractive young woman, she left to make her own way in a foreign country with a strange new language. Her personal misfortune transformed her into the Queen of Beauty.

SADE, HUGHES, MURDOCH

The Marquis de Sade's great crisis was being sentenced to life imprisonment in the dreaded Bastille, a traumatic experience for a man who revered freedom. French biographer Maurice Lever (1993) said that Sade "went into prison a man and came out a writer." He became a world-renowned writer/philosopher, which would never have occurred had Sade remained a free man.

The various crises in Howard Hughes's life were of a more personal nature. Within a two-year period while Hughes was a teenager, both of his parents died unexpectedly, as well as a beloved aunt. Hughes was eighteen when his father died and left him as the only surviving member of the family. Young Howard was distraught but assumed the responsibility for his father's business. After these three traumatic events he became a robotic manipulator of people and companies in building his industrial empire.

Rupert Murdoch had an experience similar to Hughes's when he was twenty-one. His father died while he was away at school in Oxford and Murdoch was forced to return to Australia and assume control of the small family newspaper in Adelaide. He was transformed from a frivolous schoolboy to the Boy Publisher within a few years. The early responsibility gave him the confidence in his own ability to meet disaster and win.

TESLA, MONTESSORI, PICASSO, WRIGHT

The great traumas of Nikola Tesla, Maria Montessori, Pablo Picasso, and Frank Lloyd Wright transformed them and proves that "crisis is often the mother of creativity." Nikola Tesla was near death when a Eureka-like experience gave him the inspiration for alternating current and inductive engines. Maria Montessori's pregnancy in Roman Catholic Italy came precariously close to destroying her promising career in children's education. Pablo Picasso made a Faustian-like pact with God to save his dying sister. After she died, Picasso went on a destructive rage that resulted in the creation of cubism. Frank Lloyd Wright rebuilt Taliesin after its destruction by fire. The estate would become his testimonial to freedom of form in architecture and life.

Family Tragedies

SIBLING DEATHS

There is a repeated pattern of sibling deaths in the early lives of many of these subjects, including: Napoleon, Hitler, Hughes, Picasso, Rubinstein, Sade, and Tesla. Sade had a sister, Caroline-Laure, who was born in 1737 but died at age two a year before the birth of the Marquis. When Sade, named Donatien, was born, his parents "indulged and admired" and submitted to his every childish demand, molding a character which defied all authority until the day he died. Sade's father was appointed ambassador to Cologne six months after his son's birth, leaving him in the care of many doting women. Napoleon had eight brothers and sisters, but another five died at birth or shortly thereafter. Adolf Hitler's parents had three children die before Hitler's birth, and then his brother died unexpectedly when Hitler was five. These various deaths probably had a bearing on his mother's indulgent behavior toward him throughout his youth. Howard Hughes's mother also lost a child in childbirth just prior to her pregnancy with Howard. She was then told by her doctors that she couldn't bear another child, which materially affected her treatment of Hughes, according to biographers Donald Bartlett and James Steele and psychotherapist Ray Fowler, who testified at the trial over his will. Picasso's sister Conchita died of diphtheria when he was fourteen, which had a lifelong effect on him. Helena Rubinstein's older brother died in infancy prior to her birth. Rubinstein was the oldest of eight daughters and was treated like the son that her father never had. Tesla's older brother Dane died tragically, which led to his many compulsions and obsessions.

PARENTAL DEATHS

Parental deaths or absent fathers were a frequent occurrence in the lives of these individuals. Napoleon's father died when he was eighteen and away at school in France. Duncan's father deserted the family before she was born and she only saw him one once as a very young child. Hitler's father died when Adolf was thirteen and Hitler purportedly became emotionally despondent, throwing himself on the casket in abject devotion—strange behavior toward a father who had beaten him repeatedly as a child. Hitler's adoring mother died when he was seventeen. Hughes's mother died unexpectedly when he was away at boarding school during his junior year of high school when he was just sixteen. He found a surrogate mother in his aunt Annette Gano, whom he treated poorly. His father suffered a heart attack and died unexpectedly when Howard, Jr., was eighteen. The impetuous Howard was devastated emotionally but assumed control of the Hughes Tool Company at age nineteen. He began writing his own will, convinced that he would also die young. Rupert Murdoch's father died while he was away at school in Oxford, England. In her eyes, Edith Piaf's parents "died" when they abandoned her at birth. Sade's mother had little influence on him as she was absent from his life after age four. She entered a convent when he was in his teens. He was raised by a grandmother, a debauching uncle, doting aunts, and in boarding schools.

UNHAPPY, LONELY PEOPLE

Most great visionaries appear to be unhappy and/or lonely, escaping into the fantasy of books, movies, or television. Many were first or only children and found themselves alone and insecure. Most of these fourteen started reading early in life and escaped into a fantasy world that was happy and heroic. They never lost their need to escape into books and were often more content to be alone with their own fantasies than with a group. Unhappiness and loneliness appear to be recurring themes in the lives of many powerful people, and these fourteen were no exception. They paid a dear price for success, which left little time for happiness or pleasure. Freud confirmed this experience saying "artists tend to be unhappy introverts and like other unsatisfied men, turn away from reality and transfer interest, and his libido too, to the wishful constructions of his life phantasy." Psychiatrist Anthony Storr confirms the unhappiness in creative writing, "A happy person never fantasizes, only an unsatisfied one" (*The Dynamics of Creation,* p. 20). Storr also found that "the creative person has easy access to his inner world," a common trait of the introspective individual. Gestalt psychologist Abraham Maslow wrote "self-actualizing means experiencing fully, vividly, selflessly, with full concentration and total absorption." His description aptly describes the powerful and creative in this book. Maslow went on to say, "The compulsive-obsessive person not only loses much of the pleasures of living but also he becomes cognitively blind to much of himself." "Cognitive blindness" was an affliction found in all of these subjects.

Hermann Hesse wrote in *The Glass Bead Game* of the terrible price one pays to reach the top: "He suffered the fate of all who exercise a natural and initially unconscious power over men; the power is not exercised without a certain cost to its possessor." These fourteen are classic examples of this aphorism and paid a terrible price for their success. When they were not enraptured by their cause they were terribly unhappy and miserable. Napoleon wrote, "I came to my room to dream by myself, to abandon myself to my melancholy." Napoleon's aide-de-camp Caulaincourt said that Napoleon "had acquaintances but no friends." When Napoleon's power was at its zenith, he wrote, "I love nobody. No, I don't even love my brothers. . . . I know that I have no real friends." Such is the heritage of the supersuccessful. Maria Montessori became the messiah of education, but when Hitler and Mussolini came to power they abolished her teaching methods in both Germany and Italy. Maria was forced to become a vagabond teacher, seeking refuge in Spain in 1934, and then was ousted by the Spanish Civil War, which forced her to relocate to Holland. In Holland she was soon greeted by Hitler's invasion and emigrated to India for the balance of the war. She became a homeless and wandering messiah of primary education but was never happy.

One reason for the discontent of successful people is their Promethean temperament. The Promethean is constantly striving for more and is often dissatisfied with past achievement and success. Such is the destiny of the creative geniuses who are constantly pursuing future opportunities at the expense of present contentment. The very qualities that make them great also make them unhappy and lonely. Most research instructs us that one must be very unhappy with the "existing" order of things in order to be sufficiently motivated to create the "new." Therefore, Anthony Storr may be correct in his conclusion, "I don't think any artist can ever be happy." I would be hard pressed to describe any of these fourteen individuals as happy. Hitler certainly was not, neither was Hughes, Picasso, Tesla, Rubinstein, Murdoch, or Disney. Those closest to happiness were Amelia Earhart and, ironically, Sade, yet both lived lonely tragic lives. Montessori admitted she was miserable, as did Napoleon, Picasso, Piaf, and Duncan. Isadora's life read like a Greek tragedy. The price of power is high and happiness is not often one of the rewards.

The "Bottom" Grooms You for the "Top"

Two individuals in this book dramatically illustrate how catastrophe can often become the catalyst for later success. Most of these fourteen visionaries rose like phoenixes from the ashes of their defeats to become even greater. Both Walt Disney and Edith Piaf were able to overcome tragic early lives to become the very best in their professions. Neither allowed perpetual setbacks to defeat them. They were not interested in money and consequently were often cheated by unscrupulous individuals who exploited their frailties. Those who did so never understood that Disney and Piaf had little or no interest in the material rewards of their success. Such exploitation never deterred them from pursuing their dreams since money was not the driving force behind their success. Perfection was their only goal and it ultimately became their legacy. Integrity of their art form became their gift to posterity and has proved to be their lasting memorial. These two never allowed the repeated trips to the bottom (bifurcation point) deter them from bouncing back to success. Their tenacity was awe inspiring.

Walt Disney: Catastrophe Was Around Every Corner

Disney was virtually bankrupt every other year for thirty years. He constantly flirted with financial catastrophe from age twenty-one until his early fifties. Hollywood moguls nicknamed many of his early creations "Disney's Follies." It wasn't until his plan to create Disneyland forced him to make a deal with television that he became financially secure both personally and professionally. Disney's love of perfection and fear of failure kept him from capitulating to the wills of the bankers or his brother Roy. He refused to accept the quantitative analysis of his creative ventures, always insisting on the qualitative aspects over any financial considerations.

Disney's crises began with an abusive father. His mother salved his physical and emotional wounds by reading him fairy tales, which imprinted a fantasy innocence and feigned happiness on his unconscious. His first personal trauma occurred when he was eleven: He drove a nail through his foot and was bedridden for weeks. During his recovery, he discovered comic strips, which inspired him to become a newspaper cartoonist. After he came home from serving in Europe during World War I, he opened his first business to create cartoons. This began an almost perpetual series of financial disasters that continued for three decades. These business disasters were inextricably entwined with his emotional being and contributed to eight nervous breakdowns, excessive drinking, and obsessive smoking. Disney's eight collapses occurred between ages twenty and fifty. He was always afflicted with facial tics and other symptoms of underlying anxieties prompted by fanatic perfectionism. Habitual drinking and smoking contributed to his physical problems and constant bouts with manic depression. Daily bottles of scotch and three packs of cigarettes ended in premature death. The chronological history of

Disney's battle for survival and the evolution of the Disney empire is equivalent to taking a ride on Space Mountain. His life was like a roller-coaster ride of professional and personal traumas which could be likened to a sine wave where the troughs were devastating tragedies and the crests were euphoric experiences adorned with Oscars. The following nineteen crisis stages give credence to the histrionics associated with the creation of the Disney entertainment empire.

Disney's Traumatic Flirtation with Disaster

1. At age nineteen Disney and Ub Iwerks founded Disney Commercial Artists in Kansas City. The firm lasted one month, dying from the lack of contracts or income.

2. At age twenty Disney founded Laugh-O-Grams in Kansas City. His first product was an *Alice in Wonderland* animated cartoon for Kansas City theater owners. The firm became insolvent due to selling animated shorts for too little money. It was a profound learning experience but Disney went broke before any success could materialize. He skipped town to avoid angry creditors and ended up in Hollywood a ward of his older brother Roy.

3. Disney founded Disney Brothers Studios in Hollywood at age twenty-two on October 16, 1923, with a $500 loan from Uncle Robert and $285 from Roy. With an advance of two thousand dollars from Margaret Winkler, he produced his first successful cartoon *Trolley Troubles* featuring Oswald the Rabbit. Unscrupulous distributor Charles Mintz stole Oswald, his animators, and attempted to take over Disney Studios. The naive Disney lost his only cartoon character, only revenue, plus his best animators. Broke and disconsolate, he created Mickey Mouse on the train to California.

4. At age twenty-seven Disney launched Mickey Mouse in *Plane Crazy,* an overnight sensation in 1927. By 1928 he was insolvent again when his first sound cartoon, *Steamboat Willie,* was produced; he was forced to sell his car to stay in business and finance *Steamboat,* which became a supersuccess.

5. At age twenty-nine Disney made a deal with MGM for distribution of Mickey Mouse cartoons with unscrupulous Pat Powers who stole his number one animator Ub Iwerks and refused to pay $150,000 in royalties. Harry Cohn of Columbia rescued him from certain bankruptcy after the Powers debacle and financed *Silly Symphonies,* which saved the company. Disney had his first nervous breakdown and took overdose of sleeping pills in an attempt to escape torment of corrupt businessmen. He referred to this as the lowest point in his life.

6. At age thirty-one Disney pioneered in technicolor with *Flowers and Trees* cartoon and won his first two Oscars in 1931. He ran out of money and had his second nervous breakdown. He paid his animators with promissory notes and

gold tokens. Disney risked everything on color and then couldn't make the payroll; bankruptcy seemed inevitable when licensing of Mickey Mouse for Christmas coloring books, shirts, watches, and toys saved the firm. His first steady income brought him back in 1932.

7. By age thirty-two Disney and Mickey were famous. *Three Little Pigs* from Grimm's fairy tales released in 1934 became an international hit and Disney Studios grew prosperous enough to begin producing *Snow White and the Seven Dwarfs,* known as "Disney's Folly." Roy accused him of "Trying to ruin us"; experts thought full-length animated film idea was crazy. Studio became insolvent from *Snow White* costs and Disney had his third nervous breakdown.

8. By age thirty-five (1936) Disney convinced the Bank of America to loan him $5 million to complete *Snow White,* which was finally released December 21, 1937, with overwhelming success. Twenty million patrons paid $8 million to see this film and the company had money for huge expansion. "Disney's Folly" with re-releases earned $100 million by 1990. During the final stages of production, Disney suffered another nervous breakdown. Success revived him in time to accept an Oscar and to appear on cover of *Time* in 1938.

9. At age thirty-eight Disney was flush with monies from *Snow White* profits and embarked on three herculean productions: *Pinocchio, Bambi,* and *Fantasia,* which guaranteed bankruptcy unless all three were a phenomenal success. All films were over budget, and two were delayed. Within twenty months Disney Studios was insolvent during the middle of filming *Pinocchio* and *Fantasia.* Disney bought land for Burbank Studio. Brother Roy pulled financial coup with public offering of stock in 1939, which provided cash to finish the three major features.

10. At age thirty-nine Disney released *Pinocchio* in February 1940 at a cost of $3 million (most expensive film ever produced) to rave reviews. *Fantasia* was then released and was a box office bomb while *Bambi* was delayed still further. Walt hired Leopold Stokowski who used Stravinsky's music for *Fantasia,* which contributed to box office disaster. This was the golden era for Disney Studios.

11. Walt was professionally successful by age forty but an emotional disaster. Nineteen forty-one was a disastrous year. In June his workers struck the Disney Studios, *Fantasia* bombed, and his father died, causing his most severe nervous breakdown. The company was again on the verge of bankruptcy. Roy recognized his brother's suicidal tendencies and coerced him into a three-month vacation while he settled the strike through binding arbitration.

12. After the strike in October 1941, Disney released *Dumbo* with great fanfare and it saved the company from bankruptcy. Due to financial misfortunes, he had produced *Dumbo* for $1 million in contrast to the $2/3 million cost of his other animated films.

13. In early 1942 the Defense Department confiscated Disney Studios because of its proximity to Burbank's Lockheed Aircraft. Disney was outraged by the act and announced his retirement at the ripe old age of forty-one. Bored, he returned to animated entertainment almost immediately, producing U.S. Navy training films between 1942 and 1945 to pay the bills.

14. At age forty-three in 1944 Disney Studios was once again insolvent and needed cash to survive after the failure of *Bambi*. The resilient Disney re-released *Snow White* to enormous demand and the income from a product with no cost saved him from certain bankruptcy.

15. In 1947 at age forty-six Disney was able to show the first profit in seven years but was near bankruptcy again by 1949. During this period he was emotionally distraught; he had a blatant affair with Dolores Del Rio, started drinking heavily, smoked three packs of cigarettes daily, and lost all interest in creativity. A near-fatal air disaster in Alaska with an inebriated pilot sparked his sense of mortality and reawakened his creative spirit. He used the Alaskan footage to produce *Seal Island*, which both Howard Hughes and Roy Disney recommended scrapping. He ignored their advice and it won an Academy Award in 1948.

16. Disney drew his first plans for a Mickey Mouse amusement park targeted for Burbank in August 1948. Bank debt would not permit implementation. Roy called it a "fairground" and accused his brother of schizoid behavior for such a childish idea. Walt Disney ignored both brother and the studio board, forming WED in 1951 to finance his dream park. He borrowed $100,000 on his insurance policy and sold his Palm Springs home to help finance the start-up that Roy refused to support.

17. Fortunes improved in 1950 with success of *Cinderella*, but *Alice in Wonderland* bombed in 1951. Work on *Peter Pan* and *Robin Hood* took all available cash and company was again near bankruptcy throughout 1951.

18. By 1952 Disney had hired and personally funded the Stanford Research Institute to draw up plans for Disneyland. The Disney studio board had amusement park experts review the SRI plans in November 1953 and concluded that it wouldn't work (the reasons turned out to be the very reasons for its phenomenal success) and advised Walt to save his money.

19. TV was the mortal enemy of Hollywood studios but Disney struck a deal with ABC for money to finance Disneyland in 1953. Disney got financing and ABC got the rights to the Disney film library and "Walt Disney Presents." Disney was fifty-three when the "Mickey Mouse Club" and the "Disneyland Story" first appeared on television on October 27, 1954. Disneyland opened July 17, 1955, making Disney a millionaire. The financial crises finally ended. Disney's TV show revolutionized the medium and began a long-term relationship between Hollywood and television.

Walt Disney went broke for the first time at age nineteen after opening his first enterprise to create animated cartoons. He flirted with bankruptcy virtually every year thereafter until age fifty-four when he made a deal with television and opened Disneyland. When Disneyland opened in 1955, he finally became a millionaire even though most people thought he was rich long before since he had been winning Oscars for twenty years. His sudden wealth had little or nothing to do with his creative success but was primarily based on accidental leverage created by his need to live on the edge. The board of directors of Disney Studios refused to finance the park and forced him to carry out the project on his own, which ironically made him rich. Disneyland was built from his childlike imagination and reflected his need for excellence, cleanliness, purity of purpose, and perfection. His brother insisted that Disney put up his own money and take all of the initial risk. Disney did so without hesitation as money was never high on his list of importance, it was only a means to finance his dreams. If Disneyland had failed, he would have become a pauper. Because of its success he became a multimillionaire. Walt Disney had always been willing to risk everything on his creative ventures and never allowed the negative opinions of others to deter him. He produced the original sound Mickey Mouse cartoon *Steamboat Willie* and *Snow White, Fantasia,* and Disneyland all against the advice of the experts. Proceeding without their support or money, he was always underfinanced in every project. Since he was never well financed, he was able to gamble and it was that high-risk attitude that earned him the fortune to match his fame. Without the annual threat of insolvency and such a traumatic life, Disney probably would never have made it as a big-time producer of entertainment. If Oswald had not been stolen, Mickey Mouse would never have been born, and if his board would have liked the Disneyland idea, the "Mickey Mouse Club" and "Walt Disney Presents" would never have been seen on television.

Edith Piaf: Blindness and Abject Poverty Catalysts for Success

The Little Sparrow's life was one crisis after another. Edith Gassion was born in a gutter, abandoned by her mother, weaned on wine, raised in a brothel, and began life as a street urchin. She was blind at age three, on the street at seven, singing for food at ten, and a mother at sixteen. Never having attended school, she was illiterate until age twenty-one. Her life was a constant series of tragic events that led to alcohol and drugs, although more than anything Piaf was a "man addict." She earned a billion francs in her lifetime but died in poverty because money was not important to her; it was only a vehicle to seek love, happiness, and to sing songs. Her motto was "Love conquers all" and she spent much of her life in a frenetic search for it. The Great Piaf had a manic need to find the love she never had as a child.

This petite woman of ninety pounds could outwork, outdrink, outperform, and outsing the most powerful men who entered her life. She was a diminutive tiger who could not be stopped no matter how great the tragedy. Piaf was living with her paternal grandmother in a brothel when she lost her sight and after years of unsuccessful visits to doctors her grandmother arranged a pilgrimage to the shrine of Saint Theresa of Lisieux. Shortly thereafter, Piaf regained her sight at age seven. She was convinced that restoration of her sight was a miracle performed by Saint Theresa. Piaf recalled: "I always believed that that journey through darkness made me more sensitive than other people." During her blindness she talked of dreaming of "light" and "sunshine" and desperately wanting to be normal: "Much later, when I wanted really to hear something, really *see* a song, I would shut my eyes."

Piaf's blindness molded her into the consummate entertainer. She had an empathetic and almost mystical sensitivity for the emotional needs of her audience. Her "inner feeling" and extreme sensitivity affected her stage presence. This was not a learned skill but the by-product of her tragic early life: "Blindness taught me sounds have arms, faces, gestures. A voice is like the palm of a hand, no two are alike." These qualities earned her acclaim from the media. For example, the *New York Times* reported: "Piaf sings with the anguish of a shattered life, or a sinner petitioning St. Peter for hospitality."

Such emotion on stage evolved out of Piaf's traumatic childhood. Her school had been the streets of Paris, which instilled in her the basic instincts of pragmatic success. Lack of formal voice training or music education caused her to memorize the music when she sang since she couldn't read one note of music. She was forced to resort to her "street smarts" and to concentrate on pleasing the audience through emotional communication since she had no formal training as an entertainer. Piaf could mesmerize audiences when she sang from the soul about life's misfortunes and lost love, both of which she knew firsthand. Piaf was a child of the streets where love and emotional travail were not masked. That is why she was capable of such great emotional empathy with her audience. Songs like "La Vie en rose" and "Non, je ne regrette rien" became her legacy because they described life and love from the depths of the soul. To this French chanteuse life was truly magnificent and she certainly had no regrets. This hedonistic woman was determined to live life in the fast lane in order to make up for the tragedy of her early life. The following chronology of her unfortunate life illustrates that "crisis is truly the mother of creativity."

Piaf's Tragic Search for Love and Acceptance

1. Edith's only home from birth to age seven was a brothel managed by her paternal grandmother. Her only nurturing and role models came from the prostitutes. Blindness kept her from school but when she could see at age seven the schoolmaster refused her admittance because she lived in a whorehouse. Well-meaning but stupid bureaucrats forced her to become a street urchin with her itinerant father. From age seven to fifteen Edith lived by her wits on the streets of Paris as her father's assistant and pimp.

2. Edith grew weary of singing on the streets with her father, and his sexual liaisons and left him at age fifteen. She struck out on her own as a street entertainer who sang for food, lodging, and love. Her protectors and friends were pimps, hoods, and bums.

3. At age fifteen Edith fell in love with Louis Dupont and had his baby at age sixteen. Her daughter Marcelle died of meningitis at age two and a half, which started Edith's excessive drinking. This tragic period also was the beginning of her insatiable desire for men, especially soldiers.

4. By age nineteen Louis Leplée had discovered Piaf singing on the Champs Elysees. He recognized her talent and became her mentor and substitute father, changing her name from Gassion to Piaf ("Little Sparrow"). Leplée groomed her as a cabaret singer in his Club Gerny's. He made her a star at age twenty. Edith loved Leplée like a father. Nine months later Leplée was murdered and Piaf was arrested as an accomplice due to her sordid street friends. Destitute again, she was back on the street.

5. Piaf met Raymond Asso at age twenty. He became her mentor, lover, and agent, teaching her how to read and write plus cultural and social protocol. Asso beat her while grooming her for stardom at the ABC Music Hall in Paris. Piaf became an instant sensation in her first appearance. Once successful, she spurned Asso for the refined actor and well-bred Englishman Paul Meurisse, who became her newest love.

6. Living with Meurisse at age twenty-one, Piaf met her lifelong friend, sometime lover, and confidant Jean Cocteau. Cocteau was an intellectual, a poet, playwright, writer, and artist. He wrote *Le Bel Indifferent,* in which Piaf and Meurisse starred. Piaf named this her Professor Period, which was interrupted by another great trauma, the invasion of Paris by the Germans and five-year occupation. She snubbed the Nazis but survived.

7. At age twenty-three Piaf met the Jewish songwriter Michel Emer who wrote her first great recording hit, "L'Accordeoniste," which sold 850,000 records (78s). She would sing it for twenty years, and repaid her lover and friend Emer by bribing his way into unoccupied France to escape the Nazis.

8. At age twenty-five Edith made the movie *Montmarte sur Seine* and met songwriter/publicist Henri Contet, who would become her lover, songwriter, and publicity agent. Piaf stole him from another woman, a trend that she often repeated. Malcontent, she began drinking heavily, was evicted from hotel after hotel, and lived like a vagabond. Piaf indiscriminately gave money away. Contet accused her of running a brothel. She had many love trysts, causing Contet to call her mad, a drunk, a whore, hysteric, and a nymphomaniac. She tried to make retribution to him and reform by having his baby (she was unsuccessful).

9. By age twenty-seven Edith became the Great Piaf under Henri Contet's tutelage and promotion. She lived a life of decadence and was evicted from the finest hotels for her provocative lifestyle, noise, and excessive drinking. She spent the balance of the war living with her sister Simone in a brothel. Only prostitutes could tolerate her scandalous lifestyle. She called this her Brothel Period.

10. By age twenty-eight Piaf became a slave of men and the bottle, two passions which led to her Mentoring Period. She fell madly in love with Yves Montand and groomed him to be a cabaret singer and movie actor. Five years her junior, he became her student, lover, and roommate. They made the movie *Etoile sans lumiere* (Star without Light). Montand later admitted to her and the media that "I owe everything to Edith." He said that Piaf "only sang well when madly in love."

11. Piaf's conquest of America started at the end of WWII when she was thirty-one. She tutored a group called the Compagnons and their manager Jean-Louis Jaubert became her newest lover. "Le Toris Cloches" became a big hit in France. Critics labeled her the "white dove from the slums." She befriended Marlene Dietrich in New York who introduced her to boxer Marcel Cerdan, her next lover.

12. Piaf met the married Cerdan at age thirty-three and fell madly in love with the man destined to be the Welterweight Champion of the world. They created an international scandal when Cerdan smuggled Piaf into his New York training camp via his car trunk. Cerdan upset Tony Zale (Piaf credited) and was defeated by Jake LaMotta (Piaf blamed). She begged him to visit her in the United States and he died en route in a plane crash on October 28, 1949. Part of Piaf died with him due to overwhelming guilt. Blaming herself for Cerdan's death, she resorted to stimulants to sing and depressants to sleep while drinking heavily. She was a drug addict for much of the rest of her life.

13. Piaf had her first nervous breakdown at age thirty-five in 1950 due to Cerdan's death. When she crawled home drunk and drugged at 6 A.M. her sister Simone said, "She's mad. She's going to die." Piaf met Eddie Constantine during this period and tutored him to a successful stage career. Her student, lover, and singing partner, Constantine was married and left her for his wife after using Piaf as much as she used him.

14. Driving in France with songwriter Charles Aznavour on July 24, 1951, the car went off the road and Piaf broke her arm and ribs. She convalesced on morphine to kill pain but continued use of alcohol in her search to overcome depression. She lost all friends and became a street bum, which ended in an attempted suicide. Two drug cures were unsuccessful during this traumatic and tragic period of her life.

15. Piaf met Jacques Pills in early 1952, when she was thirty-seven and he forty-seven. They married in Paris on July 29. He was unaware of her drug ad-

diction. She collapsed on their honeymoon tour in Hollywood. A four-year night-mare caused by her drug addiction, her marriage to Pills ended in divorce in 1956. She personally produced and financed a rerun of *Le Bel Indifferent* when no one would produce the play because of her instability. It flopped, costing her millions in 1956, and she was broke again at age forty-one.

16. Frenetic search for her lost youth started at age forty with boys twenty years her junior: Claude Fugus, Felix Marten, and Charles Douglas. She had amazing powers of seduction even when unstable, inebriated, or on drugs. She pursued self-destructive relationships in a desperate search for love.

17. Piaf met and fell in love with songwriter Charles Damon at age forty-five. He wrote her greatest hit, "Non, je ne regrette rien" (I have no regrets) in 1960. He wrote forty songs for Piaf but she needed drugs to walk on stage to sing them. One manager attempted to cancel her performance. Edith cried, "If you do I'll kill myself," and the audience encouraged her performance. She collapsed after the eighth song, but no one asked for money back. The Little Sparrow could still mesmerize audiences and refused to quit when dying.

18. At age forty-seven and terminally ill, she married Theo Serapo, twenty years her junior, on October 9, 1962. She lived one more year, leaving Serapo with 45 million francs of debt after having earned over one billion in her short lifetime. Her death ended a tragic existence where she used an indomitable willpower to overcome every adversity.

Edith Piaf lived a roller-coaster life of continuous tragedy and crises. Every trauma involved a different man and was followed by enormous professional success. Piaf hit the very bottom almost yearly and yet managed to rise to success. What enabled a woman with so few gifts to gain such enormous power? The answer lies in her persona. Piaf had great tenacity and some internal power to overcome adversity. She was hypomanic and drove herself beyond reason. How did she become manic? It appears this was imprinted during her life on the streets where survival is a daily necessity. This early training taught her to deal with calamitous events and conditioned her to deal with a catastrophic life.

Piaf learned early that both success and tragedy are fleeting. On September 25, 1962, she enjoyed her finest hour with a gala performance from the top of the Eiffel Tower before an audience that included Dwight D. Eisenhower, Winston Churchill, Prince Rainier of Monaco, Elizabeth Taylor, Richard Burton, Audrey Hepburn, and countless other notables. Terminally ill at the time, Piaf was still capable of rising to the occasion and brought this prestigious audience of her peers and international celebrities to its feet in a standing ovation and tribute to her greatness. Piaf's last performance was held at the Olympia in Paris where she defied her doctors' orders that she was too ill to perform. The Little Piaf was magnificent as she and the audience sensed that this was her last hurrah. Piaf called on some inner power to belt out her songs of love and tragedy with an emotional intensity that captivated this audience. Many in the audience were crying when she finished; she died less than a year later.

This tenacious woman searched the world for love, only to be denied. It was at her funeral that she finally found this tribute when she drew forty thousand weeping and adoring fans.

Summary

In Chinese the word "crises" is made up of two characters: one means "danger," the other "opportunity." That sums up the term for the creative genius. Crises is a two-edged concept where danger or trauma can be transformed into new opportunity. All systems tend toward *entropy,* which is the tendency to complexity and disorder. The Second Law of Thermodynamics dictates that all systems are either destroyed or die in "heat death." When systems or people reach this breaking point or "chaos" (Dr. Ilya Prigogine's "bifurcation point") they either die or reemerge, often reaching higher levels than before. Reaching this crisis point or entropy is traumatic at the time but appears to be a prerequisite for even greater achievement. Prigogine was able to transform the nihilism of entropy to a positive theory that he labeled "dissipative structures," which calls for all systems to reemerge as a higher order after reaching the point of crisis or instability. Creative geniuses appear to follow a similar track. They often accomplish this in a trauma state where superlearning transforms them into greater beings than they were before.

These fourteen visionaries faced continual danger and traumatic periods during their climb to fame and fortune. The debacles of Disney and Piaf are examples of the catastrophes most faced. The psychobiographies go into further detail on each individual but it is safe to say each experienced behavior modification during their formative years due to some great crisis. The personality and behavior traits that resulted from great trauma is what ultimately made them great. Some became risk-oriented, others learned to be tenacious, and others become workaholics. Most ended up as manic or Type A personalities. Since great crises can imprint inspirational positives or denigrating negatives, it appears that successful people are fortunate enough to have been imprinted positively, while failures were imprinted negatively. In the cases of these fourteen, the strongest imprints were a manic need to succeed plus an obsession for excellence and achievement. Their early imprints instilled them with the key personality characteristics for great success. Tesla was transformed into a manic overachiever by the tragic death of his brother, Dane. Montessori turned an unfortunate pregnancy, at the height of a brilliant medical career, into the Montessori method of educational reformation. Picasso made a Faustian pact with God to save his sister's life and when she died, sublimated his guilt into some of the greatest masterpieces in history. Frank Lloyd Wright was able to survive the murder of his lover and the burning of Taliesin West, sublimating this tragedy into a lifetime of iconoclastic architecture. Disney and Piaf saw tragedy as just another detour along the way to their destiny.

Family tragedies were prevalent in the lives of these fourteen and appear to have been a motivational force in their later lives. Premature deaths of parents also appear to have conditioned them for overachievement. All fourteen seem to have had an abnormal or even psychopathic need to achieve, which can be traced back to some early trauma or crisis. They appear to have been overachieving as compensation for their earlier problems and were intent on showing the world that they were special. In many hypomanic personalities the need for success overwhelms their total being. Manic and/or Type A personalities often emerge as the predominant characteristic in the creative power broker. Such individuals usually confuse achievement with self-worth and success with happiness.

For some individuals winning becomes an obsession and no price is too great to pay. Such a single focus ultimately takes its toll, even on those who reach the top, and unhappiness and loneliness result. Visiting the bottom of life's troughs is not a pleasant experience, but it appears to groom the individual for a life of great power and success. It certainly conditions a person to take higher risks, which correlates to success. These visionaries were all high risk-takers and highly resilient due to continuous bouts with catastrophe. Both Walt Disney and Edith Piaf are examples of how constant failure can often be turned into great creative success. The price these two paid was huge—nervous breakdowns; suicide attempts; drug, alcohol, and cigarette addiction—but their successes were just as huge. The spoils of such success are often delayed until death, which was the case for both Disney and Piaf. Both received far more accolades in death than in life.

When this book was being written in early 1995, boxer Mike Tyson was sitting in an Indiana prison convicted of rape. This was a traumatic experience for Tyson, stripped of everything he held dear, including the freedom to pursue his only avocation—boxing. It became apparent to me that Tyson would leave prison with a new dedication to boxing and would annihilate any opponent daring to enter the ring against him. While in prison Tyson was unable to train or keep in shape, he had no fights for two years at a critical period in his professional life, and his aging took place in an environment not conducive to success in such a physically demanding profession. Furthering this argument, Tyson had little or no financial incentive since he was independently wealthy from his past fights which left him a multimillionaire with little or no incentive to risk his person for money.

I predict that Mike Tyson will become the most successful heavyweight ever and will go on to become the most dominant heavyweight boxing champion in history, not because of his skills in the boxing ring but because of the psychological imprinting which took place in that Indiana prison. He now has an intense and uncontrollable emotional need to exorcise those inner ghosts; this need will be released in the ring against unsuspecting opponents. Every opponent will be viewed as someone blocking that inner mission and will be summarily destroyed by a maniacally driven man searching for emotional redemption.

My prediction of Mike Tyson becoming far more successful than before his incarceration was given some credence in late 1995 when he annihilated the previously undefeated Peter McNealy in the first round at Caesar's Palace in Las

Vegas. His second fight against Buster Mathis, Jr., took a little longer but ended in a similar devastating knockout of his opponent. His domination of these fighters had nothing to do with skill but a lot to do with an internal drive looking for liberation. Mike Tyson is a man on a mission of destruction, which is a manifestation of his internal needs and not external skills. The trauma resulting from being imprisoned has created a seething person whose destiny will prove emphatically that crisis is the mother of creativity and superstardom.

3

Power and Influence: "Hierarchy of Power"

Being powerful is like being a lady. If you have to tell people you are, you aren't.
—Margaret Thatcher

Philosophy of Power

All power emanates from others even though it is spawned internally. As Deepak Chopra wrote, "The deepest reality you are aware of is the one from which you draw your power." Chopra was confirming that we are only as weak as our greatest fears and repressions. Our secrets may allow us to delude others but we can never delude ourselves. Truth erupts from our actions as is seen in the character Raskolnikov in Dostoevsky's *Crime and Punishment,* the world's greatest psychological novel. The protagonist successfully killed without compassion, able to fool everyone, including the police, but he was unable to fool himself. Real power can only come from those with internal integrity. Hitler and Napoleon were successful in attaining great power apparently by duping the populace. Not so! They were guilty of perverted ethical values and morals but both men were absolutely convinced of their destiny to lead their adopted nations to redemption. They believed they were meant to lead the masses to a utopian existence and conveyed that through mesmerizing dialogue. Their belief was rewarded with great power given by the masses. It is axiomatic that such power cannot be achieved without a constituency who supplies it.

Michael Korda, author of *Power* (1975), wrote: "Power over other people is a sham." He was saying that power is earned, not taken. An example is how a baby can have such enormous power over its parents. When a baby cries, the parents jump, due to its innate dependency. Its helplessness gives it huge power based on nothing more than need. Power is a state of mind as Ram Dass wrote in *Be Here*

Now: "As long as you want *power* you can't have it. The minute you don't want *power,* you'll have more than you ever dreamed possible." The West spent forty years attempting to break down the Berlin Wall. When they gave up pursuing the power of destruction and pursued ideological freedom for all, the Wall was torn down by its own creators. In this case power was acquired through acquiescence, not aggression. The need to demonstrate power was removed thereby allowing for success in the Wall's demise.

Power comes in mysterious ways. It is often available to those who ask for it. Simply stop someone on the street and ask for help with directions or other advice. It is nothing short of amazing the aid you can get just by asking. When you subjugate your own will to others or demonstrate that you "need them," help is willingly given. Most people are too proud or shy to utilize this source of power.

Educator David McClelland has spent most of his life researching motivational power. He found that "individuals who have a high power motivation have a single goal—to feel powerful." Napoleon is an excellent example of someone who worked diligently to gain power. He wrote, "Power is my mistress," and truly believed his success was based on his ability to manipulate others. His philosophy was: "Keep on acquiring more and more power, all the rest is chimerical." Bertrand Russell defined power as "the production of intended effects." Alvin Toffler in *Powershift* (1990) described power in a sociological context where physical (force), financial (money), and knowledge (computers) powers were the dominant forms. He concluded that knowledge power would ultimately win out over force and money. Francis Bacon preceded Toffler in saying "knowledge is power." Machiavelli propounded a far more perverse definition of power which he concocted for politicians. His philosophy of power was described in his classic work on power politics, *The Prince*. Machiavelli envisioned the successful politician, now known as a "Machiavellian," as one who values ruthlessness and cunning above all else—a philosophy of "destroy or be destroyed."

Psychosexual Power

Freud felt that all power sprang from "suppressed sexual energy," which led him to conclude that "man would make no progress if he could obtain fully satisfying pleasure." He used the ascetic and unmarried Leonardo da Vinci as an example of this theory. Freud viewed power and sex as a zero-sum game where anyone sexually sated becomes lethargic with little potential for creative success. Nikola Tesla firmly believed in that thesis and refused to even date for fear it would stifle his creative powers. Hitler also believed the same. Howard Hughes was married at age nineteen but once divorced refused to allow marriage to interfere with his lifestyle until age fifty. Ironically he was impotent by age fifty and spent the balance of his life sublimating sexual energy into power. In a Freudian twist of fate, Hughes had lost all need for sex. New-Age author Michael Hutchison wrote in *The Anatomy of Sex and Power* (1990): "Sex and Power are inextricably intertwined. . . . Sex cannot only undo power, it is power." His thesis can be summarized as: Sex = Power and Power = Sex. Hutchison maintains that there is a direct link between "social dominance and sexual potency, between power and sex." He concludes that those with high testosterone—Big T personalities—are those with the highest sex drive and therefore the most powerful. Years earlier Napoleon Hill arrived at the same conclusion, which he described in his best-selling motivational book *Think and Grow Rich* (1960). After studying Napoleon, Lincoln, J. P. Morgan, George Washington, William Shakespeare, Thomas Edison, Henry Ford, Andrew Carnegie, John D. Rockefeller, and numerous other powerful people, he concluded, "The genius that was theirs undoubtedly found its source of power in transmuted sexual energy. . . . There never has been, and never will be a great leader, builder, or artist lacking in this driving force of sex."

Charismatic power is used interchangeably in this work with psychosexual energy or libidinal drive as it is hard to separate these concepts in these fourteen power brokers. The libidinal drives and psychosexual proclivities of the subjects are illustrated in figure 9. The fourteen visionaries in this book certainly exuded an irresistible sexual energy. Even those who were not sexually precocious were sexually alluring. Tesla never had a date, but J. P. Morgan's daughter, Anne Morgan, did her best to seduce him because of his animal magnetism. Numerous other women were attracted to him in the same way. His best friend was Robert Underwood Johnson. Johnson's wife, Katherine, wrote Tesla passionate letters for many years in a futile attempt at seduction. Montessori exuded a similar sensual appeal when lecturing to large audiences. Like Tesla, she never married, although her one serious love affair ended in a traumatic pregnancy. Most of the other subjects were sexually provocative. Hitler was more sadomasochistic than Sade, for whom the word was coined. The Marquis de Sade himself was notorious for his sexual depravities, primarily because he documented all of his sexual fantasies in the infamous books *Justine* and *Juliette*. Sade was a perversely driven man with enormous sexual energy. He documented his orgasms while in prison and if one is to believe him, he averaged approximately eight orgasms daily for many years. However, Sade was probably second in sexual energy and depravities to Howard Hughes. Prior to Hughes's near-fatal plane crashes and drug addiction, which made him impotent, he led a life of perversity with both sexes. His movies could not have done justice to his sexual lifestyle. During one frenetic period during the 1930s, Hughes maintained simultaneous sexual relationships with four men and three women who were the acknowledged sex gods and goddesses of Hollywood. Two of the women were married at the time of his liaisons, causing many confrontations where Hughes was relegated to climbing out windows with pants in hand or engaging in hand-to-hand combat, which was not one of his strengths. During this period Hughes engaged in weekly and often daily sexual liaisons with Ginger Rogers, Bette Davis, Katharine Hepburn, Jean Harlow, Cary Grant, and Randolph Scott. Davis and Rogers were married at the time, requiring the licentious Hughes to arrange trysts on his boat or in dingy hotel rooms. His movie *The Outlaw,* starring Jane Russell, was considered by Hollywood insiders as nothing more

FIGURE 9
PSYCHOSEXUAL DRIVE—LIBIDINAL ENERGY

Napoleon Bonaparte. Biographers portray him as having "boundless sexual energy."

Walt Disney. Disney had a Victorian morality sublimating his sexuality into the personalities of cartoon characters like Mickey and Donald. Walt's personality characteristics are clearly delineated by Mickey Mouse (Superego: humble, chaste, cerebral, asexual, and adored) and Donald Duck (Id: dark, volatile, emotional, sexual, and angry).

Isadora Duncan. Called herself "Aphrodite" and lived to fulfill that internal image of herself. She was antimarriage and an exponent of freelove, living her life in a series of scandalous love affairs which resulted in three illegitimate children by three men from different countries (Germany, America, Italy). Friend Mary Desti said she "could no more live without human love than she could without food or music."

Amelia Earhart. "America's first androgynous sex symbol," according to feminist Susan Brownmiller. Wore Gene Vidal's jockey shorts for luck on many of her record-breaking flights. Kept her maiden name when married and agreed to live in open relationship with husband George Putnam.

Adolf Hitler. Sexually perverse and sadomasochistic, requiring whipping and insults to achieve climax. Charismatic charm attracted many women, three of whom attempted suicide due to his inattention (Unity Milford, Mitzi Reiter, Eva Braun twice). His niece Geli Raubal killed herself after one of his jealous sexual rages (1930). Married Eva Braun in Berlin bunker then committed suicide in last sadomasochistic act in 1945.

Howard Hughes. Led lascivious life spending millions to satisfy his sexual fantasies. Slept with men and women indiscriminately. Sex was a game and his partners conquests until impotency at age fifty. Proposed marriage to dozens, married three (Ella Rice, Terry Moore, Jean Peters). Susan Hayward aborted his child. A perverse bisexual who used movies to satiate bizarre fantasies (*The Outlaw* filmed as fantasy of Jane Russell's breasts). Hollywood banned his movies due to sexuality.

Maria Montessori. Bore an illegitimate son (Mario) in Roman Catholic Italy; raised as a nephew. Never married in deference to son. Lived a devout life thereafter sublimating sex to education, work, and son.

Rupert Murdoch. "Tits and Bums" nickname earned for perverse headlines in Australia, London, and New York City. The "Page Three Girls" of *London Sun* made paper famous and successful. "Kinky Vicar and His Sex Slave" a typical headline that will prove to be legacy of this puritanical fundamentalist.

Edith Piaf. Started "one-night" stands at age fifteen and never stopped. Could not sleep without a man— any man. Soldiers were her passion. Had illegitimate child at age sixteen; married twice but never happy. Piaf nonchalantly engaged in ménage-à-trois, leading perverse life and seeking love in all the wrong places.

Pablo Picasso. Sex and destruction synonymous in Picasso's art and relationships. Mistress Gilot said he had "an exhaustible passion for work and sex." Picasso drove first wife to neuroses, second wife and a mistress to suicide, and mistress Dora Maar to nervous breakdown. Slept with wives of friends.

Helena Rubinstein. Always sublimated romance to work. Two marriages of convenience, not bothering to attend her second husband's funeral. Relationships only used as a source of power on her terms

Marquis de Sade. *Sadism* his legacy. A lecher who spent his life debauching. Seduced virgin sister-in-law, which led to his demise—a truly sadomasochistic act. Lived life in libidinal frenzy, culminating in his repeated seduction and sodomizing of a sixteen-year-old girl while in prison at age seventy-four.

Nikola Tesla. Attracted women by the droves, but was so obsessed with science that he felt a woman would detract from his work. Never had a date, dying a virgin, sublimating sex to his only passion—work.

Frank Lloyd Wright. A sexually charismatic visionary who abandoned his wife, six children, and successful business for married lover (Mamah Cheney). Biographer Meryle Secrest says he had "enormous sexual energy." Taliesin was nicknamed the "love cottage" because of his image as a provocative libertine.

than Hughes's vicarious escape into his sexual fantasy over Russell's incomparable breasts. The movie was banned, compelling the voyeuristic Hughes to keep it for his own private viewing. He watched it for years before suing the Motion Picture Association, winning the right to release the film for public viewing in 1946.

Psychosexual energy and charismatic power were prime ingredients in the rise to power of Napoleon, Duncan, Earhart, Hitler, Hughes, Piaf, Picasso, Sade, and Wright. Piaf's sister was amazed at the sexual attraction and power that Edith exercised over virtually every man she met. Simone said she never saw a man capable of resisting Edith's seductive power. Audiences were mesmerized and attracted to her animal magnetism and sexual energy on stage. Amelia Earhart was called "America's first androgynous sex symbol" due to her unique unisexual appeal. Hershman and Lieb (1994) said Napoleon exuded "boundless sexual energy" and his wife Josephine said, "I am alarmed at the energy which animates all his doings." Françoise Gilot, the ex-mistress and mother of Picasso's last two children, wrote, "Picasso had an inexhaustible passion for work and sex"—and this was when Picasso was approaching seventy. Frank Lloyd Wright's biographer Meryle Secrest described him as having "enormous sexual energy." Only Disney's relationship was anywhere close to being normal (even Disney had a notorious affair with movie star Dolores Del Rio). The other two so-called normal relationships in this group included Earhart, who had an open marriage, and the Marquis de Sade, who used his wife to solicit young girls for his pleasure. Piaf was by far the most sexually provocative of any in this book and even made Sade and Hughes look ascetic by comparison. Duncan, Picasso, Hughes, and Wright were highly promiscuous while Disney, Montessori, Murdoch, Rubinstein, and Tesla were quite Victorian. Even those with puritanical views about sex exuded a certain sexuality, confirming Henry Kissinger's famous aphorism, "Power is the ultimate aphrodisiac." Aristotle Onassis gave a more mundane analysis: "If women didn't exist, all the money in the world would have no meaning." These fourteen were sensuous even when not intending to be and this contributed to their charismatic power over individuals and groups.

Sources of Power and Influence

Six sources of power and influence were critical to the success of these fourteen: physical, financial, knowledge, titular, charismatic, and willpower. These six power sources are different but effective means for rising to the top of any profession. These visionary leaders used all of them at some time during their rise to fame and fortune. Each of these power sources falls into the personal, positional, or internally generated categories. Personal power is the most valuable form since it is under the control of the individual. Positional power can be given or taken away, making it less enduring. Internally generated power depends on convincing others to accept one's dream and become a disciple, which in turn creates *power* and *influence* for the originator. Cultists are infamous for this use of power.

George Gilder in *Microcosm* (1989) and Alvin Toffler in *Powershift* (1990) have made strong arguments for *knowledge power* and *technology* as the driving forces behind our changing society. Gilder was more inclined toward a "technological elite" to guide a dynamic society. Toffler saw knowledge power as the critical element for a dynamic evolving society. He sees inexorable and unpredictable shifts in power as the guiding principle behind all change. The following quote from *Powershift* sums up his three principles of power that he believes to be critical for success in any dynamic society: "For inside the world of business as in the larger world outside, *force, wealth,* and *knowledge*—like the ancient sword, jewel, and mirror . . . remain the primary tools of power."

Toffler concludes that knowledge, based on the onset of the information age and the computer revolution, is the most instrumental factor in the struggle for power. He states that knowledge, an "Information Age" fallout (software in contrast to hardware), and computer science are destined to control the ebb and flow of data. In other words, Toffler believes that high tech, and the knowledge of same, will become the key to controlling future power. He says that "physical force or muscle power" can be ultimately controlled by money or financial power and those with enough "knowledge power" can control those with the money. Physical power or force are negative in that they will ultimately destroy that which you want to control which makes it a subservient type of power. Money power is also dangerous since it has finite limitations and is ultimately exhausted. Only knowledge power is unique in that it can be constantly increased throughout life. Toffler concludes: "The control of knowledge is the crux of tomorrow's worldwide struggle for power in every human institution."

HIERARCHY OF POWER

I believe that a hierarchy of power exists and will prove to be the crux of all power. Toffler's evolution of power stopped with knowledge, which he anointed as the ultimate power source. It is apparent from this research that power emanates from various sources beyond Toffler's force, wealth, and knowledge. Creative geniuses and great power brokers prove that power is gained or lost via emotional strength, not physical strength.

From bottom to top in importance the primary powers are: physical, financial, knowledge, titular, charismatic, and willpower (see figure 10).

Great power brokers must actually begin at the top of the power stages— Will—and work their way down to the more basic forms of power like strength and guns. Recall that Hitler's experience of attempting to use physical force at the Munich Beer Hall Putsch ended in disaster and his imprisonment, and only after exercising his will, charisma, and intellect did he gain ultimate power in Germany. Those in the ghetto who resort to guns without knowledge or sense of will are destined to end up in jail—or dead. Those who start at the top of the hierarchy of power will be successful. Those who attempt to cut short the process and begin with guns and muscle are destined to become powerless. One cannot ignore the hi-

FIGURE 10
DEVELOPMENTAL STAGES OF POWER
(AN EVOLUTIONARY ANALYSIS OF POWER)

| Generalizations: | Males: | Use power to obtain sex |
| | Females: | Use sex to obtain power |

Power Type	Manifestation	Power Source
Physical Power	Strongest prevails Agrarian and male-dominated Dictators and fascists	Muscle, guns, and force
Financial Power	Economic strength Bureaucrats/managers	Money and fiscal wealth
Knowledge Power	Computer science Educational institutions Intelligentsia leaders	Mind and intelligence
Titular Power	Authority position Rank: CEOs and directors	Elected or birthright (kings); fear/dominance-oriented
Charismatic Power (Externally generated)	Psychosexual energy Cult leaders and visionaries with hypnotic attraction	Personal magnetism, Personality and behavior; love and expertise
Willpower (Internally generated)	Psychic energy Competitive aggressors	Promethean visionaries; aspiration-oriented

erarchy of power. The reason is that physical power or strength is fleeting; willpower and mental and emotional strengths are not. An example is the Eastern mind-control gurus who defy the laws of nature through control of their bodies by transcendental meditation, which is another form of willpower.

WILLPOWER

True power emanates from the inner self or mind. The highest two (charismatic and willpower) are personal powers that are a function of the individual's psyche. Titular power is positional and popularly known as authority. It is inherited or granted by others as in the birthright of kings or the inheritance of a company. Authoritarian power is obtained through the luck of the draw, election, or appointment to lead an organization or institution. Kings and queens have "positional" power due to the luck of birth. Presidents and dictators have positional power because of their personal power, the ability to get elected or seize power. The lower forms of power are physical, financial, and knowledge. They are critical to the process but can be easily controlled if one is endowed with the higher three.

The above six sources of power are often used interchangeably to create success for an individual or organization. Figure 11 depicts a simplistic outline of the

FIGURE 11
HIERARCHY OF POWER

"Invincibility is in oneself, vulnerability is in the opponent"
—Sun Tsu (*The Art of War*)

"The strong shall conquer and the weak shall perish"
—Philosophical premise of Nietzsche and Ayn Rand

STAGE 6
WILLPOWER
(Internal Drive)

Strongest wills prevail when those taking responsibility (especially in times of crisis or trauma where fear and uncertainty exist) exercise self-control and influence the weak. Awesome self-esteem is critical to this power.

STAGE 5
CHARISMATIC POWER
(Psychic energy)

External manifestation of willpower. Passionate libidinal energy and vital force of personality prevail over logic. First five stages subjugated to this personal power. Communications and selling skills critical to success.

STAGE 4
TITULAR POWER
(Authority)

Positional power where lower powers can be effective in gaining organizational control, power, and influence over subordinates. Fear is a motivational device for controlling the weak. This power is given and can be taken away, thus is a fleeting form of power and influence.

STAGE 3
KNOWLEDGE POWER
(Brains)

Smart people can dominate information-driven societies and are capable of earning money, buying the most guns, and dominating by fear. Intelligentsia and computer science control, but are ineffective without strong willpower.

STAGE 2
FINANCIAL POWER
(Money)

Secondary influence where power can be "bought" in the form of subjects, guns, knowledge, or titles. Leverage used to acquire economic power, which is fleeting since brains, authority, charisma, and willpower can get money.

STAGE 1
PHYSICAL POWER
(Muscle and guns)

Primary anthropological influence where Alpha A males gain power over weaker subordinates. Higher powers unavailable in Third-World nations where force (muscle and guns) are the most effective. This basic form of power is fleeting as there is always someone stronger or with more guns.

hierarchy or evolutionary nature of these powers. This chart outlines power from the lowest type (physical) to the highest (willpower) and describes the manifestation and source of each. Entrepreneurs, creators, and innovators, including the fourteen in this book, tend to be quite evolved in their use of power and have reached the top two. Hitler and Napoleon depended more on physical power to expand their sphere of influence than the others, but they would never have been capable of utilizing this low-stage power had they not exercised their will and charisma on the masses. Industrialists Howard Hughes and Rupert Murdoch likewise utilized personal magnetism and enormous willpower to parlay their financial base into powerful industrial dynasties.

PSYCHIC ENERGY AND POWER

Business leaders Helena Rubinstein, Howard Hughes, Walt Disney, and Rupert Murdoch were inclined to flaunt their titular or authoritarian power and often were considered tyrants as operating executives. The others gained fame and fortune through the use of their intransigent and indomitable wills. All operated at the top of this power hierarchy where personal magnetism can move mountains. They were able to use psychic energy (willpower) to get their way. Their magnetism (charisma) made them gurus (knowledge) within their professions and earned them money (financial) with which to buy their instruments of force (physical). When an individual uses his willpower (stage 6), he seems to become electrically charged with psychic energy or charismatic power (stage 5), finds it easy to acquire the titular power (stage 4) needed to employ the knowledge power (stage 3) and earn the economic or financial power (stage 2), and control the masses through physical power (stage 1). In other words, those capable of mastering an internalized or Nietzschean willpower are capable of controlling those who have the lesser powers, and ultimately rise to the very top of their professions.

Physical Power

In comparative psychology, the most powerful male in a primate group is the "Alpha male" who virtually always gets first call on food and sex and has the highest status within the pack. Maturity, muscularity, and experience become the defining attributes of power in such primitive environs. According to psychohistorian Dean Keith Simonton: "Alpha males in human societies are virile, tall, and violent." He used U.S. presidents as examples of his theory in *Greatness* (1994). These presidents tended to be taller and more attractive. According to many sources, Kennedy beat Nixon because he was taller and better looking. The taller presidents—Lincoln at 6'4", Washington, Jefferson, and Franklin Roosevelt all at about 6'2", Kennedy and Bush at 6'1"—won over their shorter adversaries. Clinton at 6'3" was two inches taller than Bush and won. The same rise to power is evident in Third-World nations where muscle and firepower are usually dominant.

The same is found in most primitive societies. Those with the biggest muscles or guns gain the greatest power.

Physical power prevails where the strong attempt to subjugate the weak by using superior physical size and strength. Males exercise this form of power over females when other variables do not interfere. The alpha male dominates in primitive but not in more advanced societies. Stranded on a desert island, the strongest male will end up with the most desirable mate and the best food. Violence and aggression are often used when physical power is employed. Force is the supreme arbiter in all physical conflicts such as street fights or war, or in social conflict. The problem with such power is that it often tends to destroy that which is pursued (an example is Napoleon and Hitler who killed in order to conquer), cheapening life in the process. Using force as the primary source of power is dangerous because it is so fleeting. There is always someone with more guns or bigger muscles who is willing and desirous of taking power. Napoleon was the most powerful leader in Europe when he controlled the most soldiers and guns, but lost power when Wellington assembled more men and weapons. Likewise Hitler expanded his sphere of influence through the use of physical power, but lost it when Eisenhower and Stalin produced more effective weaponry.

It is ironic that Napoleon came to power due to the Reign of Terror (physical power) of Robespierre, who then died from the very tyranny he created. France was left under committee rule with a corrupt Directory allowing the upstart Napoleon to gain power. The failure of physical power and bureaucratic incompetence allowed the driven and imperious Napoleon to gain power. In the absence of higher forms of power, muscle and guns will always prevail.

In gender conflicts and confrontations the male tends to resort to his anthropological heritage, striking out at his adversary since he is confident that physical power will dominate the weaker female. Women resort to their more dominant verbal skills (research indicates that women are typically more verbally proficient than men). Women will usually resort to verbal combat in any confrontation rather than put themselves at the disadvantage in using physical means to resolve the problem. Women will attempt to talk their way out of conflict, which equalizes their intergender power in more advanced societies. The conclusion is that physical power is fundamentally a male source of power and most often utilized in personal or primitive environments.

Financial Power

Economic power dominates physical power in most situations. Everyone knows that cash is king in all entrepreneurial or start-up ventures. The physically dominant (Alpha male types) described above tend to exploit the weak in order to control food, money, and wealth. But even the weak are capable of earning vast sums of money to buy the guns and ultimately wrest control from the physically strong. Howard Hughes and Rupert Murdoch are examples of individuals who used their willpower and charisma to gain wealth and then used that economic power to build vast empires. The United States did the same as these two on a grander scale. The United States became a wealthy international power as a result of its vast natural and human resources that worked in concert with the advent of the Industrial Revolution. Once its financial base was secure, it was able to exploit its economic power to build the most dominant military operation, featuring the most ships, planes, and guns.

Hitler built his German military juggernaut in the same way. Hitler's meticulous control of the money in Nazi Germany was the base for his rise to power. He convinced German industrialists like Gustav Rupp and Ernst Hanfstaengl of the threat of communism in order to finance his Third Reich. His ploy worked. His mesmerizing rhetoric was his greatest and most important power, but it was only an instrument to use in raising the vast sums of monies from the industrialists to build his military machine. He also appealed to their nationalism by promising an Aryan-dominated world.

Howard Hughes's father convinced him that financial power was the most effective form of power, which prompted young Howard to say, "I can buy any man in the world." He resorted to his financial power in buying actresses, generals, and bureaucrats. His Watergate influence and military contracts were notorious scandals spawned by his use of money to buy governmental favors.

Rupert Murdoch has built the dominant media empire in the world through the use of financial power through leverage. He used his hard-won power with far more discretion than Hughes, although Murdoch was even more risk-oriented than Hughes in business dealings. He used financial leverage far more in his numerous acquisitions, having learned early that risk and leverage are synonymous terms in business. One can expand in business through the use of leverage where current assets are pledged to finance new acquisitions. Such advice is a two-edged sword and if able to service the debt will result in enormous expansion and growth. When not successful, the business will crash as fast as it grew, just like a house of cards. Murdoch first built a strong financial base at News Corp and then began pledging his growing asset base to build a media dynasty. He created only three small operations from scratch: *The Australian,* a newspaper equivalent to *USA Today*; a cable television station in Adelaide; and the *Star* tabloid in the United States. The rest of his vast holdings were acquired through the use of his enormous financial power.

Knowledge Power

Information is the cornerstone of knowledge and therefore the ability to acquire and manipulate information becomes critical to gaining power. Knowledge is also the key to acquiring individual power since it is the basic ingredient in building self-confidence and enthusiasm. The world has become an "Information Age," in the words of Alvin Toffler, and the tools of information gathering and manipulation are the primary tools of power. Computers dominate information gathering and are indispensable in controlling the key elements of the information age: the acquisition, sorting, and manipulation of information. Computer scientists and computer literate individuals have a disproportionate amount of power due to their ability in this area. In those industries (education, market research, government) where knowledge is power, those with computer expertise become the most valuable resources.

Toffler predicts that those who control computers will hold the greatest power within organizations. Many bureaucrats and educators, including the intelligentsia, believe knowledge (intelligence) is the ultimate power and tend to pursue it to the detriment of all else. Some of this is self-serving since intellectuals congregate in educational and governmental institutions and other bureaucratic environments. Murray and Herrnstein, the authors of *The Bell Curve* (1994), predict that a "cognitive elite" will gravitate to the top and have absolute power over society. In their eyes the intellectually superior will hold power over the "cognitively deficient." They define the "cognitive elite" as white upper-middle-class intellectuals who would leave the less intellectually gifted (lower IQs) and minority groups in controlled ghettos. Murray and Herrnstein created a masterful statistical analysis on intelligence demonstrating how the cognitive elite correlates with success in higher education, earnings, job proficiency, low crime, low welfare, preferred parenting, and so forth. The furor over the book came about because people actually believe that intelligence is the key characteristic in those predestined to lead the world. On the contrary, those who lead the world will be the workaholic risk-takers who have great self-confidence, drive, intuitiveness, tenacity, and an obsession with their dreams—the same qualities found in these fourteen visionaries.

Intelligence ranks low on the list of important criteria for success in entrepreneurial, creative, or innovative endeavors. I agree that the cognitive elite is destined to become dominant in bureaucratic organizations and educational institutions. However, these individuals will never become great innovators, artists, or entrepreneurs. A dynamic world demands dynamic people, not people with a 150 IQ. Knowledge is important, as shown by these fourteen wunderkinds, but it is not everything. These fourteen probably knew more about their professions than anyone in the world, but knowledge wasn't their only power. Willpower and charismatic power were far more important. The entrepreneurs and creative geniuses with average IQs will continue to be far more powerful and influential than any cognitive elite. In Nietzsche's words, "Reason is an instrument of the Will to Power," or in the context of this argument, "knowledge is subservient to will."

Knowledge power is sexless. Both genders have an equal opportunity to utilize it, in contrast to physical or money powers, where men have a decided advantage. Tesla and Montessori are classic examples of utilizing knowledge to reach the pinnacle of their professions. Tesla was so knowledgeable in some areas of creating electricity and its distribution that industry experts were baffled by his esoteric lectures and flamboyant demonstrations. Edison was quite critical of Tesla's alternating current theories and spread rumors of death and destruction if such an energy distribution system were implemented. Tesla decided to prove the safety of his alternating current systems in one dramatic demonstration at the 1893 World's Fair in Chicago, allowing two million volts of electricity to flow through his body. Tesla's body glowed like a "live wire" and he was able to light a bulb held in his hand. It was his superior knowledge of high-voltage electricity that allowed him to perform such stunts. He knew better than Edison that high-frequency current would not electrocute him since it kept the energy at the "outer surfaces of the skin."

Maria Montessori used knowledge as a tool to gain influence and power in a similar way. She had enormous empirical knowledge from her years of experimentation with the education of preschool children. Unlike other educators, Montessori was able to violate educational traditions since she taught children considered to be uneducable and was able to experiment with real-life students. She spent day and night with her "idiot" and "deprived" children and knew their learning habits and aptitudes better than anyone in the world. She is the consummate example that knowledge is power.

Knowledge power overcoming all other power is often seen during wartime or similar crises. Higher titular power (authority) becomes subservient to knowledge power when survival is the issue. Life-and-death situations are always determinants of true power. When an army is lost in a jungle and the private knows the way out and the general does not, titular power (authority) switches from the general to the private. Of course, the general can exercise his ultimate authority and courtmartial the private when they return to a civilized world where he can exert his authoritarian power. Most of these fourteen were like the private. They began with little or no power but excelled in knowledge of their field.

Titular Power

Authoritarian power is primarily asexual although in certain organizations either gender can dominate. Women dominate the beauty professions more than men. The president of the United States has always been a male, although that may change within the foreseeable future. Authoritarian power is based on position or rank within that organization. This power is not acquired but given by rulers, owners, or voters.

Sometimes authority is maintained by using fear to control subordinates. Hitler had those who opposed his Third Reich ideology killed. Napoleon annihilated anyone who opposed his will. These men had absolute power. The others in this book were not politically inclined and in their particular professions titular power was not as important except to those running large organizations (Rubinstein, Murdoch, Disney, Hughes).

Titular power is typically given by the masses (in political power) or by the owners (stockholders and board of directors) in organizations, and can be taken away. A leader's personal power is a function of the size and economic status of the organization and the financial control he or she personally wields. Rupert Murdoch, Howard Hughes, and Helena Rubinstein were in total control of their companies. When these individuals gave orders, everyone jumped. Such power was embodied in their authority to hire and fire, give raises and promotions, and control the career and financial destiny of their workers.

In entrepreneurial organizations, authoritarian power is usually controlled by the founder, and if financial control or ownership position changes through dilution (raising capital for growth), his or her power base is diminished accordingly. An example of this turn in circumstances is illustrated by Rupert Murdoch's autocratic leadership at News Corp. He controlled the firm from its inception and made all the important decisions autonomously. When he became insolvent in 1990 due to his penchant for "betting the firm," his power diminished drastically. For a two-year period the bankers made all the important decisions. Murdoch's acquisition of Metromedia, Fox TV, and Triangle (*TV Guide, Racing Form, Seventeen*) in 1985 was responsible for his loss of control. The bankers and his shareholders thought he was crazy but history proved him right! He lost a great deal of his power and was forced to liquidate many of his pet operations to get out from under the $7.6 billion debt to 146 creditors on four continents. His ownership in Cruden Investments, the major shareholder in News Corp, went down from 46 percent to 39.5 percent after this flirtation with disaster. Ted Turner had the same experience four years earlier when he lost control of Turner Broadcasting System (TBS) due to a similar acquisition mania. Both have survived, but their titular power has dramatically diminished.

Titular power comes from the authority to control subordinates. Employees may be more motivated by fear than greed, the whip than the carrot, because they can be terminated without hesitation or cause. The affable Walt Disney fired everyone in the company during the famous 1941 strike at Disney Studios, when the employees unionized. Disney was a staunch anti-Communist and willing to close down rather than capitulate. He ultimately lost and was forced by binding arbitration to rehire them all. His titular power still proved strong when he exacted his own revenge by refusing to rehire the animator who instigated the strike, Arthur Babbitt. When Babbitt attempted to work in the industry, Disney had him blacklisted. When Babbitt entered the armed services during WW II, Disney used his influence in Washington, D.C., to keep Babbitt a private throughout the war. Crossing those with power can be dangerous, as writer Anton Wilson notes:

> Every authoritarian structure can be visualized as a pyramid with an eye on the top. This is a typical flow-chart of any government, any corporation, any army, any bureaucracy, any mammalian pack. . . . It is important to see what the Top Dogs (alpha males) see; it is inconvenient, and possibly dangerous to see what is objectively happening. (*Prometheus Rising* [1990], p. 221)

Rupert Murdoch and Helena Rubinstein were even more ruthless than Disney in their exercise of authoritarian power within their organizations. Murdoch destroyed the union at Wapping (London) in the late 1980s by automating jobs and closing existing plants. When Max Newton, his brilliant publisher of the *Australian* newspaper, didn't operate as Murdoch expected, he was fired and replaced with Adrian Deamer, whom Murdoch also fired. When Murdoch's biographer Thomas Kiernan asked him who had been his greatest publisher and editor on the *Australian,* Murdoch grudgingly admitted it was Deamer. But Deamer had been fired for not agreeing with Murdoch. Authoritarian power tends to reward allegiance more than talent or success, which ultimately results in submission and fear.

Rubinstein's longtime assistant Patrick O'Higgins said that "Madame played power games" and was a "tyrannical holocaust." He said that "fear was her instrument of power" as she ruled "imperially and dictatorially." Rubinstein was a control freak, a classic trait of Type A personalities who create their own organizations.

Hitler and Napoleon would not tolerate any insubordination. Hitler said: "Nothing happens in this movement except what I wish. . . . Whoever fails to obey my orders will be destroyed. I shall strike as soon as I have so much as a suspicion of their disobedience" (Hershman and Lieb 1994, p. 181). Authority can be devastating to those who do not have it but it is fleeting even to those who do.

Charismatic Power

The word *charisma* comes from the Greek, meaning "gift of divine grace." Those having it are considered endowed with extraordinary or magnetic powers of persuasion. They are able to influence others to do their will. Such leaders exude passion, which can move mountains. These fourteen visionaries had charismatic power. A quote by Laura Rose from *Charisma: Power, Passion, and Purpose* gives credence to such power:

> When people get involved with a charismatic's dream or vision, employees many times think that the vision was their idea. It probably wasn't, but they think that anyway. When I did my initial research, I noticed that charismatic leaders have the ability to introduce ideas, get others to implement them, and somehow think that it was their idea all along. (Buffington 1990, p. 101)

Charismatic power is dependent on the *expertise* of the leader. It is hard to convince others to follow you unless you have a philosophical tenet or special message with universal appeal. A typical example of the importance of this type of knowledge is the coach of a professional team who never played the game. Motivating players to take direction and performing it "your way" could prove very difficult in such an organization where firsthand knowledge is critical. It is a fact that great charismatic leaders are "creators of a new order." They break values in building their belief systems and creating their new dogma. Their inspiration is based on revolutionary new ideas which are usually disruptive to the social order. Charismatics are viewed as disruptive mavericks by the establishment, a reputation earned by all of these fourteen visionaries. Their power was their nonconformity.

Charismatic leaders like Alexander the Great, Catherine the Great, Napoleon, and Hitler possessed a certain magnetism that attracted disciples to follow them blindly into perverse new realms of their dreams. The Indian Maharishi Yogi had an "aura" that won him an allegiance not otherwise possible. Mother Teresa exudes this same magnetism. Individuals with this kind of power tend to attract a following of disciples not otherwise possible through the use of force, money, knowledge, or authority. These fourteen visionary leaders possessed a spellbinding talent for attracting followers who embraced their vision of reality without equivocation.

PSYCHIC ENERGY (INTERNALIZED DRIVE)

Charismatics appear to have a special kind of mental energy emanating from within. Mohammed, Joan of Arc, Jesus, and cult leaders have demonstrated the power of passion and emotional energy for a cause. Such power must emanate from an internal belief system that can be effectively communicated to a needy following. Leaders with such power are totally immersed in their cause and able to subtly, but enthusiastically, communicate their dream in such a way that their disciples adopt it as their own. Charismatic power can be used either positively or negatively, although most examples in recent history have been negative, as seen in cult leaders Jim Jones, David Koresh, and Luc Jouret of the 1994 massacre of the Order of the Solar Temple in Switzerland. These individuals led many intelligent people to bizarre deaths based on charismatic power.

Motivational scientist Amitai Etzioni says all personal powers like charisma are motivated by love, in contrast to positional powers, which are motivated by fear. Charismatics earn their power the hard way by convincing their followers of their love, then they resort to the use of fear to maintain control. They typically promise followers salvation to gain control and then threaten them with hell to maintain it.

Charismatic power is acquired via a seductive attraction of a trusting constituency where love for the leader transcends all else. Many such leaders resort to traditional brainwashing techniques where sleep and food deprivation are used to modify behavior. Jim Jones used an espionage network to uncover personal secrets and thereby convince new People Temple members that he was omniscient, scaring them into allegiance and reinforcing their dogmatic belief.

David McClelland spent his life researching power motivation. In his book *Power: The Inner Experience* he says, "Charismatic leaders are effective because they arouse power motivation in their followers" (p. 7). M. F. Rogers called this personal power "influence potential" where the leader uses his own power of inspiration to fill the needs of his followers and make them feel empowered. As McClelland found, "If a leader wants to have far-reaching influence, he must make his followers feel powerful" (p. 263).

PSYCHOSEXUAL ENERGY

Libidinal energy is a subset of charismatic power. Sexual attraction is similar to charismatic power in that people are emotionally attracted to powerful people. Many beautiful and famous women were drawn to the powerful Howard Hughes and went to bed with him even though he was disgustingly dirty and smelly. Many women tolerated Picasso's abuse to become a part of his power. Henry Kissinger gave some insight into such motivations when he told the press, "Power is the ultimate aphrodisiac." The single Kissinger was obviously implying that women were attracted to men with great power and included himself as an example. Freud believed that sex pervaded our every action. He preached that repressed sexual energies never disappear but return in other forms. His view of sex and creativity as a zero-sum game, where sexual energy was a direct trade-off with creative energy, gives credence to sexual frustration leading to charismatic sexual attraction. In other words, what is not used up in the bedroom becomes available in the boardroom. Freud felt that any person sexually sated would be incapable of making great contributions professionally since he would not be optimally motivated. Tesla, Napoleon, Hitler, Hughes, Rubinstein, and Disney confirm Freud's hypothesis. They used the opposite sex only for physical gratification or professional convenience, marrying more out of expediency than desire. Napoleon married to create a successor. Hitler never married and Rubinstein had two marriages of convenience. Disney married because it was the midwestern fundamentalist thing to do, while Tesla never bothered to marry.

Studies have shown that personal power is far more effective than positional power. Personal power is often referred to as ego-power by psychologists because of the high drive found in those with such power. Freud's belief that all power is intertwined with sexual energy is confirmed in most of these subjects. Frank Lloyd Wright's biographer described him as having "enormous sexual energy." Wright attracted women and disciples with equal aplomb. Even the highly eccentric Nikola Tesla had an amazing sexual attraction. It didn't hurt that Tesla was tall, dark, handsome, articulate, and a millionaire by age thirty-three. The Marquis de Sade was so charismatic he was able to talk his wife into becoming a party to his sexual liaisons with young girls. After he was imprisoned he was able to persuade her to smuggle sex-oriented toys into the Bastille to placate his insatiable sexual appetites.

Males often use personal power to attract women for sex. Hughes, Sade, and Picasso were especially blatant about this. Piaf used her sexual attraction in a frenetic search for love, but this ended in a fruitless series of one-night stands. Rubinstein, Duncan, Earhart, and Montessori used their femininity to open doors dominated by bastions of male power more than for any physical gratification. Piaf and Isadora Duncan were the most sexually active females. Both used their sexuality to get power just as most of the males used their power to get sex. Rubinstein married once to have children and a second time for a royal title. It is ironic that she spent her life making women more seductive-looking to men when she had little or no interest in beauty except to use it to build a business empire. These individuals give credence to the aphorism, *Men use power to get sex and women use sex to get power!*

CHARISMATIC WIZARDS

Hitler and Napoleon were the most charismatic of these fourteen visionaries. Much of the media and the German people who were caught up in Hitler's mesmerizing rhetoric were later shocked to realize that they were captivated by an ideology they disagreed with. Hitler was able to eloquently and passionately deliver his messages on a Master Race and other equally perverse concepts and gain converts who intellectually disagreed with him. He promised the people Aryan purity and national pride in return for granting him power. His audiences were so hypnotized by his magnetic appeal that they were unable to resist his doctrine even when they suspected it was ideological rationalization for the "final solution." The shocking thing about Hitler's power and influence is that he was totally devoid of any other redeeming qualities. He was lazy, inexperienced, disorganized, unattractive, overbearing, and an introverted bore. His greatest power was based on verbal enthusiasm and passion. Hitler biographer George H. Stein described his charismatic power as the "magnetism of a hypnotist . . . the force of an African medicine man or an Asian shaman." After having defected to England, Rudolf Hess wrote, "Hitler held the masses and me with them under a hypnotic spell." Nazi diplomat Joachim von Ribbentrop said that when officials spent half an hour with Hitler, they would "support Adolf Hitler's point of view with the greatest conviction, although often it was the very opposite of what they had meant to tell him." A young German hearing Hitler speak for the first time said:

> I forgot everything but the man, then glancing around, I saw that his magnetism was holding thousands as I. Of course I was ripe for this experience . . . weary of disillusionment, a wanderer seeking a cause, a patriot without a channel for his patriotism, a yearner after the heroic without a hero. The intense will of the man, the passion of his sincerity seemed to flow from him into me. I experienced an exultation that could be likened only to a religious conversion. . . . I knew my search was ended. I had found myself, my leader, my cause." (Hershman and Lieb 1994, p. 149)

Napoleon was so charismatic that his mortal enemy the Duke of Wellington said, "The Corsican's presence on the field of battle was equivalent to the force of 40,000 soldiers." Even when captured by the British, Napoleon maintained his allure. Count Balmain wrote, "The most astonishing thing of all is the influence which this man—a captive, deprived of a throne—wields on anyone who comes near him." Bored while exiled on Elba, he decided to march on Paris and regain his throne. Landing in southern France, Napoleon began his march north and was confronted by the king's army. The little Corsican convinced whole regiments to desert the king and join him in his march to power. The deaths of millions were fresh in their minds but they could not resist his hypnotic charm. Napoleon was able to regain the throne without a shot being fired, causing Balzac to write, "Before him did ever a man gain an empire simply by showing his hat?"

Willpower

Schopenhauer wrote, "Will is the master, intellect the servant," adding credence to my hypothesis that those with a strong will can acquire knowledge, money, and force. This source of power has been borrowed from Nietzsche's "will to power," which he proclaimed as the highest attainment for the consummate man—the "overman" or "superman." In *Also Sprach Zarathustra* Nietzsche said that "will-to-power" is man's basic motive in life, suggesting it was pervasive in all things. He wrote, "The only thing men (or women) want is power, and whatever is wanted is wanted for the sake of power." Nietzsche felt the acme of power could only come from the "perfect" or "self-possessed man," one who did not fear other men. He used Napoleon as an example of his hypothesis, describing him as the "synthesis of the inhuman and superhuman." He used Goethe as a model for the "overman," the archetype for the "worldly antithesis of god." He saw Goethe as a man who had "organized the chaos of his passions, given style to his character, and become creative." Nietzsche went on to emphasize the tremendous need for such "great men" in the world. Psychologist Alfred Adler was obviously influenced by Nietzsche since his thesis of man "striving for superiority and perfection" is identical to Nietzsche's philosophy of self-actualization for mankind. Nietzsche insisted that "we must become creators instead of remaining mere creatures," which is exactly what the great power brokers in this work did. They were able to rely on their will as the ultimate source of power. Using the Nietzsche argument any man in control of his willpower is capable of becoming a "superman" and thereby rising to the pinnacle of power. Such a definition indicates that these fourteen visionaries qualify as Nietzschean "supermen" and "superwomen."

POWER ACCEDES TO HE WHO TAKES IT!

Adler said, "Striving for perfection, superiority, and power" is fundamental to all mankind. These fourteen visionaries certainly substantiate Adler's view. They acquired power internally through the sheer force of their wills and often took power others had relinquished. They prove the thesis that power accedes to those who take it. People attempting to survive in a lifeboat always defer to that person willing to step up and assume responsibility. Such power emanates from within, not from without, and those who attain great power are those who feel comfortable with complexity and ambiguity and step forward to assume power. They have an indomitable internal belief system that dominates all external anxiety. True power lies in the source of guns, not in the guns; in the source of wealth, not in the wealth;

in the source of knowledge, not in the knowledge. True power brokers understand this. The self-made millionaire Andrew Carnegie had enormous power and understood its source: "You can take away our factories, take away our trade, our avenues of transportation, and our money—leave us with nothing but our organization—and in four years we could reestablish ourselves." I would go further and say the organization is also unimportant as it can be rebuilt if the leader has a well-developed willpower. People create organizations, build products, and sell them; companies don't. A corporation only exists as a legal entity and its success or failure is a linear function of its people. People with wills—not organizations—are critical to the process. People who know where they are going will attract disciples. Those who don't are destined to become followers looking for knowledgeable leaders. They are the ones with an invincible willpower.

Nietzsche's will-to-power is commonly identified with "guts" or "moxie" because those possessing it are often high risk-takers who feel comfortable with ambiguity. An example of a strong-willed individual who took power that was not his is Steve Jobs, one of the founders of Apple Computer. Jobs had no title at Apple and even though he was a principal, he had no authority within the company. Even so, he constantly drove engineers crazy by making every important decision at Apple, starting projects and changing hardware decisions. Because he assumed the power, he received it by default.

Entrepreneurs and innovators often use a gutsy or arrogant approach to dominating their business operations. They have high self-esteem and self-confidence and never allow bureaucrats to deter them. Promethean personality types have an unusual propensity for assuming power. They represent only a small percentage of the general population, yet they typically control a disproportionate amount of the power in the world. All but two of the subjects in this book were Promethean temperaments and they were able to convince others to follow them to unknown destinies.

WILLPOWER AND SELF-ACTUALIZATION

Many people are insecure and looking for leaders endowed with the conviction of their beliefs. People want to follow powerful leaders regardless of the price. Hitler and Napoleon's rise to power are prime examples. Hitler was influenced by Schopenhauer's concept of will and Nietzsche's "overman" or "superman" concept. He wrote in *Mein Kampf,* "willpower is greater than knowledge," as if he anticipated this hierarchy-of-power thesis. Hitler chose to redefine Nietzsche's "blond beast" as the Third Reich's Aryan model of the Germanic superman. Nietzsche envisioned Napoleon as an archetypical "superman," writing, "What a blessing, what a deliverance is the appearance of an absolute ruler—the appearance of Napoleon was the last great proof: the history of the influence of Napoleon is almost the history of the higher happiness." Nietzsche went on to say "God is dead" as a philosophical tenet which demanded that man find a way to survive alone, without a superior being. His "superman" was created as the savior of man left without God, who would lead man to a higher state of willpower.

Anyone striving for excellence must use the power of the "will" over "self." Creative, innovative, and entrepreneurial ventures all demand leaders with a strong will. All fourteen visionaries used their willpower to reach the top. Napoleon, Duncan, Hitler, Montessori, Piaf, Picasso, Tesla, and Wright used virtually no other resource to gain power and influence. Psychologist Carl Rogers (1959) wrote: "The mainstream of creativity appears to be . . . man's tendency to actualize himself, to become his potentialities." These visionaries were certainly self-actualized through their willpower. Details on their specific rise to power can be found in the subject chapters.

WILLPOWER IS ASEXUAL

Cleopatra, Catherine the Great, Madame Curie, and Margaret Thatcher are examples of powerful women who utilized their will to gain ultimate power. Males are more likely to resort to their will in seeking power since they have been conditioned by society to envision themselves as dominant. Men are seen as powerful and women as submissive in their traditional roles. This isn't necessarily true, but it does precondition males to be more egocentric than women. Women tend to be more relationship-driven while men are more ego-driven. If women are to optimize their power they must employ more ego or "will" in their drive to the top.

Self-Destructive Tendencies

Powerful and creative people often appear to have a propensity for self-destruction. Plato wrote: "No one desires to injure himself hence all evil is done unwittingly." It was those very attributes which made them great that caused their greatest debacles. Most of these fourteen were not consciously self-destructive but their obsessive drive and need to succeed made them so. These visionaries had such a gambling spirit they were often accused of having a death wish. Some even understood their flirtation with disaster. Napoleon wrote: "What fury drives me to my own destruction? Indeed, what am I to do in this world? Since die I must, is it not just as well to kill myself?"

Amelia Earhart and Howard Hughes are the quintessential examples of using risk to reach the top. Both were thrill-seeking adventurers who parlayed their high-risk lifestyles into fame and fortune. Both had an extraordinary passion for flying where their daredevil antics became the cause of seven major crashes. Their exploits allowed both to break many continental and intercontinental airspeed records between 1928 and 1938. What compelled these two attractive and successful people to push themselves and their planes beyond prudent limits? What drove them to go faster and farther than anyone else in a dangerous profession (there was a 75 percent fatality rate for airmail pilots during this era)? Apparently it was an internally driven need to be the very best and to satiate some internal compulsion for excitement.

Psychologist Frank Farley characterized Amelia Earhart as a thrill-seeker or Big T personality who had inordinately high levels of testosterone. Farley believes high testosterone is the key element found in all great risk-takers. Earhart and Hughes certainly qualify as Big Ts according to Farley's hypothesis. Both also met his other prerequisites of defiance, novelty, competitiveness, creativity, sexuality, and adventure.

Both Earhart and Hughes continually defied the odds by taking off in planes destined to crash. Both repeatedly gambled their lives to such a degree it was as if they had a death wish. Hughes's first flirtation with death occurred during the filming of *Hell's Angels,* when he crashed in a WW I fighter plane that he didn't know how to fly. He was pulled unconscious from the plane. During World War II, two passengers died when Hughes crashed a Sikorsky S-43 into Lake Mead on a checkout flight. Once again he was pulled unconscious before the plane sank to the bottom.

Hughes's last crash was his worst and became the cause of most of his later eccentric behavior. On July 7, 1946 Hughes functioned as test pilot for one of his fighter planes, the XF-11. Hughes was determined to push the plane to its limits to show off its superior performance to the air force. Hughes overloaded the gas tanks in violation of federal regulations and flew over Katharine Hepburn's house, in addition to numerous other violations. When told to land, Hughes continued to fly, lost control, and crashed into a West Los Angeles house. He would have burned to death if not for a courageous spectator who pulled him from the burning plane. He was precariously close to death and was rushed to the hospital screaming in pain from a crushed chest, fractured skull, displaced heart, and severe blood loss. The doctors didn't expect him to live. Hughes aged twenty years within hours of the crash and started a life addicted to drugs to alleviate the pain from an accident that should never have occurred. This crash destroyed him physically and emotionally and was a result of his own internal need to overachieve.

In many respects Amelia Earhart was more intent on self-destruction than Howard Hughes. She loved fast cars and planes. Her poem "Courage" gives insight into her need to take risks. The first line reads, "Courage is the price that life exacts for granting peace," and true to form she was never happy when not challenged. She told Wiley Post of plans to fly across the Gulf of Mexico, prompting him to say, "Don't do it, it's too dangerous." Post saw this death-defying flight from Mexico City to New Orleans as senseless. Post's warning was the type of reverse encouragement that motivated the thrill-seeking Earhart. She took off in a plane loaded with 472 gallons of high-octane fuel (which Post characterized as a "Molotov cocktail") from a potholed dirt runway in Mexico City. She succeeded in setting a record in spite of adverse conditions and extreme risk.

Earhart's greatest gamble was in attempting to break Post's around-the-world record. She became her own worst enemy by refusing to include the most basic communications equipment in order to reduce the plane's weight. She compounded the problem by knowingly hiring a confirmed alcoholic—Fred Noonan—as navigator. These were terrible decisions considering the tiny target—

Howland Island—she had to find in the South Pacific. It would be her last stop before taking off for the easy flight to Honolulu. If lost, there was no place to land, so in effect she was playing Russian Roulette. When Earhart took off from Miami, she gave her good friend Jacqueline Cochran, also a famous aviator, her lucky silk American flag, which she had always carried on her record-breaking flights. When Cochran asked her to take it with her for luck and sign it on her return, Amelia said, "No, you'd better take it now."

Strengths and Weaknesses

Ralph Waldo Emerson wrote, "Our strength grows out of weakness." Sun Tzu in *The Art of War* wrote, "Disorder arises from order, cowardice arises from courage, weakness arises from strength." These aphorisms are endemic to everyone and especially anyone aspiring to great power and influence. In respect to Sun Tzu's axiom, you must first have order to feign disorder, be brave to feign cowardice, and be strong to pretend weakness. Extroverts communicate well but don't always hear much because they are too busy talking. Visionaries live their lives in an opportunistic future and consequently miss out on the present. Hedonists endure the greatest problems, and great athletes end up with the most ravished bodies. It isn't an accident that avid tennis players get the worst tennis elbows and scientists have the worst trouble with their eyes. Most people's strengths eventually become their weaknesses and these fourteen were no exception. Figure 12 depicts the power (strengths) and its effect (weaknesses) in each of these fourteen subjects. The very trait that had made them into superstars became the instrument of their demise. The *good* in them ultimately became the *bad*. This hypothesis was never more true than in the tragic life of Edith Piaf.

EDITH PIAF

Piaf was abandoned just after birth and spent her life searching for the love denied her as a child. Her passionate search for love led to hundreds of one-night stands with strange men who used and abused her, but did not provide her with the love she so desperately needed. Her charisma and sensualness attracted men by the droves, but once she found an acceptable man she destroyed the relationship by being unfaithful. She never wanted any man she could have, only the ones she couldn't, which is why she had so many affairs with married men. She never understood that her search was futile since it was for lost childhood love that could never be supplied by a man. She destroyed every decent relationship she entered due to her fear that she would be abandoned (as her parents had). She involved each of her main men in a ménage à trois with her sister Simone. This was her way of showing she was willing to share her love and was caring, but it wasn't conducive to long-term intimacy and stability with her men. Her surrogate father and mentor Louis Papa Leplée was murdered, two lovers died in crashes, one committed sui-

FIGURE 12
SELF-DESTRUCTIVE TENDENCIES

Strengths Tend to Become Weaknesses

Creative Genius	Power (Strengths)	Effect (Weaknesses)
Napoleon Bonaparte	Manic speed and success	Outran provisions
Walt Disney	Imagination and fantasy	Unrealistic expectations
Isadora Duncan	Independence and freedom	Lacked stability
Amelia Earhart	Thrill-seeking broke records	Cost was her life
Adolf Hitler	Mania for power/expansion	Power corrupted/destroyed
Howard Hughes	Perfectionist	Obsessional delusions
Maria Montessori	Awesome self-esteem	Wrought arrogance
Rupert Murdoch	Antiestablishment tactics	Destroyed reputation
Edith Piaf	Instant passion	Destroyed all relationships
Pablo Picasso	Nihilistic philosophy	Destroyed everything
Helena Rubinstein	Indomitable and tyrannical	No friends
Marquis de Sade	Philosophical rebellion	Cost his freedom
Nikola Tesla	Obsessional achievement	Destroyed health
Frank Lloyd Wright	Macrovision	Ignored details

cide, and her daughter Marcelle died at age two, all due in part to Edith's frenetic lifestyle. Her passionate search for love made her a professional success (all of her great hits were about love and passion) but turned into personal disaster.

NAPOLEON BONAPARTE

Speed was Napoleon's forte on the field of battle, but he moved so quickly that he outran his provisions and support. His most famous conquest was Russia, but when he made it to the walls of Moscow, he discovered he had outrun his food and supplies. His strength of speed became his Achilles' heel. Another of Napoleon's strengths was his willingness to risk everything for victory. He repeatedly risked his and everyone else's life to realize the glory of his deluded dreams. He wrote in 1804: "Death is nothing, but to live defeated and inglorious is to die daily." This "enlightened despot" went on to fulfill his own perverse dreams, causing the deaths of millions because of his need to gain more power. His legacy is forever inscribed in his aphorism, "Power is my mistress." Napoleon's need for power ultimately led to the destruction of him and his armies at Waterloo.

WALT DISNEY

Walt Disney's strength was being able to immerse himself in childlike fantasy. Disney's success was based on his ability to create fantasy cartoons of happy-go-lucky characters such as Mickey Mouse, Donald Duck, and Pluto, which negated the reality of the Great Depression, when they were created. Such behavior also cost him dearly as he refused to accept the every-day reality of paying the bills. While he was lost in his private world creating monumental works of artistic genius, Disney Studios verged on bankruptcy, insolvent for most of its existence before 1955. Being unrealistic creatively is good for innovative ventures, but usually disastrous in operating a business. Disney's live-on-the-edge need for innovation was his great strength but was the firm's great nemesis.

ISADORA DUNCAN

Isadora Duncan was a free spirit whose independence destroyed her in the end. She lived a frivolous lifestyle ignoring the traditions of marriage, economics, religion, and politics. She rejected marriage proposals from some of the most eligible men of that time, notably renowned theatrical designer Gordon Craig and sewing machine heir Paris Singer. She had children by both but refused to marry either. The rebellious but masochistic Isadora finally chose to marry a mad Russian poet twenty years her junior when in her forties. He tried to kill her repeatedly and ended up killing himself. This free spirit's closing words, after jumping into a Bughatti sports car, were: "I go to glory." Moments later, her long free-flowing scarf, the symbol of her iconoclastic lifestyle, caught in the car's wheels and snapped her neck. She died as she lived, with reckless abandon.

ADOLF HITLER

Hitler's unrealistic expectations emanated from his mania for power. This insatiable need destroyed him and everything he cherished. Hitler's hypomania molded him into a great demagogue, but that same maniacal drive ultimately brought down the Third Reich.

MARIA MONTESSORI

Maria Montessori used self-esteem to revolutionize children's education. It was this total belief in her own system and supreme confidence that turned her into an arrogant know-it-all, according to her adversaries. A pompous attitude and disdain for traditional educators earned her many enemies within the very environment where she needed the greatest support.

AMELIA EARHART

Earhart spent her life being different and fighting for her freedom. She was a free spirit who valued independence, wanting to go where no one ever had. She did and was never found. Her thrill-seeking made her rich and famous, but ultimately destroyed her.

HOWARD HUGHES

Howard Hughes was a scintillating bon voyant because of his daredevil exploits in the air, movie successes, and dashing good looks. Living on the edge made him a famous Hollywood tycoon. When he crashed his XF-11 into a Hollywood Hills home in 1946, his charismatic charm ended. He became a drug addict and impotent. Ultimately his passion for perfectionism turned to obsessional delusions and he lived a terrible life in a self-imposed asylum—a hotel room in the Desert Inn, where the man who tried to control everything was unable to control himself.

RUPERT MURDOCH

Rupert Murdoch has Victorian morals but earned the nickname "Murdoch of the Mammaries" because of the sensational headlines used to build circulation in his Australian, London, and New York newspapers. His innovative approach to selling newspapers was eminently successful, resulting in his building the largest circulation English-language paper in the world—*The London Sun*. News Corp distributes sixty million papers weekly on four continents, a success by any barometer. But Murdoch's style and reputation have kept him from gaining entrance into the top markets. By being competitive and violating the established rules of decorum—a behavior that has made it impossible for him to become recognized as a great newspaper man—he has been ostracized by industry leaders.

PABLO PICASSO

Picasso was the consummate "creative destroyer." He was successful in destroying established traditions in art, which had been his objective, but his emotional rages and uncontrolled passions ultimately enveloped his very being, destroying any chance for him to live a happy or contented life.

MARQUIS DE SADE

Sade preached ideological freedom but his philosophy cost him his own freedom. Sade was unbelievably self-destructive. He lived an autonomous life, purposely violating the traditional dogmas of the Catholic religion and French society. His rebellious lifestyle caused him to spend half his adult life behind bars. Sade wrote with both conviction and integrity relative to his philosophical tenets, but religious and political adversaries sought revenge. Sade had numerous opportunities to be free, but repeatedly dared the establishment to destroy him. He was prophetic in writing, "The self-destructive power of the human race is the 'Supreme Power.' "

HELENA RUBINSTEIN

Rubinstein was an indomitable spirit who built her empire of beauty care, but she became a tyrannical boss who had no friends. Her competitive aggression got her to the top, where she remained all alone because of those very traits which had been responsible for her success.

NIKOLA TESLA

Tesla was more interested in seeing his induction motor produced than he was in getting rich. To help his friend George Westinghouse survive a financial debacle, he forgave $12 million in royalties to insure that his alternating current invention could be implemented by Westinghouse Electric. His impulsive decision caused him to live the last thirty years of his life in abject poverty, and many of his incredible inventions were never implemented due to lack of funding.

Tesla's self-destruction went beyond money. Virtually every one of his great inventions were the result of bursts of frenetic and manic energy. Every one was followed by life-threatening exhaustion and ill health. His obsessiveness resulted in great scientific discoveries, but also exacted personal trauma and ill health, including numerous nervous breakdowns. His iconoclasm and risk-oriented nature resulted in his reputation as a bizarre eccentric. Tesla often used his body as a guinea pig. He would pass millions of volts of electrical current through his body in a dramatic demonstration of the safety of alternating current. Tesla was incapable of seeing an animal hurt or injured and was a vocal pacifist. He was against all war and violence, which makes his invention of radar, radical instruments of destruction like death rays, and remote-controlled bombs even more paradoxical.

FRANK LLOYD WRIGHT

Wright is a classic example of a Promethean temperament who sees the big picture and ignores the details. His total dedication to esthetics and form was at the expense of the practical and functional. Wright created some of the most outstanding architectural buildings in history—and most of them leaked.

Biographer Meryle Secrest described Wright as having "an unconscious courting of catastrophe and ruin." He lived on the edge personally by riding fast horses and driving fast cars. This respected middle-aged church deacon and son of a Baptist minister left a successful business, wife, and six children and ran off to Europe with a mistress. Wright not only was the protagonist in this outrageous act, but was shocked that his actions were considered newsworthy by the media. Wright's strengths proved to be his worst weaknesses, but in the end he outlived his infamy.

Summary

Individuals tend to reach the top by ascending through six stages of power: physical, financial, knowledge, titular, charismatic, and willpower. *Physical power* dominates in all environments where the strong prevail, as in Third World societies. Those possessing the most money are able to buy the most muscle or guns, which makes *financial power* more powerful than force. This stage became dominant with the advent of the Industrial Revolution when those who controlled money became the most powerful individuals: Rockefeller, Carnegie, Mellon, and J. P. Morgan. In a high-tech world where information is doubling every eighteen months (according to computer scientist Dr. Jacques Vallee) the most important source of power is information, making anyone capable of manipulating data destined to hold the most power. Computer scientists become the most powerful in information-driven societies where *knowledge power* dominates. As societies progress, organizations require ever stronger leadership and *titular power* becomes an important source of power. Authority is a positional type of power where the "Top Dog," according to Anton Wilson, uses fear as an instrument to maintain control. Positional powers are fleeting since titular power always rests in the hands of others.

The highest attainments of power are the internally generated *charisma* and *will*. These two powers were used by the fourteen creative geniuses in this book to rise to power. Individuals capable of optimizing their charisma and will are capable of great accomplishment, often seducing others to follow them into new, unknown territories. These two sources of power are neutralized in a world of Social Darwinism where the strongest prevail. In a normal progression physical power becomes subjugated to financial power (money) since money can buy more muscle and bigger guns. It has been proven that those with enough knowledge will be able to dominate both muscle and money. Titular power is the province of a king or other organizational authority that can dictate to the intellectuals, financiers, and laborers. The only true powers that seldom are lost and are never taken away are charisma and will. These are personal powers that emanate from within. Charisma instills captivating attraction and will, psychic or libidinal energy.

The fourteen power brokers in this book were extremely charismatic. These individuals exercised a hypnotic influence over their followers. Their disciples often became so enraptured that they followed blindly, often to their deaths. Hitler and Napoleon were the most charismatic, with Duncan, Earhart, Montessori, Picasso, and Wright close behind. Sade, Hughes, and Piaf were the most sexually provocative. Hughes and Murdoch used their financial power to build vast industrial empires; Hitler and Napoleon utilized physical power to gain political might; and Montessori and Tesla used knowledge power in their rise to the top. Amelia Earhart and Howard Hughes proved to be the most self-destructive, while Picasso, Hitler, Hughes, and Napoleon were the most destructive to others. Most were able to identify with a Nietzschean type Will-to-Power where their "superman" nature emerged to lead them to the top. Tapping into their subconscious "wills" instilled *charisma,* which attracted disciples who granted them *authority,* enabling them to gain *knowledge,* get *money,* and control their *physical* destiny. Such is the nature of power in the world of creative genius.

Self-destruction appears to be a by-product of a risk-taking mentality in over-achievers. These individuals are prepared to sacrifice everything to achieve great success. They tend to live on the edge in virtually everything they do, which gives the appearance of a death wish. These fourteen subjects were self-destructive. Earhart and Hughes took off in planes that had a high chance of crashing. The Marquis de Sade wrote a scathing paper on Napoleon and Josephine, who then imprisoned him for life. Murdoch went over $7 billion in debt and found himself insolvent in 1990, and when out of his near bankruptcy continued with an even greater acquisition mania. Disney lived with business insolvency for thirty years but was never deterred from taking the next big gamble to realize his greatest childhood fantasies. Piaf and Hughes both became drug addicts. Virtually every one of Picasso's relationships ended in death or destruction. Tesla allowed two million volts of electricity to pass through his body to prove Edison wrong about his alternating current system of power distribution. No price seemed too great for these individuals to pay, but their greatest sacrifices were happiness and normality. From the research about these fourteen, it became apparent that virtually every subject had a strength that ultimately became their biggest weakness. Their most noteworthy asset often turned out to be their greatest liability.

4

Intuitive-Thinking Temperament: Napoleon Bonaparte and Frank Lloyd Wright

Promethean temperaments are the architects of change in the world.
—David Keirsey and Marilyn Bates

Macrovision: The Opportunities and Possibilities of Life

Individuals with an intuitive-thinking preference for operating in the world are referred to by Jungian psychologists as having a Promethean temperament. This personality type was named for the Greek mythological god Prometheus, the symbol of light and energy, who was commissioned by Apollo to bring science to man. These individuals always see "the big picture" and have a macroview of life and its many possibilities. An example is Maria Montessori, who intuitively knew that the traditional school system of Italy utilized ineffective teaching methods for many of its students. She created a Montessori method utilizing educational toys, open classrooms, parent/teacher conferences, and other motivations in a valiant attempt to improve the system. Montessori used her intuition to see the opportunities and then rationally thought out the possibilities. She saw the big picture (forest) but resorted to critical details (trees) for resolution of the problem. This is a classic Promethean at work. The Promethean attacks problems in a holistic or *intuitive* way and utilizes a rational, structured, or thinking approach.

PROMETHEANS

This *intuitive-thinking* approach allows individuals to plan in a macroway while implementing their plan in a microway. Only 12 percent of the population has this particular operating style according to those tested on the Myers-Briggs personality test (the most widely used test for assessing personal aptitudes and preferences in work and career placement). This combination of intuitive-thinking is re-

117

ferred to as a Promethean temperament. These personality types are known as the "architects of change in the world" because they see the big picture and operate on it in a definitive manner. They have a predisposition for the abstract and are attracted to the innovative and different. They tend to be culture's foremost visionaries and pioneers who seek truth and knowledge. All of the subjects in this book were intuitive-thinkers with the exception of Duncan and Piaf, who preferred operating in a more personal, emotional, *feeling* way.

Promethean personalities are often workaholics who view work as an enjoyable opportunity and not a tedious task. Even when playing, this type personality typically thinks about work. Prometheans perpetually seek knowledge and truth in all endeavors. Impatience and impulsiveness are their trademarks. Their motto in life is "be excellent in all things." They prefer quality to quantity, a sixth sense to common sense, the abstract to the known, long term to short term, qualitative to quantitative. They are more interested in the future than the past or present. They are intolerant of error and inefficiency and demand perfection from themselves as well as their associates. They are always focusing on the possibilities in life and not the potential obstructions. Unfortunately, these personality types are often oblivious to detail and the opinions of others. They tend to get caught up in life's potential to the detriment of the present. They will always mortgage the present for the future in their inextricable march to find truth and success. In their trek to the top they usually leave the details and drudgery to others; as leaders they are great delegators.

MACROVISIONARIES

The two individuals who best illustrate the Promethean personality are Napoleon Bonaparte and Frank Lloyd Wright. Both were macrovisionaries with a rational perspective. Their intuitive-thinking style became their Achilles' heel because they were often crippled by an inability to deal with trivial details. Both Napoleon and Wright are classic examples of how strengths can become weaknesses for a Promethean personality. They had a preoccupation with future opportunities instead of boring minutiae. Napoleon marched out of Paris pursuing his dream of becoming the master of Europe. He might well have succeeded had he not ignored an important detail—the Russian winter. He pursued the future at the expense of the present and it destroyed him in Russia.

Frank Lloyd Wright, like Napoleon, used his intuitive powers to become the most imaginative architect in history. He totally disregarded practical details, which hurt his reputation among his more discerning peers. Wright spent his life designing innovative buildings but disregarded what he considered to be bothersome details. Consequently, his most ingenious buildings leaked when it rained and lacked the basic needs of day-to-day living. The exciting future always took precedence over the unexciting present for him. Wright's genius resided in his holistic (big picture) view of man and machine interfaces. He anticipated Norbert Wiener's Cybernetic culture by fifty years and designed buildings to work in a world where man and machine had to coexist. Wright always anticipated the needs of man in the design of his buildings. His creations became pragmatic living and work environments, but in their creation he ignored some of the most mundane aspects of design. In aesthetic leadership he had no peers, but his buildings and personal life suffered greatly because of his intuitive-thinking style.

HOLISTIC THINKERS—RIGHT-BRAIN PREFERENCES

These subjects, especially Napoleon and Frank Lloyd Wright, were different from much of the "normal" population in that they were able to utilize both hemispheres of their brains for problem resolution. In other words, they were holistic thinkers who were capable of utilizing the strengths of the left hemisphere (which controls one's verbal, digital, logical, and micro-oriented rational actions) while employing the right hemisphere (which is responsible for the nonverbal, visual-spatial, perceptual, and macro-oriented intuitive actions). They utilized the left hemisphere for tapping into the objective and quantitative while employing the right for the subjective and qualitative. Western man since the advent of the Copernican Revolution, soon followed by the Industrial Revolution, has been biased toward a mechanistic left-hemisphere operating style as a means of surviving a quantitatively driven society that demanded "doing it by the numbers." Great creative geniuses like these subjects were able to subjugate their tedious and analytical left-brain natures in order to tap into their creative and innovative right-brain natures. Most people are incapable of suppressing the quantitative for the qualitative. These subjects were.

RIGHT-BRAIN TYPES

Napoleon was an intuitive-thinker who always saw the "forest" and not the "trees" in his vision of reality. His macrovision is a critical trait for anyone desirous of becoming a creative genius or innovator. One cannot resolve critical problems without seeing them as a whole. "Clerk mentalities" (customs agents are a prime example) tend to see reality in a limited way through their own restricted perspective. They never see the big picture and consequently are stuck in their own little compartment.

The opposite of those with intuitive vision are defined by the Myers-Briggs test as *sensors,* those people who are concerned with details and have a microvision of the world. This personality type typically sees the "trees" as the dominating feature in all things. Accountants tend to have such a detailed perspective and rightfully so. There is nothing wrong with having a sensing rather than an intuitive vision, it just does not happen to be the necessary outlook for great creative geniuses and power brokers like Napoleon and Wright. The great innovators are right-brain types who are able to suppress the left-brain control.

PERSONALITY PREFERENCES

Figure 13 classifies all fourteen subjects into one of sixteen categories of personality preference as defined by the Myers-Briggs Type Indicator (MBTI). The MBTI cate-

FIGURE 13
PERSONALITY PREFERENCES OF CREATIVE GENIUS
CARL JUNG'S ARCHETYPES AND MYERS-BRIGGS TYPE INDICATOR (MBTI)

How People are Energized:	Extroverts (Social)	Introverts (Territorial)
How People Perceive the World:	Sensors (Microvision)	Intuitors (Macrovision)
How People Make Decisions:	Feelers (Emotionally)	Thinkers (Rationally)
How People Operate—Lifestyle:	Perceivers (Spontaneously)	Judgers (Structured)

Creative Visionaries	Personality Type	MBTI
Napoleon Bonaparte	Introvert—Intuitive—Thinker—Judger	INTJ
Walt Disney	Introvert—Intuitive—Thinker—Judger	INTJ
Isadora Duncan	Extrovert—Intuitive—Feeler—Perceiver	ENFP
Amelia Earhart	Introvert—Intuitive—Thinker—Perceiver	INTP
Adolf Hitler	Introvert—Intuitive—Thinker—Judger	INTJ
Howard Hughes	Introvert—Intuitive—Thinker—Perceiver	INTP
Maria Montessori	Introvert—Intuitive—Thinker—Judger	INTJ
Rupert Murdoch	Introvert—Intuitive—Thinker—Judger	INTJ
Edith Piaf	Extrovert—Intuitive—Feeler—Perceiver	ENFP
Pablo Picasso	Extrovert—Intuitive—Thinker—Perceiver	ENTJ
Helena Rubinstein	Introvert—Intuitive—Thinker—Judger	INTJ
Marquis de Sade	Extrovert—Intuitive—Thinker—Judger	ENTJ
Nikola Tesla	Introvert—Intuitive—Thinker—Judger	ENTJ
Frank Lloyd Wright	Extrovert—Intuitive—Thinker—Judger	ENTJ

gorizes everyone by their preference for living and operating in society. It was originated by Carl Jung who created the first personality "Archetypes." Jung concocted a
theory where certain archetypes were formed in a "collective unconscious" that preordained a person to become an "extroverted" or an "introverted" personality "type"
among others. In the early forties the mother and daughter team of Myers and Briggs
organized the Jungian archetypes into four bipolar groups which could place any personality type into any one of sixteen preference scales: *extroversion* or *introversion,
sensing* or *intuiting, feeling* or *thinking,* and *perceiving* or *judging. Extroverts* are more
sociable and *introverts* more territorial. *Sensors* tend to see things in a microway and
intuitors see things in a macroway. *Feelers* make their decisions emotionally and personally while *thinkers* decide rationally and impersonally. *Perceivers* live life spontaneously while the *judgers* live life in a structured way. There is no right or wrong personality type. Carl Jung felt the intuitive-thinkers (Prometheans) were more inclined
to be innovative and creative than any other type. All but two of these fourteen subjects
had Promethean temperaments. The majority of men (five of nine) were introverts
while the majority of women (four of five) were extroverts. Extroversion and introversion does not appear to have any impact on success as the subjects were almost
evenly split in this dimension. Nine were classified as judgers and demanded closure.
They must finish whatever they started. These individual types were the power brokers
like Napoleon, Hitler, Murdoch, and Wright. They were the Type A personalities who
were always in a hurry to make decisions even when they weren't sure of the outcome.

COSMIC VISION

An intuitive-thinking style is critical for anyone aspiring to a career in creativity, innovation, or entrepreneurship. An example is Nikola Tesla who was thought to possess "cosmic vision." He was a scientist who did not resort to the "scientific method" of problem resolution. Tesla refuted Edison's trial-and-error approach (experimentation), preferring to use his intuitive powers. Einstein had the same preference for problem resolution. His theory of relativity was an elegant intuitive inspiration and was opposed by the scientific community for years since he violated their sacred methods of laboratory experimentation. Tesla had a lab and used experimentation for many of his theories but his experiments were strictly used to validate the concepts he derived through the art of intuition. When in school, Tesla thoroughly irritated his teachers by solving problems in his mind and refusing to tell them how he had derived the answers. (Amelia Earhart also infuriated her teachers in this way.) Tesla gave credit to his intuitive powers for the solution to his most revolutionary invention, the polyphase system of accelerating current. Once he had the mental picture of the solution, he proceeded to the lab to build the prototypes of his AC induction motors. He said of his breakthrough, "I could visualize with such facility . . . needed no models, drawings, or experiments, but could picture them all as real" (Cheney 1981, p. 12). The scientific community labeled him as a kook with a talent for "cosmic intuition." He certainly appeared to "know" the answers to many concepts which might not have been discovered but for his intuitive powers.

THEY RESORTED TO A "GUT FEELING"

Rupert Murdoch was fond of using his "intuition" to resolve problems in the development of his media empire. He told biographers that a "gut feel" was most responsible for his enormous success in publishing. In 1994 one of his managers told a reporter that News Corp's successful operations was an emulation of Murdoch's unique style. He said at News Corp: "We operate much more on gut." Edith Piaf wrote, "My intelligence is instinct." Isadora Duncan envisioned herself as a Greek goddess in a mad search for the truth in dance. Innovation was her style and intuition her methodology. She wrote in her autobiography, "I was possessed by the dream of Promethean creation." A testimony to Helena Rubinstein's nature is the painting by Salvador Dali who painted the empress of beauty in 1943 as a feminine Prometheus chained to a rock by her glittering emerald robes. Hughes, Picasso, Disney, Hitler, Earhart, Montessori, and Rubinstein all utilized a long-term macrovision in the pursuit of their dreams. They resorted to the exact opposite approach to problem resolution used by most bureaucrats. Bureaucrats approach everything by the numbers or "quantitatively" while Prometheans tend to resolve problems "qualitatively." The visionary plans and analyzes rationally (left brain) by thinking out potential solutions and then implements intuitively (right brain), allowing their emotions free rein to sort out solutions. They are creative because they get the left-brain structure out of the way, which allows the right brain to seek unobstructed creativity. Their power emanates from an intuitive or "gut" feel for what is important, and are never reliant on quantitative empirical evidence to govern their actions. Figure 14, the Promethean Personality Outline, gives an overview of the strengths, weaknesses, and leadership qualities of these personality types.

FIGURE 14

PROMETHEAN PERSONALITY TYPE—VISIONARIES

(Source: Carl Jung, Myers-Briggs, Keirsey and Bates)

(MBTI = INTJ, INTP, ENTJ, ENTP)

(E = Extrovert, I = Introvert, N = Intuitive, T = Thinker, P = Perceiver, J = Judger)

Preference for Dealing with Life (NT = Intuitive-Thinking)

PERSONALITY DESCRIPTION

These personality types are the architects of change. They see life as a process of acquiring knowledge and competence for its own sake. They tend to focus on patterns that appear in all things and excel at deriving new laws and principles. They value competence and quality and seek to solve problems and enigmas and admire power and genius. Intellectual stimulation is their forte and they are cultures foremost visionaries and pioneers. They are insensitive to authority as competence is their only criterion for success.

MANAGERIAL STRENGTHS

The NT Visionary manager is intolerant of error and inefficiency, and demands a great deal of himself and others. He can envision the organization ten years hence and draw a blueprint for the ten-year goals. He never says things twice. His focus is on possibility, and he is often intellectually ingenious, pioneering in technical and administrative areas. NTs have a long-range, sweeping view of things and are innovative, creative, and entrepreneurial in their perspective.

MANAGERIAL WEAKNESSES

When the Visionary manager is involved in the creative process, he has enormous drive; but once his castle is designed, he is more willing to allow someone else to take over its execution and construction. He is often insensitive to the feelings of others. His intellectual problem resolutions set high standards and he often loses patience with those not as interested in impersonal solutions. Impatience and intolerance are his greatest weaknesses, with inattention to detail a serious concern.

WAYS OF DEALING WITH COLLEAGUES

The NT manager works well with idea and new-concept managers. Communication skills are sometimes lacking as he tends to be nonconforming and ahead of the crowd. He tends to be on the growing edge of change and seldom looks back. He is an excellent decision-maker, works well under pressure, and honors commitments. Innovation and focusing on results and not procedures are his forte. Colleagues sometimes feel that he has a "my way or the highway" philosophy, but that isn't necessarily accurate.

CONTRIBUTIONS TO A MANAGEMENT TEAM

If an organization does not have a Visionary/Architect/Builder on the management team, planned change may be minimal, and sooner or later deterioration will occur. The status quo will continue, perhaps to obsolescence. The NT manager can contribute theoretical structure to the management team. These temperament types should not be in charge of accounting, just as the Sensor-Judger (Traditionalist) types should not be in charge of long-range strategic planning.

Napoleon Bonaparte: "Power Is My Mistress"

Overview

Napoleon has been universally acclaimed the greatest military genius who ever lived. One reason was his ability to succeed against enormous odds, which appears to have been due to his megalomaniacal drive and belief in his own destiny. Napoleon not only loved power, he exuded it because he believed he was divine. His delusions translated into reality and history has made him a powerbroker of herculean proportions. At the turn of the century, James McKeen Cattell called him the most eminent personality in Western civilization and ranked him ahead of Shakespeare, Voltaire, and Newton. Michael Hart ranked him thirty-fourth in a 1978 list of the one hundred most influential persons in history. During the twentieth century, no fewer than 200,000 volumes have been written about Napoleon and his times (Simonton 1994).

How did this diminutive immigrant became the leader of a nation on the basis of nationalism? A Promethean temperament had a great deal to do with it, although his hypomania, charisma, and obsessiveness were critical to his success. His great power and success had little to do with his heritage. Born in Corsica of Italian ancestry, Napoleon spoke Italian much better than French his whole life. He wrote abominably and was a commoner with few friends. He graduated forty-second out of fifty-eight from the École Militaire, although in his inimitable fashion, he graduated in half the allotted time. At best Napoleon was a mediocre student and considered quite average by most biographers of his early life. His was a classic rags-to-riches story. He was an unlikely candidate to take over one of the most powerful nations in Europe, remaking it into the predominant nineteenth-century military power. No one who knew him as a teenager could have imagined him conquering all of Europe by his midthirties.

POWER WAS HIS GOD

Napoleon's meteoric rise to fame was a mystery even to him. His manic need for power at any cost certainly contributed to his ascent. No one can ascend to great stations without believing in their own destiny, and this egomaniac certainly believed that he was deserving. He was a master of manipulation and forced many powerful nations to capitulate to his will. He even forced the pope to fall to his knees and kiss his ring when he was crowned in 1804. (In classic fashion his mother slapped his hand rather than kneel in submission to his power.) Napoleon was labeled the Champion of Death due to his need for more power. In using France as a pawn to meet his personal needs for military victories, he was ultimately responsible for the deaths of some 2.5 million men. How did an immigrant with so few credentials attain such enormous power?

PROMETHEAN VISION

Napoleon's power was a by-product of his manic energy and Promethean temperament. He always saw the total picture in everything he did. He had a holistic view of the battlefield and an intuitive vision of his adversaries' moves on it long before he set foot on the field. Napoleon fought every battle in his head before he fought it on the field. He looked upon war as a game, planning his political and military moves in the field as if they were pieces on a chessboard. He had an omniscient vision of how the game should be played and used duplicity and the unexpected to win. He was the omnipotent "mover" who always "knew" exactly what strategy should be used to outwit the enemy. Napoleon and Hitler were both successful in doing the unexpected. They violated traditional strategy and tactics of war, often shocking their enemies by showing up where least expected. What has been lost on most historians is the importance of Napoleon's swift action in defeating his enemies. Only someone with "total confidence" and "intuitive vision" can move swiftly in any profession. Napoleon had both of these traits in abundance. Whether deluded or not, Napoleon always "knew" what was best for his country and troops. His Grand Army followed him with a blind conviction of his omniscience. He believed he was gifted and that belief translated into his speech and ability to lead. He "knew" the "truth" and the "way" and that belief system attracted disciples willing to follow him to their deaths. Most leaders who lose are usually those who are indecisive or lack confidence in their actions, which causes them to hesitate until the opportunity is lost. Napoleon's supreme confidence came from his holistic knowledge of where he was going. He often said a politician must be a "dealer in hope." He always expected to win and therefore did. His positive attitude, charisma, and swift action led him to countless victories, which caused him to believe that he was invincible.

MANIC-DEPRESSIVE ILLNESS

Napoleon's bipolar illness—more popularly known as manic depression—was one of the reasons for Napoleon's swift action. When in the manic state, Napoleon was energized, talkative, an insomniac, reckless, with an expanded self-esteem and capable of the most herculean feats. He could outmarch, outride, outthink, and outwork his adversaries. He was manically driven by delusions of grandeur that inspired him to superhuman achievement. Speed resulted from his manic need to outperform his peers both in the field and in strategic planning. He won many battles because of his ability to outmaneuver his enemies or outflank them, due to his unique ability to think quicker and implement faster. Napoleon was famous for inspiring his men to perform beyond their ability. He became their role model through his own manic behavior and "superman" accomplishments, using action to motivate his troops to make a superhuman effort. They responded in kind by winning impossible battles.

Napoleon had the power of macrovision and maniacal speed. Most historians agree he would never have achieved such enormous success had he been even slightly normal. He was abnormally driven and that abnormality led to his great success. Biographers Hershman and Lieb (1994) wrote, "Mania was the secret of Napoleon's success," and he confirmed that in his memoirs at St. Helena: "My troops moved as rapidly as my thoughts." Intuition gave him superior insight, rational decision-making gave him analytical ability, manic energy gave him speed, and charisma attracted many disciples. Together these made him virtually invincible.

INFLUENCE

Prince Tallyrand, whom Napoleon had deposed and exiled, became his mortal enemy, but still paid him the ultimate tribute: "His career is the most extraordinary that has occurred for one thousand years. . . . He was certainly great, an extraordinary man. . . . He was clearly the most extraordinary man I ever saw and I believe the most extraordinary man that has lived in our age, or for many ages" (Markham 1966, p. 265). One of the few men ever to defeat Napoleon in battle was the Duke of Wellington, who proclaimed, "Napoleon was not a personality, but a principle" (Markham, p. 154). He went on to say with the utmost respect that "the Corsican's presence on the field was the equivalent of 40,000 soldiers." Chateaubriand called him "the mightiest breath of life which ever animated human clay." Madame Germaine de Stael, a writer whom Napoleon snubbed and then had exiled from Paris, became the leader of the intellectual opposition to his empire. In 1797 this adversary described Napoleon as "that intrepid warrior, the most profound thinker, the most extraordinary genius in history" (Markham, p. 133).

Early Life Experiences and Influences

Napoleon was born in Ajaccio, Corsica, of Italian (Florentine) lineage. He was the second son of a mother who bore thirteen children, only eight of whom survived infancy—Joseph, Napoleon, Lucien, Elisa, Louis, Pauline, Caroline, and Jerome. His mother was quite beautiful. His father, Carlo, a military man and guerrilla, had failed at farming, politics, warfare, and poetry, and died penniless while Napoleon was being educated in France. Carlo Buonaparte had resisted the French takeover of Corsica just one year prior to Napoleon's birth in 1769. His mother spent the last three months of pregnancy (with Napoleon) as a refugee in the Corsican mountains, helping in the fight for independence. This prenatal experience would become a part of Napoleon's legacy. General Pasquale Paoli had fought for Corsican independence and would became Napoleon's first military hero. His mother envisioned Napoleon as the savior of Corsica, but Napoleon had greater designs. Alexander the Great would later supplant Paoli as Napoleon's hero mentor.

At age five Napoleon was reckless, precocious, and steeped with feelings of nationalism and independence. At this early age he swapped a loaf of his mother's bread for military rations from a passing soldier. When asked why, he responded,

"Because it is the food I will be eating when I grow up." He wrote at St. Helena: "I grew up wild and untamable. . . . Nothing overawed me. I wasn't afraid of anybody. I struck one person, I scratched another, 'till all were afraid of me." In 1779 Napoleon was sent to boarding school in France at age nine. He first went to Autun with his brother Joseph, and then to Brienne le Château, one of twelve royal schools in France. He and his brother stayed in France for eight years without returning home. Napoleon was considered an "unpopular," "sullen," and "insolent" student who was prone to losing control at the least provocation. From St. Helena he wrote: "From the very beginning I could not bear to be anything less than first in the class," adding, "I had confidence in my power, and enjoyed my superiority." Napoleon had a special aptitude for mathematics, according to his teachers. In 1784 he was sent to France's finest military school, the École Militaire in Paris. It was there that he decided he was special: "Already I had the feeling that my will was stronger than that of others." Napoleon discovered at this early age that he could be rebellious and indifferent to the feelings of others and still prevail. This experience gave him confidence in his ability but also instilled in him the tyrannical behavior he would exhibit the rest of his life. He passed his exams at the military academy in record time, graduating in one year instead of the standard three years, an early indication of his compulsion for manic speed at the expense of precision. This is a common finding in most Promethean temperaments. In Napoleon, it was exhibited very early in life.

SOCIOECONOMIC STATUS

Napoleon was socioeconomically inferior to those attending the École Militaire and was ragged constantly for his foreign accent and small stature (5'2"). It was at the École that Napoleon was first given the nickname Little Corporal. He would never forget the snobbery and *haute noblesse* (high nobility) airs and would rant against them for years. Napoleon was probably better educated in his particular profession than any other person in this book. However, his ultimate success was more a result of his personal attributes than any particular concept he learned about strategy in military school. Luck also played a part in his meteoric rise through the ranks. The French Revolution took place just four years after his graduation and appointment as an artillery lieutenant in Valence. The Revolution would play a significant role in his rapid advancement since most of the royalists had fled the country and the guillotine. The Royalists had dominated the ranks of the military elite and their absence left the road to the top open for anyone with ambition. Napoleon qualified as ambitious. As is often the case in confrontational environments, the talented and courageous individuals are those who take overt action. Napoleon was not a royalist and in no fear for his safety, and the road to the top was cleared of a great number of talented competitors who were guillotined or expatriated. Napoleon took advantage of this void in the ranks. In the seven years after graduating from school, Napoleon traveled frequently between France and Corsica as he was enamored with the possibility of freeing his native country from French rule. His initial efforts were unsuccessful and he and his family were forced to go into exile in France in June 1793. It was at this time that he changed his name from the Italian Buonaparte to the French Bonaparte in deference to his new French citizenship.

MYTHOLOGICAL MENTORS

Napoleon was always a voracious reader and a loner—a common trait in most innovative geniuses. He attempted to view all problems from a philosophical perspective. His heroic role models tended to be great philosophers or military leaders, especially Rousseau and Voltaire whom he read passionately and quoted often. Alexander the Great was his military and political hero. Joseph Campbell said in *A Hero with a Thousand Faces* (1949) that all heroes are buried in our collective unconscious as "archetypes" and donning the right "Mask" as a "mythic image" can inspire us to greatness. Campbell believed that one must have real models to emulate for success and in *Hero* he says that "life potentialities are innately unconscious" (p. 17). Napoleon used these visions of heroes in his march to the top as a military leader extraordinaire. He first distinguished himself during the Italian campaign, at Lodi in April 1796, as chief commander of an army of 30,000 Frenchmen ordered to fight against a combined Italian and Austrian force of 70,000. He won a decisive victory with brilliant tactical maneuvers. From that day forward he believed that he was destined to be a great military genius. At St. Helena he credited this early victory at Lodi as the turning point in his life. His emotional and internalized belief in his omnipotent destiny is a consistent finding in great achievers. Many of the other subjects in this book were found to have a similar mystical revelation at some critical point in their early lives. These revelations instilled the sudden "knowledge" of a special destiny. Power and influence never trail far behind the imprint of greatness. Joseph Campbell spent his life researching the psychology of heroes. He said, "Symbolically, man will discover his true identity." Napoleon had discovered his identity and wrote of this revelation: "It was only after Lodi that I realized *I was a superior being* and conceived the ambition of performing great things, which hitherto had filled my thoughts only as a fantastic dream" (Markham, p. 42).

After Lodi, Napoleon rose in the ranks at an unparalleled pace even in a nation beset by revolution and terror. His advancement is unprecedented in the annals of military or political history. However, his internal belief in his infallibility became overtly exaggerated. This deluded sense of self helped him overachieve but would ultimately cause him to be a tyrant. His legacy to the world of psychology is the "Napoleon complex," which is defined as an egomaniac with a deluded opinion of self. Napoleon considered himself to be "destined to change the face of the world." Nothing could stop his inextricable drive to become the first emperor of France since Charlemagne.

A Promethean Spirit

As a Promethean, Napoleon saw the larger vision in battle and then *thought* out military strategy in a rational and structured approach to winning. Napoleon envisioned the battlefield and then went about planning his tactics in a calculating and left-brain manner. But when he implemented his plan, he was driven in a manic way and resorted to a right-brain approach. He envisioned the battle holistically, planned it analytically, and implemented it emotionally. His approach to life and war was impersonal, to the chagrin of his generals, relatives, wives, and mistresses. Most of his success has been attributed to his military genius. Overshadowed is the Napoleonic Code that he created and implemented as a testimony to his interest in systematic order and judicial morality. He devised this exhaustive and comprehensive legal and administrative system and executed it in every nation he conquered. It was his contribution to the Enlightenment. To his credit, this code has been influential in much of Europe and in the state of Louisiana. His great victories against enormous odds and his Napoleonic Code are lasting tributes to his Promethean temperament.

A Manic Success

D. Jablow Hershman and psychiatrist Julian Lieb analyzed Napoleon's manic drive in *Brotherhood of Tyrants* (1994) and concluded that "mania was the secret of Napoleon's success" (p. 143). The authors also found Napoleon to be "absurdly optimistic," a function of his manicness, and said that he had "boundless sexual energy" (p. 144). His manic energy allowed him to outmaneuver his enemies and reach a strategic position first, a critical factor in any military engagement. Napoleon understood the importance of his edge and said, "I will lose a man but never a moment." Austerlitz gives testimony to this talent. The battle of Austerlitz (1805) is recognized as Napoleon's single greatest military victory. Napoleon's decisive victory took place in Austria and never ceases to amaze historians. This crowning achievement was accomplished through Napoleon's manic behavior and obsession with speed. Napoleon was confronted with a combination of Russian and Austrian armies twice the size of his own which he engaged on territory of which he was totally unfamiliar. He drove himself and his men to superhuman efforts in order to outflank the enemy. By racing the enemy to a strategic position, he won the battle through sheer will and speed, allowing him to defeat 80,000 men with only 40,000 of his own.

Mania dominated Napoleon's professional and personal life. Everything in his life was accomplished at superhuman speed. He talked fast, ate fast, rode fast, thought fast, and lived fast. He even slept fast, never taking more than four hours to rest his body. He graduated from the École Militaire in one year when the average time was three. He became a general at age twenty-four, an unheard-of accomplishment. He ascended to the leadership of France as First Consul at the age of thirty and became emperor by age thirty-five. By this time he was acknowl-edged as the most powerful man in the world. He admitted the offensive against Egypt was based on his desire to emulate his hero, Alexander. When he walked into Berlin, a victor over Prussia in 1806, he had reduced the powerful Hapsburg state to a French vassal. Napoleon was still only thirty-five and had virtually con-quered Europe. He lived life in such a hurry that he left most of his peers in his wake. In the end he rushed into battles he should not have fought and his "rush-ing sickness" became responsible for his ultimate demise at Waterloo.

Napoleon's hypomania was legend. Once in a manic ride through Europe, he killed five horses in five days of nonstop frenetic riding in which he never rested or stopped. Constant, his valet, said, "I never comprehended how his body could en-dure such fatigue, and yet he enjoyed almost continuously the most perfect health," adding, "and he never even stopped to change clothes" (Hershman and Lieb 1994, p. 145). Napoleon's normal work day averaged fourteen to sixteen hours and he often never stopped to eat. He could dictate to four or five secretaries simultaneously on different subjects (a classic multitasking trait found in Type A personalities). An Eng-lish colonel at Elba said, "I have never seen a man in any situation of life with so much personal activity. . . . He appears to take much pleasure in perpetual move-ment, and in seeing those who accompany him sink under fatigue" (Hershman and Lieb 1994, p. 47). Napoleon's success was a result of the mania that I have labeled "manic success syndrome," but it was also responsible for his speedy demise. Her-shman and Lieb wrote: "The very mania that gave him such advantages in battle doomed him to waste the victories and destroy his empire" (p. 44).

Power, Influence, and Destructiveness

Napoleon was given enormous "titular power" by those enthralled by his charisma and psychic energy. He wielded a cultlike hypnotic charm that could motivate peo-ple to do his will. Most of Napoleon's power has been viewed as "physical power" or "force" since he subdued all enemies with muscle and guns. Those who resort to guns and force are intent on instilling fear to control their adversaries. The adage of absolute power corrupting absolutely must have been coined for Napoleon. Once he had absolute power he used it for destruction and for his own personal ag-grandizement.

EGOMANIA

When Napoleon was posted to Paris during the Reign of Terror, he indiscrimi-nately fired into an unruly mob at the Tuileries, gaining a reputation of someone not to anger for fear of retribution by gunfire. His famous "whiff of grapeshot" in-cident gained him a reputation as someone with total disregard for anything but ruthless nationalism. His destructive behavior, aimed at keeping the masses in line through fear, led to his promotion to commander of the Army of the Interior.

Napoleon saw himself as invincible and infallible, deserving of any and all power he could acquire. He began to see himself as Christ, Buddha, and Mohammed, and said, "I saw myself founding a religion." Everything became "I" or "me" and all glory was aimed at his own deification. He even deserted whole armies in Italy, Egypt, and Russia to save himself. During an uprising in Paris he ran through the streets with a small command of troops, shouting, "Follow me. If they resist, kill, kill! I am the god of the day!" (Hershman and Lieb 1994, p. 28).

DELUSIONS OF GRANDEUR

Napoleon always considered himself to be above the ordinary rules of society. He said, "I am not a man like other men; the laws of morality and decorum are not for me." In Italy he ordered Italian officials executed without trial and entire towns burned to the ground with all their inhabitants slaughtered if one French soldier was killed. Remember that he was of Italian ancestry not French, but France was his power base and it was to France that he pledged his allegiance. After Napoleon's defeat at Waterloo, Chateaubriand commented "Napoleon was regarded as the devil let loose upon Europe." His insensitivity and inhumanity became more pronounced as he aged. The culmination of Napoleon's destructive nature came towards the end when his empire was crumbling. He wrote, "If I lose my throne, I will bury the world beneath its ruins" (Hershman and Lieb 1994, p. 178).

POWER AT ANY PRICE

Napoleon lived and died for power, admitting, "There is only one thing to do in this world and that is to keep acquiring more and more *power.* All the rest is chimerical." This ideology drove him to attack Russia to prove his omnipotence. His Russian invasion appeared to be pure genius until he reached the outskirts of Moscow. When he reached the walls of the city on September 14, 1812, his greatest fantasy was realized as victory was imminent. He wrote later, "If I had succeeded, I would have been the greatest man known to history." This powercrazed man entered Moscow expecting pomp and ceremony as a conquering hero. Instead, the city had been set afire by the Russians, who had masterfully taken all provisions and ammunition with them, leaving a destitute and charred city for Napoleon. Napoleon went into a deep depression—the down side of his manic-depressive illness. His depression lingered during his stay in Moscow, causing him to become totally ineffective, which contributed to the destruction of his own forces. He allowed horses and humans to die of cold and hunger and was incapable of making the simplest decision during his depression. Napoleon became impotent when denied his consummate victory and remained in Moscow long after prudence dictated his retreat from the advancing winter. By delaying, he allowed the devastating Russian winter to destroy his Grand Army. Lacking food and clothing, it was exposed to attack by partisans. Napoleon became distraught. Decisions which he could have made in October were postponed until December. When he finally decided to abandon the city and retreat south, it was too late. Delays due to his depression led to his army's annihilation and two hundred thousand men perished from cold and starvation. Napoleon found reasons to leave for Paris, and abandoned his army in its long, painful retreat.

Napoleon's mania helped him win repeated victories, but also caused his self-destruction and that of his empire. Napoleon lost a total of half a million men in the Russian campaign and by 1814 one million Frenchmen were dead. When he was finally defeated and exiled as emperor of Elba on April 11, 1814, Napoleon went into another severe depression. When presented with the Treaty of Fountainbleau for his signature, Napoleon resorted to poison in an attempt to escape the humiliation of defeat. His egomania still rampant, he said "I did my best to get killed . . . rather than capitulate to inferior beings." He survived the poisoning and took refuge in Elba. Ten months later, his depression gone, he began planning his return to regain his throne.

Mania and Power: Napoleon's Waterloo

Napoleon had an uncontrollable obsession for winning at all cost and firmly believed that "death is nothing, but to live defeated and inglorious is to die daily." His philosophy was to "combine absolute power, constant supervision, and *fear*" (Christopher 1955, p. 137). His successful military strategy was, "It is the same with strategy as with the siege of fortresses; concentrate fire on a single point; when the breach is made the equilibrium is broken and all the rest becomes useless and the fortress is taken." Napoleon was successful and powerful because he had a strong philosophy of life and combined passion with intellect to defeat his enemies. He worshiped the ideology of Rousseau and Voltaire and the aggressiveness of Alexander the Great. This mythological "mask" of a larger-than-life hero instilled in Napoleon the belief that he was omniscient. He sincerely believed himself to be a mythological god who was both infallible and deserving.

CHARISMATIC POWER

Napoleon's charisma was spellbinding. One of his generals said, "This diabolical man had such power over me that I could not resist it" (Hershman and Lieb 1994, p. 144). His tyrannical outbursts were part of an overall scheme to motivate and influence those around him. He destroyed a nation, and killed and maimed millions pursuing his dream of becoming "king of the world." When his kingdom seemed in peril, he wrote, "If I lose my throne I will bury the world beneath my ruins." These were not the ethics of Rousseau, but of a driven man who could never accept losing. His ambition was to "keep gaining more and more power," and when that proved impossible, he capitulated without a word.

His charisma was never more apparent than when he decided to march on Paris to reclaim his throne. He left Elba on March 1, 1815, landing two weeks later in the south of France. It took him all of twenty days to regain power. During these days, his persona was mesmerizing and his power incarnate. He proved that the power of oratory could conquer nations. When he landed unopposed at Antibes on March 15, 1815, intent on disavowing King Louis XVIII who had replaced him as the French leader, Napoleon had been out of power for ten months. On his march on Paris, he picked up ally after ally.

Napoleon was engaged at Grenoble by a regiment of one thousand of the king's armed men. Napoleon ordered his brigade of men to trail their muskets, and shouted with supreme self-confidence, "Kill your emperor if you wish." The soldiers disobeyed their orders to fire when just one shot would have stopped Napoleon. The king's men shouted *"Vive l'Empereur"* and joined Napoleon in his march on Paris. By his own admission, this was probably his finest hour. He wrote from St. Helena, "Before Grenoble I was an adventurer; at Grenoble, I was a reigning prince."

General Ney promised the king to stop "the Little Corporal" and was prepared to shoot him if necessary. Ney was one of the many generals disenchanted by Napoleon's erratic and destructive behavior, but who was also unable to resist the charms of this mesmerizing man. Ney disobeyed the king and joined Napoleon, which insured Napoleon of retaking the throne. Employing will and charisma only, he was able to walk into Paris and reclaim power without a shot being fired. This final victory of mind over might caused the king to flee for his life. Balzac would later write, "Before him did ever a man gain an empire simply by showing his hat?"

Napoleon's misanthropic plans were never completed. He was still not contrite, even after the defeat at Waterloo. Boarding the ship *Bellerophon* to St. Helena, he was fat, middle-aged, and totally defeated. During the two-day trip he captivated the officers on board, prompting Admiral Lord Keith to comment, "If he had obtained an interview with His Royal Highness in half an hour they would have been the best of friends" (Markham 1966, p. 138). Even in defeat Napoleon regarded his career as a game, writing, "After all, I've lost nothing. For I began the 'game' with a six-franc in my pocket and I've come out of it very rich." Napoleon's life and success is a classic example of Nietzsche's will-to-power, a "superman" created out of one's imagination and capable of great achievement and power. He is living proof that "power does accede to those willing to take it."

NAPOLEON BONAPARTE
The Greatest Military Genius in History
b. Aug. 15, 1769, Ajaccio, Corsica; d. May 5, 1821, St. Helena

Dominant Trait: Egomaniac with charisma and messianic obsession with power

Motto: "Power is my mistress." "An army marches on its stomach."

Nickname: Little Corporal, the Corsican, Enlightened Despot, the Champion of Death

Vices/Hobbies: Wrote poetry and read voraciously even during arduous battles

Heroes/Mentors: Paoli (Corsican revolutionary), Alexander the Great, Voltaire, Rousseau

Philosophy of Life: "Combine Absolute Power, Constant Supervision, and Fear." "I am destined to change the face of the world." "God gave me the will and the force to overcome all obstacles."

Fantasy: To rule the world: "I wanted the kingdom of the world."

Professional Successes: Became General at twenty-four; dictator of France at thirty; emperor and most powerful man in Europe at thirty-five; created Napoleonic Code, which became the legal and administrative model for most European nations.

Power: "Keep acquiring more and more power, all the rest is chimerical." Duke of Wellington felt he was equal to 40,000 soldiers. A general said, "This diabolical man had an (irresistible) power over me."

Influence: Probably the greatest military genius who ever lived. Russian Count Balmain wrote, "The most astonishing thing of all is the influence which this man wields on anyone who comes near him."

Destructiveness: "If I lose my throne I will bury the world beneath my ruins." Destroyed 1.5 million men due to megalomania, saying, "I reign only through the fear I inspire." Killed wantonly to gain reputation.

Birth Order: Secondborn of eleven surviving children. Corsican of Italian lineage. Father named him after a cousin who died fighting the French.

Parental Influence: Father a minor noble, politician, and guerrilla fighter; mother a ravishing beauty. "I was very well brought up by my mother, I owe her a great deal." Corsican upbringing instilled nationalism.

Transiency: At age nine was sent to France for military school training in three different schools and cities. Did not return for eight years, when his father was dead. Led transient life.

Crises: Fighting and death were his heritage (Corsican fight for independence) followed by the French Revolution (1789) and Reign of Terror (1794).

Formal Education: Never liked school. Boys-only schools in Corsica followed by College of Autun, Military College at Breinne, and École Militaire in Paris. Self-educated via reading throughout life.

Libidinal Drive: "Boundless sexual energy," according to biographer. Josephine said, "I am alarmed at the energy which animates all his doings." Two marriages, two bastard sons, and one legitimate heir.

Personality: Introverted-Intuitive-Thinker-Judger on MBTI. A charismatic manic-depressive egomaniac and Type A personality. Autocratic, impatient, imperious, could not stand losing at anything.

Self-Esteem: "I had confidence in my power and enjoyed my superiority," he wrote in St. Helena.

Rebellion: A loner who admitted, "I love nobody . . . not even my brothers. . . . I know I have no real friends."

Risk Propensity: "Fearless in battle." "I consider myself the boldest of generals."

Work Ethic: Worked nonstop 14–16 hours a day, never getting tired or sick. "He had the energy of a whirlwind."

Tenacity: Couldn't live in luxury as emperor of Elba. Reclaimed his empire only to lose at Waterloo.

Optimism: "He was absurdly optimistic." "I wasn't afraid of anybody."

Manicness: "Napoleon's energy verged on the superhuman." He kept 4–5 secretaries busy simultaneously, dictating for hours. Killed five horses in manic ride. He had energy incarnate.

Frank Lloyd Wright: Shining Brow

"Truth Against the World."

Overview

Frank Lloyd Wright's life would have been unbelievable had it been a novel or movie. Ayn Rand described him best in her superlative philosophical novel *The Fountainhead* (1943), a tale about good versus evil featuring an architect as the good or "heroic man" and the establishment as evil. Her protagonist, Howard Roark (alias Wright), fought evil by destroying his creation rather than allow mediocrity to defile it. Roark and Wright's successes were inextricably immersed in what Rand labeled man's true credo for living—"rational self-interest." Rand had incredible insight into what made Wright tick, especially considering the ever-irascible Wright refused to talk to her when she first approached him. He later agreed to design her new house in California. Rand depicted Wright's iconoclasm and nonconformity accurately in the personality of Roark.

Wright's independence and "rational self-interest" were inherited from a long line of Welsh ancestors. His guile and renegade nature were imprinted very early in life by a doting mother and itinerant father. His mother, Anna, believed his birth to be a prophetic event of a future messiah. His father, William, was a wandering dreamer searching for castles in the sky. His mother expected her son to grow up to be another Christ or Lincoln. Anna Wright idolized her son and proved to be the primary influence in the development of his egoistic and arrogant personality. She was so convinced of his natural supremacy that she gave him the middle name Lincoln at birth but the independent Frank changed it to his mother's family name Lloyd at age eighteen. This was more proof of the enormous influence his mother would exact on his life.

Wright's professional life is legendary. In the early part of the twentieth century the media called him "one of the really great men of our time." Writer-physicist Mendlesohn wrote, "His genius is beyond doubt." Human consciousness guru Gurdjieff called him "a man who *knows*." Lewis Mumford, his friend and social consciousness critic, called him "the world's greatest living architect" in 1938, and by 1957 had established that observation to "Wright is one of the most creative architectural geniuses of all time." Wright even referred to himself as a creative genius in one of his many court battles. When a reporter asked him about making such a self-serving statement Wright responded without hesitation, "I was under oath, wasn't I?"

ORGANIC ARCHITECT

Just as Picasso painted a person's psychological likeness, Wright designed homes and buildings to fit the persona of their owners and environment. Wright fought tradition in a lifelong battle to meld man to his environment through architecture. His name for his creative style was "organic architecture." By "organic" he meant "green," an idea which was ahead of its time. Wright was a pioneer ecologist who designed buildings that could coexist synergistically with nature. The first "green architect," Wright was determined to marry nature and technology together with elegant style. He despised the negative impact machines were having on the American lifestyle and architectural designs, in particular the effect the automobile was having on twentieth-century urbanization. He created Broadacre City as a creative response to city sprawl and concrete ghettos. He decried skyscrapers although he built one in his later years (Price Tower in Oklahoma). Aesthetics, not function, was the driving force behind his creative designs for industry and residences.

Early Life Experiences and Influences

Frank Lloyd Wright was born at Richland Center, near Madison, Wisconsin, on June 8, 1867. He was the eldest child of Anna Lloyd Jones and William Wright, an articulate Baptist minister, lecturer, and intrepid entrepreneur. Anna was William's second wife and fourteen years his junior. William had three children by his first marriage, and with Frank and his two younger sisters, there was constant conflict within the family.

William Wright was a vagabond in constant search of his fortune, which led the family through every state in the Northeast when Frank was quite young. The family never stayed in one town more than a few years, to the chagrin of Frank's mother. After five rapid moves, Anna divorced William and raised the family in Madison. It was there that Wright got his Midwestern roots.

Wright revealed in his autobiography that his mother groomed him for a life as an architect: "The boy would build beautiful buildings . . . she intended him to be an architect" (Wright 1962). Envisioning him as a master builder, she placed wood carvings of English cathedrals around his crib in the hope that osmosis would make him a designer of great buildings. She so doted on young Frank that he later wrote, "The lad was his mother's adoration"—to his constant irritation. Anna was so immersed in his care that she flew to Tokyo to nurse him through sickness when he was middle-aged.

Motherly Influence

Anna Wright had by far the greatest influence on her son's life. It was a veritable love-hate relationship due to her incessant and vigilant doting. She was a driven woman herself and was subject to "fits of madness." She had an intellectual bent and resorted to the latest in creative learning techniques to teach him abstract problem solving. She discovered the German educator Frederick Froebel, who was the first to advocate abstract problem solving through colored blocks. When Wright was three years old, she invested in Froebel's books and used them to mold her son's abstract problem-solving abilities. Wright's biographer Meryle Secrest (1993) felt this training was highly instrumental in making Wright a great architect: "The successful nurturing of Wright's genius is due to the enlightened teachings of Frederick Froebel." Wright later admitted his early training in abstract problem resolution was key to his innovative building designs.

Anna Wright's doting turned her son into an egotist and mama's boy who never picked up after himself or helped with domestic chores. He was spoiled and a prima donna primarily because of his mother's indulgence. She successfully groomed him to be an arrogant "know-it-all" and iconoclast who suffered fools poorly. Her grooming also contributed to his becoming the most innovative architect in history. Wright totally ignored his father and suggested his father didn't love him.

TRANSIENCY MOLDED HIS CHARACTER

Wright's early transiency was responsible for molding him into a renegade nonconformist. Moving from one strange city to another as a young child between the ages of two and nine placed him in new environments and schools where he was forced to make friends from different cultures. This early nomadic experience led him from Wisconsin to Iowa, Rhode Island, Connecticut, and Massachusetts prior to age ten. During this period his indulgent mother took on the task of teaching him, utilizing Froebel Blocks instead of relying on standard school methods of instruction. This early training turned out to be a critical piece in the complex puzzle that became Frank Lloyd Wright. Being firstborn also contributed to his need for perfection and achievement and imprinted him with self-sufficiency. As a teenager he spent summers on a Wisconsin farm, which instilled the Welsh work ethic. His maternal relatives taught him the Welsh adage "adding tired to tired" when he complained of overwork. All of these early-life experiences groomed him to become an irascible egoist who wrote in his autobiography, "Individuality is the most precious thing in life."

MYTHOLOGICAL HERO/MENTORS

Frank Lloyd Wright fulfilled his mother's dream of him as a "supernatural being." Her nurturing and training paid off as he became convinced that he was "special," and he grew up with few mental limitations for success or achievement. Anna Lloyd Wright was a descendant of rebellious Welsh immigrants who were known for their independent spirit and strong will. She inherited those traits and passed them on to her famous son. Her imprints on his young psyche influenced his pursuit of the birthright she had predicted for him as a creative superman. When he was born, she predicted he would distinguish himself in the likeness of the mythological Celtic poet/savior and magician Taliesin, which means "the Shining Brow" in Welsh. She even referred to him as Prince Taliesin. Anna Wright felt so strongly that her son was predestined for eminence that she surrounded his crib with prints of great architectural buildings and drawings of art to inspire him as an infant. As he grew older, she reinforced his Herculean personal image. Young Frank lived up to her grandiose expectations and developed an audacious personality that was capable of saying, "Early in life I had to choose between honest arrogance and hypocritical humility. I chose honest arrogance."

The mythological god Taliesin became Wright's role model, although he would never admit it in public. His destiny as a superior being was Nietzschean and would one day become immortalized by Ayn Rand's objectivist philosophy, which aggrandized "egoism and individualism."

Wright was a devoted nonconformist from a very young age. His ideology didn't become apparent until his middle-age, when he placed his motto over the door of his Wisconsin estate: "Truth against the World." Wright's obstreperous behavior was based on his personal belief that he was special and could operate autonomously without considering the consequences of his actions. As a teenager, Wright became totally enamored with the story of Aladdin and his lamp adding this to his internal fantasy imagery. Like Aladdin, Wright identified with the magic of life's possibilities, seeing few limitations to his achievements. He never graduated from Madison High School, but started taking engineering classes at the University of Wisconsin. His most grounded mentor became Louis Sullivan, the father of the skyscraper, who coined the phrase "form follows function." Wright worked for Sullivan for several years and considered him his *lieber meister* (dear master). By this time he was married to his first wife Catherine and had two children.

Wright was continually dissatisfied with his own and anyone else's work. He was impatient and intolerant, and began moonlighting on the side to make more commissions, which resulted in his firing. As in many cases, this "crisis became the mother of his creativity," and he opened his own architectural practice in 1893. His mother's preaching that "nothing is so sacred as an architect" had taken hold and he was now a professional architect.

REBEL WITH A CAUSE

Wright was a daring and reckless iconoclast who always violated tradition in both design and life. He valued nonconformity in all things. This was demonstrated when he eloped to Europe at the height of his career in 1909, just after turning forty. He and lover Mamah Borthwick Cheney suddenly disappeared, with Wright leaving a successful practice, a devoted wife, and six children. He had just completed a new home for Edwin and Mamah Cheney in Oak Park, Illinois.

Wright often became friends with his clients since he created homes in their owners' psychological likeness. In this case friendship turned into passion. Mamah Cheney was an attractive, iconoclastic woman with a temperament similar to Wright's. She held a master's degree in education and was a proponent of free love.

Unable to cope with the guilt of destroying two families, Wright and Mamah Cheney surreptitiously disappeared after the birth of Wright's sixth child. Wright's scandalous act was even more shocking to the media since he was a respected member of the community and church in fashionable Oak Park, in addition to his eminent position in the architectural movement in the Midwest. Wright left his Chicago practice in the hands of an assistant (it was closed after twelve months) and didn't return to Chicago for eighteen months.

Wright was perpetually flirting with bankruptcy but had the audacity to borrow $10,000 from a Chicago friend in order to finance his affair. The two lovers took up residence first in Berlin, Germany, and then Florence, Italy, while working on a new architectural publication of his works with Ernst Wasmuth, who had commissioned him to publish his architectural designs.

The Chicago newspapers ran titillating headlines about the missing architect. The media and religious community lambasted him. Typically, Wright was nonplussed about the recriminations of "ordinary people."

While in Florence, Wright was inspired by the Villa Medici to return to America and build his dream home in Spring Green, Wisconsin. He designed a utopian estate to be named Taliesin. When it was finished some years later, it would be called Wright's "love cottage" due to his flagrant cohabitation with another man's wife.

EGOMANIA

Wright had always been an arrogant egoist, but his affair with Mamah Cheney was clearly motivated by a midlife crisis. Like most creative visionaries, he never considered the ramifications of his capricious act. He actually abandoned his business and family to pursue a fantasy.

Most of Wright's great creations were spawned by his imaginative fantasies. His favorite childhood fantasy had been Aladdin and his magic lamp. Turning forty, he convinced his lover, Mamah, to escape reality (as a vicarious Aladdin) and embark on a new life. While in Europe, he decided to divorce Catherine and complete his fantasy by starting over with Mamah at Taliesin, a secluded rendezvous in Spring Green, Wisconsin, where they could live happily ever after. Writing to his mother from Europe, he convinced her to sell her Oak Park residence and buy the land for his chateau. Anna Jones Wright disagreed with her son, but never distanced herself from him.

TALIESIN

Anna Lloyd Wright rationalized her son's bizarre behavior as the eccentricities of the gifted. Frank had grown into her vision of him and she delighted in his unconventional ideas, dress, buildings, and behavior, which she saw as the necessary baggage of an "eccentric genius." Chicago newspapers weren't quite as forgiving. For three years they published scathing editorials about his deplorable behavior. Wright tried to counter the bad publicity by hiring a reporter to suppress news about him and Mamah.

Wright embarked on the creation of Taliesin as a Celtic pantheon to his own inflated image of himself as the world's greatest architect. The chateau was completed near his birthplace in 1911. Taliesin would become part of his mythological identity. The name was destined to follow him to his grave, and it still is synonymous with Wright and freedom and truth in architecture.

ORGANIC ARCHITECTURE

Wright was highly influenced by his rural upbringing and modified this with his demand for freedom in all things. The architecture of Taliesin became Wright's signature style, which he named "organic architecture." His later creations never deviated far from the fundamental principles found in this Prairie House or ranch-style design. Wright's "organic architecture" married form and function with nature and need, which ultimately became the cornerstone of all of Wright's great architectural innovations. The Prairie House made obsolete such traditional spaces as the attic and the cellar. Taliesin became the outlet for his most imaginative creative fantasies where aesthetics were wed to freedom and the environment.

SARTORIAL SPLENDOR

Wright's agrarian, mid-American upbringing was apparent in all his creations except his style of dress. A broad-brimmed hat, cane, and swirling cape were his signature costume. "No one who ever saw him make an entrance in that regalia ever forgot him" (Secrest 1992). He enjoyed the image of an iconoclast and was a sight to behold in his sartorial splendor. He was considered a swashbuckling renegade or "weird genius" by the media, which were oblivious to his intent of self-promotion. While using both style of dress and innovative designs to make statements about the personality of a person and building, no other person approached the audacious style of Frank Lloyd Wright.

A PROMETHEAN SPIRIT

Frank Lloyd Wright was the quintessential Promethean spirit in constant search of new opportunities in architecture. Truth and freedom were his only masters, and they were the reasons for his creative genius. He violated social decorum, to the chagrin of his family, wives, and associates. Wright was an intuitive-thinking independent visionary, never constrained by what "was" and therefore was able to create what "could be."

SUPERMAN PERSONA

Wright's "superman" persona was legend in the world of architecture. It made him great, but almost destroyed him. Wright always felt he was above the mundane matters in life like paying bills, earning a profit, or meeting schedules. The artist in him refused to consider the financial concerns of business, causing him to flirt with bankruptcy most of his life. Banks constantly hounded him and even attempted to take away his most valued possessions like Taliesin. Wright never became financially solvent until his eighties.

Wright violated every rule of social decorum both personally and professionally. The only authority he gave credence to was a superbeing known as "himself." Wright was autonomous as a young man, a nonconformist in middle age, and a renegade always. His autonomy led him to dress in complete defiance of societal fashions, to violate marital traditions, and to design his buildings according to his own unique standards. He was introspective about his nature: "I am a wild bird and must stay free," validating a Promethean temperament.

Wright's unique style and talent drew devoted disciples from society and the arts. Many became lifelong friends, such as Carl Sandburg, Clarence Darrow, Lewis Mumford, Ayn Rand, Samuel Johnson, Ernest Hemingway, and Georgei Gurdjieff. These powerful personalities saw Wright as a true visionary and twentieth-century leader. Paul Goldberger of the *New York Times* wrote in 1994, "If Walt Whitman had been an architect, he would have been Frank Lloyd Wright." He also compared Wright to the great iconoclastic artists of the era: "Wright's only true equal in modern times was Picasso," a true testimony to Wright's mastery of "creative destruction." His designs would define the twentieth century in much the same way as Picasso's art, and both created psychological likenesses through their productions.

Promethean Creativity

Taliesin was the first great monument to Wright's genius. This eight-hundred-acre estate was begun in 1937 and completed in 1939. The wide-open look and freedom of the Prairie House became Wright's signature style. His need for freedom, both professionally and personally, became the essence of his design and a memorial to his genius. He had "Truth Against the World" engraved on the entrance to Taliesin as his motto.

When he completed Taliesin West in Scottsdale, Arizona, it became apparent that Wright considered himself the god Taliesin. His original Wisconsin chateau was a magnificent memorial to his creative genius and is still an acceptable contemporary domicile in the 1990s due to its clear, simple lines that are classic Wright. But Wright's intuitive and fertile imagination demanded the new and different. Ultimately he destroyed Taliesin by constant redesign of the building, in much the same way Walt Disney did with Disneyland. Disney built his amusement park and then declared it "would never be finished." Wright was Disney's precursor in that he approached all creative designs as if they were temporary, which caused the original Taliesin to be lost to posterity. His Promethean temperament also allowed him to continually destroy his creations in order to improve on their design rather than protect them as many creators. This classical Promethean trait is pervasive in all creative and innovative individuals.

CREATIVE DESTROYER

Wright's Prairie House and Broadacre City are two nonconforming concepts that made him unique. Both evoked the ire of the establishment by violating the traditional standards of architecture. Wright always refused to build two things alike, always searching for the ultimate truth in architecture. He was never satisfied with any creation even when it was world-acclaimed. Innovation was his forte. He was more interested in destroying the *existing* in order to be innovative in a *new way*. His creative destruction was demonstrated by his enthusiastic rebuilding of Taliesin not once but three times. His swashbuckling approach to life was in tune with his creative genius. It made him a unique person. The one thing that can be said about Wright is that he always lived on the edge of acceptability in everything.

MANICNESS

The finest example of Wright's manic creativity is the Fallingwater home built for Edgar Kaufmann, a Pittsburgh department store tycoon. Kaufmann commissioned Wright to build a mountain retreat at Bear Run in remote Pennsylvania. The Kaufmanns had always dreamed of a vacation home facing the falling waters of Bear Creek and commissioned Wright to build it in 1935. Wright envisioned the opposite, a home integrated with the environment, hanging precariously over the waterfall.

Wright was a philosophical architect in the same way Picasso was a philosophical artist. He had to "see" his creation in advance and it had to conform psychologically to the subject. Wright had to have a holistic vision of his work prior to starting the design. He stressed this approach to his students, saying, "Never attempt to resolve a design until the idea has taken a clear shape in your imagination" (Secrest 1992, p. 419). For this reason Wright had procrastinated over the design of Fallingwater for many months while the impatient Kaufmann kept calling for a progress report.

On one trip to Milwaukee, which was a two-hour drive from Taliesin, Kaufmann called for an update and Wright calmly said in front of his associates, "Your home is finished." Kaufmann said he would drive right over to Taliesin to review the results. The truth was that Wright had not even begun the project except to conceptualize it in his mind. No drawings were available for Kaufmann's review. Wright's associates were aghast.

Frank Lloyd Wright was always dramatic and impulsively innovative. This time he lived up to his reputation as a flamboyant creative genius. He hung up the phone, sat down with three tracing sheets, and began a marathon creative exercise that his associates described as a tour de force. Seven associates personally witnessed this herculean task of creative genius. Wright started drawing while carrying on a running commentary of his designs. He completed it with the most minute detail, christening it Fallingwater during that manic two-hour session. He even included details such as the seats from which Kaufmann and his wife could view the waterfall.

This creative masterpiece was destined to become Wright's most famous building even though it was created in less than two hours. His last-minute creation would one day be called "one of the most beautiful houses in the world" (Secrest 1992, p. 420). His associates were amazed when Kaufmann showed up, looked over the drawings, and said, "Don't change a thing."

ENERGY INCARNATE

When inspired, Wright was energy incarnate and this hypomania continued into old age. His biographer Meryle Secrest wrote: "His inventiveness and energy were prodigious and he worked ceaselessly" (p. 230). Most great entrepreneurial geniuses are capable of juggling many balls simultaneously, or multitasking. These individuals enjoy being frenetic, scheduling far more than they can possibly complete, and pride themselves in accomplishing all with precision. This talent makes them exceptionally productive, but can prove devastating to family and associates.

Wright was a workaholic and adhered to his own aphorism, "Work should be the creative and joyful essence of life." His prodigious output of architectural creations substantiates his manic need to produce. Between 1894 and 1912, Wright designed 135 buildings in addition to lecturing, operating his firm, publishing ten articles, and serving as the titular head of Chicago architecture.

Later in life he became more methodical and less social, but did not slow down in productive output. At age eighty-four he began work one morning at 4 A.M. and before breakfast had completed new drawings for three distinctly different homes. During his eighties, Wright took on three hundred new commissions, finishing what turned out to be a full one-third of the total output of his creative life. These later creative ventures included New York City's Guggenheim Museum of Art; the Price Tower in Bartlesville, Oklahoma; plus the eight-million-dollar Marin County Civic Center on 130 acres in Northern California. These masterpieces were all radically different designs in the classic Wright tradition.

Power and Influence

Wright liked to say, "Architecture receives its power from the life force and both man and his creations are in an identical state of becoming" (Secrest 1992, p. 210). Could he have been speaking of himself? Wright's power evolved out of his ability to ignore all tradition in creating the new and different. But his power was also his nemesis. His strengths became his weaknesses.

Since Wright always insisted on creating only the "new," he was never able to achieve the economies of scale of other businessmen. Being innovative proved detrimental to him financially since every new creation required the same energy and time as the previous one. Wright never capitalized on past work like other architects who replicated past creations. The first of anything is always the most costly; huge profits are the by-product of mass production. Wright never reused his designs and therefore never reaped profits from past designs. When famous later in life, he was able to charge exorbitant fees for his work and only then became successful financially. He became furious when others copied or imitated his work. Ingenious creativity was his strength but it also contributed to his constant battle with insolvency; Taliesin was repossessed several times by banks. Wright also lost many major commissions over the years due to his unpopular avant-garde designs.

LIVE-ON-THE-EDGE VISIONARY

Wright derived his power and influence from an audacious and rebellious spirit. These same qualities caused him to live insolvent for the better part of his adult life. Risk taking left him nearly bankrupt and he was in constant threat of being evicted from Taliesin by irate creditors.

Lack of interest in detail is common in the Promethean personality, since they are only interested in the big picture and bored by detail. Wright ignored minute details in all things. Wright's demand for aesthetics at the expense of detail afflicted most of his buildings with leaks, mechanical problems, and other anomalies. Taliesin burned three times, two of which were due to this gross inattention to detail. The Imperial Hotel in Tokyo could withstand great earthquakes but lacked leakproof roofs. His designs were aesthetic masterpieces but lacked the most essential items. Virtually no one ever complained about Wright's artistic taste or the "form" of his creations. But most of his clients complained about the most trivial problems that any skilled mechanic could have resolved. To Wright such petty details were not important.

CRISES AND CREATIVITY

Wright's greatest tragedy occurred on a summer afternoon in 1914. This was the day his lover and intended wife, Mamah Borthwick Cheney, was murdered, along with her two children and four staff members working at Taliesin. The murders and burning of Taliesin were committed by Wright's emotionally disturbed servant Julian Carlton. Wright was in Chicago working on a new building at the time of the murders and arson. Mamah had told Carlton and his wife that they would be let go at the end of the week for incompetence.

Wright was virtually destroyed by the tragedy and said, "All I had left to show for the struggle for freedom of the five years past" was lost. He began rebuilding Taliesin immediately since it was his one link to a glorious and romantic past. Wright was never the same after the tragedy. He had carefully planned an idyllic life with Mamah and her children after abandoning his first wife and six children. Taliesin was to have been their dream cottage, but all that was destroyed. Yet this crisis became the catalyst for his greatest creations.

PSYCHOSEXUAL ENERGY

The personal tragedies in Wright's life are the stuff of drama. He left his first wife, Catherine; his lover Mamah Borthwick Cheney was murdered; and his second wife, Miriam Noel Wright, was a malicious, power-hungry female who attempted to destroy him. Wright was vulnerable after Mamah's murder and the mercenary Miriam lured him into marriage. When he realized her intent he threw her out and filed for divorce, after which she ruthlessly planned his demise. Wright had married Miriam Noel the month of his divorce from Catherine (November 1923), after living with her since 1915. After the first six months as husband and wife, she left in May 1924, beginning six years of fighting.

Miriam was a drug addict who hid it from Wright until after they were married. She was also a borderline psychotic. Wright became engaged to Olga Ivanovna Lazovich, a Russian immigrant, in 1924. When she gave birth to his daughter Iovanna in 1924, the jealous and demented Miriam spent years attempting to have Olga deported and Wright jailed under the Mann Act (transporting an unmarried woman across state lines for the purpose of sex). Miriam resorted to court actions for four tortuous years, causing Wright and Olga to flee to Puerto Rico and to hide out in a remote Minnesota farmhouse where the ever-creative Wright began writing his memoirs. This period of Wright's life was a nightmare. Both Wright and Olga were pursued by the FBI, reporters, the U.S. Justice Department, and immigration authorities. His creative efforts came to a virtual halt until Miriam died in 1933 after ten years of harassment.

MARRIAGE AND TRAGEDY

Wright married Olga Lazovich in 1928. Olga was a strange choice for Wright: she was thirty years his junior, and came from a cultural background diametrically opposite his. Olga and Wright had met at the ballet in 1924. Wright was then fifty-eight years old, but they were not married for four years despite having a love child.

Olga was a radical disciple of Georgei Gurdjieff, the human consciousness guru. Although Olga and Wright had little in common, they probably stayed together to spite Miriam and because of Gurdjieff's enormous influence. Gurdjieff was a constant visitor at Taliesin, coaching Olga in the art of psychological survival which included her capitulation to Wright's whims.

Olga had endured Miriam Noel's harassment, during which she was imprisoned, constantly badgered, and threatened with deportation. Amazingly, the relationship lasted through such turmoil. Olga probably decided to stay with Wright at any price after such an ordeal.

Tragedy struck again when Wright's stepdaughter Svetlana (Olga's daughter by a previous marriage) died tragically in a car crash on the Taliesin estate during the thirties. Taliesin burned for the third time in 1925, causing Wright to say, "Taliesin lived wherever I stood" (Secrest 1993, p. 316). Then in 1927 the bank foreclosed on his estate, forcing him to take up residence in California.

Frank Lloyd Wright's Legacy

Wright's radical simplicity in design was his legacy to architecture. Wright's self-description of his work was "radical conservatism." He was obsessed with blending nature and truth into his designs. Truth to Wright was the marriage of nature and design of function and form. It is ironic that his style would come to be known as contemporary in the latter part of the twentieth century: Wright's architectural peers had despised his radical ideas in his youth, but later architects imitated him. The cantankerous Wright became a cynic and often referred to American architecture as "imitation by imitators of imitation."

Wright's reputation and influence have endured because of his unique aesthetic style. The Museum of Modern Art in New York City paid tribute to his greatness with an exhibition in 1994. Wright's major contributions to architecture are the Prairie House and Broadacre City, both radical departures from the traditions of the era. His Prairie House designs attempted to "destroy the box" concept of home building. With Broadacre City he endeavored to marry the automobile and other machines to the needs of man and his environment. His Usonian (modular home concept) or "self-made" home for the masses never caught on even though he spent a great deal of energy on them during his twilight years.

Frank Lloyd Wright was charismatic, flamboyant, independent, and driven to succeed in what he called "organic architecture." His anarchy and iconoclastic approach to achieving goals were never better defined than in Ayn Rand's protagonist, renegade architect Howard Roark. Roark's line in *The Fountainhead*—"The essence of the creator's power is the ability of independent rational judgment"—is quintessential Wright. Wright was always a dreamer: "I am not fond of thinking; preferring to dream—until circumstance forces me to think." Such statements are typical of the right-brain driven Promethean temperament. He spent his professional life pursuing fantasy creations that were instilled in his psyche as a child. His childhood hero, Aladdin and his magic lamp, was his fantasy model for a utopian life. Wright never veered far from fantasy in most of his creative achievements.

According to Wright's biographer Meryle Secrest, "No one could have stopped him from becoming a success because he refused to be discouraged." Taliesin and he were synonymous concepts with freedom and individualism the embodiment of him and his creations. Imagination was his forte and acceptance by others never a factor. The *new* (novel) and *untried* (innovative) were the basis for everything he did. While the *new* and *untried* made him famous, they also became the major causes of his infamy.

Wright is probably the world's best-known architect even though he was a mediocre draftsman, journeyman engineer, and inept businessman. His vision and power allowed him to create the avant-garde with style and panache. Total disregard for the establishment and tradition made him great. Had he listened to the experts, he would never have realized such success. Wright was the consummate visionary whose genius was in avoiding tradition. His business motto was, "What we did yesterday we won't do today. And what we do tomorrow will not be what we'll be doing the day after" (Secrest 1993). The media hailed him as "one of the really great men of our time" and Lewis Mumford named him "one of the most creative architectural geniuses of all time." This Promethean was charismatic, independent, and rebellious, and these traits can be seen in any of his buildings. Look at the Guggenheim Museum of Art and think of Wright as the "anarchist of architecture."

FRANK LLOYD WRIGHT
America's Preeminent Architect
b. June 8, 1867, Richland Center, Wisconsin; d. April 9, 1959, Scottsdale, Arizona

Dominant Trait: Intuitive, charismatic, flamboyant, and independent

Motto: "Truth against the World." "Life is Truth." "What a man does; that he is." "Organic architecture."

Nickname: "Prince," "The Shining Brow," "The Fountainhead," "Anarchist of architecture."

Vices/Hobbies: Fast cars and fast horses; flamboyant, bizarre clothes and beautiful buildings

Heroes/Mentors: Aladdin and his magic lamp, the Welsh God Taliesin (Shining Brow), Abraham Lincoln, Walt Whitman, Louis Sullivan (his architectural *leiber meister*)

Philosophy of Life: "Organic architecture" comes from the "inner forces of nature." "Honest labor needs no master."

Fantasy: To build "Broadacre City" (organic city); "Usonian House"—utopian house affordable for "Everyman"

Professional Successes: Taliesin (1911); Larkin office building (America's first); Tokyo's Imperial Hotel (1921); Arizona Biltmore Hotel (1930); Fallingwater (1935); Price Tower (1953); Milwaukee Greek Church (1957); New York's Guggenheim Museum (1961); Marin County Civic Center (1965)

Power: World's first "green architect." "Architecture receives its power from the life-force."

Influence: Pervasive. Has been copied and imitated. "Wright is one of the most creative architectural geniuses of all time" (Lewis Mumford).

Destructiveness: Design objective: "Destroying the box"—was followed by destruction of family, friends, lovers due to "my way or the highway" mentality. Always used the "new" to destroy the "old."

Birth Order: Firstborn with two younger sisters (Jennie and Maginel)

Parental Influence: Father, William, was an undependable, vagabond Baptist Minister. Doting mother, Anna, raised him as "supernaturally gifted omnipotent" god in likeness of Welsh god Taliesin.

Transiency: Lived in five states prior to age ten, instilled self-sufficiency and comfort with ambiguity

Crises: Tragic life of continual crises starting with fist fights to keep first job. Taliesin burned three times.

Formal Education: Mother only teacher until age nine. Poor student in high school—never graduated. Engineering classes two semesters at University of Wisconsin. Sullivan apprenticeship true teacher.

Libidinal Drive: Charisma and flamboyant self-belief gave him "enormous sexual energy." Elopement with lover Mamah Borthwick Cheney in 1909 an act of passionate frenzy.

Personality: Promethean: Extrovert-Intuitive-Thinker-Judger. Impatient, impulsive, intolerant perfectionist.

Self-Esteem: "He was a model of brazen self-confidence." "Early in life I had to choose between honest arrogance and hypocritical humility. I chose arrogance."

Rebellion: "I am a wild bird and must remain free." Welsh heritage of nonconformity.

Risk Propensity: A fearless driver and horseman. "He had an unconscious courting of catastrophe and ruin."

Work Ethic: Capable of prodigious output designing three houses before breakfast at age eighty. Workaholic who created world famous Fallingwater in two hours in a monumental burst of creative energy.

Tenacity: "No one could have stopped him from becoming a success" due to persistence.

Optimism: Reporter asked about self-description as "creative genius." Reply: "I was under oath, wasn't I?"

Manic Compulsion: "His inventiveness and energy were prodigious and he worked ceaselessly."

5

Self-Esteem, Confidence, and Optimism: Maria Montessori and Pablo Picasso

Self-confidence is the first requisite to great undertakings.
—Alexander Pope

Self-Confidence Is Mental

Sun Tzu wrote over two thousand years ago: "Victorious warriors win first and then go to war, while defeated warriors go to war and seek to win." He knew that winning first occurred in the mind and then on the field of battle. Self-esteem guru Nathaniel Branden wrote in *Six Pillars of Self-Esteem* (1994): "Self-esteem is the reputation we acquire with ourselves." He was espousing the belief that self-image is not what others think of us but what we think of ourselves.

Self-esteem certainly was the most important trait for these fourteen wunderkinds. They exuded supreme self-confidence, which allowed them to perform herculean tasks. This mental strength is what allowed them to overcome the many obstacles confronted on their way to the top. Did they inherit or acquire their self-confidence? There is no doubt it was learned from doting mothers and early role models. Early successes then reinforced their positive self-image, proving the aphorism, "Success breeds more success." Their resilient belief in themselves resulted in precocious behavior which in turn inspired further creativity and success. Once a child "believes" they are special, they are capable of ignoring authority figures and follow their own dreams. Both Montessori and Picasso were so inclined. Both refused to conform to societal rules, which turned out to be their single greatest asset in achieving power and success. Psychologist Laurence Kohlberg said, "The gifted is likely to question, challenge, or defy traditions that his peers take for granted."

Even those visionaries with deluded dreams—Hitler, Sade, Napoleon,

149

Hughes, and Picasso—utilized their self-esteem to achieve enormous power. They had bizarre ideologies but were able to convince others of their validity. The critical element in such leaders is an indomitable belief system or self-confidence. Napoleon and Hitler were so convincing that they were able to sell their deluded dreams to millions, who were then led to their deaths in war. This is an oft-repeated scenario where the "pack" is looking for an all-knowing guru who will lead them to the promised land. The pack mentality longs for someone to follow to Utopia. Most people are attracted to anyone who positively "knows" where they are going, even when the journey is to hell.

Nathaniel Branden verified the importance of self-esteem for the creative genius in his book *Six Pillars of Self-Esteem*: "Creative persons listen to and trust their inner signals more than the average." In other words, those with a feeling of great self-worth are capable of exercising their creative energies. The power brokers and creative geniuses all violate tradition; they destroy the present to create the future.

Those aspiring to reach the top must be armed with an invincible self-image and confidence. These fourteen all listened to their inner voices. If they had not, they would have been destroyed by those who viewed them as charlatans or crazy rebels. Pioneers are always alone and require resilient self-esteem to enable them to ignore those "experts" who know all the reasons why their new idea is stupid.

Plastic surgeons have known for years that self-esteem is only skin-deep. Maxwell Maltz (*Psycho-Cybernetics,* 1968) described his experiences in repairing a facial scar and discovered that he had recreated a personality. After years of repairing physical self-images, he concluded: "The most important psychological discovery of this century is the discovery of the self-image. . . . Behavior, personality, and achievement are consistent with your self-image." Abraham Maslow preceded Maltz's theory with his work on the "Hierarchy of Needs." Maslow placed self-esteem second from the top in importance for motivational achievement; only self-actualization is ranked higher. Dennis Waitley wrote in his bestselling pop psychology book *The Psychology of Winning* (1979): "Positive self-esteem is one of the most important and basic qualities of a winning human being." The all-time best-selling spoken-word recording is Earl Nightingale's "The Strangest Secret," which preached, "We become what we think." These fourteen subjects confirm Nightingale's finding. Maria Montessori and Pablo Picasso are the most dramatic examples for using self-confidence to become a creative genius.

Both Montessori and Picasso employed self-esteem to make innovations in the fields of education and art. Montessori was told that girls could only be teachers and not doctors. Even her father agreed with the authorities. Montessori was so tenacious and self-confident that she appealed to the pope to gain admission to the University of Rome's medical school. Four years later she became the first female medical doctor in Italy.

Picasso was so self-confident that he defied the masters of art and established his own movement—cubism. Jean Cocteau, the French poet, shed light on Picasso's positive self-assurance in an article he wrote describing the irascible artist: "He radiated an almost cosmic and irresistible self-confidence. Nothing seemed beyond him."

SELF-ESTEEM = SELF-IMAGE = SELF-CONFIDENCE

Self-confidence emanates from a strong *self-image,* which evolves from a resilient "internalized" *self-esteem.* All three require nurturing. Did these visionaries inherit their self-esteem? No! Did they set out to create their own enormous self-confidence? No! Most acquired their confidence from parents, family, and mentors who told them they were great. These fourteen accepted this positive feedback, never questioning the validity of the adulation. Their self-assurance enabled them to confidently take risks. Success tended to reinforce their internal images. For example, Picasso was told that he would be a great painter; his early sketches were praised although they were normal childlike pictures with one exception. These drawings were not childish since Picasso was told that he was a painter—not a child. He had been brainwashed to believe that he was great. Picasso's early successes were imprinted on his psyche, which guaranteed an adult positive self-image that bordered on egotism.

Success does beget success. Napoleon, Hitler, Wright, Hughes, and Murdoch became oblivious to all adversarial opinion because they were convinced of their own omniscient ability. People with high esteem need early affirmation, but once they have it are capable of generating their own through action.

Can we modify or rewrite the image imprinted on us as children? Absolutely! Is it easy? No! Self-image is not set in "plaster" as philosopher and educator John Dewey said earlier this century, it is set in putty. Changing it comes demands hard work and the constant rewriting of our internalized image of "success" that is stored in our unconscious. Rewriting that internal tape can be accomplished through concentrated behavior modification—reinforcing the internally stored self-image through repeated positive successes. It is sometimes changed quickly through some traumatic experience, as in the example of plastic surgery to repair a physical dysfunction.

The more practical path to changing our internal image is venturing into the unknown with confidence and then enjoying and reinforcing the resultant success. After continual reinforcement, the mind is convinced that anything is possible. Picasso, Napoleon, Hitler, and Montessori are prime examples of this approach. They were conditioned early in life by their parents, and after personal successes became convinced of their infallibility.

Many of the parents of these fourteen actually convinced their children they were "little gods." Unfortunately, often parents convince their children of their "mediocrity" (risk-averse and don't-rock-the-boat self-images), or worse yet, convince them they are "terrible little devils" with no positive attributes. Success in life is a function of believing, and all belief systems emanate from within. These fourteen subjects were fortunate to have been indelibly imprinted with a positive self-esteem at an early age.

Parental Imprinting and Modifying Self-Esteem

Overindulgent parents told Sade, Napoleon, Hitler, Wright, and Picasso that they were special and destined for greatness. It is interesting to note that these particular individuals grew into arrogant egotists and irresponsible tyrants. No one ever became great who didn't think they were worthy. "Thinking big" doesn't assure you of greatness but it dramatically improves your statistical chances. Mediocrity programs a person to average success because it fulfills that internal image. Superiority likewise is imprinted and fulfilled.

How does one who was not imprinted early with a positive self-esteem change? Self-esteem is buried deep in our unconscious—"hard-wired" in what Carl Jung labeled the "collective unconscious." Our existing self-esteem has evolved out of early conditioning. It is the portrait painted on our psyche that defines our self-worth. Without changing that portrait the long buried self-esteem cannot change. The *self-image* is not buried as deeply as the self-esteem; it lies just below the surface in our subconscious. Our self-image is what we cognitively think of ourselves, but don't necessarily admit to the general public. *Self-confidence* is observed behavior. To change self-esteem and self-image it is necessary to start with self-confidence and never allow a negative thought to enter in our lives.

No one can think positively and negatively simultaneously. Therefore, it is logical to conclude that if one thinks about only positive things there will be no room for the negative. The findings on these fourteen subjects indicate that they operated in an almost continual state of positive self-confidence. Much of their confidence emanated from youthful experiences and positive reinforcement from optimistic role models and mentors. Maria Montessori established a new psychology of education and violated all rules in education by refusing to hire a professionally trained teacher for her Children's House. Montessori was confident that she was right and believed that capitulating to traditional dogma would only detract from her research. Think of the reaction of art experts to Picasso's *Les Demoiselles d'Avignon* or his painting people with horse heads, one eye, and no arms? Most experts viewed Montessori and Picasso as rebellious nuisances and laughed at their work during their early careers. Such rejection never deterred them since both were equipped with strong self-esteem. Creators and entrepreneurs must have strong self-esteems to offset expert opinion. Experts have a psychological investment in what "is" to such a degree that they are unable to imagine what "can be," and therefore are the mortal enemy of all innovators. The only deterrent for these naysayers is a resilient self-esteem. Those who are destroyed when rejected will never enjoy great creative success or gain power.

Dysfunctional Self-Esteem

Strong self-esteem saved these fourteen from the experts. What self-esteem *cannot* do is save a person from himself. These subjects had such strong self-esteems that they were often viewed as egomaniacs. Strong egos equipped them with the freedom to pursue their dreams but also made them rebellious and antiestablish-ment. Such ego-driven behavior is the formula for all great creativity, but when the ego or self-esteem runs amok other eccentricities can emerge. Hitler, Napoleon, and Hughes were not as talented as they thought. However, all three accomplished far more than they should have because of their deluded self-belief. They were gods in their own minds, which enabled them to convince others of their invinci-bility. It is a frightening thought how close they came to fulfilling their wildest fan-tasies. Five of these visionaries—Napoleon, Hitler, Picasso, Sade, and Wright—were raised by doting mothers to believe they were superior human beings destined for greatness. Such egoism can create a monster.

D. Jablow Hershman and psychiatrist Julian Lieb concluded in *A Brotherhood of Tyrants* (1994) that Napoleon and Hitler both were manic-depressives who had a deluded sense of their self-worth. They described Napoleon as "absurdly opti-mistic" (p. 39). Napoleon believed he was invincible, claiming, "God gave me the will and the force to overcome all obstacles." This egocentric belief caused him to accomplish far more than someone and with normal self-esteem.

Hitler had an even more deluded self-image than Napoleon, saying, "For me the word 'impossible' does not exist." This was a man who never held a job and failed at everything he attempted until the age of forty! He finally concluded that he was divine and implemented his "master race" and "final solution" plans as tes-taments to his delusion. Picasso's awesome self-esteem is best illustrated by a self-portrait painted at age nineteen that he signed "I the King." Sade actually believed he was a superior being, which is self-evident from his statement, "Egoism is the primary law of nature." Wright once defended himself in court by telling the judge, "I am a creative genius." When a reporter questioned such an egoistic self-assess-ment, Wright replied with candor, "I was under oath, wasn't I?" Wright's famous quote on his personality best describes self-esteem, "Early in life I had to choose between honest arrogance and hypocritical humility. I chose honest arrogance."

Positive Role Models Instill Self-Confidence

These creative geniuses clearly demonstrate that positive role models are critical to acquiring self-confidence. Not only were they conditioned by their parents, but had role models who inspired them to greatness. These role models came in var-ious forms, including teachers, older students, first bosses, or other real-life peo-ple such as Alexander the Great or Nietzsche. More often than not mythological characters in books were the role models. These fantasy heroes and mentors were usually powerful figures who were able to magically transform harsh reality to idyllic fantasy. Hero mentors like Aladdin, Goethe, or the Saint Theresa can mo-tivate children to high achievement and creative an internal vision without limits. Impressionable children often fantasize about heroes and use their imagination to envision themselves in the same limitless context fantasy.

Psychologist Wayne Dyer, author of *You'll See It When You Believe It* (1990), espouses the belief that we "envision success prior to accomplishing it." Scientist-turned-psychologist Charles Garfield proposed the same idea years earlier in his pioneering work with the first American astronauts. Garfield found: "Almost all world class athletes, astronauts, and other peak performers are visualizers. They see it; feel it; and experience it; before they actually do it." The proponents of Neuro Linguistic Programming (NLP) have clearly demonstrated that "modeling behavior is the pathway to excellence."

John Grinder and Richard Bandler of the University of California at Berkeley used Dr. Milton Erickson, Virginia Satir, and Gregory Bateson to demonstrate that modeling the behavior of great people can improve performance. They were rewarded when the students began emulating the behaviors of these eminent individuals. Grinder and Bandler concluded that mimicking superachievers enhances success.

It appears that the success of these fourteen was helped by an unconscious use of NLP. They identified with great hero mentors while young and then allowed few limitations in their adult lives. Real-life role models included: Alexander the Great, Christ, Rousseau, Nietzsche, and Wagner. Mythological role models included: Aladdin, Citizen Hearst, Aphrodite, and Taliesin.

Montessori's role model was her uncle Antonio Stoppani who pioneered scientific positivism as a teaching technique in Italy. She idolized and emulated him, adopting his scientific style in her own work in children's education. Froebel and Séguin were her educational role models.

Picasso idolized painting masters Raphael, Cézanne, and Matisse, ensuring him outstanding models to emulate and pushing him to perfection. Nietzsche's philosophy of an "overman" armed him with the strength to follow his own maverick beliefs in direct opposition to societal mores. Nietzsche as mentor imprinted Picasso with an infinite upper limit for his egoistic drive since Picasso envisioned himself the reincarnation of Nietzsche's "overman" or "superman" who was to be the savior of mankind. Picasso saw himself as above the pack just as Nietzsche had predicted in *Thus Spake Zarathustra*.

Optimism and Positive Attitudes

Creative geniuses exude confidence, optimism, and a positive approach to their life and profession. Walt Disney believed in his innovations when no one else did. When he first created many of his greatest characters and ideas (Snow White, Pinocchio, *Fantasia,* Disneyland) his brother Roy and the Hollywood experts called them Disney's Folly. They were convinced he had allowed his imagination to interfere with practical business sense. Roy Disney despised most of his brother's creations, but capitulated when they became successful. *Snow White* was berated and Disneyland was called a carnival by the Disney Studio board of directors.

Disney never allowed dissidence to affect him or his creations. He was always positive and optimistic about any new venture, relying on his own counsel instead of listening to so-called experts. Disney ultimately found solace in the rejection of his creations, deciding that if experts liked his new innovations, they probably were too ordinary to become truly successful. If the experts despised an innovation, he felt had a potential winner. Disney learned to listen to but not be affected by his critics. His optimism could only have been possible due to an intransigent self-confidence. He even went so far as to say, "We are not in the 'art' business" to dissuade people from becoming enamored with aesthetics over concept. Disneyland, which proved to be his greatest idea, was the one most objected to by the experts. No one was capable of grasping the fantasy aspect of his theme park. Disney Studio's board of directors totally rejected the idea and then hired a market research firm to validate their decision. Disney ignored them all and personally financed Disneyland's initial designs. The success of Disneyland verifies the role played by self-confidence and optimism in his genius.

Isadora Duncan was optimistic from a very young age. At age sixteen, she barged in on a famous New York impresario urging him to hire her because "I shall be famous some day." Isadora was convinced that her self-sufficiency and self-esteem evolved from a positive and optimistic family environment: "I was never subjected to the continued *don'ts* of other children." Biographer Dorothy Rich characterized Earhart's confidence as her greatest asset. When the media asked Amelia Earhart about the possibility of crashing just before her last around-the-world flight, she responded, "I am confident of success." Howard Hughes was enormously optimistic about business projects costing millions which were in direct opposition to what industry experts believed would be successful. He continually violated all traditions and norms of the movie, airline, and casino industries in building his empire, believing himself omniscient and refusing all outside counsel. Maria Montessori was so self-confident as a child that she told her mother during a serious illness, "Don't worry. . . . I cannot die. I have too much to do." She told her biographer and friend E. M. Standing (1962): "I could have done anything." Rupert Murdoch created his vast media empire by refusing to listen to traditionalists and following his own optimistic vision of the "global village." Darryl Wardle, a school chum, characterized Murdoch as "always eminently confident." Edith Piaf used optimism to escape from a Paris ghetto to become The Great Piaf. Helena Rubinstein was so confident in her own ability that she told reporters, "Don't worry, I bring luck." A Hearst newspaper described Nikola Tesla as having "that supply of self-love and self-confidence that usually goes with success."

Maria Montessori

Education is social engineering.

Overview

Montessori relied on empirical pragmatism or what she called scientific positivism in developing her psychology of education. She found that the ages between three and six were critical in the education of the child, terming this the "sensitive" period: during this period, children are "absorbent" (highly sensitive to environmental stimulation). She maintained that children from the ages of seven to eighteen lose much of their plasticity, but are capable of building on the sensorial foundations and early skills learned during the formative or "absorbent" period.

Montessori became the preeminent authority on preschool education, utilizing techniques diametrically opposed to turn-of-the-century education. In her book *The Montessori Method* (1912), she wrote, "First the education of the senses, then the education of the intellect." This visionary had found what researchers at the end of the century were just discovering: enhanced environments stimulate learning. Montessori believed in satisfying physical needs prior to attempting to stimulate mental processes. She felt learning was inextricably bound up in science and reason, or what she called "sanity and science." She was convinced that "experiential" factors were critical to childhood learning and created environmental dynamics to optimize the spontaneity of the child's interaction with the world. Pragmatism was an important part of her creative learning materials, toys, and free-form environment. In creating such an environment, she violated existing educational methodologies by going back to Rousseau, Itard, Séguin, Froebel, and Pestalozzi. She ignored the contemporary theories of behaviorism and psychoanalysis, which touted "motivational theory" and "instinctual drive" as the determinants of learning. In her era, intelligence was still considered a genetic gift with no allowance for heuristic or empirical learning. Maria had little other than confidence in her own ability to intuitively resolve the problems for uneducable children. She ignored past dogmas and attacked the problem based on her "gut" feeling that children must feel good about themselves and be physically healthy prior to learning. She found "Education is . . . acquired not by listening to words but by experiencing the environment" (Chattin-McNichols 1991, p. 90) and "intelligence is rendered useless by lack of practice, and this practice is almost always sense education."

Montessori's methods are surprisingly in line philosophically with the findings on creative genius and power in this book. These fourteen visionaries, like Montessori's children, used an empirical approach—not theoretical maps or innate skills—to get to the top. They used the same empirical pragmatism espoused by Montessori and utilized sensorial traits—self-confidence, tenacity, work ethic, right-brain vision—to make their mark in the world. They also used a heuristic—trial-and-error—methodology in learning their professions. Montessori espoused the identical roadmap for successful education of the young as this book does for achieving great power and success in adults.

Montessori employed pragmatic learning, allowing children to explore their own potential with little or no constraints. She used the teacher as a guidance counselor and not an instructor. The children were allowed to follow their own natural path in learning skills like reading and writing. She allowed her students to build self-esteem through positive self-learned reinforcement of experiential learning. They learned to believe in themselves because they saw the positive results of their own actions.

The experts were unable to dissuade Montessori from her empirical theories, which were eminently effective, just as these fourteen subjects never allowed the experts to deter them from achieving their dreams.

Montessori first discovered the errors of teaching by rote when she was assigned to teach a ward of mentally deficient children, termed "idiots." Later, when she taught economically and emotionally deprived children, she developed the system that became the Montessori method.

These two experiences motivated Montessori to use her method to teach normal children. Her students from the San Lorenzo ghetto were considered uneducable, yet her method enabled them to start reading and writing by age four, which was unheard of in the so-called normal school system. Educators, journalists, and religious leaders from southern Europe were astounded by the San Lorenzo experiment, and within two years all of the kindergartens and orphanages of southern Switzerland were converted to the Montessori system. Within five years the United States Montessori Educational Association was formed, headed by no less an authority on specialized teaching than Alexander Graham Bell.

By age forty Maria Montessori was internationally famous. Anna Freud and Jean Piaget became her disciples. Queen Victoria invited her to London and sponsored the inauguration of the Montessori Method in England. Queen Margherita of Italy became a patron and gave her the ultimate tribute, "Her contribution to society is more important than Marconi's." Her name became synonymous with progressive education. This was the consummate tribute of acceptance by bureaucratic institutions.

This "Prophet of Pedagogy" was a paradox. As a child she avoided any thought of a career in education since she was told it was the only profession she could enter. Ironically it is the field in which she excelled. This driven woman came to be known as the "Messiah of Education," nurturing and teaching children on four continents, yet she was unable to teach her own illegitimate son, Mario, who was raised in a foster home in Florence. As a teenager she decided to become an engineer. Influence by her uncle Antonio Stoppani, she attended a technical high school. Once in college, she rebelled against the establishment by pursuing a medical career. Montessori became the first female medical doctor in Italy when she graduated from the University of Rome in 1896. She published *The Montessori Method* in 1910, *The Secret of Childhood* in 1939, and *The Absorbent Mind* in 1949. This visionary woman was nominated for the Nobel Peace Prize in 1949,

1950, and 1951. She was entertained by kings, queens, presidents, and prime ministers. She was awarded the Legion of Honor by France in 1949 as a tribute to her influence on French education. She was awarded honorary doctorates from virtually every nation in the world. The *New York Tribune* called her "a woman who revolutionized the educational system of the world . . . and the most interesting woman in Europe."

Early Life Experiences and Influences

Montessori was born August 31, 1870—the same year Italy became a unified nation. At the time of her birth, the country's illiteracy rate was second only to Portugal's. She was the only child of Alesandro Montessori, an engineer and builder, and Renilda Stoppani. The family moved to Florence when Maria was three and to Rome when she was five. Her mother was from an educated family but was refused the pursuit of education because she was female. Her liberal views on women's rights and professional latitude were stifled by the nineteenth-century subjugation of women. Her dreams would one day be realized through her daughter. Her mother encouraged young Maria's exploration into the new and unknown and raised her to be a free soul. Early liberation from traditional dogmas molded her into a strong-willed child instilled with leadership qualities. Her maternal uncle, Antonio Stoppani, was a scholar-priest who was an acclaimed writer-educator in Milan, where a monument stands today as a memorial to his scientific contributions. He became a professional role model for young Maria, who was influenced by his philosophy of scientific positivism. Emulating her uncle she became fascinated with resolving the abstractions posed by math and science, and by age eleven decided to pursue an engineering career.

Biographer Rita Kramer (1988) gave credence to Montessori's mother's early influence: "Her self-confidence, her optimism, her interest in change and her belief in the possibility of effecting it were certainly formed by the . . . child-rearing practices of her mother." Montessori was a renegade in a nineteenth-century society that discouraged women's rights. Her mother, Renilde, supported her daughter's nonconformity to the chagrin of her tradition-bound father. According to Kramer, "Renilde took a vicarious pleasure in her maverick daughter."

Montessori was enrolled in elementary school at Tolentino at age six, attended girls-only schools after the third grade, and by age ten was determined to become a female scientist. Always strong-willed, she told her mother, "Do not worry, mother, I cannot die, I have too much to do" when she became seriously ill at age eleven. The child had already acquired larger-than-life goals that would separate her from the pack. Recalling her education at Buonarroti Middle School, Montessori later wrote, "It taught but did not educate." She was the only female enrolled in Leonardo da Vinci Tech Institute at age sixteen, specializing in math and science.

Montessori graduated from the technical institute in 1890 at age twenty and changed her professional interest from engineering to medicine. When she approached Giudo Baccelli, the director of the University of Rome's Medical School, he informed her that her desire to be a medical doctor was "not only unprecedented but unthinkable" for a woman (Kramer 1988, p. 35). Montessori would not be denied and she informed the director, "I know I will become a Dr. of Medicine." Her father attempted to dissuade his strong-willed daughter but she ignored him. When admission was denied, she appealed to Pope Leo XIII who interceded and she was granted admission as the first female medical student at the University of Rome.

Once admitted, Montessori's troubles began. Male students hassled and taunted her, and some classes became intolerable. In turn-of-the-century Italy, it was unacceptable for both sexes to view a naked body together, even if it was dead. The faculty forced her to study anatomy at night and alone; she found herself cutting up cadavers in an eerie dark hall. The faculty and administration assumed this experience would discourage Maria and she would soon drop out. Maria became distraught: "My God, what have I done to suffer in this way? Why me all alone in the midst of all this death? . . . A shiver ran through my bones." One night the experience became intolerable, causing Montessori to run from the laboratory intending to quit. Walking home in a nearby park, she stopped to talk to a beggar woman who had a young baby that was playing with a red ribbon. She was mystified and inspired for some reason which she couldn't explain. The child's cherubic expression and euphoric calm, even though relegated to a deplorable state, somehow inspired her. She went through an emotional metamorphosis and returned to the lab determined to outlast her adversaries. Montessori admitted to biographer E. M. Standing (1962): "I was moved by emotions I could not explain, turned around and went straight back to the dissecting room." She graduated on July 10, 1896, and became the first female medical doctor in Italian history.

An Awesome Self-Confidence

"No one can be free unless he is independent," Montessori wrote in her pioneering work *The Montessori Method*. She lived that precept by creating parent-teacher conferences and many other revolutionary educational concepts. An indomitable self-esteem allowed her to ignore the experts in education. She had an intuitive understanding that anything new demands the "creative destruction" of the old.

Montessori used self-confidence in establishing a pragmatic system with the child in the center of the learning model. Her schools became "child-centered" institutions, not "teacher-centered" or "results-centered." The nature and needs of the child were paramount in the Montessori system.

The Montessori method has been unjustly criticized as permissive. Montessori was a strong and autocratic leader and her rules became the ultimate authority and discipline. Compliance was absolutely demanded of both teachers and students, but all her rules were aimed at the child learning, not at the teacher preaching. The essence of her educational philosophy is clearly delineated by this passage from *The Montessori Method* (1910):

> The task of the educator lies in seeing the child does not confound good with immobility, and evil with activity as often happens in the case of the old-time discipline. Our aim is to discipline for activity, for work, for good, not for immobility, not for passivity, not for obedience. (p. 93)

Montessori's ghetto school had simple but steadfastly enforced rules. She insisted that children be punctual, clean, and respect the school, and that parent-teacher conferences be held weekly to discuss the child's progress. She was always in control of the environment even when it was based on freedom and indulgence.

Manic Success

Montessori's mania for knowledge began early in life. Raised with the high expectations imprinted on an only child, overachievement and perfectionism were traits developed in a permissive family that respected knowledge. She did everything in excess, which was illustrated by her taking a math book to the theater. Further proof was shown in medical school when a snowstorm closed the school. Montessori was the only student to show up, so impressing the professor that he held the class with only her in attendance.

Montessori had a strong will and a spiritual sense of her life's mission. Her sense of creative power was enhanced by her metaphysical approach to anything new. She said in one of her lectures: "We human beings, we have a mission . . . of which we are not aware." Montessori believed she had a "destiny to fulfill." According to her biographer E. M. Standing, she had a "special mission to delve into the unfathomed depths of the child's soul." Her intense and tireless efforts toward this end started when she was appointed director of the Orthophrenic Institute in Rome in 1899. In this position she was given responsibility for nurturing and educating a group of "idiot" children who had been abandoned by their parents and subsequently institutionalized. Maria was given this position since she was female and the junior medical practitioner.

In typical manic fashion, Montessori became obsessed with educating these "uneducable" children and studied the children diligently from 8:00 A.M. until 7:00 P.M. daily. Demonstrating her type A personality, she spent each evening analyzing the results of the day in order to implement new teaching projects the next. During this period, she juggled a private medical practice and administrative responsibilities in addition to acting as the educational researcher for the "idiot" children. Work to Montessori wasn't work in the normal context; it was pleasure, just as learning for her children turned out to be a kind of "work" they enjoyed. Her mania for work became even more intense a few years later when she opened the Children's House in the San Lorenzo ghetto. When she became internationally famous, she worked tirelessly spreading the word of her teaching method on three other continents.

Success and Self-Esteem

When Montessori was appointed director of the Orthophrenic School, it was here that she first began to investigate learning techniques for young children. In this position she was given the task of educating mentally deficient children who had been labeled unteachable by Italian asylums and elementary schools. The children had histories of retardation and low IQs, and had been classified "idiots."

Montessori was never deterred by the difficult or impossible. These children had been locked up and had their food thrown at them like animals. She was given the children and allowed to experiment on them since they had been written off as lost. Montessori first changed the children's environment from an impoverished one to an enriched one and established a structure more conducive to learning. She later wrote: "I felt that mental deficiency presented chiefly a pedagogical rather than mainly a medical problem." The children responded immediately and began learning at a skill level similar to normal children. Maria was ecstatic and wrote a scathing report: "The idiot is not incapable of learning but only incapable of following the common methods of education." At the Turin Pedagogical Congress she said, "The intellectual idiot and the moral imbecile are capable of being educated and have instincts that can be used to lead them to the good. . . . In certain kinds of work requiring mechanical repetition, it is even an advantage to have imbeciles trained to do the work."

Montessori utilized a holistic approach to education. She attacked the physical and mental problems with equal intensity, but delayed addressing the mental problems until the physical ones were resolved. Her philosophy was: "First the education of the senses, then the education of the intellect." When first given the "idiot" children she found them locked in rooms and treated like animals. The children performed as would be expected: treated like animals, they behaved in kind. Self-image was ignored and therefore no self-confidence could exist. Montessori changed the environment and treatment, and the children responded with normal behavior. She said, "We should first teach the child *how,* before we make him execute a task." Montessori successfully taught them to "master skills that had been thought totally beyond their capabilities." The Montessori method took form during her experience with the "idiot" children. The media discovered her and described her as "vibrant," "erudite," and the "Messiah of education." She lectured about her findings and was found to be a charismatic speaker. Ada Negri, a poet and passionate feminist, was "moved to tears" when she heard Montessori speak on children and women's rights. After one New Woman's speech, Negri "jumped to her feet, weeping and crying 'Brava! Brava!' " Over two hundred articles appeared in Italy, Germany, France, and England on her pioneering work in educating deficient children.

CRISIS AND CREATIVITY

Montessori fell in love with her assistant, Dr. Guiseppi Montesano, in 1898 and found herself pregnant while at the pinnacle of her power and success. She was forced to quit her position as head of the Orthophrenic School of Rome and abandoned a promising career. She feared the professional repercussions from having an illegitimate child in Catholic Italy although she was able to keep her son a secret from the press until after her death. A more plausible reason for her job resignation was not her pregnancy but the rejection by her lover. She and Dr. Montesano agreed to raise the child together secretly and they agreed to never marry. The child, Mario, was born in March 1898, wetnursed in the country, and then sent to a foster home. It was at this time that Maria went on a sudden and unexplained lecture tour called "The New Woman" espousing women's rights. Montessori became a feminist, making disparaging remarks about men's treatment of professional women. Overnight, she became an advocate of women's issues and a strong feminist leader in Italy. No one suspected the true reason for such a sudden and radical change in this nurturing medical practitioner. Montessori told women to "start arguing with your brains, not just your hearts." She predicted: "The woman of the future will have equal rights as well as equal duties. . . . The new woman will marry and have children out of choice." This was certainly an emotional response to her own plight. Montessori's problems were compounded by the fact that Dr. Montesano was not only her lover but also her assistant at the Orthophrenic School. His mother refused to allow him to marry Montessori and then in 1900, he announced his intention to marry another woman despite their pact to raise their child together. This total rejection by Montesano was the true cause of Maria Montessori's sudden resignation from the Orthophrenic School and not her desire to return to school to pursue a career in education, as has been maintained by other authors.

METAMORPHOSIS TO "SUPERMAN" EDUCATOR

Montessori reenrolled at Rome University and studied anthropology, psychology, and education between 1901 and 1904. She began visiting elementary schools and analyzed current teaching methods in a passionate need to keep busy. She was in fact sublimating her need to teach her child Mario into the teaching of disadvantaged children. Montessori found the teaching methods in traditional education antiquated and called them "degrading" and "destructive," and was "appalled" at the repressive nature of the educational system.

Montessori had always been a perfectionist who pursued truth as if it were a scientific experiment. She intuitively knew that "In order to educate, it is essential to know who are to be educated," and had concluded that "what really makes a teacher is love for the human child for it is the love that transforms the social duty of the educator into the higher consciousness of a *mission*" (Montessori 1912, p. 443). She began teaching classes on the history and anthropological effects of education at the

Rome Pedagogical School from 1904 to 1908. This teaching experience and research period proved valuable for her later studies. It is truly prophetic that a woman I have labeled as Promethean with a Nietzschean "will-to-power" approach to life should later write: "Moral education . . . demands a 'Superman.' What we need to find is not a method, but a *Master*" (Montessori 1912, p. 449). Her will-to-power philosophy was the methodology she used in her rise to the top of her profession, and she was essentially prophesying her own arrival as "overman" or "master." By 1912 Montessori had become the acknowledged Master she spoke of by writing her gospel of education, *The Montessori Method*. By 1915 she had become world renowned and her schools were operating in dozens of countries based on her experimental educational work at the Casa de Bambini in a Rome tenement house.

THE MONTESSORI METHOD

The Casa de Bambini was a huge government administered home that had grown beyond control of those who had developed it. The children, who were denied entrance to ordinary schools, became tyrants and delinquents. Montessori was offered the unenviable task of attempting to open a school within the San Lorenzo ghetto to educate these incorrigibles. She accepted this not only as a challenge but with the proviso that she could incorporate her own educational teaching methods. The administrators gave her full rein expecting her to fail but happy to have someone else take over a terrible responsibility.

The first Children's House was opened January 1907 with fifty unruly children. This program differed from Maria's first experience since the children were not idiots or retarded like those in the Orthophrenic School, although they were still considered uneducable by the authorities. These children were socially and culturally deprived, living in squalor without proper schooling, food, or a decent family environment.

When Montessori accepted this new assignment, her colleagues were appalled that a doctor of medicine and a full professor could so demean herself. They felt she was degrading herself in accepting a position as a lowly teacher of ghetto children. Within two years they would be proven wrong when she became internationally famous.

Montessori's first school had fifty children, ages two to six, in one stark room in the middle of the Casa de Bambini tenement house. A few years later she would tell the press, "I had a vision and was inspired by it." The day of the school opening she predicted great success for her undertaking. She was embarrassed about her passionate enthusiasm and admitted later, "I was inflamed and said that this work . . . would prove to be very important." Her self-esteem plus an indomitable will drove her to such optimistic enthusiasm.

Montessori's grand experiment began with the hiring of Candida Naccetelli, the daughter of the building porter, as the school's first teacher. She was employed because she was uneducated, had no professional teaching experience, and arrived with no preconceived notions about how children should be taught.

Montessori indoctrinated Naccetelli in her methods demonstrating that the environment and educational materials were more important than the teacher. The teacher was only a catalyst or facilitator. The results of Montessori's free-form experiential programs were immediate and even more revolutionary than the results at the Orthophrenic School. "From timid and wild . . . the children became sociable and communicative. They exhibited new and different relationships with each other. Their personalities grew and they showed extraordinary understanding, activity, vivacity, and confidence. They were happy and joyous" (Kramer 1988, p. 113).

The Montessori Method encompassed sensor materials, spontaneous activity, work challenges, new interesting toys, and freedom to learn at a student's own pace. The children were never criticized and were allowed to make mistakes. Children began to read and write at age four, an unheard-of accomplishment even for normal children. "They worked, not out of fear of punishment, or anticipation of rewards, but for the sheer pleasure of the activity itself" (Montessori 1912, p. 117). Montessori was not permissive; she demanded discipline from the children but not in any authoritarian way. Her concepts proved far more effective than she had ever dreamed. Her innovative methods and environment proved revolutionary: parent-teacher conferences, open classrooms, educational toys, freedom to advance at varying levels, motivation to "work" not "play," child-size furniture, self-actualization techniques, and unstructured learning. Her theory that "education is social engineering" was now proven.

Montessori documented her findings one year later: "From the very beginning in my work methods . . . I used more rational [educational principles] than those in use" in regular classrooms. Rational vision and intuitive thinking predominated in the Montessori school. She described the creation of her method: "This feeling, so deep to be in the nature of an intuition, became my controlling idea" (Montessori 1912, p. 33). Her landmark book *The Montessori Method* documented the results of the Children's House experiment. It was published in Italy in 1910 and translated into English in 1912. Her *Secret of Childhood* was a refinement of her theory and published in 1939; a further elaboration appeared in *The Absorbent Mind* in 1949. Montessori became an internationally respected proponent of children's education and spent much of her later life advocating her method before her death in 1952. Her system of education can be summed up in the following five principles (Standing 1962, pp. 40–43):

1. Children are capable of sustained mental concentration when genuinely interested in their work.

2. Children love order and especially enjoy repetition of actions that they have already mastered.

3. Children prefer work to play and prefer didactic materials to toys.

4. Rewards and punishments are unnecessary to motivate children.

5. The child has a deep sense of personal dignity that is easily offended.

Power, Influence, and Destructiveness

Maria Montessori was called the "Prophet of Pedagogy," which is testimony to her use of *knowledge* as a source of power. Her success was in large part due to her *charismatic power* for communicating her theories. These two powers were merely external manifestations of her invincible willpower. Unfortunately, Adolf Hitler's will was even stronger and he convinced his puppet Benito Mussolini to ban Montessori schools, books, and programs during the early thirties. This fascist denial of the freedom of education proved to be a serious reversal for Montessori and caused her to leave Italy.

Montessori was armed with a powerful persona that never succumbed to her many adversaries. She validated her strong character by quitting a secure job, returned to school, and started at the bottom to pursue a dream. Such verve and temerity is the sign of true power. All great innovative concepts are born in the trenches of entrepreneurial risk taking. Montessori became a teacher of the indigent in order to prove her hypotheses and then went out and documented her findings for the whole world. She quit a prestigious and high-paying job and parlayed this into international fame. Her willingness to give up power resulted in her gaining more power than she could ever have attained as the titular head of the Orthophrenic School. Montessori said: "While everyone was admiring the progress of my idiots, I was searching for the reasons which could keep the happy, healthy children of the common schools on so low a plane that they could be equalled in tests of intelligence by my unfortunate children" (Kramer 1988, p. 91). This realization motivated her to give up one power so that she could gain more power as the "Messiah of Education."

A CHARISMATIC PROMETHEAN

Montessori was a true Promethean spirit who was more interested in future possibilities than present realities. She was highly intuitive, driven, and capable of passing on her dreams to others. While young Montessori was seen as a femme fatale, which helped her gain disciples for her movement. She was always capable of hypnotizing audiences, even in languages she did not speak well. Before age forty she had an irresistible combination of youth, physical charm, scientific knowledge, a medical pedigree, enormous self-assurance, and a captivating verbal ability. She could entrance an audience with her hypnotic power of speech and was effective in articulating her system to many cultures. Her charisma attracted educators from all over the world, many of whom became devoted disciples who spread her influence far and wide. Elise Braun Barnett, a follower, gave some insight into Montessori's power: "She was a fantastic personality. When she was around there was nothing else in the room. . . . We loved her and respected her. To us she was next to God. She was vain, which amused us, but we loved her for that too" (Pollard 1990, p. 51). The media described her as a "beautiful scholar" and an "erudite educator." She described herself during a period of cynical introspection, "I am not famous because of my skill or intelligence, but for my courage and indifference toward everything." A reporter, after hearing her speak, described her charismatic persona: "Maria had the delicacy of a talented young woman combined with the strength of a man." She had an intuitive feel for identifying the problem—an antiquated educational system—and the rationality to fix it via "empirical pragmatism."

INFLUENCE

Montessori's influence has been pervasive. In addition to educators who have adopted her system in many nations, she has influenced Jean Piaget, Erik Erikson, and Anna Freud in their work with children. The influence on Anna Freud was remarkable considering Montessori's system of "senses" and "experience" were diametrically opposed to Freud's fundamental thesis of "instinctual drives" and "unconscious conflicts" as determinants of behavior. Montessori hypothesized that "spontaneous interest in learning" during the "sensitive periods" were the determinants of learning. Anna Freud was able to satisfactorily resolve her father Sigmund Freud's and Maria's systems and became a true advocate of the Montessori method.

Montessori had successfully documented for the world more comprehensive evidence of positive results than any other educational system. She had living proof of uneducable "idiots" who were transformed into normal functioning adults. She then replicated the feat by taking normal children who were culturally and socially deprived and teaching them to achieve above the skill level of normal children: many learned to read and write by age four and were self-motivated far beyond that of normal children. Her embellished environment, freedom, and positive reinforcement were simple but effective. Montessori discovered a system of success not different from that used by the overachieving subjects in this book. Successful people must be allowed to try and err without penalty and to do so empirically. Montessori clearly demonstrated that attempting to control success is impossible: The more knowledge is forced, the less chance of success. Relaxing the system to allow children to achieve at their own speed is the essence of her great success as it is for the great creative geniuses of the world.

SELF-DESTRUCTION

Maria Montessori was self-destructive in that she refused to surrender her independence to the establishment. She used the entrepreneurial approach of creative destruction in her development of the Montessori method. By destroying outmoded educational dogmas, she had to deal with many adversaries.

Montessori was never deterred from her goal because she was confident that she was right and considered her detractors ignorant, even when Mussolini and Hitler banned her concepts from their totalitarian states. Her beliefs and temperament also caused tragedy in her personal life. After being jilted by her lover and associate, Dr. Montesano, Montessori never again found romance or happiness. She lived for work and to a great degree as reparation for her lack of nurturing her illegitimate son, Mario. Had Montessori married and had a family, she probably never would have created the Montessori method. Had she not been jilted by Dr. Montesano, she would not have resigned from her directorship at the Orthophrenic School and enrolled in postgraduate work to understand the psychology of educating young children. Her lifelong dedication to education had started with this great crisis and it would follow her to the grave. Maria Montessori had been willing to give up everything for her life's work and illegitimate son, and this adversity led to her power and success.

What Made Maria Tick?

Maria Montessori was a pioneer in the intellectual development of young children. Her method allowed children the freedom to find their own mental solutions to problems—to err and learn—a concept not espoused in the dogmatic educational system at that time. This intuitive woman was trained to cure people, not to educate them, but probably knew more than most educators in the world about the psychology of education. She was a classic Promethean who ignored tradition and the establishment in pursuing her dream of educational reform and is now ranked with John Dewey and other great educators of the twentieth century. Her system was based on the belief that everyone should have the right and the "freedom to learn what he likes but without any previous preparation of interest." She disagreed with techniques where classes were being trained en masse with resulting mediocrity. Her philosophy (Standing 1962, pp. 42–49) dictated that:

1. The child must learn by his own activity.

2. He must be granted a mental freedom to take what he needs.

3. He must not be questioned in his choice since the teacher should answer the mental needs of the child, not dictate them.

Montessori was the classic pragmatist, often saying, "It is not I who propagate the method which has been named after me: it is the children themselves." She felt children left to their own devices would gravitate toward their own best interest in a similar fashion to the theory of homeostasis where individuals tend to crave that which is in their physical best interest. Shakespeare wrote, "If all the week were a holiday, to play would be as tedious as to work" (Simonton 1994). This aphorism is the essence of the Montessori method. Her "education of the senses" dictates a pragmatic view of life. She liked to use metaphors in describing the philosophy of her system, once saying, "The free horse runs swifter than one motivated by either the whip or the carrot." She would often demonstrate her methods by having her instructors point a dog toward a target and then explain that the dog does not look at the target but at the finger. Her system was similar in that it was based on the experiences of the child and not on the goal.

In a 1921 speech Montessori said, "Liberty and freedom is power." This was her way of pleading for the destruction of bureaucratic structures where children often become casualties of the system. The cost of control is freedom and Montessori was against anything that removed the child's freedom to learn. She wrote, "No one can be free unless he is independent" and "education is liberty." This was her attempt to weaken authoritarian teachers who viewed education as control. Her system showed that the child had an innate and "vital instinct for work," which she believed was a critical link to learning potential. In her system "work" was more important than "play." (Her adversaries' biggest complaint is that her system allows too much freedom to play). They do not understand her basic premise of "it is work not play that organizes the child's personality." Her system can be summarized in a statement from the *Secret of Childhood* (1939): "When work has become a habit, the intellectual level rises rapidly, and organized order causes good conduct to become a habit." *Positive feedback begets more positive behavior.* This axiom was the basis of Montessori's power as it was for the other subjects in this book. They drove themselves to fulfill their childhood fantasies and their successes became self-fulfilling rewards that drove them to ever-increasing success. Maria Montessori is the personification of that behavioral approach to life. She rose to the very top of a profession she despised as a child and used her first love— science—to reform the world of education. Her self-esteem was born of her belief that "education is social engineering," and her belief made it a reality.

MARIA MONTESSORI
Medical Doctor, Feminist Leader, and Educational Innovator
b. August 31, 1870, Chiaravalle, Ancona Province, Italy; d. May 6, 1952 Noordwijik-on-Sea, Holland

Dominant Trait: Awesome self-confidence and self-esteem. Perfectionist, intuitive, and a maverick empirical scientist

Motto: "No one can be free unless he is independent." "Education is liberty in the prepared environment." "Education is social engineering." "The woman of the future will have equal rights as well as equal duties."

Nickname: "La Dottoressa—The Lady Doctor," "Prophet of Pedagogy," "Messiah of Education"

Vices/Hobbies: Reading and writing books and lecturing. Roman Catholicism

Heroes/Mentors: Uncle Antonio Stoppani (Scientific Positivism); Rousseau (*Emile*); Frederick Froebel; Psychologists Itard, Séguin, and Pestalozzi; Giuseppe Sergi (her anthropology professor)

Philosophy of Life: "The free horse runs swifter than one motivated either by the whip or the carrot." "Education is . . . acquired not by listening to words but by experiencing in the environment."

Fantasy: To see the Montessori method adopted worldwide

Professional Success: Founded Orthophrenic School of Rome (1899) and the Children's House (January 1907). Wrote innovative books *The Montessori Method* (1910), *The Secret of Childhood* (1939), *The Absorbent Mind* (1949). "Sensitive child" concept.

Power: Empirical knowledge. Believed "Liberty and freedom is Power" (1921 speech). Disciple Elisa Bennett said, "When she was around there was nothing else in the room. . . . To us she was next to God."

Influence: Pervasive: Piaget, Erik Erikson, Alexander Graham Bell. Anna Freud said, "Her work was admirable and acted as an inspiration."

Destructiveness: Implacable opinions and feminism destroyed her chance for marriage and for raising son Mario as her child. She destroyed without remorse the dogmatic teaching methods of the educational establishment.

Birth Order: Only child of Alesandro Montessori and Renilda Stoppani

Transiency: Moved to Florence at age three, Rome at age five. A citizen of the world after age thirty, living in Italy, Spain, Holland, India, the United States, and England

Crises: Illegitimate son, Mario, by Dr. Guiseppi Montesano change her life. Quit directorship and turned to education, raising son as nephew, and launched into passionate study of young children.

Formal Education: All-boys school to study math in defiance of tradition. High school (1886); Medical Degree U. Rome (July 10, 1896); postgraduate work in psychology, anthropology, and education.

Libidinal Drive: A femme fatale until age thirty-five who defied Catholicism by having an illegitimate child. She felt that an "inner force" and "passionate drive" were critical to overachievement.

Personality Type: Self-confident maverick with a "strong-will." Introverted-Intuitive-Thinker-Judger on MBTI scale.

Self-Esteem: Told her mother while seriously ill at age ten, "Don't worry. I cannot die. I have too much to do." Told biographer Standing (1962), "I could have done anything."

Rebellion: Maverick and divergent personality from childhood who studied engineering and medicine in defiance of system.

Risk Propensity: Great temerity. Never feared the unknown.

Work Ethic: "It is only in persons of exceptional power—the geniuses—that this love of work persists as an irresistible impulse." "It is by work not play that the child organizes his personality."

Tenacity: She persevered despite many political and social adversaries who attempted to destroy her.

Optimism: Nothing deterred her from her life goals.

Manicness: "The subconscious is much more important than the conscious" for childhood/adult development. A charismatic speaker who was defined as "a strange blend of the mystic and the pragmatist."

Pablo Picasso

I have the revelation of the inner voice.

Overview

Picasso had a supreme confidence in his destiny that allowed him to violate the established traditions of art and reach unprecedented heights of achievement. He has been acknowledged as the greatest painter in history and is without a doubt the most prodigious. Beyond that, his paintings have become the conscience of the twentieth century. Arianna Huffington, his biographer, labeled him "a seismograph for the conflicts, turmoil, doubts, and anxieties of his age." It was his titanic self-image that allowed him to be innovative in painting. Self-confidence made him a respected master by age twenty-five, the father of cubism by twenty-six, and progenitor of surrealism by age thirty-five. Picasso was so charismatic as a teenager that he was able to gain a following of his peers. One of these was a fellow Catalan, writer and poet Jaime Sabartes, who said, "At eighteen he could see farther than we could" and "we spoke of him as a legendary hero." Sabartes became Picasso's assistant and faithful companion for much of his life.

Picasso's power and influence were pervasive and destructive: his fascination with destruction via cruelty, sex, violence, and anarchy made him infamous. His defiance was not by chance, but planned, and it contributed to an innovative painting style that made him one of the greatest painters that ever lived. He is universally acknowledged as the most prolific painter in history, having filled a long life with a continual stream of paintings, sculptures, lithographs, linocuts, tapestries, and drawings.

Picasso's unique talent for documenting the ills and anxieties of societal trends was not accidental. He always searched for the deeper essence of the individuals he painted and every painting had an underlying psychological meaning. His professed philosophy of art was: "Portraits should possess not physical, not spiritual, but psychological likeness." Early in his career he visited prostitutes in prison at Saint-Lazare so that he could better depict their inner souls—not unlike one of his heroes, Michelangelo, who had dissected cadavers in order to better understand muscles.

His introspective style was never more poignant than in his portrait of Gertrude Stein, who he painted as he saw her becoming, not as she existed. He painted her with a mask that looked nothing like her, and when reporters said so, he retorted, "Don't worry, it will." Stein later agreed that he was right.

Picasso's *Weeping Woman* (1937) characterizes his mistress Dora Maar as an emotionally unstable female. He admitted: "I gave her a tortured appearance, not out of sadism, and without any pleasure on my part, but in obedience to a vision that had imposed itself upon me."

Picasso's most revealing painting is *The Minotaur Carries Off a Woman* (1937), which depicts him as half-man and half-bull carrying off a nude nymph,

Marie-Therese (his mistress), while his other mistress Dora Maar watches—a deep-seated fantasy of his macho womanizing. He had an inner need for women to sacrifice their minds and bodies to him as in the *Minotaur* picture.

Picasso's most psychologically provocative painting is *Jacqueline in a Rocking Chair,* which he painted when Jacqueline (his mistress, housekeeper, and second wife) was in her twenties. Jacqueline was fifty years his junior, and he was subtlety defining her role as caretaker in his old age.

Picasso viewed life through a perverted perspective where the ideal Sunday consisted of Mass in the morning, a bullfight in the afternoon and a whorehouse in the evening. His self-esteem bordered on arrogance and egoism. Work was his catharsis as he told mistress Françoise Gilot introspectively: "I sacrifice everything to my painting. . . . You and everyone else, myself included." She bore him two children and desperately wanted to be his wife but he enjoyed rejecting her. His indomitable self-esteem contributed to a fearlessness that allowed him to thumb his nose at the Nazis who had occupied Paris: "I don't care to yield to either force or terror. . . . I prefer to be here, so I'll stay whatever the cost." Although equipped with a resilient self-confidence, he was unable to permit anyone to leave him on their own terms. He abandoned each mistress after her successor was already in place. Regarding his women, he said: "I'd rather see a woman die any day than see her happy with someone else" (Huffington 1988, p. 56). Françoise Gilot said, "He refused to discard anything he ever owned—property, women, art or clothes." This deep-seated insecurity was the basis of his destructive nature. What he couldn't control, he wanted to destroy: "The painter must destroy" in order to create.

Picasso was a self-made man: his power, influence, and destructiveness were learned, not inherited. He was the product of his own internal striving for perfection in art and self-actualization. Strangely, he is the personification of the tumultuous era in which he lived. In a moment of introspection he said, "I have the revelation of the inner voice" which was his way of describing his justification for his destruction of the existing way in order to create the new. Picasso said he must "destroy it (art) to give it another life" adding, "I always try to be subversive, whatever drives me to create . . . it is only to wage war on the world." This self evaluation caused his aphorism, "It's not what an artist does that counts, but what he is. Art is not truth. Art is a lie that makes us realize truth."

Early Life Experiences and Influences

Pablo Picasso was born in Malaga, Spain, on October 25, 1881, the first child of Doña Maria Picasso and Don José Ruiz. Having been revived at birth, he was not expected to live. He was named for a deceased uncle, Pablo Ruiz, a doctor of theology who had supported Don José's painting career in spite of his lack of talent. Don José Ruiz loved painting and pursued it passionately. This intense ardor for the arts was instilled in Picasso during his formative years by his father. Paintings by great masters were hung over young Pablo's crib.

Pablo Picasso and his father were the only males in a household dominated by women: Doña Maria, four unmarried aunts, and a grandmother. By the time he was five, his two sisters, Concepción and Conchita, were born. He admitted later that "I was an angel and a devil in beauty," the focus of a family devoted to his well being and the development of his genius.

When Picasso was three years old, a devastating earthquake shook Malaga. Young Pablo was carried screaming from the burning house. Shortly afterward, a master painter, Don Antonio, came to visit Picasso's family. He arrived coincidentally with King Alfonso XII, who had come to inspect the earthquake damage. The impressionable Picasso confused the two events and grew up relating pomp and circumstance with art: he thought of artists as the most revered individuals in society. From that time on, Picasso identified "painting with glory." Remembering this event fifty years later, he suggested its great influence on his passion for painting.

Young Pablo's family encouraged him to draw and rewarded his work with dusted sugar fritters. Consequently, Picasso drew before he talked. His first word was *piz* for pencil. School was arduous for this spoiled child, who never cared to leave the nurturing environment his family. Picasso would never have graduated from grade school without tutoring and the bribing of school officials. He may have been dyslexic, which purportedly contributed to his being a terrible student. He also hated rules and anyone who criticized his work or behavior.

Picasso purposely misbehaved so that he would be isolated from the other students and allowed to draw. Painting became his means of expression. His first painting was of the Port of Malaga with a lighthouse. At age six he painted *Hercules with His Club*. He "never did any childish drawings" like other children.

When Picasso was ten, his family relocated to Corunna, Spain, so that his father could get work. Picasso had a difficult time adjusting to his new life and became rebellious. His father enrolled him in a school of fine arts to begin his formal training, but Pablo had a short attention span and was impatient with schoolwork.

At age thirteen, Picasso met his first love, a schoolmate named Angles Gil. Angles was from an aristocratic family that outranked the Ruiz family socially. Picasso was crushed when her family sent Angles away to school at Pamplona in order to avoid any romance. A reporter in later years wrote, "something very tender and profound was destroyed in him."

When Picasso was fourteen, his eight-year-old sister, Conchita, died of diphtheria. This was a traumatic event for the teenager. Picasso made a pact with God in which he agreed to stop painting if Conchita were spared. He had mixed emotions about this and became guilt-ridden when he found himself confused over wanting his sister to live or die. When she died, Picasso became infuriated with God and was laden with his own guilt over her death. Don José added to the turmoil when he gave Pablo his brushes and vowed never to paint again.

The family relocated to Barcelona to escape the tragedy of Conchita's death. Picasso was enrolled in another school of fine arts. Here he met his best friend and lifelong consort, Jaime Sabrates.

SEX AND ART

Picasso was a rebel who hated all authority. Barcelona contributed to his becoming a nihilist as it was the most anarchic city in the world, attracting existentialist painters who were enraptured with the latest philosophical trends. Picasso's first nihilistic painting was completed in Barcelona, *Christ Blessing the Devil*. Manuel Pallares, a fellow student in the Barcelona Art School, described an emerging iconoclast, "Picasso grasped everything very quickly; paid *no* attention to what the professors were saying. . . . Sometimes very excited, at other times he could go for hours without saying a word."

Picasso also discovered sex before the age of fifteen and spent endless hours in brothels. Sex and art were his main passions during his teenage years, which set the stage for the next seventy years. Frustrated with the uninhibited teenager, his father enrolled him in the Royal Academy of Art in Madrid in 1897. He became ill from continuous dissipation and returned to Barcelona without having distinguished himself at the school.

OEDIPAL COMPLEX

When young, Picasso adored his father. Don José was his first role model in the arts, but soon became a psychological rival. His father was tall, dark, handsome, and trim with an elegant gait. Picasso was short (5'3"), squat, and unattractive. Picasso rejected the man who represented to him the very essence of manhood. Picasso wrote later, "Every time I draw a man I think of my father. To me, man is Don José." It was during this period that Picasso became a bohemian and adopted his mother's surname.

Picasso's mother had been his supporter through all of his travails. When he was young, she had told him, "If you become a soldier, you'll be a general. If you become a monk, you'll end up pope." This idolatry was imprinted on the young Picasso and armed him with a resilient self-esteem. Doña Maria had created a self-absorbed individual who believed himself to be outside the bounds of ordinary behavior. From childhood on, Picasso deprecated teachers, administrators, and other authoritarian figures who dared grade his performance or criticize his work.

TRANSIENCY AND NIETZSCHE'S SUPERMAN

Picasso lived a transient life as a child. He was born in Malaga and then moved to Corunna at age ten, Barcelona at fourteen, Madrid at sixteen, and back to Barcelona at eighteen. When his work was largely ignored by the Barcelona art community, he moved to Paris before his nineteenth birthday. His life as a gypsy roaming the Pyrenees mountains and visiting the brothels of Madrid and Barcelona had resulted in syphilis. A Castillian poet wrote: "Picasso is the most gypsy of all." His life in Barcelona was centered around the young bohemian artists hung out at the cabaret El Quartre Gats. It was here that he met Carlos Casegemas, a painter and existentialist whose hero was Nietzsche. Nietzsche's will-to-power philosophy influenced Picasso and his art. Picasso became enamored of Nietzsche's concept of a "Superman" who could use his "will-to-power" to survive a world in which "God is dead." Picasso adopted Nietzsche's philosophy and his own ideology.

When Barcelona ignored his work, Picasso left for the freedom of Paris with his friend Casemegas. His bequest to his parents was a Nietzschean-inspired self-portrait that he titled *Yo Rey,* meaning "I the King." This painting is testimony to a young man with an extraordinary self-image.

PARIS, MENTORS, AND THE BLUE PERIOD (1900–1904)

Paris became Picasso's home for the rest of his life. He discovered Paul Cézanne's paintings at the Louvre in Paris and admired his work for many years. He commented: "If Cézanne had worked in Spain they would have burned him alive."

This began the blue period where Picasso typically did one painting every day. He vacillated between a passion for life and a preoccupation with death which manifested itself in nudes and shades of blue. His dominant subjects consisted of derelicts, beggars, prostitutes, sad couples, and poor families. He painted *Two Sisters*—a prostitute and a nun—depicting his divergent views of woman as both madonna and whore. In Picasso's mind his mother was perfection, all other women were flawed.

During this frenetic period of carousing and whoring, Picasso's good friend Casamegas fell in love with a Spanish model. Picasso slept with his best friend's sweetheart and was then devastated when Casemegas committed suicide after being jilted by her. This triggered Picasso's blue period paintings, beginning with *The Burial of Casamegas.* Nihilism engulfed him during this period. Personally he couldn't face death and refused to attend funerals. Yet death, destruction, sickness, and sadness permeated his work during these years of the twentieth century, including his first masterpiece *La Vie* (1903), followed by *The Tragedy, The Ascetic, The Old Guitar, The Poor Man's Meal,* and *Poor People at the Seashore.*

THE ROSE PERIOD (1904–1907)

Picasso prostituted himself in order to survive during his early years in Paris. He lived off Max Jacob, a homosexual artist and aspiring poet, and others during this time and even resorted to running phony lotteries to earn enough money for food. Arianna Huffington (1988) called this period one in which "he had contempt for morality and worshiped at the altar of genius" (p. 75). Bisexuality was pervasive in bohemian Paris and Picasso had many liaisons with artists and poets, including Max Jacob who adored and supported him during these early days of struggle.

Picasso met Fernande Olivier during the blue period and she became his first live-in mistress. Olivier pulled him out of his nihilism and the blue period came to an end when a rose glow creeped into his paintings. Picasso's women coincided with his various styles and Olivier began his hedonistic era and the rose period of art. She would later write, "his radiance, an inner fire one sensed in him, gave him a sort of magnetism which I was unable to resist." The rose period was characterized by paintings of harlequins and circus performers in this color. Horses and nude boys were prominent in his rose period paintings. *Family of Saltimbanques* (1905) was the climactic painting of this style.

CUBISM

By age twenty-five, Picasso was on the verge of greatness. His iconoclastic masterpiece *Les Demoiselles d'Avignon* was completed in 1907, which commenced the orgy of surrealism he was about to release on the world of art. This picture has been universally acclaimed as the beginning of cubism. It was inspired by his visit to an African museum where mythological masks and Negroid features made him realize that perception was reality. It was at this time that he concluded "the whole of creation is an enemy" and "nature has to exist so that we may rape it."

In *Les Demoiselles* he portrayed five prostitutes in primitive masks challenging societal morals and ethics. In like manner, the painting was challenging the morals and ethics of art. Henri Matisse called it a mockery. To Picasso, it was an exorcism of the tormented conflicts buried in his unconscious. This painting forever set him apart from his peers, and created his image as the consummate iconoclast and renegade—a rebel who despised society's traditional values. *Les Demoiselles* marked the end of his financial struggle and launched his artistic career. It defined his inner turmoil and summed up his nihilistic philosophy: "The painter takes whatever it is and destroys it. At the same time he gives it another life. . . . But he must pierce through what the others see—to the reality of it. He must destroy. He must demolish the framework itself" (Huffington, p. 118).

An Optimistic Spirit and Success

Picasso was not a struggling artist after *Les Demoiselles d'Avignon*. His work was acclaimed in America and Europe. Picasso worked harder than ever in his manic need to paint. By his thirties, Picasso was earning huge commissions and from the age of forty earned 1.5 million francs annually. He produced about three hundred paintings a year and due to his long life created more paintings than any other artist in history. When his estate was finally settled in 1977, a total of fifty thousand works of art were recorded. These did not include the numerous paintings sold or given to his barber, mistresses, friends, and doctor. His output was conservatively valued at $260 million and contained: 1,885 paintings, 1,228 sculptures, 2,880 ceramic works, 18,095 engravings, 6,112 lithographs, 3,181 linocuts, 7,089 drawings, 11 tapestries, 8 rugs, and 149 notebooks filled with another 4,659 drawings and sketches. Within twenty years these works had a value in excess of a billion dollars. In late 1995 Sotheby's sold *Le Memoir* for $20 million and *Garçonàla Collerette* for $12.1 million. Twenty-seven paintings sold for in excess of $70 million.

Picasso was a mesmerizing personality. Coco Chanel admitted to being attracted to him: "I was swept up by a passion for him. He was wicked. He was fascinating like a sparrow hawk, he made me a little afraid. . . . He had a way of looking at me. . . . I trembled." This charismatic power also made Picasso appealing to the media. He was never lost for words and would expound on any subject with a philosophical analysis justifying his art. *The Arts* magazine in 1923 quoted him relative to his "creatively destructive" approach to life and art and his renegade behavior: "Art is not truth. Art is a lie which makes us realize the truth."

Picasso's artistic success spanned many decades and his themes ranged from the controversial to the outrageous. These paintings were replete with rebellion, violence, conflict, and tragedy. These elements were pervasive in his most famous works: *La Vie* (1903), *The Old Guitar* (1905), *Les Demoiselles d'Avignon* (1907), *Three Dancers* (1925), *Nude on a Black Couch* (1932), *The Minotaur Carries Off a Woman* (1936), *Guernica* (1937), *Weeping Woman* (1937), *The Charnel House* (1945), *The Peeing Woman* (1965).

PAINTER OF EXISTENTIAL PHILOSOPHY

Many of Picasso's works included images of his friends, associates, and lovers. The *Weeping Woman* depicted his mistress Dora Maar as an emotionally disturbed woman, her face a vision of disillusionment. Poet and devoted friend Paul Eluard was entranced by this work and convinced Picasso to sell it to him just as he was finishing it. Eluard bought this picture for £250 and within decades it would become priceless.

Picasso painted his mistress turned wife Jacqueline, depicting her as a matronly little woman (*Jacqueline in a Rocking Chair*). He painted the picture when she was a sphinxlike femme fatale in her twenties. He painted her not as she was, but as he saw her becoming—his caretaker in old age.

Picasso's greatest success was his unusual ability to portray life on canvas. He had an extraordinary talent for documenting the societal and emotional ills of an age on canvas just as his friends Jean-Paul Sartre, Albert Camus, and Jean Cocteau were able to do with paper and pen.

Picasso lived and painted during the most volatile, turbulent, and destructive era in the history of mankind, including the Russian Revolution, the Spanish Revolution, the Great Depression, and two world wars. All were played out psychologically, emotionally, and physically within the purview of Picasso. He became the pictorial chronicler of a tumultuous age; his painting will be viewed by history as the biography of the twentieth century.

Picasso used five prostitutes in *Les Demoiselles d'Avignon* as a barbaric force to challenge societal mores. This picture would represent much of the first half of the twentieth century, prompting the surrealists to use it as their symbol for revolution.

In *Guernica* Picasso painted a monument to the devastation and despair of this Spanish city destroyed by German bombers where seventeen hundred perished.

This is a satanic picture depicting a horse, a bull, and a woman as the tragic symbols of the tragedy of Hitler and Franco's tyranny. Art writer Herbert Read described *Guernica* as "Picasso's great fresco . . . a monument to destruction, a cry of outrage and horror amplified by the spirit of genius" (Gardner 1993). Harvard psychologist Howard Gardner says the work "harbors intimations of horrifying experiences from Picasso's own life, particularly the memory of the chaos when his family had fled the earthquake when he was three" (Gardner 1993).

Picasso was a strange mixture of passion and perversity, rage and devastation, seduction and rape. His lifelong mistress Marie-Therese Walter endured his charm and wrath far longer than any other woman. When asked what made him happy, she replied succinctly, "He first raped the woman . . . and then he worked." She was responding to his 1937 painting *The Minotaur Carries Off the Woman*. Picasso saw himself in that image—the Minotaur was his alter ego—the embodiment of power over women and art. Picasso portrays himself as the Minotaur carrying off the nude nymph Marie-Therese while the subservient Dora Maar and his ex-wife Olga watch. They behold the master in wonderment and expectation—the wish-fulfillment of Picasso's insatiable need for adoring and helpless women. Such an introspective and destructive masterpiece led art critic Richard Klinger to say, "He reminded me of a racehorse. There was something massive and supernatural about him."

Power, Influence, and Self-Destruction

Picasso's power emanated from his enormous self-esteem and willpower. As a teenager he became enthralled with the Nietzschean concept of "will-to-power" where a "Superman" was created to cope with the absence of God. Such a romantic but mystical god-like character had great meaning for the anarchic nature of Picasso. He immediately adopted Nietzsche's "overman" as his own. When Nietzsche wrote, "I myself am fate (Superman) and have conditioned existence for all eternity," Picasso believed this to be a vision of himself. Nietzsche subscribed to the theory that great power accedes to those who take it, and this egoistic philosophy appealed to Picasso. Picasso assumed the mantle of the supreme master in art, given to him by an adoring public. His rebellion knew few bounds and like Jean-Paul Sartre he became a card-carrying member of the Communist party after the war to defy the establishments.

Picasso's charisma gained him many followers among the Paris intellectuals of the early twentieth century. Coco Chanel, Charlie Chaplin, Jean Cocteau, Gertrude Stein, Jean-Paul Sartre, Albert Camus, Guillaume Apollinaire, Sergei Diaghilev, Alice B. Toklas, and Paul Eluard were some of his confidants. Coco Chanel gave credence to his powerful magnetism saying, "I was swept up by a passion for him" and "trembled when near him." Jean Cocteau characterized his power as a "discharge of electricity . . . rigor, flair, showmanship, and magnetic radiance. He had an almost cosmic and irresistible self-confidence. Nothing seemed beyond him." Gertrude Stein also confirmed his power as a "radiance, an inner fire one sensed in him, gave him a sort of magnetism which I was unable to resist." Henri Matisse was more objective and expressed a less passionate view of Picasso and his work: "Picasso had an all-consuming urge to challenge, shock, to destroy and remake the world."

SELF-ESTEEM AND CHARISMA

Picasso's imposing self-confidence and charisma were the by-products of his indomitable will. This ability to will success set him apart. Once he produced his early masterpieces, a kind of titular power was bestowed on him by the art world. By age twenty-five, he had been hailed the "Father of Cubism," which assured his lifelong influence in the art world. Picasso rose to the pinnacle of Parisian art in his twenties, dominated European art by his thirties, and became the most influential artist in the world by his forties. Creative destruction and rebellion made Picasso and the Marquis de Sade the symbols for the surrealist movement. Guillaume Apollinaire, the first leader of surrealism, gave this insight into Picasso's power: "Picasso studies an object the way a surgeon dissects a cadaver." Art critic A. Waldeman described his work as "the cleverest of modern disquiet . . . corresponding to the collective reality of the moment, to a modern neurosis." If nothing else, Picasso's paintings, exuding both positive and negative emotions, became powerful statements of defiance that left the viewer in an internal state of emotional conflict. Biographer Arianna Huffington corroborated Picasso's power and confidence: "He radiated an almost cosmic and irresistible self-confidence. Nothing seemed beyond him."

LIBIDINAL DRIVE

Picasso's famous quote, "I do not seek, I find," defined his power and confidence. That power manifested itself in perverse and romantic liaisons. His libidinal drive and resultant conquests give credence to his psychosexual energy. Picasso had four children by three different women: his son Paul was by his first wife Olga Koklova; his mistress Marie-Therese bore him a daughter, Maya; and mistress Françoise Gilot bore him a son, Claude, and a daughter, Paloma.

For most of his life Picasso found enormous pleasure in playing his various lovers and wives off against one another. He always maintained multiple mistresses whom he used and abused. He invited his estranged wife Olga to visit the Cote d'Azur and reside in the same hotel where he was living with Dora Maar and cavorting with mistress Marie-Therese Walter. At age sixty, Picasso continued his relationships with twenty-one-year-old Françoise Gilot, Dora Maar, and Marie-Therese Walter. He had multiple sexual trysts most of his adult life and delighted in duping each woman into thinking he was her faithful lover. He continued these perverse relationships well into his eighties.

Picasso had a depraved need to create jealous conflicts among his lovers. The tragedy is the destruction he caused. Olga was turned into an emotional cripple and

Dora Maar had a nervous breakdown and was institutionalized. His son Paulo became an alcoholic and his grandson Pablito committed suicide when not allowed to attend Picasso's funeral. Both his mistress Marie-Therese and second wife, Jacqueline, were unable to cope with life after his death and committed suicide. His friend Jean Cocteau said of Picasso's influence and destruction, "Picasso sanctified defects. That is for me, the only genius. Everything else is play."

DESTRUCTIVENESS

Picasso's destructiveness knew no bounds. He had an internal conflict between a psychological need to create and a compulsion to destroy. Contemporary Henri Matisse said that he had "an all-consuming urge to destroy." Picasso admitted: "The painter must destroy" and "everything is the enemy." He felt "a good painting ought to bristle with razor blades."

Picasso's attitude toward women was pernicious: "I would rather see a woman die any day than see her happy with someone else." This was never more obvious than with his marriage proposal to Françoise Gilot after she had left him and married another artist. He even agreed to adopt their two children in order to dupe her into leaving her new husband. He promised marriage immediately following her divorce. As soon as Gilot had petitioned the courts for divorce, the eighty-year-old Picasso secretly married his current mistress, Jacqueline, purposely suppressing the news so that François would learn of his despicable deed in the newspaper. He found a sense of power in this vile act, which she described as his "evil." Because Gilot had dared leave him, he destroyed her.

Arianna Huffington described Picasso in her biography, *Picasso—Creator and Destroyer* (1988), as an "orgy of destructiveness—existentialism and nihilism in art." He justified his avant-garde art: "nature has to exist, so that we may destroy it."

Psychologist Carl Jung was shocked by Picasso's art. Comparing Picasso's work to drawings by his schizophrenic patients, he concluded: "The work expresses the recurring characteristic motif of the descent into hell, into the unconscious," adding "the ugly, the sick, the grotesque incomprehensible" in analyzing his work. Jung concluded that Picasso was schizophrenic.

A famous graphologist who treated the retarded was asked to evaluate a letter written by Picasso to his friend Paul Eluard. Eluard requested the analysis but did not disclose the identity of the letter writer when asking the graphologist to offer a psychological profile of the writer's personality. The frighteningly accurate analysis read: "He loves intensely and he kills what he loves. . . . He is sad. Looks for an escape from his sadness through pure creation."

Picasso's need to destroy bordered on evil. During the period when he was finishing *Guernica,* he invited both mistresses Marie-Therese and Dora Maar to his studio at the same time, anticipating a jealous clash. When they showed up, he purposely provoked a fight between the two women who ended up in a fistfight during which Picasso smirked but continued painting. He later said, "It was one of my choicest memories."

What Made Picasso Tick?

Picasso used his power to make sexual conquests and his defiance to create paintings. He lived to work with a manic energy that resulted in a prolific output of art. His mistresses and love life acted as a catalyst for his art and many of his liaisons ended up as diabolical sublimations in his art. He was competitive and aggressive and lived on the edge of acceptability. Joining the Communist party indicates his renegade nature: He was a capitalist but was compelled to belong to a group that was antiestablishment.

A remarkable confidence helped him gain professional and personal success. His life and art were an orgy of the destructive bordering on the bizarre. Without a formidable self-esteem, Picasso would not have achieved such enormous power and success. His innovative art was a by-product of his ability to revile the existing order of things and create the new and different. He was the most prolific and psychologically influential artist in history because he dared to be different.

Picasso had an indomitable will, an implacable self-esteem, and a charismatic power that transcended his other traits and attracted many disciples. Like the other creative geniuses in this book, Picasso's greatest strength became his greatest weakness: his extraordinary self-esteem also contributed to his arrogant egoism. His short height gave him a Napoleon complex: he was similar to the diminutive Sade and Napoleon who overcompensated for size by becoming bullies.

Picasso attracted some of the most intelligent and attractive women in Europe. His first wife Olga was a Russian ballerina. Mistress Marie-Theresa was a beautiful child-woman who bore him a child and asked nothing in return. Mistress Dora Maar was an exceptionally talented artist and an intellectual. Françoise Gilot, the mother of his two children, was a precocious twenty-one-year-old when she met the sixty-one-year-old Picasso, and she was a potentially gifted artist. She ultimately became a successful artist and married Jonas Salk, the eminent scientist.

Picasso painted "in opposition" to the establishment, while demeaning women in art and in real life. Many of his greatest masterpieces were those in which he degraded women and glorified destruction. *Les Demoiselles d'Avignon, Guernica, Weeping Woman,* and *The Peeing Woman*—all based on human destruction or psychological annihilation and suffering—are acclaimed works of art.

Picasso was never happy with his art or personal life and spent his life attempting to change both. No woman ever met his enormous expectations and no painting ever met his approval. He spent his life trying to create the absolute painting and died without achieving that goal. This frustration and search for perfection is what drove Picasso to continuously create. It was as if Picasso's self-worth were tied to artistic perfection. He had an internal fire and manic energy which drove him to seek the new and unknown in both art and women.

Picasso became a giant in the world of the visual arts because he was willing to gamble his reputation and his psyche: his belief in his own perverted vision of reality made him the most powerful and influential artist who ever lived. He was a genius the like of which we will never see again. His artistic documentation of the turbulent twentieth century is his legacy.

PABLO PICASSO RUIZ
Twentieth Century's Greatest Artist
b. Oct. 25, 1881, Malaga, Spain; d. April 8, 1973, Paris, France

Dominant Trait: Supreme self-confidence. A prolific creator with inexhaustible passion. A charismatic destroyer.

Motto: "I do not seek, I find." "I too am against everything . . . everything is unknown . . . and an enemy." "There are only two kinds of women—goddesses and doormats." "Art is not truth. Art is a lie."

Nickname: "Wonderfully Terrible Lover" by mistress Marie-Therese

Vices/Hobbies: Bullfights, poetry, pottery, bugle blowing, philosophy, and seduction of innocence

Heroes/Mentors: His father followed by Raphael, Cézanne, Nietzsche's Superman, Matisse

Philosophy of Life: "Life is only a bad novel." "We paint because we are unhappy." "Art exists to be used against the established order." "I always try to be subversive."

Fantasy: To create a universal art—the Absolute art!

Professional Success: *La Vie* (1903), *Les Demoiselles d'Avignon* (1907), *Three Dancers* (1925), *Minotaur Carries Off a Woman* (1937), *Guernica* (1937), *Weeping Woman* (1937), *The Charnel House* (1945), *The Peeing Woman* (1965)

Power: Indomitable will and confidence. Established titular power creating cubism and surrealist movements. "Portraits should possess not physical, not spiritual, but psychological likeness."

Influence: A leader who said: "I do not seek, I find." The art world followed him.

Destructiveness: "I'd rather see a woman die any day than see her happy . . . the painter must destroy." His nihilism was demonstrated in two great works: *Les Demoiselles d'Avignon* and *Guernica*.

Birth Order: Firstborn with two younger sisters, Concepción and Conchita

Parental Influence: Idolized by doting mother, aunts, grandmother. Took mother's name in defiance of father who was a journeyman painter, curator, and teacher.

Transiency: Moved to Corunna at age ten, Barcelona at fourteen, Madrid at sixteen, Barcelona at eighteen, and Paris by nineteen.

Crises: Survived earthquake at age three. Sister's death when fourteen transformed his life due to Faustian pact.

Formal Education: Terrible student with little formal schooling. Attended Barcelona and Madrid Art Academies.

Libidinal Drive: Perverse and sadomasochistic tendencies. "He had nothing but contempt for morality" and "Inexhaustible passion for work and sex."

Personality Type: Extroverted-Intuitive-Feeler-Perceiver; manic-depressive and a macho womanizer

Self-Esteem: Self-portrait at age nineteen signed "I the King." Jean Cocteau said: "He radiated an almost cosmic and irresistible self-confidence. Nothing seemed beyond him."

Rebellion: Communist and atheist in Republican and Catholic France. "The painter must destroy." "I always try to be subversive, whatever drives me to create . . . it is only to wage war on the world."

Risk Propensity: Fearless and lived life on the edge, refusing to leave Paris during German occupation

Work Ethic: Most prodigious artist in history with 50,000 works of art: 1,885 paintings; 1,228 sculptures; 2,880 ceramics; 18,095 engravings; 9,293 lithographs, linocuts,; 11,748 drawings; 11 tapestries.

Tenacity: Pursued art, friends, and lovers until they capitulated to his will.

Optimism: Personal unhappiness drove him to produce art for desperately needed acceptance and adulation.

Manicness: "I have the revelation of the inner voice." "I sacrifice everything to my painting."

6

Risk-Taking Propensity: Amelia Earhart and Howard Hughes

Change has no constituency.

—Machiavelli

A Live-on-the-Edge Mentality

Risk is the function of dealing with uncertainty, or in a behavioral sense, the art of finding comfort in ambiguity. True creative geniuses and power brokers, like these fourteen, love the new and untried: It is what drives them because they know intuitively that great success in products, art, or life is never accomplished without risking failure. This is the rule for all aspiring entrepreneurs: Find out where the experts are and go elsewhere. Trailblazing concepts are usually found in the least likely places, making it imperative to violate the norm, choose a different path, opt for a unique strategy, or pursue the bizarre or arcane. Picasso gained fame and fortune by deliberately violating all the established traditions in painting. Wright broke with traditional architecture, earning him the nickname "the Anarchist of Architecture." Rubinstein opened retail stores to sell beauty products in both Australia and England during an era when makeup was used only by actresses and prostitutes. Disney violated traditional dogmas in animation, Duncan in dance, Tesla in science, Murdoch in media, Piaf in performing, and Montessori in education. They all were willing to risk and fail, and their temerity took them to the very top of their professions. More than any of the others, Howard Hughes and Amelia Earhart defied tradition and risked everything in pursuit of their dreams.

Helen Keller put risk in perspective when she wrote, "Life is either a daily adventure or nothing." She understood that temerity is the basis for living a worthwhile and productive life. Those attempting to eliminate all risk from their ventures are working in opposition to the ultimate objective. Risk and reward are a

183

zero-sum game and when risk is removed, all potential opportunity is also removed. Risk is a double-edged concept where rewards have a linear relationship with the amount of risk taken. Bureaucrats take little or no risk and are perturbed when they never experience success. Entrepreneurs take high risks and consequently are the recipients of huge rewards.

RISK AND EMOTIONAL REWARD

Thrill-seekers are not motivated by money but by tangible rewards such as personal satisfaction and the euphoria that accompanies defying the odds and winning. The most important motivators are inherent and not extrinsic. Internal drive is what causes people to live on the edge. The elation of surviving a great adventure like white-water rafting, downhill skiing, or skydiving is an internal reward. Living on the edge professionally can create the same degree of exhilaration. Risk and reward are highly correlated, eliminating risk eliminates rewards both personally and professionally. Consider the person who is afraid of flying. He can feel safe by never boarding a plane, but he also loses out on the pleasure of seeing any difficult-to-reach foreign land. Downhill skiing demands risking broken bones and being cold. Sitting in the lodge removes those risks but also eliminates the euphoria experienced flying down a mountain.

These fourteen visionaries were content with living and working high on the risk/reward curve. The higher the risk, the greater the challenge and higher the motivation to confront the risk head-on. These visionaries thought of risk as a positive opportunity to use to their advantage. To them, it was not a negative but a positive adventure, fun and internally energizing.

RISK AND FLOW

Risk must accompany any great success, but it also must be managed. It requires diligent preparation as described by Mihaly Csikszentmihalyi in the book *Flow: The Psychology of Optimal Experience* (1990). This research psychologist argued that crossing a Manhattan street is far more risky than climbing the Matterhorn. His reasoning was based on the ability to anticipate risk and therefore control it. The Matterhorn climb is preplanned with exacting precision while the Manhattan street crossing is not. Virtually every possible risk on the climb has a planned solution while the Manhattan experience cannot be planned and muggers, wayward bikes, taxis, and other uncontrollable variables will likely contribute to an accident. The fourteen subjects in this book operated more like the mountain climber. All were very willing to risk everything, and it is what made them rich and famous. But they also carefully managed their risks.

RISK-REWARD CURVE

Amelia Earhart and Howard Hughes were the most risk-oriented individuals among the fourteen subjects. Both took crazy risks and attempted to manage them but they were so confident in their own ability that they were often negligent in leaving too much in the hands of others. They repeatedly risked their lives in airplanes in order to break speed records, accepting the possibility of crashing. Most people are unwilling to risk their lives for such notoriety. Both Earhart and Hughes pushed themselves and their planes beyond prudent limits in their pursuit of fame. They operated their businesses with the same disdain for safety.

A heuristic (trial-and-error experimentation) approach is the only way to solve great problems. Such activity is fraught with risk, but confidence and success ensue from both wins and losses. Cy Young, the baseball pitcher, has the most wins in history but also owns the record for the most losses. Picasso painted as many failures, and his masterpieces number but a fraction of his output. Some of Walt Disney's most cherished works (*Fantasia, Bambi, Alice in Wonderland*) were total failures when first released. Interviewed at the opening of Disneyland, he told a reporter, "I mortgaged everything I own for this park." He had actually borrowed on his insurance policy to finance the initial plans.

There is a saying in sports, "There is no gain without pain." The same is true in attempting to reach the very pinnacle of success in business, entertainment, the arts, or other professions. Amelia Earhart learned while young that the greatest thrills came from taking big risks. When older she preferred to drive fast cars, fly the sleekest and fastest planes, and lived life with unabashed freedom. She spent most of her adult life living on the edge, satiating an internal need to prove she could take great risks and survive the gamble.

Howard Hughes had a similar propensity for risk taking. He flew with total disregard for his own safety, often taking off in planes destined to crash because of his disdain for rules or safety. He pushed planes beyond their capability and flew in marginal conditions.

Did Earhart and Hughes have a death wish? Possibly, but it is apparent that they needed the euphoric rush from living dangerously. Neither were content living a "safe" and "comfortable" life, in the normal context of those words. Both were Big T (high testosterone) thrill-seekers who had to be the best.

POWER BROKERS AND RISK

Napoleon repeatedly led his troops in suicidal attacks. At the turn of the century, Nikola Tesla demonstrated the magic of electricity by allowing two million volts to flow through his body. In 1896 he told a friend, "I almost got killed today as I had 3.5 million volts strike me." Montessori, as the first female medical student in Italy, was forced to dissect cadavers alone at night. She questioned her sanity and almost gave up, but ultimately refused to back down from her goal of becoming the first female doctor in Italy. Rupert Murdoch "was an inveterate gambler by the time he was sixteen," according to Thomas Kiernan in *Citizen Murdoch* (p. 20): "He would gamble at anything from horse racing to finger tossing. . . . Gambling allowed him to assume a certain arrogant, cocksure attitude." When this adventurous entrepreneur was questioned by the media about his off-the-wall business acquisitions, he responded, "Business is a life of constant calculated risks." When he paid $1 billion in 1994 for the rights to televise NFL football games, he overbid CBS by $400 million. Murdoch did not see this as such a titanic risk: To him, *not* securing the NFL deal was more risky. He was convinced that Fox could not compete as a network without the NFL contract.

Not all these subjects had the money or nerve of Murdoch, Tesla, or Napoleon, but virtually every one was comfortable with taking large risks and dealing with the unknown. In fact, most of them preferred pioneering in unfamiliar terrain. It was this desire to face such challenges that led them to unparalleled heights. Without their enormous risk-taking propensity, these subjects would all have been mediocre. Amelia Earhart and Howard Hughes certainly would not have achieved early distinction and success had they not been willing to take inordinate risks. Earhart had to be restrained from flying under high-tension wires just for the thrill of the experience. Hughes almost killed himself attempting to fly a WW I fighter plane which he had never been in before.

The other subjects also took risks but not to the same degree. Edith Piaf's sister, Simone, said that "no risk was too great" for Edith and that "she had the most fantastic nerve." This was apparent when she refused to sing for the Nazis during their occupation of Paris. Picasso was also fearless and, like Piaf, refused to leave Paris or capitulate to the will of the Nazis. He expressed his philosophy of risk taking while defending his masterpiece *Les Demoiselles d'Avignon*: "Painting is freedom. If you jump, you might fall on the wrong side of the rope. But if you are not willing to take the risk of breaking your neck, what good is it? You don't jump at all. You have to wake people up. To revolutionize their way of identifying things" (Gardner 1993, p. 159).

Helena Rubinstein was told, "Try to set up a business in London and they will slaughter you." She ignored the experts and succeeded in 1909 by establishing the first cosmetic shop in conservative London. Sade never feared anything including his incarceration in the Bastille for much of his adult life. Sade lived through one of the most tumultuous eras in history, including the French Revolution, Reign of Terror, and the Napoleonic Wars. He came within feet of the guillotine and flaunted his beliefs in the face of a dogmatic society. Frank Lloyd Wright "had an unconscious courting of catastrophe and ruin" (Secrest 1992). His great loves were swift horses and fast European sports cars. He owned Jaguars, a Mercedes-Benz, and a Riley, and rode his own horse daily until in his nineties.

TESTOSTERONE AND TEMERITY

Research in psychology has shown thrill-seeking behavior to be a function of high levels of testosterone, and a factor in creativity, sex drive, and competitiveness.

Frank Farley, former president of the American Psychological Association, is the father of testosterone research. He believes "that thrill-seeking can lead some big 'Ts' [high testosterone] to outstanding creativity." All fourteen subjects were categorized as Big T personalities based on their proclivity for risk taking. In fact, Farley used Amelia Earhart as an example of the Big T personality in his research. Farley describes these personalities as endowed with abnormally high testosterone levels and "tend to be more creative, and more extroverted, take more risks, have more experimental artistic preferences, and prefer more variety in their sex lives" (Farley 1986). Harvard psychologist William James was not as specific as Farley but believed, "It is only by risking our persons from one hour to another that we live at all. And often enough our faith beforehand in an uncertified result is the only thing that makes the result come true." An even more cogent description of the Big T personality was given by George Gilder in his book *Wealth and Poverty* (1984): "The investor who never acts until statistics affirm his choice, the athlete or politician who fails to make his move until too late, the businessman who waits until the market is proven—all are doomed to mediocrity by their trust in a spurious rationality."

These fourteen got to the top because they were not averse to taking risks. One thing is clear from this study: *No one will ever catch the brass ring without risking everything for the opportunity.*

All managers and leaders fall into one of three categories: *Risk-takers* who operate with an entrepreneurial mentality; *Care-takers* who operate with a bureaucratic mentality; and *Under-takers* who lack insight, foresight, and courage to achieve. The following table illustrates risk-taking and leadership propensity. From a management perspective, everyone is either a Risk-taker (Leader), Care-taker (Follower), or Under-taker (Parasite). Risk-takers often become innovators, Care-takers experts, and Under-takers clerks.

LEADERSHIP AND RISK-TAKING PROPENSITY

Types

| RISK-TAKERS | CARE-TAKERS | UNDER-TAKERS |

Operating Styles

RISK-TAKERS (Innovators)	Visionaries with macrovision and long-term perspective
CARE-TAKERS (Experts)	Bureaucrats with microvision and short-term perspective
UNDER-TAKERS (Clerks)	Underachievers with no vision and no perspective

The following risk-reward curve (figure 15) illustrates how differently the risk-takers function from the care-taking bureaucrats. It demonstrates in graphic form how both people and businesses evolve down the curve from high-risk mentalities when new or young with little or nothing to lose, into risk-adversity when they age or accumulate more assets. Big T personalities do not typically follow the standard risk-reward curve and continue to take high risks even after they achieve success, accumulate assets, or age. Little Ts or bureaucratic personalities tend to take few risks regardless of age or assets and tend to operate at the bottom of the risk-reward curve.

FIGURE 15
RISK-REWARD CURVE
PROFESSIONAL AND PERSONAL PROPENSITY TO TAKE RISK

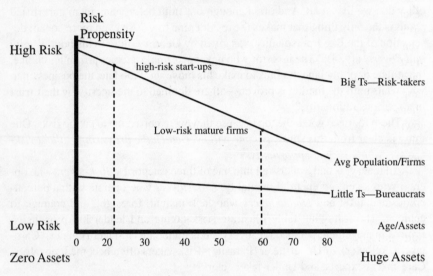

Risk-taking Axioms for Entrepreneurs and Innovators

* On average the propensity to risk declines as assets increase for both people and organizations.
* On average the propensity to risk declines with personal aging and organizational maturity.
* New start-up firms have little to lose and must take inordinate risks to equalize their competitiveness.
* Older and larger organizations tend to protect their large investment in existing products and programs and will not jeopardize existing market share or revenues thru risk. New firms should take advantage of their risk-averse mentality.
* High testosterone individuals and entrepreneurs (Big Ts) tend to operate very high on the risk-reward curve and often risk beyond their need to do so and are not affected by an increase in assets or age.
* Low testosterone individuals and bureaucrats (Little Ts) tend to take few risks even when they have little to risk due to their internalized need for self-preservation.

Amelia Earhart

Courage is the price that life exacts for granting peace.

Overview

The above quotation is the first line of the poem "Courage" written by Amelia Earhart while she sold airplanes and worked in a settlement house during the early 1920s. The second line reads, "The soul that knows it not, knows no release." This describes the woman whose temerity was acquired early in life. Later she would write that her tomboyishness saved her from serious injury at the age of six. This event occurred while she sledded down a steep hill near her grandparents' house in Atchison, Kansas. During that era it was unacceptable for females to "belly-slam" or lie facedown on a sled. Ladies sat demurely upright despite the inherent dangers. At the bottom of the hill, a horse-drawn wagon appeared in her path. There was no way to stop or turn the sled, but fortunately for her she was lying down like a boy; she put her head down and flew through the horse's legs unharmed. Had she been sitting up, she may not have survived the experience. That fact was not lost on Earhart. This early experience conditioned her that risk is everywhere and the greatest thrills emanate from the greatest risks.

David Viscott, author of *Risking* (1977), wrote on the psychology of risk taking and concludes that the greatest danger is always in *not* risking: "The driver most likely to be killed is the one who hesitates, loses his nerve, and can neither accelerate nor apply his brakes." According to Viscott, he cannot follow through on a commitment to act. This axiom defined Amelia Earhart. She "dared go where no one had ever gone and to do what no one had done," according to her biographer Doris Rich. When Earhart was preparing to leave on her last flight, husband George Putnam said, "You don't have to do this." She said emphatically, "Yes I do!"

Earhart had an internal need to prove that she could push the limits and survive the experience. Aviation was her life and nothing could deter her from proving that she was above fear and failure. She loved the very idea of going where no one had ever gone; that was part of her mystique. Anna Morrow Lindbergh spent time with her just after she and Charles Lindbergh had set their Atlantic flying records and wrote in her diary: "She is the most amazing person—just as tremendous as [Charles], I think. It startles me how much alike they are in breadth. . . . She has the clarity of mind, impersonal eye, coolness of temperament, balance of a scientist" (Lindbergh, *Hour of Gold, Hour of Lead, 1929–1932*).

In *Love of Flying* (1985), Gore Vidal described Earhart and Charles Lindbergh as the "god and goddess of flight," remembering meeting them in childhood: "They looked spookily like each other." His impression of them was "the air age beautifully incarnate." Earhart's unprecedented transatlantic flight took place on the *Friendship* just one year after Lucky Lindy's monumental flight, causing the media to label her "Lady Lindy."

Lindbergh and Earhart flew in an era fraught with danger and death. Seventy-five percent of all airmail pilots died in their planes and commercial flights were considered a success when 80 percent of the passengers were able to avoid airsickness due to low altitude turbulence.

Earhart and Lindbergh were amazingly alike in temperament as well as looks. Both were young idols with daring, lithe figures and a devil-may-care attitude toward life. When the *Friendship* landed in Burry Port, Wales, on June 18, 1928, Earhart was given the mantle which had been Lindbergh's just one year earlier. Lady Astor told the *New York Times* (June 28, 1928): "She is a remarkable girl. . . . Everyone I have talked to in England thinks this girl is a great credit to womanhood and to her own country. She has charm, intelligence, and above all character." The *New York Times* (July 1937) printed when she was reported missing: "She was in rebellion against a world which had been made, for women, too safe, too unexciting. . . . She wanted to dare all that a man would dare" (Ware 1993, p. 29).

Earhart was a daredevil in an era when 90 percent of American women were housewives and mothers. She did more for women's liberation during the Depression than any other woman with the possible exception of her friend and ardent admirer Eleanor Roosevelt. Earhart became a role model for working women by writing and lecturing on her air adventures. She was a charismatic speaker with an assertive—yet feminine—demeanor.

After Earhart's first record-breaking flight in 1928, she lived the rest of her life scrutinized by the media and promoted by her husband, George Putnam, a publisher and publicity agent. By the time she attempted to become the first woman to circumnavigate the world, her fame was legend. After she vanished in the South Pacific, she became an icon. Her parting statement to the press just prior to takeoff proved to be prophetic: "I've got only one obsession—a small and probably feminine horror of growing old—so I won't feel completely cheated if I fail to come back" (Rich 1989, p. 256). She vanished twenty-three days before her fortieth birthday.

Earhart was an independent spirit who defied conformity in all she did. Her cousin Nancy Morse said that she was a "loner with unconventional dreams" and was kicked out of prep school "for walking on the roof in her nightgown." Her marriage agreement to George Putnam was an example of her need for freedom and independence. She met Putnam while working at Denison House, a settlement house in Boston, Massachusetts. He promoted her after the 1928 record-breaking *Friendship* flight. He began an aggressive courtship and persisted until she finally agreed to marry him on February 7, 1931. Earhart gave Putnam an unusual ultimatum that she wrote in the guise of a betrothal agreement the night before their wedding. It is the consummate testimony to her independent spirit:

> I shall not hold you to any medieval code of faithfulness to me nor shall I consider myself bound to you similarly. If we can be honest, I think the difficulties which arise may be avoided should you or I become interested deeply or in passing in anyone else.

> Please let us not interfere with the other's work or play, nor let the world see our private joys or disappointments. I may have to keep some place where I can go to be by myself now and then, for I cannot guarantee to endure at all times the confinement of even an attractive cage.
>
> I must extract a cruel promise, and that is that you will let me go in a year if we find no happiness together. I will try to do my best in every way and give you that part of me you know and seem to want. (Rich 1989, p. 116)

The ever-pugnacious Putnam accepted her terms. She became Amelia Earhart Putnam legally although she would always use her maiden name professionally. When questioned by the press about her domestic duties and dual role as housewife and professional aviator, she said, "My husband . . . does not interfere with my flying and I don't interfere with his affairs."

Early Life Experiences and Influences

Earhart was born on July 24, 1897, the eldest child of Edwin and Amy Otis Earhart of Atchison, Kansas. She had one younger sister, Muriel. Her sister and mother would lean on the resilient Amelia for much of their lives. The most dominant influence on Earhart's early life was her alcoholic father whom she idolized. Her father failed at most every profession he attempted and became a lawyer late in life after he and Amy had divorced. Her father's entrepreneurial bent demonstrated to Amelia quite early that she could make it without becoming a part of the establishment.

Earhart's maternal grandfather had been a bank president and U.S. district judge. Edwin Earhart was never able to meet the high standards set by his wife and moved the family constantly in a vain attempt to find fame and fortune. This vagabond lifestyle became the basis for Amelia Earhart's need for change and discomfort with permanent roots. She found comfort in ambiguity and learned to cope with the new and the different because of this early transiency. Her thrill-seeking nature was imprinted during these early years where she was constantly faced with the new and unknown. Her highly transient youth began two days after her birth when the family moved from Atchison to Kansas City, where she lived until she started school. Then young Amelia was sent to live with her maternal grandparents in Atchison. During this period she exhibited an independence that often infuriated her teachers. Biographer Doris Rich characterized her during these years as a "gifted speaker, tenacious and impatient . . . with the eyes of a maverick."

TRANSIENCY

By the time Earhart was a teenager, the family moves became tedious. Earhart had moved repeatedly between Atchison and Kansas City and then to other states. By the time she reached high school her father had become an itinerant businessman, which forced her to attend six different high schools in Atchison, Kansas City, Des Moines, St. Paul, and Chicago. She later said, "I grew up here and there like a rolling stone" (Ware 1993). These experiences molded her into a resilient and self-reliant woman capable of coping with whatever the world had to offer. These early experiences also groomed her for the nomadic lifestyle she would lead as an adult.

INDEPENDENCE

Amelia graduated from Hyde Park High School in Chicago in 1915 but demonstrated her independent spirit by not attending commencement. In the fall of 1916 she enrolled in Ogontz College in Philadelphia where she gained the reputation as "the girl in brown who walks alone." During her second year she was elected vice president of her class and composed its motto, "Honor is the foundation of courage." During Christmas break 1917 she visited her sister in Toronto, Canada, and became so moved by four amputees returning from World War I that she impulsively quit college and enlisted as a nurse. After the war she enrolled in premed at Columbia University and took other courses at Barnard College in Manhattan.

Earhart had always been devoted to her tall, handsome, loving, and witty father. During Christmas break 1920, he would be the cause of an experience that would change her life. That fateful day in Los Angeles, Edwin bought her a ticket for a plane ride. Earhart said, "As soon as we left the ground, I knew I myself had to fly . . . knowing full well I'd die if I didn't." She dropped out of Columbia and relocated to Los Angeles to be near her father, who was now divorced and living alone. Southern California provided an ideal climate for year-round flying. It was here that Cora Kinner began giving her flying lessons.

YELLOW—THE COLOR OF "INNER CONFIDENCE" AND ENERGY

When Earhart arrived in California, she took a commercial photography course and opened a studio with a friend. When this entrepreneurial venture failed, she bought a truck and began hauling gravel for a construction company in order to earn money to buy an airplane, even though she didn't have a pilot's license. She finally received her license on December 15, 1921. Within a year she would set her first flying record.

Earhart's first plane was an open cockpit biplane that she painted yellow and named "The Canary." It was a representation of her free spirit, energetic persona, and need for independence. Amelia was wildly uninhibited in her flying and asked Cora Kinner if she could fly between two high-tension wires eight feet apart when she was just learning. Another instructor, Neta Snook, said, "She would have flown between them if I didn't watch her all the time." She experienced a number of crashes while learning, none of which injured her severely. Then she impulsively sold her dream plane, bought a car, and reenrolled in premed at Columbia. This car was a Kissel sports car that she had painted yellow and named "Yellow Peril." Color psychologists have determined that yellow, the color of both her plane and car, is the color of "spark and energy." It is the "most upbeat of all colors" and a "statement of self-satisfaction." Amelia was primed for speed and action.

SEARCH FOR KNOWLEDGE AND TRUTH

Earhart was in a constant search for her niche in life. Deciding it wouldn't be in education, she left Columbia for the second time. She took some courses at Harvard in her continual search for knowledge but felt formal education was not the formula for success. Her philosophy of education was: "Experiment! Meet new people. . . . That's better than any college education."

Earhart was similar to the other subjects of this book who detested the discipline and structure of formal education but who turned to books and were self-taught. It was in books where Earhart acquired her vivid imagination and adventurous nature. She confided: "Books have meant much to me." In June 1928 she told the *Daily Mirror* that her imaginary flights through literature were adventures as real to her as flying over the Atlantic. Her first love was still flying and she took a job as sales manager for Bert Kinner, whose daughter Cora had been her flying instructor. While she worked at Denison House in Boston, she also sold planes as the sales manager and part owner of a new airplane distribution organization. It was in this position that Earhart met George Palmer Putnam. He was immediately attracted to her both personally and professionally and encouraged her to become the first woman in history to cross the Atlantic Ocean in an airplane. She agreed to the crossing in the *Friendship* on June 17, 1928. She and two men, Bill Stultz and Slim Gordon, took off from Newfoundland and landed in Burry Port, Wales, after spending twenty-four hours and forty minutes over open ocean. Ironically, while in the air she discovered that Stultz, like her father, was an alcoholic, which would also be true of another aviator on her flight ten years later. The media and public went wild over her accomplishment, and Earhart, never one to self-promote, put the achievement in context: "only by an accident of sex" was she an international celebrity.

A Thrill-Seeking Spirit

Cora Kinner, Earhart's first flight instructor, said, "She used to scare me to death." Earhart was fascinated with fast cars and planes and loved to push each to its limit. She learned to fly in open cockpits and after she crashed her first plane was found powdering her nose when help came: "I wanted to look nice when the reporters arrived." Earhart's confidence and self-assurance was demonstrated when she bought her first plane *before* she had a license to fly it. After earning her pilot's license in 1922, the irrepressible Earhart decided to use the open cockpit Kinner Canary Airster to establish an altitude record. She took off on October 22, 1922, at Rogers Field in Southern California. With no oxygen tank in the cockpit, she climbed to fourteen thousand feet through fog and sleet until the plane's motor began to falter. Fearing a stall, she put the plane into a tailspin after having set the altitude record. The plane went into a perilous dive through the clouds. Earhart was unable to pull out of the dive until the plane was beneath the fog bank, which was below three thousand feet. On the ground a veteran pilot asked her what might have happened if the fog had reached ground level. She admitted to not having considered such a possibility as she had only focused on the objective, breaking the altitude and speed records. Safety was always a low priority in Earhart's life.

ATLANTIC SOLO CROSSING

On her record-breaking flight across the Atlantic in 1932, Earhart encountered numerous storms and life-threatening mechanical malfunctions. Her altimeter didn't work and she never knew how high or low she was flying. Since airplanes at this time were not equipped with an oxygen supply, it would have been disastrous if she had passed out from oxygen deprivation. She climbed to 12,000 feet to get above the weather but ice formed on the wings. Then the engine manifold cracked. Earhart was forced to descend below the clouds but the plane went into a spin and pulled out close to the ocean with the waves breaking just under her wings.

For ten more hours Earhart fought the elements in this death-defying flight to prove that a woman could endure the crossing. Gasoline kept dripping down her neck as the manifold fire kept pouring fumes into the cockpit, which made her sick to her stomach. The gauge to her reserve fuel tank was broken so she was flying blind relative to elevation and distance.

With the arrival of dawn, Earhart spotted a ship and knew she was near land. Paris had been her destination but it was now out of the question. Since she sensed impending disaster, she decided to land the plane no matter where she was. She landed in Londonderry, Northern Ireland, and became the toast of the international media once again. Earhart had barely survived this ghastly ordeal but never discussed this with the media. She acted as if this ordeal was just another Sunday drive in the park. Earhart later described her near-fatal mishaps in her book *The Fun of It* (1932). When a reporter asked her why she had undertaken so perilous a journey, she responded, "Because I wanted to." Her Atlantic flight was to be her greatest achievement and for which she was awarded the Distinguished Flying Cross from the United States Congress, the Harmon Trophy, the Legion of Honor from the French government, and the Gold Medal from the National Geographic Society presented by President Herbert Hoover.

RISK IS RELATIVE

It is important to view Earhart's exploits in the context of the times. She was one of the owners of Transcontinental Air Transport airlines in 1929, which became TWA with Howard Hughes as owner. Gene Vidal and Paul Collins were her partners. She was vice president in charge of public relations and piloted many of the early flights between New York, Philadelphia, and Washington, D.C. Flight records on these trips give some idea of the sad state of commercial flying during the period: "People were so sick they used rubber matting instead of carpeting on the floor of the plane. . . . They used to say passengers didn't get out of a plane, they slid out" (Rich 1989, p. 107). Will Rogers joked about his use of one sick-bag for every fifty miles of flying time. The fumes, turbulence, untrustworthy condition of runways, and lack of air traffic controls made flying adventurous at best and fatal at worst. Earhart was an adventuress during an era when flying was not for the faint of heart.

BIG T MENTALITY

Before Earhart's final flight, her good friend Jacqueline Cochran, also an expert pilot, told her, "I hope you don't go." Cochran didn't think it was possible to hit a tiny island in the middle of the Pacific Ocean. The media also questioned the flight: "responsible authorities should stop her . . . too many risks" (Ware 1993, p. 206). The British weekly *The Aeroplane* called the flight "a useless adventure" (Rich 1989, p. 197). Earhart could not be dissuaded: Her previous records were achieved because of her need for thrill and danger. She had been the first woman to cross the Atlantic in 1928 and then the first woman to cross the Atlantic alone, which also made her the first female pilot to fly the Atlantic twice. She was the first woman to fly the autogiro, a precursor of the helicopter. She was the first woman to fly solo between Honolulu and California in either direction.

All of these firsts, plus a number of cross-country speed records, were not without problems. Earhart experienced seven plane crashes, a few of which were life-threatening. But these flirtations with death never deterred her. She told her neighbor, competitive pilot Ruth Nickols, "I just don't think about crackups" (Rich 1989, p. 131). On one of her air adventures in 1932 Earhart planned to fly across the Gulf of Mexico from Mexico City in order to break a record. Aviator Wiley Post told her, "Don't do it, it's too dangerous." Her Vega aircraft was loaded with 472 gallons of potentially explosive high octane fuel. Taking off in Mexico City was a perilous task since its runway was downright dangerous. Post's warning helped her decide. She felt if the great Wiley Post thought the trip too dangerous, she would prove that she could do it. Earhart made the trip without difficulty, displaying a rare brand of courage.

FEMALE POWER

Earhart's professional life was one continual flirtation with disaster. She had always been obsessed with demonstrating that women were the equal of men both in the air and on the ground. Her determination as a self-sufficient female could possibly be the reason why she took confirmed alcoholic Fred Noonan as navigator on her around-the-world flight. This could have been an unconscious demonstration that she could conquer the air with a less-than-competent male to guide her, but this was probably her worst decision.

Earhart wrote in *The Fun of It* (1932), "I chose to fly the Atlantic because I wanted to. It was . . . a self-justification—a proving to me, and to anyone else interested, that a woman with adequate experience could do it." She used a low-key approach in stating her strong views on femininity, wielding power with dignity and grace. Earhart was one of the first women who dared wear short hair and long pants in complete defiance of the establishment. She flew before she could drive. She had a classy way of doing the opposite of what was expected, and that ability coupled with her tenacity made her great. Her motto was: "If you follow the inner desire of your heart, the incidentals will take care of themselves" (Ware 1993, p. 57). Those inner desires or "gut" instincts were her driving force whether in the air or on the ground.

Manic Success

Amelia Earhart was compelled to be different and constantly defied custom and safety. In one frenetic stretch of a Midwest lecture circuit in the fall of 1933, she delivered twenty-three speeches in twenty-five days, logging seven thousand miles by car mostly alone. In 1935 she took off in a car alone and made 135 personal lecture appearances during one six-week period. This manically driven lady of the air somehow found time to be the aviation editor for *Cosmopolitan,* appear on numerous radio shows, and design and promote her own clothing line while planning her numerous flying exploits. In addition, she wrote articles for *Redbook, McCall's, National Geographic,* and various newspapers including the *New York Times.* Earhart's first book, *Twenty Hours Forty Minutes* (1928), was about her 1928 Atlantic crossing in the *Friendship* and became a best seller. Her second book, *The Fun of It* (1932), was a random collection of various flight records between 1931–1932. During periods of respite, she found time to promote feminism. Eleanor Roosevelt admired Earhart, calling her "inspirational" and one of the "twentieth century's most influential women."

POET AND PHILOSOPHIC VIEW OF LIFE

An introvert, Earhart wrote poetry to express her most innermost feelings about life. Kay Jamison, author of *Touched with Fire* (1993), found that artists with a creative bent were those with high energy. She found many to be manically driven and independent, like Earhart. She illustrated the hypomanic natures of Lord Byron, Honoré de Balzac, Ernest Hemingway, Leo Tolstoy, Georgia O'Keeffe, and Edgar Allan Poe, concluding: "High energy levels and boldness are clearly essential to virtually all creative endeavors" (p. 114). According to Jamison, one of the characteristics of low-level manics is that they will sometime "spontaneously start writing poetry while manic—often without any previous interest in either reading or writing poetry" (p. 108). This is not to conclude that Earhart was a manic-depressive, although she certainly had many of the symptoms. She had a philosophic view of life and saw the world as a whole and not in detail.

HIGH IN TESTOSTERONE

Earhart had a classic Big T (high testosterone and thrill-seeking) personality. Frank Farley, former president of the American Psychological Association and creator of the Type T personality concept, used Earhart as an example in defining the "Thrill Seeker" personality in his research. The Big T personality, according to Farley, has a higher than normal testosterone level and is highly aroused by: uncertainty, unpredictability, high risk, novelty, complexity, ambiguity, low structure, high intensity, and high conflict. Earhart qualifies for the Big T label as she fits every one of the above traits. She had a "yen for novelty and risk" and deplored predictability, structure, and rigidity, meeting the key criteria for the Big T personality.

POWER, INFLUENCE, AND SELF-DESTRUCTION

Amelia Earhart achieved power and influence without any assistance from education, intellectual precocity, money, or socioeconomic status. Her innate power was formed during her early years. Earhart had a strong internal need to prove she was equal to any man and it was this demand for equality that drove her to achieve. She was never the world's best pilot—nor even the best female pilot—and always admitted it. Her power emerged from a quiet confidence in the face of enormous danger, and from her indomitable will and charismatic ability to convey feminine grit. Her daredevil exploits in the air were demonstrations aimed at proving that a woman could compete and succeed in a man's world. Earhart had the appearance of an attractive upper-middle-class housewife but functioned with the aggressive self-assurance of a macho male. She was an attractive woman who *did not have to act like a man,* not unlike Gloria Steinem of a later era. After her first flight, Earhart could easily have become a housewife and lived a carefree existence, but instead chose to demonstrate to the world that a woman could live and risk like a man, while maintaining the dignity of a woman. When she was lost in the Pacific in 1937, the *New York Times* said, "She was in rebellion against a world which had been for women too safe, too unexciting." Her legacy lay in her opening up the skies to women and establishing forever that a woman could be free to achieve in any arena, even one considered "for males only."

Independence and a willingness to risk everything were Earhart's greatest strengths, but they also contributed to her early demise. Self-sufficient to a fault, she never relied on anyone, especially a man. Her power was based on her ability to think as an autonomous and free woman.

This Goddess of Flight had the classic Promethean personality and often neglected important details in pursuit of the larger vision. This inattention to detail and a transcendent—even romantic—approach to her last flight were major factors in its catastrophic ending. She ignored the simplest details, which were of no interest to her. An example of this was her neglecting to install the traditional telegraph radio, a critical communications device for navigational support in that era. After crossing the Atlantic on the first leg of her around-the-world flight, she recognized her error. But by that time she was in Africa and it was too late to correct. Earhart had always preferred to navigate by instinct instead of by instruments. She was engrossed with the possibilities and opportunities of her journey; all else was relegated to the back burner. The challenge of finding a tiny Pacific atoll—Howland Island—after a 27,000-mile journey intrigued this thrill-seeker. Her around-the-world flight was ten thousand miles farther than Wiley Post had gone in his record-setting trip in 1933. It was now 1937 and Earhart was more interested in the challenge of breaking his record and surviving a death-defying gamble than anything else. Typical of her romantic approach to flying, she left behind the most basic safety navigational equipment in order to lighten her load.

Summary

Biographer Doris Rich called Amelia Earhart "pathologically optimistic." She was the consummate risk-taker who disdained anything that would compromise her freedom to function as an independent woman. When her sister, Muriel, was about to get married, Earhart told her, "I don't want *anything* all the time," and later wrote, "I think I may not ever be able to see marriage except as a cage until I am unfit to work or fly." Nevertheless she married the divorced George Putnam and gambled on marriage, even though her real desire was to remain free and independent.

Feminist Susan Brownmiller called Earhart "America's first androgynous sex symbol" (Ware 1993, p. 168). She was a tomboy from mid-America being forced to comply to societal rules. If she had lived in the latter part of the twentieth century, it is a good bet she would never have married. Bowing to pressure from family and friends, she entered a marriage of convenience with George Putnam. The marriage admittedly helped her career since Putnam was a consummate promoter, helping to make hers a household name. This independent spirit despised domesticity and never adapted to the traditional role of wife. Home was never as romantic to her as her flying, and she spent approximately 50 percent of her married life in the air or on tour.

Virtually every time Earhart took off on a flying adventure, she was living on the edge. Her high-risk gambles were made to experience the emotional high of beating the odds and proving her self-worth. The fact that she was a woman who dared to be different, competing with man on his own turf, was the crucial issue. Earhart would have been dumbfounded by the fact that not one female astronaut was selected to walk on the moon in the 1960s and 1970s. She would have been furious that women pilots were purposely excluded when the original Mercury astronauts were chosen in the late fifties. She had been the sixteenth woman in the world to receive an international pilot's license in May 1923, and she got it only after setting the first of many airspeed records in October 1922. She used a tremendous willpower and temerity to become a powerful and influential aviator during an era when women were discouraged from *any* professional career. Earhart was always objective and introspective about her talents and once admitted to a reporter questioning her skills as a pilot, "I'm not the best pilot. What I have is tenacity."

When Earhart took off at 5:56 A.M. on June 1, 1937, from the Miami airport, she had decided that this would be her last "stunt trip." The plane was a new Lockheed Electra donated by Purdue University for her equatorial around-the-world flight. She said prophetically, "I have a feeling there is just one more flight in my system . . . this trip around the world is it" (Rich 1989, p. 257). She was ill-prepared and further risked her chance of success by employing a known alcoholic as navigator. The toughest objective was to land on tiny Howland Island in the middle of the Pacific prior to embarking for Hawaii and then back to the United States.

Earhart had told Putnam a number of times, "When I go, I'd like best to go in my plane. Quickly." She was granted her wish when her plane ran out of fuel somewhere in the South Pacific near the international date line. She would die as she lived—in an airplane flirting with disaster. She had tested fate once too often, but her legacy lives on for all women who need a role model to risk and achieve.

AMELIA EARHART
Pioneering Aviator, Writer, Public Speaker, and Feminist
b. July 24, 1897, Atchison, Kansas; Declared missing July 2, 1937, South Pacific

Dominant Trait: Independence and risk taking
Motto: "Courage is the price that life exacts for granting peace."
Nickname: "Lady Lindy," "Goddess of Flight," "First Lady of the Air"
Vices/Hobbies: "Fast cars, sleek planes, and feminism." Wrote poetry ("Courage").
Heroes/Mentors: Father Edwin, Charles Lindbergh, Eleanor Roosevelt
Philosophy of Life: "If you follow the inner desire of your heart, the incidentals will take care of themselves."
Fantasy: "To go where no one has ever gone"
Professional Successes: Wrote two books: *Twenty-Four Hours Forty-Minutes* (1928); *The Fun of It* (1932). Was an independent feminist who led the way for women to fly and be self-reliant.
Power: Courage, determination, and moxie. "If to dare was to die, then she would die."
Influence: Demonstrated that a women could compete with men. Idolized by all classes of women. First woman to fly Atlantic twice and first to fly Hawaii to California.
Destructiveness: Self-destructiveness caused seven major crashes, many of which were due to "thrill-seeking."

Birth Order: Firstborn with one younger sister, Muriel
Parental Influence: Idolized her father, Edwin, an unsuccessful, alcoholic vagabond-turned-lawyer.
Transiency: Attended high schools in Atchison, Kansas City, Des Moines, St. Paul, and Chicago. "I grew up here and there like a rolling stone." "I've had 28 different jobs in my life and I hope I'll have 228 more."
Crises: Near disaster on sled at age six imprinted her with a fearless tomboy behavior that led to her success as a pilot. She enjoyed the challenge of the unknown, which caused all of her crises.
Formal Education: Graduated from a Chicago high school. Attended Columbia premed, Harvard, and Ogontz. "Experimentation is better than any college education."
Libidinal Drive: "I am unsold on marriage, I don't want anything all of the time." Called "America's first androgynous sex symbol." Wore "lucky" jockey shorts of Gene Vidal on flights.
Personality: Independent maverick; Introvert-Intuitive-Thinker-Perceiver on Myers-Briggs scale.
Self-Esteem: Self-confidence in the face of great odds was her forte.
Rebellion: Her signature long pants and short hair violated social and cultural standards. "I will not live a conventional life and I want to dare all that a man would dare."
Risk Propensity: She flew before she could drive and lived her life on the edge as a thrill-seeker.
Work Ethic: Multitasking personality, writing, flying, lecturing, and running businesses
Tenacity: "I'm not the best pilot. What I have is tenacity."
Optimism: "I am confident of success. . . . I just don't think about crackups."
Manicness: "I've got only one obsession, a small and probably feminine horror of growing old."

Howard Hughes

I can buy any man in the world.

Overview

The billionaire recluse, as Howard Hughes was called in his Las Vegas days, was an extremely shy and introverted personality who became a tiger when put in a sleek airplane or a fast car or was in pursuit of a sexual conquest. Hughes was a perfectionist and control freak, which played an integral part in his rise to fame and fortune. Most people associate Hughes with Las Vegas casinos and TWA. But he was the person most responsible for ending the daredevil era of air piloting and almost singlehandedly launched the era of commercial aviation. Hughes was a daredevil himself during the early thirties, along with Amelia Earhart, Charles Lindbergh, and Wiley Post.

When Hughes landed his Lockheed 14 on New York's Bennet Field on July 14, 1938, he changed aviation history. One year after Earhart's disappearance, Hughes successfully broke Wiley Post's around-the-world record set five years earlier. He broke it by an incredible 50 percent, taking three days, nineteen hours, and seventeen minutes to circumnavigate the world, crossing Europe, Russia, Alaska, and the United States. He had devised a methodical plan, financed it personally to the tune of $300,000, and systematically implemented his plan with no deviations.

Hughes's exploits in Hollywood and Las Vegas overshadow one of his most noteworthy contributions to society. He clearly demonstrated that commercial aviation could be a solid business with tightly scheduled itineraries that could be met with precise planning and organization. He would personally capitalize on this as future owner of TWA and Air West.

POWER AND INFLUENCE

This "eccentric madman" led a thrill-seeking and provocative life. He seduced many of the world's most glamorous women and men, "bought" governors and congressmen, mesmerized the media, and acquired what he couldn't otherwise control.

Risk taking became the basis of Hughes's power through financial leverage. He used his enormous assets as the base to acquire his financial empire, transforming him into the most powerful man in the world between the mid-fifties and late sixties. During these years he reportedly bought and sold senators, governors, Pentagon officials, and a president of the United States. According to biographer Charles Higham (1993), he was "almost comically corrupt" during the period he was building Hughes Aircraft into a powerful government contractor. No less a figure than Franklin Delano Roosevelt's son Elliot came under his influence. Hughes blatantly bought the allegiance of Elliot Roosevelt and Richard Nixon's brother

Donald (Higham 1993, p. 187; Bartlett and Steele 1979, pp. 203–204). Hughes hired actress Faye Emerson to be Elliot Roosevelt's escort during the war years when FDR was president. Hughes's intent was to secure government airplane contracts. Ironically, Emerson and Roosevelt fell in love and were married due in large part to the exotic lifestyle paid for by Hughes (Higham 1993, p. 144; Bartlett and Steele 1979, p. 126). Hughes paid for their stay at the Beverly Hills Hotel and Emerson's racetrack gambling debts, and he gave Elliot Roosevelt $75,000 in cash, according to testimony given before Senator Owen Brewster who investigated wartime government contracts in 1947. The specific contract under congressional investigation concerned the infamous *Hercules* (*Spruce Goose*) which had been awarded to Hughes Aircraft by the air force. Hughes was exonerated of any wrongdoing, which only reinforced his belief that he could use his financial power to buy influence.

MONEY POWER

Hughes became a legend in his own lifetime due to his dashing good looks and gambling lifestyle. He used an invincible willpower to build a vast business empire and then used his financial power to expand further and buy influence. His acquisition mania during the sixties eclipses any ever seen in the annals of business.

Success does breed success and Hughes learned early that he could buy what he couldn't otherwise have. His first successful conquest was the highly unorthodox purchase of screen starlet Billy Dove in 1929 when she was considered the most beautiful woman in Hollywood. Hughes wanted her both professionally and sexually and paid her husband $325,000 ($8 million in today's money) plus another $335,000 to Warner Brothers for her contract. Her professional contract called for five movies; her sexual duties lasted but a short time. His acquisition turned sour when Dove bombed in her movie roles and then sought comfort in the beds of Hollywood's finest. Hughes went crazy when he discovered her in bed with her co-star, George Raft, during the filming of *Scarface*.

Most of Hughes's acquisitions turned out better. He acquired TWA (TransWorld Airlines) through stock purchases but to the chagrin of TWA executives ran it like his own private airline. For years every TWA flight had several seats reserved for Hughes's personal friends and associates. He once arranged a flight for former lover Bette Davis where she was the only passenger. Hedda Hopper and Louella Parsons never paid for a TWA flight anywhere.

CONTROL FREAK

Hughes was a control freak who bought friends and lovers, and even went so far as to buy a hotel just to have his favorite penthouse. During the sixties, when he was becoming increasingly eccentric, he made an impulsive acquisition that would grow into a power base. Hughes was refused his favorite Las Vegas penthouse by the owners of the Desert Inn because it had been reserved by golfers Arnold

Palmer and Jack Nicklaus for the Tournament of Champions. Furious, Hughes promptly bought the property for $13.2 million and moved in on April Fool's Day 1967. He ordered all of the hotel's windows painted black, cancelled the golf tournament and the annual Easter egg hunt, and declared the top floor and penthouse his domicile. At this time Hughes didn't drink, gamble, or entertain. He was essentially a recluse, which made this acquisition strange indeed.

The purchase of the Desert Inn was but one of many that would add to Hughes's reputation as an eccentric. He lived at the Desert Inn for many years, never leaving the penthouse. He also hired Mormons as round-the-clock guards to ensure his privacy.

Hughes's need for ever-increasing power was at the root of his acquisition mania. After establishing Las Vegas as his operating base, he liked to watch television all night to satiate his voyeurism since by this time he was impotent. Because KLAS in Las Vegas didn't broadcast after midnight, Hughes bought the station and changed its broadcasting to an all-night format for his private enjoyment.

During his glory years in Hollywood, Hughes would often call up and reserve a TWA Constellation for one of his female or male conquests. Toward the end of his life, he even hired two full-time guards to catch flies in his bedroom.

To Hughes, money was only as good as what and who it could buy. He used money to control employees, lovers, and business associates.

After Hughes's successful piloting of the *Hercules* (*Spruce Goose*), the U.S. government decided to take possession of this white elephant, which ultimately would have been scrapped. The *Hercules* was Hughes's personal toy and he refused to see it destroyed. He exercised his contractual right to lease the useless flying boat, spending $1 million a year for the next twenty-five years to keep it docked at Long Beach Harbor and under his control.

TYCOON

Hughes's major achievements were in the movies, the airline industry, and Las Vegas casinos. His vast empire revolved around Hughes Tool Company, Hughes Aircraft, TWA and Air West, numerous Las Vegas casinos (Desert Inn, Sands, Frontier, Castaways, Silver Slipper, Landmark, Stardust), movies (RKO studios), gold and silver mines, and miscellaneous radio and television stations. In 1968 *Fortune* magazine listed him as the richest man in the world with a net worth of $1.4 billion. He spent $65 million in one two-year period where he acquired thirty-five hundred (35 percent) of the rooms in Las Vegas and controlled 28 percent of that city's gaming revenues (Bartlett and Steele 1979, p. 316). Columnist Art Buchwald speculated that Hughes was intent on buying up the entire state of Nevada. The Hughes influence ranged from Washington congressmen to stockbrokers who would jump on any stock Hughes was rumored to be buying because of his reputation for having the Midas touch.

Howard Hughes was an enigma. Biographers Donald Bartlett and James Steele summed up his personality as a "fanatical compulsion to control every aspect of his life and environment." His need for control was both personal and professional. It was an obsession that contributed to his great wealth and ultimately made him a slave of his own self-imposed asylum.

Hughes became very rich by making the right move when he was only nineteen: his insistence on total control of Hughes Tool resulted in the brilliant move of buying out his relatives with the firm's own assets. This was his first taste of power and it would grow in concert with his obsessions.

Hughes's behavior became bizarre as he grew older, and his idiosyncrasies transformed him into a paranoid eccentric who became mentally incompetent. Hughes had an obsession to control everything and ended up controlling nothing, including his own person. The *Chicago Tribune* described him as "power gone berserk." He had carefully nursed his image for thirty years and it was destroyed during the last fifteen years of his life when the news broke of his reclusive and eccentric lifestyle. He is now viewed with scorn and ridicule as a childish man with ten-inch-long fingernails and wearing no clothes. Nevertheless, Howard Hughes became a legend in his own lifetime due to his willingness to risk and win big.

Early Life Experiences and Influences

Howard Hughes was born on Christmas Eve 1905 to Dallas socialite Allene Gano and oil wildcatter Howard Hughes, Sr. His entrepreneurial father became his professional role model and his hypochondriac mother became his personal role model. Howard Sr. was willing to risk anything to win. He was a high-rolling gambler, incorrigible womanizer, and Type A workaholic. His mother was just the opposite. Allene Gano was told she was unable to have any more children after young Howard and devoted her short life to fulfilling her son's every wish. Allene was psychosomatic and neurotic, and feared germs and infections, a fear she instilled in her child. Her preoccupation with germs and disease taught him that feigning illness could attract attention and gain sympathy while masking problems. Hughes's biographers suggest that his mother "was obsessed with her son's physical and emotional condition . . . and helped instill in him lifelong phobias about his physical and mental state" (Bartlett and Steele 1979, p. 45). As a teenager, Hughes supposedly contracted polio and spent months in a wheelchair. He miraculously recovered when the doctors could find nothing wrong with him. As an adult Howard found illness a convenient way to escape day-to-day problems, and developed a habit of jumping into an airplane alone and disappearing, sometimes for months at a time. It was his mental health therapy. His most notorious disappearances occurred during his three nervous breakdowns in the mid-thirties, early forties, and early fifties.

Young Howard closely bonded with his mother during his early years since his father was often absent. Like most entrepreneurial geniuses he had a transient childhood and spent a great deal of time alone. His rambunctious father moved from one oil strike to another to seek his fortune. Oil would not be the brass ring, but oil bits were. His father moved the family to Shreveport, Louisiana, when young Howard was eighteen months old. It was there that Howard Sr. created the oil tool bit on November 20, 1908, which would become the foundation of the Hughes fortune. During this period relatives remembered young Howard "idolizing his mother," while Howard Sr. was busy developing the Rock Eater Tool Bit.

When Hughes was three, his family moved back to Houston where Howard Sr. formed the Hughes Tool Company to manufacture and distribute the oil tool bit. Hughes began his schooling at the private Prosser Academy. He demonstrated some mechanical aptitude in school, which was encouraged by his father, but he showed little interest in normal schoolwork. At age ten Hughes was enrolled in a New York State summer camp where he learned to cope on his own for the first time. At age fifteen he entered Fessenden, a preparatory school in Boston, Massachusetts. He was good at math and became skilled at golf. On a trip to Fessenden, his father lost a bet with him on a Harvard football game, and this wager had a major impact on young Howard's life. He was fifteen years old when Howard Sr. paid off the bet by taking him for a ride in a Curtiss seaplane. This exhilarating experience spawned a lifetime passion in Hughes which was never satisfied.

HOMOSEXUALITY, BRIBERY, AND CRISIS

Howard Hughes, Sr., decided that Boston was too far from his expanding business in California. In 1921 he decided to enroll his son in the Thacher School in Santa Barbara, California, which was close to the Southern California oil industry and to the family's new home on Coronado Island, San Diego.

In many ways this move would have a profound impact on Hughes's life. His uncle Rupert Hughes was a screenwriter who introduced young Howard to the exotic life of Hollywood. He also introduced him to bisexuality by seducing the fifteen-year-old.

Howard Sr. added another negative dimension to his son's character by bribing Anson Thacher to admit young Howard to a school that was already full. His father offered to build the school a new dormitory if Howard were accepted.

While Hughes was at Thacher, his mother died from what historians have labeled an unnecessary operation after she suffered hemorrhaging from the womb. His despondent father removed sixteen-year-old Howard from Thacher prior to his graduation and enrolled him at the California Institute of Technology in Pasadena. Since his son had not earned a high school diploma, Howard Sr. donated money to the school's scholarship fund in return for his son's acceptance at Cal Tech.

Hughes's father persuaded his sister-in-law Annette Gano to act as mother to her nephew, and she moved in with the family. She complained that "they [Cal Tech] were bribed to let him in" and she disapproved of young Howard's being taught to buy his way through life using financial power. Howard's father then decided to move the family back to Houston. Once again he resorted to influence, convincing Rice University officials to accept his son as a student.

Just over a year later tragedy struck again when Howard Sr. dropped dead of a heart attack on January 14, 1924. It had been less than two years since his mother's tragic death. Hughes suddenly found himself alone at age eighteen. One month later he dropped out of Rice University and started planning his future. He was already obsessed with death and in a state of shock over losing both parents. His inheritance amounted to $450,000, all in the form of Hughes Tool stock, of which he owned 75 percent. The precocious teenager evaluated his options and within four months of his father's death decided to buy out his relatives in order to have absolute control of Hughes Tool. With unusual insight for a youth, he resorted to leverage by using company funds amounting to $325,000 to pay off his relatives. Hughes had learned well from his father: He didn't want any partners, especially relatives whom he would have a tough time controlling.

Hughes was intent on becoming the master of his fate and, to prohibit anyone from challenging his control over Hughes Tool, he petitioned a judge to have himself declared "of full age." The judge granted his petition, but leaving nothing to chance, Hughes ensured his adult status by proposing to Ella Rice, a descendant of the founders of Rice University. He had attended kindergarten with Ella and felt that her status as a debutante would contribute to the image he needed as chief executive officer of a major corporation. He was not about to have a guardian tell him how to operate his business.

Because of his obsession with disease, Hughes avoided traditional bachelor parties and spent his entire engagement period preparing a ten-page will in which he created the Howard R. Hughes Medical Research Laboratory. Such preoccupation with death is not normal behavior for a nineteen-year-old about to be married.

Ella Rice and Howard Hughes were married on June 1, 1925, and moved to Los Angeles, where they bought a Rolls-Royce and took up residence at the Ambassador Hotel. This is where the legend of Howard Hughes begins.

A Live-on-the-Edge Lifestyle

Hughes was shy, polite, and introverted. Only when he was behind the throttle of a plane did he become an aggressive extrovert. Despite his inclination for solitude, he found comfort in uncertainty and risky ventures: It was his way of releasing internal stress and energy. His first ventures in the movie industry were not for the faint-hearted. Hughes fit in well and directors, actors, and actresses soon learned of his obsessive perfectionism. He hired and fired on the set and ultimately became the producer, director, and costume manager for most of his early films. He made his first movie, *Everybody's Acting,* at age twenty-one. No one in Hollywood took him seriously except himself. The impulsive and impatient Hughes lost millions learning the ropes in Hollywood, but total control of the creative process and 100 percent ownership were always more important to him than the return on his investment.

OBSESSIVE ENTREPRENEUR

After arriving in Los Angeles, Hughes started taking flying lessons and planes soon became his passion. He was fascinated with World War I flying aces and their fighter planes, which motivated him to finance and produce two flying movies during the twenties: *Two Arabian Knights* about the western front in WWI, which won an Academy Award in 1928, and *Hell's Angels.* Hughes became so obsessed with the movie *Hell's Angels* that he purchased eighty-seven vintage fighter planes for the film, making him the proud owner of the world's largest private air force. Only the United States, Britain, and France had larger air forces.

In a scene that would be repeated throughout his life, Hughes couldn't resist jumping into the cockpit of one of the planes used in filming. It was a Thomas Morse fighter and he decided to take it for a spin even though he had no idea of how to fly it. At four hundred feet the plane went into a spin and crashed at Mines Field in Inglewood, California. Hughes was pulled unconscious from the crumpled plane and suffered a crushed cheekbone that required surgery.

Three pilots died during the filming of *Hell's Angels,* and one of these fatalities was due to Hughes's preoccupation with perfection. He decided to film a burning German bomber in a death dive. The two pilots on the plane were to parachute to safety after putting the plane into the dive. Pilot Phil Jones was not able to get out of the bomber. Little did movie audiences realize that the scene they saw in the theater actually showed a man perishing in the spectacular crash.

TYPE A PERSONALITY

After Hughes spent eighteen months and $2 million on the production of *Hell's Angels,* Al Jolson's sound movie, *The Jazz Singer,* was released in 1927, making silent movies obsolete overnight. Coming so close to its release, most people would have been discouraged, but the irrepressible Hughes became more determined to produce the world's greatest air movie. He set out to find a sultry-voiced female lead and settled on Jean Harlow, who he made a star. He then gambled another $1.8 million in producing a talking version of the movie, bringing its total cost to $3.8 million. *Hell's Angels* was released in 1930 and lost $1.5 million, but established Hughes as a big-time Hollywood producer. It also proved that he was a risk-taker of the first order.

The production madness of *Hell's Angels* would be repeated often. Hughes's style was to produce expensive movies, dominated by sex and frenetic action, but with little or no redeeming philosophical message. His obsession with perfection and control were becoming obvious to anyone who worked with him. Biographer Charles Higham (1993) wrote: "He had to dominate in everything" (p. 34). As both producer and director, Hughes often worked twenty-four to thirty-six hours straight without rest, demonstrating his Type A behavior. He seldom left the studio, leaving his wife, Ella, alone in their hotel room, which cost him his marriage within two years.

Hughes lived on the edge in cars as well as in the air, and drove with reckless abandon. He was responsible for the death of one pedestrian during this period, but once again was able to get himself out of this crisis.

A DEATH-WISH MENTALITY

In September 1935 Hughes had his second brush with death while setting a speed record with his personally designed H-1 air racer. He broke the French record of 314 miles per hour set by Raymond Delmotte on September 12, 1935, in Orange County, with a speed of 352 miles per hour; Amelia Earhart was one of the judges. Carrying a small fuel supply to save weight, Hughes pushed the plane and himself beyond reasonable limits. He refused to bail out for fear of destroying his pet plane and crash-landed it, jeopardizing his own life. The aviation world was captivated by his sleek air racer design. They were also appalled at his bravado in staying with the plane. Hughes would repeat this behavior often.

Hughes's next major crash occurred in May 1943 while test piloting a Sikorsky seaplane intended for the air force. When asked by an FAA (Federal Aviation Agency) official why a business tycoon was piloting the craft, Hughes responded, "Why should I pay somebody else to have all the fun?" The Sikorsky crashed and sank in 165 feet of water in Lake Mead near his future home in Las Vegas. Hughes was badly hurt with multiple lacerations and was in severe shock when pulled out of the water. He had escaped serious injury while passengers Richard Felt and William Cline were killed and aeronautics inspector Charles Rosenberg suffered a shattered spine. The crash was attributed to miscommunications between Hughes and the ground crew with incorrect loading that altered the plane's center of gravity according to a federal investigation.

In his last crash, Hughes was also flying as test pilot and this time the air force found him guilty of pilot error. Flying an XF-11 at Culver City, California, on July 8, 1946, Hughes violated numerous FAA regulations, causing a crash that the air force concluded could have been avoided had he "attempted an emergency landing" instead of pushing the new plane beyond reasonable limits. "This accident was avoidable after propeller trouble was experienced" (Senate War Hearings, August 1947, p. 20) had Hughes exercised reasonable caution. But that was never Hughes's style. He loaded the plane with twice the required fuel; retracted the landing gear, which was not supposed to occur until the second test flight; and committed numerous infractions including a violation of the forty-five-minute flight test limit.

Hughes crashed an hour and fifteen minutes into the flight. He could have avoided the disaster had he landed the plane in a field or on a road. The obstreperous Hughes refused to do this and it almost cost him his life. The plane went out of control, crashed into a house in Los Angeles, and caught fire. Hughes was trapped in the plane, suffering a collapsed lung and his heart pushed to the other side of his chest cavity. When pulled from the wreck, Hughes was in severe shock. On the ambulance trip to the hospital, he was screaming in pain. He spent days hovering near death, and his recovery was short of a miracle.

No one in the emergency room thought he would live. Hughes was irate when the air force refused to allow him to pilot the next version of the XF-11 just one year later. He flew it anyway on April 5, 1947, for ninety minutes in Culver City. He then flew to Washington to appeal their ruling and agreed to "pay the government $5 million if the plane crashed with him at the controls"! He would never again fly as a test pilot since this last crash had taken its toll on his body and neurological system. He was never content living a safe life which augmented his swashbuckling image but also contributed to his demise. His injuries also caused him to become addicted to morphine and codeine, and this addiction was the cause of his impotency. Within five years of the crash, Hughes became incapacitated both mentally and emotionally. His live-on-the-edge lifestyle had made him into an icon but would lead him to become a reclusive eccentric.

Obsessive-Compulsive Personality

Howard Hughes never did anything in moderation: everything was done in excess, obsessionally, compulsively, impatiently, and impulsively. He had a manic-depressive personality and owed much of his success to the manic side of that illness. This iconoclast would interview beautiful young women for movie roles and his own titillation. Never one to abide by normal business practices, he refused to allow them to wear makeup in order to better judge their true beauty. An eccentric with a social conscience, during his youth he sold his Rolls-Royce because it polluted the Los Angeles air, a move thirty years ahead of its time. When he filmed *Hell's Angels,* instead of renting planes, he purchased eighty-seven vintage aircraft in his manic need for control.

Hughes's compulsions and obsessions were often bizarre. He was an insomniac who slept but a few hours at a time. For years he ate the precise same food for dinner and never varied: a medium rare steak, twelve peas (no more, no less), and vanilla ice cream for dessert. This meal was never varied or the cook was fired. During the day he ate Hershey Bars, pecans, and drank whole milk. No wonder he was always constipated and once spent forty-eight straight hours sitting on a toilet, holding business meetings during his vigil.

Hughes suffered three nervous breakdowns that appear to have been caused by severe anxiety and obsessive need for perfection and control. When unable to control a situation, he would disappear or become physically ill or, in the case of the TWA debt, have a nervous breakdown. He ordered sixty-three jetliners worth over $400 million from Convair and Boeing and was unable to pay for them. He exhibited bizarre behavior just prior to his breakdowns and in this case, talked ten hours without stop with Bob Hummel, the chief engineer at TWA.

Often Hughes would get in a plane and just disappear. His most bizarre vanishing act occurred in 1946 during the TWA debt quandary. Hughes turned up missing after he and a group landed a plane in Shreveport, Louisiana. (This was possibly a nostalgic regression since he had lived in Shreveport as a child.) He was discovered in jail, having been arrested as a vagrant. A week later he mysteriously disappeared in Florida and was not found for a period of three months. When he reappeared at the New York Plaza Hotel, Hughes was dressed in a tuxedo and sneakers and carried two douche bags and a dental drill in a black bag. Such bizarre behavior contributed to his image as an eccentric billionaire.

Hughes's obsessive-compulsive behavior bordered on pathology. An example is the following excerpt he wrote as instructions for removing his hearing aid cord from a cabinet:

> First use six or eight thicknesses of Kleenex pulled one at a time from the slot in touching the doorknob to open the door to the bathroom. The door is to be left open so there will be no need to touch anything when leaving the bathroom. The same sheaf of Kleenex may be employed to turn on the spigots so as to obtain a good force of warm water. This Kleenex is then to be disposed of. . . . The hands are to be washed with extreme care, far more thoroughly than they have ever been washed before, taking great pains that the hands do not touch the sides of the bowl, the spigots, or anything in the process. (Ludwig 1995, p. 128)

ENTREPRENEURIAL MADNESS

Hughes was not yet thirty when he disappeared for months and was discovered masquerading as an American Airlines pilot by the media. He had adroitly decided to carry out his own market research. There was usually a hidden agenda to Hughes's strange behavior.

Hughes had a remarkable memory and a true entrepreneurial bent. In this instance, he had applied at American Airlines in order to get inside their corporate operations and find out the nuances of the commercial airline industry. He was first hired as a lowly baggage handler and was promoted to copilot. Hughes was contemplating the acquisition of TWA and wanted to understand the commercial airline business from the ground up. He earned $250 a month using the name Charles Howard as an alias. As soon as his identity was known, American terminated him. A few years later he began buying up TWA stock.

Megalomaniac on a Mission

Hughes was manically driven in all he did. When he made movies, he worked day and night and was inconsiderate of associates. When he decided to break speed records, he was intolerant of the least little item left unplanned. This manic perfectionism contributed to his success at breaking flying records, making epic movies, and in analyzing new business opportunities.

Hughes was also manic about his sexual conquests, and repeatedly proposed to Hollywood starlets on the first date, once offering Elizabeth Taylor a million dollars to marry him. He fantasized about female breasts, giving credence to an oral personality. His obsessive behavior was never more blatant than in his making of the movie *The Outlaw*, starring Jane Russell. He spent many sleepless nights designing brassieres that would pass the support test while achieving maximum exposure for Russell's movie part. To his credit, his designs proved quite innovative technologically and anticipated the modern era of bra-making.

Biographer Charles Higham (1993) describes Hughes's film-making obsessions as a "masturbatory frenzy": "No other individual in commercial Hollywood had so completely released his sexual urges on the screen, and nobody would for decades" (p. 98). *The Outlaw* was banned by the movie censors, but the tenacious Hughes would not be denied. He was rich enough to fight the system and shelved the film, releasing it in 1946 in complete defiance of the film industry's ban. The film was approved after he filed in San Francisco a five-million-dollar lawsuit against the Motion Picture Producers for interference with trade. He won his suit when the judge found nothing disgusting about breasts.

PSYCHOSEXUAL DRIVE

Hughes's manic lifestyle was most pronounced in his pursuit of women. His depravity exceeded that of the Marquis de Sade. Hughes loved group sex and perversity. While in bed recovering from spinal meningitis at age twenty, he had an affair with a young starlet. His wife, Ella, caught him in the act and he beat her black and blue, which caused her to leave him (Higham 1993, p. 36). Hughes always preferred fellatio with either sex. An affair with Carole Lombard finally ended his first marriage. He asked women to marry him on the first date, whether they were married or single, and without any intention of keeping his promise. He had an obsessive need to own women or he didn't want them. He often engaged in concurrent sexual trysts with both women and men. He would sleep with one woman at lunch, another at dinner, and a third on his yacht that evening. His stable of lovers included the most ravishing queens and kings of Tinseltown, including Carole Lombard, Ginger Rogers, Jean Harlow, Katharine Hepburn, Bette Davis, Tyrone Power, Cary Grant, and Randolph Scott. He was sleeping with all of these stars during the same period in the mid-thirties. Hughes asked all these women to marry him. He succeeded in impregnating Susan Hayward and Rita Hayworth, and married Terry Moore aboard his yacht which he had deceitfully floated outside the legal limits at twelve miles. Jean Peters finally got him to the altar after he was fifty and impotent. His other sexual conquests included Lana Turner, Jean Simmons, Ava Gardner, Billy Dove, Linda Darnell, Ida Lupino, Debra Paget, Gene Tierney, Mitzi Gaynor, Barbara Hutton, Barbara Payton, Marlene Dietrich, Yvonne de Carlo, and Joan Fontaine, as well as numerous show girls and anyone else who happened to be attractive and available. The number of attractive and talented women who slept with him because he was powerful is amazing since they often admitted that he was disgustingly dirty and unkempt. This is a sad commentary on power and the women who succumb to it.

Hughes's mania and obsessive need for control became his Achilles' heel. He used and abused women, and never had one become his friend or companion.

When he became mentally incompetent and a prisoner of his self-imposed asylum in the Desert Inn, he had no one to turn to for help. He desperately needed someone to help him escape his deluded world of drugs and emotional trauma. The only people within his inner circle were those very people who would benefit by his incapacity: his guards and administrators. Hughes had created his own self-imposed sanctuary where his guards kept him safe but insured his slavery.

Power and Influence

Charismatic charm and financial power defined the early Howard Hughes. His debonair good looks and charm were instrumental in his rise to power. After his many risk-taking antics in airplanes and his movie successes where he "made" stars, he became enormously powerful and influential. When charismatic power failed, he resorted to economic power.

Hughes's flamboyant image was real and often dramatized by the media. His daredevil escapades, renegade lifestyle, off-the-wall acquisitions, and rebelliousness attracted the media in droves and Hughes very carefully manipulated them to suit his own needs. His air crashes and governmental fights only added to his scandalous but romantic image. Shyness and introversion were positive traits for such a dynamic tycoon and caused everyone to listen when he did speak. His tirades before Congress were headline events with the masses applauding his audacity for standing up to the bureaucrats in Washington. Public opinion formed by his well-honed image helped him win many battles that would have otherwise been lost.

Hughes was a master manipulator of the press and used the media with more insight than almost anyone during his era. Columnists Hedda Hopper and Louella Parsons always traveled free on TWA and were met by block-length limousines on their arrival. Effectively bribed, they ensured that his pristine image remained intact.

Hughes's suave demeanor and dashing good looks helped him circumvent rules others were forced to obey. When building his Las Vegas gambling empire, he knew Nevada needed his right-wing conservative image in a town known to be operated by gangsters. Hughes's will and charisma made him financially successful and when his economic base was established he deftly used his financial power to dominate the opposition. Publicity helped Hughes create his image as the most powerful man in the world, but in the end it earned him the more accurate reputation as the world's greatest kook.

Financial Power

Howard Hughes built his industrial empire through the use of financial leverage in much the same way Ted Turner and Rupert Murdoch do today. Using his asset base to finance new acquisitions was the tool he used to create his empire. He developed very little from scratch but methodically bought those elements that appealed to his dream and intuitive vision. Hughes's industrial empire was acquired, with the exception of his early entrepreneurial ventures in Hughes Tool, the movies, Hughes Aircraft, and TWA. His early ventures earned him a reputation as a pioneering innovator, but in reality he bought the majority of his companies. He bought control of TWA, RKO, Air West, and owned his mining and real-estate interests outright. Hughes could not stand losing and was willing to spend whatever it took to accomplish his objectives. Control and perfectionism were his forte. He always placed excellence above monetary considerations. Whatever Hughes did was with complete dedication and perfection, regardless of cost. History has vindicated his actions and his risk-taking mentality made him rich and famous.

Hughes spent $300,000 during the Great Depression to break the around-the-world speed record. In the middle of the Depression, this was seen as an arrogant and wasteful act of a wealthy playboy. It was, in fact, a pathfinding effort financed privately.

Numerous air exploits and foolhardy investments added to the image of "The Eccentric Billionaire." He was an innovative movie producer who had a knack for selecting neophyte talent like Jean Harlow, Paul Muni, and Jane Russell and turning them into famous stars. Hughes was a master manipulator of financial and human resources and had a unique intuitive sense of timing and need. He was great at creating new organizations, but totally inadequate at running them. Hughes Aircraft and TWA were testaments to his manic drive to be the very best but he could never have worked in these firms. His flying boat, the *Hercules* (*Spruce Goose*) was the one creation which fit his egomania. He intuitively knew this plane would never fly and had zero commercial value, but his strength was in building it just for the publicity value.

SPRUCE GOOSE—A PUBLICITY WINDFALL

The *Hercules* (the official product name used in government contracts) had been touted as a savior in World War II when in 1942 German submarines were sinking ships faster than American industrialist Henry Kaiser could build them. Kaiser concocted the idea of a flying boat that could safely transport men and supplies to Europe. Kaiser knew he was incapable of building the plane and recommended it be built by the entrepreneur Howard Hughes. The huge plane appealed to Hughes's ego since it was the largest ever built. (It had eight engines, was three stories high, had a wingspan longer than a football field, and weighed two hundred tons—three times the weight of any airplane in existence.) It so appealed to Hughes that he was willing to invest $50 million of his own money in addition to $22 million in government funding. With the war over and the plane not needed, Hughes was contractually committed to turn it over to the air force. Instead, he leased it back and spent another $25 million for storage at $1 million per year. No one understood such economic logic, including his executives. The ever-astute Hughes knew the plane's enormous publicity value. He also was entranced by the idea of being the creator and the only man to have ever flown it. The plane was a testament to his own ego.

Hughes's logic was lost on the bureaucratic congressmen who accused him of bilking the taxpayers out of millions of dollars to build the *Spruce Goose,* knowing it would never be used. Senator Ralph Owen Brewster became Hughes's worst adversary in Congress and began crusading against Hughes. Brewster forced the reclusive Hughes to appear before Congress on November 2, 1947, to prove he did not purposely cheat the government in building the *Spruce Goose.* Brewster was convinced Hughes would not appear and suggested Hughes be fined for building a white elephant. The congressional hearing occurred only one year after Hughes's XF-11 crash, which almost cost him his life. Hughes shocked everyone by appearing before the committee, defending himself and the *Spruce Goose* in his flamboyant style. He told reporters: "If the plane is judged a failure I will probably leave the country and never come back."

The irrepressible Hughes used his charisma to win the support of the press and the public who saw him as a champion of individual rights. The audience continually cheered him on during the hearings and Hughes was buoyed by its support, arrogantly declaring, "Goddamn the Senators."

In typical Hughes fashion, he flew back to Long Beach, intent on proving that his prized possession could fly. On November 1, 1947, he personally flew the *Hercules* and had it airborne for a mile over Long Beach Harbor. This was the first and last flight ever for the ill-famed flying boat.

WILLPOWER

Willpower was the dominating ingredient in the success of Howard Hughes. He inherited a firm (Hughes Tool) that he could not manage himself, but was smart enough to hire those who could after buying out those who could have opposed him. He then proved wrong those who predicted his early demise in Hollywood. When TWA tossed him out, he persevered to earn an unprecedented $547 million by selling his 6.5 million TWA shares on May 3, 1966. It was this huge windfall gain and potential tax liability that caused Hughes to move to Las Vegas in order to avoid California taxes. This was just another example of his will to determine and control his own destiny. He then went on to use those monies to build his Las Vegas gambling casino empire.

A testimony to Hughes's willpower and entrepreneurial flare was the *Spruce Goose* project. No corporation could have ever achieved what Hughes did with the *Spruce Goose*: No one would have taken the initial risk and no board of directors would have sanctioned the contract or the plane's design or construction. Self-preservation and a preoccupation with the balance sheet are the guiding principles of all mature organizations. But Hughes had a larger vision and used the *Hercules* as a vehicle to achieve his larger objective for building Hughes Aircraft into a strong competitor of Lockheed and other aerospace conglomerates. The *Spruce Goose* helped him acquire a reputation as the creator of radical new concepts and an enterprising individual who could deliver on high-risk projects. It was this reputation which allowed Hughes Aircraft to become the preeminent contractor for satellite and missile development, which made the firm dominant during the "Star Wars" years. Hughes singlehandedly created the innovative image that was responsible for winning those huge contracts.

Hughes was perceived as an individual capable of doing the impossible since he dared to be different. His risk mentality worked in concert with his irresolute willpower. In Hughes's case, it was his reputation that made him successful and powerful. History has shown him to be right as Hughes Aircraft, now owned by General Motors, is the preeminent space industry manufacturer.

A Paradox

Howard Hughes was not afraid to risk his life in wild flying escapades, yet was scared to death of a housefly. An introvert, he could also be extremely aggressive and vocally competitive. He was personally frugal but professionally wild with money. He had earned a reputation as a spendthrift who repeatedly blew millions on airplanes, movies, women, and casinos while personally living an ascetic lifestyle.

Hughes always spent money with abandon but never without a master plan. When a project did not meet his long-term objectives, he refused to spend a dime. He had a dashing playboy image of a man who could make stars and buy companies with abandon, yet he was shy and taciturn when confronted at a party. His power attracted women in droves, but they soon became disenchanted when they found him uncouth, dirty, thoughtless, and totally self-indulgent.

Robert Maheu was able to gain power vicariously through the use of the Hughes name. He bought and sold millions in Las Vegas real estate and casinos without having met Hughes. Using his name was enough. Maheu's power was "titular": It was given by Hughes and then taken away, and Maheu was destroyed in the process. Hughes had hired Maheu by phone. Maheu, a former FBI agent, handled many of Hughes's problems like leaning on those who would expose him and showing up in those places Hughes refused to go. Maheu said: "He was the poorest man as well as the richest in the world" (Higham 1993, p. 193). Hughes had another long-term employee, Bill Gay, terminate Maheu, not having the guts to do it personally, which instigated a $50 million lawsuit for breach of contract.

The power of Howard Hughes was never more evident than with the Clifford Irving fake biography. Irving worked under the assumption from information received from Maheu that the reclusive Hughes would never come out of his self-ordained asylum to deny the integrity of the book. Irving was so convinced of this that he was able to convince the conservative McGraw-Hill publishing house of its authenticity. Hughes had been secluded for fifteen years, giving Irving reason to believe the stories of his inability to function in public. When McGraw-Hill announced to the press the "absolute authenticity" of the book, Hughes agreed to a multinetwork radio interview with reporters from the Associated Press, the *New York Times,* the *Los Angeles Times,* the *Chicago Tribute,* United Press International, and NBC from his hideaway in the Britannia Beach Hotel in the Bahamas, which took place on Friday, January 7, 1972. On Monday morning, January 10, the exposé of the hoax was headlines across the nation. Clifford Irving confessed and was sentenced to two and a half years in prison and fined $10,000.

Hughes's renegade image also accounted for so many fake wills surfacing after his death. Intriguing stories of a fortune being left to a gas station attendant could only have occurred with someone with Hughes's reputation.

Destructiveness

Howard Hughes was a destructive person who destroyed not only others but also himself. After he had successfully created stars like Carole Lombard, Jean Harlow, Paul Muni, and Jane Russell, he was able to use that reputation to his own advantage. Every attractive young female became fair game for this chauvinist who signed budding stars to long-term contracts and then closeted them away for years.

Many of Hughes's high-risk ventures often resulted in losses as well as profits. His manic need to control was usually responsible for these losses. He once gambled and lost $100 million on a helicopter project at Hughes Tool. Scam artist John Meier duped Hughes out of $20 million in worthless mining properties. Hughes ultimately won a $7.9 million judgment against him, but Meier escaped to Australia and Hughes was left with a lot of worthless Nevada real estate.

The acquisition and destruction of Air West was classic Hughes. The airline was popularly known as Air Worst when Hughes parlayed his TWA reputation to entice the stockholders to accept his takeover at a time when the firm was verging on bankruptcy. He offered the company $89 million or $22 per share and adroitly wrote in fine print that the price would change based on stock price changes and the effect on the balance sheet. The naive shareholders sold out to Hughes. The stock and balance sheet declines allowed Hughes to pay only $33 million or $8.75 per share—37 percent—of what had been agreed to. Many people were destroyed by engaging in business with this ruthless business tycoon.

Even though he was a vocal adversary of nuclear testing in Nevada, Hughes was inadvertently to blame for the premature deaths of a number of top Hollywood stars due to radiation contamination. He fought the government testing, but when he lost and it was time to shoot film footage near the nuclear site in northern Nevada, he sent the unfortunate stars on location. The nuclear test took place in 1963 and John Wayne, Susan Hayward, Agnes Moorehead, and other crew members were on-site. All these stars died of cancer contracted while filming *The Conqueror* for Hughes.

Hughes's greatest destruction was to himself. Seven air crashes took their toll on him both physically and mentally. His last crash in 1946 apparently did irreparable damage to his emotional and mental faculties. He vacillated between life and death and became addicted to demerol, codeine, and valium, which destroyed his kidneys. He spent the last twenty years of his life deprived of everything he loved. He became impotent in his early fifties and was no longer capable of socializing or negotiating the business deals that were his lifeblood.

After his last crash, Hughes became a slave of his paranoid delusions and a recluse with bodyguards watching his every move. His reckless lifestyle had caused him to become incapable of fornicating, flying, golfing, or negotiating. At a time when he was acclaimed the most powerful man in the world, he was incapable of going out to a movie. This master manipulator of women, business, and people ended up unable to control his own self, including his bowels. Paranoia, germs, and delusions governed his life. He lived his last fifteen years as a slave to drugs, alone except for his bodyguards. His power had led him to a barren existence where he was king of everything and nothing.

Risk—A Double-Edged Sword

Howard Hughes was blessed with good looks, money, and a resilient spirit. He gambled away most of these gifts for power and influence. His success made him into one of the world's richest and most powerful men. By the time he had reached the pinnacle of success and power, he was in his fifties and impotent. He had long since lost all friends, including his lover Cary Grant. Hughes became an emotional cripple incapable of the most basic acts. He had gambled and won the battle of business and lost the war of life.

Virtually every other subject in this book started in life with less of everything than Howard Hughes, but none ended up with so little. Even the tragic Edith Piaf and the despotic Adolf Hitler ended life better than Howard Hughes. Hughes learned early that he could buy influence. That education proved unfortunate as he spent his life trying to buy things that were not for sale like love, friends, pleasure, integrity, and happiness.

Taking gambles while young created Howard Hughes's mystique but destroyed him physically and mentally. When he could no longer fly, he resorted to the vicarious pleasure of buying airlines. When he could no longer make love, he lay in bed and fantasized over illusory female conquests in old movies. Mormon guards were hired because of their ascetic lifestyle and honesty, yet he didn't trust even them. Toward the end of his life, Hughes attempted to satiate his need to make deals and squandered millions on phony silver and gold mines because he was incapable of managing his own affairs. He would not have been so bamboozled had he been capable of monitoring these investments. Being a recluse in his own private asylum—a Desert Inn room on the Las Vegas strip—made him dependent and vulnerable. Had he understood the motivations of people like he knew machines he would have been able to survive by giving equity incentives to a lover or associate or even Jean Peters. They would then have had an incentive to support him.

Hughes used people and money to fit his own perverse sense of reality. The sad fact is that he ended up with only one real friend whose friendship was not based on business or sex. That was Jack Real, a Lockheed executive and pilot whom Hughes had hired toward the end of his life. The self-serving Hughes even slighted Real in addition to his own family members by refusing to sign a will. His egocentric need for control never allowed him to admit that he needed anyone or anything, and consequently he died alone and desperate.

The Hughes Medical Institute was established in Miami as his personal tax dodge. It was never used to help anyone except Hughes during his life. It is appropriate that this institute has invested $500 million on education during the 1990s.

Hughes always had a perverse obsession with wills, sickness, and death. This risk-taking entrepreneur was capable of the most audacious personal and professional ventures yet was never able to tolerate so much as a housefly on his person. High risk made him into a powerful tycoon but it cost him his sanity and physical well being. "Power and influence are fleeting," and Howard Hughes is proof of this axiom.

HOWARD ROBARD HUGHES
Aviator, Business Tycoon, and Movie Mogul
b. December 24, 1905, Houston, Texas; d. April 4, 1976, Acapulco, Mexico

Dominant Trait: Obsessive risk-taker, compulsive perfectionist, and control freak

Motto: "I can buy any man in the world."

Nickname: "Sonny" (childhood), "Eccentric Madman" (media), "Eccentric Billionaire Madman"

Vices/Hobbies: Flying; women; movies; golf; homosexual affairs; cigarettes; addiction to codeine, valium, and demerol

Heroes/Mentors: Father and Uncle Rupert, bisexual movie writer who introduced him to homosexual lifestyle

Philosophy of Life: "I want to become the world's number-one golfer, top aviator, and world's most famous motion picture producer, then the richest man in the world."

Fantasy: Medical industry savior and most powerful man in world

Professional Successes: Around-the-world flight record. Made stars of Jean Harlow, Paul Muni, Jane Russell. Owned TWA, Hughes Aircraft, Hughes Tool, and 30 percent of Las Vegas casinos.

Power: Money, dashing image, and very handsome. *Chicago Tribune*: "Power gone berserk."

Influence: Bought newspapers and government officials. Midas touch image caused the world of business and finance to jump at his every move. If he couldn't have his way, he bought it (Desert Inn).

Destructiveness: Most of seven plane crashes caused by his violation of rules. Perpetually lived on the edge with personal and professional death wish. Killed pedestrian, bought freedom.

Birth Order: Only child of Howard Hughes, Sr., and Dallas socialite Allene Gano

Parental Influence: Inherited $600k Hughes Tool started by incorrigible father. Mother had neurotic preoccupation with disease, making him a hypochondriac.

Transiency: Born in Houston, moved at age two to Shreveport, and back to Houston at age three. In boarding schools from age ten in Boston (Fessenden) and California (Thacher).

Crises: Everyone he loved died during his teen years: mother died when sixteen; Aunt Adelaid hanged herself aboard ship six months later; father died of heart attack when he was nineteen.

Formal Education: Houston (Prosser Academy), Connecticut (Sanford), Boston (Fessenden), and California (Thacher). Never graduated but father bribed his way into Cal Tech and Rice.

Libidinal Drive: Led life of perversity with kings and queens of Hollywood: Billy Dove, Carole Lombard, Jean Harlow, Ginger Rogers, Katharine Hepburn, Bette Davis, Tyrone Power, Cary Grant, Randolph Scott, Susan Hayward (had abortion), Ava Gardner, Rita Hayworth, Lana Turner. Married Ella Rice, Terry Moore, and Jean Peters. A libertine bisexual.

Personality Type: Introverted-Intuitive-Thinker-Perceiver; Type A manic-depressive and phobic. Obsessive-compulsive

Self-Esteem: Image was everything and used public relations to gain success professionally and personally.

Rebellion: A reclusive iconoclast who hated the establishment. A renegade ruled by paranoia who lived for eighteen years in bedroom without clothes and without wife Jean Peters.

Risk Propensity: Seven major plane crashes contributed to his physical and mental deterioration and drug addiction.

Work Ethic: Repeatedly worked sixty hours at a stretch without sleep.

Tenacity: Never gave up even when disaster struck, namely on *Hell's Angels* movie when talkies came in: he scrapped the film and started over when most people would have quit.

Optimism: Biographer Higham (1993) said, "There was no doubt in his mind he was Genghis Khan."

Manicness: "He was obsessed with everything as though he were God."

7

Rebellion: Marquis de Sade and Isadora Duncan

> Who would be a man must be a nonconformist.
> —Ralph Waldo Emerson, *Self-Reliance*

Ignore All Experts

Powerful and influential people are nonconformists who seldom listen to experts. Their willingness to break the rules accounts for their phenomenal success. The gifted have the strong self-esteem needed to resist useless conformity. They often live with rejection early in life and as they grow older, refuse to allow others to dictate their behavior or direction. In many respects, independent people are rebels because they are not guided by tradition. They are mavericks with a propensity for destroying the present in order to create the future.

Success comes to the gifted because they dare to be different and in doing so ignore the experts. An expert is someone who has a psychological investment in what "is" to such an extent that they are never able to see what "can be." Anyone desirous of being a pioneer or an innovator must be prepared to tread in unknown waters, which is where all new creative ideas and concepts originate. Innovators and entrepreneurs must be prepared to ignore the know-it-alls who are intent on defending their own doctrines. An expert is someone who "knows" beforehand what will or will not work. They are what I like to refer to as the "belts and suspenders" types who are so afraid of losing their pants they are unable to trust just one apparatus.

According to New Age writer Anton Wilson: "The authoritarian personality is 'always right' and tends to seek positions of power. They are obsessed with facts and figures. . . . I think it was men of this type who killed Socrates." These fourteen subjects were aggressive and competitive but never authoritarian know-it-alls.

221

They were the first to declare their own products obsolete or play devil's advocate with their own new ideas.

Individualists are often considered eccentric because they differ from the norm and violate traditional paradigms. Thomas Kuhn wrote in *The Structure of Scientific Revolution* (1962) that "all new paradigms were resisted by experts for approximately thirty years—a whole generation." Kuhn was the first to preach that an old generation must die off before mass acceptance of any new paradigm. He found that the worst offenders were the experts within an industry who would resist anything that differed from their accepted dogma. He concluded that the new would never gain wide acceptance in any society until these so-called experts died off.

Kuhn's theory has been validated in recent times. Milo Farnsworth invented the television during the twenties and it was not in mass use until the fifties. The birth control pill had a similar incubation period. Maria Montessori's revolutionary educational reforms took even longer since she was fighting a bureaucracy and for a time Fascists Mussolini and Hitler. Frank Lloyd Wright's innovative "ranch style homes" took fifty years to be accepted.

Marilyn Ferguson confirmed Kuhn's theory in her 1976 book, *The Aquarian Conspiracy*: "New paradigms are nearly always received with coolness, even mockery and hostility. Their discoveries are attacked for their heresy." Arthur Schopenhauer was even more insightful: "All truth goes through three stages: It is ridiculed; then it is radically opposed; and only much later will it be accepted as self-evident." He concluded that 97 percent of the population go through stage one (ridicule) and stage two (violent opposition), while only a select 3 percent have the temerity and perspicacity to reach stage three, when truth becomes self-evident. These fourteen were in that select group.

Stages of Truth, New Ideas, Products

According to Thomas Kuhn, innovation will be resisted by the masses, therefore anyone attempting to bring about change should be prepared for rejection and confrontation. New ideas will never be accepted unless the creator is prepared to fight resistance: Only a resilient and rebellious champion of new ideas is ever able to achieve great success.

The masses jump on new concepts when they become self-evident, but by that time all opportunity for success has long since passed as the law of supply and demand takes over. Entrepreneurs face an uphill struggle convincing bankers, officials, or investors of their idea because these risk-averse individuals are part of the majority who will not believe. It is imperative that innovators and entrepreneurs recognize they will be attacked by everyone, including their families, while in the development stages of their creations. By stage three they will be vindicated, but the road to success is often strewn with corpses.

It is important for the innovator to find out where the experts or competition are mentally, and go elsewhere. According to psychologist Carl Rogers, "Creative man is a loner; and so is the innovative man, for once he departs from consensus he is on his own." Machiavelli wrote: "Change has no constituency." Educator Erik Winslow went even further, saying in 1989, "Innovators (and creators) are, at best, mildly sociopathic, and at worst completely insane." These definitions have evolved because it is virtually impossible to create anything totally new and great within the confines of the establishment.

CREATIVE GENIUSES MUST BE STUPID

It appears that creative geniuses and great power brokers should never be too smart; in fact, they are better off being neophytes. Most great innovations have emerged from those who were not experienced in the profession in which they made their greatest contribution. It is often best not to know too much since knowledge can prove inhibiting. This hypothesis was best described by Sigmund Freud's disciple, Carl Jung, who believed all creative work emerged out of the unconscious where "It is not Goethe who creates *Faust,* but *Faust* which creates Goethe."

Michelangelo was a sculptor, not a painter, but he was forced to paint by the Medicis and the pope. He was not constrained by too much knowledge about artistic structure or its limitations. His unconventional approach to painting is why the Sistine Chapel is one of the world's masterpieces.

The buildings of Frank Lloyd Wright and the movies of Howard Hughes are prime examples of creators not knowing too much about the subject. Disney's ignorance of amusement parks caused the experts to predict that Disneyland was destined for disaster. It turns out that all reasons they gave for its failure are those that have made it such a success.

CREATIVE DESTRUCTION—THE FORMULA FOR SUCCESS

Philosophers often discover the essence of life before others. Nietzsche discovered that genius demands nonconformity: "Whoever wants to be a creator in good and evil, must first be an annihilator and break values. Thus the highest evil belongs to the greatest goodness; but this is—being creative" (*Thus Spake Zarathustra*). Joseph Schumpeter of Harvard University accurately described innovation as "creative destruction." He understood that one must be prepared to destroy what exists in order to create. A new home cannot be built on a lot unless the old one is destroyed. As Picasso said, "The painter must destroy. He must destroy to give it another life." Frank Lloyd Wright was so destructive that the *New York Times* labeled him the "Anarchist of Architecture." Hitler used the concept by convincing the masses that he could only create the new Master Race of pure Aryans by implementing the Final Solution. The even more depraved Sade wrote: "The self-destructive power of the human race is the Supreme Power."

CREATIVE REBELLION

Isadora Duncan and the Marquis de Sade are the two subjects who best exemplify the creative rebel. Duncan is a classic example of one who hated the establishment: "I was always in revolt against puritanical tyranny." She was against all forms of tradition and dogma, and defied societal mores while living, loving, and working in Europe. She violated the traditional values of early twentieth-century America by having three children by three different men in three different countries. Her first child, Dierdre, was born out of wedlock in 1905. The father was artist Gordon Craig, who had eight children by three different women prior to meeting Duncan. Duncan then had a son, Patrick, with Paris Singer, who had already fathered five children by his American wife.

The Marquis de Sade was even more rebellious. He defied both the authority of the Roman Catholic church in religion-dominated France and the laws of French society, in an act of defiance aimed at promoting Rousseau's societal freedom. He invented the word "Isolism" to describe nonconformity: "All creatures are born isolated with no need of one another" (*Juliette*). Sade's rebelliousness was blatant: He was an atheist in Catholic France, a destroyer of values during the Enlightenment, a nonconformist in an era dominated by conformity, and a nobleman during the French Revolution. His defiance would lead to his destruction.

RENEGADES

The other subjects in this book were not as rebellious as Duncan and Sade, although Tesla biographer Margaret Cheney (1981) described him as "an arch conspirator against the established order of things." He was ridiculed much of his life because of his eccentricities; his metaphysical theories about the derivation of energy were criticized; he never married because of his compulsive and obsessive behavior. The media were highly critical of him because they never understood him. Frank Lloyd Wright touted "Truth against the world" as his philosophy. Wright's rebellion was displayed in his dress and his architectural creations. Author Ayn Rand modeled her protagonist in *The Fountainhead,* Howard Roark—an independent spirit who revered "rational self-interest"—on Wright. Helena Rubinstein lived and worked listening to no one but herself. She built a beauty empire by ignoring the experts. Picasso actually utilized insurrection and rebellion in his approach to art. His success as the greatest painter in the twentieth century was based on his avant-garde approach to painting. Picasso believed that all painters must "destroy" what "is" to create the "new": the artist "must destroy to give it (art) another life."

MAVERICKS ON A MISSION

Edith Piaf was a rebel who was denied a religious funeral by the Roman Catholic church because of her heretical lifestyle.

Napoleon Bonaparte, France's Man of Iron, by the French painter Paul Delaroche.
(AP/Wide World Photos)

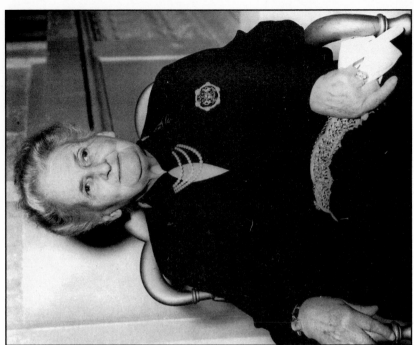

Renowned medical doctor, feminist, and innovative educator Maria Montessori. (AP/Wide World Photos)

Called "the anarchist of architecture," Frank Lloyd Wright was one of the greatest architectural geniuses of all time. (AP/Wide World Photos)

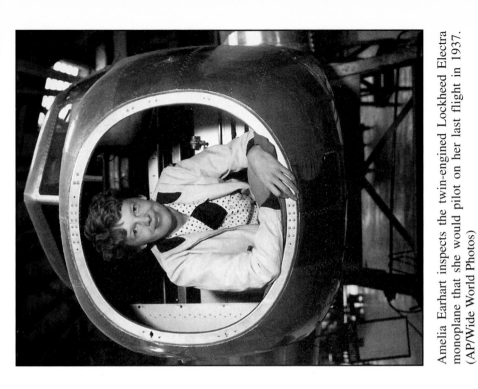

Amelia Earhart inspects the twin-engined Lockheed Electra monoplane that she would pilot on her last flight in 1937. (AP/Wide World Photos)

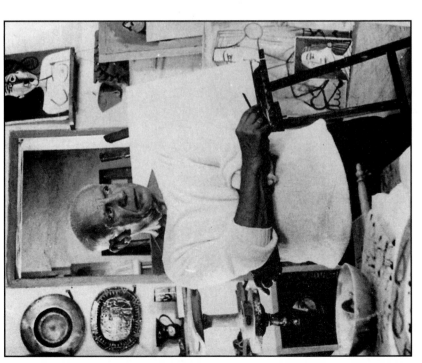

Avant-garde artist Pablo Picasso in his studio at Vallauris, Southern France in 1953. (AP/Wide World Photos)

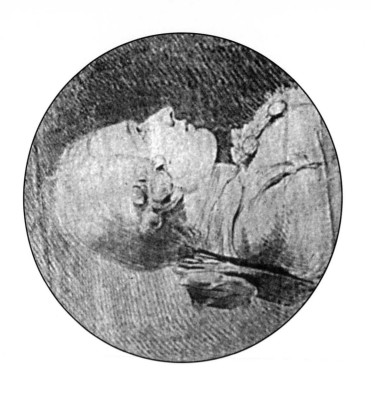

Portrait of the Marquis de Sade at the age of twenty by the French painter Charles Amédée Philippe Van Loo. (Jean-Jacques Lebel Collection, Paris)

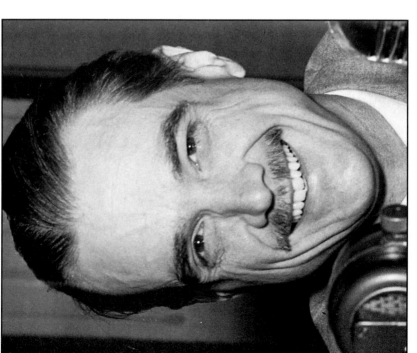

Howard Hughes smiles as he sits in the witness chair at a 1947 Senate war investigations subcommittee probe of his aircraft dealings with the government. (AP/Wide World Photos)

Nikola Tesla, brilliant inventor in the fields of engineering, physics, medicine, and science, was considered a "mad scientist" by colleagues and the public. (AP/Wide World Photos)

Isadora Duncan, founder of modern dance, was a free spirit whose life mirrored Greek tragedy. (AP/Wide World Photos)

"First Lady of Beauty" Helena Rubinstein in her Fifth Avenue office, New York City. (AP/Wide World Photos)

Official portrait of Reich Chancellor Adolf Hitler in 1937. (AP/Wide World Photos)

French chanteuse Edith Piaf upon her arrival at LaGuardia Airport, New York City, in 1955. (AP/Wide World Photos)

Rupert Murdoch addressing the Television Critics Association in Universal City, California, in 1994. (AP/Wide World Photos)

Walt Disney after receiving an honorary Master of Arts degree from Harvard University at the 1938 commencement. (AP/Wide World Photos)

Fox TV network testifies to the maverick in Rupert Murdoch, who has despised the establishment since his college days. The nonconformist Murdoch put a bust of Lenin in his room at Oxford University to display his antiestablishment persona. He has taken on the establishment on four continents in building his media empire, and has never allowed convention to stand in the way of his circulation-building approach to reporting the news. His huge success is a result of his defiant stance against the status quo.

Maria Montessori was a maverick at a very young age. She violated Italian tradition by pursuing engineering and medical careers. She challenged the authorities, including her tradition-bound father, to get into Rome's medical school, finally petitioning the pope to gain acceptance. Montessori became the first female medical doctor in Italian history and then violated church dogma by having a son out of wedlock.

MAD ECCENTRICS

Independence, nonconformity, and rebellion are the most universal of the personality traits found in these fourteen visionaries. Their success appears to have been attributed in large part to their ability to ignore traditional dogmas and experts and they perpetually defied the establishment. Their greatest talent was an internal need to "creatively destroy" the existing order of things.

The media labeled Howard Hughes an "eccentric madman." This description was not even close to defining his idiosyncrasies or enormous hatred for the establishment. Not surprisingly, Adolf Hitler was highly rebellious. He wrote in *Mein Kampf:* "The creative genius stands always outside the circle of experts" (Hershman and Lieb 1994). Amelia Earhart worshiped independence, claiming, "I will not live a conventional life" (Rich 1989). She proved it by wearing long pants and short hair when neither were in vogue. The renegade Earhart kept her maiden name in an era when that was not done and violated all convention in her drive to the top. Walt Disney refused to allow the word "art" to be used at Disney Studios and would not hire anyone with an art degree. He was convinced that professional artists were not innovative enough to become creative. Napoleon violated all the rules in his rise to the top. He once wrote to his brother Joseph when he was a young officer in the army: "I have never paid the least attention to the plans sent to me by the Directoire."

Marquis de Sade

The self-destructive power of the human race is the Supreme Power.

Overview

Sade was the consummate iconoclast and one of the first writers to attack the establishment in a creatively destructive manner while in search of philosophical truth. He would one day become the model for the surrealist movement and the symbol of the French Revolution because of his refusal to abide by societal rules. Sade's French biographer Maurice Lever (1993) wrote: "Sade does not merely embody the Revolution, he is the Revolution" (p. 397). Sade wrote from the Bastille, "Kill me or take me as I am, because I will not change." This defined his rebellious nature, which he "knew" was critical to living a life of intellectual integrity. He clearly demonstrates that creativity can be negative as well as positive.

FATHER OF SADOMASOCHISM

The Marquis is most notorious for having fathered the concept of sadomasochism. His name became synonymous with the term "sadism" due to his writings on the subject. The word "sadism" was coined by Richard von Krafft-Ebbing in *Psychopathia Sexualis* to describe sexual pleasure emanating from physical or mental pain.

The French philosopher Albert Camus claimed: "The history and the tragedy of the modern world began with Sade." In 1909 the French poet Guillaume Apollinaire said that Sade had the "freest mind" the world has ever known. This description was spawned by the surrealism movement, which became the symbol of revolution in art and literature. This movement adopted Sade as its model because of his philosophical desire to free the world of written and sexual hypocrisy. He was the consummate "sexual intellectual" who believed in freedom of expression socially and personally, especially in the arts (writing, plays, and painting).

Sade proved to be his own worst enemy because of his need to *prove* the absurdity of social and religious dogma. His obsession with sexual perversity didn't help his cause. Truth was always important to him and he paid the price for fighting the establishment's need to maintain the status quo: He himself was never able to experience personal freedom as he was incarcerated for 50 percent of his adult life for defying societal rules. Frustrated, he wrote a poem while incarcerated in the Bastille in 1887 called "The Truth" in which he "denied all forms of religion, virtue, and morality" (Thomas 1992, p. 191).

CREATIVE DESTROYER

Sade was devoted to the destruction of all social and religious dogma which he saw as limiting personal freedom. This crusade for unabashed freedom of mankind was destined to destroy him. His blatant effrontery toward social and religious mores cost him his freedom, which he found mystifying and about which he concluded: "The cause of my misfortunes is not the way I think; it is the way others think." Because of his bizarre sexuality, Sade has been largely ignored for almost two hundred years as a philosophically gifted and influential writer. It is apparent that he was the precursor of the existential movement and had strong influence on Nietzsche, Sartre, and Camus. The only difference between Sade and these existentialist writers is that he felt he "knew" the difference between good and evil—he didn't choose to abide by any moral standard imposed by the proletariat. The existentialists insisted that it was impossible to "know" the difference between good and evil.

PERVERTED INTEGRITY

Sade has been noted for one thing—his sexual depravity. This interpretation is not entirely correct. Sade had a wife and three children whom he treated normally. There is *no* record of sexual depravity in Sade's relationships with his wife, mistresses, or lovers. He had a strict moral and ethical code of right and wrong, good and evil. It was through prostitutes that he realized his unconscious libidinal fantasies: He fully expected to carry out his wildest fantasies with these women because he had paid for their services.

Sade's sexual depravity bordered on the grotesque and was aptly named sadomasochistic. He relished writing eloquent but perverse plays, not dissimilar to morality plays, in which he could play various roles and enact his most bizarre sexual fantasies. These plays had sex rather than morals as their theme, but were philosophically meaningful and perverse. They became Sade's vehicle for realizing his sexual depravity both intellectually and physically.

TRUTH = POWER

Although behavior is often inappropriate, it is virtually never bad. It is okay to scream at a football game, not in church; to shoot in a war, not in a home; to have indiscriminate sex with consenting adults, not to force affections on a partner. Sade was often guilty of engaging in inappropriate behavior. He was a philosopher who wrote dialogues (plays and books) in metaphor using fiction as his medium. Most people envision the "truth" of creative genius to be positive. However, it can be negative as is the case with Sade. This is not a defense of Sade's morality, but a justification for his right to believe in freedom within the context of his code of morality as long as no one is hurt in the process. Sade did not differentiate between moral right and wrong but felt that integrity was important whether it was negative or positive. Sade, Picasso, Hitler, Napoleon, and Hughes are all negative il-lustrations of this point. Sade demanded sexual freedom and the right to explore the depths of depravity in writing or through his own perverse experiences. These demands led to his imprisonment since he violated social dogma.

Sade's work should not be labeled good or evil, virtuous or immoral, positive or negative. These words are "absolutes"—are value-laden concepts that blind the reader to objectivity on success in life. Hitler, Hughes, Napoleon, Picasso, and Sade were monsters who destroyed many people, but their ability to gain power and influence were enormous accomplishments. The focus of this book is to iso-late the derivation of power and influence from creative genius whether it be pos-itive or negative. These five were rebels who violated traditional norms of be-havior in their drive for power. Their success did not make them right but one cannot deny that they were powerful. Sade believed all behavior was acceptable as long as the individual performing the deed did so with integrity: He believed that "truth was power," and in that sense he was right.

Many tyrants in history, including Napoleon and Hitler, have been self-right-eous in their sadistic and fiendish actions. They lied to the constituency about their true intent, and rationalized about killing and abuse to preserve their own selfish interests. Regardless of what one thinks of Sade, he was honest about his evilness. He wrote: "I am a libertine, I admit it." Most evildoers like Hitler, Stalin, Napoleon, or Picasso were self-righteous in public and sadistic in private. Napoleon and Sade were both atheists. Napoleon denied his atheism to gain power over a devout Roman Catholic nation; Sade flaunted his atheism in the face of his adversaries. Napoleon killed millions and contended it was in their best interest; Sade would never have done such a thing. To gain power in Germany, Hitler ad-vocated his Master Race plan, using ethnic cleansing to achieve this. His Final So-lution was a justification for killing the Jews he hated for other reasons. Sade would have detested such actions. He violently opposed capital punishment and saved many innocent lives during the Reign of Terror when he was a judge.

Napoleon imprisoned the sixty-one-year-old Sade and kept him incarcerated for the rest of his life, primarily because of Sade's atheism and because he dared to write disparaging remarks about Josephine.

Sade saw through the hypocrisy of religious dogma that had been used dur-ing his era as an excuse for tyrannical acts like the Inquisition. He admitted to his need for sodomy but believed it to be his right as a "free" man. He said, "My way of thinking is the fruit of my reflections. . . . I am not the master who can change it, and if I were I would not." He never deviated from the truth even when it re-sulted in his arrest, ruined him financially, and destroyed his image. Sade never de-luded himself or others with anything other than the truth.

CREATIVE LEGACY

Some noteworthy writers in history have discovered Sade. Simone de Beauvoir wrote: "Sade went into prison a man; he came out a writer." Charles Baudelaire credits Sade for his objectivity in evaluating the essence of life and its dark side: "One must always return to Sade to observe mankind in its natural state and to understand the quality of Evil." Sadism as a modern phenomenon was most clearly delineated in Marcel Proust's *Du cote de chez Swann* (1913). Proust thought that Sade brought "virtuous awareness" to the world. Gustave Flaubert called Sade "the one ultra-Catholic writer." French writer Maurice Lever feels that Sade's *Justine* "remains one of the most striking creations of French literature"; it also became the absolute symbol of evil and the birth of Sadean mythology. "In his rage for the absolute, Sade lacerated language and shredded the rhetoric of the usual 'alcove writers'" (Lever 1993, p. 385). Surrealist writer Paul Dobson says Sade is the "Unique One"—"the man who rises above nature and arrogates to himself the creative and destructive capacities of nature."

Early Life Experience and Influences

The Marquis de Sade was the son of Jean Baptiste, Comte de Sade, a soldier-turned-diplomat. This nobleman had seduced a lady-in-waiting, Marie Elenore, who attended Princess Caroline at the Conde Palace in Paris. The tragic death of their first child, a daughter who died in infancy in 1737, preceded the birth of Donatien Alphonse Françoise Sade on June 2, 1740. The daughter's death had a decided effect on Donatien's childhood. His parents decided that he would be an only child and he was surrounded by doting females who indulged him. His early life was dominated by his mother, aunts, and other females at the court. They worshiped him and made him into an "idol" for the first four years of his life. Children often grow up to fulfill their internal images of themselves and in Sade's case this was true. His childhood molded him into a creative genius and an arrogant egoist. Sade wrote years later: "As soon as I was able to believe anything at all, I concluded that Nature and Fortune had combined to shower their gifts upon me. And I believed this more firmly because of the stupid way in which people were always assuring me of it" (*Aline and Valcour* [1795]).

PAMPERING, TRANSIENCY, AND REBELLION

Early feminine adoration spawned Sade's flagrant disrespect for females in later life. This was not unlike Picasso's early deification by females, which created an adult who destroyed women. Sade's indulgent mother, aunts, and grandmother molded him into a precocious child with strong self-esteem but also arrogance. Sade was embraced by four aunts who were cloistered in convents near Paris, becoming the object of their unfulfilled affections. His father's influence was different. The Comte de Sade became his son's role model—albeit a negative one—and became the primary influence on his intellectual and literary development. Sade's biographer Maurice Lever (1993) described his father as a lecher, describing his amorous activity as having "no limits" and including "mistresses beyond counting."

MALE BONDING

The young Sade identified with his father and had little affection for his mother: "I love my father with distraction, and feel that I hate my mother" (*Philosophy in the Boudoir* [1795]). His mother first doted on him, then repudiated him when he became incorrigible. His father, by contrast, was fondly affectionate and constant in his feelings toward his son. Maurice Lever (1993) has suggested that Sade had a reverse or negative Oedipal complex, aligning himself with his father rather than killing him: the young Sade "forges an alliance with him (father) and turns his powerful hostility against his mother" (p. 14). According to Lever, this caused him to "develop an all-consuming hatred of matriarchal values" for the rest of his life. If true, these feelings would be reinforced during the years he spent living with his debauching uncle, the Abbé de Sade.

INCORRIGIBLE

By age four Sade had become incorrigible and was sent away from the palace. This was prompted by young Donatien's aggressive and brutal attack on his playmate, Prince Louis-Joseph. Sade was sent to live with his paternal grandmother at Avignon, where he was once again indulged beyond belief. He would write that she also contributed to his egoistic and tempestuous behavior: "she succeeded in strengthening all my faults." He had stayed at Avignon only one year when his behavior became so intolerable that his grandmother sent the "little wretch" to live with her son, the abbé, in Provence. Jacques-Françoise Abbé de Sade was not so tolerant of his nephew's behavior and became a deplorable role model. He lived openly in a sexual alliance with a mother and daughter, and had frequent visits from prostitutes to gratify his insatiable sexual appetite. The abbé traveled extensively and took young Sade with him throughout France and southern Europe. This transient life and freedom instilled Sade with a vagabond spirit. He learned independence and nonconformity from the experience. During these years he was molded into a renegade visionary who believed he could defy all rules.

ROLE MODELS/MENTORS AND SEXUAL DEPRAVITY

Sade had virtually no parental guidance after age four. He soon became convinced that he was not bound by any rules. His godlike self-image made him confident as well as self-sufficient at a very early age. When it was time to start school, his father had him returned to Paris. Until age ten he had been with the abbé who was a scholarly influence since he was surrounded by books and intellectual dialogue. At the age of ten Sade was enrolled at the College Louise le Grand, a Jesuit school in Paris, where he stayed for four years with little supervision. This was the time he learned how to manipulate women. His training in debauchery began at the tender age of thirteen. His father set him up in an apartment of his own and encouraged his seduction by one of his own mistresses, Madame de Vernouillet.

She was Sade's favorite. This woman would became a substitute mother to him, as would Mesdames de Raimond and de Saint Germaine. All three women contributed to molding this handsome young royal into a depraved libertine.

CHARISMATIC POWER

Sade had a hypnotic effect on women. They were captivated by Sade and were protective of him. Sade eventually destroyed their faith in him, but usually he was able to convince them to engage in the most bizarre acts.

His father removed Sade from school at age fourteen and enlisted him in the army so that he could pursue a military career. By 1758 Sade had risen to the rank of captain but spent much of his time partying and seducing women. He was never able to differentiate between the personal and professional or sex and work. He proudly wrote that he had learned German from a woman who was his "mistress of education." Sade, like Napoleon, was 5'2" and fearless, but dedicated only to satisfying his libidinal desires.

Break-the-Rules Mentality

Sade was a revolutionary spirit: Rebellion defined everything he did. He predicted the French Revolution in his book *Aline and Valcour,* which was written in 1788, one year prior to the storming of the Bastille. Although *Aline and Valcour* was not published until 1795, Sade foresaw the Revolution: "Your modern Babylon will destroy itself. . . . It will vanish from the face of the earth as did the flourishing cities of Greece" (Lever 1993, p. 406).

Sade lived his life in opposition to society, yet never comprehended why he was not understood or allowed to live an unfettered life. He wrote from prison, "I prefer death to the loss of my liberty," but always seemed to find a way to create his own misery and end up back in jail. At every opportunity he had to straighten out his life, he would devise some imbroglio that would destroy any chance of freedom.

BLASPHEMY

One of the first examples of Sade's self-destructive behavior took place after his marriage. To his chagrin this was an arranged marriage, the bride, Renee-Pelagie de Launay, had a sizeable dowry and he was expected to follow through with his father's selection of a bride. The dejected Sade was twenty-three and did everything possible to prevent the marriage. He contracted a venereal disease one month prior to the ceremony. The night before the wedding he arranged an orgy with a group of prostitutes. After the wedding, Sade kept his own apartment and was rarely home.

When his wife was five months pregnant, Sade had his first run-in with the police over the mistreatment of a prostitute, Jeanne Testard. He was arrested for blasphemous behavior. Sade was always delighted to find a prostitute who was devoutly religious as it was doubly titillating for him to have sex while desecrating the church's most cherished icons. Testard reported that during their sexual encounter he screamed "God does not exist" while ejaculating into a chalice. He then inserted two hosts into her vagina and proceeded to enter her, shouting "If thou art God, avenge thyself" (Lever 1993, p. 119). Jeanne Testard resisted his attempts to have her engage in sodomy or whipping. She reported him to the authorities, not for his sexual perversity, but for his blasphemy. The only two criminal acts in this case were sodomy and blasphemy, and he had not engaged in sodomy with Testard. He was arrested on October 29, 1763, and released when his ambassador father appealed to Louis XV. Sade spent fifteen days in prison before the king exonerated him. It was the first of many such incidents.

DEFIANCE, SODOMY, AND SPANISH FLY

Sade's second arrest, in 1768, resulted from his selection of a woman, Rose Keller, who succumbed to his entreaties but who disavowed being a prostitute. Once again the charges were violations of religious rather than criminal statutes. He was charged with whipping Keller, who had agreed to be his chambermaid, a sexually provocative occupation at the time. His more grievous offense was having committed the act on Easter Sunday, the holiest day for French Roman Catholics. Sade served five months in jail but was released with a pledge to reform.

Sade's next legal skirmish occurred in the French port town of Marseilles when a warrant for his arrest on poisoning charges was issued in July 1772. Sade had always fashioned himself a playwright. It was his most consuming ambition and allowed him to combine creativity and perversity into a cultured medium. He had written an erotic play while on holiday in Provence, which included a number of characters performing sexual acts. He had his valet Latour arrange for prostitutes to act out his fantasy play. In his enthusiasm for putting the prostitutes in the optimum passionate mood, Sade gave them chocolates laced with the aphrodisiac Spanish Fly. Two of the women became violently ill and reported him to the authorities, claiming he had attempted to poison them. Already recognized as a sexual deviant, Sade was charged with attempted murder. The evidence against him seemed weak since the women regained their health as soon as the effects of the pills wore off. However, this charge triggered his downfall, leading him down a path of destruction and lifelong incarceration.

Sade was less guilty in this case than in any other in his life, but his rebellious nature caused him to flee the country, making him appear guilty and arousing the wrath of his mother-in-law, Madame de Montreuil. Sade fled to Italy rather than face a charge he thought unfair. He later wrote of this indictment of his character: "Yes, I am a libertine, I admit it. I have thought of everything that can be thought of in that line, but I have certainly not done everything I though of, and surely never will. I am a libertine, but I am not a criminal or a murderer" (Lever 1993, p. 204).

SISTER-IN-LAW SEDUCTION

When Sade fled to Italy under the assumed name, the Count de Mazan, he asked his wife to bribe the two Marseilles prostitutes so they would not testify. She was successful and Sade might have lived a free man, he had a penchant for creating his own disasters.

Sade had persuaded his sister-in-law, Anne Prospere, to join him on his flight to Italy. He had seduced this nineteen-year-old virgin while he was in hiding from the Marseilles charges. She traveled with him to Italy, posing as his wife. Along with his valet, Latour, they set up housekeeping at Savoy, where they remained for six months.

Sade's biggest mistake was not in fleeing, but in seducing his wife's sister. Madame de Montreuil would punish him the rest of his life for this sexual misdeed. Sade's mother-in-law exercised her enormous influence to have Sade apprehended and returned to France.

Sade may still have managed to elude disaster. However, instead of keeping a low profile while awaiting trial, he had his wife arrange for a number of young women to take up residence with the Sades at La Coste and participate in his sexual fantasies. His wife in essence became his pimp, hiring these women for household and sexual duties. One of the women hired by his wife was Catherine Treillet, a twenty-two-year-old hired as a maid, who would be immortalized as Sade's his famous heroine Justine. Renee-Pelagie had finally decided that her husband was an incurable debaucher and felt if he was going to dally, he might as well do it in their residence.

Sade performed sadomasochistic rituals with these girls; when they returned home, the marks were clearly visible and their stories shocking to their families. Many pressed charges against Sade while he was awaiting his hearing on the attempted murder charges. These new charges of sexual perversity, whippings, and sodomy resulted in his imprisonment once again. Sade wrote from prison of his latest indiscretion, "My stupid childish amusements always cost me my freedom."

BASTILLE IMPRISONMENT

Sade's faithful wife, Renee-Pelagie, arranged to pay off the La Coste women in order to clear her husband's name. But Sade's seduction of his sister-in-law proved to be his ultimate undoing. Madame de Montreuil had arranged a marriage for Anne-Prospere to a member of the prominent Beaumont family of Paris. The family was vaguely aware of Sade's role in Anne-Prospere's recent past. They made a pact with Madame de Montreuil to have Sade removed from society under the guise of the lettres de cachet. The Beaumonts would agree to the marriage if she could arrange for "Sade to remain in prison forever." Madame de Montreuil also wanted Sade out of the way because by then she had become the guardian of his three children and did not want them to have any contact with their father.

The tenacious and influential Madame de Montreuil arranged with the authorities, who loathed the Marquis, for King Louis XV and his successors to sign the necessary lettre de cachet for his incarceration. These letters signed by the king were a legal device to allow a family to imprison a member if they were judged a potential menace to society and were equivalent to present-day law allowing a family to have a member declared mentally incompetent. The family member so appointed had to pay for the cost of imprisonment and had absolute authority. Ironically, Madame de Montreuil used Sade's own money to keep him locked up for the next fourteen years.

The lettre de cachet was arranged without Renee-Pelagie's knowledge. She was furious and attempted to dissuade her mother, but to no avail. Sade was served on July 5, 1775, and imprisoned shortly thereafter. He was thirty-seven years old and would not be a free man until he was fifty, when the French Revolution made lettres de cachet illegal.

Sade's rebellious nature and need to pursue his passion on his own terms had cost him his freedom. It also made him into a sexual intellectual as he went into prison a libertine and came out a philosopher and writer. He sublimated his incredible sexual energies into writing. Starting with his incarceration in the Bastille, he wrote manically for the rest of his life.

Hypomania and Obsessions

When Sade was free, he was a manically driven person. He was a bundle of libidinal and hypomanic energy, impatiently living for his next conquest. He was frivolous with money, spending vast amounts of money on women and pleasure, and exerting enormous amounts of energy writing plays and creating fantasy scenarios to appease his need for sexual perversity. Sade's endless seductions are impossible to track. Everything he did was in excess. Even when imprisoned he was excessively driven to sex, persuading his wife to smuggle him phallic and vaginal-like instruments to satiate his excessive drives.

His mania reached its zenith on July 14, 1789, when he hung out his cell window, screaming through a handmade megaphone at the milling crowds below. He urged the insurrectionists to storm the Bastille. He had a sympathetic audience and his taunting proved such a threat that the alarmed prison officials had him moved to Chareton mental hospital. He wrote: "I stirred up the spirit of the people from my window. . . . I warned them . . . and urged them to tear down this monument of horrors" (Thomas 1992, p. 194).

Even though Sade was a Type A personality, he was a classic loner in everything he did. He drove himself but was unable to control his own needs and obsessions. He was impatient and intolerant but charming. He never liked women but needed them to fulfill his fantasies.

While in prison, Sade developed an obsession with numbers. No one understands the strange compulsions that Sade enumerated in his prison diaries. Psychologists have speculated that such compulsions helped him survive years of confinement. This cryptomania was based on his obsessional need to guess the dates of his release, thinking it was coded in his wife's letters.

Sade was a workaholic in prison and completed fifteen volumes of fiction, kept a detailed diary, wrote thousands of letters, and read volumes of Voltaire and Rousseau. He documented everything in a compulsive need to maintain his sanity. One of his more provocative habits was to journalize (*Almanach illusionair*) all of his orgasms while in prison. He reported in December 1780 of having 6536 "orgasms by masturbation" and "introductions" (anal sex) over a period of twenty-seven months, a phenomenal number of sexual experiences for someone incarcerated. At age seventy-four Sade reported having sodomy eighty-eight times in four months and documented his daily sexual encounters with the sixteen-year-old Madelaine LeClerc. He was planning a future with this girl and her mother in a ménage à trois upon his release.

Power, Influence, and Success

Sade's power included a vast store of psychic energy and charismatic charm. His influence has come out of his philosophically based novels and their arguments against religious and social tyranny. Sade worshiped freedom, which is ironic in that he was seldom free. Many of his writings were destroyed when the Bastille was captured at the height of the Revolution, but his adversaries also destroyed what they considered pornographic writings. His major surviving works are: *Misfortunes of Virtue* (1787), *Justine* (1791), *Aline et Valcour* (1795), *Philosophy in the Boudoir* (1795), *Juliette* (1797), and *120 Days of Sodom,* which was written in the Bastille and found in the possession of a French family in 1904. These works were banned in France and elsewhere for two hundred years. The writings dealt with sexual perversity in total defiance of societal and religious dogmas. They were written in a philosophical venue since "Sade believed in the immortality of his genius" (Lever 1993, p. 387). Sade aimed to destroy the hypocrisy of the legal system to allow absolute freedom of sexual relations between consenting adults. He wrote in *Juliette*: "Without laws and religion, one cannot imagine the degree of glory and grandeur that human knowledge might have achieved."

INFLUENCE

Sade has been called the "Most absolute writer who ever lived" due to his dedication to the "veracity" and the "authenticity" of man's passions. He first gained wide recognition when the *Universal Dictionary* listed "sadism" in its 1834 edition. Krafft-Ebbing gave Sade's name psychological significance half a century later by coining the word "sadomasochism." British writer Algernon Charles Swinburne helped create a more positive picture of the man by describing Sade as the most influential writer in modern history. He was precise in his view of Sade as a man who "saw to the bottom of gods and men." French author Guy de Maupassant was so enthralled with Sade's writing that he named his driveway "Avenue Sade." French writer Gustave Flaubert acknowledged Sade as "the one ultra-Catholic writer" because Sade focused on Roman Catholic icons such as the crucifix, rosary, and Mary statues. Sade lived during the Enlightenment and was the antithesis of that puritanical period when the church became sacrosanct in its dogmas.

The irony of Sade's reputation for destruction is that he was made a judge for a brief period after the French Revolution and jeopardized his own safety and life by being too lenient with those who had been his mortal enemies. Testimony to his strong ethical sense and moral integrity is the fact that he could very well have become vengeful during the Reign of Terror when he had the power to destroy his enemies. He was truly a man who believed in the integrity of truth at all costs, including his own freedom. Sade was a pacifist opposed to capital punishment and refused to have anyone killed even though his own sexual passions were aroused through pain. This man who had been virtually destroyed by his in-laws jeopardized his own freedom during the Reign of Terror to protect them.

SELF-DESTRUCTION

Sade was a man who was in opposition to the world. That he saw the power manifested in his internal energy is shown by this quote from his biographer Maurice Lever: "Donatien was thrilled by his own impatience because he saw in it a reflection of his power" (Lever 1993). His need for seduction became his destruction. He could never control his enthusiasm for new conquests since he was a dedicated hedonist. Everything else wilted in comparison to that driving force in his nature. He did everything in absolute violation of that which could have enabled him to live a normal life. Such is the nature of power and influence that begets self-destruction. A free man after many charges, he could not control himself, sneaking into Paris, which resulted in his arrest and imprisonment.

Every time that Sade was close to resolving his legal problems, he would create new ones. This is best illustrated when he was finally freed in 1890 after spending fourteen years in prison. He was released on April 2, 1790, after the lettres de cachet were made illegal. He remained free for ten years, during which time he was a model citizen. But Sade could not refrain from writing about his religious beliefs and the rights of man. He published *Aline et Valcour* in 1795, which included the view: with the phrase "Religion is nothing but the instrument of tyranny. . . . To banish kings without destroying the religious cult is to cut off but one of the hydra's heads." He continued to extol the virtues of reason and rational behavior, to his own detriment. But Sade could not and would not live a low-profile life: "If atheism wants martyrs, let it say so, and my blood is ready." Robespierre took him at his word and attempted to have him beheaded, but Robespierre fell from power as Sade was at the foot of the scaffold awaiting death.

LITERARY EXPRESSION—THE FINAL NAIL

Sade published *Justine* in 1791 as a pornographic novel strictly for money to survive. Then he wrote *Juliette* in 1797 as a philosophical expression of the need for sexual freedom. Although Sade needed the money from these books, it is also fair to say that he never strayed from his rebellious need to expose hypocrisy.

On January 8, 1794, his publisher, Girouard, was guillotined for selling *Justine* and other such works. Sade should have been alerted by this, but associated it with the Reign of Terror and not society's disdain for his material. He wrote *Juliette* in complete defiance of the moral climate of eighteenth-century France. This book totally violated the sensibilities of the Committee that was governing France in 1797. By 1801 Napoleon was in power and his lieutenants saw Sade as unfit to live free to write his pornographic books. These officials considered Sade a man of great depravity and perversity. He was arrested for the seventh and last time and charged with writing pornography.

More than anything else, Sade's horrible reputation had destroyed him. He was declared to be psychologically incompetent and suffering from "chronic libertine dementia," incorrigible and afflicted with incurable sexual obsessions. On April 27, 1803, Sade was committed to the mental hospital at Charenton in rural Paris. His only offense was to have written a revolutionary book on the rights of man in violation of social morals and religious dogma.

A Rebellious Sexual Intellectual

The Marquis de Sade was a sexual intellectual who was obsessed with destroying the dogmatic myths of religion and society. He was ineffective in the era in which he lived, although he became notorious during his own lifetime. He was made into a martyr by the surrealists and reborn in the turbulent 1960s as a symbol of rebellion. American International Films released *De Sade* in 1969. It was one of the pioneering X films which exploited his name. This was another case of individuals using the Sade name and reputation to further their revolutionary cause. Peter Weiss's play *Marat/Sade* depicted him as a cynical philosopher to contrast Marat's idealism. Sade was, in fact, a spiritual man and had a towering sense of moral right and integrity. Sade was introspective and honest about his morality and insatiable drives. While in the Bastille, he wrote a poignant self-description to his wife: "I am imperious, angry, furious, extreme in all things, with a disturbance in the moral imagination unlike any the world has ever known—there you have me in a nutshell" (Lever 1993, p. 313).

French author Chateaubriand characterized Sade as a "fatal prodigy." He obviously understood the overt self-destructiveness of Sade. Biographer Donald Thomas (1992) attempted to put Sade's life and literary contributions in perspective: "In a different context and in a different age, the mere cruelties of Sade's fiction might have seemed visionary rather than obscene" (p. 256). It certainly is easier to view Sade from the perspective of the twentieth century. In today's world he would have been middle-of-the-road relative to pornographic expression.

There is no question that Sade was a bizarre personality with an insatiable appetite for sexual perversion. He also had a talent for self-destruction that appears to be a necessary element in the highly creative and entrepreneurial personality. In many respects Sade is emblematic of the rebellious and creatively destructive visionary. He destroyed himself in the pursuit of truth and contended to his death that religious, social, and legal factions should not be allowed to control man's freedom of expression. This consummate revolutionary furthered truth in philosophy and writing. He dared to be different. Sade left us a legacy of perversity but also gave us integrity of thought. He violated societal and religious dogmas in quest of "revolutionary truth," which has proven a boon to the creative visionaries of the world.

DONATIEN ALPHONSE FRANÇOIS COMTE DE SADE
Infamous Writer, Philosopher, and Sadist
b. June 2, 1740, Paris, France; d. December 2, 1814, Lunatic Asylum, Charenton, Paris

Dominant Trait: Rebellion and libidinal energy, sexual perversity and debauchery (sodomy), devout atheist

Motto: "Kill me or take me as I am, because I will not change"; "Laws are simply useless or dangerous."

Nickname: "Sadistic Libertine," "Sadism" (Krafft Ebbing), "Father of Surrealism" (Apollinaire)

Vices/Hobbies: Libertine and debaucher. Loved theater and sex, and combined the two in perverse plays.

Heroes/Mentors: Voltaire and Rousseau. Early mentor and role model Uncle Abbé de Sade.

Philosophy of Life: "One cannot create virtues for oneself . . . one is no more the master, free to adopt this or that taste than one is . . . to make oneself brunette when one is born a redhead."

Fantasy: To write and act in theatrical productions that satiated his wildest fantasies (blasphemy).

Professional Success: *Misfortunes of Virtue* (1787), *Justine* (1791), *Aline et Valcour* (1795), *Philosophy in the Boudoir* (1795), *Juliette* (1797), and *120 Days of Sodom.*

Power: Blatantly fought the establishment over right to think, write, and act. Martyr of surrealism; "Sade does not merely embody the [French] Revolution, he *is* the Revolution."

Influence: Model for surrealists and writers. "The history and tragedy of the modern world began with Sade" (Camus). "Freest mind the world had ever known" (Apollinaire).

Destructiveness: "The self-destructive power of the human race is the 'Supreme Power.' " Seduction of virgin sister-in-law was a self-destructive act that resulted in lifelong imprisonment.

Birth Order: Only child of noble Parisian family. Sister born year earlier died.

Parental Influence: Father Jean Baptiste Comte de Sade, a womanizing ambassador to Cologne. Raised by indulgent females who told him he was "incarnation of Jesus, marvel, miracle, idol and superior being." Wrote "I love my father with distraction, and feel that I hate my mother."

Transiency: Paris to Provence at age four, lived with Abbé de Sade from age five and traveled Europe.

Crises: Imprisoned for half of adult life, the inspiration of his writing.

Formal Education: No school until age ten. Poor student who quit at fifteen, never graduating. Voracious reader.

Libidinal Drive: Awesome psychosexual drive. Daily sex with teenager in prison at age seventy-five.

Personality Type: Extrovert-Intuitive-Thinker-Judger; Charismatic rebel with symptoms of hypomania, sexual fantasy.

Self-Esteem: Confident to the point of egomania; Wrote in prison: "The cause of my misfortunes is not the way I think; it is the way others think" and "Egoism is the primary law of nature."

Rebellion: Violated rules of church and society. Loner and iconoclast who didn't feel bound by societal rules. An atheist in a Catholic society, a rebel in a dogmatic nation, a noble during the French Revolution.

Risk Propensity: Thought himself invincible with a death-wish approach to life. Perpetually lived on the edge.

Work Ethic: Worked and debauched with equal intensity. Insatiable libidinal energy.

Tenacity: Died believing he was right and never capitulating to will of authorities.

Optimism: Believed he was a superior being. "I act in accordance with my thoughts good or bad."

Manicness: Imperious and obsessed in all things; "Obsession" his forte regardless of consequences.

Isadora Duncan

I'm a revolutionist.

Overview

Isadora Duncan was one of the world's most rebellious women. She was inspired early in life to be a radical and lived to fulfill that image: "The dominant note of my childhood was the constant spirit of revolt" (Duncan 1927, p. 20). Isadora was convinced of her destiny quite early in life since she was born under the astrological star "Aphrodite" (Duncan 1927, p. 10). She believed "that whatever one is to do in one's after life is clearly expressed as a baby" (Duncan 1927, p. 11). Her life gives credence to my thesis of childhood fantasies turning into adult realities. This renegade claimed, "I was possessed by the dream of Promethean creation" (*My Life* [1927]) and was the personification of a Promethean goddess who stole not fire from the gods to bring science to man, but Greek mythology from literature and philosophy to bring to modern dance. Duncan spent her life in a struggle against established traditions and artforms like the ballet. She decided quite early in life to combine dance with the Greek classics, art, music, poetry, and sculpture, and spent her entire life attempting to fulfill that dream. She was a renegade both professionally and personally. Duncan spent her life fighting the established order of things. She identified with revolutionaries: "I am indeed the daughter of Walt Whitman" (America's renegade poet).

RENEGADE SPIRIT

Duncan was influenced by Walt Whitman's "personal freedom" in poetry, Nietzsche's philosophy of superiority ("Superman"), Rousseau's social justice, Rodin's natural organic beauty, and the antiestablishment music of Beethoven and Wagner. Her nonconformity encompassed dancing, art, religion, love, and life itself. Freedom in dance was her passion, but it spilled over to her lifestyle. Duncan spent her short life exploring the inner essence of dance intellectually, psychologically, and philosophically. A rebellious spirit earned her the reputation of a renegade artist. It also led her to the very top of her profession. Rodin was enthralled when they first met. He was an old man at the time and Duncan was a ravishing beauty in her twenties, but her "dance of freedom" captivated him. He called her "the greatest woman the world has ever known," even though his romantic advances had been rejected by the "Puritan Pagan," as she referred to herself in this period of her life.

INFLUENCE

Daniel Boorstin called Duncan "the barefoot Contessa" in his epic work, *The Creators* (1992). He described her as the "beginning of a new outlook. . . . She was the first to *dance* the music and not dance *to* the music." He wrote: "Anyone of any age could duplicate 'what' she did but not 'how' she did it. When she raised her arms it was an incredible experience. She could stand still—and often did—but it was an alive stillness and it was dancing" (Boorstin 1992, p. 498). Choreographer Agnes De Mille described Duncan's influence as critical to the innovation of dance. She said "Isadora cleared away the rubbish. She was a gigantic broom. There never has been such a theater cleaning." Duncan's friend and biographer Mary Desti (1929) described her passionate performances: "No religious experience has ever moved its believers to a higher ecstacy than did Isadora's dance" (p. 17). *Time* magazine described Duncan as a "talented, bizarre, intelligent, scandalous, extraordinary woman." Ilya Ilyich Schneider became the principal of Isadora Duncan's Moscow School of Dance after her death. Schneider was a Russian art critic, choreographer, director, and producer of ballets. Her description of Isadora's influence on dance gave credit to the critical part personality played in her success: "Her appearance in the world of art produced the effect of an exploding bomb not only because she had given up ballet costume and danced barefoot in a light tunic, but also because she dared to perform her dances to the music of great composers" (Schneider 1968).

Duncan was an innovative genius. Her major influence was in showing the world that "individual personality" and "passion" were important and that "tradition" should not interfere with the creative process. She was convinced that the essence of dance emanated from the unconscious—the "central inner force"—of the soul. That is the way she performed on stage and in life. Her life resembled a Greek tragedy, which is ironic since she spent a great deal of her time, money, and energy desperately trying to unite the Greek classics with dance. This revolutionary defied the establishment in order to remake the world of dance. Her work did not go unnoticed and she was called the "the goddess of dance," a reputation earned through many years of arduous work and pain. When she was tragically killed in Nice, France, the driver screamed "I've killed Madonna! I've killed Madonna!" According to those who knew her best, the driver was astute in his observation.

Early Life Experiences and Influences

Isadora Duncan was born in San Francisco on May 27, 1878, the fourth child of two musicians, Joseph Charles Duncan and Dora Gray. She only met her father once in her life and always lived in awe of his flamboyant lifestyle as poet, teacher, entrepreneur, and adventurer. He was a dashing but irresponsible womanizer her mother had divorced just after Isadora was conceived. Ironically, and to her mother's everlasting grief, Duncan grew up to be much like her father. Dora Gray became a vitriolic, antimarriage agnostic who instilled her strong beliefs in all her children, but most of all in young Isadora. Duncan liked to say, "I learned to dance in my mother's womb probably as a result of the oysters and champagne—the food of Aphrodite." Dora Gray said, "This child will not be normal," and when

Isadora was born, said, "You see I was quite right, the child is a maniac!" thereby preconditioning Duncan to a renegade lifestyle.

Young Isadora grew up thinking that marriage was a heinous institution and promised as a very young girl never to marry. Dora Gray was an accomplished pianist and became Duncan's role model, mentor, and accompanist. Duncan became a free soul due to the permissiveness of her iconoclastic mother. She was allowed complete freedom to explore the streets of San Francisco, which she claimed was totally responsible for her later creative achievements. Duncan was raised in a family that was intellectually stimulating, revered the arts, and was permissive beyond the norm. She had total freedom to go where she wanted, when she wanted, and never felt any shackles of restraint: "I owe the inspiration of the dance I created" to childhood freedom.

Transiency and Moxie

Duncan wrote of the frightful parents who groomed their children for mediocrity by locking them up emotionally and physically. She described her early life as a latchkey child as a romantic and learning experience that programmed her for success. In her view, "freedom to experience life—to try and fail—and live by your wits" was paramount in molding self-sufficiency and success. Her family was destitute and young Isadora learned early how to survive. When the family could not afford food, she would volunteer to approach the baker and butcher for credit since she was the youngest, thinnest, and gutsiest. She confided in her autobiography: "I was the most courageous and when there was absolutely nothing to eat in the house, I was the volunteer who went to the butcher and through my wiles induced him to give me mutton chops without payment" (Duncan 1927, p. 20). A testament to her self-sufficiency, at age six she started giving dance lessons for money to neighborhood children.

The Duncan family was so poor that they never stayed in one apartment for more than a few months, causing young Isadora to experience what she later termed a "nomadic childhood." The family moved every time the rent was due, an experience most parents would find disastrous, but for young Isadora it proved to be a positive learning experience. Early transiency groomed her for a pioneering lifestyle where she would compete in a foreign language and culture and unaccepted artform. The new or foreign were never a concern for her as she had experienced them constantly as a child. Children with such a background have a built-in advantage over those from a protected environment.

Freedom to Err—Formula for Success

By age ten, Duncan had quit school and opened an informal dance school to teach other children in the neighborhood. She also taught dance to the children of the wealthy in late nineteenth-century San Francisco. She wrote in her autobiography: "I pitied the children who were given everything they needed, who would never learn how to cope when they grew up." Duncan added an admonition: "The finest inheritance you can give to a child is to allow it to make its own way, completely on its own feet." She concluded: "In comparison to these children of millionaires, I seemed to be a thousand times richer in everything that made life worthwhile" (Duncan 1927, p. 21). Duncan described the overprotected children with governesses and nurses: "What chance of life have they?" . . . "My brothers and I were free to follow our own vagabond impulses." She gave total credit for her later success and creativity to this early training. It is difficult to refute her logic as her experience is replicated in more dramatic fashion by Earhart, Disney, Hughes, Hitler, Piaf, Sade, Tesla, and Wright. Duncan was convinced that overprotective parents are the bane of creativity and success: "It is certainly to this wild untrammeled life of my childhood that I owe the inspiration of the dance I created, which was but the expression of freedom. I was never subjected to the continual 'don'ts' which it seems to me make children's lives a misery" (p. 11).

Duncan grew up a free soul who explored life holistically. She taught herself poetry, dance, and philosophy. Her search for the "truth" in dance and life groomed her to be a rebel. When Duncan was very young, her mother was brutally honest with her about Santa Claus so that she wouldn't expect presents. When young Isadora started school, her teacher said that Santa had brought the class candies for Christmas. The rebellious Isadora told the teacher, "I don't believe lies. . . . There is no Santa Claus." The teacher punished her for disrespect. Isadora never received her candies but was proud of her integrity. She maintained that rebellious honesty throughout her life, insisting on her freedom and independence despite the consequences. After the Santa Claus incident, friends and family started calling her a maverick. Duncan began living her life in a way to fulfill that early image of herself. She wrote of her diverse image: "I was considered amazingly intelligent and at the head of my class, or quite hopelessly stupid and the bottom of the class." She hated school and believed that "My school was the dance" and "When I could escape from the prison of school I was free. I could wander alone by the sea and follow my own fantasies." Duncan was convinced "that whatever one is to do in one's after life is clearly expressed as a baby. I was already a dancer and revolutionist" (Duncan 1927, p. 11). She began organizing neighborhood children into dance classes at age six and by ten had so many students she informed her mother she was quitting school to pursue a career in dance. In order to appear older than ten, she wore her hair up and claimed that she was sixteen.

SELF-TAUGHT BUT ERUDITE

During Duncan's teens, her mother scraped up enough money to give her a ballet lesson. When the teacher told her to stand on her toes, she asked him why. He said, "Because it is beautiful." She replied with conviction, "It is ugly," and left the class after one session. That was the extent of her formal dance education. When reporters asked about her dance education, she responded emphatically: "Terpsichore taught me to dance." Although her formal education in both academics and dance were limited, Isadora Duncan was probably one of the more erudite subjects in this book.

When she left school she started reading Dickens, Thackeray, Shakespeare, and everything else she could find that was philosophically in line with her values. Her tastes expanded to Walt Whitman, Voltaire, Nietzsche, Schopenhauer, Rousseau, and the Greek classics. She was a voracious reader throughout her life. She wrote a novel as a teenager and kept a journal her whole life. When she arrived in Chicago at age sixteen to seek a dance career, she spent all of her free time in art galleries and museums. She did the same in New York, London, Paris, Berlin, Moscow, and Athens. She could not stop searching for truth in life, philosophy, and the dance.

CHARISMATIC POWER

Duncan was charismatic. People found it difficult to refuse her. She was able to persuade her whole family to follow her to faraway places in pursuit of her dreams. She talked her mother into leaving her native San Francisco and moving to Chicago. After she talked her way into a theater engagement in New York City, she talked the whole family into joining her and then convinced them to follow her to London, Paris, and Greece. In Chicago they encountered the realities of creative hardship. They virtually starved and were lucky to survive. Duncan's charismatic power came to the rescue. She read an article in the *Chicago Tribune* that the great Augustin Daly was coming to Chicago with his theater troupe. She brazenly walked in on him at the theater and said in nonstop staccato: "I have discovered the dance. I have discovered the art which has been lost for two thousand years. . . . I bring you the idea that is going to revolutionize our entire epoch. . . . I am indeed the spiritual daughter of Walt Whitman. . . . I will create a new dance that will express America. I bring to your theater the vital soul that it lacks, the soul of the dancer" (Duncan 1927, p. 31). Daly was speechless, but offered this impetuous and passionate young lady a part in a New York City pantomime he was producing. In classic Duncan style, she wired her brothers and sister in San Francisco and told them to meet her in New York because she had finally made it in show business.

In New York City Duncan gained valuable experience but it wasn't what she had in mind. She was just seventeen and had no theatrical clothes or place to live. She invited her family to view her great success only to find out that she had a secondary part in the show that paid little. The family found lodgings on 180th Street in Manhattan and her rehearsals were on 29th Street. Duncan didn't have money for food or transportation and walked to and from rehearsals daily, a total of 300 blocks. She reflected in her autobiography: "I didn't eat lunch because I had no money, so I used to hide in the stage box during the lunch hour and sleep from exhaustion" (Duncan 1927, p. 35). Such is the basic training of creative geniuses.

A Rebellious Promethean

Duncan was independent and passionate in everything she did. The establishment was taken aback by her radical views on marriage, religion, dance, and politics. As a young child she had concluded marriage was not for her. In fact, she vowed to fight for the emancipation of women so that they could live with men outside marriage and have children without loss of virtue. An even greater example of her rebellion occurred when she was just starting out in Paris. A German producer from the largest music hall in Germany had seen her perform in the elegant parlor of one of her rich patrons. He offered to bring her to Berlin for an engagement that he thought would make her a star. At the time of this offer Duncan was destitute. She survived these low periods in her career by focusing on her dreams. She would retreat into her own internalized world and later recalled: "I can remember standing for hours in our cold, bleak studio waiting for the moment of inspiration to come to me to express myself in movement." It was this movement that she wanted to express for art, not entertain in a music hall for money. To Duncan, art was more important than food, and in a moment of passion she refused this offer which could have made her rich since he had offered her one thousand francs—a veritable fortune to the destitute Duncan. This rebellious Promethean was interested only in pursuing her dreams. Stubborn adherence to this philosophy made her famous but also kept her impoverished much of her life.

INTELLECTUAL INTEGRITY AT ANY COST

In her first major performance in Berlin, Duncan gave a lecture on the "art of the dance of liberation." She ended her lecture with a speech on the right of women to love and bear children without marriage or permanent relationships. Her speech was received with gasps of shock from the women in attendance and "scandalous" reviews when she contended that "any intelligent woman who reads the marriage contract and then goes into it, deserves all the consequences" (Duncan 1927, p. 181).

Duncan always said what was on her mind and that honesty cost her dearly throughout her life. It cost her monetarily in fees and destroyed many of her romantic relationships. Once it cost her both a man and security. This occurred in March 1917, at the outbreak of the Russian Revolution, when Duncan performed at the New York Metropolitan Opera House. She danced to the "Marseillaise" with what she described as a "terribly fierce joy." Then she threw caution to the winds and danced to Wagner's music, when the United States was in deadly combat with the Germans. She followed that attention with "Marche Slav," which offended many in the audience since the Bolsheviks were considered enemies of the West and capitalism. Her lover and father of her child was in the audience—Paris Singer, the son of sewing machine magnate Isaac Singer, and a consummate capitalist who hated both Russia and Germany. He was her benefactor and the man who had promised to finance the Duncan School of Dance. Without Singer, Duncan would be destitute. Singer walked out of her life that evening, forcing her to pawn a diamond necklace he had given her to finance her trip home to France. The introspective but self-destructive Isadora reflected later, "My art impulse was too strong for me and I could not arrest it even to please one I loved" (Duncan 1927, p. 225).

Revolutionist, Not Communist

Duncan was the consummate revolutionary. She was sympathetic to the Russian Revolution because she had danced in St. Petersburg and Moscow a number of times. During the early twenties she established a dance school in Moscow and married a Russian poet who reminded her of her dead son. The media constantly badgered her about her political philosophy and Communist leanings. The truth was that Duncan was apolitical her whole life and only true to her art. She believed that all great creative endeavors were destined to destroy existing dogmas. In her opinion, the establishment and experts were there to be ignored. She told the media: "I am not an anarchist or a Bolshevist. I'm a revolutionist. All geniuses worthy of the name are. Every artist has to be one to make a mark in the world" (Duncan 1927, p. 118). She loved to say, "I was always in revolt against Puritanical tyranny" as a dig against dogmatic people or systems. When the philanthropist Paris Singer offered to finance her dream school in New York City, she was ecstatic. He paid $250,000 for a down payment on a full city block costing $5 million to show his dedication to her school. When he took her to see the site, she said, "I can't work here. It smells of horses."

Impulsive and Impatient Renegade

Duncan's most controversial views were on the institution of marriage. Not only did she not believe in marriage, she detested it and advised courting couples that they were making a terrible mistake.

Duncan approached all the major decisions in her life with unabashed disdain. She never bothered to review contracts or consider the financial implications of her major ventures. When she opened her first school of dance in Berlin in 1904, there was no consideration about how to finance it. She admitted later, "It was the most rash undertaking imaginable," adding, "This was quite in keeping with . . . other undertakings most impractical, untimely, and impulsive."

Whenever Duncan received a financial windfall, she would spend the money foolishly on some dream. In one of her first mistakes she impetuously bought a mountain in Athens, Greece, fully intending to establish a school of dance here and make it her permanent home. She did open a school of dance across from the Acropolis, featuring Greek children who in the tradition of Sophocles pranced across the stage barefoot. The grand plan failed miserably, costing her a fortune since her mountain had no water and could not be made habitable. Duncan never considered such fundamental things, yet she and her brother Raymond spent a fortune over a ten-year period in a vain attempt to build a school on her property.

Psychosexual Drive and Crisis

Duncan had her first love child, Dierdre, in 1905 by Gordon Craig. Craig was a gifted stage designer and son of her friend Ellen Terry. She had met Craig in Berlin and had a passionate relationship with him for two years. Their tempestuous love affair didn't last, but her reputation did. She had made a mockery of American puritanical codes by her romantic liaison with a married man. America ignored her professionally because of this behavior, while Europe found her avant-garde behavior refreshing.

Duncan marched to a different drum beat. She appealed to the art community and the wealthy. The rest of the world ignored her art. When she met Paris Singer and ran away with him on his yacht, he was already married and had five children. Their affair grew to scandalous proportions as the couple raced uninhibitedly across Europe defying moral traditions.

Duncan had her second child, Patrick, with Singer in 1910. She stopped touring and had the child in Belgium. She would have a third illegitimate child, but this time it was planned. Her two older children, Dierdre and Patrick, were tragically killed when a chauffeur lost control of her car, sending it into the Seine River, killing both children instantly. Duncan claimed to have had a premonition of this tragedy while dancing to Chopin's Funeral March in April 1913 during which the envisioned "two blond heads enshrouded in black" (Duncan 1927, p. 269). Duncan was distraught and close to an emotional collapse. She went to Italy to recoup with her friend Eleanora Duse. While there in 1914, she methodically seduced a sculptor in an attempt to replace her lost children. It was not to be. The newborn died, probably affected by her weakened emotional and physical state. This new tragedy only added to Duncan's grief. She never fully recovered from these multiple tragedies as she repressed the tragedy.

CAPITULATION TO MARRIAGE

At age forty-four, Duncan finally broke her lifetime vow not to marry. She fell passionately in love with a twenty-six-year-old Russian poet who was mad. Sergei Esenin was a blond Adonis who reminded her of her dead son, Patrick. In fact, Esenin was not much older than her son would have been. He was unable to leave Communist Russia unless he was married to someone on traveling business, so Duncan agreed to marry him for the sole purpose of having his company on her tour of Western Europe and the United States. This impulsive decision would prove disastrous. The marriage ceremony in Moscow involved nothing more than a ritualistic sharing of vows. Esenin was an epileptic and prone to violent rages. He was probably the worst possible choice for Duncan who needed stability in her life. One of her motivations could have been Esenin's resemblance to her father, who was also an audacious and lecherous poet.

Duncan was mesmerized by Esenin's youth, beauty, and genius and was not repulsed by his epileptic fits and uncontrollable rages. Their marriage became a violent and turbulent relationship. During their marriage, he had threatened to kill her almost daily. Tolerating such behavior gives credence to her self-destructive personality.

Esenin was as perversely driven and depraved as the Marquis de Sade. While in America and France, he destroyed many hotel rooms and was deported from both countries for disruptive behavior. He destroyed property everywhere he went and spent money with abandon, leaving Duncan to pay. When she ran out of money because of his random destruction, he left her destitute in Paris and returned to Moscow. They never divorced and she stood by him even when after he had illegally married Leo Tolstoy's granddaughter. Duncan forgave him but never lived with him again. Esenin finally hanged himself in 1925.

Manic Success

Duncan was defined by her psychic energy and manic passion. She was a driven perfectionist who would dance all night at a feverish pace, oblivious of time, food, or fatigue: "I was so interested in my work that I got into . . . a state of static ecstasy." Psychologists now call this the "Zone" or "Flow"—a euphoric state bordering on transcendental behavior where "people are so involved in the activity that nothing else seems to matter." According to Mary Desti, a friend and confidant who lived with her in Europe, Duncan didn't sleep when in one of her manic periods: "She acted like a person demented." "Nothing could stop her. . . . Isadora would not sleep a wink and was in a state of the wildest excitement. . . . She decided not to go to bed but to go from restaurant to restaurant, night club to night club, anywhere and everywhere for excitement" (Desti 1929, p. 133).

Duncan perpetually lived life on the edge. Such an existence tends to create its own turmoil and manicness. She was never bothered by personal rejection, and lived her own life rejecting all tradition and the establishment. She did so with a manic-type persona that is personified by her Dance of the Future, a style aimed at redefining Walt Whitman's rejection of tradition and in her case, the rejection of ballet. Her dance Primavera was based on the Botticelli painting. Her free-flowing robes, bare feet, and dancing to the great composers Wagner and Beethoven became her signature. Her Russian School of Dance was a real coup at the time. Duncan passionately wanted to found her own school of dance, was never able to convey her own unique style of dance, which was difficult to replicate.

Power, Influence, and Destructiveness

Isadora Duncan was internally driven by a psychic need to achieve and be different. She persevered because of her strong willpower that demanded she dance in her own unique style. By violating traditional dance modes she was able to create her own niche in the world of art. Her avant-garde approach to theater and her stage persona gave her power.

Talent alone is seldom the deciding factor of success in the arts or any other endeavor for that matter. Madonna, Edith Piaf, and Amelia Earhart were not even close to their peers in talent but were immensely successful. Duncan's power grew out of her passionate psyche, which erupted in a unique style that gave her enormous appeal to audiences. Her captivating style and presence on the stage never veered far from her internal demand for independence and freedom. She was driven to act in a free and unobstructed way.

IMPULSIVE AND IMPATIENT

Duncan's success was often contaminated by impetuousness. One example was her impulsive move to Moscow to open her dance school. The Russians had promised to establish a permanent school of dance for her in Moscow at their expense. She accepted their verbal offer and immediately sold off her belongings, leaving for Russia with no written agreement. This is consistent with Type A personalities, who expect other people to fulfill their part of the bargain. Isadora left friends, family, and all possessions to move to a Communist country just after a major revolution. When she arrived in Moscow and called Lounarcharsky, the Soviet Minister of Public Instruction, he informed her that the government was still considering her proposal. Duncan was devastated and found herself in a hotel with no bed, no water, and without money.

PSYCHIC ENERGY AND ITS PRICE

Duncan wrote: "Nothing seems to exist save in the imagination." She seems to have been able to tap that inner energy to revolutionize dance. She constantly wrote of her "Inner-Self" and "Spiritual Vision": "I feel the presence of a mighty 'power' within me which listens to the music and then reaches out through all my body, trying to find an outlet for this listening. Sometimes this power grew furious, sometimes it raged and shook me until my heart nearly burst from its passion." (Duncan 1927, p. 224). Her charismatic power grew out of this internalized energy. Choreographer Martha Graham often acknowledged Duncan as the one who broke the ground for the advancement of dance. Like all great pioneers, Duncan paid a horrific price for her success. Her greatest tragedy was losing both children in a tragic accident. She was not at fault, but it has been suggested that this would never have happened had she been a full-time mother and a part-time dancer. Isadora lost all of her great loves for the same reason.

THE TRAGIC LIFE OF A CHARISMATIC

Much of Duncan's life was a Greek tragedy unfolding. She was so driven, so immersed mentally and physically with her need to achieve that she lost everything she loved and much of it tragically. Every love affair in her life ended in disaster.

An illustration of her ability to overcome disaster occurred in New York City when the Hotel Windsor burned to the ground, destroying all her possessions. She found herself homeless and broke. In classic Duncan style, she resorted to her charismatic power to survive. She blatantly approached the wealthy in New York

City for fare to London, England, using an alias—Maggie O'Gorman. It was approaching the turn of the century when Duncan raised enough money to book passage to London for her family on a cattle boat. This proved a low point in her life but she saw it as part of the struggle to realize her dream. In London the family found themselves starving on a park bench. The irrepressible Duncan marched into the Dorchester Hotel near Hyde Park and in her words, "I informed the night porter that we had just come on the night train, that our baggage would come from Liverpool . . . and to order breakfast to be sent up to us" (Duncan 1927, p. 52). She and her family lived in this prestigious hotel like royalty for two days, and then disappeared into the night.

FREEDOM AND DESTRUCTION

Duncan's free spirit was never more apparent than in Nice, France, when she was a poor and aging star with a dismal future. She met a car salesman in a bar and this impetuous Aphrodite asked for a test ride in his exotic Bughatti sports car. Isadora was never reticent to tell her dreams to anyone and expressed interest in owning her own Bughatti. She made an appointment to be picked up outside a popular hotel where she could impress Paris Singer, who had been avoiding her. Mary Desti described Duncan as someone "always looking for a man and not afraid of anything." She informed Desti of her date with the car salesman. Her parting but prophetic words were, "I'm off to the moon, so don't be surprised if you don't see me again."

Duncan was dressed in her usual free-flowing dress with trailing six-foot-long scarf. This was her signature dress of the time as it connoted freedom and independence of spirit. Jumping into the rear seat with the convertible top down and waving to her adoring friends, she said, "*Adieu, mes amis. Je vais a gloire*" (Farewell my friends. I go to glory). The driver drove the high-powered sports car into the balmy Nice evening. Duncan's scarf got caught in the rear axle and in one terrible bone-crunching instant snapped her neck, killing her instantly. She died as she had lived—in a frivolous but violent style that demanded freedom.

What Made This Rebellious Spirit Tick?

Isadora Duncan was unpredictable. She would agree to a dinner date and when the gentleman arrived expecting a romantic interlude with Duncan, she would be immersed in a perverse group that included a beggar, a poet, an artist, an actress, and a vagrant. She was never interested in pedigrees. She believed that "truth" in anything was inextricably imbedded in the unconscious. She often said that "life is a dream," a "spiritual vision" where the "inner self" becomes the driving force of life: "I enthusiastically believed that it was only upon awakening the *will* for beauty that one could obtain beauty" (Duncan 1927, p. 174).

Duncan fulfilled her early dreams of life and dance, and considered her great success as a "fantasy" that she had "improvised" to fit her needs at the time. She was self-taught, but was a workaholic in perfecting her art. She was a perfectionist who refused to accept mediocrity and attacked dance with a passionate vengeance. Her methods included studying Beethoven, Wagner, Nietzsche, and the Greek classics in an attempt to find truth in her craft. She felt that in truth she would find excellence. Isadora Duncan's life was like a Greek tragedy because she was willing to pay any price to be the best—and did.

Duncan reached the pinnacle of success in her profession and was idolized by millions. But the price she paid for that success was enormous. She became estranged from her mother, lost most everyone who meant anything to her—friends, lovers, children—and ultimately lost her own life.

Duncan pursued truth in dance and was willing to go anywhere to find it. Money was unimportant to her and consequently she never had any because she spent it frivolously. Her struggle to found a permanent dance school was heart-wrenching. She tried first in Athens and failed due to cultural and financial barriers. When she opened a school in Berlin, it was closed down because of her reputation (by then she had her first child out of wedlock and made her infamous speech "art of the dance of liberation"). Schools opened in Paris and London were both closed due to lack of money. Paris Singer offered to finance her school in New York City, but his help failed to materialize when she performed her revolutionary dance at the New York Opera House. With a promise from the Russians, she sold everything and went to Moscow in a desperate attempt to open a permanent school of dance.

Isadora Duncan had always been willing to sell her soul for the dance. In the end it was the great "Isadora" herself—not any school—that was destined to become her legacy. Her name is synonymous with "revolution" in dance and her free-form approach became the precursor of modern dance. Duncan was the consummate rebel and arguably one of the most successful women who ever adorned a stage.

ISADORA DUNCAN
Founder of Modern Dance
b. May 27, 1878, San Francisco, California. d. September 14, 1927, Paris, France

Dominant Trait: An independent spirit who worshiped freedom. The consummate iconoclast and rebel.

Motto: "I'm not a Bolshevik, only a Revolutionist." "I am a Puritanical Pagan." "What one has not experienced one will never understand."

Nickname: "Princess Pub," "Dorita," "Aphrodite," "Topsy" (nicknamed by lover Gordon Craig)

Vices/Hobbies: Writing and reading poetry/philosophy, Greek classics, and visiting museums.

Heroes/Mentors: Walt Whitman, Nietzsche, Rousseau, Rodin, Beethoven, and Wagner's renegade music

Philosophy of Life: "I was possessed by the dream of Promethean Creation." "I'm a revolutionist."

Fantasy: To combine dance with art, sculpture, music, and the Greek classics

Professional Success: Spectacular performances at Carnegie Hall, Berlin, London, Paris, Moscow. Rodin called her "The greatest woman the world has ever known." Acknowledged creator of modern dance.

Power: Charismatic stage presence. A vital force of free-form personality attracted men and fans.

Influence: Martha Graham acknowledged her as the one person who made modern dance possible.

Destructiveness: Her life was a Greek tragedy. Her rebellion negated marriage and then led her to marry a madman. She gave birth to three illegitimate children, who all died.

Birth Order: Lastborn of four children; musician parents divorced after she was conceived

Parental Influence: Mother, Dora Gray, was a rebel, agnostic, and antimarriage feminist who was permissive with her children. Isadora was a latchkey child who credited her success to early freedom saying "Finest inheritance you can give to a child is to allow it to make its own way."

Transiency: Nomadic childhood, moving dozens of times before age ten. Sought fortune in Chicago at seventeen, New York at eighteen, London at twenty, Paris at twenty-two, and then Greece.

Crises: Abject poverty as child, constantly evicted. Lived by wits most of life.

Formal Education: Dropped out of school in fifth grade to start dance school. "Terpsichore taught me to dance."

Libidinal Drive: Three illegitimate children by different men. Finally married poet who reminded her of dead son.

Personality Type: Classic Promethean temperament: Extrovert-Intuitive-Thinker-Perceiver on MBTI scale

Self-Esteem: Awesome self-confidence. Told theater impresario at age sixteen: "I shall be very famous one day."

Rebellion: "I was always in revolt against Puritanical tyranny." "I'm a revolutionist. All geniuses worthy of the name are. Every artist has to be one to make a mark in the world today."

Risk Propensity: Lived life on the edge like a Greek tragedy. Fearless!

Work Ethic: Pursued dreams of perfection in dance oblivious of time, food, or others.

Tenacity: Never capitulated to adversaries in lifestyle, dance, or politics. Bounced back from worst adversities to regain power and success.

Optimism: Positive attitude: "I was never subjected to the continued '*don'ts*' of other children."

Manicness: "I was so interested in my work that I got into . . . a state of static ecstasy (Flow)"; "Life is a Dream, Spiritual Vision, Inner Self"; "I followed my fantasy and improvised."

8

Obsessive Will and Manic Energy: Nikola Tesla and Adolf Hitler

> Creativity, as seen in both artists and scientists, does not come from a sudden inspiration invading an idle mind and idle hands but from the labor of a driven person.
> —Anne Roe, *The Making of a Scientist*

Manic Success Syndrome

Psychoanalyst Alfred Adler believed that man's primary need in life is to "strive for superiority, perfection and power." The fourteen subjects of this book fit Adler's model. They had a manic need for power and success which in some cases became delusive. Jacques Barzun wrote in *The Paradox of Creativity*: "Mad passion or passionate madness is the reason why psychopathic personalities are often creators and why their productions are perfectly sane." High energy and obsessional behavior are predictors of achievement. These subjects were obsessively driven far beyond the norm. They were hyper, unreasonable, impatient, and impulsive personalities. Mania so dominated their lives that I coined the term *Manic Success Syndrome* to describe their behaviors.

Nikola Tesla and Adolf Hitler best personify the obsessive personality. Both had an internal vision of themselves as a "superman," in Nietzsche's vernacular, and a maniacal willpower need to achieve. Both were charismatic, psychosexually driven and seriously hypomanic. They were steeped in fantasy during their formative years and often became lost in their own dreams of grandiosity. Their mythological hero mentors gave them inspiration to chase impossible dreams and build fictional castles in the sky. Idiosyncrasies and egoism defined them. Their obsessions and psychic energy helped them overcome any obstacle. High energy led them to the top, but became their Achilles' heel.

253

HYPERACTIVE AND DYSFUNCTIONAL PERSONALITIES

All fourteen subjects were energy incarnate, manic, and often dysfunctional. Many were Type A workaholics with an obsession for achievement. Most worked beyond the capability of normal beings, at times driving themselves two or three days without sleep, and normally working eighty hours per week. This hyperenergy often overcame their other deficiencies. It certainly was the key factor in the transformation of Napoleon, a Corsican immigrant, into the emperor of France. It transformed Hitler from an unemployed loser into the most powerful dictator in Europe. In *A Brotherhood of Tyrants* (Hershman and Lieb 1994) the authors describe the manic depression of Napoleon and Hitler. They were convinced "Mania was the secret of Napoleon's success," basing their conclusions on the fact that "Mania increases the speed at which a person thinks." They also characterized him as a supreme "charismatic" whose mania and charisma "served him like a secret weapon" (p. 146). Napoleon's success as the world's greatest military genius was inextricably tied to his manic and charismatic behavior, which allowed him to seduce millions with his grandiose dreams. Hitler was often as manic as Napoleon, but he rose to the top on the strength of his passionate oratory. His manic delusions of a Master Race and personal invincibility were bought by a needy constituency who elected him as their führer (leader).

Tesla, like Napoleon and Hitler, employed psychic energy to become the greatest inventive mind in history. His megalomania caused him to sleep but two hours a night for much of his life and drove him to take unbelievable risks in validating his theories on the nature of electricity. Howard Hughes utilized the mania part of his manic depression to outwork and overpower his peers. According to Hershman and Lieb: "In some manic-depressives like Howard Hughes, manic grandiosity and depressive withdrawal from society coexist" (p. 33). Where did these individuals acquire such enormous manic energy? It appears to have emanated from their obsessive need to self-actualize themselves into Adler's "ideal man" where superiority, perfection, and power were paramount. All of the manic-depressive subjects (Napoleon, Disney, Hitler, Hughes, Piaf, Sade, Tesla, Rubinstein) were energized with the classic symptoms of euphoria, racing thoughts, sleeplessness, and grandiose ideas. They validate the Manic Success Syndrome as a key element in the super successful.

Manic Need for Superiority

Napoleon could have been included in this chapter with Tesla and Hitler since he personifies Adler's definition of man's passionate need to be superior. Napoleon actualized his need for superiority through mania. He was driven beyond description. Napoleon's valet, Constant, described his "iron will" as a weapon in his arsenal for the seduction of mankind. New Age writer Anton Wilson wrote, "The future exists first in the *Imagination,* then in *Will* and then in *Reality.*" Wilson implores us to use "imagination" to create dreams, then commit these dreams to "will" in order to have them "realized." In this scenario internal belief always precedes success. Impossible dreams turn into improbable success because the will deems it so. Napoleon admitted at St. Helena that his wild dreams of power were useless until the battle of Lodi: "It was only on the evening at Lodi that I realized I was a superior being, and conceived the ambition of performing great things." After that night he went through a psychological transformation, believed in his destiny, and never equivocated until he became the emperor of France.

Manic Vision

Contemporary psychologists confirm Napoleon's mystical transformation. It is now understood that "we become as we think." NASA researcher Dr. Charles Garfield found that all world-class athletes, astronauts, and other peak performers were those capable of visualizing their success before performing: "They see it, feel it, and experience it before they actually do it."

All of the subjects in this book visualized themselves as superior beings long before their success. All were instilled with a strong Nietzschean will-to-power mentality.

Tesla had such a powerful internal belief system that his biographer Margaret Cheney concluded that *he* was his greatest invention: "a self-made Superman and producer of marvels." A reporter described Tesla's accomplishments as being "like the dream of an intoxicated god." Tesla's college professor wrote to his father asking that young Nikola be removed from school because "he was in danger of killing himself from overwork." The professor had seen the signs of the megalomania in this teenager. Tesla worked nonstop for days, admitting that the solution to a problem was "a matter of life and death" for him. He was a Type A personality who had to finish anything he began as a matter of personal satisfaction. He once finished one hundred volumes of Voltaire because he had started them and could not bear not to finish.

Hypomanic and Obsessional Behavior

Hypomanic energy was found in all of these subjects. They were obsessed with success and would compulsively drive themselves to exhaustion in their need for achievement. They were so impatient with completing a project that they became tyrannical until it was finished to their satisfaction. Their obsessions and manicness were exhibited in different ways. Eight of the fourteen (Napoleon, Disney, Hitler, Hughes, Sade, Piaf, Tesla, and Rubinstein) had the classic symptoms of manic-depressive illness: insomnia and immense productivity. Five (Disney, Duncan, Hughes, Sade, and Tesla) were obsessive-compulsives and were often unable to control certain habitual behaviors. Five (Earhart, Duncan, Murdoch, Picasso, and Wright) were hypomanics. The hypomanic person has been described thus:

The hypomanic person is often extremely busy; he has enormous energy and can continue his activity day and night. Work may become very easy as ideas flow. He sleeps little if at all, writes many long letters, keeps a diary and makes numerous phone calls. . . . Hypomanic patients are often sexually excitable, promiscuous and may develop erotic delusions. They often rationalize their bizarre behavior by claiming medical, marital, or employment problems . . . and develop delusions of grandiosity, divinity, of being descended from a noble family, or possessing great wealth. (Hershman and Lieb 1994, p. 205)

Both Napoleon and Hitler had an egocentric view of the world which infused them with the power to perform herculean feats. They were living examples of Nietzsche's hypothesis that *power accedes to those who take it.* Nietzsche's "Superman" concept in *Thus Spake Zarathustra*) precisely described these two political despots. Hitler actually bastardized Nietzsche's philosophy to fit his own vision of the world. This book's premise is echoed in his words: "Will and power is how to win the masses" (Stein 1968, p. 68). His will enabled him to gain enormous power.

MANIA FOR DESTRUCTION

These subjects all had a messianic vision of themselves, which attracted many disciples who were willing to follow them anywhere—even to their deaths. Kay Jamison wrote on creativity and manicness in *Touched with Fire* (1993): "Manic-depressive illness is one that confers advantage but often kills and destroys as it does so" (p. 240). Hypomania is prima facie evidence for intellectual and artistic achievement because: "Who would not want . . . elevated and expansive mood, inflated self-esteem, abundance of energy, less need for sleep, intensified sexuality, and—most germane to our argument here—'sharpened and unusually creative thinking and increased productivity' " (Jamison 1993, p. 103).

Fantasy Obsessions of Childhood—Adult Realities

Childhood fantasy heroes became inspirational mentors for these visionaries (see chapter 1). They often identified with larger-than-life heroes and heroines from books and these figures became their fantasy mentors. When children fantasize about Alexander the Great (Napoleon's hero), Aladdin (Wright's hero), or Voltaire and Mark Twain (Tesla's heroes) they see themselves as that individual in fantasy and therefore envision few if any limitations to their greatness. They become immortalized in their own minds. When they grow up they tend to have fewer limitations on achievement than those who choose a more normal fantasy mentor to emulate. It seems that the more exotic, superhuman, and grandiose the hero, the more inspirational the impact. Tesla wrote that the book *Abafi* was the inspiration that "awakened my dormant powers of will" (Cheney 1981, p. 10). Hitler had such experiences which were documented by his teenage friend, August Kubizek. Hitler and Kubizek frequently attended operas in Vienna as teenagers and on one occasion, returning form Wagner's *Rienzi* in 1908, Hitler became "emotionally frenetic and passionate," yelling, "I have been inspired. . . . I will lead Germany out of servitude to heights of freedom." Hitler later said, "Wagner is the greatest genius the world has produced," and he emulated Wagner's nationalistic and majestic power. Hitler told Kubizek in 1939, "In that hour it began" (Hershman and Lieb 1994, p. 59).

Psychic and Charismatic Energy

The obsessiveness and manicness that pervaded these individuals emanated from within. It was a Freudian-type vital energy that erupted from their unconscious and drove them to achieve beyond any normal expectations. Tesla was probably the greatest inventor in history because of his enormous psychic energy. In his autobiography and other writings, Tesla often referred to his inner vision and mystical energy. He acknowledged that it was the basis of his enormous drives and obsessions and the reason for his success. Tesla was precognitive, which came from his highly developed senses. Biographer Cheney says "he could hear the ticking of a watch three rooms away" (p. 22). A *New York Times* reporter had dinner with Tesla and a Slovakian boxer and was shocked at the "psychic energy" between the two, writing that it "made his skin itch."

Adolf Hitler could rouse himself into such high levels of hyperactivity that he would consume everyone around him. He referred to it as his "black magic," learned from the mystical Thulists and taught by his political mentor Dietrich Eckart. Hitler became the most powerful and influential man in the twentieth century due to this mystical power. He was capable of mass hypnosis through hypomanic dialogue.

Carl Jung wrote: "Magic is just another term for psychic." Magic to most people connotes a negative, like black magic. Jung was convinced there was nothing dark and mysterious about magic. He thought it was simply a unique ability to control and enhance the "human energy potential" of man.

SECRET BEHIND HITLER'S GREAT ENERGY

Hitler was inspired by the Thulist movement, a group that practiced magic and various mind control techniques. His mentor, Dietrich Eckart, met him in 1919 and decided to use Hitler to prove his theories of mind control through the use of mental energy. Hitler was trained in the human-potential ideology of the Thulists. This was the genesis of much of Hitler's anti-Semitic ideas as Eckart was highly educated but a devout anti-Semite. Eckart's success was incredible since he was able to transform a shy, introverted loser into one of the most mesmerizing speakers in history. After Eckart's training, Hitler was capable of bringing audiences to tears through the power of speech. Dietrich wrote to a friend in 1923: "Follow Hitler! He will dance, but it will be to my tune. We have given him the means to maintain contact with them (the Masters). Don't grieve for me. I have influenced history more than any other German" (Schwarzwaller 1989). Alan Bullock, Hitler's biographer, characterized him as having the "magnetism of a hypnotist": *What* Hitler said was immaterial, it was *how* he said it that drove crowds into a passionate frenzy. Elsa Bruchman, a socialite, recalled meeting Hitler: "I simply melted away in his presence. . . . I would have done anything for him" (Stein 1968, p. 58). A young German, hearing Hitler speak for the first time, said: "I forgot everything but the man. . . . The intense will of the man, the passion of his sincerity seemed to flow from him into me. I experienced an exultation that could be likened only to a religious experience. . . . I had found myself, my leader, my cause" (Hershman and Lieb 1994, p. 149).

Nikola Tesla

Throughout space there is energy.

Overview

Nikola Tesla was nicknamed the "electrical sorcerer" and "poet of science" by the media and was arguably the greatest inventive genius who ever lived. Some called him mad, others a genius, but everyone agreed he was an enigmatic superman. Tesla was one of the giant visionaries of any era. He was a linguist, poet, connoisseur of fine wine and music, philosopher, fluent in eight languages, and a brilliant inventor. He created some of the most innovative and revolutionary products in history. He was the first person to demonstrate the fundamental precepts of robotry, fluorescent lighting, radio wave transmission, computer-controlled missiles, satellites, microwaves, and nuclear fusion. The first electric clock and fluorescent light were built by Tesla. He transmitted radio waves before Marconi. But Tesla's most astonishing accomplishment was the invention of an electrical distribution system known as alternating current and the induction motor which runs on it. This electrical current is used in every home, factory, and office in the Western world. Before this there was only Thomas Edison's direct current system, which made the Wizard of Menlo Park Tesla's greatest adversary. Tesla had made obsolete Edison's dynamo, causing the great man to expend enormous energy and money to destroy Tesla.

INTUITIVE POWER VS HEURISTIC POWER

Tesla was to Westinghouse what Thomas Edison was to General Electric. Neither company would have become an industrial giant without the technology created by these two eminent inventors. Ironically, the two worked together for a period in the 1880s and then became bitter enemies when Tesla sold his patents to Westinghouse. Edison was an inventor who enjoyed the entrepreneurial process and died a rich man. Tesla refused to get involved in the commercialization of his inventions and this scientific genius died a pauper. Edison took a pragmatic path to uncovering scientific mysteries while Tesla embarked on an intuitive path relying on macrovision to create. Tesla was a genuine scientist and refused to prostitute his work for the sake of money while Edison refused to create any product that didn't have practical commercial value. Edison used experimental techniques heuristically—by trial and error—to create products such as the light bulb, which he used to launch General Electric. Tesla was more interested in finding out what made the universe tick. He used a remarkable intuitive vision to make innovative products like the electric clock, but was never motivated to pursue the financial rewards of building consumer products to sell. Tesla's reward was the personal euphoria experienced in resolving a problem, and he was willing to rely on firms like Westinghouse for the commercialization process.

ECCENTRIC GENIUS

Tesla was hypersensitive, hypermanic, and an obsessive-compulsive. He sensed the deaths of both his sister and mother and documented these extrasensory experiences, which he kept secret much of his life. He could not eat a meal without computing the cubic contents of the soup, coffee, and contents of every portion prior to eating. Germs and flies were his nemeses. If a fly landed on his table, he would have the waiter bring a whole new order. Eighteen napkins were neatly arranged at his personal table at the Waldorf Astoria and Delmonico's for cleaning and polishing the silverware before each meal. His compulsions were strange. He counted footsteps as he walked to an engagement and would only stay in a hotel room with a number divisible by three. He never lived in a house or apartment, preferring the spartan existence of hotel life.

Tesla was a towering intellect, well over six feet tall, handsome, articulate, and elegantly attired with a cultured charm. He and Frank Lloyd Wright had the same predilection for sartorial splendor. Tesla's normal clothing was a Prince Albert coat with a derby hat and silk handkerchiefs, which he wore both for dinner nightly and to work. The only time he changed from this prim dress was to don formal wear if he were going to embark on some mystical electrical experiment for his friends or the media. He wore a new silk shirt, tie, and gloves just once and threw them out. His weight never varied more than one pound in thirty-five years. Tesla almost always dined alone and never in his life allowed himself to dine alone with a woman. His phobias and obsessions included a violent aversion to women's hair, pearls, and earrings.

ENIGMATIC VISIONARY

Tesla was an enigma even to those who knew him. He would walk down Fifth Avenue and in one sudden burst of superhuman energy, jump in the air in an athletic somersault and land on his feet. This giant of a man would then keep on walking as if this circuslike act was normal behavior. He purportedly could do these feats into his sixties. His technological exploits in the world of electronics and science were even more amazing. Tesla's life was spent working in the mysterious world of the arcane where electronics was still in the realm of black magic. His experiments and lectures at the turn of the century were usually beyond the comprehension of the average person. Even the top scientists of the day had difficulty conversing with this dazzling visionary. Since most were unable to grasp his concepts, they would often denigrate him.

ENERGY INCARNATE

Tesla was a man of enormous appetites and energy. He was obsessed with the unknown in the universe. He was precognitive and had numerous experiences of extrasensory perception, once sensing his sister's serious illness and telegramming friends before he definitely knew she was ill. He had premonitions of disaster and after a party in 1890 asked his guests not to take a train which then crashed, injuring many on board. Tesla was highly opinionated; he was a perfectionist who would criticize anyone overweight or dressed inappropriately.

To Tesla, no risk was too great if it meant success. When Thomas Edison was attempting to discredit his alternating current system as too dangerous, Tesla stood on a podium at the Chicago World's Fair in 1893 and passed one million volts through his body, lighting a light bulb in his hand and then melting a wire to authenticate his invention.

RIGHT-BRAIN MACROVISION

Tesla's intuitive powers were exceptional and were in opposition to the scientific method embraced by traditional scientists. Einstein had the same type of intuitive insight into problem resolution as did Tesla, which Edison despised. Tesla said: "I could *visualize* with the greatest facility. I needed no models, drawings, or experiments. I could picture them all in my mind. . . . The inventions I have conceived in this way have always worked. . . . My first electric motor, the vacuum tube wireless light, my turbine engine and many other devices have all been developed in this way" (O'Neill 1968, p. 257). This introverted visionary spoke eight languages fluently and was a flamboyant and mesmerizing speaker in any of them. He was extremely gracious, but his intellect was of such enormous power that he could be intimidating. The *New York Times* science writer Waldemar Kaempffert branded him "an intellectual boa constrictor." Tesla had once embarrassed Kaempffert with a caustic response when he had insolently accused Tesla of creating an instrument of war in his remote boats. This angered Tesla since he was an avid pacifist.

PRODIGAL GENIUS

Most science writers idolized Tesla. They were in awe of his intellectual precocity and intrigued by his ability to demonstrate his wildest theories in the simplest terms. The New York science-fiction writers Kenneth M. Swezey and John O'Neill worshiped him. O'Neill, writing his biography, *Prodigal Genius,* thought of Tesla as a god. B.A. Behrend was a renowned engineer in his own right and was awarded the Edison Medal at the same time as Tesla. Behrend summed up Tesla's enormous contribution to the world of science: "Were we to seize and eliminate from our industrial world the results of Mr. Tesla's work, the wheels of industry would cease to turn, our electric cars and trains would stop, our towns would be dark, our mills would be dead and idle. . . . His name marks an epoch in the advance of electrical science. From that work has sprung a revolution" (Cheney 1981, p. 217). Lord Kelvin, an early adversary of Tesla's, gave him a similar tribute: "Tesla has contributed more to electrical science than any man." In 1956 when Gardner Dales of the Niagara Mohawk Power Corporation was addressing the American

Institute of Electrical Engineers, he gave Tesla the ultimate tribute: "If there ever was a man who created so much and whose praises were so little sung—it was Nikola Tesla. It was his invention, the polyphase system, and its first use by the Niagara Falls Power Company that laid the foundation for the power system used in this country and throughout the entire world today" (Cheney 1981, p. 89).

Tesla's enormous contributions in science, engineering, and physics caused him to have several nervous breakdowns, and left him little notoriety and no money. He magnanimously gave away millions in royalties to further the implementation of his AC system by Westinghouse Electric, which left him without the funds to implement some of his greatest inventions.

Early Life Experiences

Tesla was born the fourth child of the Orthodox priest Milutin Tesla and Duka Mandic in the small Yugoslavian village of Smiljan in the province of Croatia. His childhood was one of intellectual stimulation. His family prided themselves on their exceptional feats of memory. Nikola was groomed to be a priest by his father who took special care in developing his communication and memorization skills. Tesla wrote that he had inherited his photographic memory and inventive genius from his uneducated mother who had memorized whole volumes of classic European poetry. His father wrote poetry and had some published, and this influenced Tesla to write poetry much of his life. At age five he built a waterwheel and attempted to fly in a homemade plane. When a village firehose wouldn't work, the venturesome youth dove into the river and resolved the problem to the delight of the village. Tesla retold this story in his autobiography: "I was the hero of the day." He also recounted emotional and physical crises with near-death experiences during his youth.

CHILDHOOD TRAGEDY

His older brother Dane, a gifted child and the family favorite, died tragically at age twelve. This event would cast a dark spell over young Nikola and affect him for the rest of his life. Nikola was five at the time of his brother's death, and one story claims that Nikola pushed his brother down a flight of stairs to his death. There may be some truth to this account since Tesla became emotionally afflicted with strange phobias and obsessions dating from that period in his life. He was a different person after this tragedy and began experiencing strange flashes of light anytime he became "agitated or greatly exhilarated."

FANTASY IMAGES AND MENTORS

Tesla wrote in his autobiography: "Up until the age of eight years my character was weak and vacillating." It was during this period that he became obsessed with books and would often read all night. His parents became alarmed over his manic behavior and took away his candle. Young Nikola then taught himself to make candles and would secretly read all night, hiding the evidence from unsuspecting parents. It was in his precious books that Tesla discovered a mythological hero who became his fantasy mentor. Tesla credits the book *Abafi* with its hero, Son of Aba, with molding his strong will. This book "awakened my dormant powers of will and I began to practice self-control." He attributed many of his later successes to this fantasy hero who he was convinced imprinted him with the need to become a superior being. Nikola spent his teens in a life-and-death struggle with a mysterious ailment that the doctors claimed was incurable. After one such bout the doctors gave up on him. During his vigil in bed, Tesla was given a book written by Mark Twain and later credited Twain for his miraculous recovery.

Tesla experienced strange phenomena during this period. When excited or in deep concentration, he experienced strange flashes of light. Science writers later labeled his strange flashes as his "cosmic vision." When in this state, Tesla would embark on imaginary journeys and experience intuitive visions of new concepts. Intuitive vision was one of his great gifts. He almost was kept back in school due to his prodigious memory and intuition. He used these powers to solve problems but seldom bothered with the mundane tasks of writing down solutions. He solved problems in his head, like memorizing logarithmic tables allowing him to intuit solutions to the most complex problems. He never supplied his methods to teachers who accused him of cheating and were no more impressed than Einstein's had been.

TRANSIENCY AND MANIA

Tesla moved a great deal while young. When he was seven, the family moved to Gospic where he attended grammar school. He attended middle school in Karlstadt, Croatia, where he contracted malaria and then cholera. He entered the Austrian Polytechnic School in Graz in 1875. He was sent to live with another family for two years in an attempt to control his obsessive behavior. This did not deter him as he completed the courses in half the time expected, causing further concern for his health. In 1879 he left Graz for the University of Prague. He would study from three in the morning until eleven each night. Tesla wrote that he dedicated four hours in bed to rest but spent two of those thinking about solutions to his problems. This habit of sleeping only two hours each night would last most of his life.

FORMAL EDUCATION OF A TYPE A

Tesla's Type A behavior as a student groomed him for overachieving later in life and it ultimately took its toll on his health. The dean of the university wrote to Tesla's father that after his son's first year, he had completed 50 percent more work than assigned: "Your son is a star of the first rank but should not return for fear he will kill himself with his obsessive work ethic."

One example of Tesla's obsessive need to achieve was his discovery of

Voltaire. Once Tesla started a book, he could not stop until it was finished. He discovered that Voltaire had written one hundred volumes. He could not stop reading until he had finished all one hundred volumes, which he did in one semester in addition to his schoolwork.

Tesla said, "I had a veritable mania for finishing whatever I began." He finished the first year of college with honors, but during the second year his father died, leaving no money to continue his formal education. It was during this second year that Tesla conceived of the idea for the induction motor. He told Professor Poeschl of his idea for utilizing accelerating current in motors. Poeschl told him the idea had no merit, saying, "Mr. Tesla may accomplish great things, but he will never do this," and accused him of proposing a "perpetual motion machine—an impossible idea." That was all Tesla needed. He had the solution within twenty-four months, although the intense thought process almost killed him. When he finally solved the problem, he proclaimed it as "A mental state of happiness about as complete as I have ever known in my life" (Tesla 1982, p. 65).

MANIC SUCCESS

The Tesla Polyphase System was destined to revolutionize the industrial world. Science writer John O'Neill (1968) said it best: "In a single mighty burst of invention he created the power of today; he brought into being our electrical power era, the rock-bottom foundation on which the industrial system of the entire world is built" (p. 5). As in most great breakthroughs, it was accomplished through great sacrifice and pain. Tesla accepted his first job in Strassburg, Austria, in 1882 and it was there he built the first working model of the induction motor. By 1883 he was an employee of Continental Edison and offered this company his great invention for the price of long-term employment. He was turned down even though the company was affiliated with Thomas Edison, which was his reasoning for taking the job in the first place.

Tesla immediately set out for the United States to discuss his invention with the great Thomas Edison. All of his possessions including his clothes were stolen prior to boarding ship, but Tesla arrived unperturbed in New York City in 1884. He went immediately to Edison and enthusiastically described his invention. Needless to say, the AC system was received with veiled contempt. However, Edison was perceptive enough to realize Tesla's genius and hired him to refine the direct current dynamo at ConEdison in New York City. Tesla accepted the job but continued refining his own system and was finally issued the first patent for his alternating current generation system on October 12, 1887. He was twenty-nine years old. On May 16, 1888, he was given his first opportunity to demonstrate his invention before the American Institute of Electrical Engineers. In the audience was George Westinghouse. From that day on, Nikola Tesla would be known as one of the greatest electronic engineering geniuses of all time and Westinghouse Electric would become a world leader in power-generating plants.

Will and Manic Power

Tesla was obsessive-compulsive and much of his success emanated from his manic need to achieve at any cost: "I work in a frenetic passion" and then "I sink into a nearly lethargic state which lasts half an hour." His biographer John O'Neill was convinced that Tesla's power lay in his manic nature: "his greatest creation was himself . . . as Superman!" Tesla could become so intense in resolving a mentally taxing problem that he would collapse from emotional exhaustion. He had several nervous breakdowns because he constantly pushed himself beyond reasonable limits in his need for perfection. He described this as a life-and-death internal struggle: "With me it was a sacred cow, a question of life and death. I knew that I would perish if I failed" (Cheney 1981, p. 22).

Tesla's willpower was the overriding factor in many of his most successful creations. While walking in a park and reciting from Goethe's *Faust,* he had an intuitive experience. He remembered, "While reciting these inspiring words the idea came like a flash of lightning and in an instant the truth was revealed." He concluded: "The incessant mental exertion developed my powers of observation." Mania was Tesla's greatest asset *and* his most devastating enemy, emotionally and physically.

Tesla used visualization to create new products and concepts. Often, during intense concentration for resolution of a problem, he would go into a trancelike state during which he would see flashes of light. At times he worked in such a feverish manner he would collapse. The maids who cleaned his hotel room reported finding him standing in a trance and cleaned around him without his moving a muscle. Tesla made note of one of these trances when he was refining his radio transmitter in 1892: "I worked unremittingly and I was at the point of breaking down, nature applied the preservative, inducing lethal sleep." He referred to these occasions as "mists of oblivion" and was never quite sure how long he was out of touch with the real world.

Psychic Inspiration

Tesla was in the middle of one of his periods of nervous exhaustion when he found the inspiration for the induction motor. He was so hypersensitive during this period that he could hear a train whistle twenty miles away, which made his chair vibrate wildly. He stated: "I had the sense of a bat and could detect the presence of an object at a distance of twelve feet." His pulse fluctuated wildly from subnormal to 260 beats per minute. His doctors gave up in their attempt to find a cure for the physical symptoms that obviously had an emotional base.

At the height of his emotional trauma, Tesla said, "The idea came like a flash of lightning, and in an instant the truth was revealed." It was 1882 and would be another six years before the world would know about this scientific breakthrough. When the solution came, Tesla said: "It was a mental state of happiness about as complete as I have ever known in my life. . . . Ideas came in an uninterrupted stream.

. . . In less than two months I evolved virtually all the types of motors and modifications of the system." In one gigantic creative effort he had revolutionized the distribution of electricity to homes and businesses and simultaneously created the motor that could be driven by such a system. This system of motors included polyphase induction, split-phase induction, polyphase synchronous, and the whole polyphase and single-phase motor system for generating, transmitting, and utilizing electric current. Tesla had revolutionized electromechanics. He was only twenty-six at the time of this creation and by age thirty-three would be a millionaire.

WORKAHOLIC CREATION

When Tesla invented his polyphase system, he had no money to commercialize either the system or motors. It was at that time he decided to leave for America and present his ideas to Thomas Edison. Edison would not give him any support and actually demeaned his idea since it was diametrically opposed to his invention. However, Edison hired Tesla to refine his direct current dynamos and Tesla worked feverishly at the project since Edison had promised him a $50,000 bonus. Edison ultimately refused to pay the bonus (Cheney 1981, pp. 32–33). In fact, he had given the manic Tesla a task that he felt was impossible to accomplish. After this the two became bitter enemies, not just over the money, but because Edison did everything possible to destroy Tesla's AC creation. Tesla found himself broke and unemployed. He decided to never work for anyone again and became an entrepreneur forming the Tesla Electric Light Company in Rahway, New Jersey. Financially backed by James Carmen, he opened his new company in April 1887 with an initial capitalization of $500,000, to design, build, and implement AC systems, plus develop other electronic concepts.

WESTINGHOUSE

George Westinghouse, the inventor of the railroad air brake, was fascinated by Tesla's presentation at the American Institute of Engineers. He told Tesla, "I believe your Polyphase system is the greatest discovery in the field of electricity," and offered him one million dollars for the alternating current patents plus royalties. Tesla responded, "If you will make the royalty one dollar per horsepower, I will accept the offer." Within a matter of minutes these two giants of industry shook hands and Tesla was destined to become the richest man in the world. Based on Tesla's forty-one U.S. patents, this offer, although attractive, came only to $25,000 per patent. Within four years the agreement would be worth $12 million, which Westinghouse couldn't pay. In fifty years this contract would have been worth billions.

Tesla, like all visionaries, was never motivated by money. His only interest was in seeing his alternating current system and induction motor commercialized. The record of the royalties exists in the Westinghouse archives, and if this contract had remained intact Tesla surely would have become one of the richest men in history.

As part of his agreement with Westinghouse, Tesla agreed to work as a consultant in the commercialization of his patents, for which he received $2000 per month. One legacy from Tesla's work at Westinghouse was his insistence on the United States standard—a sixty-cycle system for alternating current. Tesla and Westinghouse collaborated in the lighting of the 1893 Chicago World Exposition using alternating current. Edison was by then an outspoken critic, and the flamboyant Tesla lectured extensively and allowed two million volts of electricity to flow through his body to refute newspaper claims by Edison that alternating current would electrocute anyone who installed it. A short time later Westinghouse successfully installed the first major power-generating plant in the United States at Niagara Falls, which transmitted alternating current power twenty-two miles to Buffalo.

TRAGEDY

On July 30, 1891, Tesla became a U.S. citizen, which he called one of the "happiest moments of his life." He kept this certificate in his office safe, but threw his honorary degrees in drawers.

Tesla's royalties grew enormously during the first few years. After four years, Westinghouse owed him $12 million but couldn't pay. The company had expanded without the necessary capital and Westinghouse was forced to go to J. P. Morgan for capital. Morgan told Westinghouse to "get rid of that royalty contract" with Tesla if he wanted help. George Westinghouse went to Tesla and explained his dilemma: if the royalty agreement was not canceled, he would be forced to file for bankruptcy and Tesla's AC system of electrical distribution would never be commercialized. Tesla, in the inimitable style of a Promethean inventor, ignored the dire financial implications of his decision and said, "Mr. Westinghouse, you have been my friend, you believed in me when others had no faith, you were brave enough to go ahead and pay me a million dollars when others lacked courage. . . . Here is your contract and here is my contract—I will tear both of them to pieces. . . . Is that sufficient?" (Cheney 1981, p. 49).

John O'Neill, Tesla's friend and biographer, described this impulsive decision best: "Probably nowhere in history is there recorded so magnificent a sacrifice to friendship as that involved in Tesla's stupendous gift to Westinghouse of $12,000,000 in unpaid royalties." Tesla had a few years of funding to pursue his great ideas, but would spend a great percentage of the rest of his life raising funds for research instead of researching. According to his friend O'Neill, he was incapable of funding the fundamental research on radios, electron microscopes, fluorescent lighting, wireless energy, or solar engines because of limited financial resources. Westinghouse paid Tesla a one-time fee of $216,600 for the outright purchase of all forty-one patents. Tesla would regret his decision as he spent the later part of his life destitute and unable to finance his creative ventures.

GOLDEN YEARS OF CREATIVITY

Despite Tesla's business naiveté he became a world-famous scientist while still in his thirties. One of his first inventions was a gas-filled tube light that he used to light his laboratory in 1893. It was the forerunner of the fluorescent light bulb and would not appear on the market for another fifty years. Tesla thought it very practical but refused to pursue its commercialization partly due to limited capital. He then built and demonstrated the first radio wave transmitter in 1893. He was years ahead of Marconi who would become rich from his radio patents. During the 1890s, Tesla was a pioneer in the field of X-rays and cosmic rays, which would later be refined by Marie and Pierre Curie many years later. In 1891 he received the patent on a carbon-button lamp that became the precursor for the 1939 electron microscope. Early in the 1890s he adapted his polyphase system to create the world's first electric clock, which worked on AC current. He was too busy to commercialize this creation also. Tesla discovered some therapeutic benefits of electrical energy flowing through the body due to his own experiments. This work was the basis for diathermy some fifty years later.

On March 13, 1895, a fire destroyed Tesla's laboratory and with it a lifetime of research. He had lost many of the experiments and documented research on the radio, X-rays, wireless transmission of sound, energy transmission, and guided vehicles.

After a short respite in which Tesla was forced to borrow funds, he came up with the idea of controlling the sun's energy to create steam in his "solar engine." This was another concept he created, refined, and demonstrated but never commercialized. In 1897 he demonstrated two remote-control model boats in Madison Square Garden to the delight of thousands of onlookers. He was the madman of invention, creating a prodigious output of revolutionary products and concepts before age forty.

ENERGY IS PERVASIVE

By 1898 Tesla had became fascinated with the possibility of controlling weather. He moved to Colorado Springs where he set up a laboratory. His main objectives were to create lightning in the laboratory and generate the highest voltage of electricity ever produced by man. These experiments were controversial and proved many of Tesla's theories, except for his idea that the world is a gigantic "energy conductor." One of Tesla's goals was to harness the power of the sun which could then be channeled to control the world's weather. Another idea was the transmission of energy without wires. Tesla believed that 90 percent of all energy was wasted between the generation station and its ultimate destination and blamed this loss on wires. He spent five years of his life (1898–1903) attempting to resolve this esoteric scientific problem.

MAD SCIENTIST

Tesla claimed his greatest invention was the electrical transmitter built in the Colorado Springs lab, which was capable of generating one million volts of electrical power. During these experiments, he successfully generated manmade electrical storms, earning him the appellation of mad scientist. Horses grazing a half mile from his experiments often became frightened. Many saw his experiments as science fiction.

On July 3, 1899, Tesla created what he described as "experimental evidence of a truth of overwhelming importance for the advancement of humanity" (Cheney 1981, p. 142). He demonstrated that "it was practicable to send telegraphic messages to any distance without wires, as I recognized long ago, but also to impress upon the entire globe . . . to transmit power, in unlimited amounts to any terrestrial distance and almost without loss." In one final experiment he was able to generate twelve million volts in a laboratory environment which would not be duplicated for many decades.

Tesla had made the world dance to his electrical tune and was now revered as a mythological wizard who could alter the world. The media described him as being not centuries ahead of his peers, but millennia. Unfortunately, he gave the press remarkable stories about his ability to create and distribute energy, infuriating traditional scientists.

The major product that evolved from his eighteen months in Colorado was the Tesla coil. Tesla used this device to produce high-frequency and high-voltage electrical current. In 1899 he produced an electric spark 135 feet in length and lit two hundred lamps more than twenty-five miles away without the use of wires. This resulted in a proposal to build the World Wireless Center on Long Island in 1900, to be financed by J. P. Morgan. When Morgan pulled out, the project died. Tesla was now on a manic mission to create even more esoteric products.

MANIC ENERGY

Once on a project, Tesla would drive himself to such a degree that he would burn out and be forced to take a rest cure. His work habits even startled the notorious workaholic Thomas Edison, who was his first American employer. When working for Edison, Tesla started each day at 10:30 A.M. and ended at 5:00 A.M. the following morning. He did this seven days a week. If he was close to the solution of some esoteric problem, he would work for two or three days without sleep. Edison gave him the ultimate tribute: "I have had many hardworking assistants but you take the cake." Edison was seriously joking when he promised Tesla $50,000 to rework every dynamo in New York City, because he thought such a task was physically impossible. Tesla worked in a manic frenzy, scarcely sleeping while redesigning and reworking all the dynamos. When finished, he proudly told the shocked Edison and learned the realities of the cruel world of business.

Power, Influence, and Destructiveness

Tesla had a resilient will and charismatic power. His Balkan accent gave him a mysterious air. He had flair, an attractive persona, and a huge intellect. Franklin Chester wrote in the *Citizen* (1897): "When he talks you listen. You do not know what he is saying, but it enthralls you" (Cheney 1981, p. 78). John O'Neill, the Pulitzer Prize-winning science fiction editor of the *New York Herald Tribune,* became Tesla's fan and biographer. He described Tesla as a man with an "ethereal brilliance" who had "created the modern era." Science writer Julian Hawthorne, the son of Nathaniel Hawthorne, was fascinated that such a technological genius could also be a sensitive poet, philosopher, and connoisseur of fine wine and music. Hawthorne wrote that when this "Titan spoke one could grasp the future in his face," adding, "His psychic energy was awesome." During a Manhattan dinner with Tesla and Freddie Zivic, the welterweight boxing champion of the world, Hawthorne recalled, "the energy zinging between them made my skin itch and tingle." O'Neill likened Tesla to a ten-pound diamond: "No one would question the value of the stone, but who would be in a position to purchase it or make any use of it?" (p. 73).

ICONOCLASTIC GENIUS

Tesla's dominant will was in many ways identical to some of his great inventions: Both were almost beyond comprehension. Tesla's willpower emanated from deep within his psyche and his creations were laden with the same transcendental-like quality. This unique persona caused him to live life as an eccentric loner. His many idiosyncrasies only added to his reputation as a brilliant iconoclast. The prognostications that emanated from this brilliant mind can only be compared to those of Leonardo da Vinci. Both were able to predict scientific progress with amazing accuracy.

Tesla delighted in shocking his friends, including Mark Twain, by lighting himself up with a million volts of electricity in his Manhattan laboratory. He would glow like a Christmas tree to the delight of his audience. This feat was possible since he kept the frequency very high, which kept the current on the outer portions of his skin, otherwise he would have been instantly electrocuted. He knew this even though the greatest scientists in the world did not. His prescient knowledge added to his charismatic power, and in the last part of the nineteenth century earned him the reputation of an "electrical sorcerer" who used black magic in his creations.

CREATIVE DESTRUCTION

Tesla was famous for the creation of oscillators. In 1898 he attached a tiny electro-mechanical oscillator to an iron pillar on a loft building located on East Houston Street in Manhattan. He flipped the switch and was waiting for his test results when buildings miles from his lab began to shake and hordes of people descended on the streets in panic. Police were immediately dispatched to the mad inventor's house to investigate the cause. By the time newspaper reporters arrived, Tesla had destroyed the oscillator as even he became concerned that it might bring down some large building. Tesla often boasted that he could destroy large buildings: "I could drop the Brooklyn Bridge in less than an hour" (Cheney 1981). He boasted to science writer Alan Benson of having the power to split the earth with a big enough oscillator and precise timing. He once told reporters that he could walk over to the Empire State Building and "reduce it to a tangled mass of wreckage in a very short time" with an oscillator small enough to slip into his pocket. Such power gave Tesla a reputation as a "mad scientist," when in fact he was a pacifist and a very gentle man.

SELF-DESTRUCTION

Tesla lived on the edge in everything he did. His work in science, physics, engineering, and medicine were all concepts ahead of their time. He never worried about the risk involved in his work or the effect it had on existing traditions. He frightened the establishment and thereby contributed to his own self-destruction. He would not surrender his principles, no matter how much it hurt him. Refusing to accept the Nobel Prize with Thomas Edison struck a mortal blow to a man who desperately needed the prestige it would have given him in order to raise monies for research. Tesla never forgot being cheated by Edison, and was even more incensed at Edison's refusal to accept alternating current as a viable concept. He could never come to terms with sharing such a prestigious award with someone who denied the truth. His refusal cost him credibility within the scientific community in addition to many engineering grants. His eminent work became lost to posterity when the name Tesla should be better known than Curie, Rutherford, and Edison.

Tesla's Promethean temperament also contributed to his self-destruction. He persisted in being a loner and refused to document or share his work with others in the scientific community, which resulted in great losses to him and mankind. When his lab caught fire in 1895, years of pioneering work and many great inventions were lost. A more traditional scientist would not have been so devastated. This crisis drove Tesla into a depression and near breakdown. He spent his later life struggling to survive and died a pauper when he should have died a wealthy man. Money was never important to him but in the end it kept him from realizing many of his dreams.

LIVING ON THE EDGE

Tesla's need to excel led to numerous breakdowns in his life. His manicness allowed him to create wondrous things for society but it took its toll on his health and at other times almost killed him. His closest brush with death took place in Colorado Springs. He had turned a switch off and it accidentally kicked back on while he was lying on his back repairing an instrument. High voltage electrical streamers, which had the power to incinerate a person with seconds, filled the room, bouncing everywhere. Tesla recalled: "The primary carried 50,000 volts and

I had to crawl through a narrow space with the streamers going. The nitrous acid was so strong I could hardly breathe." Tesla barely survived this brush with death.

TRUTH AND INTEGRITY PERSONIFIED

Tesla was a courteous and humble man who loved and nurtured pigeons his whole life, treating them as if they were his intimate friends. He would not have hurt anyone. His wild experiments however, earned him a reputation as a mad scientist. Telling the press that he was able to destroy the Empire State Building or Brooklyn Bridge with his infamous oscillator did nothing to improve his image. When he told the press that he was capable of splitting the earth he furthered his reputation as an eccentric. The coup de grâce occurred when he told the *New York Times* that he had a "death beam" which could destroy ten thousand airplanes at a distance of 250 miles and one million soldiers at one time. Tesla was crying out for recognition but a fearful public never knew if he was serious or bragging. Tesla was a compassionate and caring individual whose real talent was intellectual power. He never used superior knowledge as a destructive force or to gain power. His only desire was to pursue truth, but his arrogance and superior intellect was his downfall. He created fear in a public that could never comprehend his concepts. It is interesting to note that many of Tesla's outrageous quotes took place at the time when Orson Welles's broadcast "War of the Worlds" caused such a panic over a presumed Mars invasion. Tesla had often said he was able to communicate with Mars and these stories only contributed to his bizarre reputation.

Tesla's Legacy

Tesla is the most important but least known scientist in the history of the world. This visionary had utopian ideas of creating a world without hunger and communication without wires. He dared control the weather and sought to create limitless energy. He was a giant intellect who was the real father of radio, fluorescent lighting, robotry, guided vehicles, automated robots, and solar engines. He revolutionized the world of power distribution and created the motors which run the industrial world. His solar engine was announced to the *Mining and Scientific Press* on January 15, 1898, as "a method of producing steam from the rays of the sun." This one of many ingenious inventions that Tesla never commercialized.

Tesla once said "Throughout space there is energy. . . . It is a mere question of time when men will succeed in attaching their machinery to the very wheelwork of nature." Scientists are just now beginning to understand the meaning of his remark. His dream of transmitting power from station to station without wires caused the media to call him a madman, with one headline reading, "Tesla Electrifies the Whole Earth." He created more media excitement by claiming he was close to communicating with Mars, claiming that "communication with Martians was a statistical certainty."

Biographer John O'Neill called Tesla a "self-made Superman" and "the greatest invention of the greatest inventor of all time." O'Neill's description of him as a superman gives credence to my theory that he was driven by a Nietzschean "Will to Power." One thing is certain: Nikola Tesla's success was based on an obsessive need to create and overachieve. He drove himself until he was sick, but his mania resulted in monumental achievements. His legacy can be seen in the context of his monumental contribution to mankind. Every powerhouse in the world, every dynamo, every motor which drives every machine are monuments to his obsessional need to create. Tesla virtually gave away his patents for the accelerating current induction motors. He also failed to pursue the commercial aspects of many of his most noteworthy inventions like the radio, fluorescent lights, guided missiles, X-ray technology, and electric clocks. He was not selfish and willingly shared his most precious inventions. Marconi received credit for the invention of the radio when Tesla actually preceded Marconi in every aspect of the fundamental research on radiowave transmission. Tesla sued Marconi in 1915 and was given certification of his prior art for his work on radio transmission. He declared: "Let the future tell the truth, and evaluate each one according to his work and accomplishments. The present is theirs, the future, for which I really worked, is mine." In 1943 Tesla was finally awarded the rights of creation of radio transmission by the Supreme Court of the United States.

Tesla realized that his "visualization" had kept him "poor in a monetary sense though it made him rich in the raptures of the mind." It is commonly accepted that all great innovative geniuses downplay the financial considerations of their inventions. Tesla operated as a classic Promethean by living on the edge technologically and financially. Science-fiction editor Kenneth Swezey said Tesla "plunged into the unknown. He was an arch conspirator against the established order of things." Science editor Hugo Gernsback gave Tesla his proper due: "without a shade of a doubt Nikola Tesla is the world's greatest inventor, not only at present but in all history. . . . His basic as well as revolutionary discoveries, for sheer audacity, have no equal in the annals of the intellectual world." Biographer John O'Neill called him "A God whose ethereal brilliance created the modern era." Probably the most renowned quote came from *New York Herald Tribune* science writer Julian Hawthorne: "Tesla's brain compared with those of most of his contemporary scientists [Edison, Lord Kelvin, Marconi, the Curies] is as the dome of Saint Peter to pepper-pots."

NIKOLA TESLA
Inventor of AC Induction Motor and Engineering Visionary
b. July 10, 1856, Smiljan, Croatia, Yugoslavia; d. January 7, 1943, New York City

Dominant Trait: Psychic energy, obsessive-compulsive, eccentric

Motto: "Throughout space there is energy"

Nickname: "Electrical Sorcerer," "Poet of Science," "Father of Radio"

Vices/Hobbies: Poetry, gambling (billiards and cards), pigeons, voracious reader. Sartorial splendor matched Wright.

Heroes/Mentors: Son of Aba, Mother Duka Mandic, Anital Szigety, Mark Twain, and George Westinghouse

Philosophy of Life: "Intuition—I could visualize, needed no models, drawings, experiments."

Fantasy: "Wireless transmission of intelligence." "World as energy conductor."

Professional Successes: AC induction motors (1884), first wireless (radio) transmission (1893), fluorescent lights (1893), solar engine (1898), Tesla coil (1898), VTOL (1915), and concepts inspiring the electron microscope, cosmic rays, guided missiles, and radar. Predicted satellite TV reception in 1915.

Power: Charismatic flare for describing his intuitive brilliance. Frightened people with creative genius.

Influence: Pervasive through fields of engineering, physics, science, and medicine. A true renaissance man,

Destructiveness: Type A personality who drove himself into creative frenzy with "periods of tortured concentration." Nervous breakdown 1884, amnesia 1891. Obsessive-compulsive and megalomaniac behavior.

Birth Order: Second son who became only son when he killed brother Dane accidentally. Younger sisters Mikla, Angelina, Marica. Dane's traumatic death by his hand at age five emotionally affected him for life.

Parental Influence: Autocratic Orthodox priest father, Milutin, and inspirational mother, Duka, who he idolized. "I inherited my photographic memory and inventive genius from my mother."

Transiency: Family moved at age six. Nikola left home for school as teenager, never to return.

Crises: Brother Dane's death tormented him for life. Doctors gave Nikola up for dead three times. Came out of nervous breakdown to invent AC induction motors.

Formal Education: Voracious reader who taught himself four languages (English, French, German, Italian); attended Polytechnic University in engineering but did not graduate for lack of funds.

Libidinal Drive: Sublimated to work; never married despite charismatic appeal. Saw women as distraction from work.

Personality Type: Introvert-Intuitive-Thinker-Judger on MBTI. Had "cosmic intuition," saying, "Ideas came like a flash."

Self-Esteem: Enormous self-confidence in his own ability confirmed by a Hearst writer who said, "He has that supply of self-love and self-confidence that usually go with success."

Rebellion: Loner who media called "an arch conspirator against the established order of things."

Risk Propensity: Gambled to raise money for college. Put one million volts through his body as an experiment.

Work Ethic: Type A workaholic who could work days without rest. Edison called him hardest worker ever knew. College professor asked him to be removed from college over obsessive work ethic.

Tenacity: When father took away his reading candle, he made his own candles in order to read all night.

Optimism: Inveterate optimist who believed he could accomplish anything including many bizarre experiments.

Manicness: *New York Times* wrote his "flashes of psychic energy" were amazing. He saw any achievement as a "question of life and death. I knew that I would perish if I failed." Computed the cubic contents of food at every meal, hotel rooms had to be divisible by three.

Adolf Hitler

Right only exists through power and force.

Overview

Adolf Hitler achieved more power with less talent than anyone in history. He had no qualifications for leading the German nation or even heading the National Socialist German Workers party (Nazi party). This dictator had no experience, little education, no redeeming qualities, no social consciousness, and few talents other than a charismatic power of speech. He was a rabble-rousing political hack who took advantage of a desperate nation with weak leaders during a worldwide depression. This opportunist saw Germany's weaknesses and carefully manipulated them to his advantage. Hitler used nationalism and Aryan superiority to win over a disgruntled constituency by promising them racial purity and redemption from economic chaos. Hitler frightened them with the specter of communism. They bought into his deluded dream. Hitler was a demigod who used Versailles Treaty and Depression to sell his demonic dreams of redemption. Using his gift of oratory, he seduced the minds of many Germans who became his faithful disciples. He was a political chameleon who changed into the common man for the socialists, a gracious host with women, an anti-Semite for the hate mongers, capitalist for businessmen, and a shy compassionate friend for children. He was even capable of becoming a Communist when that image met his needs. Never has a major nation relinquished so much power to someone less deserving or qualified.

POWER OF SPEECH

Hitler never rose above the rank of corporal during WW I, yet in 1921 he was able to have himself appointed führer of the emerging Nazi party and then Reich chancellor in 1934 after former President von Hindenburg's death. Hitler rose to the very pinnacle of power in the German Republic on a platform of nationalism, yet did not have one drop of German blood!

During the first forty years of his life, Hitler had not achieved one positive thing. He was a dismal failure in regular school, failed two entry exams to art school, failed as a painter, and never held one responsible job his whole life. He was a bum and an Austrian draft dodger who by an accident of fate ended up in Munich when the Great War broke out. Serving as a soldier in World War I was his only legitimate occupation, and there he never made it past corporal even after distinguishing himself for bravery.

How could someone with no talent or qualifications get to the top strictly through the power of speech? Charisma can be hypnotic with small numbers of disciples, but Hitler raised the art of mass brainwashing to a new level. His first successful experience took place just after he joined the German Workers party on his release from the army. The party had a platform that fit his fanaticism and psychic energy, allowing him to bully his way up within the organization to a position of leadership. The Nazi party was a radical group to begin with, but after Hitler's influence it became tyrannical. The Nazi party became the embodiment of Hitler's philosophy, which was expounded in *Mein Kampf*. This book was Hitler's one and only creative contribution. It was written when he was incarcerated in Landsberg Prison at age thirty-six, serving time for leading the Nazis' 1924 Munich Beer Hall Putsch. It was an attempt at a coup d' êtat, but was both premature and amateurish. Hitler learned much from the experience and used the crisis as a motivator to gain power.

STRUGGLE FOR POWER

The "triumph of the will" was Hitler's rallying cry. *Mein Kampf* ("My Struggle") was intended as an autobiography to rationalize Hitler's personal failure in life. He wrote that he was raised poor, which was not true. He claimed he failed in art school because of Jews which was also untrue. Every philosophical tenet in the book led to justification and rationalization of his ineptitude and failures in life. One of his insights, which all cult leaders understand, is that one common goal or adversary must be chosen as a rallying call to the masses. In *Mein Kampf* Hitler chose the Jews as that adversary and used bigotry to enjoin the German masses in the cause to create a pure Aryan or Master Race. Hitler truly believed he was chosen to lead the German people against the Jews and to destroy communism. In *Mein Kampf,* Hitler dwelled on fear and destruction. It ignored the evidence that his failures were caused by indolence, lethargy, and inability to get along with people. He said that "Struggle is the father of all things," and this became his legacy. Struggle was something a depression-bound society could identify with: it would become the motto of the Nazi party.

Mein Kampf was barely readable and contained little useful philosophy or literary facts, except that plagiarized from Nietzsche and Schopenhauer. It clearly postulated Hitler's view of life and his dreams for a Third Reich. He bastardized Nietzsche's "Will to Power" and Schopenhauer's "Blind Will" to fit his own demented philosophy. His "Might makes Right!" and racial prejudice were adopted from Nietzsche's highly ethical "superman" concept of rational self-interest. His plea to the German people was: "Submit to the party's will." In other words, subjugate their "will" to his, which, unfortunately, they did.

Early Life Experiences

Hitler was born in Braunau am Inn, Austria, on April 20, 1889. He was the first son of Alois Hitler and Klara Poelzl, Alois's niece and housekeeper. Klara had three other children die prior to his birth, which contributed to her indulgence with her new son. Hitler's father was a womanizer. He had two prior marriages and was fifty-two when Hitler was born. Alois, Jr,. and Angela were Hitler's half brother and sister who were six and seven years old at the time of his birth. Edmund and Paula were born after Adolf. Edmund died of measles when Adolf was eleven, leaving him to carry on the family's name and his mother's dreams. Hitler's father was a self-made man who rose from extreme poverty to achieve respectability as a customs agent. Alois was an autocratic father who beat young Adolf regularly. His mother would salve his wounds after the beatings and he was consoled by an older and younger sister. Hitler loved his mother passionately and carried her picture with him constantly, keeping her picture at his bedside until the end of his life (it was found in the Berlin bunker after his suicide).

EDUCATION

Hitler attended primary school in Fischlheim, followed by a Benedictine monastery school where he was a choirboy. When Hitler's younger sister was born, his half brother Alois ran away from home to get away from their abusive father. The family moved to Passau, Austria, when Hitler was three, and then moved again to Linz where he attended a science school. Hitler was always a poor student due mainly to his lethargy and total disregard for authority. His father died suddenly when he was fourteen and his mother doted on him more than ever. She gave him anything and everything he wanted. He dropped out of school in 1905 because of a strange illness that went away after exam time. His half brother Alois described Hitler's childhood in an interview in 1948: " He was imperious and quick to anger from childhood onward and would not listen to anyone. . . . If he didn't get his way he got very angry. . . . He had no friends, took to no one and could be very heartless. He could fly into a rage over any triviality" (Toland 1976, p. 9).

MAMA'S BOY

After his father's death, Hitler took advantage of his indulgent mother. First he dropped out of high school and then decided to become a composer. Convinced of his intentions, she used precious funds to buy him a piano that he never played. She then financed his move to Vienna to study art. He and August Gustl Kubizek, the only true friend he would ever have, shared an apartment in Vienna. Hitler became apprenticed to Alfred Roller, a stage scenery painter, until he became bored and applied to the Vienna Art Academy. His friend Kubizek passed the entrance exam, but Hitler failed, not once, but twice. He met with Academy President Siegmund l'Alemand and, learning l'Alemand was Jewish blamed that for his failure.

Hitler loved Vienna and never returned home. It was here that he formulated his philosophical and political ideology. Having inherited eight hundred crowns after his father's death, Hitler bought elegant clothes and an ivory-handled walking stick, and attended the opera every night. Wagner's Nietzsche-inspired operas became his favorites with their omnipotent themes. For a while he pursued architecture and then decided to become a freelance artist. Being spoiled and lazy, he failed at these also.

CRISIS, TRAUMA, AND INSPIRATION

The death of Hitler's mother in 1907 was devastating to him. As a teenager, he was now on his own. Kubizek was his only companion and Hitler became very possessive, insisting that is friend speak to no one else. Kubizek spoke of Hitler's emotional outbursts where he would "rage and pontificate" on subjects of interest: "Such rapture I had only witnessed in the theater . . . as though a demon had possessed him . . . he never tired, he never slept." These are classic manic-depressive symptoms.

Kubizek recalled that one evening in 1908 Hitler became enraptured by Wagner's opera *Rienzi.* On leaving the operahouse, Hitler told Kubizek he had never been so inspired and planned to "lead Germany out of servitude to heights of freedom." As Führer, he would invite Kubizek to the Reich Chancellery in 1939 and tell him, "In that hour it [his power] began."

Kubizek went home, leaving Hitler alone to find his way. Hitler became a bohemian street person. He tried painting postcards but was not diligent in production or effective in his art. Rejected in other trades, he began a life of abject poverty. The more he failed the more he railed against those he felt responsible for his failure. It was during this period that he developed the nihilism that permeates *Mein Kampf.*

Psychic Energy Incarnate

Hitler was naturally exuberant, which bordered on bombastic. His overt enthusiasm was a symptom of his hypomania. His mentor, Dietrich Eckart, was able to transform his animated behavior into charismatic rapture, which made him a spellbinding speaker. Eckart was an intellectual publisher and anti-Semite who belonged to the German Workers party before Hitler joined. They met in 1919 after Hitler returned from duty in WW I. Eckart was everything Hitler was not. He was an erudite, wealthy, and hard-drinking Bavarian. He published his magazine *In Plain German* to promote his radical nationalism. His poetry and plays followed the same theme. He was a devotee of occultism and black magic, and active in the Thule Society.

WILL EQUALS MIGHT

Eckart introduced Hitler to the Thule society. Followers believed in *Thule,* a legendary island like Atlantis in the North Atlantic and purportedly the home of a race of Aryans. The society's ambition was to build a race of supernatural beings and eradicate what it considered to be inferior races.

Eckart had married many of the Thulian concepts with those of Carl Jung and was a disciple of consciousness expansion. Eckart invited Hitler into his inner circle, and began indoctrinating him in the psychological techniques of mind expansion. Eckart's chief aim was to optimize Hitler's human energy potential. For the first time in his life Hitler became an excellent student since the material appealed to his perverted sense of ego. He mastered the techniques of oratory. The result was what Alan Bullock referred to as "the magnetism of a hypnotist." Shortly before his death in 1923, Eckart wrote: "Follow Hitler! He will dance, but it will be to my tune (Schwarzwaller 1989, p. 60).

PRAGMATISM PREVAILS

On meeting Hitler for the first time, a member of the German Workers party said: "I felt I had come face to face with God." Hitler was not only a hypnotic speaker, he suddenly believed himself to be the savior of Germany. He declared: "I am the greatest German of all times," when he wasn't even German. He wrote, "I shall become the greatest man in history. . . . I have to gain immortality even if the whole German nation perishes in the process" (Hershman and Lieb 1994, p. 185).

After his release from Landsberg prison in 1924 Hitler staged a power play to become party leader, taking the title *der führer* (the leader). He had learned from the beer hall debacle, where the party almost perished, never to use force to gain political power. He then created the SS, a racially elite police force, for his personal protection. This group was made up of many aristocrats who were blindly obedient to Hitler and as fanatic as their führer. Under Heinrich Himmler, the SS were put in charge of all security including the prisons and extermination camps. Hitler used the SS as a buffer against the uncontrollable SA, the storm troopers.

Hitler decided that power was best acquired with popular support. Legal elections were far safer and more enduring. He used his influence to bend the rules to become a German citizen, thus becoming eligible to run for election. Hitler adroitly used his newly acquired power of speech to gain supporters and ultimate election into the Reichstag Congress. He received 33 percent of the vote in 1932. His strong showing wasn't enough and he lost to the aging von Hindenburg. There were seven million unemployed in Germany, and Hitler ranted and raved, promising jobs. Von Hindenburg capitulated on January 30, 1933, and made him president. In August 1934 Hitler abolished the office of the president after von Hindenburg's death and appointed himself "Führer and Reich Chancellor." He felt by exercise of his "will," anything was possible.

CHARISMATIC POWER

Once in power, Hitler resorted to force to expand and preserve that power. He carefully surrounded himself with needy people with great ambition. Many were from the fringe element of society who saw the opportunity with Hitler to implement their renegade and often sociopathic drives. Refusing a salary when elected chancellor, Hitler endeared himself to the working classes in a masterful public relations coup. He knew that the person who controlled the Nazi party's money would be the one to control power, so he surreptitiously controlled the pursestrings of the Nazi party. His business manager and confidant, Max Amann, managed the money and only Hitler knew the source or use of the funds. Hitler raised vast sums for the party and felt he was entitled to spend it as he saw fit. He concentrated his charm on the wives of Germany's industrialists. Women were captivated by Hitler's charisma and love of the arts. They became his conduit to their husbands' wealth. Some of the Führer's more enthusiastic supporters were Helen Hanfstaengl, Winifred Wagner, Elsa Bruckman, and Helene Bechstein. One industrialist whom he carefully cultivated was Gustav Krupp, who had married Germany's richest heiress. Both Krupps were enamored by Hitler's magnetism and became ardent Nazis. Hitler's financial strategy worked and by 1932 this man who never had a legitimate job in his life had become a millionaire and, more importantly, controlled the finances of the Nazi party.

WILLPOWER

Hitler was able to convince people to surrender their will to him. This enormous power was born of psychic energy and his own intransigent will. He said: "If the economic experts say this or that is impossible, to hell with economics. What counts is *will* and if our will is hard and ruthless enough we can do anything" (Bullock 1971, p. 82). The West saw this trait in Hitler and naively decided to use him and his party to curb the advance of bolshevism. Hitler responded in kind and used the West's greatest fears for his own ends.

Hitler surrounded himself with fervent disciples who believed in his immutable destiny. He adroitly selected individuals from each economic and political sector to appease the broadest constituency. Ernst Rohm had been a soldier. Rudolf Hess and Hermann Goering were both ex-officers. Joseph Goebbels was a pseudointellectual who had been unsuccessful in business but a natural to head Hitler's public relations effort. Publicist Heinrich Hoffman was his photographer and confidant Max Amann his business manager. Propaganda Chief Herman Esser was a libertine and anti-Semite. His bodyguard was Ulrich Graf. These men became the nucleus that led the party through the difficult days of the 1920s and into political power. Hitler inspired these men with a steady stream of messianic dialogue aimed at motivating them to follow his every command. He told them, "If the party once falls to pieces, I shall shoot myself without more ado," and philosophized, "I have not come into this world to make men better, but to make use of their weaknesses."

TH FÜHRER

Hitler assumed power in January 30, 1933, when President von Hindenburg appointed him Reich Chancellor after he received 37 percent of the electoral vote.

In March he received 44 percent of the vote, the most ever received in a free election. He realized ultimate power was when von Hindenberg died in August 1934 and he appointed himself dictator with the title Führer. From that day forward Hitler was the supreme commander of the armed forces and began a military buildup for the conquest of Europe. He violated the Versailles Treaty when he occupied the Rhineland in March 1936. He used the *Anschluss* (German for "annex") to annex his homeland, Austria, on March 13, 1938, but it was an expropriation by fear. He then occupied the Sudetenland in September 1938, after which he organized the first programs against the Jews of Germany. His enormous success prompted his decision to invade Czechoslovakia in March 1939 and Poland on September 1, 1939. The Allies declared war to stop Hitler's onslaught, but his momentum could not be stopped and he conquered Belgium and the Netherlands with little resistance in spring 1940. By the end of summer he was in Paris and France had fallen under the Nazi juggernaut. By April 1941 Yugoslavia and Greece had fallen and by mid-1941 Hitler was at the zenith of his power.

DELUSIONS OF GRANDEUR

By 1942 Hitler was indisputably the most powerful man in the world and started believing he was invincible. His overconfidence led to his demise. His first two major blunders took place in 1941. His invasion of Russia in June was too easy and he, like Napoleon, reached the outskirts of Moscow with little or no resistance. By December he was delirious with power and fully thought he had defeated Mother Russia. He then made his biggest mistake by declaring war on the United States in December 1941. Hitler was no longer rational. He personally took command of the army when it was unable to take Moscow. In January 1942 he crossed all bounds of rationality, implementing an unconscious urge to destroy, by implementing the Final Solution. By summer 1942 Hitler's power had peaked. He was now deluded with power: "Extraordinary geniuses permit of no consideration for ordinary mankind." Albert Speer said "he trusted his inspirations no matter how inherently contradictory they were." Hitler believed that "One must listen to an inner voice and believe in one's fate." His psychic energy had brought him success, but it would ultimately destroy him along with his beloved nation.

A MANIC CHARISMATIC

Hitler's hypomania was probably the factor most responsible for his rise to power. Dr. Hermann Rauschning, president of the Danzig Parliament, said, "he neither tires or hungers; he lives with morbid energy that enables him to do almost miraculous things." According to one of Hitler's early supporters, Alfred Rosenberg: "He had a fanatical belief in his own mission which, toward the end, actually became incomprehensible . . . and was frequently derailed by sudden outbursts of passion." Hitler was always more comfortable speaking to thousands than attending a small party. He was shy, introverted, and uncomfortable around proficient people. His animated behavior was a ruse to offset feelings of inadequacy. France's pre-war ambassador to Germany was convinced Hitler was a raving lunatic. He wrote of a meeting when he and Hitler were talking and Hitler suddenly burst out with a violent diatribe that was not pertinent.

> He burst forth into a harangue. . . . His arguments gathering speed and volume . . .
> he roared and thundered as though addressing thousands of listeners. . . . These
> "fits" would last ten minutes or even three-quarters of an hour. Then suddenly . . .
> it was as though his batteries had run dry and he lapsed into inertia. (Hershman
> and Lieb 1994, p. 151)

Such was the nature of the impatient and impulsive Hitler whose attention span never allowed him to concentrate on just one topic. He had the multitasking ability found in great entrepreneurs and creative geniuses. He could simultaneously juggle two or three conversations yet amazingly keep them separated. He was the consummate autocrat and paranoid personality who took all the responsibility and trusted no one. He had become deluded into believing he was divine and omniscient and demanded control of everything and everyone. He said: "The work that Christ started but could not finish, I Adolf Hitler, will conclude." In his madness he must have forgotten that Christ was Jewish.

PSYCHOSEXUAL ENERGY

Psychic energy is characterized by enormous libidinal drive. Hitler had an animal sexuality that attracted females far beyond physical factors. His nickname was King of Munich, earned during his early sexual conquests in southern Germany. During that period Hitler had numerous mistresses that he used to satiate his sadomasochistic needs. Power was his forte, and many women are attracted to powerful men. He used charismatic appeal to attract money, votes, and women. Hitler had numerous mistresses, many of whom attempted suicide over him. Like Nikola Tesla, he felt that women and power were incompatible and carefully avoided any permanent relationships during his reign of power. His abnormal sexual practices were well concealed by the Nazi party. He felt strongly that his image should remain as a spartan single man without distraction. He committed to never marry while in power.

LIBIDINAL DRIVE

After Hitler came to power, screen star Renate Mueller became one of his favorite actresses. According to Hitler's biographer Wulf Schwarzwaller, one night she was invited to the Reich Chancellery, fully expecting traditional sex. While undressing, Hitler threw himself on the floor and insisted Renate beat him. Horrified, she refused, which spawned a furious tirade from Hitler, who humiliated himself, saying that he was her slave and totally unworthy of her love. Renate ultimately capitulated and beat him with his riding crop, causing Hitler to become aroused and to masturbate while being beaten. After his orgasm, they had a glass of wine and he bid her a cordial good evening, as if this were his nightly ritual. Hitler's bizarre sexual needs were corroborated by his henchman Gregor Strasser. He confirmed Hitler's sadistic and sadomasochistic tendencies, but was killed by the SS on June 30, 1934. Hitler's friend and financial supporter, Putzi Hanfstaengl, often claimed Hitler was incapable of normal sexual intercourse. Eva Braun's diary and other resources indicate he was capable of normal sex but preferred the more perverse variety.

Power and Influence

Hitler is considered a political genius who altered the course of the twentieth century through his willpower. Had he died in late 1938, many historians believe he would be remembered as the greatest German political leader who ever lived. His work programs and military buildup restored economic vitality to Germany and his nationalism and expansionism gave the German people someone to idolize. He offered peace with the Munich Treaty while secretly preparing for war. He used financial power to finance a military war machine and his charismatic power to maintain total control over the nation. He skillfully instilled an esprit de corps in the people through the use of flags, marches, and melodramatic dreams of a thousand-year Reich. He made Marxism and Jews the enemies of the German people.

Charisma enabled Hitler to mesmerize the people into supporting his dreams of Germanic destiny. His power of persuasion was exercised not only on the uneducated or the naive. Hitler charmed the likes of industrialist Ernst Putzi Hanfstaengle, a German American who became his friend, confidant, financial supporter, and foreign press secretary. Hanfstaengle had been sent to Germany by an American military attaché and became so captivated by Hitler's fiery rhetoric that he became a member of the Nazi party. After the Munich Beer Hall Putsch, Hanfstaengle's wife, Helen, took away the revolver with which Hitler intended to commit suicide. She lived to regret that action. Hermann Goering was another bright and competent individual who fell under Hitler's spell. Goring was a highly decorated WW I fighter pilot who heard Hitler speak in 1922 and immediately joined the party. Winifred and Siegfried Wagner, the son of composer Richard Wagner, also became members of the party and financial supporters after hearing Hitler in the early twenties. Shell Oil magnate Sir Henri Deterding also came under Hitler's spell and supplied early seed monies for the party.

MAD DEMIGOD

Hitler was actually surprised at the ease of the party's expansion and his own rise within it. He described it as "miracle," admitting he did not understand the cause. Hitler was the consummate pragmatist, always ready and willing to adopt any platform or resort to any ruse to gain power and influence. He used unemployment, communism, Jews, inflation, nationalism, the Versailles Treaty, and disenchantment as tools to gain power. But his primary instrument was his magnetic power of speech over the masses: "If you wish the sympathy of the broad masses, then you must tell them the crudest and most stupid things." He wrote in *Mein Kampf* that "lies were important" to gaining power and the use of "vehemence, passion, fanaticism, are the great magnetic forces which alone attract the great masses" (Bullock 1971, p. 38). Confirmation of his belief in the power of dialogue is seen from his comment: "The greatest revolutions of the world have never been directed by a goose-quill! . . . The broad masses of the people can be moved only by the power of speech (Stein 1968, p. 49). His madness grew until he forced the German youth to worship him like a god. They were required to take an oath that sounded more like a prayer: "I consecrate my life to Hitler, I am ready to die for Hitler, my savior." Hitler always used passionate words effectively in his speeches (psychologists have found passionate words most effective in communications). He acknowledged selecting key words like "force," "smash," "hatred," and "ruthless" in a deliberate attempt to raise audiences to hysteria. Alan Bullock wrote in *Hitler—A Study in Tyranny* (1971) that his strategy worked: "Men groaned or hissed and women sobbed involuntarily caught up in the spell of powerful emotions of hatred and exultation." When he achieved total power, Hitler declared, "Whoever fails to obey my orders will be destroyed."

MEGALOMANIC IDEOLOGY

Hitler's hypnotic magnetism and enthusiasm were his instruments for gaining power over the German people. Once in control he resorted to physical force to maintain power and expand his sphere of influence. The Nazi party followed the Führer's philosophy to the letter and became fanatical and passionate in carrying out his orders. Hitler had a hair-trigger temper and was capable of violent rages. No one in his entourage dared to disobey him and carried out his most perverse orders. His methodology for gaining power was based on two nationalistic concepts: "destruction of the Jews" and "more living space." Both ideologies were widely accepted by the German people since one eliminated competitors for valued jobs and the other offered an expanded power base for the nation. The Jews of Germany were the intellectual elite who dominated merchandising and distribution of goods. Most Germans could agree with Hitler's diatribes during the Great Depression when the middlemen (Jews) were seen as the ones reaping profits from basic commodities. Hitler had skillfully drafted an agenda with universal appeal. Both programs justified a build-up of a military elite and the creation of the feared SA (storm troopers), which he formed in 1921 to maintain order. Hitler was able to gain both revenge and power with the same platform.

PSYCHIC INFLUENCE

Every person in the twentieth century was influenced in some way by this pernicious man. Hitler ranked as the thirty-fifth most influential person in Michael
Hart's 1989 book, *The 100—A Ranking of the Most Influential Persons in History*.
Hart equated Hitler's influence as equivalent to that of Napoleon and Alexander
the Great. Unquestionably he was the most popular leader in Europe during the
mid-thirties and was considered a political genius at the time. His influence, like
his power, was mostly negative. The only positive thing that can be learned from
Hitler's rise to power is that the human will and charismatic power can be pervasive and awesome. The power he attained and the influence he exercised were
based on nothing more than his ability to enthrall masses of people through the
power of speech. His personal power over people radiated from within his psyche.
He knew how to move the masses with mesmerizing orations, which were often
pointless diatribes but always appealed to the fears of his audience. If Hitler had
used this talent differently, he might have achieved more positive ends.

DESTRUCTIVENESS

Hitler's wartime destructiveness resulted from his messianic belief in his invincibility. Hitler had delusions of grandeur, a typical symptom of manic-depressive illness.
He believed he "knew" the way to greatness and the German people followed him.
The trail ended up in destruction unparalleled in history. Some forty million people
died as a result of his power. The shape of Europe and the Cold War resulted from his
madness. Ironically, he was responsible for the spread of communism, which he
hated. Hitler's destructive power sprang from his need to justify his personal deficiencies. He was prepared to destroy everything and everyone to maintain his position as Führer. Hitler used his power negatively. His destructive nature was spawned
by a need to exorcise both a tormented childhood and a failed adulthood. He needed
to blame someone for his bungling past and the Final Solution was the result.

Hitler's destructiveness will outlive the thousand years he had predicted for
the Third Reich. One need only go through the Holocaust Museum in Washington, D.C., to understand the full impact of Hitler's madness: He was responsible
for the deaths of approximately six million Jews and the displacement of eight
hundred thousand more. His megalomania resulted in the deaths of an additional
twenty-five million Russians and Poles, seven million soldiers and civilians, plus
seven hundred thousand Gypsies. In total, forty million lives were lost, with
countless millions more were effected. In 1939 Hitler was asked about his intentions. He responded: "Do I intend to eradicate whole races? Of course I do!"

Hitler's destructive nature even soured his love relationships. His niece and
lover, Geli Raubal, committed suicide after his jealous rage at her affair with his
chauffeur, Emil Maurice. Another mistress, Unity Mitford, shot herself in a suicide attempt. Mistress Mitzi Reiter also attempted suicide, as did Eva Braun twice.
Braun joined him in a double suicide in their Berlin bunker in 1945.

Legacy of a Madman

Hitler was an enigma, having none of the qualities associated with becoming a great leader. Yet between 1939 and 1945 he was the most powerful man in the world. In 1934 Hitler received an unprecedented 84 percent of the popular vote, which was highly influenced by the SA. By 1942 this despot had control of Europe and North Africa. He ruled the National Socialist German Workers party with an iron fist between 1921 and 1945. His total belief in the redemption of Germany appealed to the masses. His fanatical belief that he could "will" anything gave him an enormous power. How did he accomplish this? Mostly by seduction of the masses with his charismatic power. His mastery over his own will was the first step in controlling others.

Hitler was a manic pragmatist who never allowed any adversary to deter him from reaching the top. It is significant that after his defeat at Stalingrad in 1943 he became a recluse. Defeat had drained him of his enormous psychic energy, which was fed by the adulation of his disciples and military victories. He would make only two more public speeches. Hitler became a sad sight as an emotional cripple who had turned an ideology of national supremacy into national degradation. Although a negative role model, we can learn from Hitler's manic need to succeed.

Symbols such as flags, crests, and emblems build esprit de corps and become important visuals in building a following. People need and desire to identify with emotional imagery. Visual images can be used in recruiting disciples and motivating them to pursue radical causes. Hitler understood this principle of leadership and chose the swastika in 1921, an esoteric symbol found in many cultures, as the symbol of the Nazi party. The swastika was probably one of the most psychologically powerful symbols ever created for a nation. Evolving from Hitler's work with the Thule sect, its crimson background symbolized socialism and passion. The white circle denoted nationalism. The black swastika was placed inside the white circle to represent the "victorious struggle of the Aryan race." Hitler reversed the swastika's right-handed orientation to left-handed, clockwise to counterclockwise. This change was subtle but effective. He took a positive right-handed concept representing white-magic, light, and creativity and transformed it into a negative left-handed concept symbolic of black magic and destruction. This should have alerted the world to the nihilism latent in Hitler and his party.

Hitler's megalomania was largely responsible for his rise to power. He was certainly a manic-depressive, as were other famous despots such as Alexander the Great, Napoleon, and Stalin. The manic half of this affliction became his tool for gaining power. The classic symptoms of hypomania are fearlessness, euphoria, racing thoughts, sleeplessness, grandiose ideas, promiscuity, and belief in one's own divinity. Hitler had these symptoms in abundance and they all played a key role in his rise to power. Hershman and Lieb (1994) state that all tyrants (including Hitler and Napoleon) are ruled by three forces: "unlimited egoism, the compulsion to control everything, and . . . manic-depressive delusions, particularly grandiosity and paranoia" (p. 198). Hitler fit their description when he proclaimed, "I shall become the greatest man in history. . . . I have to gain immortality even if the whole German nation perishes."

ADOLF HITLER
German Führer and Founder of the Third Reich
b. April 20, 1889, Braunau am Inn, Austria; d. April 30, 1945, Berlin, Germany

Dominant Trait: Hypnotizing charismatic orator extraordinaire spawned by manic personality. Obsessed madman.

Motto: "Right only exists through power and force." "One must listen to an inner voice and believe in one's fate." "Struggle is the father of all things." "Submit to the 'will' of the Nazi party."

Nickname: "Wolf," "The Führer," "King of Munich"

Vices/Hobbies: Poetry, Wagner's operas, fast cars, kinky sex, and a lifelong passion for art

Heroes/Mentors: Richard Wagner, Schopenhauer, and Nietzsche. Wagner's opera *Rienzi* his inspiration at age nineteen. Mentor Dietrich Eckart molded him into hypnotic speaker through "mind control."

Philosophy of Life: "Might makes right." "I have no bourgeois scruples." "I believe very deeply that destiny has selected me for the German nation." Promised Germans redemption, power, and purity of race.

Fantasy: Master Race of Aryans in Third Germanic Reich cleansed via Final Solution.

Professional Successes: Politics and writing *Mein Kampf* (1924). Creator of Third Reich to rule Germany for 1000 years. After he assumed leadership in 1933, it lasted but twelve horrifying years.

Power: Came precariously close to ruling world through "triumph of the will" philosophy. Used charismatic power to wield enormous influence over millions which led to the deaths of some 40 million souls.

Influence: Altered twentieth century more than any other man. Worldwide devastation, including Final Solution.

Destructiveness: Monster of destruction who destroyed many mistresses: Geli Raubal (died), attempted suicides by Unity Milford, Mitzi Reiter, and Eva Braun. Responsible for deaths of forty million in WWII: 6 million Jews, 7 million Allies, 17 million Germans, 700,000 Gypsies, and 10 million Russians.

Birth Order: Firstborn of father, Alois, who married niece Klara. Two older half-siblings and younger sister, Paula

Parental Influence: Permissive mother and authoritarian father who beat and abused him. Mother doted on Hitler, molding him into an egocentric. Idolized mother; kept her picture at bed entire life.

Transiency: Moved at age three to Passau and at six to Linz. In teens left home for Vienna and life of art.

Crises: Three older siblings died prior to Hitler's birth; brother died when Hitler was five. Father's abuse instilled psychotic rage and need for revenge. Father died when Hitler was thirteen, mother when he was seventeen, became bohemian bum at nineteen. Nervous breakdown and suicide attempt after Geli Raubal's death.

Formal Education: High school dropout. Blamed Jewish headmaster for Vienna Art Academy rejections.

Libidinal Drive: "Women's gushing adulation carried to the pitch of religious ecstasy." Sado-masochistic tendencies.

Personality Type: Introvert-Intuitive-Thinker-Judger. Sadistic and masochistic. Manic-depressive.

Self-Esteem: "Hitler believed that whatever he desired would come to be." "He had a demonic belief in his ability."

Rebellion: "The creative genius stands always outside the circle of experts" (*Mein Kampf*). Half-brother Aloise said, "He had no friends, took to no one, and could be very heartless."

Risk Propensity: Risked everything daily for the redemption of his own deluded dream of reality. Had a death wish.

Work Ethic: Kubizek said, "He had an ecstatic dedication and activity. He never tired, he never slept."

Tenacity: "We shall not capitulate! No never! We may be destroyed, but if we are we shall drag a world with us, a world in flames." "He who resigned . . . lost his right to live."

Optimism: "For me the word 'impossible' does not exist."

Manicness: Biographer Stein wrote: "He had the magnetism of a hypnotist, the force of an African Medicine man."

9

Work Ethic: The Type A Personality: Helena Rubinstein and Rupert Murdoch

Even if you are on the right track, you'll get run over if you just sit there.
—Will Rogers

Type A Personality

Twelve of these fourteen visionaries were Type A personalities. Type A individuals are obsessed with winning at all costs because they believe their self-worth is a reflection of their accomplishments. Type As are afflicted with a kind of *rushing sickness,* marked by their impatience and impulsiveness. They are generally intolerant of mediocrity and do not understand why other people are not so driven. Most cannot bear not having complete control over their destiny. Such personalities cannot relax without feeling guilty, in contrast to the Type B person who is more patient and capable of relaxing and enjoying life. Type Bs are capable of playing a game without having to win at any cost; Type As cannot.

Most successful entrepreneurs and creative geniuses are Type As. They speak rapidly, walk and drive fast, and typically receive an inordinate number of traffic and speeding tickets. They take early flights and use taxis instead of shuttles. High energy and drive are their forte. They tend to be early for meetings and have a short attention span. Most must complete what they start and will finish a book even if they hate it. Completing tasks is exhilarating for these people. They avoid lines and nonproductive conversations. The Type A personality is multitasking and can read a book, watch TV, and hold a conversation simultaneously. They worry about work or resolving problems even while playing golf or attending a ball game. Such people feel guilty on vacation or when relaxing. Ironically, they are seldom ill or miss work other than when they have pushed themselves to exhaustion. They literally don't have time for sickness or injury until their bodies and emotional systems

289

rebel and collapse. Walt Disney and Nikola Tesla were repeatedly forced to abandon work and relax to avoid a complete physical collapse.

PRODIGIOUSLY PRODUCTIVE

Types As are those irritating people who insist on finishing others' sentences. They do so because they are thinking ahead, anticipating the speakers intent, and are incapable of waiting. Most are ridiculously early for appointments unless their overcommitted schedule delays them. They annoy others socially by interrupting their conversations in a desperate need to make their point. Type As tend to schedule more than is possible or reasonable, pushing themselves to overachieve by setting impossible goals. They are obsessed with winning. Success is based on the score, not in the play. They will sacrifice valuable relationships to win the game (more true of males than females). These individuals are perpetually in a hurry as if they were double-parked on the street of life. Most never check bags on plane trips because they feel it a waste of their valuable time and won't relinquish control of their bags. They have an insatiable need to control everything in their lives, professionally and personally. Their achievements can be sensational because they have set such high standards for themselves and others in their employ. These personality types are driven to great achievement and feel guilty when not in pursuit of their dreams. Artist Vincent Van Gogh declared: "My work is my body and soul, and for it I risk my life and my reason." Composer Peter Tchaikovsky exclaimed: "Without work life has no meaning for me." Prodigious output and achievement are the goals of the Type A personality.

Work Ethic—A Formula for Success

The only two subjects in this book who were not Type A personalities were Amelia Earhart and Maria Montessori, but even these two were workaholics who drove themselves far beyond the norm. All the others were workaholics who rose to the top by outworking their competitors. The two individuals who best personify the workaholic personality are Helena Rubinstein and Rupert Murdoch. Both achieved enormous success but were so driven that they had little time for friends or family. Like the other subjects, neither took time to enjoy the fruits of their success or power.

WORK IS FUN AND PLAY TEDIOUS

The majority of these fourteen individuals worked an average of twelve hours a day, seven days a week, and slept an average of four to six hours per night with Tesla the most driven at two hours per night. Work has a negative connotation to most people, but as Shakespeare said, "If all the week were holiday, to play would be as tedious as work." To these creative geniuses their excessive time on the job was not work, it was their passion, and they would have been perturbed if someone told them to spend less time doing what they enjoyed. Nikola Tesla was so immersed in his work he slept only two hours every night, although he admitted to staying in bed for an additional two hours to think about his work. He arrived at his lab every morning at 10:30 A.M. and left at 5:00 A.M. the following morning. He did take time for a long dinner when not absorbed in some revolutionary invention. When working on the alternating current invention, he said, "I knew I would perish if I failed" and "I had a veritable mania for finishing whatever I started."

Pablo Picasso answered, "I never get tired" in response to those who couldn't understand his passion for work. He was blessed with an inexhaustible vitality, which he explained by saying, "That's why painters live so long. While I work, I leave my body outside the door, the way Moslems take off their shoes before entering the Mosque." Picasso was still a workaholic in his eighties and told reporters, "I have less and less time and more and more to say." At age ninety he told a reporter, "I am overburdened with work. I don't have a single second to spare, and can't think of anything else."

ENERGY AND SUCCESS

Helena Rubinstein and Rupert Murdoch owe their success almost entirely to hard work. Murdoch biographer Jerome Tuccille (1989) characterized him as "a prototypical workaholic. If the word didn't exist, it would have to be coined to fit him." Murdoch slept only fours each night right into his sixties. Helena Rubinstein was similarly driven: "Sleep has never been important to me. I often worked . . . way into the night" (Rubinstein 1972, p. 46). One of her favorite sayings was: "Work is your best beauty treatment." At age eighty-eight she wrote of her early days getting started in Australia: "I worked twenty hours a day, every day, including Sundays. I swear if I had to do it all over again, I would sooner kill myself." During her heyday, the *Saturday Review* labeled her a "human whirlwind." A typical work day for media baron Rupert Murdoch at age sixty consisted of breakfast in New York and dinner in London, during which he was on the phone buying or selling a business in Australia or Asia. This frenetic activity is the rule for those driven to achieve at all cost. Their wives seldom relate to this behavior. One of Murdoch's partners in an Australian airline said, "I am a normal businessman, but he is a phenomenon. Rupert is well above all of us in capacity and speed. I have never seen anyone working so fast and so precisely. He can cover so much ground—no other human being in the world could do it" (Shawcross 1993, p. 216).

Competitive and Aggressive Behavior

Most of these visionaries were so competitive they would lie and cheat in order to win. To these individuals, their profession was a game and they played it with the same gusto. Money wasn't the major consideration, winning was. They often sacrificed money, health, and marriage to win. Consider Nikola Tesla's decision to rip up a legal contract from Westinghouse worth $12 million so that his alternating current invention would replace Edison's direct current system. Biographer William Shawcross was shocked by Rupert Murdoch's competitiveness. Murdoch was not a good athlete but when playing tennis was a tiger. Shawcross wrote, "Murdoch always played tennis as if the world hung on his winning." Even the soft-spoken Maria Montessori was driven. Although not a Type A, she was described by her good friend E. M. Standing (1962) as "possessing a driving ambition." Howard Hughes had to beat the competition at any cost. He was determined not to lose control of TWA, and his tenacity and competitiveness won him a court award of $547 million in 1964. Walt Disney was so competitive during the famous Disney Studio strike in 1941 that he fired everyone, almost bankrupting the company in the process. Napoleon was notorious for cheating at cards. One biographer said that Napoleon "was unable to accept losing so much as a chess game." He treated all battles as a game, declaring at Elba, "I've lost nothing. For I began the game with a six-franc in my pocket, and I've come out of it very rich." Even so, he went on to lose his empire because he was incapable of standing on the sidelines and jumped back into the game only to lose everything at Waterloo. Frank Lloyd Wright resorted to a fistfight to keep his first job and almost killed his co-worker when he resorted to lethal weapons in defending his position.

Impatience, Impulsiveness, and Intolerance

These power brokers were intolerant of mediocrity, quick to fire incompetents, and irritable with anyone who did not agree with their master plan. Edith Piaf was labeled a tyrant by her sister, Simone, because she was so impatient and intolerant. Her impetuousness was legend. She would step out for a drink and come back two days later. According to Simone, "she lived as though each day would be her last." Isadora Duncan was driven to perfect her dance style and would dance all night without food or rest when a certain mood or feeling would hit her. Her friend and roommate, Mary Desti (1929) describes one frenetic and impulsive period: "She acted like a person demented, that nothing could stop. . . . Isadora would not sleep a wink and was in a state of the wildest excitement." (p. 133). Duncan was always impulsive and on her first visit to Greece bought a mountain in Athens to open a school of dance without inquiring whether the land had water. It didn't and she lost a fortune. Her impatience led her to make a similar error in accepting an offer to open a school in Moscow after the Russian Revolution. She was unsuccessful and forced to return to Paris.

Most of these visionaries had similar experiences due to their impatient and impulsive behaviors. They would enter into major contracts with a handshake. This need for speed made them eminently successful since they were able to spot and act on new opportunities and leave the competition at the gate. It also caused them great problems as speed does not always allow time for excellence. They were able to move swiftly because they were extremely knowledgeable about their given professions. Those who hesitate are usually afraid of making a mistake and refuse to act because of their basic insecurity. None of these subjects lacked confidence or knowledge and allowed their impulsive natures to take precedence over detailed analysis.

Rushing Sickness

All of these individuals were addicted with a kind of "rushing sickness." They ate, talked, drove, slept, and lived fast. Picasso was so impetuous when he arrived in Paris at age nineteen that he painted a new work each day. An art dealer warned him that he would ruin the market for his art. Picasso proved more right than the art dealer because he was able to reinvent his art every decade. He ultimately produced fifty thousand works of art—the most prodigious production in the history of art. When Hitler was a teenager, his friend August Kubizek said, "He had an ecstatic dedication and activity. He never tired, he never slept." Napoleon was energy incarnate. He worked nonstop fourteen to sixteen hours a day, living on three to four hours of sleep. His valet Constant said, "He had the energy of a whirlwind." Everything Napoleon did was at an accelerated speed. He graduated from college in half the normal time and became the most powerful man in the world by age thirty-five. Nikola Tesla had a similar propensity for speed, allowing only two hours a night for sleep in his mad dash for achievement. Both these men were in a hurry to finish whatever they started and their speed allowed them to leave the competition in their wake. Walt Disney had a serious case of "rushing sickness." Disney would embark on work binges for many months and then would collapse. He slept on the couch at his studio almost half his working life since he didn't want to waste the time commuting. After months of feverish work he would break down both physically and emotionally.

Those in a hurry often are too impatient and impulsive to worry about the repercussions of their behavior. They are often eminently successful but the rushing madness takes its toll on their bodies. Disney, Hughes, Napoleon, and Tesla were all prone to nervous anxiety due to their frenetic work habits. Each experienced emotional breakdowns following periods of prodigious output. Frank Lloyd Wright in many ways was as prolific in architecture as Picasso was in art. He completed three hundred commissions during his eighties, which amounted to one-third of his life's output. He completed his most famous design, Fallingwater, in a two-hour burst of energy that left his assistants flabbergasted. Meryle Secrest, his biographer, said he worked "ceaselessly" throughout his life in a passionate drive to create. Even Sade was afflicted with "rushing sickness" in his sexual liaisons, even while in prison. He recorded in his diary 6,536 orgasms by masturbation or "insertions" over a twenty-seven month period while in the Bastille.

Insecurity, The Father of Overachievers

Most of these subjects forced themselves to succeed because they didn't dare fail. Their innate need to achieve negated any chance they wouldn't. Edith Piaf was literally born in a gutter. She worked day and night to make sure she never returned to the Paris streets. When twenty, this chanteuse worked all day and then changed clothes for her nightly cabaret appearances. Her sister, Simone, said Piaf even worked when eating, "She would look around and listen, and she got her ideas out of everything." Piaf had a deathly fear of being alone and spent many hours each day making sure a man would occupy her bed.

Disney had an "obsessional preoccupation with death," which is one of the things biographer Marc Eliot contends drove him to overachieve. Disney was so afraid of artists stealing his concepts that he refused to hire any at his studio. Nikola Tesla felt insecure because of a talented older brother: "I grew up with little confidence in myself." He always felt his accomplishments were "inconsequential to [those of] his dead brother." Tesla's fear of failure became an obsession that made him ill but also contributed to his enormous inventiveness. Tesla developed an obsessive-compulsive personality as a defense mechanism against potential failure. Howard Hughes, like Tesla, had a neurotic dread of germs. He feared premature death, which drove him to fill each day with more and more activity. His intense fear of disease and dying is especially strange in that he regularly risked his life in aerial exploits. Hughes's fear of failure drove him to spend days without rest in a mad rush to finish a movie or refine an airplane engine. He spent millions on maintaining the *Spruce Goose* because it was a symbol of his superiority in building unique aircraft. He spent $1 million a year for twenty years just to store this useless plane because he was afraid of losing his valued reputation.

Multitasking

These visionaries had such drive and energy that they often did many things simultaneously. They could carry on a conversation while reading a book or listening to a radio or television. They could talk on the phone while planning. Biographer Meryle Secrest (1993) called Frank Lloyd Wright a "champion juggler" due to his ability to keep "many balls up in the air simultaneously." Wright once designed three totally different homes before breakfast while in his eighties. Napoleon dictated to four secretaries simultaneously on different subjects. Maria Montessori was the director of the Orthophrenic School in Rome at the same time she carried on a medical practice, taught classes, and lectured. Each evening she would analyze classroom results and create new programs for the next day. Even after she became highly successful, Montessori had at least three different projects running simultaneously in different parts of the world.

Rupert Murdoch is the king of juggling different companies located on various continents. He is the key operating executive in all of his television, newspa-

per, magazine, movie, cable, airline, book publishing, and computer graphics industries. He is the master puppeteer in the game of media madness, manipulating
a gigantic media empire that stretches over four continents. Helena Rubinstein
maintained a similar juggling act running a fashion/cosmetics empire in Australia, London, Paris, Germany, and the United States. She pulled all of the strings
and made every decision.

Helena Rubinstein

In this business you must work twenty-four hours a day and three hundred years in a lifetime.

Helena Rubinstein, or Princess Gourielli as she preferred to be called later in life, was the queen of beauty during the first half of the twentieth century. She was the consummate self-made woman and preceded Elizabeth Arden, Coco Chanel, Estée Lauder, and Mary Kay. This First Lady of Beauty dominated the cosmetics industry not only in the United States, but also in Australia, Britain, Germany, France, and Italy. Her name was synonymous with beauty and skin care. *Vogue* magazine described her as "an adventurous soul who deviates from established routes." Rubinstein's power prompted *Life* magazine to speculate, "She is perhaps the world's most successful businesswoman" and an "effective autocrat." *House and Garden* (November 1992) characterized her as having "a monstrous vitality," adding that she "worked ceaselessly and slept little" with a talent for being "fantastically idiosyncratic." Rubinstein's dominant trait was a Type A personality that gave her a need to control everything in her life, including her "gofer" husbands. Her first husband, Edward Titus, finally left: "Nothing will ever change you, Helena, your business is your life."

HUMAN DYNAMO

Rubinstein was a workaholic, always willing to sacrifice everything for her business, including sleep: "Sleep has never been important to me" as "I often worked in my kitchen way into the night, even after a party, until I could no longer keep my eyes open." She was convinced that work was critical to all business success: "In this business you must work eighteen hours out of every twenty-four . . . and three hundred years in a lifetime." She admitted, "My own success is due primarily to a combination of luck, hard work, and perseverance." She lived by those standards, working every day until she died a wealthy dowager at age ninety-four.

TYRANNICAL HOLOCAUST

Patrick O'Higgins worked, lived, and traveled with Rubinstein for the last fifteen years of her life. When they first met, she was introduced to him as Princess Gourielli. She interviewed him at the Colony and a colleague at *Flair* magazine warned him, "Eat what she eat; otherwise she eat you!" Rubinstein had a well-earned reputation around Manhattan as a "tyrannical holocaust," a name coined by *Life* magazine. During this first meal with O'Higgins, Rubinstein, fifty years his senior, ate twice what he ate and finished it before he even got started. He recalled, "I had to wolf down my food in order to catch up with Princess Gourielli." On the ride to the theater, he was asked to pay for the cab as the frugal princess never paid unless there were some residual benefits to her.

FRUGAL CONTROL FREAK

Rubinstein was notorious for cutting everything in half during negotiations, including employee wages. Such behavior helped this matriarch build one store in Melbourne, Australia, into a $100 million beauty empire. Her frugality was legend. Despite her great wealth, she insisted on a brown-bag lunch. Patrick O'Higgins describes her habit of buying clothes in Manhattan bargain basements in order to save money, only to embark on annual around-the-world trips costing tens of thousands of dollars. O'Higgins described her as "imperial" and "dictatorial," adding that she was an obsessed "control freak." He characterized her as "favoring quick action, spirited, independent, ruthless." She spent frivolously on homes, art, and image clothes (outer garments for effect) spent almost nothing for undergarments. Rubinstein was infamous in New York City for paying slave wages while demanding unreasonable work. Her sisters managed most of her enterprises and she treated them as shabbily as she did anyone else.

Early Life Experiences

Helena Rubinstein was born on Christmas Day 1870 in Cracow, Poland. She was the first of eight girls born to Augusta and Horace Rubinstein. Helena had one brother who died in infancy, which caused her father to treat her as the "son" in the house. Horace Rubinstein ran a wholesale business in the food industry, buying eggs from peasants and selling them to merchants at a profit. He was a major influence on young Helena, both positively and negatively. She named her son after him, one indication of his influence on her early life, and she spoke highly of him in her autobiography. After the birth of eight daughters, Rubinstein gave up on having a son and looked upon Helena as his heir apparent.

MAGICAL BEAUTY CREAM

Helena Rubinstein credited her mother as the one who instilled her with a sense of beauty. She wrote of her mother's ability to maintain her looks and beauty despite having a child every year. Her mother preached to her the importance of beauty in the life of a woman: "Beauty will give you the power to control your own life." Her mother's actress friend visited the Rubinstein home when Helena was quite young. She introduced the family to a skin cream purchased from a Hungarian chemist, Dr. Jacob Lykusky. This was a compound blended from herbs, almonds, and extracts from the bark of the evergreen tree. Her mother insisted the girls use this magical cream nightly before bed with the admonition, "It will make you beautiful, and to be beautiful is to be a woman." Young Helena never forgot this advice nor the beauty cream destined to become her life's work.

Rebellious Eagle

As the eldest of eight daughters, Rubinstein was in charge of the household after her parents. Because she exhibited an authoritarian temperament by age twelve, her sisters nicknamed her the "eagle." It was her father who instilled the business work ethic in young Helena. She watched him buy and sell eggs for a profit and often assisted him with his books. In his eldest daughter, he saw the son who had died, and confided in her on many business matters. When she was fifteen, he sent her to speak for him when he was too ill to keep an important meeting. Her mother gave her sage advice prior to this meeting: "If you want to be really clever, listen well and talk little." Rubinstein took her mother's advice and was a success in her first venture with mature business men. This early success made a lasting impression on the young girl.

Australia and Independence

Her father was so impressed by young Helena's exceptional verbal talents that he enrolled her in a technical high school to prepare her for a career in medicine. She grew dizzy at the smell of antiseptics and did poorly in science. She enraged her father by dropping out of school and he immediately arranged for her marriage to a wealthy thirty-five-year-old widower. An authoritarian, he expected her to be a housewife with babies if she was not a professional. But he had molded Helena into a strong-willed and rebellious teenager who was not about to become chattel. She turned down the suitor in defiance of her father and at age eighteen fled the household. She wrote to Eva, a cousin in Melbourne, Australia, for permission to live with her and an uncle, Louis. Eva had lived with the Rubinsteins and the two girls had become friends. Rubinstein packed her belongings, including twelve jars of her precious skin cream, and embarked on the three-month trip.

Rubinstein had no money, spoke no English, had no skills or profession, and was going to a foreign country to make her way in the world. On the long voyage she learned a smattering of English and met Helen MacDonald, who would be instrumental in establishing her beauty business. She didn't even know her uncle, who turned out to be a problem. Uncle Louis was single, and he took advantage of her loneliness, attempting to force his affections on her and even suggesting matrimony. Rubinstein put it gracefully in her autobiography, "He took liberties." This eighteen-year-old needed him for security, not for romance. She became despondent and decided she had to leave his home. Lacking money and skills, her only knowledge lay in the beauty cream from Poland. The Australian outback was harsh on the complexion and everyone wanted to know her secret for beautiful skin. She decided to tell them.

CRISIS AND CREATIVITY

When Rubinstein first arrived in Australia, she found a ready market for her skin cream. She sold her total supply to women whose skin suffered the effects of the arid Australian climate. When she found herself alone in Melbourne and needed a means of survival, she turned to the beauty cream. With the rudimentary knowledge of merchandising learned from her father, Rubinstein decided to open a beauty salon to sell her skin cream. Her shop would be the first such retail establishment in the world. Rubinstein had a flair for marketing and was a workaholic. What she needed was the funding to open her store. She contacted the woman she had befriended aboard ship, Helen MacDonald, and asked for a loan. Miss Mac-Donald lent her $1500 to open her first salon. This was to be her first and only loan, which she repaid within months. Rubinstein's only product was Creme Valaze, but her store became an overnight success.

ENTREPRENEURIAL GENIUS

Rubinstein was oblivious to the difficulty of succeeding as an entrepreneur and the risk attendant to it. She was not only an innovator, but she was opening a business with little capital, no experience, and only one product. She relied on instinct only in pursuing her dream. On paper, she lacked the qualifications to succeed. However, once her store was open, Rubinstein became a terror. She often went without food and worked day and night to survive.

A retailing empire arose from this one-room storefront in Melbourne. Rubinstein's only real assets were her indomitable will and work ethic. It was ironic that she was in a business of making women attractive to men while she personally led a nonsexual existence. She was a celibate workaholic who worked eighteen hours a day seven days a week. She wrote in her autobiography how strange it was for her to become a purveyor of beauty to women when becoming seductive and provocative to men was unimportant to her. She also admitted to having missed many a beau during these early days in Melbourne. This early lifestyle became imprinted on her and she was never able to change.

THE ELIXIR OF BEAUTY

The first Helena Rubinstein Beauty Salon opened on Collins Street in the heart of Melbourne in the 1890s. She had only one product, Dr. Lykusky's Creme Valaze. Rubinstein painted the walls of her shop, designed her own logo, purchased the inventory, demonstrated and sold the product, mopped the floors, and opened and closed the store. She experimented with the creation of new creams aimed at people with different skin types. Becoming popular with actresses and Australia's chic crowd, Rubinstein was interviewed for a Sydney newspaper. The woman reporter was enchanted with Rubinstein's enthusiastic demonstration of skin care and her products. Her article recommended the store and creams.

Instant Success

The newspaper article created an avalanche of calls and new clients from all over Australia. Rubinstein suddenly had more business than she could handle. She wrote to Dr. Lykusky, the creator of Creme Valaze, and invited him to Australia to teach her to formulate her own line of creams. She credited her success to him but later changed the name of the product from Creme Valaze to Wake-Up Cream. With his help she developed a new line of products for oily, dry, combination, and normal skin types. Business was booming and she brought one of her younger sisters, Ceska, to Australia to help her run the store. Within twenty-four months, her store was so successful that Rubinstein considered its expansion.

Manic Success

Rubinstein's was a rags-to-riches story. This petite Polish entrepreneur worked very hard and saved every penny, living like a pauper, to build her beauty empire. She was a workaholic with an iron will that allowed nothing to interfere with her business. Rubinstein defined the European work ethic, always preaching that work was the cure-all for every business problem. Her early achievement reinforced her belief in work as the formula for all success. She was manically driven, placing hard work before all else. Ultimately, it did not make her happy or loved, but it made her rich and powerful.

Romance

Within the first two years of opening the salon in Melbourne, Rubinstein repaid the $1500 loan to Helen MacDonald and banked £12,000 ($50,000 U.S.), which was a king's ransom at the turn of the century. Within ten years she had accumulated $100,000, enough to finance a European trip to learn more about the science of beauty. But Rubinstein had another motivation for her trip. Now in her mid-thirties, she had met a man and was in fact trying to escape his hold on her emotions.

Edward Titus was an American newspaperman of Polish heritage who started courting her in Melbourne. Titus was an intellectual and flamboyant extrovert who passionately pursued the elusive Helena. Her trip to Europe was a flight from Titus after he told her, "Helena, I can see you are determined to build an empire. Marry me and we will do it together." Frightened, she left for Europe, promising him an answer on her return.

Rubinstein visited Paris, Vienna, and London. While in London, she decided to open a salon there. She had little intention of returning to Melbourne.

London

Rubinstein decided to open a salon in London. In 1908 she met with London beauty experts to learn about their culture and the machinations of that market. She was astonished to find the conservative British women afraid of any product aimed at improving their looks. Makeup was considered taboo and used only by actresses and prostitutes.

British upper-class women were the most demanding in the world. Rubinstein's friends told her, "Try to set up a beauty shop in London and they'll slaughter you." As a true entrepreneurial risk-taker, she was only challenged by such advice. Having correctly analyzed the London market, she opened her first store in the Mayfair district to serve London's carriage trade. Instead of being slaughtered, her store was an instant success and would become the base of her burgeoning empire. She had her eye on the Continent and London was the perfect city from which to launch her business. While in London, Isadora Duncan became one of her clients. Rubinstein wrote in her autobiography that she and Duncan were iconoclasts with similar needs for freedom.

MARRIAGE

Just before Rubinstein was about to open her Mayfair salon, Edward Titus strolled in one day. He had followed her from Australia, intent on winning her over. Rubinstein wrote that "marriage had never entered into my scheme of things," but capitulated to his charms. He was a fellow Pole and a welcome respite from her workaholic schedule. Titus took her to the ballet and courted her with unrestrained passion until she agreed to marry him in a small private ceremony at the London Registry Office in 1908. She retained her maiden name since it was already well known. Their children were named Titus.

The newlyweds resided over the London store so Rubinstein could be near her work. She would continue this practice for the next two decades. Titus wrote ad copy for the salons. The autocratic Rubinstein allowed him few other duties so Titus embarked on a career as a literary agent. In the salons he was never more than a gofer. Titus gained notoriety as the Parisian literary agent for Ernest Hemingway and James Joyce.

Rubinstein had her first child, Roy, in 1909. She called on her sister Manka to move to London as manager of the salon, freeing Helena to mother Roy and plan her beauty empire.

A PARISIAN WORKAHOLIC

Rubinstein lived for work and ruled her salons with an iron fist. She fully expected those in her employ to have the same work ethic. The First Lady of Beauty insisted on involvement in every decision. She drove herself unmercifully, causing the *Saturday Review* to characterize her as a "human whirlwind." Everything in her life was secondary to her business, including husbands and children.

Always looking for the next big opportunity, Rubinstein decided that Paris would be the next market for her salon. The city was a world-renowned fashion and art center with Picasso, Duncan, Hemingway, Fitzgerald, and Joyce in residence and Coco Chanel embarking on her fashion business.

Rubinstein admitted, "I could not enjoy the pleasures of domesticity for which millions of other women yearned." Her son Roy was two when she moved the family to Paris, once again residing over her new shop on the Rue St Honore. Anticipating her role as the chief executive of an emerging industry she had another sister, Pauline, manage this salon. During her stay in Paris, Rubinstein bore a second son, Horace, in 1912.

Hypomania and Success

At this time, the whirlwind started calling herself Madame. Rubinstein now had three stores but remained a restless, hypomanic personality. It became the catalyst for her enormous success and the basis of her horrid reputation as a tyrannical boss. She was never satisfied with herself, her sisters, or employees. A typical Type A personality, she confused self-worth with business success. Rubinstein was always in a hurry and recognized her mania: "The beauty business always came first with me. . . . I chided myself for my restlessness." Later she would write, "The truth is that my heart has always been divided—between the people I have loved and the ambition that would not let me rest" (Rubinstein 1972, p. 35). She truly believed in a philosophy of "work is your best beauty treatment." Rubinstein earned the title "World's most successful businesswoman" from *Life* magazine through hard work and high energy.

QUEEN OF AMERICAN BEAUTY

Rubinstein and her family were living in Paris when the First World War broke out. Concerned for the safety of their children, she and the American-born Titus planned to seek refuge in the United States. Rubinstein had long thought of America as the land of hope and opportunity—and a new market. They landed at Ellis Island in January 1915.

Respectable American women wore no lipstick and only a little rice powder on the nose; it was believed that only loose women resorted to makeup and lipstick. Everyone trusted to God to make them beautiful, according to Rubinstein, and she intended to change that. She opened her first American salon in a Manhattan brownstone on 49th Street in the summer of 1915. Once again, the family resided over the salon. However, the ambitious Rubinstein had larger aspirations than New York City.

AN EMPIRE BUILT ON BEAUTY

In the next two years Rubinstein opened salons in San Francisco; Boston; Philadelphia; Washington, D.C.; Los Angeles; Chicago; and Toronto, Canada. She sent for her sister Manka to help her with these openings and in classic Rubinstein style, worked as if her life depended on the outcome: "Eighteen out of twenty-four hours we were either traveling between one city and another or actively working. We lived out of our suitcases like actresses in a theatrical touring company. But with the excitement and stimulus we were never conscious of being tired."

By 1929 Rubinstein had opened salons in Milan, Vienna, and Rome. In 1929 she opened her flagship salon at 715 Fifth Avenue in New York City, which was the culmination of her life's achievement. By this time Rubinstein touted her salons as bastions of "scientific beauty" and staffed the Fifth Avenue store with physiotherapists, make-up and skin-care experts, dieticians, gymnasts, a medical doctor, and coiffeurs. It became a one-stop shop for beauty and featured her "skin-food" or Wake-Up Cream.

The Rubinstein creams were now mass-produced and merchandised through thousands of shops and department stores. They were the nucleus of the firm's revenues. The salons were an image front established to give credibility to her products and the Rubinstein name. Already widely known as "the beauty queen," she used the media and self-promotion to reinforce that image.

Rubinstein was now an incurable workaholic. She ignored her family, especially her husband. Titus subsequently engaged in many affairs for companionship. Rubinstein's Paris manager told biographer Patrick O'Higgins that his roving eye was not his fault but hers: "She never gave him a moment. God only knows how she found time to have two sons." Her husband told her, "Nothing will ever change you Helena. Your business is your life." They were divorced in 1930.

CHEAP FREAK

Madame Rubinstein never lost the frugal values acquired in her poverty-stricken youth in Poland. She had a "horror of waste" that was reinforced during those early years in Melbourne. Yet, she was a paradox. This wealthy woman would take around-the-world trips on a whim, but eat on park benches to save money. She was famous for arguing with cab drivers over minuscule fares. At age eighty-six she took a three-month trip to visit salons from Australia to Vienna with a side trip to Tel Aviv. According to Patrick O'Higgins, she admonished each manager for waste and inefficiency and was so obsessed with saving she would walk down three flights of stairs so as not to waste electricity on the elevator. She would sit up all night in trains rather than spend money on a sleeper. Rubinstein felt that eating out was for show and ate at her desk most of her life. She never spent money or engaged in any meeting unless it had commercial value. If it benefitted her business or her, then it was an acceptable venture. This habit made her into a master self-promoter.

FINANCIAL POWER

Rubinstein's financial power enabled her to buy estates, art, clothes, jewelry, and companionship. Her most noteworthy purchase was her second husband, Prince Gourielli, whom she met and married in 1938. The prince came with a title and was twenty years her junior. Patrick O'Higgins said, "He was one of her better possessions," even though she began treating him as a possession. When he died, she refused to return from her European vacation to attend his funeral. When her lawyer asked if she would return, she replied, "He's dead. What good? Why waste the money?"

From the twenties through the fifties, Rubinstein crossed the Atlantic six to eight times a year in an effort to maintain tight control over her international network of salons. Her first trips were made before World War II, when crossings were arduous sea voyages. She maintained homes in Paris, London, the South of France, New York, and Greenwich, Connecticut. New York became her home base and although a United States citizen, she was really a citizen of the world.

WILLPOWER

In 1950 Rubinstein was voted one of the ten richest self-made women in the world. She accomplished this through work and tenacity coupled with a manic obsession for achievement. She also was endowed with a resilient willpower that manifested itself in a mania for success. Rubinstein was impatient, impulsive, and could be ruthless during her march to the top. She was afflicted with "rushing sickness." She didn't ask for power; she took it and dared anyone to stop her. She had believed in the therapeutic value of Creme Valaze since childhood and this belief gave her confidence. She proved that work and enthusiasm for an idea can produce success. Rubinstein exuded grace and beauty when young and supreme confidence when older. She was shy and reticent personally but powerful and charismatic professionally.

MY WAY OR THE HIGHWAY

Rubinstein radiated an air of authority. As a corporate executive she could be tyrannical and used her financial power to buy people and influence. She was autocratic with a "my way or the highway" mentality. Patrick O'Higgins was her long-term secretary, lover, bodyguard, and social director. He described her operating style as "Business must come first." He felt she used her money as a tool of power and persuasion where she "artfully, even cruelly, manipulated each and every step made by her seven sisters, two husbands, two sons, and anyone who crossed her path—including me" (O'Higgins 1971, p. 224). O'Higgins said her greatest power was "manipulating money wisely." She left an estate in excess of $100 million that included five homes plus an extensive art collection that included some of the world's great masterpieces.

CHUTZPA—THE ULTIMATE POWER

Rubinstein had what she called chutzpa—supreme self-confidence—and used it with aplomb. Like Howard Hughes, she often resorted to buying what she was denied. When looking for a permanent home in Manhattan, she finally found the ideal apartment. It consisted of three floors, thirty-six rooms, including a gigantic master bedroom and penthouse, and was ideal for housing her vast art collection. She made an offer and it was refused. When the owners refused to negotiate, the real estate agent took her aside and told her the truth: They did not want to rent to a Jew. The invincible Rubinstein bought the building, fired the management, and moved into the penthouse.

Competitor Elizabeth Arden was so envious of Rubinstein's successful sales record that she hired away her whole sales team. This was probably not too difficult since Rubinstein was infamous for paying her employees low wages with enormous expectations. She immediately retaliated by hiring Arden's ex-husband, T. J. Lewis, as her national sales manager.

TYRANNICAL WHIRLWIND AND RETIREMENT

Patrick O'Higgins wrote that Rubinstein drove herself and her employees, even her sisters, beyond belief: "to the very end, she continued driving herself, and all those around her, unmercifully" (p. 109). Rubinstein was never concerned about offending those who could not help her either personally or professionally. She lived by the dog-eat-dog rules of business; morals or ethics never interfered with her objectives.

This diminutive woman outmaneuvered a major Wall Street investment firm and did so with ruthless malice. The Rubinstein company was at its zenith in 1929 and Lehman Brothers made Rubinstein an acquisition offer she couldn't refuse. She accepted their offer of $8 million in cash for the business. The purchase included only her U.S. salons and trade revenues. Rubinstein agreed to return to Europe where she had salons and homes and take early retirement. She admitted, "My decision was a quick one. I accepted Lehman Brothers' offer" but "I knew they would make a mess of things. What do bankers know about the beauty business?"

FINANCIAL COUP

Rubinstein returned to Paris, bought a new chalet, and divorced Titus. But this shrewd woman grew restless operating on such a limited scale. After talking with her American customers and learning that they were unhappy, she started planning to get her company back. Her timing couldn't have been better since the stock market had crashed six months after her sale to Lehman Brothers, driving the price of Rubinstein stock down to record lows. She recalled: "I began to buy back some of the stock on the open market until eventually I held one-third of it. Then as a substantial shareholder I wrote Lehman Brothers, registering a strong complaint." The corporate executives ignored her and then compounded their blunder by underestimating her chutzpa. This petite tiger began writing letters to shareholders saying the Rubinstein business was being jeopardized and urged them to complain to management. Her ploy worked. The stock dropped even further as her letters triggered shareholder fears precipitating further stock sales. Rubinstein stock had gone from $60 to $3 per share within months. Rubinstein then offered Lehman 15 percent of what they had paid her less than a year earlier. Frustrated and fearful, the company accepted her offer. This uneducated but shrewd lady had made $7.5 million in twelve months by outmaneuvering a giant Wall Street investment banker. Money was king to Rubinstein and she had an intuitive flair for making and keeping it.

DESTRUCTIVENESS

Rubinstein's independent and at times destructive nature was demonstrated in April 1958 upon the death of her younger son, Horace. She had refused to interrupt a vacation to attend Prince Gourielli's funeral two years earlier, electing to sit for a Picasso portrait instead. Rubinstein was in Paris once again in 1958 when Horace died of a heart attack suffered in an automobile accident. She was distraught but stayed in Paris, refusing to return for his funeral. She told Patrick O'Higgins that she was deathly afraid of her own mortality. It was her distaste for any negatives in life and her egocentric fear of her own death, rather than Horace's death, that upset her. Rubinstein and Horace had been estranged since he refused to be controlled by his mother.

Rubinstein remained a Type A, which caused her to have a most unhappy personal life. Her frenetic style, while often self-destructive, contributed to her enormous success.

A FEARLESS WORKAHOLIC

Helena Rubinstein admitted, "I drove myself relentlessly for most of my life" and "I am very difficult to please." She always set impossibly high standards for herself and her employees. These high expectations helped make her the best in her profession but also the least liked. She was the most powerful and influential executive in her industry for over half a century. O'Higgins said "The impact of her personality was almost smothering. . . . She played power games." This was never more evident than when she became the target of a major robbery at the age of ninety-four. Rubinstein had a reputation for keeping millions of dollars worth of art and jewelry in her New York apartment. Three hoodlums decided the aged lady was an easy mark and broke into her Manhattan apartment intending to steal her money and jewelry. What defense would a ninety-four-year-old woman have against three young gangsters? Madame showed them!

The three broke into Rubinstein's bedroom at 8 A.M. before her secretary and servants arrived at her apartment. They threatened to kill her if she didn't give them the key to her safe. Rubinstein distracted the youths with idle chatter. She then dropped to her knees and pretended to pray. They said, "What are you doing?" "I'm praying for you," she responded. This strong-willed woman refused to capitulate: "I'm an old woman. You can kill me, but I'm not going to let you rob me. Now get out." During this exchange, she surreptitiously slipped the key to the safe from her purse and dropped it down her ample cleavage. The thieves discovered her purse and emptied its contents on the bed. They snatched up a hundred dollars in bills but in their haste missed the baubles which included a pair of earrings worth $40,000. Rubinstein hurriedly covered the earrings with tissues and the crooks never discovered them in their frenetic search for the keys. When her secretary entered the room and fainted, the thieves became alarmed and fled with the hundred dollars, leaving millions in art and jewels.

MODERN PROMETHEUS

This competitive and aggressive woman was also impatient, impulsive, and intolerant. Rubinstein lived for work and so personified the Promethean image that Salvador Dali immortalized her in 1943 by painting her as a feminine Prometheus, chained to a rock by her glittering emerald robes. Nothing could have been more befitting this independent, self-made woman who drove herself to be the best. The word "no" did not exist in her vocabulary. She knew her business and was ever confident in her ability to succeed even when the experts decried her reasoning. She skillfully manipulated the media to gain notoriety. *Life* magazine declared, "Rubinstein's greatest promotion is undoubtedly herself." Rubinstein carefully nurtured her image as the queen of beauty, and then used that reputation to build an empire with her at the center of all activity. She became wealthy and powerful in the process. This visionary started in Australia with nothing but a dream, and used an obsession for work and a passion for perfection to change that dream into reality.

HELENA RUBINSTEIN
Beauty Tycoon
b. December 25, 1870, Cracow, Poland; d. April 1, 1965, New York City

Dominant Trait: Type A workaholic, competitive, aggressive, and impatient

Motto: "I bring luck." "If I don't keep busy, I'll go mad." "You must believe in yourself."

Nickname: "Madame," "First Lady of Beauty," "The Princess," "Princess Gourielli"

Vices/Hobbies: Fine clothes, jewelry, fine art, and money

Heroes/Mentors: Dr. Lykusky, creator of Creme Valaze

Philosophy of Life: "Work is your best beauty treatment."

Fantasy: To control the world of beauty

Professional Successes: *Life* magazine called her "perhaps the world's most successful business-woman" (1941). Built empire employing 30,000 in fifteen countries. Left estate of $100 million.

Power: Used human weakness for beauty to achieve power. Her willpower evolved into financial power, using fear to gain power and dominate beauty in four continents.

Influence: Revlon, Elizabeth Arden, Estée Lauder, and Mary Kay have imitated her beauty-in-a-jar merchandising.

Destructiveness: Labeled "A tyrannical holocaust" by her assistant O'Higgins who said: "She's a hydra . . . eight heads are constructive, one destructive." A "ruthless" businesswoman who used fear to gain power.

Birth Order: Firstborn of eight daughters by Horace and Gertrude Rubinstein.

Parental Influence: Father was a Jewish merchant who instilled expertise in merchandising; mother instilled need for beauty.

Transiency: Fled Poland for Australia at age eighteen and then left uncle's home for Melbourne a year later.

Crises: Forced to flee family at eighteen when father insisted she marry a thirty-five-year-old. She had no knowledge, training, education, money, and couldn't even speak the language. She had only bravado for survival.

Formal Education: High school dropout. Later studied dermatology in Paris under Dr. Berthelot.

Libidinal Drive: Sublimated sexual energy into work. First husband, Edward Titus, divorced her: "Your business is your life." Two marriages of convenience. Didn't bother to attend second husband's funeral.

Personality Type: Introverted-Intuitive-Thinker-Judger. Workaholic who was tyrannical, impatient, impulsive, ruthless.

Self-Esteem: Supremely confident. Never questioned ability to excel even in areas where she was ignorant.

Rebellion: A maverick who never listened to experts, or anyone else, in maniacal drive to the top.

Risk Propensity: Risked constantly due to strong self-image.

Work Ethic: "I worked 18 hours out of every 24." Worked daily until age ninety-four. "I believe my own success is due primarily to a combination of luck, *hard work,* and perseverance."

Tenacity: O'Higgins said "the word 'no' just didn't exist in Madame's vocabulary." When denied right to buy a Manhattan apartment because she was Jewish, she bought the building and fired management.

Optimism: She believed and it led her to the top.

Manicness: *Saturday Review* characterized her as "a human whirlwind." O'Higgins described her as one who "made every decision, ruled imperially, and dictatorially."

Rupert Murdoch

I think what drives me are ideas . . . and having a little smidgen of power.

Rupert Murdoch is one of the most powerful and influential men in the world. *Forbes* magazine in 1995 said, "Rupert Murdoch is arguably the most powerful private citizen in the world." Murdoch gained such power through hard work, temerity, and tenacity. He works harder than his competitors or employees, views risk as a positive adventure, and never capitulates in the face of imminent disaster. When asked why he was willing to lose $150 million in the first year (1994) on broadcasts of National Football League games, he responded with the insight of one who knows: "You're not a network without the NFL." Murdoch is a nonimposing man who is driven to dominate whatever industry he enters and to control each and every enterprise. He has been enormously successful in building the most pervasive network of print and visual media throughout Australia, North America, Europe, Asia, and Latin America. In late 1995 he launched a conservative weekly, *The Standard,* which prompted an American news authority to comment, "I think he's aiming for political stature commensurate with his financial stature."

Much of Murdoch's enormous success has been based on his philosophy, which he espoused early in his career: in "the struggle for freedom of information, technology not politics will be the ultimate decider." *USA Today* reported, "Politicians are more afraid of Rupert Murdoch than he is of them. . . . He's like the puppeteer who's pulling strings behind the scenes." In most venues Rupert is a powerful man who has limitless energy and an insatiable need to grow and acquire. The September 1995 issue of *Vanity Fair* listed Murdoch as number one on the list of persons most influential in the burgeoning information age, with Bill Gates number two and Michael Eisner of Disney number three.

Sensationalism

Rupert is a paradox in that he is steeped in Victorian morality yet built his vast newspaper empire based on "sensationalism" and "vulgarism." His flagship papers in Australia, England, and the United States were all built via flagrant headlines that flaunted sex, murder, rape, and gore for the express purpose of building circulation and beating the competition. When he started running pictures of barebreasted women (Page Three Girls in London), he was nicknamed "Murdoch of the Mammaries." To this conservative, puritanical Presbyterian, provocative headlines and bare breasts were only the means to an end and had nothing whatever to do with morals or ethics. He repeatedly argued that the provocative headlines were what the majority of readers wanted in their local papers. He transferred his titillating headlines for provocative themes on the small screen with Fox. In 1995 he launched *Medicine Ball,* featuring a lesbian gunshot victim whose nipple ring wouldn't come off and a forty-one-year-old man who sought a circumcision. To Rupert the end always justified the means.

WORLD'S DOMINANT MEDIA MOGUL

Murdoch is a pragmatist who is determined to find out what the general public wants to read and then gives it to them with unabashed passion and candor. If the end product is irritating to the establishment and shocking to the moral right, he does not care. In fact, Murdoch thrives on controversy and risk. He told Barbara Walters in an interview when selected as one of 1994's Ten Most Fascinating People, "Combat is good for the soul." It is such combativeness that has likened him to Citizen Kane, based on William Randolph Hearst, the man who dominated America's newspaper industry during the first half of the twentieth century. He has also been compared to Joseph Pulitzer, the award-winning journalist who is the acknowledged father of media advertising. Hearst and Pulitzer were powerful and influential media moguls, but both pale in comparison to the high-powered, risk-taking Rupert Murdoch. Adjusted for inflation, Pulitzer's media empire in 1994 would have been valued at some $300 million. The same assessment of the Hearst empire would have been $700 million. News Corp, Murdoch's Australian holding company, grossed $20 billion in revenues in the mid-nineties, had well over $20 billion in assets and $1 billion in profits (more than 40 percent higher than Hearst's highest revenues). *Forbes* magazine in 1994 ranked News Corp the second largest corporation in Australia and Murdoch the richest man in his homeland with a net worth of $4 billion. He was also ranked as the sixth-richest person in the world.

WINNING MOTIVATES MURDOCH

"Business is War" is Murdoch's motto. Despite his enormous financial success, Murdoch said "I'm not about making money." Like most great entrepreneurs and creative geniuses, Rupert was far more interested in beating the competition than getting rich. Power and money are the by-products of winning or becoming the very best in your field. Murdoch is a living example of that axiom. His holdings and influence are imposing when compared to all other media giants. He is not only dominant in his homeland but is an international power broker of unprecedented power and influence. He is no longer considered an Australian but an international media magnate with multinational influence. News Corp publishes sixty million newspapers each week in the United States, Australia, Europe, and the Pacific Rim. In Australia alone he controls 70 percent of the news print circulation plus numerous TV stations and 50 percent of Ansett airlines. In Great Britain he controls one-third of the press, including ownership of the *Times, Sun, News of the World,* Times Books, HarperCollins Publishing, Sky Channel Cable TV, Reuters News Service, and Pearson P.C. The *Sun* has the largest circulation of any English-language paper in the world—4 million daily.

Fox TV—Flagship to Immortality

Since the 1970s Murdoch has made the United States his base of operations. His U.S. holdings include Fox TV, the fourth television network; Twentieth-Century Fox Studios; the *Boston Herald*; *San Antonio Express News*; *New York Post*; *New York* magazine; *TV Guide*; the *National Star* tabloid; Harper and Row Publishing; Salem House; New World Communications; Zandervan; and numerous television stations (eighteen as of 1995). In 1993 Murdoch bought control of the most widely broadcast Pacific Rim television operation, Star TV. Star is headquartered in Hong Kong and dominates satellite programming to China, India, Malaysia, and most of Asia. This archconservative defended these Far East acquisitions: "satellite TV is an unambiguous threat to totalitarian regimes everywhere." His adversaries accuse him of spreading "American Cultural Imperialism" by distributing Fox programming throughout his vast media network, which is ironic since he is of Australian heritage. Murdoch has recently expanded his media empire to include Latin America. Without a doubt Rupert Murdoch has used his intuitive vision and manic energy to create a dynasty in news and entertainment. He is unquestionably the most powerful media mogul in history. With Fox producing and distributing his shows, he is also arguably the most influential.

Competitive Aggression

Rupert Murdoch got to the top by being in a hurry. He built his empire in record time due to impatience and the use of logic-based "gut" decisions. He set out early to build an international media empire. Biographer William Shawcross gives some insight into Murdoch's success, describing him as a man who hates to lose—the consummate competitor: "Murdoch always played tennis as if the future of the world hung on his winning. . . . His life has been an endless assault on the world. . . . Incessantly moving, questing, searching, striving, fighting, cajoling, bullying, demanding, charming, pushing always for more—newspapers, TV, space, power" (Shawcross 1993, p. 4).

Murdoch hires executives in his own image—aggressive individuals who have emulated his operating style. He has had an intuitive feel for attracting management who have his renegade nature. Interviews with his chief lieutenants elicit responses like "possessed" and "win at any cost." Many adopt his frenetic operating style and competitiveness. Maury Povich was recruited to Fox from another network and was stupefied by the difference between Fox and the others. He described what he found as "sheer audacity. . . . They were fearless; Murdoch's daredevil squadron heading into the unknown without parachutes."

Type A Success

Newsweek remarked in June 1994 that Murdoch "has turned the industry upside down. This deal [Fox network's outbidding CBS for NFL football] is so unprecedented, it's absolutely brilliant."

Murdoch's tireless work ethic is shocking even to his wife, Anna. She doesn't understand his obsessive need to acquire more and more by working harder and harder. She told reporters in 1984: "I wish he would slow down . . . but I don't think that's going to happen."

When Murdoch made his deal with Walter Annenberg in 1988 to acquire Triangle Productions, it proved to be the largest media purchase in history. The acquisition of Metromedia (Twentieth Century Fox) and Triangle Publications (*TV Guide, Seventeen,* and *Racing Form*) was a shock even to Annenberg. After closing the sale, Annenberg described Murdoch as "an immense gambler. A determined dedicated fellow and a fearless competitor . . . and after having Fox and Metromedia I sensed he wanted the whole ball game." Kelvin MacKenzie, the editor of the eminently successful London *Sun,* said "The boss achieves more in half an hour than any other human being achieves in a whole day. He's smart as a wagonload of monkeys."

Early Life Experiences

Rupert Murdoch was born March 11, 1931, on Cruden Farm, thirty miles south of Melbourne, Australia. He was the first son and second child of Keith Murdoch and Elizabeth Greene. His sister Helen was two years older. Two younger sisters, Anne born in 1935 and Janet in 1939, were never as close to Rupert as Helen. Keith Murdoch was a publishing legend who built the Melbourne *Herald* into the foremost newspaper in Australia. He was an entrepreneur during his younger days and a freelance writer who settled down later in Melbourne to raise a family. He was in his mid-forties when Rupert was born and a major role model. Murdoch was first attracted to the publishing industry as a youth when he recognized the power his father wielded. Young Rupert received his Victorian ethics and morals from his paternal grandfather, who was a Presbyterian minister.

Murdoch was named for his maternal grandfather, the irascible Rupert Greene. Rupert Greene was a hard-drinking, gambling, woman-chasing scallywag who many people think has been the greatest (and worst) influence on Murdoch. Grandfather Greene would encourage his namesake to drive his car when young Rupert could barely reach the pedals. He was also instrumental in many other pranks and rebellious activities which delighted young Rupert and his sisters.

His mother, Dame Elizabeth, was probably the most influential in instilling independence in the youth. Every summer she expected her son to spend every night alone in his tree house: "I thought it would be good for Rupert to sleep out. It was pretty tough. He was more than halfway up the tree. He had no electric light." Rupert never agreed with her opinion that this experience built character. However, such experiences instill independence and self-sufficiency, often imprinting the young with self-survival skills necessary to compete alone against the elements and win. Independence, self-sufficiency, and temerity are the very traits that have made Rupert Murdoch into a successful business tycoon.

YOUTHFUL ENTREPRENEUR

As a youth Murdoch caught hares, rats, and rabbits and sold their skins for play money. He gathered manure from the farm and sold it for gambling money. His older sister Helen was his closest companion while growing up and described him as "a bit of a cat who walked alone." At age ten he was enrolled in a boarding school, Geelong. He hated Geelong with a passion but his mother defended her decision to send him there: "I thought that boarding school taught you to live with other people and be more unselfish." What she may not have known is that it is a great environment for instilling entrepreneurial traits. (Fred Smith [Federal Express] and Ted Turner [CNN] attended boarding schools and also hated the experience). Such schools groom the young to be independent, self-sufficient, and to survive in a competitive environment. Students learn to cope in new environments. The experience builds character, responsibility, and independent decision making. Murdoch recalled: "I felt a loner at school and was ostracized a lot and bullied" and "it made me realize that if you're going to do your job as a publisher or a principal in the media, you've got to be your own person and not have close relationships which can compromise you." School friend Darryl Wardle said Murdoch "was eminently confident" and that "he was always going to be involved in newspapers." Rupert's antiestablishment convictions were formed during his Geelong years.

A GAMBLING RENEGADE

Murdoch graduated from Geelong in 1948 and spent time working at the Melbourne *Herald*—his father's paper—as a cadet reporter. He was then sent to Worcester College at Oxford in 1950 where he studied politics, economics, and philosophy, but not journalism. It was at Oxford that Murdoch became a true radical, keeping a bust of Lenin in his room to show his dislike of the establishment. Rupert was a free spirit who delighted in nonconformity. As a student he was cocky, rich, and a Communist—not endearing traits in conservative Britain. He was blackballed when he attempted to join the Cricket Club. Rohan Rivett, a friend of Murdoch's father, became his best friend during his student days. Rivett wrote to Sir Keith Murdoch about his son: "I am inclined to prophesy that he will make his first million with fantastic ease." Murdoch was a poor student with a penchant for bravado. On a visit to a friend of his father, Murdoch arrived in a Rolls Royce, explaining, "I rang up Rolls and told them that if they lent me a Roller for the weekend, I'd review it for one of our papers." Not everyone appreciated such brashness. The school paper *Cherwell* described him as "Turbulent, travelled, and twenty-one, he is known . . . as a brilliant betting man with that billingsgate touch." Murdoch became enamored of gambling while young and it never left him.

THE BOY PUBLISHER

Tragedy entered Murdoch's life during his senior year at Oxford. Sir Keith Murdoch died suddenly leaving his only son with the management responsibility for the family's two Australian newspapers in Brisbane and Adelaide. Both were moderately successful small town papers which made no money. On advice from a friend, Dame Elizabeth sold the Brisbane paper. Young Rupert was furious as he was anxious to oversee these papers as publisher. He wrote to the management of the *Adelaide News* for all financial details and assumed titular control from England during his final term at Oxford. He barely passed his final exams and was given a third-class degree in 1953. He spent some time working at the *London Times* to gain needed knowledge of the business. He arrived in Adelaide to take over the *News* in September 1953. Murdoch became chief executive officer of the small paper, which was virtually insolvent due to a pitiful circulation of 75,000. Murdoch came in like a flash, worked in every department, and earned a reputation as the Boy Publisher by age twenty-two. His amazing energy proved infectious as suddenly everyone had to work faster and harder just to keep up with this human whirlwind. Adelaide's other paper, the *Advertiser,* operated by his father's old firm, decided to put the *News* out of business and went to great lengths to destroy it. Murdoch met every competitive move with a stronger one. The *Advertiser* wanted Murdoch to sell out and go away but finally capitulated to his energy and drive and agreed to a merger, leaving the Boy Publisher at the helm.

EMPIRE BUILDING

Murdoch's first flirtation with expansion began in 1956 when he acquired a Melbourne weekly magazine called *New Idea*. After turning that paper around financially, he acquired the Perth *Sunday Times*. This purchase caused dissension on the *Adelaide News* board of directors since Perth was some fourteen hundred miles from Adelaide and would prove difficult to manage. Murdoch was determined to prove the board wrong and personally went to Perth and turned around this foundering paper. It was in Perth that he first earned his reputation as a sensationalist publisher. "Circulation at any cost" became his motto. Lurid headlines such as "Leper Rapes Virgin, Gives Birth to Monster Baby" became typical. His strategy worked like a charm and the paper leaped to number one in that market.

LEVERAGE AND EXPANSION

Murdoch soon realized that he could use leverage—using other people's money for expansion—to his advantage and began an expansion strategy of buying up foundering newspapers, turning them around, and using the expanding asset base to acquire even more. A banking relationship was needed to further such an expansionist strategy. Banks love equity loans and this ruse allowed him to expand without the use of cash. Murdoch approached the Commonwealth Bank of Sydney, which proved to be an ingenious move. This aggressive bank saw Murdoch as a young tiger with ambition and acumen and backed him from the start. It was not long before he was able call them on the phone, ask for $150 million in cash, and receive verbal approval over the phone. General Manager Jack Armstrong said, "He has never, ever not performed with his banks as he said he would. He always meets every payment, therefore we have ultimate faith in Rupert." This relationship with the Commonwealth Bank armed Murdoch with immediate and almost unlimited credit and became the basis of the unprecedented growth of News Corp.

TELEVISION

In 1956 Murdoch met and fell in love with Patricia Booker, a pretty blonde airline hostess. True to his style, he spent much of his honeymoon inspecting some newly acquired businesses. The couple had a daughter, Prudence, in 1959, but his family obligations never deterred him from work.

Murdoch was becoming fascinated with the new entertainment sensation TV, which had finally made its way to Australia in the mid-fifties. Murdoch foresaw that this new technology would become an important fact of the media. The first Australian TV broadcast took place in Adelaide in 1957 and Murdoch decided to own his own station. He recalled, "In the 1950s you had to be in TV and to be in TV you had to be into America." Rupert put in a bid for Channel 9 in Adelaide and then left for America to learn the inner-workings of the industry and to buy programming for his new station. His first stop was Las Vegas where he fell in love with American culture and the Strip. Murdoch's first business mentor was Leonard Goldenson, the trailblazing president of ABC television. Goldenson had just made a deal with Walt Disney and was looked on as a man with the magic touch. The two risk-taking entrepreneurs became fast friends and made numerous deals. Murdoch sold Goldenson 6 percent of News Corp in exchange for immediate programming and long-term distribution of ABC's programs in Australia. He later admitted that "Goldenson was in many ways a role model, though we came from very different backgrounds. . . . Leonard's success was always an inspiration and encouragement. He proved you *can* buck the odds."

HYPERSUCCESS IN SYDNEY

Murdoch returned to Australia inspired by the exciting prospects of television and with plans to create an Australian version of *TV Guide.* He launched his magazine coincident with airing on Channel 9 in September 1959. The station was an instant success and earned enough money to allow the impatient and impulsive Murdoch to expand at an ever-increasing rate. During this period he became fascinated with big-city publishing and moved "out of Adelaide and into the major markets Sydney and Melbourne." His first move was into Sydney, where he purchased the insolvent *Sydney Mirror.* Sydney was the largest market in Australia and the toughest to penetrate. The "good old boys" owned the market and were convinced that they would slow down the Boy Publisher by selling him a lemon. Murdoch allowed them to take advantage of him but insisted on using leverage once again. He paid $7.5 million, with only 30 percent down, to acquire the Sydney paper from the Fairfax Group, the largest and oldest publishing house in Australia. They fully expected him to default on the loan within the year since they had not been able to make the paper a success. Murdoch resorted to his tried and true tactic of sensational headlines and aggressive marketing campaigns, boosting circulation with headlines such as "Tennis Star Shocks Priest" and "Girl 13 Raped." His success pulled the paper out of the red and proved for once and all that Rupert Murdoch was not to be reckoned with lightly.

THE AUSTRALIAN—FIRST NATIONAL PAPER

Murdoch began to dream about creating his own paper from scratch, which would be bigger than anything else in Australia. While undertaking this massive project, he acquired a defunct Sydney UHF TV station, WIN 4, to supplement his Sydney operations, where he had just moved his family. Murdoch was only thirty-three when he embarked on an enterprise that was destined to become his crowning achievement in publishing. He chose the city of Canberra due to its central location and proximity to the seat of government. He hired a publishing legend by the name of Max Newton as editor, which started a love/hate relationship that would last for years. Newton later wrote, "In those terrible hours and days . . . Rupert showed some of the steel, the gambler's recklessness and the foresight that have since grown to such immense maturity on the world stage" (Shawcross 1993, p. 118).

This idealistic venture started Murdoch in big-time publishing and was truly innovative. He was many years ahead of *USA Today* when he launched the *Australian* on July 14, 1964. Max Newton said, "His energy seemed to *will* the *Australian* into existence." The paper lost money for many years, but it was an image paper that Rupert had personally founded; he stuck with it and made it the success it is today.

Murdoch was just thirty-three but a seasoned risk-taker and workaholic. Launching the *Australian* paper kept him away from home for weeks at a time. He had left his family in Sydney while he was working in Canberra and commuted to other far-off places. Murdoch later admitted his marriage was failing, reflecting, "I was probably too young and married on the run." Murdoch went through a messy divorce, winning custody of his daughter, Prudence. After his divorce, he met and fell in love with Anna Torv, a cadet reporter in Sydney who was both beautiful and ambitious. Anna, who ultimately became an author, recalled that upon meeting Murdoch, "He was like a whirlwind coming into the room. It was very seductive." They married in April 1967.

GLOBAL VISION

By the late sixties Murdoch had conquered the major markets in Australia when he received an unexpected offer to expand outside Australia. A college friend,

Stephen Catto, called Murdoch and asked if he would consider making an offer for a London paper called *News of the World*. In London the paper had come to be known as "News of the Screws," as it was Britain's most salacious Sunday paper despite being one of the oldest. Robert Maxwell was attempting to acquire the paper and Murdoch was offered the paper to shut out Maxwell. This chance to demonstrate his prowess to the arrogant English who had demeaned him in college was too much for the ambitious Murdoch to turn down. Despite the fact that Anna was pregnant with their first daughter, Elizabeth, Murdoch acquired the paper and moved his family to London.

Mania and Success

Murdoch answered a reporter's question, "What makes Rupert run?" with, "It's the challenge of the game. It gives me a great thrill and it would be very wrong to deny that it is emotional." Biographer William Shawcross(1993) observed: "His acquisitiveness is like a madness. . . . He finds it virtually impossible to relax. . . . In his early sixties he is still a man possessed . . . with invincible energy." His long-term editor and associate Max Newton said of his dynamic behavior: "The biggest asset Rupert's got is his own intellectual and emotional energy." Murdoch used that energy to dominate the news media.

Murdoch arrived in London in late 1968 to negotiate for the Sunday paper *News of the World*. Once in control of this paper, Murdoch became a hurricane of activity and interfered with the paper's day-to-day operations. Editor Sir William Somerfield was perturbed when Murdoch paid Christine Keeler nearly $100,000 for her memoirs of her affair with John Profumo. Murdoch responded in classic style, "I didn't come all the way from Australia not to interfere. You can accept it or quit." Somerfield quit.

LONDON IMPRESARIO

Within twelve months of his arrival in London. Murdoch engaged in another takeover battle with his now archenemy Maxwell and beat him once again in the acquisition of the *London Sun*. Both the *London Sun* and *News of the World* were purchased on leverage and both were struggling for survival when Murdoch bought them. *News of the World* was virtually bankrupt and Murdoch turned it around and put it in the black almost overnight. Then he acquired the *Sun* for no other reason than to keep Maxwell from purchasing it. He made these newspapers the financial backbone of his empire. His critics in Britain saw it differently. They were appalled by his salacious operating style which had created the infamous Page Three Girls in the *Sun* launched on November 17, 1970. The *Sun* became a sensational tabloid under his direction and ultimately the largest-selling English newspaper in the world with a daily circulation of four million. His titillating promotions earned him the nickname "The Dirty Digger" and the wrath of the British establishment.

IMPLICATIONS OF YELLOW JOURNALISM

Murdoch resorted to his time-proven tactic of yellow journalism to revive both London papers. On November 17, 1970, he first placed topless girls on page three, earning a reputation that would follow him for life. He used blatant sexual pictorials and ghoulish headlines to build circulation, but it also became known as the most scandalous paper in history. Rival papers, the *Mirror* and *New Statesman,* started referring to his paper as "Murdoch's shit sheet" and he earned the wrath of clergy, government officials, and social purists. Elizabeth Murdoch questioned her son's moral integrity and demanded he justify his prurient headlines. He explained to her: "The poor Brits had to have such entertainment—their lives were so wretched." After publishing the Christine Keeler memoirs in the *Sun,* he was summarily berated by David Frost in a TV interview. The ever-combative Murdoch exacted revenge by exercising his enormous financial power, buying Frost's parent and summarily firing him. Frost reflected on the experience: "You definitely don't want to get on the wrong side of him." Murdoch's tactics worked despite the criticism and circulation increased dramatically at the *Sun.* The paper was named Newspaper of the Year in 1971 and soon became the cash cow of News Corp. By 1983 it was earning a staggering $50 million a year.

AMERICA

Murdoch now mimicked the fictional Citizen Kane in his manic need to dominate the media world, and looked across the Atlantic for expansion. Anna Murdoch had disliked life in Britain and was ecstatic about a move to the United States. British critics were outraged by Murdoch's antiestablishment views and with his headlines screaming "Pussy Week in the Sun." His newspapers were banned in libraries and he was persona non grata in London.

Murdoch relocated to the United States in fall 1976. He immediately acquired three San Antonio papers for $20 million. He then launched the *National Star,* a supermarket tabloid to compete with the *National Enquirer.* By the 1980s this paper boasted a circulation of four million and an annual profit of $12 million. He then bought the *New York Post*—America's longest-published newspaper—for $30 million and by the end of 1976 had completed a hostile takeover of *New York* magazine and the *Village Voice,* both published by Clay Felker. Felker was destroyed and blamed Murdoch's motivations on his need to "beat his father, Keith. And to run the world." He purchased the *Boston Herald* from Hearst Publishing Corp. in 1982 for $16 million, which was to begin his political fights with Edward M. Kennedy.

AMERICAN CITIZEN

Murdoch established his headquarters in New York City and moved his family there in order to be close to his new prized possession, the *New York Post.* During this period Murdoch would often have breakfast on one continent, dinner on another, while buying or selling a business on a third. After he bought the *Boston Herald,* he considered U.S. citizenship since Sen. Edward M. Kennedy began questioning America's papers being owned by a foreigner. Murdoch became a U.S. citizen in 1985. His timing was crucial as his citizenship was badly needed to gain the Securities and Exchange Commission's approval for his acquisitions of Metromedia and Triangle. His wife, Anna, told the *New York Times*: "I was shocked. I never thought he'd do it. I realized then how strong his ambitious drive was." Murdoch and his wife loved the United States, especially New York City where they lived until 1992. He decided that entertainment was the avenue of growth for News Corp. He moved his operations and family to Southern California to be near to Twentieth Century Fox and Fox television.

RISK-TAKING MANIA

Murdoch embarked on his expansion of News Corp in the eighties when he was middle-aged. There was no decrease in his enormous energies and he continued taking risks. The risks paid huge dividends as Murdoch's empire grew sixfold during the eighties—a multibillion-dollar citadel built on debt. In 1985 Murdoch acquired Metromedia and Twentieth-Century Fox for $2.6 billion increasing his debt to over $2.3 billion. In May 1985 the *New York Times* observed: "Rupert's a man who's always thrilled with a new challenge. He's always ready to climb Mt. Everest. He has a broad attention span. Very broad." Not deterred by the huge debt, he then spent $3.8 billion for Harper and Row in 1988. The debt for News Corp grew to astronomical proportions frightening the bankers. Murdoch was never hindered by risk or debt as he had confidence in his ability to leverage his way out of tight spots. No risk was too great. Barry Diller characterized his operating style as "being best when he's cornered."

COMPETITIVE AGGRESSION

Murdoch's magic touch even worked outside the media industry. He bought Ansett Airlines—the second largest Australian airline company—for $80 million in 1979. By the mid-eighties this acquisition was worth $500 million. He was not only a purchaser but a fearless owner. One example was his battles with unions, which culminated the Wapping war in London. Murdoch showed his tenacity and courage in this dispute. The unions had a death-grip on business during the sixties and seventies. Murdoch methodically planned this battle to undermine their control. He built an automated newspaper plant at Wapping in 1986 without revealing to anyone his real intent. He spent eighteen months attempting to reason with union demands while building the plant. London unions were highly nonproductive, which irked this consummate capitalist. Murdoch had plenty of comparative data to use when he accused the Fleet Street newspaper unions of running a "protection racket and a lunatic asylum." At the time, Murdoch's San Antonio papers employed four men to a press, Chicago had five, New York and Sydney six. London had eighteen or three times the people to perform an identical job. In addition, the English union workers had salaries 100 percent above the national average. Murdoch decided to automate every facet of the production process, thus eliminating the need for the union workers. He spent millions of dollars purchasing the latest American computer-aided typesetting equipment and had it secretly shipped and set up in Wapping. When he opened the new plant the union workers, as expected, went on strike in January 1986.

CREATIVE DESTROYER

On the night of January 25, 1986, Rupert Murdoch knew that his papers had to go to press or the union would win and he would be virtually out of the newspaper business in London. He personally took over the management of the Wapping plant and became a human dynamo, working alongside nonunion men to produce the paper that would break the union stranglehold on the newspaper industry. He donned a cardigan sweater and sneakers and ran through the plant motivating, cajoling, operating, and doing whatever else was necessary. His workers saw him with a cape and crimson *S* emblazoned on his chest as he singlehandedly destroyed the union stronghold on business. That historic night Murdoch's plant successfully printed four million papers, which effectively destroyed the unions. He had singlehandedly liberated Fleet Street. Drexel Burnam estimated that his gamble on beating the union raised the value of his two London papers from $300 million to $1 billion.

GAMBLING MENTALITY

By 1990 this visionary had leveraged himself into $7 billion in debt with $2.3 billion of it short-term. This number terrified the bankers. It came very close to wiping out his empire as News Corp was basically insolvent. Murdoch was near bankruptcy during 1990 to 1992. Ann Lane of Citibank was placed in charge of reducing Murdoch's debt. Project Dolphin was Lane's code name for the Murdoch bailout. She spent months with him and characterized his operating style as "An Australian Red Baron who operated by the seat of his pants." She said he was so deep in debt that one phone call could have ended his whole life's work. Lane got to know the real Rupert Murdoch and was quite impressed: "He worked harder and more determinedly than anyone she had ever met and knew he would never give up, say 'I can't' do it anymore." To his credit, he sold off some of his most precious possessions—*Seventeen, New Woman, Mirabella,* and *Racing Form*—for $650 million in order to placate the bankers and improve cash flow. He worked feverishly and with Lane's help saved his media empire. In keeping with his gambling mentality, once he saw that the empire would not break up, he started acquiring at a faster pace than before. To the amazement of his business associates and family, he actually took more risks after this crisis than before.

CLEVER LIKE A FOX

The reason for Murdoch's continual flirtation with disaster was his dream of creating a fourth network under Fox. He had set the stage for this network in 1985 with the acquisition of Metromedia and Fox. He officially launched the new network on March 1, 1987, but it was not a serious contender with ABC, CBS, or NBC in terms of programming or advertising dollars. Murdoch was a true entrepreneur and willing to do anything to bring credibility to Fox. First he lured Joan Rivers from NBC and paid her $5 million to compete with Johnny Carson. This effort turned into a miserable flop, cost him millions. Maury Povich was then hired to host "Current Affair." The show became a huge success, making $25 million in 1989. Povich gave credit to Murdoch's tactics: "The sheer audacity of it all. Nobody mentioned focus groups, or consultants or marketing research. These guys were so casual, as if nothing could be easier. They were fearless: Murdoch's daredevil squadron, heading into the unknown without parachutes" (Shawcross 1993, p. 429).

"THE SIMPSONS"—A RENEGADE SUCCESS

The Fox network gained further momentum in 1989 when Murdoch launched the antiestablishment cartoon "The Simpsons." It became an overnight sensation. Bart Simpson, the brainchild of Matt Groening, is a counterculture character in many ways like the antiestablishment Rupert Murdoch with the exception of achievement. Murdoch is the classic overachiever and Simpson the classic underachiever. Both are renegades intolerant of acceptable behavior, street-smart, determined, aggressive, strong-willed, and dislike rules. Both can be charming and are capable of manipulating people. Fox then followed the Simpson success with "America's Most Wanted" and "Married With Children."

OPTIMISTIC RISK TAKING

When Murdoch emerged from his 1991 cash crunch, he moved faster than ever in his quest to build a network to compete with ABC, CBS, and NBC. In 1994 he shocked CBS and the media world by offering the National Football League $1.6 billion for the rights to broadcast league games for four years. CBS had broadcast the games for over forty years and had bid a competitive $400 million. Murdoch was more interested in using the NFL to gain credibility and was prepared to lose $150 million a year to legitimatize Fox as the fourth network. CBS had resorted to a short run and bureaucratic-induced bid while Murdoch envisioned the long-run implications and won the bidding war easily. He then outbid CBS for the rights to the National Hockey League broadcasts at $155 million for five years, including the Stanley Cup finals. He shocked the Professional Golfers' Association by offering to finance a world golf tour. Not to slight tennis, he offered Wimbledon $120 million for the rights to broadcast that tournament worldwide for four years. Murdoch was betting that his vast network of distribution on four continents would give him the wherewithal to pay the exorbitant fees for programming. He then offered Ron Perlman, billionaire owner of New World Communications, $500 million in exchange for switching twelve TV affiliates to the Fox network, which was coupled with fifty new affiliates giving them a total of 188 stations. This compared favorably to CBS at 215, NBC at 214, and ABC at 225. Murdoch is not afraid to put his money where his mouth is, which is everywhere in an effort to be competitive in the U.S. television wars. A gambling instinct is at the heart of all his decisions.

Power and Influence

Rupert Murdoch is a self-made man who exudes high energy and tenacity. A resilient willpower allows him to focus on objectives and act with decisiveness. He is never tentative. He made the deal with John Werner Kluge for Multimedia within minutes of having met the man, a $1.8 billion decision. This would have been impossible in a typical corporate environment. This entrepreneurial bent is what makes Murdoch a powerful man. When faced with fighting the resourceful Robert Maxwell, Murdoch always won due to his competitive spirit. A reporter asked about his bouts with Maxwell and the candid Murdoch said, "He'd (Maxwell) said some rather nasty things about me to the press. And some nasty things about Australians in general. I couldn't let him get away with that."

FINANCIAL POWER

Murdoch is an introvert and loner, but when it is needed can turn on the charm to gain an edge. His understanding of leverage—using other people's money for expansion—has proven an advantage. Murdoch used leverage to acquire the various compatible ventures he envisioned important in forming his media empire. He is confident enough to jeopardize existing assets to finance new acquisitions. His concern is growth and sustaining that growth with a positive cash flow. If any deal fits those particular criteria, he is willing to gamble. In the end it is his willpower that allows him such flamboyant and audacious moves in an international market.

LEVERAGE AND SUCCESS

Risk has played an enormous role in Murdoch's power. He is willing to take major risks for those enterprises he feels will build his empire. Big bets, when right, bring huge rewards. Rupert has had some enormous wins (*Sun,* Ansett Airlines, Fox) and losses. Murdoch's reputation as a gambler is legend. Taking huge risks and working hard to mitigate those risks is what has made him enormously successful. He had the temerity and tenacity to play for bigger stakes than his competitors. His wife, Anna, told the *New York Times,* "If Rupert was a pilot, I would not board the plane—he cuts too many corners." One such flirtation with disaster occurred when he offered Newt Gingrich, the Republican Speaker of the House, $4.5 million for two books to be published by HarperCollins. This offer in early 1995 created a furor in the U.S. Congress since it implied the purchase of political favoritism in the impending investigation of News Corp's (an Australian firm) ownership of U.S. television stations. The NAACP and NBC filed complaints with the Federal Communications Commission against Murdoch complaining that he was a foreign owner which was not only illegal but also politically incorrect. Murdoch was a U.S. citizen, even though news Corp was still an Australian-based enterprise, but it wasn't Murdoch's citizenship but his success that these bureaucrats could not understand. Stock analyst Dennis McAlpine commented "All it is, is a harassment. It's getting tough out there." What was lost in this whole controversy was the fact that the complaints were self-serving and had no validity in law and were ultimately dismissed by the U.S. courts as having no merit.

INTERNATIONAL INFLUENCE

Murdoch recently admitted: "I guess I enjoy most of all what little influence there is in publishing papers. I'm not about making money." He had been influential in helping bring down the Conservative party in Australia during the 1970s when he supported Labor party leader Gough Whitlam. When Whitlam won the election, Murdoch said, "I singlehandedly put the present government into office." Later he admitted: "I should have had more reserve, but I got emotionally involved." Rupert was even more instrumental in the election of Margaret Thatcher in Britain some years later. Thatcher owes her rise to power as much to Murdoch as to anyone. Both were antiunion, and he endorsed her in all of his publications. He gave similar support to John Major, Ronald Reagan, and George Bush. The *New York Times* (December 10, 1984) quoted Jack Kemp: "Rupert used the editorial page and every other page necessary to elect Ronald Reagan president."

Murdoch dines regularly with presidents and royalty. His power and influence are so pervasive it has become his single largest problem in expanding his media empire. Governments and corporations fear him for his ability to influence legislation and elections. His power is awesome with News Corp employing over thirty thousand people and publishing over sixty million papers each week. Murdoch papers dominate 70 percent of the Australian press and 33 percent of the British press, and Fox TV which reaches over ninety million homes. He owns Sky Television in Britain which broadcasts to over three million homes. News Corp is the largest publisher of English-language Bibles through its Harper and Zandervan divisions. News Corp earned just under a billion dollars in 1994, which is being used to expand programming and the Fox network.

DYNAMIC RENEGADE

Murdoch has always been antiestablishment. This visionary has always been willing to destroy the old to create the new, to sacrifice a mediocre present for a greater future. Murdoch makes no apologies for his "my way or the highway" operating style. Disgruntled employees and bureaucratic adversaries have called him a destructive fiend with no heart, but this man's integrity is based on the understanding that he is the boss and the boss always gets to call the shots. He has been accused of being interested in control and power at the expense of others. In his defense, Murdoch is driven by what Ayn Rand called "rational self-interest," the driving force of all great men: "The man who produces an idea in any field of rational endeavor—the man who discovers new knowledge—is the benefactor of humanity."

Murdoch is powerful, influential, and threatening to those who attempt to maintain the status quo. It is impossible to be productive and innovative in a dynamic world without being creatively destructive. The old must go and protecting inefficiency for the new is counterproductive to the process. Rupert Murdoch knows this better than most.

MEDIA BARON WITHOUT PARALLEL

Murdoch is a media baron with the mentality of a high-stakes gambler. He is tenacious, strong-willed, and a compulsive workaholic. His tenacity was most evident when he kept the *Australian* running for fifteen years without a profit. He wasted no time in reversing the losses at the London *News of the World*. Both the *News* and the *Sun* were insolvent when he acquired them, but he turned them both around within months. He then duplicated this feat with the *New York Post*. Murdoch is now prepared to risk his whole empire to make Fox the fourth network if the risk-averse bureaucrats do not interfere with his plans. Biographer Jerome Tuccille described Murdoch as "Visionary. A man who would not be deterred. Someone who knows exactly where he is going." One of the most surprising compliments came from his enemy Robert Maxwell, who told financial journalists on May 16, 1989: "He is a genius. There's no question that he has achieved a tremendous amount all over the world." *Forbes* magazine did a cover story on Murdoch during the mid-eighties in which Thomas O'Hanlon characterized him as "part accountant, part gambler, brilliant marketer, part shrewd journalist," and concluded: "By the time Rupert Murdoch retires to his Australian farm in the twenty-first century, his current vulgar image will have faded, and he will be regarded as a sage who followed opportunity where it led and put together a global empire in what may be the twenty-first century's greatest industry, communications."

In November 1994 Murdoch was voted the Most Powerful Person in Entertainment by *Entertainment Weekly* and *Premiere* magazines. *USA Today* (September 14, 1995) observed: "Rupert Murdoch has established the norm for the worldwide, vertically integrated strategy" in the communications industry. John Malone of Tele-Communications says, "Other companies are trying to catch Murdoch." *Vanity Fair* (September 1995) characterized him in a Hearstian way, "You provide the pictures and I'll provide the war," in supporting their ranking of him as the most powerful median baron in the world. Ken Aulette did a PBS special on Murdoch on November 7, 1995, characterizing Murdoch as either a "visionary or villain" and concluded by saying: "When history is written, Rupert Murdoch will be viewed as a giant."

Murdoch is using Fox to create a worldwide media empire that owns each stage of the production and distribution of entertainment from Hollywood production to distribution in Asia, South America, Europe, Australia, and North America. In 1995 he told *USA Today,* "Fox will be a marathon runner in sports broadcasting" with his eye on the Sydney Olympics. That dream is his personal crusade. He risked his personal fortune in stealing the NFL from CBS, the NHL from ABC, and in pursuing Wimbledon, the PGA, and Professional Baseball for Fox. Murdoch plans to broadcast the 2000 Olympics from Sydney through Fox and his other subsidiaries.

Murdoch has an edge in bidding for such international events due to the broadcasting power of his multinational distribution network. He can simultaneously air programs to many nations on five continents and share the cost among his affiliates. Few corporate adversaries can match his risk-taking entrepreneurial style. News Corp is now postured for enormous growth in the distribution of entertainment to an international audience. Murdoch's philosophical macroperspective will make him a dominant force in the international media wars. He has the necessary intuitive vision to dominate satellite television and expand his empire ever further. His work ethic ensures that no one will be more diligent in the pursuit of excellence and his risk taking will be impossible to match.

RUPERT KEITH MURDOCH
World's Most Powerful Media Baron
b. March 11, 1931, Melbourne, Australia

Dominant Trait: Type A Workaholic with propensity for highly leveraged and risky deals. Driven.

Motto: "In the struggle for freedom of information, technology not politics will be the ultimate decider."

Nickname: "Boy Publisher," "Dirty Digger," "Mad Dog Mogul," "Eclectic Media Mogul," "Red Rupert"

Vices/Hobbies: Tennis, skiing, gambling, horseracing, whitewater rafting, hot air balloons

Heroes/Mentors: Rupert Greene, maternal grandfather (gambling scallywag); Arthur C. Clarke (Clarke Ring of satellite fame); Walter Annenberg; Lord Beaverbrook; and Citizen Kane (Hearst) professional mentor.

Philosophy of Life: "As the world is modernizing, so it is Americanizing"—a refutation of "Cultural Imperialism." "A man who is not a socialist at twenty has no heart, while one who is a socialist at forty has no head."

Fantasy: To become "global media emperor": "I'd like to rule the world."

Professional Successes: Grew a tiny Adelaide paper into most powerful media empire in history; News Corp @ $20 billion largest in world and second largest firm in Australia. Richest man in Australia; Fox fourth network. Controls publication of 60 million papers each week in America, Australia, Europe, and Pacific Rim

Power: Indefatigable willpower earned him financial power, which he wields with wild abandon.

Influence: Brought down Conservative party in Australia; Helped elect Margaret Thatcher in Britain. Fox TV influenced American children with antiestablishment Bart Simpson. Influence pervasive.

Destructiveness: Fired employees heartlessly if they were ineffective. Destroyed labor at Wapping plant. Always willing to destroy the mediocre present for a dominant future. Tabloid sensationalism his forte.

Birth Order: Eldest son of Dame Elizabeth and Keith; older sister, Helen, and two younger sisters, Anne and Janet

Parental Influence: Father Keith (entrepreneur and publisher), grandfather Rupert Greene (wild, gambling renegade), and doting mother Dame Elizabeth

Transiency: To Geelong Boarding School by age ten and Oxford at seventeen. Traveling Europe with abandon.

Formal Education: Geelong Boarding School (prep school equivalent to Eton); hated it. Oxford Worcester College at seventeen, graduated in 1953; poor grades in political science. School much too confining.

Crises: Twenty-one when father died. In twenties, when yacht went aground stranding him on reef for two days, said: "I bet if I was going to be shot at dawn, I could get out of it." Debt of $7.6 billion in 1990 threatened empire, but escaped unscathed.

Libidinal Drive: Victorian morals except in business where tabloid sensationalism will be his journalistic legacy

Personality Type: Introverted-Intuitive-Thinker-Judger. Rebel with entrepreneurial risk-taking mentality. A workaholic.

Self-Esteem: Darryl Wardle, a Geelong alumnus, says: "He was always eminently confident."

Rebellion: This maverick who identified with the antiestablishment Bart Simpson: Both bent on shock and renegade behavior. A radical Leninist at Oxford turned to conservative right by age forty.

Risk Propensity: "Business is a life of constant calculated risks": NFL—$1.6 billion, overbid CBS by $400 million (1994); Harper and Row, $2.8 billion (1988); Fox Multi-Media, $2.6 billion (1985).

Work Ethic: Works 100-hour weeks claiming "They'll carry me out of here." Editor MacKenzie of *Sun* said: "He achieves more in half an hour than any other human being achieves in a whole day."

Tenacity: On brink of bankruptcy in 1990, never gave up and expanded empire to present state.

Optimism: Mother Elizabeth: "The ultimate aim of Rupert is to achieve . . . there is that implacable drive in him."

Manicness: A "man possessed" who finds it "impossible to relax" with "acquisitive madness" and "manic drive"

10

Tenacity and Perseverance: Walt Disney and Edith Piaf

Creativity is 99 percent perspiration and 1 percent inspiration.
—Thomas A. Edison

Persistence Prevails

Creative geniuses never give up and therefore seldom succumb to the vagaries of change and innovation. Winston Churchill was invited to speak to a graduating class at a popular university and the students anticipated an inspirational speech. Churchill stood up and said, "Never, Never, Never, Never, Never, Never, Never give up" and sat down. He had made his point to these new graduates on how to plan for a successful career. There are selling axioms that prove Churchill's point even more. Eighty-five percent of all sales are made after the salesperson has made five sales calls on the customer. However, only 20 percent of salespeople ever make five calls. Therefore, 85 percent of all sales are made by just 20 percent of the salespeople, and these tenacious individuals earn 85 percent of the commissions. This begs an aphorism of the four Ps: "Persistence Propels Potential to Perfection." The two individuals who personify perseverance in this book are Walt Disney and Edith Piaf. The others had this trait in abundance but not to the degree of these two tenacious visionaries.

DISNEY PERSEVERED

Powerful and innovative people doggedly pursue their dreams despite adversity. When the successful encounter unexpected roadblocks, they are seldom distracted and tend to view detours as normal on the road to success. Such persistence makes winners of losers and pushes the mediocre to excellence. Walt Disney was at best a mediocre artist who knew his limitations and therefore never allowed the word "art" to be used at Disney Studios. In fact, no artist could be hired during the early years. Disney intuitively knew that innate artistic skills would become equated with innovative designs and detract from creative performance. Artists would therefore become counterproductive to creativity, so he refused to hire trained artists as animators.

When Disney drew the first Mortimer Mouse, later Mickey Mouse, many of his associates, including his brother Roy, laughed at his creation. They did the same for *The Three Little Pigs* and *Snow White and the Seven Dwarfs*. Both productions were labeled "Disney's Folly." His Disneyland idea was ridiculed as a "carny" idea from a man with a "Barnum and Bailey" mentality. Disney never allowed expert opinion or adversity to stop him from creating what he discerned as innovative children's entertainment. His perseverance allowed him to build an animation empire and the world's foremost amusement park.

PIAF HAD TENACITY

Edith Piaf's tenacity was even more intense than Disney's. Edith was literally born in a gutter. She was abandoned by her mother as a child, weaned on wine, raised in a whorehouse, and was a street urchin in Paris. At age three she lost her eyesight and regained it four years later. School administrators wouldn't allow her to attend school with proper children since she lived in a brothel. She spent her teen years with an itinerant father, working as a street entertainer. She had an unwanted pregnancy followed by the death of the child at age two. Piaf couldn't read music but resorted to memorizing the lyrics and tunes. The little girl with the big voice had little talent but a huge heart and used her will to become the Great Piaf. She used passion and audience empathy to become Europe's greatest chanteuse. Tenacity defined her. Disney and Piaf never gave up despite horrible adversities and ended at the top of their respective professions. Adversity, a crutch for most, was their catalyst to fame and fortune.

Heuristic Learning

Edison was the quintessential example of learning through trial-and-error experimentation. One must find out what doesn't work in order to find what does. Anyone who believes that great success can be had without numerous problems is badly mistaken. As hair stylist Vidal Sassoon noted, the only place success comes before work is in the dictionary. Soichiro Honda of Honda Motor fame defined heuristic learning best in his acceptance speech at Michigan University in 1974. This humble creative genius told his audience: "Many people dream of success. To me success can be achieved only through repeated failure and introspection. In fact, my success represents the one percent of the work that resulted from the 99 percent that was called failure." All fourteen of these visionaries were heuristic learners. They were willing to repeatedly try and fail and then try again until they achieved success.

PERSISTENT ARCHITECT

Frank Lloyd Wright had every reason to quit a profession that derided his most basic work. His innovations were repeatedly ridiculed by the architectural profession and the media for defying tradition. They labeled him an "architectural anarchist" for his renegade approach to life and building. When Taliesin was burned to the ground, he rebuilt it bigger and better. His intended was murdered, but he would remarry twice. If nothing else, Wright was a tenacious man. His biographer Meryle Secrest (1993) observed: "No one could have stopped him from becoming a success because he refused to be discouraged."

TENACIOUS SCIENTIST

Tenacity defined Nikola Tesla. When he learned to read, he would read all night, causing his parents to be concerned for his health. They took away his candle so the youngster would not hurt his eyesight. The irrepressible Tesla taught himself to make candles and continued his habit of all-night reading. When Tesla's college professor told him his idea for developing an induction motor was "impossible," he went on to prove he was right. Tesla refused to give up on his revolutionary idea and his frenetic search for a solution caused him to have an emotional collapse. It then took ten years for him to sell the idea to Westinghouse for commercialization. Any less of a commitment and he would never have succeeded.

BEAUTY AND PERSEVERANCE

Helena Rubinstein encountered many detours on her road to the top of the cosmetic profession. She concluded: "You have to work three hundred years in a lifetime to be successful in the beauty business." Rubinstein worked every day to the age of ninety-four. She would not be denied in any endeavor. When she decided to open a beauty salon in 1909 London, the experts told her "they will slaughter you." She proceeded anyway and became a success. When the owners of a Manhattan penthouse refused to accept her purchase offer because she was Jewish, this iron-willed woman bought the building and dismissed the bigoted management.

PERSISTENT MEDIA MOGUL

Rupert Murdoch was on the brink of bankruptcy in 1990 when he owed $7.6 billion in debt to 146 different institutions in ten different currencies. Bankers told him to liquidate or they would force him to. News Corp was functionally insolvent. Sheer bravado on Murdoch's part allowed him to survive the crisis. Citibank's Ann Lane helped him placate the banks and survive his greatest business crisis. She summed up his tenacious style: "I knew he would never say, 'I can't do it anymore.' "

MENTAL TOUGHNESS

Maria Montessori was fearless in her fight to bring innovation to education. Her friend and biographer E. M. Standing said her persistence was incredible. She had a "strength of character and mind compared to the 'superhuman' ability of Napoleon." Her persistence is illustrated by her acceptance of a lecture tour to India at age seventy-nine.

Howard Hughes was so tenacious he was called bull-headed and sometimes schizoid over his refusal to give up on an idea. When he finished producing and directing *Hell's Angels* (the most expensive movie in history in 1929), it became immediately obsolete due to the advent of sound. Al Jolson's *Jazz Singer* had been released as the first "talkie" just as Hughes was completing his masterpiece. Most people would have given up and cut their losses, but not the resilient Hughes. He immediately started over, bet on an eighteen-year-old unknown named Jean Harlow, and invested another $1.8 million in producing a classic that dazzled the critics.

Amelia Earhart never gave up in the pursuit of a goal or feared any challenge. She was introspective and when questioned about her flying expertise, told reporters candidly: "I'm not the best pilot in the world. I'm not even the best female pilot. What I have that you can write about is tenacity."

DESPOTIC RESOLVE

Hitler's friend August Kubizek recalled: "Hitler did not know what resignation meant. . . . He who resigned he thought lost his right to live." Hitler himself said in a 1931 speech, "For me the word impossible does not exist. . . . I intend to set up a thousand-year Reich." His tenacity lasted to the very end when he said, "We shall not capitulate—No never! We may be destroyed, but if we are we shall drag a world with us—a world in flames."

Napoleon could not stand living in luxury as emperor of Elba. His tenacious need to be at the top drove him to march on Paris to win back his throne. Once back in power he made a final attempt to dominate Europe through war. Napoleon refused to capitulate until he was so badly beaten he had no choice.

A PERSISTENT APHRODITE

Isadora Duncan was a determined artist who survived by resorting to her wits. She learned perseverance as a child when she was forced to persuade the butcher and baker into extending credit to her poverty-stricken family. When her family were all living on a park bench and starving in London, she boldly walked into the city's finest hotel and told the concierge their baggage was on its way and to please provide them a suite. The hotel complied and she ordered a banquet to the room. They spent two days avoiding the management and bathed, ate, and slept like royalty until they skipped out in the middle of the night.

This tenacious woman persevered while living a vagabond existence as she searched for fame and fortune. She went to San Francisco, Chicago, New York City, London, Paris, and finally Berlin before she was able to gain any recognition. Most people would have given up long before that. She spent a great deal of her life in an unsuccessful attempt at founding a permanent school of modern dance. She tried in Berlin, London, Paris, New York, Athens, and finally in Communist Russia. Duncan was still trying to establish her school when she died tragically in Nice at age forty-nine.

TENACITY MEANS NEVER LISTENING TO AN EXPERT

Walt Disney was friends with Frank Lloyd Wright whom he asked to preview his movie *Fantasia*. Walt's brother Roy had already labeled the movie a failure. Wright agreed with Roy Disney, calling the film "absurd." Disney ignored them both and released what would be recognized as a creative masterpiece. *Fantasia* was a box office flop in 1940, but critics praised it. Peyton Boswell, art critic and editor of *Art Digest,* described *Fantasia* as "an aesthetic experience never to be forgotten." During this same period, Howard Hughes owned RKO Studios and was the distributor for Disney's films. Hughes and Roy Disney told Walt that his movie *Seal Island* was destined to become a commercial "disaster" and advised him to scrap it. Disney ignored their advice and produced *Seal Island.* It won the 1948 Oscar for Best Short Subject. Even those productions that failed had lasting quality and emerged later as movies or on video as huge hits.

The fourteen visionaries in this book never listened to the experts and had the temerity and tenacity to try and try until they succeeded. Tenacity ensured the positively driven individuals success. In the case of the negatively inspired subjects, it led to their demise. Tenacity became an instrument of destruction for Sade, Napoleon, Hughes, and Hitler. It should be noted that all these individuals were most persistent in pursuing their childhood fantasies or self-images. They were driven to become what people expected of them or what they expected of themselves and worked feverishly to fulfill those internal images.

Walter Elias Disney

We are not in the art *business.*

Overview

Walt Disney understood the essence of creativity better than most. When he said
that "Disneyland will never be finished," he had an intuitive understanding about
the fickleness of the buying public and the need for "creative destruction" and continual innovation for new entertainment concepts. Disney was not formally educated but had an intuitive feel for the entertainment needs of children and adults.

Disney spent his formative years on a Kansas farm and had a fundamentalist
Midwestern upbringing that he never lost even after years in dog-eat-dog Hollywood. He once said, "I prefer animals to people," meaning that he preferred working with a docile animal, which was predictable and never dishonest. He detested
the brutal and vicious tactics practiced in business and often regressed into a fantasy world where honesty and purity existed at the stroke of his pen. His father's
abuse had been indelibly imprinted on his sensitive psyche and he spent his life
attempting to exorcise this pain.

DYSFUNCTIONAL INNOVATOR

Disney had all the symptoms of a manic-depressive personality. He went into periods of manic creativity, which were always followed by severe depression, anxiety, or nervous exhaustion. He would be prolifically creative and then have to take
extended vacations to recover from physical exhaustion and depression. During his
life Disney suffered eight nervous breakdowns in a frenetic existence that saw him
either at the top of the industry receiving an Oscar or fighting for his very existence. His battles with bankruptcy and those who thought he was a dreamer caused
much of his emotional distress, but even so he was still able to build the greatest
children's entertainment industry in history. Mickey Mouse and other Disney
characters have become institutions on three continents. The imagery Disney has
created in the minds of both adults and children is unparalleled. His cartoon characters help people regress into the freedom and happiness of childhood fantasy
where one can remove the burdens of adult reality.

CREATIVE FANTASY—DISNEY'S ESCAPE

Psychologists have proven that fantasy is the genesis of all creativity. Disney
lived vicariously through his characters. Imagination and fantasy were his escape
into a world that was pure and pristine. He was driven to fulfill his own internalized images of himself and did so by creating Mickey, Donald, Pinocchio, and
other characters. Disney so identified with his characters that he unconsciously

imbued most of them with his own personality. This humanization of his characters made them more real to his audiences. Mickey Mouse and Donald Duck were make-believe but psychologically believable. Disney preferred working with innocent children and animals to the dog-eat-dog world of Hollywood. Even when relaxing, he escaped into his own fantasy world in his backyard where he had built a model train complete with engine and caboose. He spent hours alone driving his model train in order to escape the real world. Disney expressed his true feelings about life and art when he said, "If all the world thought and acted like children we'd never have any trouble." The Disney empire was built on fantasizing about life and is the consummate story of imagination winning out over rationality.

CREATIVE SUCCESS

Disney was prodigiously productive during his life. He made approximately seven hundred films in fourteen different languages. Disney was interested in money only as something needed to finance his creations. But money tends to be the barometer of the successful. As of the mid-nineties, one billion people have paid admission to see his films. The Disney empire passed the $10 billion revenue mark in 1994 with record profits exceeding $1 billion. On August 1, 1995, Disney shocked the world by buying its onetime Disneyland backer, ABC, for $19 billion in what the *Wall Street Journal* said would make "show business a whole new world" and what *USA Today* characterized as "a match made for the twenty-first century." Walt Disney had created the preeminent entertainment empire and would have been proud of the magnitude of his mouse's pervasive influence. In the *Wall Street Journal*'s words, "The mouse has roared."

Over 65 million visitors have passed through the gates of Disney's theme parks in the United States, Japan, and France. Mickey Mouse watches and comic books from the 1930s have became collector's items. When first introduced in the middle of the Depression, they sold in the millions. It is ironic that they were created not for artistic or marketing reasons, but to save Disney Studio from bankruptcy during the thirties. Disney merchandise today is sold through a chain of retail outlets in every major mall in America. Disneyland and EPCOT Center are further testimony to Disney's vision and genius. His cartoon characters are all permanent fixtures in the fantasy world of today's children.

DISNEY'S FOLLY: *SNOW WHITE*

What is amazing is that most of Disney's greatest innovations were denigrated by industry experts, friends, and collaborators, including his brother Roy. Movie moguls and bankers and Roy Disney were absolutely convinced that *Snow White* was a creative and business blunder, labeling it "Disney's Folly." Disney refused to listen to them and produced it despite their predictions that it would fail miserably. The movie came close to bankrupting Disney Studios but also became one of the great Hollywood masterpieces. When first released, *Snow White* received rave reviews. Even the most callous critics acclaimed this work a masterpiece of artistic perfection. The *New York Herald Tribune* critic enthused: "After seeing *Snow White* for the third time, I am more certain than ever that it belongs with the great masterpieces of the screen, one of those rare works of inspired artistry." The film went on to win a special 1938 Academy Award "for significant screen innovation which has charmed and pioneered a great new entertainment field for the motion picture cartoon." Disney had proved that a movie without actors and actresses, featuring only fantasy cartoon characters, could draw audiences to the big screen. *Snow White* played before twenty million movie patrons when first released in 1937 and by 1993 had grossed $100 million in revenues. In its 1994 release on videotape, it broke all records with twenty-eight million sold in the first thirty days.

CREATIVE LEGACY

When Disney died in 1966 he had earned in excess of seven hundred citations, honorary degrees from Harvard and Yale, twenty-nine Oscars, four Emmys, the Irving Thalberg Award, the Presidential Freedom Medal, and the French Legion of Honor. His wife received a telegram from then governor-elect of California, Ronald Reagan: "There just aren't any words to express my personal grief. The world is a poorer place now." Richard D. Zanuck, vice president of Twentieth Century Fox, said, "No eulogy will be read or monument built to equal the memorial Walt Disney has left in the hearts and minds of the world's people." The *New York Times* summed up his life and work in a December 16, 1966, obituary:

> Starting with very little save a talent for drawing, a gift of imagination that was somehow in tune with everyone's imagination, and a dogged determination to succeed, Walt Disney became one of Hollywood's greatest entertainers. He had a genius for innovation; his production was enormous; he was able to keep sure and personal control over his increasingly far-flung enterprises; his hand was ever on the public pulse. He was in short a legend in his own lifetime.

Early Life Experiences and Influences

Walt Disney was born December 5, 1901, in Chicago to Elias Disney, an itinerant contractor and aspiring entrepreneur, and Flora Call. Disney was named after Walter Parr, a Chicago minister, who had named his son Elias. His mother, Flora, was a church organist and both parents were steeped in fundamentalism. Born eight and a half years after his brother Roy, Walt was raised like a firstborn child. He was the apple of his mother's eye and she doted on him during his early years. His father was an authoritarian and humorless man who felt physical punishment was the best teacher of children. Elias was a failure at everything he attempted and moved continually to find his niche in life. He ran orange groves, worked at motels and manufacturing, tried farming, had paper routes, and proved unsuccessful at them all. He often took out his frustrations on his children. When beaten by his father, young Walt would turn to his older brother Roy for comfort. Roy became his substitute father, salving his physical and emotional pains.

FANTASY AND TRANSIENCY

When he was young, his mother would read Walt fairy tales. Disney was able to escape into these mythical fantasy stories, which made him happy. He often fell asleep envisioning a frog turning into a prince or a stepchild becoming a princess. The fictional heroes of many of these stories became imprinted on the psyche of young Walt.

Disney was five years old when his father purchased a fifty-acre farm in Marceline, Kansas, and the family moved there from Chicago. It was on this farm that Disney developed a love for the animals that would fill his imagination for the rest of his life. Young Walt was too small to ride a horse like his older brothers so he started riding the pigs instead. His favorite hog was nicknamed Porker, which he captured in his early drawings. No art supplies were available on the farm so the tenacious child resorted to using coal on toilet paper to draw his favorite animals. Porker became the model for the Foolish Pig in *The Three Little Pigs*. Disney said later, "I did the preliminary sketch from remembering Porker and I was practically weeping with nostalgia by the time I had finished." He drew for fun but was thrilled when the family doctor bought one of his pictures when he was eight. The ever-industrious boy then learned to swap drawings with the local barber in exchange for a haircut.

After two years of crop failures, Elias sold the farm and moved the family to Kansas City. Disney was eight at the time and enrolled in Benton Grammar School. He took a newspaper route in Kansas City to earn money for art supplies and candy. By this time his brother Roy had had enough of their authoritarian father and ran away from home at age eighteen. Young Walt and his little sister, Ruth, were now the only children left at home.

Disney was a lonely child and often lost himself in books. His favorite authors were Charles Dickens and Mark Twain and he enjoyed reading about an adventurous hero named Jimmy Dale. Charlie Chaplin and the "Little Tramp" were his screen heroes. At age twelve Disney accidentally drove a nail through his foot and was forced to stay in bed for some weeks. While convalescing he started reading comic strips and began to dream of becoming a creator of cartoons or writer of newspaper comic strips.

Elias Disney's newspaper route failed and he sold it for ten thousand dollars and returned to Chicago. Flora Disney worried that such a move would not be in Walt's best interest and arranged for him to remain in Kansas. At age fifteen Walt lived with his two brothers Roy and Herbert until school was out while his parents and sister, Ruth, relocated to Chicago. He liked it so much that he stayed over the summer and lied about his age to get a job selling soft drinks on trains traveling through six states. Disney acquired a love for railroading at this time and learned about the world from the traveling salesmen he encountered on board the Midwestern trains. This proved to be a great learning experience for the teenager, who learned to cope in a world of strangers where the imagination knew no bounds.

FORMAL EDUCATION

Roy was a role model and substitute father for young Walt during much of his teen years. When the school term was over in Kansas, Disney reluctantly moved to Chicago in the fall of 1917 and enrolled in McKinley High. He also enrolled in a night class at the Chicago Academy of Fine Arts paid for with money he earned working in his father's jelly factory for seven dollars per week. He became the school cartoonist and finished his freshman year in 1918.

Disney was a romantic and a dreamer and idolized his older brother Roy who had enlisted in the army during World War I. He received letters from Roy and became excited about the life of a soldier traveling through Europe. The sixteen-year-old Disney lied about his age and tried to enlist. He was turned down by the army but was accepted by the Red Cross. Disney spent his seventeenth birthday in Saint Cyr, France, as an ambulance driver for the wounded. He continued drawing cartoons and regularly submitted them to U.S. magazines, which all rejected him. Upon his discharge, Disney decided to return to Kansas City and apply for a job as a cartoonist for the *Kansas City Star*. To his surprise, he was hired immediately but then fired after just one month for his "singular lacking of drawing ability."

CARTOON ENTREPRENEUR

Another aspiring artist, Ub Iwerks, was hired and fired the same day as Walt. The two were unemployed but ambitious, and decided to form a partnership called Iwerks-Disney Commercial Artists. Both young men worked diligently but were unsuccessful in securing business contracts. They received but one contract for $135 and the partnership ended as fast as it started. Walt then took a temporary job at Kansas City Advertising until he and Iwerks had the money and clients to start their first real business venture, which they called Laugh-O-Grams. This was Disney's first viable business operation and became his basic training ground for producing animated films. Disney and Iwerks lacked money and experience and were forced to be innovative or starve. Their studio was in a garage and was equipped with the most primitive equipment. Disney purchased a hand-crank camera and began a trial-and-error approach to producing cartoons. The two worked day and night perfecting the process of creating lifelike animated cartoons.

The two aspiring entrepreneurs had more guts than savvy. Iwerks was more talented an artist than Disney who was more the businessman. Disney convinced some local businessmen to invest $15,000 in Laugh-O-Grams, and then entered into an agreement with a local theater group to produce one-minute Laugh-O-Gram cartoons for thirty cents per foot of film. He was not aware of or concerned with the cost of production—an error he would repeat many times during the next thirty years—and soon discovered the cost of production was $25 per foot or some $24 more than he was being paid. Not deterred by such details, Disney was inspired to produce a cartoon version of *Little Red Riding Hood,* a fairy tale his mother had read to him as a child. Iwerks and Disney spent most of their financial resources on producing the *Riding Hood* cartoon feature and sent it off to New York City for approval of their distribution company. It was immediately rejected. When Disney started Laugh-O-Grams, he was living rent-free with brother Roy. Roy contracted tuberculosis and had to leave for a cure at a West Coast Veterans hospital. Disney was suddenly alone, without money, and came close to starving.

CRISIS AND CREATIVITY

Undeterred by the rejection of *Little Red Riding Hood,* Disney and Iwerks decided to gamble everything on the production of *Alice's Adventures in Wonderland.* Disney spent his life dreaming up wonderfully romantic and innovative ideas that were not economically viable. In this case, he employed six-year-old actress Virginia Davis for the role of Alice and jumped right into production. He wrote to his New York distributor, Margaret Winkler, "I've just discovered something new and clever in animated cartoons! . . . A new idea that will appeal to all classes and is bound to be a winner . . . a clever combination of live characters and cartoons." Winkler wrote back asking to see the finished film. Always the optimist, Disney and Iwerks started working day and night in a frantic attempt to finish the project. Money ran out long before they could even get close to finishing.

During this period, Disney often resorted to mischievousness to distract himself from the problems of their business. His sense of humor was often lost on the more serious Iwerks. Disney would put mice in Iwerks's pockets and guinea pigs in his desk and then crack up at Ub's reaction. It was Disney's way of breaking the tension when they were desperately poor and on the verge of starvation. He was living on bread and water and said later, "It was probably the blackest time of my life. I really knew what hardship and hunger were like. . . . It was a pretty lonely and miserable time of my life." He had bet everything on *Alice* and had lost. This would be a recurring practice for the next thirty years. Disney and Iwerks closed the business and Walt skipped town to avoid angry creditors.

HOLLYWOOD CRAWL OF FAME

Disney decided to join his brother Roy in Los Angeles where he was recuperating from tuberculosis. He sold his camera for the forty dollars needed for a first-class train ticket to Hollywood. Halfway to Hollywood a passenger on the train asked Disney about his destination and he responded, "I'm going to Hollywood. I'm going to direct motion pictures." Such was the optimism of the young man who had just failed twice in business, was broke, had limited talent, but who was equipped with an indomitable will.

Roy was concerned about his brother's future and offered eighty-five dollars of his monthly military pension to subsidize his start in the animated cartoon business. Disney was buoyed by the support and immediately wrote Margaret Winkler in New York advising her he had relocated his operations to Hollywood and was producing *Alice* there. Winkler responded by offering him fifteen hundred dollars for each negative he produced and agreed to pay for six of them in advance. Disney was ecstatic and launched his new firm known as Disney Brothers. He rushed to the hospital to tell Roy of their good fortune and informed him they would be partners if Roy could come up with an additional $200. He also approached his Uncle Robert who lived in Los Angeles. Robert agreed to a five-hundred-dollar loan but refused to become an equity holder of the new enterprise. Roy's investment of two hundred dollars would ultimately make him one of the wealthiest men in Hollywood. Uncle Robert's reluctance to buy stock cost him and his heirs a potential billion dollars over the next sixty years.

Disney's first six *Alice* negatives were a flop and Margaret Winkler came to California to cancel their contract. The irrepressible Disney insisted that Winkler review his new animated shorts, which were much better than the ones she had rejected. She was furious with him but politely listened and watched as he demonstrated his new animation techniques. Winkler was so impressed that she wrote him a check for two thousand dollars and left for New York with the new film clips. *Alice's Spooky Adventures* became Disney's first commercially produced cartoons. *Alice* made her debut in New Jersey in March 1924 and was shown in theaters from New Jersey to Washington, D.C., with moderate success.

During the production of the *Alice* series, Roy Disney introduced his brother to a new employee in the inking department, Lillian Bonds. Roy was about to be married and Lillian was his fiancée's best friend. Walt and Lillian witnessed Roy's wedding, and then Walt proposed to her. They were married in the summer of 1925. Disney proposed to Lillian with the same impulsiveness with which he created cartoons. He borrowed forty dollars for a new suit and asked Roy for a $120 advance for his wedding. At age twenty-four he had a new bride and Disney Studios was in business.

A Persistent Spirit

Walt Disney was relentless in his drive to the top. If he hadn't been, he would have been finished in the business before he was thirty. Disney Studios was insolvent every eighteen months for the first thirty years of its existence. The firm came precariously close to folding on numerous occasions and Disney's refusal to accept defeat helped to avoid financial disaster. One of the first of these crises occurred when Margaret Winkler married a shrewd and unethical businessman named Charles Mintz. She turned over all her business operations, including the Disney cartoon contract, to her new husband. This proved disastrous for the Disney brothers.

Oswald the Rabbit

Mintz met with Disney and encouraged him to develop a completely new character to compete with the very popular Felix the Cat. The new character would be called "Oswald the Lucky Rabbit" and Mintz very shrewdly insisted on exclusive distribution rights for Oswald. He then negotiated an attractive distribution deal for this character with Carl Laemmle of Universal Pictures. Universal launched Oswald who became an overnight sensation and rivaled the success of Felix the Cat. Oswald's first cartoon hit was called *Trolley Troubles*. It received rave reviews, prompting Laemmle to renegotiate his deal with Mintz for more money and more cartoons. Mintz came to Disney with an offer to produce a new Oswald skit every other week at $2250 per skit. This was more money than Disney had ever dreamed possible. Unfortunately, Disney's contract with Mintz was due to be renegotiated within a few months and he was unaware of the character flaws in Charles Mintz: the unscrupulous Mintz was intent on stealing Disney Studios from Walt and Roy.

Oswald's Disappearing Act

Mintz surreptitiously hired away all of the animators who had worked on Oswald the Rabbit—Rudolph Ising, Hugh Harman, Friz Freleng, and Carman Maxwell—and proceeded to make an offer he thought Disney couldn't refuse. He offered a long-term contract in exchange for 50 percent of Disney Studios, explaining to Disney that he already owned the distribution rights for Oswald and that he already employed all of his key animators. Mintz stated that he wasn't interested in starting a cartoon animation company but would do so if Disney did not agree to the new contract. Disney was thunderstruck. He had never been interested in the distribution side of his work, only in creating innovative animated cartoons. His fundamentalist mentality never considered that anyone would steal his creations for profit.

The Disney brothers felt that they had no choice but to go out of business. Walt Disney walked into Mintz's office, threw a drawing of Oswald at Mintz, and said, "Here, you can have the little bastard! He's all yours, I don't want him any more! Just trying to draw him after all this would make me sick to my stomach! You can have him—and good luck to you!" He then added, "Don't worry there are plenty more characters where he came from" (Mosley 1986).

Genesis of a Mouse

Walt and Lillian Disney were in despair when they boarded the train in New York to return to California. They had no idea how they would survive this devastating loss. On the train, Disney started sketching a new character which he named Mortimer. It was a mouse with big ears, a big nose, and a mischievous personality not unlike his own.

The origin of Mortimer was in Kansas City. Disney's caricature reminded him of the mice he had played with and placed in Ub Iwerks's pockets. Working late at night, Disney would find mice in the trash can: "I lifted them out and kept them in little cages on my desk. One of them was my particular friend." Lillian thought the name Mortimer sounded too sissy and suggested the name Mickey. Mickey Mouse was born and would become the cornerstone of an empire.

Upon returning to California, Disney showed his creation to Ub Iwerks, who he had enticed to move to California. Iwerks studied the preliminary sketches of the little rodent and commented, "Looks exactly like you—same nose, same face, same whiskers, same gestures and expressions. All he needs now is your voice." Disney agreed and for the next twenty years was Mickey's voice for the sound versions.

MICKEY MOUSE DEBUTS

In 1928 newspaper headlines were trumpeting Charles Lindbergh's Atlantic crossing in *The Spirit of St. Louis.* Disney decided to take advantage of the media craze and set Mickey's first cartoon in a plane, naming it *Plane Crazy.* This animated short made its debut in May 1928 and Mickey Mouse became an instant star. Disney followed that success with *Gallopin' Gaucho* and *Steamboat Willie,* the first Mickey Mouse cartoon with sound. Mickey Mouse soon became Disney's alter ego and the storylines told of a mouse that had the personality of its creator. Disney would later say, "The life and adventures of Mickey Mouse have been closely bound up with my own personal and professional life. . . . He still speaks for me and I still for him."

Producing Mickey with sound was more costly than planned and the company became insolvent during the production of *Steamboat Willie.* Disney came face-to-face with disaster and was forced to sell his car to make payroll. *Steamboat Willie* proved to be a great investment as it became an instant smash hit when released on November 18, 1928. It was given rave reviews by *Variety* and the *New York Times* which called it "ingenious" and a "good deal of fun." At age twenty-seven, Disney was fast becoming the star of an industry saturated with unsavory people.

DISNEY'S ALTER EGO

During the financially tough days filming *Steamboat Willie,* Disney had to sell his beloved Moon four-seater when his brother Roy told him, "It's either the automobile or Mickey Mouse." This was an easy decision for this visionary who was always willing to sacrifice anything for his beloved work.

Universal Pictures distributed Disney's cartoons and asked for copyright to Mickey Mouse. Still smarting over the Mintz debacle, Disney adamantly refused. Mickey was his baby and he would *never ever* give away the right to Mickey Mouse for any price.

Mickey was Walt's alter ego. Both were brash, impudent, mischievous, kind to old ladies, and polite to all women in general even if they were chauvinists at heart. One psychological profile of Mickey and Disney depicts the mouse as his *superego*: chaste, humble, cerebral, asexual, in control, and adored. His *id* was symbolized by the personality of Donald Duck: dark, volatile, emotional, sexual, out of control, angry. Disney's fantasies, whether internal or external, unconscious or conscious, were always closely intertwined.

CRISIS STRIKES AGAIN

The dark side of Disney's personality came to the forefront when Pat Power, the distributor of Mickey Mouse and the *Silly Symphonies* cartoons, proved to be as unsavory as Charles Mintz. Power attempted to use his distribution expertise and vertically integrate by stealing Walt's best friend and chief animator Ub Iwerks. He cheated the Disneys out of $150,000 in unpaid royalties through a distribution ploy similar to the one Mintz had used. Power formed a new company, hiring away Iwerks to head the new venture to compete with Disney in producing animated cartoons. He took the Universal contract and effectively wiped out Disney Studios. Harry Cohn of Columbia Pictures saved Disney by financing the production of the *Silly Symphonies* and distributed them through his company.

This was the second time the naïve Disney had lost money and key employees and the experience made him vengeful, paranoid, and suicidal. The truth is that creative talent cannot be stolen.

Iwerks lived to rue the day he left Disney to work for Power since his firm lasted only five years. Disney rehired Iwerks but the two were never again close. Ironically, the stock which Iwerks forfeited by going to work for Power would have been worth $500 million in 1990.

This crisis in 1931 shattered Disney's emotional system and he suffered the first of eight nervous breakdowns. Lillian found him unconscious from an overdose of sleeping pills and the doctors saved his life by pumping his stomach.

MANIC DEPRESSION AND THE CREATIVE PROCESS

Disney could never understand how people that he trusted and for whom he had fulfilled all his obligations could resort to ruthless and unsavory tactics just for money. He was never motivated by money and couldn't relate to anyone who was. Disney once told reporters, "I've always been bored with just making money." After his best friend Ub Iwerks had betrayed him, Disney went into a severe depression.

Disney spent his life swinging between periods of euphoric creativity and abominable depression. During the thirties, he reached the peak of his creative productivity but was afflicted with manic depression much of the time. He often worked all night and slept at the studio at least half the time. Despite hard work, Disney Studios was continually on the brink of financial disaster, which drove him to nervous exhaustion. He wrote of the Power period: "I guess I was working too hard and worrying too much. In 1931 I had a nervous breakdown. Each picture we made cost more than we figured it would earn. First we began to panic. Then I cracked up. I couldn't sleep. I reached the point when I couldn't even talk over the

telephone without crying. I was in a highly emotional state." This is a typical statement from anyone suffering from bipolar or manic-depressive illness. Disney was
twenty-nine and said that he felt fifty-nine. Even though he had been nominated
for two Academy Awards for Best Short Subject, failure lurked around each corner. When he lost Iwerks and the $150,000, he was at his wit's end.

A COLORFUL SUCCESS

Walt Disney was resilient and persevered when things looked to be their worst. He
seemed to find new inspiration from each crisis and this brought him back stronger
than ever. After the Power debacle Disney threw all his energy into producing
Flowers and Trees, the studio's first Technicolor cartoon. Disney was awarded two
Oscars in 1931 for *Flowers and Trees.*

The *Three Little Pigs* was released in December 1933 in concert with the birth
of his daughter Diane Marie. Both events were high points in his life. The cartoon
was enormously successful and spawned a worldwide musical hit, "Who's Afraid
of the Big Bad Wolf." It also won him another Oscar in 1933. Bankruptcy, however, was always around the corner.

During this period, the firm was saved by a clever merchandising idea from a
Philadelphia man who convinced the Disney brothers to allow him to sell the
Mickey Mouse character in coloring books and watches. In 1932/33 Walt's characters—primarily Mickey and Minnie Mouse—sold 97,938 coloring books and a
half-million Mickey Mouse watches. These revenues rescued Disney Studios from
impending financial disaster. Every time the firm escaped bankruptcy and became
financially stable, Walt would use the money to produce another one of his inspirations. This time his inspiration would prove to be one of his greatest creations.

SNOW WHITE: DISNEY'S FOLLY

In 1934 Walt Disney decided to produce a full-length feature film—*Snow White
and the Seven Dwarfs*—utilizing only animated cartoon characters. The industry
was aghast. How could a fairy tale hold the interest of an audience through seven
reels of action?

Disney's innovation was considered a brilliant stroke of genius by only a few,
but the act of a raving madman by most. Few had his vision including his brother
Roy who told him, "You're trying to ruin us."

Disney never gave up his dream of producing this story of a fantasy princess
whose innocence wins out over the wicked witch. Virtually everyone called it
"Disney's Folly" and the bankers refused to fund it. The company was out of
money half-way through filming, and the pressure and anxiety caused Walt to suffer his third nervous breakdown in 1935.

Disney never capitulated to those wanting him to stop this project. Finally, in
mid-1935 he convinced the Bank of America to loan the company $5 million to
complete the film. The film almost destroyed Disney's marriage as he often slept

at the studio during its creation. A reporter wrote: "All his social activities, his sports, his family, everyone and everything play second fiddle to his work."

THE GOLDEN YEARS

Snow White exemplified the "Good versus Evil" theme which had become the Disney trademark. Disney had successfully blended his fundamentalist upbringing with the studio and his creations. He loved creating endings where Good always won out over Evil. When Disney first proposed *Snow White,* Roy's first comment was: "How much will it cost?" This was an important question for Roy, who was responsible for paying the bills. For Walt Disney it was never important and he didn't care about the cost within certain parameters. This mentality was the reason for his consummate success and the cause of the firm's continual financial insolvency.

The release of *Snow White* inaugurated the Golden Era of Disney. Between 1936 and 1941 Disney produced some of the greatest animated movies in history. The studio was also precariously close to bankruptcy due to the exorbitant production cost of *Snow White.* Disney's perfectionism did not help. Roy responded: "Why can't we just stay with Mickey Mouse?" The Hollywood gurus of the time like Louis B. Mayer, Jack Warner, and Harry Cohn all scoffed at the idea of a ninety-minute cartoon movie. They predicted Disney's demise, with Mayer cynically remarking, "Who'd pay to see a drawing of a fairy princess?" and "Who'd pay to see . . . a fairy princess when they can see Joan Crawford's boobs for the same price at the box office?"

Twenty million saw the movie during the first eighteen months after its release. *Time* magazine hailed it as a masterpiece and *Variety* called it an "all-time box office champ." It earned $8 million at the theater when tickets sold for twenty-five cents each. By 1990 *Snow White* had earned an unprecedented $100 million. Shown in eight languages, audiences were enthralled and came away humming the Seven Dwarfs' refrain, "Heigh, ho, heigh, ho, it's off to work we go." Disney had succeeded in making Dopey, Grumpy, Doc, Sneezy, Bashful, Happy, and Sleepy into stars.

Disney was now at the peak of his creative genius and received honorary master of arts degrees from Harvard and Yale. Buoyed by his success and funded by *Snow White,* he quickly commenced production on a series of animated films. *Pinocchio* was released in 1940, *Fantasia* in 1940, *Dumbo* in 1941, and *Bambi* in 1942. During this period, Disney worked incessantly in a manic drive to fulfill his every childhood fantasy. He drove himself to exhaustion and often collapsed, to be nursed back to health by his ever-faithful wife. Sometimes they would escape on a European vacation and Disney would return relaxed and renewed.

Disneyland

Just after World War II Walt Disney became obsessed with the idea of a "clean" and "family" amusement park that would appeal to both kids and adults. He began drawing plans for a Mickey Mouse park to be built in Burbank in 1948. Roy Disney thought the idea ridiculous and dissuaded him from pursuing it since the firm was in the midst of the expensive *Alice in Wonderland* production. *Alice* turned out to be a box office bomb, which further delayed Walt's dream park but he was not deterred. He spent the next few years visiting amusement parks all over Europe and the United States. After a visit to New York's Coney Island, he became even more convinced of the need for a clean amusement park for the whole family. He ignored his brother's advice and borrowed $100,000 on his personal insurance policy to have the plans drawn up. He then showed total commitment by selling his Palm Springs home to raise money to finance the implementation of Disneyland.

Disney hired the Stanford Research Institute to finalize the plans, select the final site, and complete the market research for presentation to the Disney board of directors for approval. The board turned him down flat. He immediately formed a new company called WED (Walt Elias Disney Company) in 1951 and began plans to find financial backing for his project. Stanford Research Institute completed its in-depth analysis with amusement park experts in Chicago in 1953. In reviewing a model of Disneylandia (the park's original name), featuring five themed areas beginning with Main Street and proceeding through Fantasyland, Tomorrowland, Adventureland, and Frontierland, the experts advised the Disney brothers not to proceed. Their reasoning was based on those ideas that were not then employed in existing parks. These experts resorted to a bureaucratic mentality pointing out that the park diametrically opposed all of the economic and entertainment principles by which a park then operated. Their reasoning for Disneyland's certain failure was wrapped up in their own psychological investment in their knowledge; it had nothing to do with attempting new and innovative ideas. Their objections included:

1. The park did not have enough ride capacity.

2. It had too many nonproductive areas (free entertainment like costume characters) which were not revenue producing.

3. Newfangled rides like Space Mountain were too costly to build and to maintain.

4. A year-round park was impossible to maintain.

5. A single entrance with one price was impossible; parking and congestion unwieldy.

IGNORE THE EXPERTS

Disney was not deterred by the experts' assessment since their objections were the exact items he felt were wrong with existing parks. The experts were merely defending the inefficiencies existent in traditional parks, plus they feared anything not previously attempted. Ironically, their objections turned out to be those most responsible for Disneyland's enormous success.

Roy Disney believed the experts. He concluded that Walt had finally lost all logic and was intent on self-destruction. He refused to allow the company to be part of his brother's latest folly. Roy described Disneylandia as a carnival or fairgrounds in the likeness of Barnum and Bailey. In one emotional flare-up, Roy exclaimed, "What kind of crazy crap is this, anyway? Pirates? Red Indians? Walkways? Jungle adventures? Space rides? . . . It's a fantasy and won't work" (Mosley 1986, p. 233). He further insisted, "We're a film studio not an amusement park company." Walt disagreed and saw Disneyland as an extension of bringing childhood entertainment to mass consumers.

CHILDHOOD FANTASY

Disney also had great insight into the faddish nature of entertainment. He predicted from the very beginning: "Disneyland will never be finished, something I can keep developing, keep plussing, and adding to. It's alive. It will be a live, breathing thing that will need changes. . . . I can't do that with a picture. It's finished and unchangeable before I find out if the public likes it or not" (Mosley 1986, p. 230; Thomas 1994, p. 244).

Disney's dream included a precise replica of the main street in Marceline, Kansas, where he grew up. A miniaturized version of that street to the last detail became Disneyland's Main Street. He wanted the street to fit the "remembered perspective of a child's eye." Every brick, shingle, and gas lamp was built to exacting specifications—precisely five-eighths of normal size. From this Main Street customers could embark on a fantasy trip to Frontierland (Wild West), Adventureland (Robin Hood-like forest); Fantasyland (fairy tales); and Tomorrowland (Science-fiction futuristic). Disneyland was the realization of Walt Disney's ultimate fantasy to return to a safe land where he could escape from the real world.

WED ENTERPRISES

In order to see this park built, Disney was forced to use his own money. His own brother and company would have nothing to do with the project and refused to allow the name Disney to be associated with his fantasy. Disney became energized by this resistance and formed WED Enterprises (his initials) and had the brilliant idea to use his "mortal enemies" as the financial medium for his park. Television networks were viewed by Hollywood film makers during the early fifties as their mortal enemies who were trying to put them out of business. Movie studios refused to have anything to do with television production at that time and wouldn't have dreamed of offering them a vehicle to gain a foothold in family entertainment. Television was considered only a news, finance, sports, and public affairs medium at the time but with prospects of becoming an entertainment medium. Disney had been courted by various networks for his vast film library and decided to approach them to fund his park.

"WALT DISNEY PRESENTS"

Disney jumped on a plane with his model of Disneylandia and took it to New York City for presentation to the big three networks. The executives insisted on calling his park a fairgrounds but they were interested because of Disney's huge film library. He asked for $20 million in return to build his park. During the negotiations, NBC turned him down flat because "television will never be a medium of entertainment." CBS considered his proposal but could not get approval from their board of directors. Leonard Goldenson was the entrepreneurial head of upstart ABC, which was then known as the "Peanuts Network." He was a visionary and interested in making a deal with Disney, but didn't have the $20 million. Goldenson offered $500,000 in cash and a guarantee for $15 million in bank loans in exchange for 35 percent ownership in Disneylandia. In addition, ABC would receive 100 percent of the park's food concessions for ten years. In return, Disney would give ABC an eight-year programming commitment for the film library to be hosted by Walt Disney himself in a one-hour weekly series to be called "Walt Disney Presents." Walt Disney agreed and was paid $5 million a year for his TV appearances. Roy and the board of Disney Studios became fearful that they would be left out in the cold and made peace with Walt. Disney Studios acquired one-third of the WED stock and for the first time in his life Walt Disney was a millionaire.

"MICKEY MOUSE CLUB"

The Disney/ABC deal proved beneficial for both television and Hollywood. It changed television forever and was a catalyst for Hollywood becoming a production facility for the networks. The deal transformed ABC from the "Peanuts Network" into a big-time competitor of NBC and CBS. The first Disney show aired on ABC on October 27, 1954. *Time* magazine reported the show was "a bang that blew Wednesday night to kingdom come for the other two networks." Over 30 million viewers watched that first show. The Disney show became a phenomenon that would never be equaled. It became the longest-running network TV series while changing the face of television during the next three decades. Family entertainment on TV became a reality. How ironic that Disney would acquire a struggling ABC some thirty years later for $19 billion.

Disneyland Park opened at Anaheim, California, on July 13, 1955. Its existence will always be a tribute to the tenacity and willpower of Walt Disney. The grand opening was televised by ABC while 15,000 guests and employees were entertained by Mickey and his cohorts. During the first seven weeks more than a million visitors paid admission to Disneyland. Fifteen years later Walt Disney World would open near Orlando, Florida. EPCOT—The City of Tomorrow—and Disney's ultimate fantasy opened in October 1982 at a cost of $1.2 billion. Walt Disney didn't live to see these Florida extravaganzas, but would certainly have been pleased by their success. The Disneyland parks are the consummate entertainment fantasies of both children and adults on three continents. Their existence is testimony to Disney's tenacity.

PERSONALITY, POWER, AND INFLUENCE

Disney's success emanated from his willpower, fierce temerity, and perseverance. He refused to give up even when failure appeared inevitable. He was an introvert with an intuitive vision. He had confidence in his ideas and made rational decisions. He learned early not to trust the judgment of others and philosophized that if management or experts liked his projects, he seriously questioned proceeding. If they hated his ideas, he would proceed immediately on the premise that his idea was a winner. Disney's power was inextricably tied up with his great self-esteem, which allowed him to proceed contrary to expert opinion. He didn't always produce winners, but when he did they were blockbusters. Experts told him not to make *Snow White, Pinocchio, Fantasia,* and Disneyland. He ignored them and the Disney empire was built as a result of his tenacity. His macrovision was often lost on his brother and most of his contemporaries.

One of Disney's great ideas was in producing features that were "timeless." He insisted on eliminating any topical or age references in his films. This gave the films a transcendental feel allowing audiences to escape into a fantasy motif. It also allowed them to be re-released every decade without fear of being dated. This resulted in a brilliant economic coup for the Disney company. Re-releases of the Disney film library contributed millions in profits to the company for the next fifty years. There was virtually no cost attendant to a re-released film like *Bambi,* which had bombed in its initial release in 1942 and then earned an astounding $2 million in 1957. *Snow White* was purposely re-released every seven years in order to hit each new generation. When it was offered as a videotape in 1994, the film sold twenty-seven million copies within thirty days.

COMMUNIST CONSPIRACY

Disney's autocratic nature was never more apparent than during the Burbank Studio strike in 1941. Disney was furious when his employees refused to cross the picket line and fired them all. He would have closed down operations entirely had it not been for Roy who convinced him to take a more prudent approach. Arthur Babbit, principal animator on *Fantasia* and the creator of Goofy, was a key perpetrator of the strike and became the target of Disney's wrath. When *Fantasia* bombed, the effervescent Babbitt said, "*Fantasia* lacked balls" in a statement aimed at Disney's contribution to the film. Disney considered his actions "treachery." Their verbal battles precipitated an already festering situation at Disney Studio. Disney was notorious for giving little or no recognition to the actual creators of many of the studio's most cherished productions. He paid his employees low wages, which was a by-product of his Midwestern frugalness. He was also burdened with the paranoia of training people who might become his competitors. He had operated the company as a mom-and-pop enterprise, which caused him to refuse recognition of the Cartoonists Guild Union. His employees struck on May 28, 1941. Disney saw the strike as a "Communist conspiracy" and was prepared to fight it to the death. Disney was a virulent anti-Communist and saw a connection between unions, communism, and economic strife. He had close ties with Washington since he had served J. Edgar Hoover as an underground FBI informant.

TENACIOUS AUTOCRAT

The Disney animators picketed outside the Burbank studios with signs reading, "Snow White and the 600 dwarfs; one genius against 600 guinea pigs." They told the press that Disney was an "egocentric paternalist" who lived off the success of his workers. He certainly fit their description but money was never a factor in any of Disney's decisions, for the employees or himself. Disney was furious and called the National Labor Relations Board for assistance, to no avail.

Disney was booed entering his plant on the first day of the strike—the first time in his life he had encountered such treatment. He became obsessed with washing his hands and exhibited other signs of an impending nervous breakdown. Roy recognized all the signs and came to his rescue. He elicited the assistance of J. Edgar Hoover who arranged a government-sponsored trip for Walt and Lillian Disney to South America. With his brother out of the country, Roy agreed to binding arbitration and settled the strike. Disney was not pleased and on his return told reporters, "I have a case of the D.D.'s—disillusionment and discouragement" (Mosley 1986, p. 196). He commented, "I have capitulated but, believe me, I'm not licked—I'm incensed . . . I was accused of rolling in wealth. That hurt me the most, when the fact is that every damned thing I have is tied up in this business."

All the workers were allowed to return to work but Art Babbitt, who Disney personally fired in violation of the rules of the arbitration agreement. Disney was forced to hire him back but showed his vindictive nature by having Babbitt blackballed during the war. When Babbitt returned from military service, Disney made his life so difficult that he quit. Disney had a destructive side which was more often directed inward, but in this case he destroyed an employee that he considered unfaithful.

DYSFUNCTIONAL PROMETHEAN

Disney had a Promethean and hypomanic personality. These traits caused him to pursue opportunities with unabashed passion. He was inclined to mortgage the present for the future and loved the possibilities of creating the new and different while seldom worrying over the financing of his productions. These traits allowed him to create animation masterpieces and some of the most cherished films of all time, but it also kept the firm near bankruptcy for thirty years. During this period there were never more than eighteen months in which the company was financially solvent. Disney had no interest in creating financially successful movies, only creatively successful ones. He would produce a hit and then follow it with a bomb.

Disney's business and personal lives were like a continual rollercoaster ride where he would reach the pinnacle of success only to descend into the depths of disaster within months. This up-and-down life of perpetual crisis started in 1920 when he was nineteen and just getting started and continued until the 1954 opening of Disneyland. He experienced manic periods followed by periods of severe depression in a neverending cycle. The success and failure of Disney Studios was correlated to his bouts of euphoria and depression (see chapter 2). However, he insightfully viewed his crises as catalysts: "You may not realize it when it happens, but a kick in the teeth may be the best thing in the world for you" (quote displayed at Disneyland).

EXTREME HIGHS AND DEPRESSING LOWS

Disney's suicidal tendencies were apparent to his brother and wife and they would force him to take vacations. Sometimes he would drink to escape or regress into youthful fantasy by riding his built-to-scale train for days at a time. His most creative periods typically followed his most tragic lows. When he was "up" he was a Type A workaholic of the first order. He would work nonstop and often all night. He would sleep at the studio when pressured to finish work. Once these projects came close to failing or approached completion, Disney would suffer depression or completely collapse. He endured eight nervous breakdowns during his career.

Each disaster experienced by Disney was followed by a success. The enormously successful *Snow White* was followed by bombs—*Pinocchio* and *Fantasia*—which were then followed by the success of *Dumbo,* and it went on and on like this for years. When *Bambi* was released in 1943 and bombed at the box office, Disney was saved by the re-release of *Snow White* a year later. He was then inspired with the idea to resurrect *Alice in Wonderland.* The studio received windfall profits from his re-release of *Snow White* and he felt financially secure to embark on *Alice,* which wiped out the company's reserves with a $2 million loss. Disney became deeply depressed, started drinking, and stopped working, which compounded the business problems. Then *Peter Pan* bombed as well and Disney came close to another breakdown. Within a few years Disneyland would rescue the firm from this incessant up-and-down existence and give Disney himself some needed stability and cash flow.

DISNEY AND HUGHES SYMBIOSIS

There was a strange symbiosis between Disney and Howard Hughes. Hughes had collaborated on numerous transactions with Disney during the late 1940s when Hughes owned RKO.

In one of Disney's periods of financial insolvency, Hughes gave him a million-dollar loan, interest free, in return for the noncommercial rights to his film library and RKO owned the distribution rights for seventeen years. In 1953 Hughes offered to give Disney RKO plus $10 million just to get the company out of his hair. Hughes never took advantage of the opportunity to use Disney's film library and both remained friends until Disney's death in 1966. Both men were manic-depressives who were also inclined to be obsessive-compulsive. Both were born in the Midwest, were the same age, and headed large business enterprises that included film production. Both were afflicted with eye-twitching and nervous tics and experienced repeated numerous nervous breakdowns. They were chainsmokers and arch right-wingers who were strongly anti-Semitic and anti-Communist. Disney and Hughes hated governmental controls and were manically driven. They were workaholics, control freaks, and perfectionists. Their major difference was that Disney revered his family while Hughes detested family life.

An Imaginative Success Story

The power and influence of Walt Disney is seen in the Mickey Mouse T-shirts seen in airports in every city in the world. His theme parks in Anaheim, Orlando, Tokyo, and Paris are the most successful ventures of their kind in the world with over 65 million visitors annually. Orlando is called the "Town that Mickey built," and when looking at the business climate of that burgeoning city it is difficult to refute that claim. Walt Disney World, MGM, and EPCOT alone attract some 30 million visitors annually and have catapulted Disney into a business conglomerate beyond its founder's wildest imaginings. In 1995 the company employed some 100,000 people and shocked the financial world when Michael Eisner announced on July 31, 1995, the acquisition of ABC. The $19 billion purchase made Disney the most powerful entertainment force in the world, dominating broadcasting, sports (Los Angeles Angels and Ducks), film and TV production, and theme parks. The purchase of ABC was fitting since this was the network that helped make Disneyland a reality in the mid-fifties.

By the mid-nineties Disney had become an entertainment conglomerate that dominated production for movies, television, and home video. For a five-year period starting in 1988, Disney was able to exploit the film library that Walt had built. During this time Disney received awesome sums of money from movies that had been bombs when first released: *Fantasia* produced over $25 million in revenues, *Bambi* $29 million, *101 Dalmations* $61 million, *Pinocchio* $19 million, and *Snow White* $41 million. Of this $175 million, two-thirds resulted from movies that were considered losers on first release. Walt Disney would have been especially pleased with the $4 billion in 1994 revenues earned from sixty films. The firm that spent so many years flirting with bankruptcy earned in excess of $500 million in profits. When *Snow White* was released on videotape on October 25, 1994, it immediately became the all-time best-selling video—a great tribute to "Disney's Folly."

Walt Disney insisted on producing works of innocence, fun, and fantasy. The name Disney is synonymous with good clean fun. It is often used in conveying purity, as in the aphorism "Apple Pie, motherhood, and Disney." Liberal actor Kirk Douglas was considering a lawsuit against Disney during the early fifties for using some home film scenes of Douglas and his children on the Disney TV show. Douglas finally capitulated, telling reporters, "You can't sue God." Disney's demand for a wholesome image and for integrity in business was responsible for that reputation. He worked hard to earn it and is deserving of such accolades. His characters were created within the context of his own pristine fundamentalist personality. Disneyland became grounded in his own Victorian beliefs for clean, family entertainment. Disney was always polite and courteous although he never lost his need for pranks; Disneyland is the embodiment of his personality, which is exemplified in his retort: "I think of a newborn baby's mind as a blank book."

While his characters were extensions of Disney's own personality, they did not emulate his manicness or depression. He was also a compulsive smoker and indulged in excessive drinking much of his life. Neither contributed to his physical or emotional well being. His excesses never reached print during an era when the media tended to protect its heroes instead of destroying them. His affair with actress Dolores Del Rio was widely known about Hollywood but suppressed by the gossip columnists. Mickey Mouse had made Disney as pure as he had made Mickey mischievous.

The success of the Disney empire was never more incisively put than in Disney's own comment to the media: "The thing that makes us different is our way of thinking, our judgment and experience. We developed a psychological approach to everything we do here. We seem to know when to *tap the heart*" (Thomas 1994, p. 278).

WALTER ELIAS DISNEY
Innovative Genius in Animated Films and Disneyland
b. December 5, 1901, Chicago, Ill.; d. December 15, 1966, Hollywood, Calif.

Dominant Trait: Tenacious, intuitive, and confident perfectionist. Probably manic-depressive.

Motto: "I prefer animals to people." "Be sure you're right, then go ahead." "We are not in the *art* business."

Nickname: "Uncle Walt"

Vices/Hobbies: Model trains, bowling, golf. Heavy drinker and smoker (three packs a day).

Heroes/Mentors: Mark Twain, Charles Dickens, and Charlie Chaplin (Little Tramp)

Fantasy: Utopian life as a happy child in fantasyland

Professional Successes: Created Mickey and Minnie Mouse, Donald Duck, Goofy, Pluto, Three Little Pigs, and Disneyland plus 700 feature films the most famous of which were: *Snow White* (1937), *Pinocchio* (1940), *Fantasia* (1940), *Dumbo* (1941), *Cinderella* (1950), *Alice in Wonderland* (1951), *Peter Pan* (1953), *Davy Crockett* (1955), *Lady and the Tramp* (1955), *Sleeping Beauty* (1959), *101 Dalmations* (1961).

Power: Tenacious determination to create his fantasy dreams through willpower alone. Resorted to childlike images for vicarious entertainment. His sheer force of will made Mickey Mouse and Disneyland.

Influence: Imitators copied his style. He proved "the pen is mightier than the personality of the greatest star." *New York Times* wrote on his death in 1966: "He was a legend in his own lifetime."

Philosophy of Life: "I've never made pictures for a child audience alone."

Destructiveness: A death-wish mentality; constantly lived on the edge of financial collapse. FBI informant who fired anyone not in agreement with his fundamentalist or political beliefs. Anti-Semite and prejudiced. Excessive alcohol and cigarettes killed him prematurely.

Birth Order: Raised as firstborn; Roy 8.5 years older, Ray 10 years older, Herbert 13 years older, sister Ruth, 2 years younger

Parental Influence: Abusive contractor father, Elias, beat him. Sympathetic mother, Flora, would soothe him with fairy tales. Childhood fantasies became foundation for creation of: Three Little Pigs, Donald Duck, Mickey Mouse, and Disneyland's Main Street.

Transiency: Moved from Chicago to Kansas to Kansas City to Chicago. Rode rails at age fifteen.

Crises: Bedridden from traumatic accident at age eleven, which was genesis of cartoons. Bankrupt at age twenty. Main character Oswald the Rabbit stolen in 1927, the genesis of Mickey Mouse. Numerous emotional breakdowns and suicidal over unscrupulous Hollywood promoters who stole his concepts.

Formal Education: High school dropout in. Attended Academy of Fine Arts at age sixteen but did not complete.

Libidinal Drive: Sublimated sexual needs into fantasy cartoon characters: "The life and adventures of Mickey Mouse have been closely bound up with my own personal and professional life."

Personality Type: Introverted-Intuitive-Thinker-Judger. Manic-depressive, obsessive-compulsive, and perfectionist.

Self-Esteem: Indomitable belief in himself and his creations even when other did not believe

Rebellion: Anti-Communist, anti-Semite, antiestablishment, and FBI informant.

Risk Propensity: Twice bankrupt in early twenties. Faced insolvency eight times. Perfection more important than money.

Work Ethic: Eight nervous breakdowns due to overwork. Lived and worked for months at studio and Disneyland.

Tenacity: Ridiculed for Mickey, scorned for *Snow White,* and derided for *Pinocchio, Fantasia,* and Disneyland.

Optimism: "If management likes my projects, I seriously question proceeding. If they disdain them totally, I proceed immediately."

Manicness: Walt was frenetic overachiever who drove himself to perfection, which took its toll on him physically and emotionally, culminating in many emotional collapses.

Edith Piaf

Non, je ne regrette rien (No, I have no regrets).

Overview

Edith Piaf was a petite French chanteuse with a huge voice who overcame enormous odds to reach the top of her profession. No one in this book even came close to her "rags-to-riches" story. She persevered when others would have given up. Her life began as a Greek tragedy and got a lot worse. Piaf's tragic life defines the word "tenacity." She was born in a gutter, weaned on wine, blind at age three, raised in a brothel, was a street singer at age seven pimping for an itinerant father, and accidentally became a mother at age sixteen. She survived this horrid childhood to become the Great Piaf—a legend during her own lifetime. When she died in 1963, forty thousand mourning Parisians turned out to follow her coffin to its final resting place. This woman who feared to be alone and pleaded for love her whole life, a woman who had been abandoned with virtually no family, suddenly had thousands who loved her. Her motto was "Love conquers all" and she had finally realized her dream of being loved. Actress Marlene Dietrich attended the funeral and was astonished at the adulation, commenting, "How they must have loved her."

"NO, I HAVE NO REGRETS"

No matter how bad her life was, this little dynamo never complained that life had not been fair, although she sang passionately of sadness and travail. One of her most popular songs came near the end of her life, "Non, je ne regrette rien." It became an international sensation, a tribute to a volatile life without remorse. When Charles Dumont first showed her this song, she shouted, "That's absolutely me. That's just what I feel, just what I think . . . it's what I believe."

Artist Sacha Guitry did a cast of Piaf's hands for posterity during her last days. On finishing the casting, Guitry commented: "Her life was so sad that it was almost too beautiful to be true."

Piaf had a way of mesmerizing those whom she touched. One of those she captivated was no less a personality than the great French poet and playwright Jean Cocteau. He wrote to her six months prior to her death on May 25, 1963, just after he survived a heart attack:

> My Edith
> I don't really know how
> I escaped death, it's a habit
> of ours. I embrace you
> because you are one of the
> seven or eight people I think
> about lovingly each day.
> Jean Cocteau

Piaf was first introduced to Cocteau when she was twenty-one and illiterate. Once she learned to read, she still was incapable of understanding Cocteau's writing. Cocteau was fascinated with her and they became lifelong friends. He wrote a play for her called *Le Bel Indifferent*. Cocteau died while preparing to read her eulogy on French radio, October 15, 1963, the day after her funeral. He was buried the next day.

Early Life Experiences and Influences

Edith Giovanna Gassion was born on a Paris street, the rue de Belleville, on December 19, 1915. She was named after Edith Cavell, an English spy who had been shot by the Germans a few days prior to her birth. Both her mother and father were circus performers who had met under the big top and married. It was wartime and her father, Louis Gassion, was at the front at the time of her birth. Her mother, Anita Maillard, kept her for a short time before leaving the unwanted child with her equally apathetic parents. Maillard then wrote to Gassion, who was in the French infantry, ending the brief marriage and informing him that their daughter could be found at her parents.

SWALLOW OF THE SLUMS

Piaf's grandparents laced baby Edith's bottle with red wine. They said water would make her sick but wine was more nourishing. They also took the baby to bars where she spent the night alone listening to the music. Later in life she recalled singing to the bar tunes, especially one that went, "They called her the swallow of the slums. She was nothing but a poor tart."

When Louis Gassion returned on a leave, he was appalled at her miserable condition. She was so filthy he couldn't touch her and she had rickets from malnutrition. Louis Gassion was a street person with no room in his life for a baby. But he did have compassion and pleaded with his own mother to take the child. Grandmother Louise ran a brothel that was located in Bernay, Normandy. She took on the challenge since a child was considered good luck to the prostitutes who led a life devoid of children. The prostitutes were delighted when Edith showed up. They made rag dolls for her and gave her much needed love and affection.

BLINDNESS AND METAPHYSICAL CURE

The brothel was not the ideal place for a child, but it did supply an environment filled with high-class, well-dressed, educated gentlemen. Young Edith was the center of attention as the prostitutes displayed her as their pillar of respect. Everyone in the brothel was shocked when she suddenly went blind at age three. Her loss of sight was apparently caused by the deplorable nutritional and hygienic environment of her early childhood. She was taken to different doctors, all of whom diagnosed her blindness as incurable.

Piaf recalled that three-year period with insight: "I always believed that that journey through darkness made me more sensitive than other people" (Berteaut 1973, p. 20). "When I really wanted to see a song, I would shut my eyes. And when I wanted to bring out a sound from my guts, deep down, as if it were coming from very far away, I would shut my eyes." She remembered perpetually dreaming of lightness and sunshine.

After a while, the prostitutes decided to go on a pilgrimage to the shrine of Saint Theresa. They burned candles and prayed for Piaf to regain her sight. On August 19, 1921, she regained her sight at age seven. Piaf was sitting at a piano and the keyboard was the first thing she saw. The women were awestruck and credited Saint Theresa with a miracle. The whores fell to their knees in homage and the brothel was closed for a day. Piaf went to her grave believing that Saint Theresa had cured her.

STREET ENTERTAINER

Once Piaf's vision was restored, she was enrolled in the local school. Shortly after her enrollment, the headmaster called the brothel demanding to see her father. He told Gassion that it was scandalous to have young Edith living in a brothel and demanded she be removed immediately. She was removed but this proved far more detrimental to her life than living with prostitutes. Louis Gassion was a street entertainer who slept wherever he found companionship or free lodgings, which more often than not was the street. Piaf was not only deprived of an education, she was forced into a life devoid of nurturing. Gassion lived by his wits as a street minstrel and taught his daughter those skills but little else. She was a cute, petite blonde with few inhibitions and attracted an audience for her father's act.

Piaf began passing his hat at age seven, which evolved into her singing for money by age nine. She later recalled these dreadful days being dragged from "dance halls to bistros, from alleys to squares, from towns to villages": "My job was to take up the collection" but her father often used her to entice the more attractive female patrons for seduction. Piaf recalled: "I never wanted for female company. He was always changing women." Her female role models were never mothers, wives, or women with traditional value systems. They were lonely, insecure women looking for companionship. Once her father became too ill to perform and young Edith took to the streets alone, singing to buy food and medication. Piaf reflected on this part of her life as a positive experience. She was never ashamed of it: "I learned freedom, rebellion, and independence." As a street urchin, she led a vagabond existence from age seven to fifteen. By fifteen she struck out on her own as a street entertainer. Shortly thereafter she met her half sister, Simone Berteaut, and persuaded the younger girl to become her assistant. The two worked the streets together while dodging the authorities.

STREET SMARTS

Young Edith and Simone were inseparable. Piaf nicknamed her sister Momone and they became friends and companions for the next thirty years. They worked together, slept together, and shared everything, including Edith's men. The two sisters moved from district to district carefully avoiding the police who would have placed them in detention homes or an orphanage. Their friends were pimps and other nefarious individuals who made up the Paris underground. The two girls lived by their wits sleeping wherever they could find shelter or with whomever made them the best offer. They were not alluring since they had but one set of clothes at any one time and never bathed or brushed their teeth. Both admitted later they were pretty disgusting and many men refused their entreaties because of their appalling appearance and sickening odor. Money was not abundant and whatever they earned they spent, a habit Piaf would continue even when earning $100,000 a night. Piaf learned her profession on the streets of Paris and when asked about her formal training, proudly responded, "My music school is the street." When theatrical agent Raymond Asso insisted she take voice lessons and learn to read music, she adamantly refused. She felt such training would detract from her intuitive feel for what audiences wanted to hear.

BEATNIK FALLS IN LOVE

Piaf's description of her teen years was, "We must have been the first beatniks. We wore skirts and sweaters, nothing more. . . . We bought new ones when the others got too dirty to put on again. . . . We never washed anything. . . . We had fleas. The boys used to look us up and down and reject us, no doubt because we were dirty."

Piaf fell madly in love with Louis Dupont. Dupont moved in with the two sisters and the three slept together in the same bed. Within two months Piaf found herself pregnant but refused to change her lifestyle. Dupont tried unsuccessfully to have her get a legitimate job or stay at home. She continued to do what she knew best—singing in the streets. Dupont also attempted to domesticate Piaf but with no success. He suggested she do dishes, but Piaf broke them instead and bought new ones. He admonished her to act like a wife and mother, but Edith never had a domestic bone in her body.

At age seventeen Piaf gave birth to a baby girl named Marcelle. Louis was delighted with the baby, but not enough to ask Edith to marry him. All four slept in their one bed. Dupont worked while the two young women and baby spent the day on the streets of Paris singing and dancing. Nothing ever deterred Piaf from living on her own terms; a baby or man never interfered with her need to sing and party. She came home when she wanted, sometimes not showing up for days. Piaf was able to get a job singing in a clip joint named Lulu's. It was a hangout for prostitutes but had a stage and the semblance of professional entertainment.

Simone and Louis watched the baby while Piaf worked two jobs—the Parisian streets by day and Lulu's by night. Louis became disenchanted with

Piaf's hedonistic lifestyle and took Marcelle to live with his parents. At age two and a half Marcelle contracted meningitis and suddenly died. Piaf was nineteen and started drinking heavily to drown the sorrow. She felt guilty and remorseful and never forgot this tragedy. She had spent her youth searching for love around every corner and now she felt it was lost forever. She decided to forget about any permanent love relationship and to pursue a professional singing career. Crisis had armed her with a strong resolve.

The "Little Sparrow" Is Born

Although Piaf never learned to read a note of music nor learned to read or write, she had a special talent for learning lyrics and music. If someone played a song one time she was able to commit it to memory. She told the media this talent resulted from her blindness.

One day Piaf made an impulsive decision to leave the ghetto area of Paris and sing on the Champs-Élysées. She had always avoided this area because she did not feel comfortable around sophisticated people. Piaf was singing in her flamboyant style where emotion and passion ruled over melody. A highly respectable café owner wandered past and was caught up in her performance. Louis Leplée placed a note in her hand along with a franc, saying, "See me at Le Gerny's." Leplée owned Le Gerny's, which was *the* place for the Paris elite. Located on the elegant Champs-Élysées, it was packed every night with wealthy and literate people trying to forget the Depression.

Mentor and Surrogate Father

Louis Leplée was taken with this street urchin and bent on making her a star. She became his protégée and for one of the first times in her life she listened to someone else's advice. Leplée saved her from a sordid life and gave her the chance to be a star. It was Papa Louis as she called him who changed her name to "Piaf," slang for "sparrow." The name caught on and she kept it the rest of her life. Leplée functioned as both her manager and employer. She sang in his cabaret and he found her other singing engagements.

Le Gerny's was the chic Parisian nightclub at the time and Leplée took a chance putting this inexperienced nineteen-year-old on his stage. He believed in Piaf's talent more than anyone else at the time. But he was shocked by the extent of her ignorance. Piaf was steeped in survival on the street. Appropriate dress, basic hygiene, and the simplest social skills like holding an intelligent conversation were lost on the Little Sparrow. She had never even been taught how to bathe. Papa Louis taught her style.

Piaf was incapable of following the piano music. She expected the piano to follow her. Frustrated at her first rehearsal, she shouted: "I'm the one that's singing, not him, I wish he'd shut up." Piaf felt in control on the street and could not relate to any other way. She would always be independent. The sensitive Louis took on the task of teaching her manners, grooming, and social intercourse.

OVERNIGHT SUCCESS

Piaf's opening night at Le Gerny's was a roaring success. She captivated an audience that included Maurice Chevalier, who said, "That kid's got what it takes." Leplée offered, "The kid's made it."

Piaf loved Leplée as a friend and substitute father and he loved her as a daughter. He was a homosexual who helped her because of who she was and not for any sexual favors. She had never known anyone who willingly gave without wanting sex in return, an ethical system she had learned in the brothel and on the street.

Leplée arranged her public debut at the Cirque Medrano on February 17, 1936. She was twenty at the time. A short time later she cut her first record, "L'Etranger," for Polydor and made her radio debut. The radio engagement was so successful the one-night booking turned into a six-week run. Leplée then booked her in Cannes on the Cote d'Azur.

Piaf's seven-month rise to stardom suddenly crashed with the death of Leplée on April 6, 1936. Leplée bragged about making a large sale worth fifty thousand francs and was overheard by two sailors. They assaulted Leplée and finding no money on his person killed him in frustration. The authorities never caught the assailants but Piaf was implicated because of her long association with questionable people from the Paris underground. The charges were unfounded but the resulting scandal nearly destroyed her burgeoning career as the murder made the headlines for many months.

Crisis and Creativity

The police interrogated Piaf because they were convinced she knew who had committed the crime. Her sister, Simone, was placed in a reform school for two-and-a-half months. Newspapers reported that Piaf was implicated in the murder and unfortunately she wasn't sophisticated enough to refute the allegations. She found herself out of work and back on the streets of Paris. No one would hire her and she started drinking heavily. She was booed in the few shows she could arrange. During one commitment in Brussels, she was so drunk she couldn't perform. It was during this low period in her life she met the man who would make her famous.

RAYMOND ASSO: MENTOR #2

Piaf met theatrical agent Raymond Asso by accident in an artists' café. He was the secretary to the famous singer Marie Dubas. He was looking for new talent to represent and was an ex-legionnaire; Piaf could never resist any soldier. He told Piaf:

"I'm going to help you. You're finished with pimps and drinking." Asso was shocked at her lack of knowledge but took on the task of transforming this street urchin into a professional entertainer. Piaf's sister, Simone Berteaut, said, "Leplée had discovered Edith, but it was Asso who first made her great." Asso guided her with an iron hand, which is exactly what such a free spirit needed. Piaf had never learned to read or write and knew nothing of the simplest social graces. Asso recalled: "She didn't know how to eat, she didn't even know how to wash." The married Asso became her mentor, lover, and manager, but most importantly, taught her to read and write.

Asso taught her the art of performing with grace and style, instilling her with the stage presence that made her special. He coached her in the social graces and in on- and offstage behavior. When she was ready, he booked her at the most prominent show house in Paris, the ABC Music Hall. At her debut at the ABC in 1937 Piaf mesmerized the audience and they responded with a rousing standing ovation. At age twenty-two, she was an overnight show business phenomenon. The next morning's paper contained a story that proved prophetic: "Yesterday evening on the stage of the ABC we witnessed the birth of a great singer." Piaf was on her way.

PERSONALITY OF A STAR

Edith Piaf was an off-the-chart extrovert who couldn't stand silence or being alone. She was also incapable of sleeping alone and went to great lengths not to. One-night stands were not the exception but the rule in her life. She was highly intuitive and knew it, saying, "My intelligence is my instinct." Her intuition and emotions guided her in her choice of men. She was very impatient and impulsive, and could be a raging tyrant one moment and a gracious companion the next. Piaf was a Type A personality whose self-esteem was inextricably tied to her success on stage, but also caused her to lead a frenetic lifestyle.

MY WAY OR THE HIGHWAY

The Little Sparrow was not formally educated and had no knowledge of music. Piaf insisted on learning everything there was about show business (typical of Promethean temperaments).

Piaf was generous to a fault. She had no sense of money and continually gave it away to anyone who asked. Money was to be used to eat, drink, and be happy; it had no other significance. Many leeches took advantage of her generosity and when the money disappeared, so did they.

Piaf's raucous lifestyle led to constant evictions from hotels and apartments. She never had a home or wanted one. She loved the life of a nonconformist where there were no rules or commitments. No one was able to change her iron-willed resolve to live life on her terms. It was either her way or no way, which led her to countless relationships.

MADAME PIAF

Raymond Asso made Piaf into a professional entertainer, but he had a sadistic side and beat her regularly. She came to expect the beatings in a masochistic way, accepting the inferior role. When she met and fell madly in love with English actor Paul Meurisse shortly after her success at the ABC, she missed Asso's cruel treatment and goaded Meurisse into beating her. Meurisse was too cultured and refined a gentleman to resort to physical abuse. Once when he refused to fight with her, she told her sister, "I'll make him forget his upbringing. He'll beat me yet, you'll see. I want him to beat me." She harassed him until he finally walked out on her.

Piaf began associating with many successful and talented people. Poet and playwright Jean Cocteau became her friend, confidant, and lover. He called her "the poet of the streets" and told her, "*Petite Piaf,* you're a very great person." He was enchanted by Piaf's charismatic power and wrote the play *Le Bel Indifferent* specifically for her. Cocteau would later write: "Madame Piaf is a genius. She is inimitable. There has never been an Edith Piaf before, there will never be another. . . . She is a solitary star burning in the still night sky of France" (Berteaut 1973, p. 178). Such was the power of the Little Sparrow.

PSYCHOSEXUAL ENERGY

In 1939 Piaf fell in love with Jewish songwriter Michel Emer. When he played "L'Accordeoniste" for her the first time, she was enthralled. "L'Accordeoniste" became her first big hit and she sang the song for twenty years. In its first year the 78 record sold 850,000 copies. Within the year she would repay Emer for writing this great hit for her by bribing his way out of Nazi-occupied Paris.

Piaf then met and fell in love with Henri Contet, a public relations expert and songwriter. They became lovers and he gave a tremendous boost to her image and career with a media blitz that made Piaf a household name. But Piaf drove Contet crazy with her obsessive needs for men, music, and alcohol, all of which she pursued frenetically. Contet called her "mad, a drunk, a whore, a hysteric, and a nymphomaniac." In a valiant attempt to placate Contet and to exorcise the memories of her dead daughter, Piaf agreed to have his child. She was admitted to a clinic to have a fertility operation so that she could get pregnant. She and Simone disrupted the clinic with their drunkenness and were thrown out without Piaf having the operation, which destroyed her delicate relationship with Contet. It was the first and last time she considered becoming a mother. Such behavior was common to Piaf's life where libidinal energy dominated her very existence.

The Great Piaf

Piaf insisted on leading a frenetic and manic existence. She was perpetually broke, spending money as fast as she made it. During her lifetime Piaf earned over one billion francs but lived day-to-day spending in the most frivolous way imaginable. She never led what could be considered a normal lifestyle. She appeared intent on repeating her vagabond childhood as if attempting to validate her circus heritage. She went from man to man in a manic need to find the love she never had as a child. To avoid rejection, she would always dump her lover before he had a chance to dump her. During World War II, she was evicted from so many hotels that she was finally forced to take refuge in a Paris brothel. Her manic lifestyle kept resurrecting her pathetic past.

LIBIDINAL DRIVE

Piaf was libidinally driven. When she met a new man, Piaf felt she could not truly understand him until they had sex: "You only really know a man when you've been to bed with him. You learn more about a man after one night in the sack than you do in months of conversation. When they talk they can fool you as much as they want, but they can't kid you in bed" (Berteaut 1973, p. 201). When Edith was interested in a man, her first move was seduction in order to discover what made him tick. This philosophy is what probably led her to sleep with every songwriter or agent with whom she came in contact. "Love conquers all" was her motto and she felt that Yves Montand was a man to conquer.

YVES MONTAND

Piaf reversed her role with Yves Montand and became his mentor. She devoted two years of her life to Montand as lover, mentor, and showbiz ally. They met when he was in his early twenties and she was twenty-eight, but she had a vast edge in experience. Yves Montand later said, "That woman's a genius. . . . I owe everything to her." She made him a star and he never forgot. In a moment of insight he accurately described her insatiable need for passion: "Edith only sang her best when she was madly in love." Fortunately for the world, Piaf was often in love and belted out her innermost passions on stage.

LOVE CONQUERS ALL

Bereft of love as a child, Piaf searched vainly for it her whole life. "C'est magnifique" became her biggest hit and it defined her life. She was magnificent and never felt remorse for an early life devoid of love. Her sordid youth instilled her with a need for freedom and independence and armed her with resilience. She learned to cherish freedom and even though she craved companionship, she craved freedom even more. In a moment of introspection she told reporters: "My life when I was a kid might strike you as awful, but actually it was beautiful. . . . I was hungry, I was cold, but I was also . . . free not to get up in the morning, not to go to bed at night, free to get drunk" (Lange 1981, p. 27).

Piaf was a pragmatic survivor. She sang what she wanted to whom she wanted. When Joseph Goebbels demanded she perform for the Nazi elite, the defiant Little Sparrow showed up two hours late. She defied the Nazis like everyone else in her life. During the Nazi occupation, she was once reprimanded for singing French nationalist songs and told to stop. Fearlessly she told the Germans: "No, I won't. . . . Forbid me, but all Paris will hold you responsible."

CERDAN, DEATH, AND DRUGS

One of the most devastating experiences in Piaf's life was her tragic relationship with boxer Marcel Cerdan. Cerdan was married with a family. They became lovers after the war and carried on an affair that was a scandal. They made international headlines when he sneaked Piaf into his Catskill training camp in the trunk of his car. This prank occurred while he was in training for his world championship fight with Tony Zale. After Cerdan won the world championship, the papers gave Piaf credit for inspiring him. After he lost the championship one year later to Jake LaMotta, she was held responsible. The media ripped her to shreds with headlines like "Edith Piaf Brought Cerdan Bad Luck."

In October 1949 Piaf had an engagement at the Versailles in New York City and pleaded with Cerdan to leave his French training camp to come visit her. He never made it. His plane crashed in the Azores on October 28, 1949, and Edith became wracked with guilt. She insisted on performing that night in New York City. Blaming herself for his death she said, "I killed him, it's my fault," and told the audience, "There must be no applause for me this evening. I'm singing for Marcel Cerdan, and for him alone." From that day forward Piaf believed Cerdan had been the great love of her life and resorted to drugs to kill the pain of his loss. She used stimulants to enable her to perform and depressants to help her sleep. She eventually turned to morphine and heroin and alcohol. Her physical and emotional life paid the price of drug and alcohol abuse, which ultimately destroyed her at the young age of forty-seven.

AWESOME WILLPOWER

Piaf's power emanated from an "inner force" which Nietzsche called a "will-to-power." On one of her tours of the United States the *New York Herald* reported: "Her vocalism is styled and powerful." The entertainment critic for the *New Yorker* wrote: "She devastated everybody within range with one of the canniest and most beautifully executed routines in show business." After this tour in the early fifties, Piaf went in for her first of many drug cures.

On the rebound after Cerdan's death, she met actor Jacques Pills who she married in Paris on July 29, 1952, after a whirlwind courtship. While on their honeymoon in Hollywood, she collapsed onstage. It would be the first of many such collapses. The marriage was destined for failure from the beginning because of Piaf's drug addiction and her manic need to exorcise her guilt over Marcel Cerdan. The marriage ended in divorce after five years.

Critic Monique Lange gave credence to Piaf's captivating power when she wrote: "A thousand years from now Piaf's voice will still be heard." Her onstage passion which emerged from the depths of her soul was magical. She drove audiences to tears and delirium by baring her soul in song.

Charlie Chaplin came to see Piaf perform in Hollywood. She recalled that when told he was in the audience: "I sang for him. I gave it everything I had, and he must have realized it." She had collapsed the night before and was a walking zombie, but onstage she became the Great Piaf. She was a powerhouse of passion that night and mesmerized Chaplin: "He gave me the ultimate compliment saying I made him cry."

In 1956 Piaf accepted an engagement at Carnegie Hall to celebrate her freedom from Jacques Pills. She was so weak the doctors had forbidden her to perform. She had collapsed the previous week and was in a state of physical and mental exhaustion. Typical of her inner power, she ignored the doctors and brought the house down. She belted out twenty-seven songs. The normally cynical New York crowd went wild and gave her a seven-minute standing ovation. It was a supreme triumph of willpower over addiction and a ravaged body. This diminutive powerhouse repeatedly captured the hearts of millions through charisma and will. She sold three million records in 1956, causing her friend Marlene Dietrich to say, "Her voice has a power of seduction."

HYPOMANIA

Piaf was a bundle of psychic energy much of her life. Her mood was either up or down and she was continually hypomanic. She had an irresistible energy for life and a penchant for hedonism. She was convinced she would die young and was in a hurry to fit all the life she could into that short time. Her sister Simone said, "She wore you out by forcing you to adapt to her own crazy lifestyle. She typically went to bed at eight in the morning. No one could keep up with her. . . . Even the hardiest athletes became no more than a shadow of themselves at the end of six months" (Berteaut 1973, p. 157). Piaf burned herself out due to her manic need for more and more. When ill she refused to relax or go to bed. Obsessions and compulsions started dominating her life, especially when she didn't have a man in her life. For example, she became obsessed with the movie *The Third Man,* which she saw nineteen times. Maurice Chevalier saw her perform and predicted her early demise: "Flying in the face of all opposition, she's running full tilt towards the abyss, horrified, I see looming ahead of her" (Berteaut 1973, p. 360). The Little Sparrow was dead within three years of his prediction.

The Little Sparrow was manically driven and always in a rush. Simone said, "She lived every day as if it was her last." She gradually lost emotional control of her own moods, relying on drugs to help her perform and alcohol to relax her. Her Type A behavior became more pronounced and she became a slave to her own hypomania. When famous she became obsessed with perfection and work. Simone recalled: "She drove the accompanists like slaves. That little slip of a woman was a tyrant when she got down to work . . . the work sessions often began in the afternoon and ended at dawn."

CHARISMATIC POWER

Piaf had a unique ability to charm powerful people. Such was the case with Jean Cocteau. She entertained Princess Elizabeth and the Duke of Edinburgh. Presidents asked to meet her and the elite of show business gave her the ultimate tribute by going out of their way to see her perform.

Piaf made up in charisma what she lacked in social graces. She was able to transform her weaknesses and use these to further her career.

Piaf's charismatic power was developed on the streets and it helped get her out of the slum. This magnetic charm allowed her to seduce any man who crossed her path and also helped her seduce audiences with equal aplomb. Simone wrote that men and audiences alike were unable to resist her. Such was the case when she was dying and gave her last great performance at the Eiffel Tower for Dwight D. Eisenhower, Winston Churchill, Lord Montgomery, Lord Mountbatten, and the shah of Iran. Also present among the hundreds of notables were Princess Grace of Monaco, Elizabeth Taylor, Sophia Loren, Ava Gardner, and Richard Burton. All were mesmerized by this petite woman who was dying of cancer and drug abuse. They gave her a tumultuous standing ovation after she belted out song after song with unrequited passion. She would be dead within two years of this awesome demonstration of charisma onstage.

A DEATH WISH

Edith Piaf was self-destructive and a manic-depressive with a penchant for obsessional behavior. Toward the end, her friend Jean Cocteau wrote: "Madame Piaf is burning herself out." When doctors told her she would die if she insisted on singing, Edith told them, "I want to die young." When they said "to sing is suicide," she responded, "I like that kind of suicide." Her manic need for more catapulted her to the very top of her profession but in the end it killed her prematurely. Before she died, she married one last time. Theo Serapo was a young Greek god who was twenty years her junior when he married her on her deathbed. Edith knew she was dying but could not resist using her charm to attract a beautiful man.

Perseverance and Panache

Ironically, Piaf's most famous song was written by the ex-mistress of Raymond Asso. Marguerite Monnot had written the music for Piaf's first commercial hit song, "L'Etranger." When Monnot brought her "La Vie en rose," Piaf recorded it and it became an overnight sensation and her theme song. Nightclubs even opened under the name La Vie en Rose.

Piaf sold three million records in the first year alone. The Little Sparrow had the power and influence of a Venus. When she sang, it was always her "will" winning out over matter and reason. Her songs were of heartbreak and grief of which she was *the* expert. She was a powerhouse onstage but possessed neither a superior voice or any special training. Her talent was not in her voice but in her delivery.

An American critic wrote: "Edith Piaf, the little French Isolde, goes on bravely dying of love. She dies five hundred times during dinner, and five hundred times afterwards, and always in that marvelous voice. The loudest voice coming out of the smallest body." According to another journalist: "Edith Piaf is the best champagne saleswoman in the United States, as soon as she starts to sing in a club your throat is parched with emotion."

In 1960 Piaf was terminally ill with cancer but sang as if her life depended on it—and to her it did. The manager at her last performance was so concerned by her ill health that he started to clear the theater to cancel the show. She begged him not to: "If you do that I'll kill myself. Please let me sing." Piaf knew she was dying and desperately wanted one last day in the sun. The manager capitulated and allowed her to perform. And perform she did. Clinging to the piano, in a desperate resolve of pure will, Piaf cried to the audience, "I love you, you're my whole life." She was desperately crying out to be loved and the only way she knew to convey her passion was through song. The audience knew the horrible truth and gave her a standing ovation. They screamed, "Come on, Edith, you can do it. Keep going." She responded in kind as long as her drug-ridden, emaciated body could stand it. Everyone in the audience was in tears when she collapsed during the eighth song and was carried from the stage. It was Piaf's last performance.

Edith Piaf's perpetual bouts with crises made her impervious to life's most callous events. *Absence of parental guidance* made her self-sufficient and tenacious. *Blindness* instilled her with hypersensitivity and empathy. *Singing in the streets* imprinted self-confidence and an awesome work ethic. *Poverty* made her treat money with frivolous abandon. A *loveless childhood* made her into a passionate zealot as well as an insatiably driven seductress.

Piaf's good friend Jean Cocteau once wrote: "Piaf is a genius. She is inimitable." He was right. She had used tenacity to overcome unbelievable adversity in order to reach the top of the entertainment world. She showed great insight in saying "a song is a story." Her genius was in knowing how to communicate that story with emotional verve. Tenacity is her legacy to the world. Her life gives credence to her greatest lyrical phrases "I have no regrets" and "Life is magnificent."

EDITH (GASSION) PIAF
French Chanteuse
b. December 19, 1915, Paris, France; d. October 14, 1963, Paris

Dominant Trait: Tenacious Type A personality, probably manic-depressive. Extremely extroverted.

Motto: "Love conquers all." "A song is a story." "I have no regrets."

Nickname: "La Mome piaf" (The little swallow), "Auntie Zizi," "The Great Piaf"

Vices/Hobbies: Alcohol, drugs, flagrantly promiscuous (soldiers her weakness), loved soirees.

Heroes/Mentors: Father, Louis Gassion; Louis Papa Leplée; entertainer role model Marie Dubois; lover Raymond Asso; social graces mentor Jacques Bourgeat; Jean Cocteau (theater)

Philosophy of Life: "I can't stand being alone." "Luck is like money, it goes away faster than it comes."

Fantasy: Eternal love with adoring soldier

Professional Successes: Songs: "L' Accordeoniste," "La Vie en rose," "C'est magnifique," "La vie, l'amour," "Non, je ne regrette rien." Play by Jean Cocteau: *Le Bel Indifferent.* Movies: *Montmartre sur Seine, Etoile sans lumiere, Neuf garcons—un coeur.*

Power: "Madame Piaf is a genius. . . . There has never been an Edith Piaf before, there will never be another" (Jean Cocteau). Sang from the soul with unrestrained emotion that moved people to adulation.

Influence: Most powerful star in Europe. "Dramatic Power" and "inner fire" her force. Drove audiences to tears and delirium, a euphoric experience.

Destructiveness: Sought solace for unrequited love as child in soldiers, leeches, alcohol, drugs. Suicidal drug addict and alcoholic. Said "I want to die young" when doctor told her "to sing is suicide." Responded: "I like that kind of suicide."

Birth Order: Only child of singer Anita Maillard and street acrobat Louis Gassion. Half-sister Simone Berteaut.

Parental Influence: Virtually none. Abandoned by mother, weaned on wine, raised in brothel. Street entertainer with her itinerant father who had nineteen other children through casual affairs with women.

Transiency: Three homes by age two with mother, both grandmothers (one in brothel). No home from age seven on, living by wits on street with vagrant father. Sang for food and shelter.

Crises: Life one continual catastrophe: blind at three, cured at seven, pregnant at sixteen (Marcelle who died at two). Mother died from cocaine overdose, mentor Papa Leplée murdered, and true love Marcel Cerdan died in tragic plane crash in 1949. Drug addict from that day on.

Formal Education: Less than one year, illiterate until age twenty-one. Never learned to read one note of music.

Libidinal Drive: Began "one-night stands" as teenager and never stopped. Spent life searching for love with hundreds of men. Ménage à trois relationship including half-sister. Every hit song was about passion or tragic love.

Personality Type: Extrovert-Intuitive-Feeler-Judger on MBTI. "My music school is the street, my intelligence is instinct."

Self-Esteem: Fearless and believed "she could do everything." An awesome self-confidence.

Rebellion: Shock was part of her persona. Loved renegade image.

Risk Propensity: Earned billion francs yet died broke. No risk too great. "She had the most fantastic nerve" (sister).

Work Ethic: Type A workaholic who "Worked the streets by day and the clubs by night."

Tenacity: "Edith always got her way" no matter what it took.

Optimism: Supremely optimistic even during catastrophic times: "I've always believed that journey through darkness made me more sensitive than other people."

Manicness: Manic energy drove her to euphoria and depression: "She lived each day as if it were her last." A compulsive who saw *The Third Man* nineteen times. Impatient and impulsive in everything. "Everyone sucked dry by her single-minded passion." Possessed an irresistible energy for life.

11

Power, Success, and Personality

Man's opinion of "self" and the world influences all his psychological processes.

Alfred Adler

Personality played the largest role in the power and success attained by these four-teen subjects. It proved to be the only variable that differentiated them from the pack. Their unique personalities were a direct result of early nurturing, life expe-riences, role models, and crises and give validity to the hypothesis that we all live to fulfill our internal image of ourselves. These images are not required to be valid or logical. These fourteen often acted out images that were illusory (Hitler) or mythological (Wright) or survival-oriented (Piaf), which were imprinted on their unconscious by books, mythological mentors, role models, and often by great trauma or crisis. As children they saw themselves destined for greatness and never allowed anything or anybody to interfere with fulfilling that dream. It appears that all success is a self-fulfilling prophecy resulting from early expectations of our-selves. Hitler, Picasso, Napoleon, and Wright were unable to differentiate their real selves from their delusions of self. They actually came to believe themselves to be the reincarnation of Christ, Taliesin, Alexander the Great, or, in virtually every case, Nietzsche's "Superman." Their enormous power and success were the by-product of those internal images imprinted on their psyches while young. It wasn't important how and where such imprintings took place as it was that they did. Based on this study, it appears axiomatic that we all *live our lives fulfilling our in-ternal self-images—whether good or bad!* Assuming this to be true, we should fol-low Mark Twain's sage advice: "Be careful of your dreams. You might just wake up one day and find yourself there."

Transformation of Stars into Superstars

A metamorphosis takes place when certain people achieve supersuccess. A "success imprint" or "failure imprint" occurs which is indelibly stamped on the psyche and preordains the person to live out that image. With success the world suddenly treats you differently, a subtle acknowledgment that you are different and deserving of respect, reverence, or adulation depending on the level of accomplishment. This adoration is deeply imprinted on the psyche of the achiever and a new *superman persona* is born. When Rupert Murdoch salvaged a little Sydney newspaper, he was transformed into the Boy Publisher. With two similar successes, he turned into a publishing icon in Australia and became invincible in his own mind. After the battle at Lodi, Napoleon, a talented general, was recast as an invulnerable messiah. The cubism created by *Les Demoiselles d'Avignon* changed Pablo Picasso's egoism into omniscience. The *Friendship* flight turned Amelia Earhart into an American icon, which imprinted an image of the Goddess of Flight on her psyche. Oswald the Rabbit's success inspired Walt Disney to create Mickey Mouse, Donald Duck, Pluto, and Disneyland. The Charnley House inspired Frank Lloyd Wright at age twenty-four. Teaching "idiot" children transformed Maria Montessori from a medical doctor into an educational matriarch. Wresting control of Hughes Tool from his family turned eighteen-year-old Howard Hughes into a megalomanic power broker. Success reinforced the egomania of these subjects, transforming them into Nietzschean "Supermen" with unlimited potential for greatness. It armed them with an indomitable willpower and changed them from stars into superstars. After their transition, power and success were easy.

Computer as Metaphor for Personality Development

People, like computers, are programmed to perform specific tasks in life. Some personal individuality is hard-wired (inherited) in humans like gender, height, eye color, and some innate instincts of survival (Jung's collective unconscious). Most other characteristics are developed along the way. A computer is similarly equipped as man with prewired features which cannot be changed (PC's operating structure). A computer can be loaded with various operating programs or high-level software and applications programs to enhance its performance. Humans have the same potential for programming. Left- or right-handedness in humans is imprinted prenatally just like a computer comes preloaded with MS-DOS to control its operating behavior. Carl Jung described such inborn attributes as archetypes of a "collective unconscious"—innate qualities inherited from the experiences of past generations. It is now apparent that Jung's inherited instincts and other critical traits are enhanced or modified through learned interactions with life and people.

Traits like charisma and self-esteem are alterable. If you don't like being shy and reticent like Hitler was, you can, like him, change your persona through behavior modification techniques. Such change is never easy but it certainly is possible. In other words, cognitive behavior (personality) can be altered just like a computer can be reprogrammed to fit certain professional requirements. Reinforced behavior becomes ever more difficult to alter or reprogram, but with determination and work one can become more charismatic, intuitive, and/or Type A in personality. These are learned traits, and what is acquired can be modified or changed. Figure 16 illustrates the evolution of personality as "success imprints" or other enhancements which upgrade the individual for ever-higher performance.

FIGURE 16
DYNAMIC NATURE OF PERSONALITY
Using PC as Metaphor
(Both have enormous enhancement options}

PERSONAL COMPUTER		HUMAN PERSONALITY	
	FUNCTIONAL CHARACTERISTICS		
Systems Enhancements		Human Enhancements	
STAGE I			
IBM PC/Apple Mac	Hardwired Features	Gender and Race (Eye color)	Genetic Qualities RNA/DNA
STAGE II			
Board Upgrades	Modem/Memory	IQ, Drive, Fears (Extroversion/Introversion)	Hard-Wired Imprints (Jungian Archetypes)
STAGE III			
Systems Software	MS-DOS	Will, Vision, Mania (Obsessions/Compulsions)	Cultural Imprints (Crises/Metamorphoses)
STAGE IV			
Operating Software	Windows	Self-Esteem, Charisma Independence, Rebellion	Experiential Imprints (Parental and Environmental conditioning)
STAGE V			
Applications Software	Wordperfect LOTUS 123	Resiliency, Temerity Competitiveness, Energy	Cognitive Experiences (Success imprints from Transiency, books, etc)

Creative Personality Traits Instilled Through Programming and Experiential Imprints

Personal Computers and power brokers evolve similarly through repeated moldings and experiential imprints. The above evolution depicts the self-actualization route taken by both the PC and the creative genius or entrepreneurial power broker. Both are continually reprogrammed in a ever-higher level of scripting for superior performance.

TRAITS VS SOFTWARE

Personality traits are analogous to a PC's operating and applications software programs. Drive is to success as Wordperfect is to text editing; neither result is possible without the prior programming. In the context of this book manic behavior is to power as a desktop publishing program is to printing a classy brochure. Each is critical to exceptional performance. The computer's software program determines its operating effectiveness just as a person's life experiences determine his cognitive behavior. Unique behavior traits such as extroversion, optimism, and self-confidence are learned during prenatal survival to adulthood. They are not genetic and unchangeable, but until reprogramming takes place will remain fixed as the individual's dominant personality. Personality traits are acquired through experiential programming just as MS-DOS enhances the operating effectiveness of the PC.

People go through vulnerable stages of growth and change where they learn to be an extrovert or an introvert, learn how to be charming (charismatic) or reticent (shy), prefer risk taking (temerity) or risk-aversity (safety), or acquire a macroview (forest) of life or a microview (trees). People are programmed very early to perform in context with their survival needs. I am convinced that many live to fulfill their internal images of themselves. A person's programming is changeable, just like a computer, although the more comfortable one becomes with existing programs, the more difficult it is to change them. The more a person has to lose by changing, the less likely it is he will change. Individuals with the most assets and greatest investment in what "is" are the least likely to opt for "what can be."

POWER BROKERS: PROGRAMMED AUTOMATONS

The seven traits that are most critical to success in these fourteen were programmed early in life. Their behavior traits were far different than those found in the "normal" population. These subjects were so programmed with a need for perfectionism, self-actualization, and superiority that they became manically driven to achieve their goals. Most were unable to control their obsessional need to pursue power and success. Craving peanut butter and disliking spinach have more to do with positive and negative conditioning while young than any innate desire. These acquired behavior characteristics are imprinted on the subconscious. What is seen on the surface are the conscious manifestations of that programming: optimism, fear, risk propensity, tenacity, self-esteem. These manic overachievers were programmed to become risk-taking workaholics not because of their genes, but because of their childhood interfaces that created those internal programs in their unconscious. Once they were programmed this, they externalized their internal needs for self-actualization. Like computers, they were highly predictable automatons who were manically driven to become the best they could be.

Origin of Creative Genius and Power

How were these fourteen imprinted with such high drive and an obsession for power and success? Inherited IQ or advantageous socioeconomic factors (family influence and/or money) were not critical. As discussed above, manicness and drive were acquired during the myriad of experiences in their youth. Being firstborn contributed to their success and appears to have imbued them with a heavier burden of responsibility, but it was not the only variable in their success. Frequent childhood transiency also contributed far more than might be supposed. Placing children in foreign environments by frequent moving or traveling instills in them strong wills and self-sufficiency. Such individuals are seldom intimidated when confronted with the unknown as adults. Pioneering in foreign habitats or finding themselves alone or out in front of the pack are never intimidating to adults who faced new cultures, people, and languages as children. Parents often are reluctant to move their children to strange new places, but research indicates such an experience conditions them for success as entrepreneurs and innovators. They learn early that the unknown is to be feared but that it is a function of learning how to cope and can often be quite exciting. Boarding school education has this kind of effect on children and appears to instill independence, temerity, and self-sufficiency in them.

CHILDHOOD IMPRINTS

These subjects were adequately intelligent but not geniuses in terms of IQ. Most were firstborn (79 percent) and grew up independent and endowed with a belief in their destiny as leaders. All led early lives of transiency. They moved far beyond the norm and learned to cope in their new environments. None were formally educated in their fields and were required to try harder because of their lack of pedigree or formal instruction. Many sought escape in books and found companionship in fictitious heroes who often became fantasy role models. They grew up with few limitations since they saw themselves emulating their larger-than-life heroes and heroines. Many believed anything was possible. Such children often view the world through rose-colored glasses where possibilities and opportunities are limitless. Figure 17 shows the "success imprints" which had a significant impact on their later success in life.

POSITIVE ROLE MODELS

Most of these subjects were blessed with positive role models who taught them to believe in the impossible. They also were fortunate to have been raised in permissive households where they were given freedom to explore. Virtually all were blessed with self-employed and highly independent parents. Entrepreneurial and autonomous parents instill children with the knowledge that they can make it on their own without selling out to a paycheck.

Their early training taught them to follow their own dreams despite tradition or expert opinion to the contrary. They learned to risk and fail without fear of retribution and were encouraged to explore new concepts without fear of ridicule. Many of the men who rose to the most powerful positions were treated as virtual deities when young. Most envisioned themselves as special when young, which conditioned them to become self-confident optimists as adults and at times arro-

FIGURE 17
SUCCESS IMPRINTS

Visionary	Metamorphoses Experience
Napoleon Bonaparte	Went into battle in April 1796 at Lodi against Italian/Austrian forces of seventy thousand at age twenty-four with only thirty thousand men. An improbable victory caused him to reflect: "I am a superior being." His belief was deluded but changed him into a megalomaniac who changed history.
Walt Disney	Fairy tales by mother therapeutic balm from father's abuse at ages five to eight. Oswald the Rabbit stolen, forcing Disney to create Mickey Mouse. From that time forward he saw crisis as a catalyst to creativity.
Isadora Duncan	Fictional heroes became her solace, especially the Greek goddess Aphrodite who altered her dismal life of poverty and inspired her to become the mother of modern dance. Quit school at age ten to found dance school.
Amelia Earhart	Wild sled ride imprinted risk as daring fun at age six. Success imprint of "risk" as "adventure" molded her into a daredevil who had to "go where no one else had ever been."
Adolf Hitler	*Rienzi* inspiration as teen: "In that hour it began." During WWI became blind from mustard gas attack and while recovering from the trauma exclaimed, "The idea came to me that I would liberate Germany, that I would make it great."
Howard Hughes	When father died, he boldly "took power role" assuming control of Hughes Tool at age nineteen; developed a "success through power imprint" including his invincibility.
Maria Montessori	Birth of illegitimate child in Catholic Italy destroyed medical career at age twenty-five, launching her into childhood education, a psychological substitution, thereby transforming her into "Messiah of Education."
Rupert Murdoch	Mother forced him to live in tree house as boy, imprinting independence and self-sufficiency at an early age. Father died when he was twenty, catapulting him into proprietor of Adelaide paper where he was molded into the "Boy Publisher."
Edith Piaf	Miraculous recovery from blindness at seven while sitting at piano imprinted her with music as salvation.
Pablo Picasso	Sister's death launched art career and need to exorcise inner demons and rage against the world and religion at age thirteen. *Les Demoiselles d'Avignon* (1907) created from inner guilt and "success imprint" catapulted him into father of cubism.
Helena Rubinstein	Fight with father and flight from Poland to Australia the catalysts which launched her into the international queen of beauty.
Marquis de Sade	Messianic imprints by doting relatives created licentious adult who defied all authority from age two. Imprisonment molded him into a great surrealistic philosopher while destroying the man.
Nikola Tesla	Brother's tragic death when five molded him into obsessive-compulsive and manic-depressive personality who had to create to survive.
Frank Lloyd Wright	Witnessed tragic building collapse at nineteen, which instilled "success imprint" and inspired him to become the *Fountainhead*. Taliesin tragedy instilled tenacity and immortality of architecture

gant egotists. The majority were armed with indomitable self-esteem and grew into fearless risk-taking adults. Their dauntless self-images made them believe in the impossible and eager to risk. They saw risk as an exhilarating and positive experience in contrast to most people who view risk taking as threatening and negative. Crises were found to be pervasive in their backgrounds. The experience made them more obsessionally driven than they would otherwise have become.

MOLDING OF A POWER BROKER

Empirical interfaces with life, not genetic endowments, are the keys to molding the creative and innovative personality. Such people are bred not born. Money, formal education, intelligence (IQ), and socioeconomic status are not important variables in success or the formation of the driven personality. The acquisition of power is a function of the key ingredients that form the critical traits of the power broker (see figure 18). These eight elements are instrumental in the development of the overachieving personality.

FIGURE 18
CRITICAL FACTORS IN FORMING A CREATIVE PERSONALITY

"Children grow up to fulfill their internal images and fantasies."

Life Factors	Behavior By-Product of Experience
Adequate IQ	A slightly above average IQ appears to be the ideal for achieving success in creative or entrepreneurial endeavors. Too high or too low an IQ can be counterproductive. Intelligence is helpful but not critical to achieving success.
Birth Order	Firstborn children are groomed for a life of high expectations and perfectionism. They carry the mantle of leadership for the family and are instilled with great drive.
Transiency	Instills self-sufficiency, independence, perseverance, and risk taking; children become comfortable with ambiguity and learn to cope with the unknown and learn to risk with alacrity.
Lack of formal education	Instills a need to overachieve; insecurity makes them try harder. Single-sex schooling and boarding schools provide excellent role models and environments for fostering independence, self-confidence, and self-sufficiency.
Fantasy hero/mentor	Imprints children with unconscious feelings of omnipotence and removes all limits for potential achievement. Everyone should have a mythological hero or heroine as a "bigger-than-life" mentor.
Positive role models	Independent and self-employed parents instill autonomy and demonstrate that success is not tied to a paycheck. Security is personal, not organizational.
Permissive family	Indulgent parents instill a positive risk mentality by supporting trial-and-error learning. The freedom to explore new horizons via a heuristic approach to problem resolution is critical to grooming successful adults.
Crisis	Traumatic events such as the death of parents or siblings, personal, or near-death experiences condition individuals to overachieve. Manicness and obsessional drive are instilled in those who reach the "chaos" stage. They die or are reborn greater than before the trauma. Great risks are always easier after great crises.

Crisis: The Mother of Creativity and Power

Crisis can be a major determinant in developing creative and entrepreneurial success. The backgrounds of these fourteen individuals illustrate how great traumas and crises can imprint the child with an abnormal need for achievement. Individuals with a history of trauma or crisis operate with a unique perspective in resolution of problems. Lack of money is a crisis for someone who has always had money, but to someone who has faced death or starvation the lack of money is not such a big deal. People facing chaos operate differently than ordinary people. They take higher risks with less hesitancy. It appears that the greater the crisis, the greater the imprint for drive and risk taking. Crisis is a key concomitant for creativity and success.

CHAOS AND RENAISSANCE

The pioneering work of Dr. Ilya Prigogine gave credence to the belief that personal crisis can lead to personal success. Prigogine was disenchanted with the nihilism and negativity associated with the Second Law of Thermodynamics, which said all systems are in the process of burning up and dying. He proposed a concept called Dissipative Structures, which said once a system reaches the Bifurcation Point (chaos) it can reemerge into a higher order. Prigogine concluded that complexity and chaos will cause either self-destruction or renaissance. Those who go through a renaissance tend to go through a metamorphosis and emerge stronger than before the crisis. These fourteen individuals confirm Prigogine's thesis and emerged with more determination and indomitable will. These visionaries were beset with many crises, but came out of them inspired and fearless. Most emerged manically driven and instilled with vigor and psychic energy.

VISIT THE BOTTOM TO GET TO THE TOP

Based on the lives of these fourteen it is plausible to conclude: *you cannot reach the top without having visited the bottom.* Their many traumas conditioned them for success. Chaos was a weekly event for most of them. Their turbulent lives were akin to a roller coaster ride or analogous to a sine wave of troughs (disasters) and peaks (successes). When at the bottom, they were usually distraught and willing to bet everything to survive. They would then engage in some high-risk venture which brought them success. Continual crises conditioned them to take higher risks than the average person. Las Vegas gamblers know that big wins are impossible without big risks and these high-rollers are willing to lose big in order to win big. Small bets were of no interest to them. They emulated the Las Vegas high rollers, but it appears they were so inclined because of their many traumas. These experiences armored them with tremendous resolve and a risk-taking propensity.

PSYCHIC ENERGY OUT OF CHAOS

When a person survives chaos or trauma, they tend to have a unique vision that is different than the normal population. They are destroyed by the experience or return more driven than before. It appears these fourteen subjects rose out of their chaotic periods with great psychic energy, unbelievable drive, and an obsession to succeed. Montessori's unfortunate pregnancy and the death of Picasso's sister destroyed them emotionally but imprinted them with psychic energy and a passionate need to succeed. Sade could never have written such strong prose had he not spent fourteen years in the Bastille. Hitler's blindness from mustard gas inspired him as a political leader. Four years of blindness undoubtedly made Edith Piaf into a highly sensitive and empathetic entertainer. Childhood starvation was the catalyst for Isadora Duncan as was perpetual flirtation with bankruptcy for Disney. The tragic death of Tesla's brother at his own hand and his own serious illnesses transformed him into a maniac on a scientific mission. The death of Hughes's parents had a similar effect on him. Each of these individuals rose from defeat and psychological ruin with a fanatical drive and a reenergized will that defied description. The will becomes highly charged during periods of trauma or chaos. It is my contention that these subjects were programmed with their *manic drive* and *willpower* during their periods of trauma and chaos.

Seven Key Success Traits of the Creative Genius

Seven Key Success Traits were found to be the primary determinants of success for these fourteen visionaries. It was these personality traits that were molded by the eight early environmental influences previously discussed. These Seven Key Traits became the driving force behind their rise to fame and fortune. Most subjects had all seven traits but some were particularly endowed with one that was clearly dominant over the others. Such was the case of Amelia Earhart who was a thrill-seeker beyond description, therefore risk taking was used in describing her rise to fame. Both Earhart and Howard Hughes were clearly risk-takers who lived on the edge to such a degree they could have been said to have had a death wish. Both were endowed with the other six traits but "risk" is what defined them. Earhart felt that "tenacity" was her strongest trait but she never saw her dangerous flying adventures as risky. She was also intuitive, independent, self-confident, and a workaholic, as was Hughes. Montessori and Picasso were selected as the prototypes for "self-esteem." Picasso's self-confidence bordered on egomania, Montessori's on arrogance. Both were also high risk-takers, intuitive, obsessive, and tenacious, and could easily have been used to describe those traits. Napoleon and Wright were the most "intuitive" and the prototypes for the right-brain macrovisionaries. Who could have been more rebellious than Isadora Duncan and the Marquis de Sade? Or more manically driven than Nikola Tesla and Adolf Hitler? All exuded the Seven Key Success Traits and were imprinted and/or conditioned with them during their formative years. A summary of the seven traits and the individual subjects best personifying that particular trait is illustrated in Figure 19.

FIGURE 19
SEVEN KEY SECRETS OF POWER AND CREATIVE GENIUS

INTUITIVE   Napoleon Bonaparte and Frank Lloyd Wright

Prometheans (intuitive-thinkers) are supercreative due to their ability to see the opportunities and possibilities in life. They utilize "gut" (qualitative) not "mental" (quantitative) judgment in all endeavors. They have a macrovision and view life as a forest, not just trees, arming them with holistic insight. They subjugate their left-brain to the right, freeing their creative juices.

SELF-ESTEEM   Maria Montessori and Pablo Picasso

Self-Esteem = Self-Image = Self-Confidence. Very early in life the unconscious is programmed as saint or sinner, winner or loser, and it dictates one's self-image. Self-image and self-confidence are then reinforced by early successes. Freedom to risk and fail without criticism is critical. Overachievers are instilled with a feeling of innate infallibility and omnipotence, which manifests itself in optimistic attitudes.

RISK PROPENSITY   Amelia Earhart and Howard Hughes

A living-on-the-edge nature is found in all creative geniuses. Some even appear to have a death wish. No success is possible without great risk. The creative genius has a high tolerance for ambiguity, which was imprinted early by permissive and independent parents and reinforced by tolerance for risk taking. Powerful people do not perceive risk as dangerous but as an exciting adventure.

REBELLIOUS   Marquis de Sade and Isadora Duncan

The powerful and creative must be different. Masterpieces are created by mavericks who are seen as renegades by the establishment. They have a propensity for destroying the present in order to create the future in contrast to bureaucrats who always sacrifice the future for the present. Creative geniuses ignore experts, avoid the pack, and dance to their own tune. They are pioneering iconoclasts.

OBSESSIVE   Nikola Tesla and Adolf Hitler

Creative geniuses are dysfunctional personalities who are manically driven to achieve. Most are driven as a result of some early trauma or crisis. Great success is often a function of manic behavior, hence "Manic Success Syndrome." Obsessional drive correlates with success, normal behavior with mediocrity, and abnormal behavior with great achievement. Charismatics are seldom normal.

WORKAHOLIC   Helena Rubinstein and Rupert Murdoch

Powerful and creative people are usually Type A personalities since a strong work ethic is endemic to overachievement. Powerful people are internally driven and confuse self-worth with winning. Work is not a chore to these people, it is a pleasure and gratifying. They are manics-on-a-mission whose only solace is producing and working. Eighty-hour work weeks are the rule, not the exception.

TENACITY   Walt Disney and Edith Piaf

An indomitable will is critical to the achievement of power and creativity since perseverance is required to overcome adversity. Persistence is the difference between mediocre performance and excellence and the average performer versus the superior. Tenacious people never give up and therefore achieve their goals and ultimate victory. Most people give up within sight of the finish line; winners never do.

Hierarchy of Power

The path to the top for these fourteen visionaries was dictated by their ability to acquire and maintain power. Each took a different path but all were strongly driven to excel. They were highly endowed with psychic energy, which ultimately led to their great success. These self-actualized individuals were steeped in what Nietzsche called a *Übermenschen* ("Overman" or "Superman") qualities. Nietzsche said that a "superman" persona is inculcated with a superhuman *Will-to-Power* "by sublimating his impulses and employing them creatively." "What man desires most is power" and being a "superman" "consisted in the ability to withstand great suffering." It appears that the suffering for these fourteen helped inspire them with those qualities critical to obtaining great power. These traits then allowed them to overcome their enormous adversities on the way to the top. *Willpower* and *charismatic power* are at the pinnacle of the power hierarchy (see table below). Both can open many doors closed to those with physical, money, knowledge, or authoritarian power. An indomitable *will* can overcome many adversities and act as the catalyst in one's rise from mediocrity to greatness. Genetic limitations can be overcome with a sufficient *willpower* or *charisma* but the reverse can never occur. All of the talent in the world will not overcome a lack of initiative and drive. The subordinate powers of muscle, money, IQ, and authority are always dependent on a strong will and charisma. The following table summarizes the sources and manifestation of the power hierarchy as explained in chapter 3:

STAGE	POWER	SOURCE	MANIFESTATION
6	Willpower	Internal	Psychic Energy
5	Charismatic Power	External	Psychosexual Energy
4	Titular Power	Position	Authority or Fear
3	Knowledge Power	Mental	Information/Expertise
2	Financial Power	Economical	Wealth and Money
1	Physical Power	Personal	Guns, Muscle, and Force

Poets of Power

What motivated nihilists like Hitler and Napoleon to write poetry? It could have been a release for inner feelings and hypersensitivity. The subjects who wrote poetry were passionate types who were highly driven. It was surprising at first to find so many creative power brokers who wrote poetry, thus the reason for this section. Eight of the fourteen (over 50 percent) wrote poetry: Napoleon, Duncan, Earhart, Hitler, Picasso, Sade, Tesla, and Wright. These individuals not only wrote poetry, but many wrote good poetry and wrote it often and with passion. Some wrote for their own enjoyment while others published and were quite serious about their writings (Duncan's autobiography is adorned with her poetry). In most cases, their poetry was a kind of exorcising of inner ghosts and a method of expressing a zealous philosophy. Napoleon wrote a poem during his teen years in response to Goethe's *The Sorrows of Young Werther.* The intensity of Napoleon and his obsessions is quite evident in his words. His "Young Werther" was a soliloquy that gives credence to his manic behavior:

> Always alone in the midst of men, I come to my room to dream by myself, to abandon myself to my melancholy in all its sharpness. In which direction does it lead today? Toward death. . . . What fury drives me to my own destruction? In-

deed what am I to do in this world? Since die I must, is it not just as well to kill myself? . . . Since nothing is pleasure to me, why should I bear days that nothing turns to profit? How far men have got away from nature! How cowardly they are, how vile, how rampant! . . . Life is a burden to me because I taste no pleasure and all is pain to me . . . because the men with whom I live, and probably always shall live, have ways as different from mine as the moon from the sun. Thus I cannot pursue the only way of life that could make life tolerable—hence distaste for everything. (Herold 1986, p. 31)

Amelia Earhart wrote "Courage" just prior to her first Atlantic Ocean crossing in the *Friendship*. This poem is psychologically significant in uncovering what made her tick. Her need to live on the edge is clearly evident in this poem:

> Courage is the price life exacts for granting peace.
> The soul that knows it not, knows no release
> From little things.
> Knows not the livid loneliness of fear
> Nor mountain heights where bitter joy can
> Hear the sound of wings.
>
> How can life grant us boon of living, compensate
> For dull gray ugliness and pregnant hate
> Unless we dare
> The soul's dominion? Each time we make a choice, we pay
> With courage to behold resistless day
> And count it fair.   (Rich 1989, p. 48)

Isadora Duncan lived her life poetically. She used the same lyrical style in writing letters and books. A letter she wrote to her lover Gordon Craig demonstrates this lyrical style:

> In Amsterdam by
> Rotterdam
> They dam the Dikes—
>   O
> Dam Dam Dam—
>
> affinity-affinity-Elective Affinity-I have found my Mate—
> You are he—
> And you can not Escape me—Don't try—
>
> Your Dora
>   (Steegmuller 1974, p. 95)

POETIC SCIENTIST

Nikola Tesla memorized epic poems like Goethe's *Faust* as a teenager. He wrote poetry his whole life, an interest learned from his minister father who also loved to write and recite poems. Tesla arrived in America with nothing but some of his technical drawings of the induction motor and his valued poetry. He then solved the problem which would led to his greatest invention while reciting lines from *Faust*:

> Ah, that no wing can lift me from the soil
> Upon its tract to follow, follow soaring!

Tesla said these lines inspired him and "in an instant the truth was revealed." At the age of seventy-eight he wrote the poem "Fragments of Olympian Gossip" for his friend George Viereck, a fellow poet and German immigrant. Poetry was Tesla's most revered form of communication and enhanced his ability to communicate his esoteric ideas.

POETIC PAINTER

Pablo Picasso was a frustrated poet/philosopher. His best friends were poets: Guillaume Apollinaire, Jean Cocteau, and Paul Eluard. Picasso once predicted that after his death encyclopedias would describe him thus: "Picasso, Pablo Ruiz— Spanish poet who dabbled in painting, drawing, sculpture." Picasso eschewed accuracy and punctuation, and preferred writing in a "stream of consciousness" with a surrealist bent due to the influence of Apollinaire and Cocteau. Paul Eluard's said Picasso "held in his hand the fragile key to the problem of reality," which is testimony to Picasso's highly sensitive nature that allowed him to become the documenter of the twentieth-century psyche. Picasso was able to delve into the world's nature through the synergy of painting, philosophy, and poetry. An example of Picasso's poetic talent for description was written to his ever-faithful manservant, Sabartes:

> Live coal of friendship
> clock which always gives the hour
> joyfully waving banner
> stirred by the breath of a kiss on the hand
> caress from the wings of the heart
> which flies from the topmost height
> of the tree of the fruit bower
> (O'Brian 1976, p. 301)

Philosophers of Power and Success

Philosophers love wisdom and knowledge. These fourteen visionaries pursued knowledge with a passion and lived by philosophy that was fundamental to their success and power. It is apparent that all aspiring creators, entrepreneurs, and innovators should have a clear-cut philosophy of life. Without this, success and power will prove difficult, if not impossible, to achieve. These visionaries passionately pursued truth and knowledge, which endowed them with a unique overview of the world and their particular place in it. Most lived and died by their philosophical beliefs, many of which are outlined in figure 20.

MULTIDIMENSIONAL MENTALITIES

All philosophers have a macrovision of the world which makes them multidimensional. So do entrepreneurs and creative geniuses because they all have a passionate need to know what makes the world tick. These visionaries are classic exam-

FIGURE 20
PHILOSOPHY OF POWER

"Knowledge itself is power."
—Francis Bacon

"Power accedes to him who takes it."
—Nietzsche and Ayn Rand

"The control of knowledge is the crux of tomorrow's worldwide struggle for power."
—Alvin Toffler

David McClelland said we all have a need for "power [control], achievement [drive], and affiliation [interpersonal relations]" (*The Achieving Society,* 1961). He saw power as a function of personal motivation. French and Raven said there are five sources of power: coercive (fear-based), reward (incentives), expert (special skills or knowledge), legitimate (authority), and referent (charisma). They saw power in a sociological context. Michael Hutchison in *Anatomy of Sex and Power* argued that power and sex are inextricably intertwined. Nietzsche said "God is dead" and proceeded to create an internalized "Superman" ideology for man to survive alone without an omnipotent being as protector. Nietzsche's insinuation of a "superman as psychic energy" or "supernatural being within" is the driving force for creative and entrepreneurial genius. Powerful people certainly attract a huge constituency due to their enormous and hypnotic charismatic power and psychic energies. These fourteen power brokers give credence to Nietzsche's power source—both positive and negative.

Napoleon Bonaparte. "Power is my mistress." "Combine absolute power, constant supervision and fear." "Keep acquiring more and more power, all the rest is chimerical."
Adolf Hitler. "Right only exists through power and force."
Howard Hughes. "POWER—I can buy any man in the world." *Chicago Tribune* described him as "Power gone berserk."
Maria Montessori. "Liberty and freedom is power."
Pablo Picasso. "Painting isn't an aesthetic operation, it is a way of seizing power."
Marquis de Sade. "The self-destructive *power* of the human race is the Supreme Power."
Rupert Murdoch. "I'd like to rule the world."
Nikola Tesla. "Throughout space there is energy [power]."
Edith Piaf. To her, power was "Love conquers all."
Walt Disney. CBS observed: "His imagination was more powerful than all the psychiatrists in world."
Isadora Duncan. "I had three great masters; Beethoven, Nietzsche, Wagner . . . Nietzsche was the first dancing philosopher."
Amelia Earhart. Friend and competitive aviator Jacqueline Cochran said: "She had psychic powers."
Helena Rubinstein. "Work is power."
Frank Lloyd Wright. "Architecture receives its power from the life-force."

ples of the self-actualized philosopher who can never be labeled single-dimensional. Napoleon, for example, was a general who wrote poetry and created the Napoleonic Code of law and government. His Napoleonic Code of Legal Administration is still used in much of Europe and in the State of Louisiana in the United States. Isadora Duncan was a dancer who wrote poetry, books, and studied the Greek classics. Maria Montessori was a medical doctor-turned-educator who was a devoted feminist. Amelia Earhart was America's queen of the air but found time to write three books, write columns for *Cosmopolitan* and *McCall's,* and publish poetry, while operating her own fashion design company. In addition, she lectured extensively on flying and feminism and was a principal in numerous entrepreneurial ventures. One of these was an investment in the airline partnership which became TWA. Helena Rubinstein was the Queen of Beauty but also a connoisseur of great art, dress, jewelry, and fine homes, which she collected with abandon. Walt Disney was an accomplished polo player and erected his own backyard railroad while working eighteen hours a day running Disney Studios. In addition to science, Tesla was an accomplished billiard player, a voracious reader, gambler, poet, and sartorial host to New York City's famous four hundred. Howard Hughes excelled in golf, and investment banking, in addition to being a test pilot, movie producer and director, Las Vegas real-estate tycoon, and gold and silver mining entrepreneur.

Philosopher Heroes and Mentors

All of these individuals had a highly refined philosophy of life and knew where they were going and why. Most people don't. Even when their goals were deluded, they were geared to success. These individuals were passionately interested in life and its nuances. It is amazing how many of these subjects chose philosophers as their mythological mentors. Nietzsche was the favorite of Duncan, Hitler, Picasso, and Wright. Hitler added Schopenhauer to his love of Nietzsche and proceeded to borrow their concepts for his ideology documented in *Mein Kampf.* Voltaire and Rousseau were heroes revered by Napoleon, Duncan, Montessori, Sade, Tesla, and Wright. Even the nonliterate Edith Piaf counted as her closest friend the poet, writer, and philosopher Jean Cocteau. Rupert Murdoch considered Arthur Clarke his hero.

Don't Confuse the Map with Territory

All the subjects were inquisitive and highly interested in the why and how of life. Most never confused the map with the territory or the symptom with the sickness—a critical factor in becoming a creative genius. Everyone should have a philosophy of life with a clear picture of where they are headed both professionally and personally. No matter what is said about these unique subjects, they had a clearly delineated philosophy of life which they passionately pursued. They give credence to Plato's admonition: "There will be no end to the troubles of states . . . till philosophers become kings."

Political Party Preference

Half the subjects were right-wing Republicans, including all those involved in business enterprises. Disney, Hughes, and Murdoch were radically right and both Disney and Hughes were FBI informants and fervent anti-Communists. Frank Lloyd Wright was equally anti-Communist and was labeled an "anarchist" by the *New York Times*. Duncan and Picasso, both artists, were leftist and joined the Communist party. Both held radical views on life and art and considered themselves revolutionists first and Bolsheviks second. Neither followed the Marxian ideology of a dictatorship of the proletariat or communal living. Duncan attempted to explain this subtlety to reporters: "I'm not a Bolshevik, only a Revolutionist." Tesla and Piaf were apolitical. The rest were middle-of-the-road politically. Napoleon and Hitler were politicians and right-wing dictators.

PRAGMATISTS

For the most part, these subjects were political only in as much as it affected them. Other than Napoleon and Hitler, few were politically active except to the extent it proved beneficial personally or professionally. Hughes used politics to gain an advantage in his business dealings and paid off politicians to get what he wanted. Rupert Murdoch used power of the press to either destroy or make politicians. He was more responsible for Margaret Thatcher being elected prime minister than any other individual in England. He also influenced Australian elections plus those of Ronald Reagan, George Bush, and John Major. His highly publicized and controversial involvement with Republican Newt Gingrich had more to do with countering Sen. Edward M. Kennedy's attempt to have Murdoch's media empire restricted because of foreign ownership than it had to do with politics.

PACIFISTS AND RIGHT-WINGERS

Most of the fourteen subjects were conservative. Amelia Earhart, Maria Montessori, Nikola Tesla, and Frank Lloyd Wright were pacifists. Wright earned the nickname "the Anarchist of Architecture" both for his revolutionary building designs and his antiwar activities during World War II. Wright wrote pugnacious diatribes against entering the war and influenced his employees to become conscientious objectors. The FBI investigated his activities, resulting in a 1943 *New York Times* headline describing him as "the Revolutionist as Architect." Wright heavily influenced one disciple, Davy Davison, who served a jail sentence for draft dodging. Davison's parents implored the FBI to prosecute Wright for sedition due to his influence on their son. Walt Disney was an FBI informant and friends with J. Edgar Hoover. He believed the unions at Disney Studios were Communist-inspired and became a virulent anti-Communist during and after the strike at Disney Studios. He had a vendetta to destroy both communism and the unions. In October 1940 Disney became an FBI Special Agent in Los Angeles District and filed numerous reports on "subversive" activities. He testified against many Hollywood stars and executives and was one of the key reasons his one-time hero Charlie Chaplin fled the United States. In February 1944 Disney was elected vice president of the Motion Picture Alliance for the Preservation of American Ideals and fought both communism and Franklin D. Roosevelt with a passion. Rupert Murdoch gained notoriety in 1995 with his proposed $4.5 million book contract for Republican Newt Gingrich.

FIGURE 21
POLITICAL AND RELIGIOUS PREFERENCE

Creative Genius	Political Preference	Religious Preference
Napoleon Bonaparte	Radical Republican	Catholic/Agnostic
Walt Disney	Right-wing Republican	Fundamentalist Christian
Isadora Duncan	Socialist/Communist	Agnostic
Amelia Earhart	Democrat Pacifist	Episcopalian/Agnostic
Adolf Hitler	National Socialist (Nazi)	Catholic/Agnostic
Howard Hughes	Right-wing Republican	Agnostic
Maria Montessori	Capitalist/Pacifist	Roman Catholic
Rupert Murdoch	Right-wing Republican	Protestant Evangelist
Edith Piaf	Apolitical	Catholic
Pablo Picasso	Communist	Catholic/Atheist
Helena Rubinstein	Republican	Jewish
Marquis de Sade	Royalist/Republican	Catholic/Atheist
Nikola Tesla	Apolitical Pacifist	Christian/Buddhist
Frank Lloyd Wright	Republican Pacifist	Unitarian Spiritualist

Religious Preference

Virtually all fourteen visionaries were spiritual if not metaphysical, even those who were nonreligious. Six were raised Roman Catholic and four of these—Napoleon, Hitler, Picasso, Sade—became agnostic or atheist. Nine of the fourteen (64 percent) spurned religious dogma. Of these, only Earhart and Tesla believed in a spiritual being while the rest were agnostics, atheists, or, in Tesla's case, Buddhist. Six had an immediate family member (father, uncle, or grandfather) who was a minister (Hughes, Murdoch, Picasso, Sade, Tesla, Wright) and Walt Disney was named for a Chicago minister. Seven were overtly antireligious but these were the ones raised in a strictly dogmatic religious environment.

MYSTICAL SPIRITUALISTS

Isadora Duncan was a lifelong atheist. Even so, she was highly spiritual with a transcendental quality about her. Duncan revered the Greek mythological gods and created many dances in their honor. She described herself in her autobiography, "I'm a Puritanical Pagan." Isadora was sensitive and always felt she was precognitive. She claimed to have had premonitions about the deaths of her two children and then sensed the start of World War I. Like Piaf and Tesla, she was superstitious and a believer in astrology. Edith Piaf was extremely superstitious and spent years trying to communicate with her dead lover Marcel Cerdan through séances. Tesla grew up indoctrinated with religious dogma as his father was an Orthodox minister, and as the second son, he was being groomed for the ministry. He had a *cosmic spirituality* about him that mystified his friends and the press. Like Duncan, he claimed to be precognitive.

PERSONAL DEIFICATION

Both Napoleon and Hitler believed they were divine. Napoleon was not religious but refused to acknowledge his true feelings in public since he was the leader of a Roman Catholic nation. He professed to follow Roman Catholicism but later wrote that it was a political ruse. However, his upbringing influenced him enormously as his speeches and writings were infused with the concept of a supreme being: "God gave me the will and the force to overcome all obstacles," although in his deluded mind *he* was God.

Hitler had similar attitudes toward the church and himself. He was steeped in mysticism with himself as the omnipotent power. Examples of his delusion include such statements as "I never make a mistake," "I hereby set forth . . . the claim of political infallibility," and "I am more godlike than human" (Hershman and Lieb 1994, p. 182). He then created a pledge to be recited by the young: "Adolf is the real Holy Ghost . . . I pledge my life to Hitler; I am ready to die for Hitler my savior."

ATHEISTS

Picasso was raised as a Roman Catholic but opposed the church's dogma after he decided that God had allowed his sister to die. He had a lifelong ambivalence about God and while claiming to be an atheist, depicted Christ's crucifixion at every crisis point in his life. His friend Apollinaire introduced him to the occult and he spent his life preoccupied with passion and death. Don Juan and Krishna were his mythical role models and existentialism his ideology. He interpreted coincidences as evil destiny and allowed them to dictate his lifestyle. In mid-life, Picasso became a Communist which fit his atheism and nihilism. Sade was the most ardent atheist and ironically the one most influenced by religion. He was reared in a monastery by a priest. Sade's incarcerations had far more to do with religious blasphemy than they had to do with breaking society's laws. The laws Sade broke outlawed sodomy and defamation of religious icons. Influenced by Rousseau, he disagreed with any law that did not fit his ethical system, arguing against laws promulgated by religious prelates. Sade actually had the highest moral and ethical values of anyone in this book. He refused to sentence people to die when he was a judge during the Reign of Terror, and actually jeopardized his own life for those who later incarcerated him. Sade's crimes were all against the church's dogma and its icons. He desecrated the cross, rosary, and holy sacraments by using them in his perverse sexual plays. Ironically, Napoleon was not any more religious than Sade but was enraged when Sade wrote a degrading paper about Josephine and had Sade imprisoned for life based on his crimes against God.

THE DEVOUT AND PIOUS

Walt Disney, Maria Montessori, Edith Piaf, Rupert Murdoch, and Frank Lloyd Wright were the most religious. The three men were raised in America's conservative Midwest while Montessori was a devout Italian Catholic. Montessori lived a lonely and sad life due to her accidental pregnancy in Roman Catholic Italy, but never lost her faith. Edith Piaf was strongly steeped in Catholic dogma but paid a dear price for her faith. She sang to Jesus, prayed to Saint Peter and adored Saint Theresa. She firmly believed that Saint Theresa had performed the miracle which restored her eyesight. When she died, this pious woman who had regularly worshiped God was refused a Catholic mass by Rome due to her having "lived in a state of public sin." Rupert Murdoch was the grandson of Patrick Murdoch, a minister of the Church of Scotland. Always religious, he became friends with Billy Graham. Murdoch was also obsessed with astrology, insisting that horoscopes be printed in all his papers. A Pisces, he believed in his fortune: "Your poetic approach rings the bell of success" (Shawcross 1993, p. 118).

MESSIANIC ARCHITECT

Most of these visionaries created dogma instead of following it. They believed more in themselves than in a higher being, but typically maintained a highly developed sense of spirituality. Frank Lloyd Wright was raised to believe he was the personification of the Welsh god Taliesin. He was the son of a Baptist minister and reared as a God-fearing person. Wright was steeped in mysticism and used his estate at Taliesin as his center of spiritual development. Later in life, he held group therapy sessions for his disciples to develop the mind, soul, and body. Wright's third wife, Olga, was a devout believer in Gurdjieff's mysticism and convinced her husband to follow some of his ideologies. Most of Wright's architectural works have a surreal or transcendental quality about them. Albert Bush Brown wrote in the *Atlantic Monthly* after Wright's death: "His themes are nineteenth-century themes. First there is a hero, of Wagnerian dimensions, capable of great public service, as Plutarch would have him. . . . This hero, a Messiah in the image of Christ, a philosopher like Lao-tse, owes his strength to nature; his parables come from the field; his metaphor is the root of flower, never the machine." Wright's religion was similar to that of the other subjects: it was a spiritual embodiment of their own egos. Their religion had a Zen-like quality where their soul and work became the inextricably tied to their spirituality.

Life Span: A Function of Lifestyle

A long life appears to be tied to having a profession that is a labor of love. Richard Wagner created all of his great masterpieces between ages fifty and seventy. Copernicus was seventy when he wrote *On the Revolutions of Heavenly Spheres.* Cervantes wrote *Don Quixote* at age sixty-eight. *The Brothers Karamozov* was finished by Dostoevsky when he was fifty-nine. Victor Hugo completed *Les Miserables* at age sixty and Freud didn't finish *Civilization and Its Discontent* until age seventy-three. P. T. Barnum opened his famous Barnum Circus at age fifty-six and created "The Greatest Show on Earth" at age sixty-seven. Consider Nelson Mandela ascending to the leadership of South Africa at age seventy-five. Dean Keith Simonton, author of the excellent psychohistory *Greatness* (1994), wrote: "Creative individuals can be more productive in their 70s than they were in their 20s." Psychologists have recently demonstrated that those without a reason to live, die.

Too Busy to Die

The visionaries in this work who were not self-destructive lived very long lives. They had no time nor inclination to worry about their mortality. They were driven to create and achieve even until old age. Picasso said that the reason painters live so long was a function of their minds, not their bodies. He wrote: "While I work, I leave my body outside the door, the way Moslems take off their shoes before entering a Mosque." At age ninety he told a reporter: "I am overburdened with work. I don't have a single second to spare, and can't think of anything else." He lived and painted until he was ninety-three. Frank Lloyd Wright produced a full third of his total life's output after age eighty. He created some of the world's great buildings during his old age including Fallingwater in Pennsylvania, the Greek Orthodox Church in Milwaukee, the Price Tower in Oklahoma, the Marin County Municipal building in California, and the Guggenheim Museum in New York City. He rode his horse until age ninety and was designing revolutionary new buildings until the day he died at age ninety-three. Helena Rubinstein was not an artist like Picasso and Wright, but she lived longer than anyone else in this book. She also worked till the very end of a long and productive life. Rubinstein ruled her beauty empire with an iron fist until the day she died. Vanity and pride never permitted her to reveal her age.

Eighties

Maria Montessori lived to be almost eighty-two and was lecturing in foreign countries right up to the end of her life. She embarked on a two-year lecture tour of India at the age of seventy-six and didn't publish her last book, *An Absorbent Mind* (1949), until age seventy-eight. At seventy-nine she embarked on a lecture tour through Norway and Sweden. She was planning even more work when she died suddenly at age eighty-one. Nikola Tesla was still researching new electronic concepts when he died in his eighty-sixth year. He worked until the end, but had been forced to close his lab earlier for lack of funds.

SEVENTIES

The Marquis de Sade lived over half his life in prison but at age seventy-four still had plans for his future. The profligate Sade concocted a perverse plan to be released from prison and take up residence with a mother and daughter in a ménage à trois. This remarkable man was still sex having daily with a sixteen-year-old before he died.

Howard Hughes suffered severe physical injury in his 1946 Los Angeles airplane crash, but did not succumb until age 70. Hughes's iron will kept him alive after that horrible crash where his heart was pushed to the opposite side of his body and his skull crushed. After this accident Hughes became impotent and a recluse, living the rest of his life on drugs and in a self-created asylum of hotel rooms.

SELF-DESTRUCTION AND PREMATURE DEATH

Half of these individuals died prematurely due to their live-on-the-edge lifestyles. Three of them died violently: Amelia Earhart was lost at sea at age thirty-nine, Isadora Duncan died in a car accident at age forty-nine, and Adolf Hitler committed suicide in a Berlin bunker at age fifty-six. Four others died due to their own lifestyles. Edith Piaf was forty-seven when she passed away from cancer and the effects of drug and alcohol addiction, which exacerbated her cancer. Napoleon's death is still controversial. Some historians believe that the British had him poisoned to eliminate the cost and embarrassment of his detention on St. Helena. Other historians say that cancer was the reason for his early demise at age fifty-one. Based on his lifestyle, it appears likely that he contributed to his own death due to a manic need to live on the edge. Napoleon drove himself like a madman and it must have taken an immense toll on his body. Walt Disney also destroyed his body through excessive drink and cigarettes even though this didn't exact its toll until he was sixty-five.

Based on these findings, it appears a workaholic lifestyle and fierce dedication to your profession is a prescription for a long life if you are not self-destructive. Half of these subjects lived far longer lives than the average. The other half killed themselves prematurely through self-destructive lifestyles. Figure 22 lists the fourteen subjects relative to life span, profession, and cause of death for those who died prematurely.

FIGURE 22
LIFE SPAN: A FUNCTION OF LIFESTYLE

Lived into Nineties

Helena Rubinstein	94 years	Businessperson
Frank Lloyd Wright	93 years	Architect
Pablo Picasso	93 years	Artist

Lived into Eighties

Nikola Tesla	87 years	Inventor
Maria Montessori	82 years	Educator

Lived Into Seventies

Marquis de Sade	75 years	Philosopher
Rupert Murdoch	Still living (64)	Businessperson

Died Prematurely Due to Self-Destructive Lifestyle

Amelia Earhart	39 years	Plane crash
Edith Piaf	48 years	Drugs and alcohol abuse
Isadora Duncan	49 years	Car accident
Napoleon Bonaparte	52 years	Questionable
Adolf Hitler	56 years	Suicide
Walt Disney	65 years	Alcohol and cigarettes
Howard Hughes	70 years	Plane crash injuries and drugs

Manic Success Syndrome

Mania breeds success! High energy can overcome many obstacles on the road to the top. It was the key to the enormous success of these subjects. Their high energy was not inborn but learned. Their vital energy and drive were external manifestations of some inner force that demanded they achieve at all cost. How did they develop such a manic need to achieve? Why are some people more active than others? How can some individuals work intensely for sixteen hours while others are fatigued after six? This is all mental and emotional, not physical. Manically driven people have an unrelenting need for work. Work to these people is fun and emotionally gratifying, not a chore. They find work as invigorating as most find it drudgery. The creative genius views work positively. Such is the mental influence of the hyperactive. Hypomanics are mentally and not physically driven. They are energized by an unconscious need for perfection and superior achievement. Their psychic energy emanates from a passionate need that is the "vital force" described by George Bernard Shaw or the "mad passion" described by Jacques Barzun in *The Paradoxes of Creativity*. According to Barzun: "The genius's goal rivets his attention and becomes an obsession."

MANIA AND CREATIVITY

Hershman and Lieb, the authors of *The Key to Genius* (1988), say: "Mild mania and depression are the best states for creativity because they increase both the quantity of completed work and its quality" (p. 197). Nietzsche was aware of his need to be manic: "I used to walk through the hills 7 or 8 hours on end without a hint of fatigue, my creative energy flowed most freely" (Hershman and Lieb 1988). George Sand wrote of Chopin's hypomania: "His creation was spontaneous, miraculous. It came to him without search or prescience. . . . He hurried back to hear it by throwing it on the piano, but then began the most heart-breaking labor I have ever seen. . . . He would shut himself in his room for whole days, weeping, walking up and down, breaking his pens, repeating or changing a measure a hundred times. . . . He would spend six weeks on a single page" (Hershman and Lieb 1988). Such is the genesis of creativity and power. A manic success syndrome exists in the psyches of the creative and powerful. Hyperactivity defines them.

WHAT PRICE MANIA?

Would a submissive, calm, and reserved individual be willing to become a hypomanic in order to achieve? Would they pay the price for greater success? If willing, anyone can learn to be more of a Type A and speed up their emotional reaction time. Drugs can make us hyper but exact too great a price. Modifying behavior is easier but still exacts a toll. Compulsive behaviors are passionate, and passion exacts its own price. One cannot be driven and relaxed simultaneously. Hyperactivity and relaxing are a zero-sum game and the price for getting one is losing the other. Passionate people pay a high price for their success. Not everyone is willing to pay that price.

ENVIRONMENTAL STIMULI ENHANCE PSYCHIC ENERGY

Research has shown that the human brain responds to external stimuli. People who drive too fast are either late, anxious, or have a kind of rushing sickness. Sometimes ordinary people drive excessively fast when listening to a fast song on the radio. Hostility and aggressiveness can cause people to drive recklessly or fast or both. Adrenaline released in such a state causes people to drive faster. Songs with a fast beat have the same effect as they can stimulate the brain to release chemicals that speed up the reaction time and need for speed. When the unconscious is stimulated by a strong passion, regardless of its source, the body secretes chemicals (serotonin, endorphins, and adrenaline) to enhance energy (Seyle's flight or fight syndrome). It is now possible to purchase energy-altering drugs that are both legal and illegal. But the driven people in this book had the ability to generate their own insatiable energy from within. Earl Nightingale said, "We become as we think." If we think fast, we will act fast. These fourteen were internally energized and their obsessive needs for action and completion resulted in the term "Manic Success Syndrome." They were externally energized because they were first internally driven, not the reverse. In other words, thinking fast made them operate faster, which in turn became the catalyst for their success.

RUSHING SICKNESS

Great visionaries tend to be average people with abnormal drive. They have what I call a "rushing sickness." They walk, talk, drive, eat, and think faster than most. They are in a hurry to finish at any cost whatever they begin. Visionaries are megalomaniacs on a mission. Many are hypomanic personalities with obsessive-compulsive or manic-depressive afflictions. Their achieve because of intense focus, impatience, and impulsiveness. If they moved at a "normal" speed they would never have achieved such outstanding success. Top athletes like to say "speed is king" since they use speed to outrun their mistakes. The swiftest always beats the slower, whether in sports, dominating a new market, or successfully winning a business contract. Napoleon proved this conclusively on the field of battle. Being able to outrun your mistakes is a trite motivational technique used by college coaches, but it is also true in all creative and entrepreneurial ventures. Productivity and overachievement result from rushing sickness. Power brokers and over-achievers always accomplish more than their peers because they cannot stand to be last or not to finish a project. They are always willing to sacrifice sleep, food, or family in a mad dash to accomplish the impossible. Part of their elation comes from being first.

Dysfunctional Personalities

It's okay to be different. Normal people, as expected, do normal things that often turn out to be mediocre. Fanatical people create the bizarre, which is also expected but not often admired. These fourteen individuals were not only different, they were dysfunctional as were many of the world's other great creative geniuses. Eleven of the fourteen subjects (79 percent) were hypomanic and eight were manic-depressive. This is a consistent finding in the creative personality. Anthony Storr, a researcher on the creative personality, says, "Psychopathology is indispensable to the highest achievements of certain kinds." He also wrote in *The Dynamics of Creativity* (1993): "Many of the most valuable human beings who have ever lived have shown evidence of considerable psychopathology; of schizoid traits, obsessional symptoms, and manic-depressive illness." He discovered that the great tend to be different. In other words, it takes an *abnormal* personality to achieve *abnormal* results. Normal drive and goals ensure normal achievement. These superstars had abnormal dreams and therefore achieved improbable success.

Genes versus Will

David McClelland, professor-turned-author, wrote in *Power: The Inner Experience* (1978) and *Motivating Economic Achievement* (1993) that motivation is a positive force for self-actualization. He demeaned the negative predeterminist philosophies which tout genetics as the father of all success. McClelland said that Darwin was a scientist who "showed that man was a by-product of a process of natural selection over which he certainly had no control." He saw Marx as "placing man in a context of desires and aspirations as if they were wholly determined by economic conditions." He accused Freud of making man a slave of his "unconscious forces." McClelland then cynically asked, "Where in all this picture of social determinism was there a place for man as a creator rather than a creature, as an actor rather than a reactor, as an agent of change rather than a product of historical, social and personal history?" Man has always been and always will be a free spirit, limited only by his imagination and drive. Will is the only predeterminate of destiny, not genes.

Nietzschean Supermen

The creative geniuses in this book were self-made and self-determining. They refused to abide by the deterministic tenets of Darwin, Marx, and Freud. These visionaries were *not* successful due to any deterministic genes but because they were driven to outperform their peers. They used willpower or psychic energy to rise to the top and became self-actualized due to an inordinate need to be the very best they could be. They had a vital energy that emanated from an indomitable will. Most drew their power from an inner force that transformed them into supermen and superwomen. Nietzsche was correct in saying that "man can yet raise himself above the beasts." His *superman* (will-to-power) hypothesis is far more crucial to rising above the pack than any genetic factors. Will is the difference between success and failure, the genius and the derelict. These subjects used willpower to gain power and to keep it. It was their indomitable will that allowed them to assume power that they didn't have. Most people have not mastered the art of self-motivation. These fourteen did! They learned how to energize themselves through introspection. Alvin Toffler said, "Many things that are attributable to biological pre-wiring are not produced by selfish, determinist genes, but rather by social interactions under non-equilibrium conditions" (*Chaos to Creativity* [1980]). These fourteen validate Toffler's remark. They used *super willpower* to become successful.

Frederich Nietzsche was the son of a Protestant minister, yet espoused a "God is dead" theory and then created the "superman" to allow man to survive in such a world. Nietzsche's premise was that a superhuman individual would possess the *will-to-power* that would make him impervious to the lower beings, allowing him to reinvent his own superior image. These fourteen were able to indoctrinate themselves with a Nietzschean "superman" persona which made them think and act bigger than life. They molded themselves into a "higher kind of man [woman]," a "Dionysian" or "Overman" in Nietzsche's words—a "half saint, half genius." While most power is fleeting, especially muscle, money and authority, the *willpower* is not. These wunderkinds knew they were the controllers of their own destiny. They intuitively knew power and success was a function of their own internalized willpower.

Gender, Power, and Success

Figure 23 quantifies the aforementioned variables of success and power for the nine men and five women. Seven of the men and four women (79 percent) were firstborn of their gender. Most men were introverts (54 percent) and a vast majority of women (80 percent) were extroverts giving validity to the argument that women are more verbally proficient than men—among the superachievers. Seventy-nine percent were charismatic with little difference between the genders. Hitler and Napoleon led the men in this trait while Montessori and Piaf were the most alluring of the females. All were thrill-seeking (Big T) personalities who were delighted to pioneer and take risks. All of the men were Type A personalities, while only two of the women were. Six of the nine men were manic-depressive or hypomanic personalities. Only two of the women were so afflicted, although both are far above the norm.

High sex drive was prevalent among the men with six of the nine considered sexually hyperactive. Sade, Picasso, Piaf, and Hughes were off the scale in this area. Piaf was even more promiscuous than the males and her libidinal drive bordered on nymphomania. The majority of the males were nonreligious (67 percent) as only three (Disney, Murdoch, Wright) had affiliations with an organized church. Three (Hitler, Picasso, Sade) were agnostic or atheist. Only two women were highly religious (Montessori and Piaf), and both were Roman Catholic. All of the women were highly spiritual even when not members of an organized religion. All but two (95 percent) were intuitive-thinkers (Promethean temperament) on the Myers-Briggs Type Indicator of personality preference. All of the men had a Promethean-type temperament while only two women did not (Duncan and Piaf). These two were both "feelers," not thinkers.

TRAIT SUMMARIES OF FORTY CREATIVE GENIUSES

Subjects from my two previous books—*Profiles of Genius* (1993) and *Profiles of Female Genius* (1994)—have been compiled in Figure 24 to afford a larger sample for ascertaining "What makes the great tick?" Combining the subjects from three books gives a much larger cross-section of contemporary and historical genius and it also increases the female sample to a level more in line with the males. This analysis of behavior characteristics has a total of forty subjects which comprises eighteen females and twenty-two males—a far better barometer of power and success. Notice that the forty power brokers have been segregated by gender and categorized into nine traits or behavior characteristics. The intent is to determine if any similarities and differences are prevalent in the creative and powerful personality.

This analysis illustrates that being firstborn is far more important for the male (92 percent) than the female (69 percent). This gives credence to the hypothesis that males are more burdened in carrying the mantle of responsibility for

FIGURE 23
SUMMARY OF KEY BEHAVIOR CHARACTERISTICS

Fourteen Male and Female Power Brokers by Gender

Males	First-born Gender	Extro-verts	Big Ts Thrill-seeker	Charis-matic Charm	Type A Person-ality	Manic-depres-sive	High Sex Drive	Relig-ious	Intuitive-Thinker Promethean
1 Napoleon	No	Yes	Yes	Yes+	A+	Yes	Yes	No	Yes
2 Disney	No	No	Yes	No	A	Yes	No	Yes	Yes
3 Hitler	Yes	No	Yes	Yes++	A+	Yes	Yes	No	Yes
4 Hughes	Yes	No	Yes	Yes+	A+	Yes	Yes	No	Yes
5 Murdoch	Yes	No	Yes	No	A+	No	No	Yes	Yes
6 Picasso	Yes	Yes	Yes	Yes+	A	No	Yes	No	Yes
7 Sade	Yes	Yes	Yes	Yes+	A	Yes	Yes	No	Yes
8 Tesla	No/Yes	No	Yes	Yes	A–	Yes	No	No	Yes
9 Wright	Yes	Yes	Yes	Yes+	A	No	Yes	Yes	Yes
Totals/%	7/78%	4/44%	9/100%	7/78%	9/100%	6/76%	6/76%	3/33%	9/100%

Females	First-born Gender	Extro-verts	Big Ts Thrill-seeker	Charis-matic Charm	Type A Person-ality	Manic-depres-sive	High Sex Drive	Relig-ious	Intuitive-Thinker Promethean
1 Earhart	Yes	No	Yes	Yes	B	No	Yes	No	Yes
2 Duncan	No	Yes	Yes	Yes	A	No	Yes	No	No
3 Montessori	Yes	Yes	Yes	Yes	B	No	No	Yes	Yes
4 Piaf	Yes	Yes	Yes	Yes	A+	Yes	Yes	Yes	No
5 Rubinstein	Yes	Yes	Yes	No	A+	Yes	No	No	Yes
Totals/%	4/80%	4/80%	5/100%	4/80%	3/60%	2/40%	3/60%	2/40%	3/60%

Grand Total Units	11	8	14	11	12	8	9	5	12
Percent	79%	57%	100%	79%	86%	57%	64%	36%	86%

Firstborns: Males and females (firstborn of gender) about the same—material at 79%
Extroversion: Not important for males but more important for females (80%)
Big Ts:
  (High testosterone) All of the subjects exhibited thrill-seeking behaviors
Charismatics: Most (80%) had an alluring appeal which became the basis of their power and influence
Type A Personalities: All males and three of five females were Type A personalities
Manic-Depressives: Eight of fourteen were bipolar (significantly higher than normal population)
High Sex Drive: Six of nine males (67%) were libidinally driven—females less so
Nonreligious Two-thirds of subjects nonreligious although all were highly spiritual
Promethean
  Temperaments: All males and three of five females were intuitive/thinkers (Prometheans)

the family. Extroversion is far less important for males (46 percent) than for females (69 percent), adding validity to the theory that females are more verbally proficient than males. Ninety percent (36) of the forty subjects were Big Ts (high testosterone and thrill-seeking) with the males slightly more inclined to take high risk than the females. Seventy percent (28) of the subjects were considered charismatic with little difference by gender. Males are clearly more inclined to have a Type A personality than females. All of the men were so inclined while just over half of the females were classified as Type A. Hypomania, as expected, is a male oriented trait.

The majority (55 percent) of the men were afflicted with manic-depressive symptoms while only five (28 percent) of the women were. Both figures are much higher than societal norms. The males (77 percent) were more libidinally driven than the females (61 percent), which is to be expected since there were more Big T males in the sample. But the women scored much higher than would be expected in the normal female population. More females (56 percent) had strong religious convictions than males (32 percent), although the majority (23) did not belong to an organized church. Thirty-four of the forty subjects (85 percent) were inclined to use an intuitive-thinking approach to managing their lives and careers. All of the men and two-thirds of the women were intuitive-thinkers (Prometheans).

Summary: Power, Success, and Personality

These findings indicate high energy is the formula for success. It is what drove these fourteen subjects. It didn't come from some genetic physical endowment, but it emanated from a deeply rooted emotional need to prove their superiority. Were they overcoming internal insecurities in their manic overachieving? In many cases yes! Most were deathly afraid of failure, but more blatant was their obsession with winning which manifested itself in what I have termed a "Manic Success Syndrome." The individuals were so driven that they were willing to sacrifice families, friends, health, and happiness to realize their dreams. No sacrifice was too great. When in their manic state, they were able to accomplish herculean feats. They found themselves in the "zone" or "flow state" more often than most due to their single-focused obsession with their dreams. An indomitable willpower and focus enabled them to block out the rest of the world. Obsessive drive made them successful, but it often made them sick. It was their instrument of power as well as their tool of self-destruction.

Drive and Psychic Energy = Power and Success

What is the derivation of high drive, manic behavior, and psychic energy? Is it learned or inherited, acquired empirically or by the luck of the draw? There is no absolute proof either way, however the findings on these subjects would indicate they acquired their unique personalities and drives during their formative years or

FIGURE 24
SUMMARY OF KEY BEHAVIOR CHARACTERISTICS

Fourteen Male and Female Subjects from *Profiles of Genius* (1993) and *Profiles of Female Genius* (1994)

Males (*Profiles of Genius*)	First-born Gender	Extro-verts	Big Ts Thrill-seeker	Charis-matic Charm	Type A Person-ality	Manic-depres-sive	High Sex Drive	Relig-ious	Intuitive-Thinker Promethean
1 Marcel Bich	Yes	No	Yes	Yes	Yes	No	Yes	Yes	Yes
2 Nolan Bushnell	Yes	Yes	Yes	Yes+	Yes	No	Yes	No	Yes
3 Bill Gates	Yes	No	Yes	No	Yes	Yes	No	No	Yes
4 Howard Head	Yes	Yes	Yes	Yes	Yes	No	Yes	No	Yes
5 Soichiro Honda	Yes	Yes	Yes	Yes	Yes	Yes	Yes	No	Yes
6 Steven Jobs	Yes	No	Yes	No	Yes	Yes	Yes	No	Yes
7 Arthur Jones	Yes	No	No	Yes	Yes	No	Yes	No	Yes
8 Bill Lear	Yes	Yes	Yes	Yes+	Yes	Yes	Yes	No	Yes
9 Tom Monaghan	Yes	No	Yes	No	Yes	Yes	Yes	Yes	Yes
10 Akio Morita	Yes	Yes	Yes	Yes+	Yes	No	Yes	Yes	Yes
11 Sol Price	No	No	No	No	Yes	No	No	Yes	Yes
12 Fred Smith	Yes	Yes	Yes	Yes+	Yes	No	Yes	No	Yes
13 Ted Turner	Yes	No	Yes	Yes	Yes	Yes	Yes	No	Yes
Totals/%	12/92%	6/46%	12/92%	9/69%	13/100%	6/46%	11/85%	4/31%	13/100

Females (*Profiles of Female Genius*)	First-born Gender	Extro-verts	Big Ts Thrill-seeker	Charis-matic Charm	Type A Person-ality	Manic-depres-sive	High Sex Drive	Relig-ious	Intuitive-Thinker Promethean
1 Mary Kay Ash	Yes	Yes	Yes	Yes+	No	No	No	Yes	No
2 Maria Callas	No	No	Yes	Yes	Yes	Yes	Yes	Yes	No
3 Liz Claiborne	Yes	Yes	No	No	No	No	No	Yes	Yes
4 Jane Fonda	Yes	No	Yes	Yes	Yes	No	Yes	Yes	Yes
5 Estée Lauder	No	Yes	Yes	Yes	Yes	No	Yes	Yes	Yes
6 Madonna	Yes	Yes	Yes	Yes	Yes	Yes	Yes	No	Yes
7 Golda Meir	No	Yes	Yes	Yes+	Yes	No	Yes	No	Yes
8 Ayn Rand	Yes	No	Yes	No	No	No	Yes	No	Yes
9 Gloria Steinem	Yes	No	No	No	No	No	No	No	Yes
10 M. Thatcher	No	Yes	No	Yes	No	No	No	Yes	No
11 Lillian Vernon	Yes	Yes	Yes	No	No	No	Yes	Yes	Yes
12 Linda Wachner	Yes	Yes	Yes	No	Yes	Yes	No	No	Yes
13 Oprah Winfrey	Yes	Yes	Yes	Yes+	Yes	No	Yes	Yes	No
Totals/%	9/69%	9/69%	10/77%	8/62%	7/54%	3/23%	8/62%	8/62%	9/69%

Compilation of Key Behavior Characteristics—Forty Power Brokers and Creative Geniuses

Forty Power Brokers from Three Books	First-born Gender	Extro-verts	Big Ts Thrill-seeker	Charis-matic Charm	Type A Person-ality	Manic-depres-sive	High Sex Drive	Relig-ious	Intuitive-Thinker Promethean
22 Males	19 86%	10 45%	21 95%	16 87%	22 100%	12 55%	17 77%	7 32%	22 100%
18 Females	13 72%	13 72%	15 68%	12 67%	10 56%	5 28%	11 61%	10 56%	12 67%
40 Total Percentage	32 69%	23 58%	36 90%	28 70%	32 80%	17 43%	28 70%	17 43%	34 85%

through traumatic periods. Their early experiences far outweighed any biological determination. If genetics were the basis for their success, why don't the myriad of people with identical endowments achieve the same success? There are millions of people with similar genetic gifts who are miserable failures. There is little in the backgrounds of these fourteen that would justify any argument for genetics playing a role in their success. They were all from different backgrounds but most were reared in indulgent households featuring intellectually stimulating activities. They experienced identical parental and environmental experiences and encounters with trauma and crisis. Only two (Hughes and Murdoch) had fathers who were accomplished in their fields. Most had parents who were less than successful.

GENIUSES BRED, NOT BORN

Early experiences like birth order, crises, transiency, parental role models, mythological mentors, and early freedom to explore the mysteries of life endowed these individuals with unique personality traits that caused them to be creative and successful. Even Herrnstein and Murray (*The Bell Curve* [1994]) admitted finding such individuals in their research. They touted intelligence and a "cognitive elite" as the reason for all success but admitted to many exceptions, including idiot savants. The most inexplicable were successful track betters who were highly skilled at computing parimutuel betting odds with remarkable precision and speed. These individuals were capable of performing exceptional mathematical feats with complex betting systems. When Herrnstein and Murray tested these individuals they were found to have below average IQs but with superior aptitude to function in a field where brighter and more qualified people normally operate. Other data substantiate this same finding. James Flynn's 1991 study, *Asian Americans: Achievement beyond IQ* (quoted in Murray and Herrnstein 1994) found that the real explanation for higher academic success by Asians, including their superior IQ scores, was based on a driven need to overachieve.

The French have been pioneers in the study of the born versus bred issue starting with Itard and Séguin's landmark work on the "Wild Boy of Aveyron," which Montessori used extensively. Montessori was one of the first to show that children classified as "idiot" and "emotionally and culturally deprived" by the educational system could be trained to function like "normal" children. She concluded that placing children in "enhanced environments" in contrast to "impoverished environments" entirely changes their ability to learn and compete in life. This has since been confirmed by many other scientists. Her ghetto children often outperformed normal children. The same is true for these fourteen subjects. A 1991 French study by Plomin and Bergeman demonstrated that a shift in home environment could produce as much as a twenty-point improvement in IQ scores. This is not surprising since these fourteen individuals were more successful due to being raised in an environment favorable to development of those traits most responsible for their success. They were successful despite normal genetic and intellectual gifts. From this research it is evident that "nurture" not "nature" is the root of all great achievement. Figure 25 lists twelve principles of instilling creativity in children, based on the childhood imprints of successful individuals.

WHAT MAKES THE GREAT TICK?

Creative geniuses are architects of change. They see life as a process of acquiring knowledge and competence for its own sake. They tend to focus on patterns that appear in all things (philosophical) and excel at deriving new laws and principles. They value competence and quality while seeking to solve problems and enigmas. Such individuals are competitive to a fault. Intellectual stimulation is their forte making them society's foremost visionaries and pioneers. They are insensitive to authority since competence is their only criterion for success. A succinct definition of their personality characteristics might read: The creative genius is an obsessively driven intuitive-thinker with high self-esteem, armed with a Type A personality who loves risky environs, is tenacious, and viewed as a renegade by the establishment.

The above behavior characteristics were found in these fourteen subjects and in most great creative and entrepreneurial geniuses or power brokers. How do people develop such a personality? Most are conditioned and imprinted through environmental and family influences which can be summarized as: The creative genius is often the firstborn child with a slightly above average IQ and a fair share of testosterone reared by an indulgent and doting mother and self-employed father. High transiency and life crises molded their temperaments along with mythological hero/mentors and positive role models. Formal education was not critical to their success.

WHAT PRICE GLORY?

These fourteen paid a high price for power and success. Was it worth the cost? Faust sold his soul to the devil for youth, knowledge, and power. These fourteen sold their souls in order to pursue their dreams. Both were questionable bargains which resulted in power. Was the price worth the rewards? They thought so! These fourteen destroyed families and friends and a few destroyed themselves. Their mates did not understand their bargain but they were placating psyches that had been conditioned for overachievement. In pursuing their dreams, they paid the price of a normal family life, happiness, and contentment. They were never bored and became the best they could be, which Alfred Adler said is the innate need of all men. All were self-actualized. By Adler's and Abraham Maslow's definition, these individuals made it to the highest possible position accessible to mankind. But were they happy? No, they were not in the classic definition of the word. But they achieved enormous success and power, which was a form of happiness to them. Such personalities seldom conform to society's definition of happiness. This is why everyone pursuing power and success must first come to grips with a well thought out philosophy of life. Power succumbs to him who takes it. Make sure you want it because all power comes with an exorbitant price tag.

TWELVE PRINCIPLES OF INSTILLING CREATIVITY IN CHILDREN

"Children grow up to fulfill their internal images of themselves."

It appears from the research on powerful and successful adults that childhood imprints from environmental influences are critical to later achievement. The gifted child is intolerant of useless conformity and demands a stimulating and challenging environment. Gifted children left in impoverished or non-stimulating environments often grow into average adults. Conversely, average children placed in enhanced or embellished environments are often endowed with the tools of greatness. Montessori's success in this area was dramatic and recent brain research at Berkeley and UCLA in rats has cast light on the importance of environment in optimizing an individual's ability to reach his maximum potential. Overprotective mothers and authoritarian fathers are the bane of creativity while doting and indulgent parents appear to mold creative and entrepreneurial offspring:

Indulgent and Doting Parents. Treating a child as unique and special instills strong self-esteem and builds personal confidence. The danger is in creating an arrogant and egoistic adult. Such is the price of molding an indomitable will and optimistic persona.

Demonstrate Independent Action. Entrepreneurial or venturesome professional activities by parents mold the child with similar behavioral styles. Independence is born of experience, not security. Children of self-employed parents learn they can make it in the world without capitulating to a nine-to-five job in a corporate organization. Independence and self-sufficiency result.

Extensive Travel or Transiency. New cultures and acquaintances are positive influences in building temerity, coping skills, and learning to be comfortable with ambiguity. An around-the-world trip with a year off from school is a prime example of such a trade-off for the gifted child.

Freedom of Movement and Actions. Encourage living on the edge without allowing disaster. The child must be allowed to explore while the parent monitors the activity so the child survives the new experience. Instills risk taking without fear or rejection.

Ban "No" from Vocabulary—Reinforce All Actions Positively. Magnify strengths and ignore weaknesses. Optimism should be paramount in all behavior imprints. Never allow negativity or rationalization to rule.

Preach that "Being Different" Is Okay. Leaders are different. Mimicking the pack only grooms followers, not leaders. Leaders break new ground and by definition are renegades. Children should be encouraged to risk and fail, to experiment and learn from the failures.

Games of Abstract Problem Solving. Legos, erector sets, jigsaw puzzles, video games, and ham radios are the tools of genius. Heuristic problem solving build holistic and intuitive skills.

Books, Movies, and Fantasy Heroes. Fictional and mythological heroes are excellent fantasy mentors who tend to remove limits to achievement and channel energies. Books and voracious reading play a key part in success.

Knowledge and Inquisitiveness Should Be Revered. Knowledge builds enthusiasm. It should be pursued relative to the arts, sciences, journal writing, poetry, and philosophy.

Surround with Stimulating Challenges. The unconscious is absorbent and we do become a by-product of our environment. Avoid impoverished environments and seek embellished ones.

Hyperactivity and Mania. An extremely beneficial trait. High energy and speed wins and hyperactive children should be monitored, not drugged or punished. Such behavior should be managed not changed. Most power brokers were hyperactive children.

Imagination Should Be Encouraged. All adult creative endeavors are borne of childlike fantasy that is the by-product or right-brain and holistic vision. Intuition is golden.

In the final analysis, everyone is better served to follow Joseph Campbell's admonition to "Follow your bliss." This axiom is further validated by creativity psychologist Paul Torrence who found that "happiness and good mental health consist primarily of using one's capacity to the fullest." Torrence found that creative people are happy only if they "are free to create." Success, therefore, will accrue to those willing to pursue their dreams whatever the cost.

Bibliography

Adler, Alfred. *Superiority and Social Interest*. New York: Norton and Co., 1979.

Alexander, John. *Catherine the Great*. New York: Oxford Press, 1989.

Amabile, Teresa. *Growing Up Creative: Nurturing a Lifetime of Creativity*. New York: Crown Publishing, 1989.

Barzun, Jacques. "The Paradoxes of Creativity." *American Scholar* (Summer 1989): 337.

Boden, Margaret. *The Creative Mind*. New York: HarperCollins Publishing, 1990.

Boorstin, Daniel. *The Creators*. New York: Random House, 1992.

Branden, Nathaniel. *Six Pillars of Self-Esteem*. New York: Bantam Books, 1994.

Brigham, Deidre. *Imagery for Getting Well*. New York: Norton and Sons, 1994.

Buffington, Perry. "Star Quality." *Sky* (September 1990): 101–103.

Campbell, Joseph. *The Inner Reaches of Outer Space*. New York: Harper and Row.

———. *Transformations of Myth Through Time*. New York: Harper and Row, 1990.

Cantor, Dorothy, and Toni Bernay. *Women in Power: The Secrets of Leadership*. New York: Houghton Mifflin, 1992.

Cappon, Daniel. "The Anatomy of Intuition." *Psychology Today* (May/June 1993): 41.

Clark, Barbara. *Growing Up Gifted*. Columbus, Ohio: Merrill Publishing, 1988.

Estes, Clarissa P. *Women Who Run with the Wolves: Myths and Stories of the Wild Woman Archetype*. New York: Ballantine Books, 1993.

Farley, Frank. "World of the Type T Personality." *Psychology Today* (May 1986).

Farrell, W. *Why Men Are the Way They Are*. New York: McGraw-Hill, 1986.

Ferguson, Marilyn. *The Aquarian Conspiracy*. Los Angeles: J. P. Tarcher, 1976.

Frankl, Viktor. *In Search of Meaning*. New York: Pocket Books, 1959.

Freud, Sigmund. *On Creativity and the Unconscious*. New York: Harper, 1925.

Fucini, Joseph, and Suzy Fucini. *Entrepreneurs: The Men and Women Behind Famous Brand Names and How They Made It*. Boston: G. K. Hall, 1985

Gardner, Howard. *Creating Minds*. New York: Basic Books, 1993.

———. *Framing Minds: The Theory of Multiple Intelligences*. New York: Basic Books, 1983.

Ghislin, Brewster. *The Creative Process*. Berkeley, Calif.: Berkeley Press, 1952.

Gilligan, Carol. *In a Different Voice: Psychological Theory and Women's Development*. Boston: Harvard University Press, 1982.

Goleman, Daniel. *Emotional Intelligence: Why It Can Matter More than IQ*. New York: Bantam Books, 1995.

Goleman, Daniel, Paul Kaufman, and Ray Michael. *The Creative Spirit*. New York: Dutton, 1992.

Gornick, Vivian, and Barbara Moran. *Women in Sexist Society: Studies in Power and Powerlessness*. New York: New American Library, 1971.

Gray, John. *Men, Women and Relationships*. HIllsboro, Ore.: Beyond Words Publishing, 1993.

Guiles, Fred L. *Norma Jean*. New York: Bantam Books, 1969.

Halamandaris, The Brothers. *Caring Quotes*. Washington, D.C.: Caring Publishing, 1994.

Hart, Michael. *The One Hundred: A Ranking of the Most Influential Persons in History*. New York: Citadel Publishing, 1978.

Heatherton, Todd F., and Joel Weinberger. *Can Personality Change?* Washington, D.C.: American Psychological Association, 1993.

Herrnstein, Richard J., and Charles Murray. *The Bell Curve: Intelligence and Class Structure in American Life*. New York: Free Press, 1994.

Hershman, D. Jablow, and Julian Lieb. *A Brotherhood of Tyrants: Manic Depression and Absolute Power*. Amherst, N.Y.: Prometheus Books, 1994.

———. *The Key to Genius: Manic Depression and the Creative Life*. Amherst, N.Y.: Prometheus Books, 1988.

Hirsh, Sandra, and Jean Kummerow. *Life Types*. New York: Warner, 1989.

Hutchison, Michael. *The Anatomy of Sex and Power*. New York: Morrow, 1990.

Jamison, Kay. *Touched with Fire: Manic-Depressive Illness and the Artistic Temperament*. New York: Free Press, 1994.

———. *An Unquiet Mind: A Memoir of Moods and Madness*. New York: Alfred Knopf, 1995.

Johnson, Robert. *Inner Work: Using Dreams and Active Imagination for Personal Growth*. San Francisco: Harper, 1986.

Jung, Carl. "The Stages of Life." In *The Portable Jung*. New York: Penguin, 1976.

Keirsey, David. *Portraits of Temperament: Personality Types*. Del Mar, Calif.: Prometheus Nemesis Book Co., 1987.

Keirsey, David, and Marilyn Bates. *Please Understand Me*. Del Mar, Calif.: Prometheus Nemesis Book Co., 1984.

Korda, Michael. *Power: How to Get It, How to Keep It*. New York: Random House, 1975.

Kroeger, Otto, and Janet Thuesen. *Type Talk at Work*. New York: Delacorte Press, 1992.

Landrum, Gene. *Profiles of Female Genius*. Amherst, N.Y.: Prometheus Books, 1994.

———. *Profiles of Genius*. Amherst, N.Y.: Prometheus, Buffalo Books, 1993.

Lear, Frances. *The Second Seduction*. New York: Harper, 1992.

Leman, Kenneth. *The Birth Order Book*. New York: Dell Publishing, 1985.

Lemann, Nicholas. "Is There a Science of Success? (An analysis of David McClelland's life work on motivation)." *Atlantic Monthly* (February 1994).

McClelland, David. *Power: The Inner Experience*. New York: John Wiley and Sons. 1978.

Mackinnon, Donald. "Personality and the Realization of Creative Potential." *American Psychologist* (1965).

Mahar, Maggie. "No Bull Advice." *Working Woman* (October 1992).

Maslow, Abraham. *The Farther Reaches of Human Nature*. New York: Viking Press, 1971.

Moyers, Bill. *Joseph Campbell—The Power of Myth*. New York: Anchor Books, 1987.

Ornstein, Robert. *The Psychology of Consciousness*. New York: Penguin, 1972.

Pearsall, Paul. *Making Miracles*. New York: Avon Books, 1993.

Plomin, Robert, and Gerald E. McClearn. *Nature, Nurture and Psychology*. Washington, D.C.: American Psychological Association, 1993.

Prigogine, Ilya. *From Being to Becoming*. San Francisco: Freeman and Co., 1980.

Prigogine, Ilya, and Isabelle Stengers. *Order Out of Chaos*. New York: Bantam Books, 1984.

Segal, Robert. *Joseph Campbell: An Introduction*. New York: Mentor Books. 1987.

Silver, David. *Entrepreneurial Megabucks: The 100 Greatest Entrepreneurs of the Last 25 Years*. New York: John Wiley and Sons, 1985.

Simonton, Dean Keith. *Greatness*. New York: Guilford Press, 1994.

Stibbs, Anne. *A Woman's Place*. New York: Avon Books, 1993.

Storr, Anthony. *The Dynamics of Creation*. New York: Ballantine Books, 1993.

Taylor, I., and J. Gretzels. *Perspectives in Creativity*. Chicago: Aldine Publishing, 1975.

Toffler, Alvin. *Power Shift*. New York: Bantam Books, 1990.

Troyat, Henry. *Catherine the Great*. New York: Berkeley Books, 1980.

Walsh, Anthony and Grace. *Vive la Difference: A Celebration of the Sexes*. Amherst, N.Y.: Prometheus Books, 1993.

Wolf, Naomi. *The Beauty Myth*. New York: Anchor Books, 1991.

Napoleon Bonaparte

Geyl, Pieter. *Napoleon For and Against*. New Haven, Conn.: Yale University Press, 1949.

Herold, J. Christopher. *The Mind of Napoleon*. New York: Columbia Press, 1955.

Hershman, D. Jablow, and Julian Lieb. *A Brotherhood of Tyrants: Manic Depression and Absolute Power*. Amherst, N.Y.: Prometheus Books, 1994.

Markham, Felix. *Napoleon*. New York: Penguin Books, 1966.

Seward, Desmond. *Napoleon and Hitler: A Comparative Biography*. New York: Viking, 1988.

Walt Disney

Eliot, Marc. *Walt Disney: Hollywood's Dark Prince*. New York: Carol Publishing Co., 1993.

Hinman, Catherine. "Disney Becomes Movie Monarch" *Orlando Sentinel*, April 24, 1994, p. 1–A.

Mosley, Leonard. *Disney*. New York: Stein and Day Publishing, 1986.

Thomas, Bob. *An American Original: Walt Disney*. New York: Hyperion, 1994.

"Walt Disney." *Current Biography*. 1940.

Isadora Duncan

"The Creators: Barefoot Contessas." *U.S. News and World Report*, September 7, 1992, p. 101.

Desti, Mary. *The Life of Isadora Duncan*. New York: Horace Liveright, 1929.

Duncan, Isadora. *Isadora Duncan: My Life*. New York: Liveright, 1927.

Schneider, Ilya Ilyich. *Isadora Duncan: The Russian Years*. New York: Da Capo Press, 1968.

Steegmuller, Francis. *Your Isadora: The Love Story of Isadora Duncan and Gordon Craig*. New York: Random House, 1974.

Amelia Earhart

Rich, Doris. *Amelia Earhart: A Biography*. New York: Dell, 1989.

Ware, Susan. *Still Missing*. New York: Norton Publishing, 1993.

Adolf Hitler

"Adolf Hitler." Current Biography. 1942.

Bullock, Alan. *Hitler: A Study in Tyranny*. New York: Harper, 1971.

Gay, Peter. *Adolf Hitler*. New York: Anchor Books, 1988.

Hershman D. Jablow, and Julian Lieb. *A Brotherhood of Tyrants: Manic Depression and Absolute Power*. Amherst, N.Y.: Prometheus Books, 1988.

Martin, Gilbert. *Holocaust*. New York: ADL, 1978.

Petrova, Ada, and Watson, Peter. *The Death of Hitler*. New York: Norton and Company, 1995.

Schwarzwaller, Wulf. *The Unknown Hitler*. New York: Berkeley Books, 1989.

Seward, Desmond. *Napoleon and Hitler: A Comparative Biography*. New York: Viking, 1988.

Shirer, William. *The Rise and Fall of the Third Reich*. New York: Simon and Schuster, 1960.

Speer, Albert. *Inside the Third Reich*. New York: Macmillian and Co., 1970.

Stein, George H. *Hitler*. Englewood Cliffs, N.J.: Prentice Hall, 1968.

Toland, John. *Adolf Hitler*. New York: Doubleday, 1976.

Howard Hughes

Bartlett, Donald, and James Steele. *Empire: The Life, Legend and Madness of Howard Hughes*. New York: W. W. Norton and Co., 1979.

Dietrich, Noah. *Howard: The Amazing Mr. Hughes*. Greenwich, Conn.: Fawcett, 1972.

Higham, Charles. *Howard Hughes: The Secret Life*. New York: G. P. Putnam and Sons, 1993.

"Howard Hughes." *Current Biography*. 1941.

Ludwig, Arnold. *The Price of Greatness*. New York: Guilford Press, 1995.

Maria Montessori

Chattin-McNichols. *The Montessori Controversy*. Albany, N.Y.: Delmar Publishers, 1992.

Kramer, Rita. *Maria Montessori: A Biography*. Boston: Addison-Wesley, 1988.

Montessori, Maria. *The Montessori Method*. New York: Schocken Books, 1912.

Standing, E. M. *Maria Montessori*. New York: Mentor-Omega, 1962.

Rupert Murdoch

Adams, Bruce. "Fox Outgrows the Bart Simpson Jokes." *San Francisco Examiner,* November 3, 1995.

Bart, Peter, "Rupert's Rumblings." *Variety*, February 15, 1993, p. 5.

Donaton, Scott. "Citizen Murdoch." *Advertising Age,* June 13, 1994, p. 6.

Evans, Craig. *Marketing Channels*. New York: Prentice Hall, 1994.

Kiernan, Thomas. *Citizen Murdoch*. New York: Dodd, Mead and Co., 1986.

Martzke, Rudy. "Fox Sports Set to Rival ESPN." *USA Today,* November 1, 1995, p. 2.

Reibstein, Larry, and Nancy Hass. "Rupert's Power Play." *Newsweek,* June 6, 1994, p. 46.

Roush, Matt. "Murdoch: Portrait of a 'Pirate.' " *USA Today,* November 7, 1995, p. 3D.

Sandomir, Richard. "Murdoch and Fox." *New York Times,* September 4, 1994, sec. 3, p. F1.

Shawcross, William. *Murdoch*. London: Pan Books, 1993.

Sivy, Michael. "Murdoch is Back on Top." *Money*, March 1994, p. 60.

Tuccille, Jerome. *Rupert Murdoch*. New York: Donald Fine, 1989.

Edith (Gassion) Piaf

Berteaut, Simone. *Piaf*. New York: Penguin Books, 1973.

"Edith Piaf." *Current Biography*. 1950.

Lange, Monique. *Piaf*. New York: Seaver Books, 1981.

Piaf, Edith. *My Life*, edited by Margaret Crosland and translated by Jean Noli. London: Owen, 1990.

Pablo Picasso (Ruiz)

Boorstin, Daniel. *The Creators*. New York: Random House, 1992.

Crocker, Catherine. "Twenty-seven Picassos Up for Auction This Fall." *Naples Daily News,* November 5, 1995, p. 4.

Gardner, Howard. *Creating Minds*. New York: HarperCollins, 1993.

Gilot, Francoise and Carlton Lake. *Life with Picasso*. New York: McGraw Hill, 1964.

Huffington, Arianna. *Picasso: Creator and Destroyer*. New York: Avon Books, 1988.

O'Brian, Patrick. *Picasso*. New York: Norton and Co., 1976.

Helena Rubinstein

Collins, Amy Fine. "The Reign of Helena Rubinstein." *House and Garden,* November 1992.
"Helena Rubinstein." *Current Biography.* 1943.
O'Higgins, Patrick. *Madame.* Lake, Dell Books, 1971.
Rubinstein, Helena. *Helena Rubinstein: My Life For Beauty.* New York: Paperback Library, 1972.

Marquis de Sade

De Sade, Marquis. *Juliette.* New York: Grove Press, 1968.
Lever, Maurice. *Sade,* translated by Arthur Goldhammer. New York: Farrar, Straus, and Giroux, 1993.
Thomas, Donald. *The Marquis de Sade.* New York: Carol Publishing Co., 1992.

Nikola Tesla

Cheney, Margaret. *Tesla: Man Out of Time.* New York: Barnes and Noble, 1981.
O'Neill, John J. *Prodigal Genius.* London: Neville Spearman, 1968.
Tesla, Nikola. *My Inventions.* Williston, Vt.: Hart Bros., 1982.
Wise, Tad. *Tesla.* Atlanta: Turner Publishing, 1994.

Frank Lloyd Wright

Filler, Martin. "More on the Master." *House Beautiful* (January 1994).
"Frank Lloyd Wright." *Current Biography.* 1941.
Gill, Brendan. *Many Masks: A Life of Frank Lloyd Wright.* New York: Ballantine Books, 1987.
Goldberger, Paul. "Not an Urbanist, Only a Genius." *New York Times Magazine* (February 13, 1994).
Margolies, Jane. "Remembering Mr. Wright" *House Beautiful* (June 1992).
Secrest, Meryle. *Frank Lloyd Wright.* New York: Harper Perennial, 1992.
Wright, Frank Lloyd. *An Autobiography.* New York: Horizon Press, 1977.

Index